Life of Thomas Attwood

C M Wakefield

BIBLIOLIFE

Copyright © BiblioLife, LLC

This book represents a historical reproduction of a work originally published before 1923 that is part of a unique project which provides opportunities for readers, educators and researchers by bringing hard-to-find original publications back into print at reasonable prices. Because this and other works are culturally important, we have made them available as part of our commitment to protecting, preserving and promoting the world's literature. These books are in the "public domain" and were digitized and made available in cooperation with libraries, archives, and open source initiatives around the world dedicated to this important mission.

We believe that when we undertake the difficult task of re-creating these works as attractive, readable and affordable books, we further the goal of sharing these works with a global audience, and preserving a vanishing wealth of human knowledge.

Many historical books were originally published in small fonts, which can make them very difficult to read. Accordingly, in order to improve the reading experience of these books, we have created "enlarged print" versions of our books. Because of font size variation in the original books, some of these may not technically qualify as "large print" books, as that term is generally defined; however, we believe these versions provide an overall improved reading experience for many.

INTRODUCTION.

GEORGE GROTE, the historian of Greece, speaking at the banquet given at the Mansion House in honour of Thomas Attwood and the Birmingham Deputation, on Wednesday, May 23rd, 1832, upon the occasion of the passing of the great Reform Bill, said:

"But if, Gentlemen, I were required to name the person whose services I appreciate highest, and whose feelings I envy most, throughout this momentous period, I should not hesitate to pronounce the name of Thomas Attwood. It is to him more than to any other individual that we owe the success of this great measure. He has taught the people to combine for a great public purpose, without breaking any of the salutary restraints of law, and without violating any of their obligations as private citizens. He has divested the physical force of the country of its terrors and its lawlessness, and has made it conducive to ends of the highest public benefit."

The poet Campbell followed with a glowing compliment to "that patriotic individual Mr. Attwood, who has pre-eminently, even among eminent patriots, distinguished himself on the present occasion in the cause of Reform."

"Twenty-five years ago," wrote the *Birmingham Journal* in 1856, "there was no more popular man in the British Empire than Thomas Attwood. As the creator of that public opinion which is now omnipotent he was a power in the State. The leader of the most formidable confederacy that the kingdom ever saw, with no weapons but the will of the people, he used that power with wisdom, temperance, and firmness, and brought the nation safely through a crisis as perilous as that which was consummated at Runnymede or Edge Hill, at the death of Cromwell, or the flight of the second James."

Elihu Burritt, in his *Walks in the Black Country*, page 17, says :

"Very few thoughtful men of the nation can now doubt that the storm would have burst upon the country with all the desolation of civil war, if Thomas Attwood and the men of Birmingham had not drawn the lightning out of the impending tempest by the rod of moral force, which was grasped and wielded by his steady hand."

Attwood himself, in a letter dated November 15th, 1838, says : "I have lived to see some changes. I began the war against the East India Monopoly. I saw its downfall. I began the war against the American Orders in Council. I saw their abolition. I began the late war against the Boroughmongering Parliament. I saw its *Reform*."

The public services of Thomas Attwood having been of the stupendous character briefly indicated by the foregoing extracts, it must appear strange to every one that not only should no memoir or biographical notice of him have ever appeared, but that the historians of the period should have assumed that he took but an insignificant part in the passing of the great Reform Bill. The distinct and decided testimony of the historian of Greece is, however, quite sufficient to settle this point definitely.

The people have treated the memory of Attwood with their customary forgetfulness, and the proverbial ingratitude of the populace has been equalled by the negligence, carelessness, or jealousy of historians. The sons and grandsons of the very men who bawled themselves hoarse in his honour have almost forgotten his name, whilst Alison, Martineau, and Molesworth scarcely give him credit for any important actions whatever in their respective histories.

Historians appear to have proceeded upon the principle that only those persons who have inherited ancestral estates, or those who have received titles, honours, and rewards from the Government, are worthy of commemoration in their pages, but should a man have been foolish enough to serve his country for nothing, they seem to have thought him unworthy of notice. That Tory historians should have written under such an impression is not, perhaps, surprising, but nobler and juster views of historic truth might have been expected from those who profess the Liberal creed.

Amongst all the historians to whom I have alluded, the conduct of Mr. Molesworth is the most extraordinary, for that gentleman informs us that he writes under the patronage of the Right Honourable John Bright, and that eminent politician himself states, in an extract prefixed to Mr. Molesworth's work, that he believes the book to be "honestly" written. Mr. Bright has represented Birmingham for twenty-five years, and must surely know something of the deeds of his great predecessor, and how he can state that he believes a book to be "honestly" written which professes to give the history of the Reform Bill, and yet scarcely mentions the name of Attwood, is indeed a mystery.

Of course, all this ingratitude is of no consequence whatever, so far as Thomas Attwood himself is concerned. He has gone from the scene of his labours, and posthumous fame was the very last thing he troubled himself about. He who despised rank, wealth, and honours during life might easily enough have acquired fame after death, had he cared for it. But it has appeared to me to be a sad pity that his own relatives should possess absolutely *no* record of his extraordinary life, and that, in particular, his younger descendants should grow up in total ignorance of the splendid public services, and especially of the unselfish patriotism of their great, but unfortunate and ill-requited, ancestor. For these reasons, although possessing no literary experience whatever, and having passed my life in avocations very different indeed from those of an author, I have endeavoured to put together the following pages, and should only a dozen of my relatives, or even only my own children, appreciate the trouble and expense I have incurred in collecting the materials for them, I shall be satisfied.

There is one painful subject to which I feel that candour and fairness demand that an allusion should be made. Where so much has been said of the great deeds of Thomas Attwood it does not seem to be right to pass over in silence the fact that at the failure of the firm of Attwood, Spooner & Company in 1865, many inhabitants of Birmingham censured the conduct of certain members of the Attwood family, and that even the illustrious memory of Thomas Attwood did not escape some cruel and unjust reflections. I am told indeed, and I hope correctly, that a juster and more grateful spirit now prevails in Birmingham, and that the true causes of that unfortunate disaster are now pretty generally understood. But, be that as it may, I hold it sufficient to say here, that whatever any one may choose to think respecting the commercial catastrophe referred to, it can form no possible reason or excuse for consigning to ungrateful oblivion the record of such a life as that which I have endeavoured to narrate.

In compiling the following pages, I have not attempted to write a smooth and readable biography. Even if my literary abilities had been equal to the task, I think I should have preferred the method I have chosen. My object has been rather to show what Attwood himself thought, and what his contemporaries thought of him, than what I think about him myself. I am aware that the plan adopted renders a memoir somewhat broken and tedious, but I think that the defects are more than counterbalanced by the advantages. There is another reason why I have wished in many cases to preserve the *ipsissima verba* of eye-witnesses, even when their diction appears awkward at the present day. The popularity of Attwood was so extraordinary, and the affection with which he inspired the masses so altogether unprecedented, that unless I produced contemporary evidence of the fact in the very words of those who experienced it, I should be suspected of exaggeration.

This little work has presented greater difficulties than are at first apparent, owing to the premature deaths of the whole generation intervening between myself and my grandfather. My recollections of him are only those of a child, and I have never had the advantage of consulting any one who worked with him in his prime. It must be confessed that his letters, on the whole, are disappointing, and it is not difficult to discover the reason. The man was incorruptible, and the Ministers and every one else knew it. He had the most utter abhorrence of anything approaching to an intrigue—of anything secret or underhand. The Whig Ministers openly courted his alliance, and he, as openly, declined it. Henceforth there was no room for any of that confidential intercourse which often renders the correspondence of great men most interesting when it is most discreditable, and hence it arises that the letters of many a fawning courtier, of many a selfish place-hunter, are better suited to the public taste than those of the self-denying patriot.

I have generally left the politics of Attwood to speak for themselves, and have inserted the criticisms of his opponents as well as the encomiums of his friends; but I think I may venture to make one remark. It has generally been supposed that Liberals and Radicals *alone* have reason to revere the memory of Thomas Attwood. But I think the time has arrived when moderate men of *all* political parties must admit their obligations to him for his conduct in 1832. All historians, even those who unworthily omit the name of Attwood, agree that if the first Reform Bill had not been passed in a peaceful, legal, and orderly fashion, a violent revolution would have ensued, and it is more than probable that the aristocracy and the Church and possibly the Crown itself, would have gone to pieces in the struggle. We cannot tell what is in store for us in the immediate future, but it seems to me that the Church of England and the House of Lords owe an additional lease of at least fifty years' existence to the founder of Political Unions. Surely, then, Conservatives as well as Liberals should admit their obligations to his memory. With respect to his proceedings subsequent to 1832, it is, of course, only Radicals, and extreme Radicals too, who can be expected to approve of them, but even here men of all parties must admire his unselfish integrity.

I shall now close my remarks upon Attwood's character with the following brief summary. During forty years he devoted himself with unwearied energy to the public service. He published fifty pamphlets and more than a hundred long printed letters upon his favourite subject of the Currency; he ruined himself and his family by his close application to public business; he underwent the colossal and exhausting labour of founding the Birmingham Political Union, and of repeatedly addressing at length, in the open air, the largest meetings ever assembled in England; he represented Birmingham for seven sessions in Parliament; and, finally, he was admitted by the majority of his countrymen to have saved England from revolution; and for all these unparalleled services he never received *one penny of the public money, or any title, office, pension, decoration, or distinction of any kind from the Government, either for himself, his family, or his friends.*

It now only remains for me to thank Mrs. Attwood, my wife, and other relatives and friends who have assisted me in the compilation of this memoir, and to express a hope that they will be interested in the perusal of it.

C. M. WAKEFIELD.

BELMONT, UXBRIDGE,
December 11th, 1884.

SINCE this work went to press I have discovered a few errors which I take the opportunity to correct. Matthias and Ann Attwood were married at Rowley Regis Church, and not at St. Kenelm's, as stated on page 3. Matthias Attwood, M.P., appears never to have actually sat for Fowey. He was returned for that borough, but soon after unseated upon a petition. The prayer on page 74 seems to have been composed by Thomas Attwood, not with reference to his own illness, but to that of a relative.

I must also venture to remark that the present critical and humiliating state of our relations with Russia affords a singular and melancholy proof of the correctness of the views held by Thomas Attwood with respect to the unscrupulous and aggressive tendencies of the great northern Power. Had the solemn and repeated warnings of the Attwoods been listened to, England would now have nothing to fear from Russia.

May 9th, 1885.

CONTENTS.

CHAPTER I.
Birth and Parentage—Probable Descent—Description of Hawne—Early life and education ... 1

CHAPTER II.
Joins the firm of Attwoods & Spooner—Serves as a Volunteer—Drills at Warwick—Early letters to Miss Carless—His marriage—Brief account of the Carless family—The Leasowes—Letters to 1812 ... 9

CHAPTER III.
Thomas Attwood, High Bailiff of Birmingham—His great popularity—The artisans offer him their thanks—Revocation of the Orders in Council—Letter of B. Cook—Richard Pratchett—Sir Charles Mordaunt ... 25

CHAPTER IV.
Great Speech of Thomas Attwood against the renewal of the East India Charter ... 33

CHAPTER V.
Letters from London in 1813—Mr. Attwood is presented with a silver cup by the artisans of Birmingham—Extraordinary character of the presentation—Letters to 1815—*The Remedy, or Thoughts on the present Distresses*—Letter to Lord Liverpool—Mr. Brougham presents petition drawn up by Attwood from 17,000 inhabitants of Birmingham—Cobbett's remarks—Correspondence with Brougham and Arthur Young ... 49

CHAPTER VI.
Letters during 1818 and 1819—Mr. Peel's Bill for the resumption of cash payments—Matthias Attwood calls meeting to oppose it and is supported by Sir Robert Peel—Correspondence with Lord Liverpool and Sir John Sinclair—Matthias Attwood returned for Callington—Letters during 1820 ... 66

CONTENTS.

CHAPTER VII.

Charles Attwood's letter on the subject of Queen Caroline—Evidence of Thomas Attwood before Agricultural Committee—Death of Miss Sarah Carless—Harborne Sunday School—Letter from Brougham—Thos. Attwood visits France—Letter from Wilberforce—Debate on the Currency between Huskisson and M. Attwood—Their speeches highly praised by Alison—Death of Richard Pratchett—Letters to end of 1824—Poem by Thomas Attwood ... 79

CHAPTER VIII.

Correspondence during 1825—The Great Panic—Important services rendered by Attwood—Ingratitude of the Government—Commencement of the great case of Small v. Attwood—Letters during 1826—Visit to Rouen—Letters of Peel and Liverpool—Caricature by Cruikshank—Correspondence with Sinclair, Finlay, and Gladstone—Death of Lord Liverpool—Letters—John Attwood's trial—*The Scotch Banker*—Attwood's estimate of Cobbett—Conduct of Matthias Attwood in Parliament 97

CHAPTER IX.

Commencement of the great period of Attwood's life—Elihu Burritt's opinion of his services—Birmingham Currency Petition—Great Meeting on May 8th, 1829—Attwood's speech received with extraordinary enthusiasm—Letter from Cobbett—Contemptuous rejection of the Currency Petition—Attwood determines to found "The Birmingham Political Union"—Immense sacrifices necessary—First meeting of friends for the purpose on the 14th December, 1829—Cobbett's remarks—Matthias Attwood ... 119

CHAPTER X.

Establishment of the Political Union on January 25th, 1830—Extraordinary success of the movement—Objects, Rules, and Duties of the Union—Its first declaration signed by Attwood, Scholefield, Muntz, and 33 others—Lord Blandford joins the Union—First Meeting of the Union on May 17th—Grandeur of the spectacle—Thomas Attwood is presented with a gold medal by the members—Speeches of Attwood, Scholefield, Hadley, and others, and unqualified success of the first meeting—Attwood's letters from London—Sir Francis Burdett visits Harborne and presides at the first Annual Meeting of the Union—Alison on the Parliamentary proceedings of M. Attwood—Deaths of George IV and Huskisson—Grand dinner at Birmingham on October 11th, 1830, to celebrate French Revolution—Unprecedented magnitude of the entertainment—Town's Meeting of December 13th in support of Earl Grey—Triumphant speech of Attwood—Spread of Political Unions throughout Britain—Petition of Rights—Charles Attwood founds the Northern Political Union 131

CONTENTS.

CHAPTER XI.

Influence of Attwood felt everywhere—Lord John Russell introduces the Reform Bill—Meeting of March 7th, 1831, to support Ministers—The King dissolves Parliament—Excitement in Birmingham—Letters—Lord Radnor and Sir Francis Burdett—Proceedings of Charles Attwood at Newcastle—Letter from James to Benjamin Attwood on Russian and Polish affairs—Matthias Attwood—Earl Grey—Extraordinary petition from the Union presented by O'Connell—Letters of Thomas Attwood to October, 1831 ... 156

CHAPTER XII.

Progress of the Reform Bill—First grand open-air meeting of the Political Union on October 3rd, 1831—100,000 persons present—Extraordinary order, magnificence and regularity of the proceedings—Speech of Attwood—Gratitude of Ministers—Lord John Russell's famous letter—Letters from Lord Althorp and Sir T. G. Skipwith—Stormy discussion in the House of Lords—Fame of Attwood—Abandonment of organisation of the Union—Mr. Attwood's letters—Mr. Thornton's account of meeting at Studley—Gloomy aspect of affairs—Small *v.* Attwood—Matthias Attwood 172

CHAPTER XIII.

The year 1832 the most important in Attwood's life—Letter from Lafayette—27,000 men solemnly pledge their obedience to Attwood—Mr. De Bosco Attwood's narrative of the crisis—Great Meeting of May 7th—Enormous assemblage of the people—Mr. De B. Attwood's *Call of the Unions* sung by 200,000 persons—Speech of Thomas Attwood setting forth the solemnity of the occasion—Resignation of Earl Grey—Indignation of the people—500 men of substance join the Union—Great spontaneous meeting of May 10th—Gloomy and serious aspect of affairs—" Solemn Declaration" against the Duke of Wellington—The Duke resigns—Earl Grey reinstated—Excessive joy of the populace—Mr. Parkes's letter—10,000 men assemble at Grove House and escort Mr. Attwood to Birmingham, where a third great meeting is held on May 16th, amidst the most extraordinary demonstrations of popular gratitude 189

CHAPTER XIV.

Mr. Attwood arrives in London—His interview with Earl Grey—He declines to accept any reward for his services—His final threat of calling together a million of men upon Hampstead Heath—Magnificent reception at the Guildhall—He is presented with the Freedom of the City—His eloquent speech on returning thanks—Banquet at the Mansion House—Testimony of Grote, Campbell, and others to his vast services—Letters to his wife—Return to

CONTENTS.

Birmingham on the 28th of May—His public entry into the town and extraordinary reception by the people—Flags, banners, and decorations in Birmingham 215

CHAPTER XV.

Passing of the Reform Bill—Attwood and the Secret Committee on the Bank Charter—G. De B. Attwood's candidature for Walsall—Thos. Attwood's address to the Electors of Birmingham, June 29th, 1832—Third annual meeting of the Political Union—Famous Discussion between Cobbett and Attwood on the Currency—Matthias Attwood, sen., and East Worcester Election—Birmingham Polish Association—Defeat of G. De B. Attwood at Walsall—Attwood and Scholefield are returned without opposition as the first members for Birmingham—The Chairing on December 17th—Lord Lyndhurst's decree in Small *v.* Attwood—M. Attwood returned for Whitehaven and Chas. Attwood defeated at Newcastle-on-Tyne—Letters of Campbell and Lafayette 243

CHAPTER XVI.

Parliamentary failure of Thomas Attwood—His Irish Policy—His motion for a Select Committee to inquire into distress of the country—Letters of Campbell, Niemcewicz, Plater, Western, Lafayette, Dwernicky, and Barrot—Death of Rev. Edward Carless—Letters—Great Meeting of May 20th, 1833—Cobbett's motion against Peel—Charles Attwood and Lord Durham—Cobbett's account 260

CHAPTER XVII.

Last letters from Lafayette—Grand dinner to Attwood and Scholefield on September 15th, 1834—Attwood's speech—Death of Mrs. Ann Attwood—Letters—Address to Electors—Election of 1835—Attwood and Scholefield returned by immense majorities—Last letter from Cobbett—Correspondence to close of 1835 276

CHAPTER XVIII.

Address and Petition drawn up by the Political Union, January 18th, 1836—Benjamin Disraeli's letter to Thomas Attwood—Great Reform Dinner at Birmingham, January 28th—Dinner of non-electors, February 1st—Letters—Death of Matthias Attwood, senior 293

CHAPTER XIX.

Anxieties of Mr. Attwood during 1837—He presents address to the Princess Victoria—Second movement of the Birmingham Political Union—Death of the King—Correspondence with Sir H. Taylor—Proclamation of the Queen and extraordinary compliment paid by the people to Attwood—Address to Electors—Attwood and

Scholefield again returned—M. and M. W. Attwood returned for Whitehaven and Greenwich—Letters of Thomas Attwood to the close of 1837 ... 301

CHAPTER XX.

Attwood and the Chartists—Visit to Scotland and grand reception at Glasgow—Great Meeting at Holloway Head, August 6th, 1838—Death of Mrs. Mary Carless—Her exemplary life—Small v. Attwood—Decision of the Lords in John Attwood's favour—Letters for the year 1838 ... 326

CHAPTER XXI.

Return of Mr. Attwood to Birmingham—Address of the Female Political Union—Discord in the Political Union—He presents the great National Petition, June 14th, 1839—He is heard at length in support of it, contrary to the rules of the House—His motion rejected, July 12th—Lord Palmerston and Russia—Mr. Attwood's address announcing his resignation—His private letters during 1839—Letters from Lords Melbourne and Western ... 341

CHAPTER XXII.

Mr. Attwood's resignation—Proposed monument in his honour—Death of Mrs. Attwood—Birmingham Loyal and Constitutional Association—Mr. Attwood returns from Jersey and proposes Mr. Scholefield at the election of 1841—Correspondence with Sir Robert Peel ... 371

CHAPTER XXIII.

Recollections of Thomas Attwood—Grove House, Harborne—16,000 inhabitants of Birmingham implore him to return to public life, September 29th, 1843—His reply—The "National Union"—Its failure—Letter to Sir Robert Peel—Letters from Lord Palmerston—Letters to the *Times* and *Morning Post* ... 381

CHAPTER XXIV.

First appearance of Mr. Attwood's fatal illness—His second marriage, June 30th, 1845—Visit to Germany—He leaves Harborne—Residence at Scarborough—Removes to York and Harrogate—Residence at Handsworth—Last appearance in public at the election of 1847—Removes to Allesley—Deaths of Peel, Wellington, and Matthias Attwood, junior—Deaths of George and G. De B. Attwood—Thomas Attwood removes to Ellerslie, Great Malvern, and dies there, March 6th, 1856—The *Birmingham Journal* on his death—Mrs. Attwood's lines ...

LIFE OF THOMAS ATTWOOD.

CHAPTER I.

Birth and Parentage—Probable Descent—Description of Hawne—Early Life and Education.

THOMAS ATTWOOD was born at Hawne House, in the parish of Halesowen and the county of Salop, on the 6th October, 1783. He was the third son of Matthias Attwood, and his mother was Ann Adams, of Cakemore, in the same parish.

The name of Attwood is of great antiquity in the county of Worcester, but none of the Attwoods at present existing are able to prove their descent from the ancient family of the same name, although the Attwoods of Hawne have always had a tradition that they were so descended, and many facts concur to render it almost certain. I do not propose to swell the present memoir with any account of these elder Attwoods, more especially as the subject of it stands in no need of illustrious ancestry, merely observing that the first of the name was Laurentius de Bosco, who resided at Trimpley at a very early period, as by a deed without date appears, and that his descendants lived for several centuries at Trimpley, Wolverley Court, and Perdeswell, and that they bore for their arms: Gules —a lion rampant double-queueé, argent.

George (son of George and grandson of George, all of Rowley Regis, in the county of Stafford), the grandfather of Thomas Attwood, who married Rachael Maria Gaunt of Rowley Regis, appears to have purchased the estate of Hawne about the middle of the last century, and his son Matthias removed thither to reside with him about 1778. Concerning the maternal ancestry of Thomas Attwood but little need be said. The

Adamses were simple yeomen, and amongst the last in the neighbourhood of that admirable class. They had been tenants of the Lytteltons from time immemorial, and shortly after the building of Hagley Hall purchased their small property from the first lord of that name. Although the farm of Cakemore never contained, I believe, more than fifty acres, its owners contrived to live upon it not only with comfort and hospitality, but to acquire a high reputation in the parish for charity and benevolence—a state of affairs which appears incomprehensible at the present time.

Matthias, the father of Thomas Attwood, was a man of considerable ability and much force of character. He was generally reputed to be a hard and stern man, but was capable of inspiring much affection in many of his dependents, as some touching anecdotes preserved by his son Charles show. He was a steel manufacturer, and also engaged in the nail trade and other industries. In 1791, in conjunction with Isaac Spooner, he established the well-known firm of Attwoods, Spooner & Co., which subsisted in high reputation until the sad failure of 1865. He was the owner of Hawne, The Leasowes, and various other considerable estates, and a deputy-lieutenant or magistrate for the counties of Salop, Stafford, Worcester, and Warwick, but took no part in politics, though he appears to have been a decided Conservative.

Matthias and Ann Attwood had the following children:—

Mary, born April 17th, 1776. Died February 14th, 1777.

George, the banker of Birmingham. Born December 19th, 1777. Died May 24th, 1854.

Matthias, the banker of London, M.P. for Fowey, Callington, Boroughbridge, and Whitehaven. Born November 24th, 1779. Died November 11th, 1851.

Mary Ann, born October 14th, 1781. Died July 30th, 1872.

Thomas, the subject of this memoir. Born October 6th, 1783. Died March 6th, 1856.

James Henry, born July 25th, 1785. Died July 14th, 1865.

Susanna, born November 6th, 1787. Died October 27th, 1819.

Edward, born February 22nd, 1789. Died October 19th, 1866.

Charles, Chairman of the Northern Political Union, Founder of the town of Tow Law, &c. Born January 25th, 1791. Died February 24th, 1875.

Rachael Maria, married William Mathews. Born April 26th, 1792. Died August 9th, 1881.

Benjamin, the well-known philanthropist. Born January 31st, 1794. Died November 22nd, 1874.

The parents were married at the interesting little chapel of St. Kenelm, on Clent Hills. Omitting the two daughters, one of whom died in infancy and the other at an early age, it will be seen that the remaining nine children attained an aggregate age of more than 723 years, something over an average of eighty years each—an extraordinary instance of longevity. I have somewhere read an account of nine children who attained an aggregate of 738 years, but these were a family of farmers, whilst the Attwoods were immersed throughout life in the weightiest cares, both of business and politics.

Hawne House, the birthplace of what, in spite of all their faults and failings, must be conceded to have been an extraordinary family, is a rambling, dilapidated old house situated on a steep hill overlooking the valley of the Stour, and just a mile from the town of Halesowen. In former times it must have been a picturesque and desirable residence, but it has shared the fate of many other old mansions near the Black Country, and the gradual approach of collieries, ironworks, and smoky chimneys has rendered it almost uninhabitable. When I last saw it, its neglected condition for many years, and the rapid growth of ivy and other creepers, gave it an appearance of much greater antiquity than it really possessed. I should think the older portion of it may be about 250 years old. A wing was added by the Pechells about 1700, and another by Matthias Attwood about 1790. I remember that on one of the bedroom windows there were some interesting verses addressed to a Miss Pechell, and dated, I think, 1704. The garden was very old-fashioned, without glass or other modern accessories, and the cherries produced by the old orchard of five acres were celebrated for several miles round. The small estate attached to the house contained about 150 acres, and some of the land was very fertile, producing heavy crops before it was spoilt by the smoke of the Black Country. In 1872, the forlorn appearance of the old house attracted the notice of a writer in the *Leisure Hour*, who thus describes his impressions:—

"But we have spoken of the miners; let us walk down towards the pits. No one would think we are so near them. A quiet country lane, with ferns, honeysuckle, and sweetbriar nestling in the banks, and hedgerows shaded with well-grown chestnut trees, and flanked by meadows well-wooded and divided by high old-fashioned hedges, seems more likely to lead us to some ancient-looking farmhouse with drowsy outbuildings and grass-grown courtyard, whitewashed walls, diamond panes, and heavy porch, where everything has gone quietly to sleep under the influences of a summer's day, and the silence is unbroken save by the soft cooing of pigeons sunning themselves on the barn-ridge, or the creaking of a crusty old weathercock that grumbles with every breeze. And standing a little back from the road on our right, we see just such an old-fashioned mansion, with its gardens, courtyards, and outbuildings. But it stands there a mere relic of the past, a waif just as it were above high-water mark on the shore of a busy sea, whose rising tide of grimy pits, unsightly heaps of slag, clanking foundries, heated furnaces, and smoky chimneys, has swept away green fields, perfumed meadows, waving woods, and sparkling streams, and whose busy sounds break in ceaseless echoes on the ear. We again stand on the borders of the Black Country."

The late Mr. Charles Attwood, in a paper left by him, thus speculates upon the origin of the name of Hawn:—

"In Sir Walter Scott's romance *The Monastery* is the following, note O, on 'The Pedigree of the Stewart family':—'The acute pen of Lord Hailes, which, like the spear of Ithuriel, conjured so many shadows from Scottish history, had dismissed among the rest those of Banquo and Fleance, the rejection of which fables left the illustrious family of Stewart without an ancestor beyond Walter, the son of ALLAN, who is alluded to in the text. The researches of a late learned antiquary detected in this Walter the

HAWNE HOUSE.

descendant of Allan, the son of Flaald, who obtained from William the Conqueror the Castle of Oswestry in Shropshire, and was the father of an illustrious line of English nobles by his first son, William, and by his second son, Walter, the progenitor of the Royal Family of Stewart.' The above note refers to the following passage at page 347 of the text : '"I bend to the honours of the house of Douglas," said Murray, somewhat ironically : "I am conscious we of the Royal House have little right to compete with them in dignity. What though we have worn crowns and carried sceptres for a few generations if our genealogy moves no further back than to the humble ALANUS *Dapifer.*"' Now, Hawn House, as it is now called, my birthplace, in the parish of Halesowen, in the said county of Shropshire, and for a long time the seat of the family of the Pearsalls or Pechells—(for it is spelt both ways)—the last Baronet of which name died a prisoner in the Fleet for debt, but to whom Captain Pechell, M.P., claims some relationship, and the quarter of the said parish in which it is situated, ' Hawn quarter,' derived their names, as I have often heard my father say, upon, I believe, the authority of his title deeds, from one Allen or Allan, who had been formerly, at a remote period, sole or chief proprietor of that part at least of the parish, and whose name, pronounced broadly, was called Aln, and at last Awn or Hawn, and probably, as it seems to me, the latter part of the name of the parish Halesowen itself may be either derived from that of the man (Allan) or that of the man from that of the parish of which he was entirely or in great part owner ; and that Owen is the same as Allan or Allen (Alanus in the monkish Latin), being the same as, or a translation of, Owen) : the more likely as Owen is in its own British (Salopian or Welsh) pronunciation properly Auen or Awen, which is exactly Awn or Hawn without the modern and certainly improper aspirate."

After having belonged to the Attwoods for nearly a century, all connection between them and the estate of Hawne finally ceased, in August, 1872, on the death of Miss Attwood, its last occupier of the name.

I regret that very scanty memorials have been preserved respecting the boyhood and youth of Thomas Attwood. He was the last man in the world to write an autobiography, or even to keep a diary. He was so incessantly occupied with elaborating schemes for the welfare of others, that he never had the slightest thought of perpetuating his own memory. With the rest of his brothers he was sent, as a day scholar, to the neighbouring Grammar School of Halesowen, about a mile distant from his father's residence. After a few years he was removed to that of Wolverhampton, where he finished the slender education which was then considered necessary for a boy intended for commercial pursuits. His eldest brother

George was intended for the Church, and sent to University College, Oxford, but Matthias Attwood does not appear to have had any idea of highly educating his other sons. Concerning the time which Thomas Attwood spent at Wolverhampton School, I gather a few particulars from his obituary notice in the *Birmingham Journal* of March 8th, 1856:—

"Mr. Lawson was then the head master, of whom his pupil in after life always spoke highly, as a man possessing by force of character great authority over his sometimes unruly pupils without being at all severe, and as being admirably qualified for the important position of a teacher of youth.

"For several years Thomas Attwood continued under his tuition. He was, even at that time, a thoughtful boy. Distinguished by a high feeling of conscientiousness and honour, he never joined in the indiscretions of garden robbing and other similar offences in that day common at that and almost every school. Much of this high sense of honour which was so early implanted in the breast of the boy is no doubt due to his mother. The character of a parent often influences very greatly that of a child, and, in this instance, the axiom seems to have found another illustration, Mrs. Attwood being a lady of great piety and strong common sense, who took the utmost pains to instil into the mind of her son those strict principles of duty which governed him through the course of a long and busy public life. This conscientiousness gave him a high position even among his youthful companions, who looked up to him as monitor, as the arbiter of their disputes, the settler of their differences, as their rule of propriety and good conduct. He was the school authority in this respect, and his aptitude in English composition—in which he was at the head of the school—and the kindhearted disposition to relieve distress, which uniformly distinguished him in after life, and which led him to part readily with his pocket money whenever a suffering fellow-creature was thrown in his way, although no actual appeal might have been made to his charity, gave him a position of another but no less elevated kind."

I can remember that he used to speak in terms of strong reprobation of the horrible cruelties practised upon animals by the school-boys of his day, and said that he always did his best to oppose and check such proceedings, a fact which I can readily believe, for, next to his unselfish devotion to mankind, nothing distinguished him so much as his affection for the brute creation. I never recollect him speaking of either hunting or shooting save to express his pity for the victims. To possess a deer forest, a grouse moor, or a salmon river was the very last object of his ambition. As a boy he shot a little, rather as a naturalist than a sportsman, but as he grew older he became disgusted with the sport. Such humanity is common enough in these days; the virtue has become fashionable. But it was *not* common in Thomas Attwood's day, and the lords and commons with whom he afterwards associated must have considered him a strange fellow indeed who could not appreciate their most cherished amusements. When I reflect that in those days Birmingham and its neighbourhood were generally supposed to be the headquarters of bull-baiting, cock-fighting, dog-fighting, and other cruel pastimes, I am the more astonished that a man bred up amongst them should have possessed such a singular quality, which was, however, shared by all his brothers.

I cannot ascertain what age Thomas Attwood was when he left Wolverhampton School, but I should think he could not have been more than sixteen or seventeen. He never acquired, and indeed, under the circumstances, it was scarcely possible that he should acquire, much classical knowledge. He could quote Latin, however, appositely upon occasion, and he always had a keen appreciation of the grandeur of ancient history, a fact, no doubt, attributable to the close resemblance of antique patriotism to his own. I remember him saying that when young and foolish, and, no doubt, infected by the French republican ideas which were then spreading over England, he thought Brutus was justified in killing Cæsar, but that he soon changed his mind and regarded the deed in its true light, as an infamous parricide. He had a great admiration for the character of Marcus Aurelius, and named two of his sons after him. In after years it was the fashion of some of his political opponents to insinuate that he was an illiterate man, simply because he belonged to Birmingham, and had never been sent to Oxford or Cambridge. Such a notion would, of course, be scouted nowadays, when we have seen two bishops, both intimately connected with Birmingham, raised to the primacy. Yet the late M. D. Hill informs us that in his day it was considered an audacious thing for a Birmingham man to aspire to be a barrister!

That the idea in question was a mere vulgar prejudice

against non-University men, I can confidently assert from a careful perusal of his letters extending over a period of forty years. Accurate writing was not so common then as it is now, but in point of grammar, spelling, and composition, his letters will compare with those of Liverpool, Brougham, Peel, Althorpe, or O'Connell, whilst his beautiful handwriting is not approached by any of those famous men. I have experienced no trouble whatever in reading the quantity of letters left by him, though many were written in the greatest hurry, but I have found it very difficult indeed to decipher many of those addressed to him.

Upon leaving school, Thomas Attwood at once entered his father's bank in New Street, Birmingham, and at the same time took up his residence in that town, with which his name was to be so indissolubly associated, and which he was destined to raise to a degree of power and weight in the councils of the kingdom which, previous to his time, its inhabitants had never ventured to dream of.

CHAPTER II.

Joins the Firm of Attwoods & Spooner—Serves as a Volunteer—Drills at Warwick—Early Letters to Miss Carless—His Marriage—Brief Account of the Carless Family—The Leasowes—Letters to 1812.

IN commencing to narrate the adult life of Thomas Attwood I am reluctantly compelled to pass over a space of from three to four years without recording a single fact. I have done my best to obtain information relating to this period, but have been unable to procure any. I assume that he entered the bank about 1800, and I suppose that his elder brothers George and Matthias joined the same business some years previously, though I have not been able to ascertain when the latter first established himself in London. The earliest document which I have relating to Thomas Attwood is dated February 28th, 1803, so that a considerable time remains to be accounted for. I would not venture to assert that he was altogether free from the follies of youth during this period, but from the early age at which he soon afterwards appeared as one of the leading men of Birmingham, I think he cannot have been wasting his time. No doubt he was silently preparing himself, and commencing to study his favourite and intricate subject of the Currency. At the date just mentioned he was drawn as a militiaman, and I copy here the certificate as follows:—

Warwickshire.—This is to certify that Thomas Attwood, of Birmingham, Banker, hath been duly chosen by Ballot to serve in the Militia of the said County; and that on the twenty eighth Day of February instant, Richard King, of Atherstone, Hatter, was duly inrolled to serve in the said Militia as Substitute for the said Thomas Attwood.—Dated the twenty eighth Day of February, 1803.

THOS WILMOT,
Clerk of the General Meetings.

The formal rupture of the peace of Amiens took place on the 17th May, 1803. Bonaparte threatened the invasion of England

and the whole nation flew to arms to oppose him. Birmingham was not behind the rest of the country. A public meeting was called by the High Bailiff, on August 8th, 1803, and £4,600 was subscribed for the purpose of equipping volunteers. To this sum, Spooner & Attwoods contributed £315, and Isaac Spooner £105. On this occasion Thomas Attwood, then not twenty years old, made his first appearance in public life, and was gazetted a captain in the Third Battalion of Loyal Birmingham Volunteer Infantry. Mrs. Attwood has the sword which he then wore, and Mrs. H. Freeman the pistols and accoutrements. His commission, which is on parchment, and sealed with a good impression of Lord Warwick's arms, is now in the possession of Mrs. Attwood, of the Boynes, and runs as follows :—

*By the Right Honourable George Earl Brooke and Earl of Warwick
To Thomas Attwood, Esquire.*

By Virtue of the power and authority to me given by a Warrant from His Majesty under His Royal Signet and Sign Manual, bearing date the twenty second day of May 1804, I the said George Earl Brooke and Earl of Warwick do, in His Majesty's name, by these presents, constitute appoint and commission you the said Thomas Attwood to be Captain of a Company of the third Battalion of the Regiment of Loyal Birmingham Volunteer Infantry, but not to take Rank in the Army except during the time of the said Corps being called out into actual service ; you are therefore to take the said Company into your Care and Charge, and duly to exercise as well the Officers as Soldiers thereof in Arms, and to use your best endeavours to keep them in good Order and Discipline, who are hereby commanded in His Majesty's name to obey you as their Captain, and you are to observe and follow such Orders and Directions from time to time as you shall receive from His Majesty, your Colonel or any other your superior officer, according to the Rules and Discipline of War, in pursuance of the Trust hereby reposed in you. Given under my Hand and Seal the ninth day of September in the forty third year of the reign of our Sovereign Lord George the Third, by the Grace of God, of the United Kingdom of Great Britain and Ireland, King, Defender of the faith and so forth, and in the year of our Lord one thousand eight hundred and three.   BROOKE & WARWICK.

This commission is endorsed by Thomas Attwood as follows :—

Sent in my resignation to Colonel Lord Dartmouth as per the within Copy on 8 March 1805. T. A.

With respect to the mass of his correspondence, which I have copied chiefly from letters kindly lent to me, I am puzzled what course to pursue. The most trifling minutiæ will be, or ought to be, interesting to his descendants, but others might think such insignificant details tiresome. As, however, it is improbable that any one beyond the circle of his immediate relatives will care to read this memoir, I have resolved to insert the greater part of it.

The earliest of his letters which I have seen is dated Birmingham, September 12th, 1803, and is addressed to Miss Elizabeth Carless, of Grove House, Harborne, whom he married in 1806, and I find by a subsequent note that this was the very first letter he ever addressed to her. From this time down to her death in 1840, a tolerably complete collection of his private letters has been preserved. In this first letter occurs the following passage, which seems to show that, even at that age, and amidst the universal martial enthusiasm, he had not much taste for military glory :—" This curs'd military business incapacitates a man for all rational employments, but I hope it will soon come to an end, or I am afraid one half of the wise ones engaged in it will."

The three next letters, addressed to the same, and dated September 20th, October 12th, and October 13th, do not contain any reference to matters of particular importance, and it appears that he was ill with a fever at that time.

Birmingham, Oct. 15th, 1803.
. . . I hope you have not forgotten our intended walk to Frankley Beeches, and if fortunately you should be well enough, I should be very happy to accompany you there on Wednesday, this being just the right time of the year.

To Miss Carless, at Mr. Pratchett's, High St., Birmingham.
Halesowen, Nov. 5th, 1803.
I assure you, my dear Eliza, we have been very gay at Hawn since I saw you last. When I came home on Thursday evening I found Miss Ann Biggs and my cousin Bessy, who with my sister Mary Ann made me some very pretty company, the pleasure of which was greatly enhanced the next morning by the appearance of Miss Helen Male, and at 2 o'clock by the addition of a very polite and agreeable selection of personages from Halesowen, whose entertaining small talk and very droll disputes would (if anything could) have made me for a moment almost forget I was absent from my Eliza. . . . At $\frac{1}{2}$ past twelve the good people dispersed. . . .

To the same address.

Warwick, 23rd May, 1804.

We arrived here yesterday about 3 o'clock, after a very pleasant walk. I have taken some pleasant lodgings with Mr. Lardner, at Mr. Hickling's, Jury St., where you will please to direct to me in future. I am very much afraid that your cold is worse, but hope to receive a letter at the Head Qrs. Pray write to me as you promised and take care that they are good long letters abounding with all kinds of information, advice, etc. Lardner has brought with him a good collection of books. Of couse I shall make use of them whenever I please but am apprehensive I shall not have much time at liberty.

To the same. (No date.)

Warwick itself is at no time much better than its jail. . . . It is in fact a good deal like the "Deserted Village."

Warwick, 2 June, 1804.

I have just received upon Parade your letter of yesterday, and am glad to perceive you are in such good spirits; with me it is, in truth, very different. In the short time that I have been here I have seen little to amuse and much to torment. I have heard nothing but the hideous roaring of the drum and the long shriek of the fife, sounds which though irritating at first soon cloy upon the ear and lose their effect. . . . I have determined you shall play upon the tambourine. I have a great partiality for that instrument, and will take care to procure a good one. It is the most fashionable and the most easy music, and I do entertain myself a good deal in the idea that I shall soon see you play and hear you sing to it. Lord Warwick is not now at the Castle nor has he been since we have been here, he has however behaved very politely to us, given us the use of his park, where we have exercised every day, and given orders to his gamekeepers that we should be supplied with fish every day during our stay for our mess dinner, which orders are very liberally attended to. I have understood that it was his intention, if possible, to dine with us at the Castle, on the King's birthday, and to have filled Guy's porridge pot with punch for the men, but I believe he will not be able to leave London. Our landlord at the Warwick Arms (who once lived with the celebrated Mrs. Leigh the camphire lady) has offered 140 gallons of ale to the men, which they will be very glad of.

I have seen a good many sights in Warwick, some of which would have entertained me 18 years ago. The felons in the jail distressed me very much. God bless you, thought I, as I left their court, and show you and your persecutors more mercy in the other world than they are willing to show you in this. Several of them were very young, and I thought that one or two of them were almost as miserable as I was before I was sure of my Eliza.

Warwick, 9th June, 1804.

. . . I was very much concerned that I could not write to you yesterday, but though we had no review, we remained on the field so long that the Post was gone before we returned. Yesterday I had the pleasure of dining with a Mr. Tomes together with my noble and renowned associates He

DRILLS AT WARWICK.

gave us a most grand dinner, and was so free with his wine that after having dispersed all the company except two or three old warriors, he was obliged to give it in. I had likewise the pleasure of attending at a Ball which was given last night by some of the officers to the nobility of the neighbourhood; it was a very delightful evening, and if my Eliza had been there I am sure she would have been well pleased. Your shadow, that you have heard me speak of, was there, and I had the pleasure of dancing with her. The angelic likeness seemed to think there was something strange in my behaviour to her, and asked Mrs. Thomason if there was not a similitude between herself and the lady to whom I was engaged. There is, in truth, a very great resemblance, at least she resembles you as far as human nature can resemble you. Her name is "Lloyd," but no relation to the little quaker. She comes from Highgate near London. . . . .

Warwick (no date).

. . . I dined with Lt. Aston at his father's yesterday, about 5 miles from town, and owing to the letters being delivered to the drum major, who was not to be found, I did not get yours till this morning, soon after which I was particularly pleased to receive another by Mr Lardner. The Astons are a very pleasant family, the two daughters at home almost reminded me of my Eliza. . . . The house is a fine old abbey, and the grounds about it are delightful. We took a walk after dinner and after tea, and I could not help fancying that if you had been there, it would have been difficult to have believed you were not the three fabled beings we have heard so much of. . . .

Major Stratton of the Bloxham and Banbury Cavalry, who are on duty here, gave a grand ball at Leamington last week at which I was present, and a most miserable presence it was. The company, to the number of about 20 couple, first of all danced on the bowling green to the great entertainment of the natives, and afterwards adjourned to tea, &c., then danced again, then adjourned to supper, and danced till after 4 o'clock. I left them at 12 o'clock, immediately after supper, after having danced two dances with a very pleasant partner, a Miss Dews, who formerly lived at Hagley. I was very glad to get away from them, and brought Lardner and one of the little Triangles with me (our Bird was there). We had been very nearly losing his little brother Triangle that morning, he had unfortunately fallen into a great tub full of grains, and if I and one of the other Triangles had not been present, he would most certainly have been drowned. I have no doubt but you will soon be able to play upon the Tambourine without a teacher. The drums now beat for our grand parade in the square, where we shall fire 3 vollies in honour of his Majesty. . . .

Per favor of Mr Francis. (No date).

. . . We have not yet given a ball to the natives, and I believe we shall not give one at all I have done all I could to prevent it. Nevertheless the good people of the town are about to give the men a grand dinner on Friday next, and I am told something of the kind is intended to be offered to the officers . .

To Miss Carless, Grove House, Harborne.

Birmm. Nov. 7, 1804.

. . . I shall therefore content myself with and most probably you with remarking that I shed more tears in parting with old Haden last night than I did on Monday, albeit there was a good deal of distress visible on that day, and the iron faces of the mutes seemed "soft as sinews of the new born babe." My poor grandfather and father hung over the coffin of their wife and mother, even my uncle James melted at the sight, but I, like old Pharaoh, had hardened my heart, and with my brother Matthias still preserved my composure. Here we had full time to prepare ourselves, but old Haden quite took us by surprise, and Matthias himself turned away his head from the trial. My uncle Aaron would accompany the funeral, but sunk down at the sight of the coffin, and was left behind. He has been in a morbid melancholy ever since his daughter's death and I believe cannot survive it. . . .

. . . Here would arise an interesting speculation, when so much dormant virtue may lie hidden in a man all the days of his life; *whether* Providence in the final judgment will take into account what he *would have been* had he been mingled with the world and placed in circumstances to call forth that virtue and *vice versâ*. But how have I gone on giving you an account of the funeral, and lo! the idea of writing to you has almost restored my original brilliancy, so much so that I could now edit a thousand such epistles as this, when oh hard fate! I am forced to conclude, and have not room for another idea. . . . Oh, but amidst these funereal distresses, I had almost forgot to inform you of those most important personal grievances which afflict me, unhappy man that I am. That unprincipled enemy to health, Dick Wood (not Tomlinson), this very morning "fighted me and fighted me till with his wicked fist he knocked out my precious tooth," a varied pleasure, my Eliza, and so fare thee well, my dear friend, till to-morrow evening.

Birmingham, Nov. 10, 1804.

. . . Having accomplished one of the most perilous journies that was ever performed by the son of man, I shall now, according to promise, trespass for a few moments upon your and my time in giving you a true and correct account thereof. But in truth my heart almost fails me at the recollection, so many ghastly sights and miserable adventures did we meet with in our progress. All the powers of darkness and Apollyon himself seemed combined against us, but at length by the blessing of providence and your uncle's perseverance we overcame them all, and arrived at Wednesbury Iron Works, from whence we fought our way through fire and smoak to the habitation of Waltho, with no other injuries than my having broken one leg in being overturned by a coal cart, and your uncle's having lost his left hand (by chance) under the iron shears at Wednesbury. Having fixed upon the proper place for pitts and arranged everything in these parts, we ordered our chargers and drove off full speed. We met with little opposition on the road, and soon reached Wednesbury Church, but now we were come to the real enemy, an enemy, in your uncle's opinion, threatening more than all our preceding difficulties. The name of this foul fiend was "Hunger," and dreadful indeed he did seem, for he imprisoned us for two hours in a loathsome dungeon, during all which time we heard nothing but the clanking of chains and such like hideous noises. At last by the exertions of my brother Jim we escaped, and right well were we rejoiced, and heartily did we congratulate ourselves when we arrived safe in Birmm. about 9 o'clock. I wish you would endeavour to find me out a tune for the undermentioned words. It is the "Pas de Charge" of the French, and their words seem to speak it.—

"Oh, Bonaparte, et toi, Moreau,
Noms chers à la victoire
Quel est le sublime pinceau
Que peindra tant de gloire."

As I have already noticed, Thomas Attwood resigned his commission as captain in the Birmingham Volunteers on the 8th March, 1805, and a short note from Lord Dartmouth accepting his resignation is preserved. I have often thought his brief military career interesting, for it seems to have foreshadowed his future life. It was not with material weapons that *his* victories were to be gained. In laying aside his sword, he must have little thought that he was destined to win as great a victory as soldier ever won, and that it was to be achieved, too, over the greatest captain of the age, without shedding a drop of blood or causing a single tear. It was reserved for him to show, by an extraordinary example, the superiority of moral over physical force. In this year he appears to have visited London for the first time—at least I can find no earlier mention of his going there. Londoners in those days mercilessly ridiculed provincials, so it is not surprising that the latter should retaliate by occasional bitter remarks. In the letters of 1805, also, I find the first mention of the well-known Richard Spooner, with whom, as friend, partner, and political antagonist, he was to be so intimately connected throughout life. Richard Spooner was born at Erdington in 1783, in the same year as Thomas Attwood, though he long survived him. He was the ninth child of Isaac Spooner, of Elmdon Hall, and of Barbara his wife, daughter of Sir Henry Gough, Bart., of Edgbaston Hall, and sister of the first Lord Calthorpe. He married, in 1804, Charlotte, fourth daughter of Nathan Wetherell, D.D., Dean of Hereford, &c. His name will very frequently occur in the course of this memoir. I shall now insert some extracts from Thomas Attwood's letters for 1805.

To Miss Carless, at T. F. Bricknell Esqre's, Little Gate, Oxford.

London, April, 1805.

. . . I have settled the business with the India Co., about which I principally came to town, to my satisfaction, but now I have an opportunity, I cannot leave here until I have made myself acquainted with the London banking business, which is very different from the Birmm., and, I think, rather more complicated. . . . We were in Kensington Gardens yesterday, and I saw an immense crowd of ugly people. I sincerely wished you had been there, though from the deformity of every one else, I am apprehensive the creatures would have mistaken you for a vision or a meteor. There positively was not a tolerable looking woman in the whole gardens. Satan seems equally to have taken up his abode in the hearts and appearances of the Londoners. . . .

To the same. (No date).

Grove House, Harborne.

. . . As you seem so pleased with long letters, if time allowed, I wd. talk politics to you, a subject which I know you love and respect, and which, in time, I have no doubt you will make a greater proficiency in than ever your quondam favourites Pitt or Melville did. But I must not forget to beg you will, if possible, take a few lessons on the Tambourine from that same philosopher in the Beech Lane. Geo. Biggs has taken to the Halesowen living, which is worth about 2 or 3 hundred a year. If I can, I mean to come soon enough on Thursday evening to take a walk. Pray do not take cold in the interim, and give my love to Sarah. I hope Ned is well. Write to me if you can, and write in your own way, not after the fashion of any one else. I had sooner you would imitate a monkey than any human being who is alive in these vile days. If I can, I shall purchase the great man in wax work who may be deemed an exception.

To Miss Carless, Hawn House, near Halesowen.

Birmingham, 1st Augt., 1805.

. . . I suppose you will dine at Cakemore to-morrow, and I am very sorry I cannot meet you there. Pray do not be negligent in walking there and back again, or you will be very liable to take cold. I would have you take Jim with you, in whose company alone I am quite sure that you will contract no bad principles. . . . Mr. and Mrs. R. Spooner are very anxious to see you at Moore Green, but I wish you would consult Jim upon this before you decide. His arguments are very ingenious. If you are perfect, says he, you can get no good, and if you are not, you may get harm, for harm abides in *every* corner of the world, and though varnished and glossed over with a thousand gay deceits and fashionable follies, yet it is harm, and the more deeply it is concealed the more dangerous it is. You will have heard that Sir Robt. Calder has had a drawn battle with the French and Spanish fleets, which have, nevertheless, been rather worsted. I have met with a gentleman who was intimately acquainted with Lord Edwd. Fitzgerald and Counsellor Emmett. I find as I have told you that they were most humane and liberal minded men, and almost adored by the people. Another disturbance is much to be apprehended in Ireland very shortly. The Mohawk chief that I told you of some time ago, can get no attention paid to his requests. This will probably cause a war in Canada. I know you love politics right well, or I would not tell you these things.

(*No date or place, but in* 1806).

. . . I have seen old Green and if . . . should be a bankrupt, we shall have the house at 130 guineas per annum, but this is not certain. . . . You may see that Austria is now reduced to a necessity of making war against Russia, as are likewise Prussia and Turkey, all serving for the aggrandisement of France. Bonaparte tells his people in his exposé that he has done nothing yet in comparison of what he has to do, intimating, no doubt, as I have often told you, the conquest of the whole world. This will most assuredly take place, and the great labour will be, not in conquering it, but in organising and uniting in peace and amity its jarring interests.

Birmingham, 21 *April,* 1806.

Having occasion to transact some business at Hawn, I shall not be able to come to Harborne before to-morrow evening, when I will certainly come. I do not much mind whether we are married with a special license or not, everything shall be done in the manner most agreeable to yourself. . . . I wish I could walk with you round the reservoir this evening, but, as I cannot, I hope you will have made Sarah my substitute. Sarah is become of late so strong in mind and body, that if you do not take care, there is reason to believe she will soon overtake you. She is grown very subtle too. In argument, I would sooner encounter the serpent of Eve than her little tongue. I should be sorry to see her tumble into foolish hands, for there is somehow such a natural hostility between wisdom and folly (which the latter is enabled to support by superiority of numbers) as would assuredly lead her to suicide, false doctrine or some other deadly sin. . . .

Thomas Attwood married Elizabeth Carless, at Harborne Church, the ceremony being performed by the Rev. Edward Carless, his wife's brother, on the 12th of May, 1806. It may be of interest to her descendants to subjoin here a short account of her family, of which some particulars have been preserved by the Rev. Mark Noble, F.S.A. The Carlesses were of Birmingham, where they had held a respectable position for a considerable period, but without claim to any great antiquity. The first of the line who can be traced with certainty is Richard Carless, who was buried at St. Martin's, Birmingham, on the 15th March, 1669-70. There has always been a tradition in the family, unsupported by any direct proof, that this Richard was a brother of the famous Colonel William Carless, the hero of Worcester and Boscobel, and they have always used the remarkable arms granted to him on 21st May, 1658, and which were: Or, on a mount in base, vert, an oak tree proper, over all on a fesse, gules, three regal crowns of the field. Crest: A sword, argent, hilt and pomel or, and a sceptre of the last in saltire, enfiled with an oaken civic crown, vert. Motto: "Subditus fidelis Regis et Regni salus." A curious seal, still preserved in the family, and said to have been given to Colonel Carless by Charles II, is the only corroboration of this relationship. The eldest son of Richard was Samuel Carless, constable of Birmingham in 1686, who retired to Wood's Green, Staffordshire, where he acted as a magistrate. His second son, Joseph (baptised January 24th, 1687-8), purchased Corbyn's Hall, in the parish of Kingswinford, Staffordshire, and made it his residence. He married Mary, daughter of Richard Knight, the well-known ironmaster of Bringwood Forge, Herefordshire, another daughter of whom was married to Abraham Spooner, and by her had his sixth son, Edward, who resided at Bilston. Edward married Elizabeth Tomkys of Nechels, and their only surviving son, William, married (June 10th, 1779) his first cousin, Mary Pratchett of Bilston. William Carless, of The Ravenhurst, Harborne, died on the 24th June, 1787, at the early age of thirty-four, and left the following children:—

1. The Rev. Edward Carless, Incumbent of Wolstanton, Staffordshire, who married Anna Maria, daughter of the Rev. Mark Noble.—2. Elizabeth, married to Thomas Attwood.— 3. Mary Ann, married to John Freeman, father of E. A. Freeman, the historian.—4. Sarah, who died single.

Elizabeth Carless is admitted by all who knew her to have been a lady of great beauty, and she possessed what was then regarded as a considerable fortune for her station in life. At her father's death, her mother removed to Grove House, Harborne, where Thomas Attwood afterwards resided until 1845. The young couple took up their residence at The Larches, Sparkbrook, where they remained for several years.

It was in this year (1806) that Matthias Attwood, the father of Thomas, first acquired possession of The Leasowes, the famous estate of the poet Shenstone, and a property which has probably been as much celebrated in prose and verse as any other in England. For a long period, although of small size and without any costly ornament, it ranked with Hagley and Enville as one of the show places of the neighbourhood. As so many well-known writers, such as R. Dodsley, Hugh Miller, and Elihu Burritt, have employed their pens in describing its beauties, it will not be necessary for me to dwell much upon them. I shall merely note that a full description, with a plan by Dodsley, is to be found at the end of the second volume of Shenstone's works, published in 1764. Whatever may have been the merits or demerits of the Attwoods in other respects, it cannot be claimed for them that they were desirable custodians of The Leasowes, as the place was always neglected during their ownership. On the other hand it must be remembered that they were exceedingly generous in allowing nearly everybody to walk over the grounds, and even to fish in the beautiful waters, a liberality which I understand has not been imitated by their successors. The Leasowes remained in the possession of Matthias Attwood and his descendants down to 1865, when it was purchased by the late Mr. B. Gibbons.

I shall now continue my extracts from the letters of Thomas Attwood.

To Mrs. Attwood, Grove House, Harborne.

The bearer, William Evans, is the man whom I have hired for a servant. 12th June, 1806. T. ATTWOOD.

This was the William Evans who was so faithful and highly valued a servant to T. Attwood for many years, who attended him during the triumphs of 1832, and who is figured behind his carriage in the plate of "The Gathering of the Unions." He left before my time and kept a respectable hotel in Birmingham, but I can well remember him coming to see his old master several times, once at Allesley.

From a letter not dated, but evidently written in the early part of 1807, it appears that Matthias Attwood was already thinking of entering Parliament in that year, although he did not obtain a seat until 1819:—

It is likely that Matthias may not be able to go to Malden, if so I shall come down in a few days. These things never appear in the public papers. They are transacted before a Committee of the House of Commons which you may see appointed in the papers of last Tuesday fortnight. There were three candidates at Malden. The one that was not successful has petitioned against one of the two which were returned on the ground of bribery, which petition has now been before the Committee, I think, fifteen days, and will no doubt succeed. If the Committee determine that the petitioner shall be the sitting member, then there will not be a new election and Matthias has no chance. But if it is determined to have a new election, then Matthias is sure to succeed. The Committee heard all the pleadings last week and intended to have determined to-day, but are prevented by the illness of one of their members. It will pretty certainly be determined to-morrow or the next day, after which if there is no election I shall come to you immediately. If there is an election I shall be detained in London eight days until the return is made, during which time Matthias will be absent from London.

London, 3rd Feb., 1807.

The Malden Committee determined last evening that Western should be the sitting member, consequently there will be no new election there at present. The electors will probably petition against Western, in which case Matthias is sure to come in.

No date (? 1807).

I am under the necessity of going to Hawn immediately to consult with my father about the Worcester Bank and the dissolution of Parliament which took place yesterday. John Richards from Stourbridge dines at Hawn to-day who wishes to be a partner in the Bank at Worcester, and I wish to get to Hawn before he goes this evening or would have sent for you to go with me. I shall certainly return to you to-morrow, and if we should determine to offer ourselves for Stafford or elsewhere I will take care that George shall take you over to Hawn in the gig to-morrow.

Thomas Attwood's eldest son, George de Bosco, was born at The Larches on March 15th, 1808, and privately baptised by the Rev. J. Darwall, Minister of Deritend and Bordesley, on the following day.

I have no letters for 1808, 1809, and 1810.

His second son, Thomas Aurelius, was born at The Larches on the 4th March, 1810, and privately baptised by the clergyman just mentioned on the 11th.

The Larches, Sunday morning (? 1811).

I am glad that my little son Bosco is well. Tell him that I have cut a canal for him and that he may sail boats upon it when he returns. I have also made the pool hold water for him to keep a great monster pike in.

To Mrs. Thomas Attwood, The Leasowes, Birmingham.

There is so much mobbing and rioting going on here that I do not think it proper that I should be absent from Birmingham until it has subsided. The soldiers from the barracks are just now gone to Edgbaston, where the rogues, I am told, are plundering Wheeley and others, and there is no knowing what a parcel of hungry Burdettites may take into their heads. . . .

Thomas Attwood appears to have removed from The Larches to The Crescent, Birmingham, in 1811. I believe that some years afterwards he pulled this house down and erected the one No. 11, which on his death was sold to my wife's uncle, Mr. G. R. Collis, and occupied by him for many years. Mr. Edwards, writing in 1879, says:

"The Crescent at that time was not the woe-begone place it has since become. It was planned on the model of the famous Crescent at Bath, but the plan was never fully carried out. It then was completely outside the town: indeed I have frequently heard the late Mr. Thomas Upfill, who had bought a house there for his own occupation, say that his wife objected to go there to live because it was so far in the country."

I remember hearing Thomas Attwood frequently speak of the extraordinary comet which apparently covered half the heavens in this year, but do not know when it first became visible.

I have now reached the period when my grandfather suddenly appeared as the foremost man in Birmingham, but owing to a paucity of material I am unable to explain how he acquired such great popularity in so short a time. It was, I suppose, in the October of this year (1811) that he, then only twenty-eight years of age, was elected High Bailiff of Birmingham, and he was, I imagine, the youngest chief officer the town has ever had, either before or since, although I believe the present Right Hon. J. Chamberlain was Mayor at a very early age.

The next year, 1812, was an exceedingly busy and important one.

Thomas Attwood threw himself into public matters with the greatest possible spirit, and the objects which chiefly engaged his attention were the revocation of the Orders in Council and the termination of the monopoly of the East India Company. Dr. Langford says:

"On March 4th a meeting was held 'to take into consideration the present state of the manufactures and commerce of the United Kingdom, and the propriety of petitioning both Houses of Parliament to discontinue such parts of the East Indian Charter as exclude British merchants from trading to the East.' Thomas Attwood, Esq., the High Bailiff, opened the business with a long and interesting speech, of which a more than ordinarily full report is given; and the meeting resolved that 'the commercial monopoly of the East India Company must be abolished.'"

I regret that I have no report of the speech here alluded to, which seems to have been his first celebrated one.

In the spring of this year he headed a deputation of merchants and manufacturers who went to London to endeavour to obtain the repeal of the Orders in Council which had suspended British trade with the United States. Mr. Edwards says:

"He was examined by a Committee of the House, and in the course of his examination, which extended over several days, he so clearly and forcibly demonstrated the impolicy of the measures, as to be mainly instrumental in obtaining their repeal. His efforts, however, although successful, were too late to prevent a collision; the declaration of war and the notice that the obnoxious orders were withdrawn crossing each other in mid-ocean."

I now give a few extracts from his letters to my grandmother, which allude to his proceedings in London.

Bedford Coffee House, 4th April, 1812.

We arrived here last night about 5 o'clock and have been very busy to-day in consulting with Lord Valentia and others.

Birmingham, Monday.

I am sorry to say that I cannot come over to Leamington unless Sarah should be very ill indeed, because I am necessitously concerned every moment of the day, and almost of the night, in the agitation of measures of momentous consequence, not only to the country but to myself and my family. I never did, I never will, undertake anything in which I will not succeed, but in addition to my exertions in the East India question, I am now called upon to conduct proceedings relative to the Orders in Council. I will assist my townsmen with my advice in the drawing up of their petitions, etc., but I will not have any concern in the conduct of their future proceedings.

Bedford Coffee House, 10th April, 1812.

We seem to be going on very well, but we have a great deal of work to do, and it must be done if we are to succeed.

Bedford Coffee House, 17th April, 1812.

I am sorry to inform you that of all the members I have yet seen, there is but one that can be called "decent," and that is Huskisson.

Bedford Coffee House, 14th April, 1812.

With regard to your coming to Barming when I come again to London, I will think of it, and will endeavour to accommodate you. I do not know why you should be so anxious to know who is the chairman at our grand meetings unless it is that you expect me to be the chairman. There were however persons much higher in rank and office than myself to whom I very properly yielded, but in return they have done me the honour to make me chairman of their committee of deputies appointed to conduct the negociation with Government, which committee concentrating the intellect and knowledge of the whole body of deputies is I assure you by no means a committee that can be easily rivalled The Lord Provost of Glasgow is the chairman of our grand meetings as you call them. The committee are to have an interview with Mr. Perceval to-morrow, when I doubt not that if he will leave the business to be settled by argument we shall easily substantiate all that we want, viz, an unshackled trade to India and China. In the event of our not being able to convert the Ministers, Mr Canning and Mr. Huskisson will be our leaders in the House of Commons, and we shall have a very hard contest, but shall, I expect, succeed.

To Mrs. Thos. Attwood, The Leasowes

Bedford Coffee House, 24 April, 1812.

Mr Perceval has promised to bring forward his resolutions about the India trade in the beginning of the next week. It is then likely that I shall be at liberty to come down for a week or two, which I shall be very happy to do, but I shall write to you a few days before I leave London. We are going on very well, and I expect shall succeed to the extent of our wishes or nearly so. . . .

I called the other day to see Mr. West's celebrated picture and found it equal to my expectations. There is the picture of a sick child, about as old as Tommy in June last, that would deeply affect any man who ever had a sick child. I had rather perish than ever see Tommy again in a similar situation.

London, 28 April, 1812.

I am very sorry to hear my celebrated speech censured by such competent authorities I had no idea of its ever making quite so much noise in the world, but when I came to London I found it had been in the hands of all the members of the Government, and, as far as I could judge, had reached and affected every political or commercial man in the kingdom. I know Dr. Parr is not a great favourite of yours, but he is such an enthusiastic admirer of me and my speechifying that I think your feelings towards him will be ameliorated. He told Rd. Spooner at the Duke of Norfolk's the other day, speaking of me.—" His name has never been out of my heart, or off my tongue since I read his speech," and bestowed upon me such a host of compliments and praises as would make me as proud as the prettyest of my beauties, were I not proof against all such stuff.

London 30 *April*, 1812.

The business of the Orders in Council is now taken up by the House of Commons so warmly that I expect Ministers will find it necessary to postpone the India question until the next session, and in that case I shall be able to leave London in a few days. Upon the former subject I was examined last night by the House for two or three hours, and other witnesses will be examined every night, I suppose, for a month or two. Such a set of feeble mortals as the members of both Houses are, I did never expect to meet with in this world. The best among them are scarce equal to the worst in Birmingham. In the India question we seem to have gained everything but the China trade, and I have no doubt we shall get that in the end. At any rate we shall never cease our exertions until we do get it. I have been very well ever since I came to London and am so now.

London 2 *May*, 1812.

It appears that the Ministry have at length determined to side with us against the India Co., and are now settling with them, for the Company to possess a monopoly of the article of *Tea* only, leaving everything else open to the country. The Ministry have also determined to put off the India Bill till next session, on account of the Orders in Council, so that I should set off home to-night, but that I have received a summons to attend the House of Lords on Tuesday evening about the Orders in Council. I shall, however, leave London on the Wednesday and reach Birmingham on the Thursday next week, so that I shall be glad if you can come to the Crescent by that day, that is to say if Bosco is well enough.

(No date).

I shall have a young owl come from the Leasowes in a day or two which must be sent to the children.

From a letter addressed by Thomas Attwood to the *Times* on February 5th, 1844, I take the following :—

In the year 1812 I had the honour of several interviews with the late Marquis Wellesley in promoting the abolition of the East India Commercial monopoly. Upon one occasion our discourse turned from Indian affairs to those of Spain and Russia, then pressing with extreme anxiety on the public mind. The Marquis then addressed me in the following words, which I have often had occasion to remember and repeat :—" I saved India, Sir, and my brother will save Spain, if the Ministers will let him; but if they give him a deficient commissariat, and starve him with a miserable economy, he will lose his armies as Burgoyne and Cornwallis did."

CHAPTER III.

Thomas Attwood, High Bailiff of Birmingham—His Great Popularity—The Artisans offer him their Thanks—Revocation of the Orders in Council—Letter of B. Cook—Richard Pratchett—Sir Charles Mordaunt.

THE small number of private letters preserved by Mrs. Attwood do not enable us to form a very clear idea of the important events of this remarkable year, and I am sorry that the few public documents which I have been able to procure do not afford much information to supply the deficiency. No doubt, the evidence of Thomas Attwood before the Committees of both Houses must be in existence somewhere, and the few Birmingham papers for 1812 must contain some valuable facts, but circumstances prevent me from searching the public libraries of that town, and I have hitherto failed to procure the papers elsewhere. This is the more to be regretted as it is evident that the year 1812 was, next to 1831 and 1832, the most interesting in my grandfather's life. In it his talent, his eloquence, his handsome appearance, the bold confidence with which he advocated his opinions, and, above all, the noble unselfishness which made him regard the wrongs of others as his own, seem to have carried by storm the hearts of all, and to have raised him at a bound to a position which few men acquire without a lifetime of painful labour. In 1812 he must have given promise of attaining still greater eminence than it was his lot to acquire twenty years later.

I shall now give a few extracts from Langford's *Century of Birmingham Life*, premising that that work, valuable and painstaking as it undoubtedly is, does but scant justice to Thomas Attwood. The author appears to have relied almost exclusively for his information upon the carefully preserved files of *Aris's Birmingham Gazette*. This paper is the oldest in Birmingham, but it has always been a Conservative organ, and almost entirely devoted to advertisements. Hence its reports of Liberal political triumphs have invariably been meagre and grudging in the extreme. It is true that Thomas Attwood at this time ranked amongst the moderate Liberals, but the boldness and liberality of his views must have been very displeasing to Tories of the old school.

"*Revocation of the Orders in Council*

In 1807 was issued the Order in Council prohibiting all trade between England and the parts occupied by the French. In 1809 further orders were issued which placed still greater restrictions on trade. The early part of 1812 was marked by great disturbances in the manufacturing districts. Mills were burnt, machinery was destroyed, and many murders committed. The merchants and manufacturers agitated for the repeal of the fatal Orders in Council Meetings were held in Birmingham, and very decided resolutions were passed on the subject. The agitation was so far successful that in June the orders were revoked, so far as the U.S. of America were concerned.

The next extract to our mind records a most important event It is the first instance we have of the artisans taking any part in public life—unless we look upon their doings at the riots of 1791 as having a prior claim. This first appearance in public life is honourable to their sense of right, and is an instance of the gratitude which working men have always manifested towards those who have rendered them a service. This report is also noticeable as being the first which we have met containing the name of George Edmonds. It was published in the paper of June 22 :—

" 'At a numerous and respectable Meeting of the Artizans of Birmingham, held pursuant to public advertisement, at the Shakespear Tavern, in this town, this 17th day of June, 1812, "to consider the best Means of expressing their gratitude to those Gentlemen of Birmingham who have so laudably exerted themselves to restore the suspended Trade, and also to those who have so benevolently subscribed to the relief of the Poor of this Town ;"

Mr. John Steer in the chair :

Resolved unanimously,—That they who endeavour to promote the Commercial Prosperity of the Country, upon which its Welfare and Happiness so materially depend, deserve the lasting gratitude of the People

Resolved unanimously,—That we have seen with great satisfaction the laudable exertions of our principal Merchants and Manufacturers to call the attention of Parliament to the present deplorable state of Trade, and the consequent distresses of the labouring Mechanics.

Resolved unanimously,—That being deeply impressed with a sense of our obligations to those our fellow townsmen, we beg them to accept of our most cordial and heartfelt Thanks.

Resolved unanimously,—That in particular we would offer our unfeigned thanks to Thomas Attwood, Esq., High Bailiff of Birmingham, for his invaluable services in this cause ; services which it were needless to recapitulate, as they are without doubt engraven on the Memory of every Mechanic of the town.

Resolved unanimously,—That, as farther expression of our gratitude to Thomas Attwood, Esq., High Bailiff, a subscription be immediately entered into to defray the expence of a Piece of Plate, with a suitable Inscription, to be presented unto him ; and as we consider it desirable to have numerous rather than large subscriptions, that no person be allowed to give more than sixpence.

Resolved unanimously,—That the thanks of this Meeting be given to Thomas Phipson, Esq , Low Bailiff, for his hearty co-operation with his worthy colleague.

Resolved unanimously,—That the especial thanks of this Meeting be given to Richard Spooner, Esq., for the Firmness and Eloquence which he has displayed on various public occasions when the Interests of the Mechanics have been concerned.

Resolved unanimously,—That we should consider ourselves wanting in gratitude did we not embrace the opportunity of expressing our acknowledgments for the very liberal contributions made by the wealthy Inhabitants of this Town for the Relief of the Poor ; and we request them to accept our thanks for their beneficence.

Resolved unanimously,—That the following persons be appointed a Committee to carry the above Resolutions into effect, with power to add to their number as they may think proper :—

John Steer,	William Jennings,	Thomas Taylor,
Joseph Wood,	James Connard,	William Latham,
James Boyce,	Samuel Thorpe,	William Bailey,
John Lane,	Joseph Bower,	William Dent,
Charles Kelk,	William Wight,	Jabez Aston,
John Bourne,	William Cox,	Edward Crowder.
John Hinks,	George Edmonds,	

Resolved unanimously,—That these Resolutions be advertised in such Newspapers as the Committee may think proper.

John Steer, Chairman.

Mr. Steer having left the Chair,

Resolved unanimously,—That the thanks of this Meeting be given to Mr. John Steer, for his able and impartial conduct in the Chair.

George Edmonds.'

Here is the next appearance of our artisans in public life :—

Revocation of the Orders in Council.

July 6, 1812.—The Artizans of this town being informed that Mr. Richard Spooner and Mr. Thomas Potts (two of the deputies sent from hence to procure this important measure) would return from London on Wednesday, they were determined to meet them near the town, and shew them that respect the conduct of the Deputation merited from their townsmen. Accordingly they assembled at the Shakespear Tavern, in New-street, early in the afternoon, and at four o'clock, notwithstanding the heavy rain which fell, and continued almost without intermission during the remainder of the day, they formed in procession, preceded by a band of music playing the loyal national air of 'God save the King,' and paraded through the principal streets, and reached Camp Hill, the spot where it was expected to meet the deputation at about five o'clock. After waiting about half an hour, the approach of the Deputies was announced, and the Committee of Artizans, with their chairman at their head, proceeded to meet them The carriage, which was drawn by four horses adorned with blue ribbons, contained Messrs. Spooner and Potts. The horses were taken off, and the carriage drawn by the multitude, rending the air with their acclamations.

After proceeding in this manner for a few hundred yards, to that part of the road where the Committee of Artizans and the band were endeavouring to press through the crowd, the carriage halted, and the Chairman of the Committee addressed the Deputation in a suitable speech. After the address the procession was formed, and proceeded to the town in the following order :—

PROCESSION.—Joint bands of two regiments of the Warwickshire Local Militia, in full uniform. Flag—'Friends of Commerce.' The Committee of Artizans three abreast. Flag—'Birmingham has done its duty.' Reverse—'Grateful Artizans welcome the Deputation.' The Committee as before. Flag—'Attwood, Phipson, Spooner, Potts, and the Deputation.' The carriage drawn by the populace.

The procession thus formed moved through the principal streets of the town, the windows of which were thronged with inhabitants, who congratulated the deputies as they passed along, and arrived at the Shakespear Tavern about eight o'clock, where the High and Low Bailiff and a number of other gentlemen were assembled to receive them. Mr. Spooner and Mr. Potts severally addressed the persons assembled in animate and appropriate speeches (which we regret our limits will not allow us to insert), at the conclusion of which the immense multitude collected on this joyful occasion quietly and peaceably dispersed

There was great rejoicing in the town over this victory. At a public meeting all those noblemen and gentlemen who had assisted in procuring the revocation of the Orders in Council were warmly thanked. Mr. Brougham was especially singled out 'for the great Zeal, Ability, and Perseverance he had so fully evinced by his unparalleled and successful exertions in obtaining a Revocation of the Orders in Council, and for his truly eloquent appeal to the House of Commons, on the 16th Inst., on Behalf of the Manufacturing and Commercial Interests of the United Kingdom.' On August 1 the triumph was celebrated by a Public Dinner."

Thus far Dr. Langford I think it must have been upon this occasion that my grandfather first became acquainted with Lord Brougham, from whom I shall presently insert several letters, though he does not mention him till some years later.

I now give two letters addressed to Thomas Attwood in the course of 1812:—

"SIR,
Well knowing that you are a true Friend to Commerce and to all Mankind, allow me to hand you the annexed lines, which are due to your merit, and are the production of, Sir,

Your obedt. Servt.,
13th June, 1812.   JOSEPH FAULKNER.

Lines respectfully addressed to Thomas Attwood, Esq., High Bailiff of Birmingham.

Her course restrain'd, bid Commerce wide expand,
And British Genius waft to ev'ry land ,
Her spreading sails, at thy proud wish unfurl'd,
Extend triumphant to the Eastern world !

Relax shall labour, yet awhile to raise
Her voice to thee, in grateful peals of praise.
Thy mind enlighten'd, on the Senate broke,
And Statesmen wonder'd, while an ATTWOOD spoke ;
Who nobly toil'd to serve the poor distress'd,
With all the patriot glowing in his breast ;
Whose tender heart, to each fine feeling true,
Mourn'd those sad scenes which it with pity drew :
That sacred spark, that with our wants began,
Alone exalts and dignifies the man !

The world survey, with philosophic eyes,
And teach the proud—no being to despise,
The various states, at Nature's pow'rful call,
Form one grand union for the good of all."

(Endorsed by T. A., " B. Cook, Summer of 1812.")

"DEAR SIR,
You certainly form too *low an opinion* of that class of mechanics who have determined to hold that meeting we talked about—that they are a race of men who have no sentiments of gratitude—that they are a class of beings incapable of originating sentiments that do honour to the name of man. But that what is admirable must have been taught them, is, what I must assure you, not their character. There are, Sir, in their natures, many of them, germs of noblest ideas. True, they have not been favoured with the education necessary to call forth to life and excellence those sentiments and sensations, but yet—rude and uncouth their appearance, yet this is the outside covering—

'Bright sparkles the diamond within '—

That this idea originated with themselves I can most positively assert to be the case. I am known to thousands of them, and I believe that no other master in town knows anything of the subject, unless it has been since, from their meetings it has got abroad. They did apply to me, but it was after their

. determination was fixed. I might perhaps have dissuaded them from it at the outset, because I do think I possess as much influence as many do over them, but should I have done right to have done so?—No. I was glad to see a spirit of that nature—for the whole mass, thousands, as if they had been touched with the spear of Ithuriel, started up—to men—altho' groaning under oppression—I say started up to men—and were determined to exhibit to the world that in their bosoms dwelt gratitude, the noblest of all the passions that warm the human heart. Could I check such a disposition? could I use my influence (I had none in this matter) to hinder them from showing their gratitude to a man whom all respect, whom they were determined to show to the world they respected, and whom I was convinced merited their respect? No, my dear friend! it is impossible to hinder them meeting in some way or other; and I most solemnly again assert it proceeds from themselves alone, for no master in Birmingham, even to this hour, is privy to it, except as I before stated. There will be no resolution—that the relief was for the mechanics—but the poor—and again, as I appear to know so much about it, you may suppose I have been at the bottom of it all, but had I, I should not think it a dishonour, but I will not so far sink them down in the scale of beings as to take to myself any credit, for none is due, neither will I arrogate to myself the power of stimulating eight to ten thousand men to do an act— which may be blamed by the man whose pride may be hurt that he does not partake of their feelings—but who must confess they are deserving of praise. I am sorry I named the thing to you, for you alone are acquainted with it, before it has in any manner become public. At all events it must now go on. I should not like to discourage, nor would it be right to do so, a sentiment of gratitude from servants to their masters. In *haste*, dear Sir,

Yours truly,

B. COOK."

At the end of May, 1812, the first Royal Mail Coach set out from Birmingham for London, "from the Swan Hotel, at four o'clock, the bells of St. Martin's Church ringing, and thousands of spectators assembled on the occasion, greeting it as it passed with cheering shouts.

"About two o'clock the same day the coach, attended by eight mail guards in full uniform, adorned with blue ribbons, paraded the streets, under the direction of Mr. Hart, stopped at the residences of the High and Low Bailiff, the several banks, and many of the principal inhabitants; the procession closed after it had remained some time at the house of Mr. Pratchett, High Street, where, as at the other resting places, the attendants were liberally supplied with wine, biscuits, sandwiches, &c. The carriage, horses, and harness were in a style of splendour and excellence we had not before witnessed, and reflect great credit upon our spirited townsman, Mr. Dunn; public patronage, we doubt not, will amply repay him and the other Contractors for the expense and risque they have incurred in this attempt to afford greater facilities to the commercial intercourse between this town and the metropolis, both by gaining an additional hour to answer letters by return of post, and enabling the public to insure places in the mail to London, instead of waiting as formerly for a vacancy, the chance of which was always very precarious."

The Mr. Richard Pratchett mentioned in the above extract was the uncle of Mrs. Thomas Attwood, and although only a chemist in High Street, was a man possessing great influence in the municipal and political affairs of Birmingham. As a town-commissioner he was indefatigable in promoting improvements, and we shall see that his energy in this respect was appreciated by his fellow-townsmen. He was an ardent Tory and high churchman, and as such exposed to the satirical wit of the opposite party, who, says Dr. Langford, accused him in rhymes of no very lofty character of a great partiality for expending public money on his own part of the town. The following squibs have been preserved referring to some building operations of his :—

> "To Pratchett, a friend of the true Church !
> A friend ? Aye, he is, and a bold one ;
> Why, he's stopped up a road to the New Church,
> But he's opened all ways to the Old one !"

Another squib of the day was—

> " Sing to the praise of Richard Pratchett,
> A name so great that none can match it."

I find preserved in Mr. Aurelius Attwood's scrap book the following extract from a newspaper which appears to have escaped the notice of Dr. Langford :—

"Birmingham, Oct. 7, 1812.
"At a most numerous and respectable meeting of the Freeholders, Merchants, Manufacturers, and other Inhabitants of the town of Birmingham, duly convened by the High Bailiff, pursuant to the above requisition, and held at the Royal Hotel in Birmingham, on Wednesday, the 7th of October, 1812 :
The High Bailiff in the Chair ;
Resolved, dissentient only four,—
That Sir Charles Mordaunt, Bart., by his great inattention upon various occasions, when applications have been made to him as a Representative of the County of Warwick, on subjects of great commercial importance to this town and neighbourhood, particularly by the indifference which he manifested to the interests of his constituents, when he presented to the House of Commons a Petition from Birmingham against the Orders in Council, bearing

fourteen thousand signatures, and by his non-attendance during the examination of evidence, in support of the allegations contained in that petition, has been guilty of a dereliction of his duty as a Member of Parliament, and has rendered himself unworthy of the confidence of his constituents.

Thomas Attwood, Chairman

The High Bailiff having retired, and Timothy Smith, Esq , being called to the chair,—

Resolved unanimously,—

That the thanks of this Meeting be given to the High Bailiff for his unremitting attention to the best interests of the town, and for the very great impartiality he has evinced this day in the chair.

Resolved,—

That the resolutions of this meeting be printed in such papers as the High Bailiff shall think proper.

Timothy Smith."

Angela (my mother), elder daughter of Thomas Attwood, was born on the 12th of November, 1812, at The Crescent, and was privately baptized by the Rev. J. Darwall on the 10th of December following. Upon the expiration of his year of office, Attwood's partner, Richard Spooner, was elected to succeed him as High Bailiff of Birmingham. The two friends who were to be so remarkably associated together during their long and eventful lives appear, at this time, to have worked together amicably upon all public questions, though, curiously enough, Attwood was *then* the moderate Liberal, and Spooner the Radical.

CHAPTER IV.

Great Speech of Thomas Attwood against the Renewal of the East India Charter.

THOMAS ATTWOOD did not long rest upon the fame he had acquired in 1812. His family now amounted to three, and his domestic expenses must have been heavy and increasing. But public duty was ever uppermost in his mind, and he commenced the year 1813 by a determined onslaught upon that monstrous abuse, the monopoly of the East India Company. He was ably seconded by Richard Spooner, who, as High Bailiff, summoned a meeting of the inhabitants of Birmingham at the Royal Hotel on January 9th, to protest against the renewal of the East India Charter. Here my grandfather delivered a famous speech, of which a full report is fortunately preserved, and as it is the earliest speech of his which I possess, and as Mr. Edwards, an impartial authority who never knew him, calls it "a masterpiece of reasoning, clear and convincing in style and crushing in its denunciations," I propose to reprint it here at length as follows :—

MR. HIGH BAILIFF,

About twelve months ago I had the honour to address this assembly from the Chair which you now fill, with so much credit to yourself, and so much satisfaction to all your townsmen. The subjects which I had then occasion to enlarge upon were the deplorable situation of trade, and the necessity of abolishing the commercial monopoly of the East India Company.

Sir, I revert with agony to the melancholy picture which I was then compelled to draw. Most happy should I be if *truth* had changed the scene, but it is not so, the melancholy picture yet remains—remains with accumulated horrors.

Sir, I will not harrow your soul with a recital of those details, with which my heart is full. I will merely remark, that on whatsoever side I turn my eyes, throughout the whole commercial world, I can perceive nothing but indigence, and indolence, and poverty and despair. If I look to the East, or the West, or the North, or the South, I can see or hear nothing but those terrible and appalling symptoms which precede the moral earthquake, and which threaten, ere long, to burst into such vehemence of action, as may shake the bottommost foundations of society.

Sir, I turn with satisfaction from these painful reflections to the exhilarating spectacle which the report of your Committee exhibits.

A great period is dawning in the history of commerce. Three-fifths of the Globe, which have been *shut* from the beginning of time, shall be *shut no longer.* Commerce, the best friend of man, the parent of all our arts, and all our knowledge, is about to spread her vivifying influence over kingdoms, and empires, and continents, where the foot of an English merchant never trod. The consequences that must result from this great change are not to be measured ; I will assert that its effects, moral, commercial, and political, will be felt by the latest posterity in the remotest corner of the world.

Sir, at the town's meeting to which I have alluded, I ventured to predict that "the public voice would be heard in a way that will never be resisted." My anticipations have been more than confirmed. The United Kingdom rises as one man to vindicate its rights and interests, which have so long been trampled on with impunity. England, Scotland, and Ireland, in this great work, seem animated by *one* soul. All parties and all distinctions are levelled here. The rich and the poor, the Pittite and the Foxite, like their great leaders in the tomb, forget *here* all the jealousies and all the animosities of their lives. All descriptions of men unite together with one heart and one hand, and with a voice of thunder, which echoes round the land, demand the destruction of this hateful monopoly.

In the midst of this general expression of the public mind, and of the public determination, I cannot but regret that the City of London, outraging every principle of public justice, and reason, and patriotism, has been induced to come forward and petition Parliament in DEFENCE of the *East India Monopoly!!!*

Some individuals there, it seems, are apprehensive, that the *destruction of Monopoly will endanger the safety of our empire in the East, and diminish the trade of the Port of London !!* As if *Monopoly* could possibly be necessary to *Empire !* As if it could possibly be otherwise than *injurious* to the moral and physical strength of all nations, and of all sovereigns ! As if the odium and disgrace of contending with merchants in the sale of £500,000 per annum of merchandise, could possibly be necessary to the strength of an empire supported by two hundred thousand bayonets, by the British Navy, and by a permanent revenue of SIXTEEN MILLIONS sterling per annum, equal as it is in value, to at least *sixty millions* sterling per annum in England !!! To what absurdities will not the human passions stoop, when common sense refuses its assistance? But is the sale of £500,000 per annum of merchandise all the benefit we derive from our "*Empire in the East ?*" *It is.* And is it for this that twenty thousand British soldiers are at this moment rotting in the plains of Bengal, when their bayonets are so much wanted at the foot of the Pyrenees? *It is.*

And how does the question of the port of London stand? A man, ignorant almost of the first principles of commerce, if he have the natural intellects of a man, will instantly perceive, that the trade of the port of London will be far greater under an open trade than it ever has been, or ever can be, under a Monopoly.

If commerce is to be beneficial, if commerce is to be extensive, it must be unshackled. Commerce operates upon too weighty, too tender interests to endure the least restraint; and like the fabulous Deity of the poets,

" . . . . . . At sight of *legal* ties,
Spreads its light wings, and in a moment flies."

As well might you controul the sun-beams, and command them to operate here, and to operate there. You may obstruct, but you cannot controul them. So it is with the operations of commerce. Give commerce its natural liberty, and it will find scope for its exertions in every corner of the world. But if you attempt to controul it, you obstruct it, you *destroy* it. Better for commerce is the curse of an enemy, than the blessing of such a protection as this.

Nature, Mr. High Bailiff, presents obstacles enough to the operations of commerce, without our calling in the aid of *legal* obstacles, a thousand times stronger than all which nature ever made. How shall commerce, whose very essence is liberty, endure to be confined to this port, or to that port, still less to be subjected to the controul of a body of twenty-four individuals, who have *great* and *permanent interest in its destruction?*

Interested in its destruction they certainly are, for the Act of 1793 has condemned and compelled the Court of Directors to seek no profits in commerce, but to waste all its profits in PATRONAGE. Thus their own commerce can never flourish, and is it likely that they will permit the commerce of their rivals to flourish, when subjected to their own controul, as it must be, if confined to the port of London? By the Act of 1793 the Proprietors of East India Stock are *virtually insured* in a dividend of ten and a half per cent., whatever may be their *losses !!!* And by the same Act they are *precluded* from sharing more than ten and a half per cent., whatever may be their *profits !!!*

Thus is the genius of the Company changed. Thus are the Proprietors and the Court of Directors banded together, in a mutual imposition upon the public. The Proprietors are bribed to neglect the conduct of the Directors, and of their own concerns, and the Directors are compelled to seek a reward for their labours, *not* in the legitimate dividends upon their *two thousand pounds stock*, but in lavishing their profits and their immense revenues among their *friends and dependents*, and in a sacrifice of the best interests of India and of England. Sir, I shall for ever lament that this Act of Parliament should exist a memorial among the statutes of England. I shall for ever lament that the public should so long have endured an Act of Parliament which has cancelled the labours and concentrated the errors of two hundred years, which, whilst it has on the one hand deprived the people of the natural right which they possess of trading to all countries at peace with England, and compelled them to pay a monopoly price for East India goods, as the *purchase money of their own injuries*, has, on the other hand, retarded the civilization of the Eastern world, and deprived England of *all* commerce, and of all revenue, the only legitimate ends of *all* empire.

If ever the Court of Directors shall forget the nature of man, and the first principles of human action, if ever they shall consent to *save for the public* what they now *waste for themselves*, and from *that saving* shall be able to repay a debt of THIRTY-FIVE MILLIONS STERLING, and to PAY OFF TWELVE MILLIONS OF THE NATIONAL DEBT ; they will *then*, and not till *then*, have the power of *encreasing* the dividend of ten and a half per cent , by dividing among the proprietors ONE SIXTH PART ONLY of the surplus profits of the Company.

By the Act of 1793, the other FIVE SIXTHS of the surplus profits, after having *effected* all these *uneffectible* objects, will then go to the public, in aid of the CONSOLIDATED FUND.

It is thus that the Court of Directors are condemned to neglect all commerce, which to *them* and to the *Proprietors is*, and *can be, no gain*, and are compelled to waste all their immense revenues among their friends and dependents.

Their genius is PATRONAGE and not GAIN. Profit and loss are both the same to them. Money *borrowed*, is to them the very same as money *gained*. Money *expended* in paying off a just debt is to them just as much money *lost* as if it had been thrown into the sea !!!

Well may the East India Company apply to Parliament in one year for TWO MILLIONS and a HALF of the public money, and in the next year for THREE MILLIONS and a HALF of the public money. All the money in England, all the wealth and the strength of England would not long be sufficient to prop such a system as this.

Under these circumstances, can it be doubted that although justice be done, and the trade of the East be thrown open ; can it for a moment be expected that the trade of London will not materially encrease ?

The whole exports of the East India Company to all their immense continents and oceans amount now to only one million, six hundred thousand per annum, rather less than is annually exported to the negroes of Jamaica.

About one-half of this sum may consist of stores for their civil and military establishments, and that part of the exports will still be confined to London. *Nothing* will be taken from London to which London has a *right;* but in the vast encrease of commerce which must take place, from a change in this dreadful system, London will necessarily be benefited in common with the rest of the empire. London will still be the great emporium of Indian commerce, and will still contain a large proportion of the commercial intellect and capital, and a still larger proportion of the Eastern knowledge of the country. These advantages will still ensure to London a full share in all the benefits to be derived from the freedom of Eastern commerce.

In the import of Tea, probably, some diminution may be expected to take place in London ; but that diminution will be amply counterbalanced by the tenfold increase which *must* take place in the export and import of all other articles. Why, Mr. High Bailiff, but two centuries ago, in the reign of the First James, the whole commerce of England was *confined to the port of London, by monopolies and exclusive companies*, and yet that commerce was *nothing*, and London itself was little better than a village ; but no sooner were these *odious* monopolies destroyed, than the commerce of England encreased a thousandfold, and *London itself*, instead of being injured by the rivalship of the out-ports, suddenly grew up into a mighty city, and has now evidently derived more benefit from the DESTRUCTION OF ITS OWN MONOPOLIES THAN EVEN THE OUT-PORTS THEMSELVES.

See also in your own experience, what a prodigious effect the energies of the human mind have, when operating *freely* and without *controul*. Call to mind, Sir, that since the beginning of the late unfortunate war, England has sustained the loss of the French, and the Dutch, and the German, and the Spanish, and the Italian, and the Baltic, and the Turkish, and the American trades; *all* and *each* of which were very considerable, and then constituted the whole commerce of England, and yet, the energies of the human mind remaining, and *having a free operation, new sources of trade, external and internal,* have been developed, and the commerce of England, though suffering most severely, is not totally destroyed !

What would have been our situation had the commerce of England been confined to the port of London, and to an exclusive company?

Certainly, we should have had no foreign commerce at all.

London *itself* would have been reduced to a desert

But let these events turn out how they will, they cannot possibly affect the bearings of this great question. Will those individuals in the City of London, who are foremost to raise their voices against corruption and sinecure places, and undue advantages, now stand forward in defence of a monopoly, more unjust, more unnatural, more injurious, and more odious than all? Will they, when they think their own interests may be a little concerned, have the audacity to obtrude those paltry interests as an obstacle to justice, and the great interests of the British people? No—this can never be. The City of London might as well claim a monopoly of the American trade, or of the West India trade, or of all trade, as of the East India trade. The City of London has been beguiled by the East India Company, but the City of London will quickly awake to a sense of justice, and honour, and true interest, and duty.

And what interest has the East India Company had in thus influencing the City of London? Not an interest in the legitimate profits of commerce, which neither their *constitution*, nor *habits*, as a commercial company, nor the *very Charter* under which they exist, will permit them to obtain or enjoy; but a baleful interest, confined to the Court of Directors, and their immediate friends and connexions, in all manner of *patronage*, and in all manner of *waste* and *profusion*. This baleful interest it is which foresees its own destruction in the destruction of Monopoly, and whilst struggling almost in the agonies of death, grasps at any, the smallest assistance which the weakest and basest passions of humanity can give. This baleful interest well foresees, that when the commerce of the East is opened, very soon will the revenues of India be made available for the service of England ; very soon will a great part of that SIXTEEN MILLIONS per annum, which is now squandered away in almost a PEACE ESTABLISHMENT, be deposited annually in the treasury of England. Then, indeed, will our empire in the East be of some use to England—hitherto that empire, bought and maintained by the fleets and armies of England, has never yet contributed one single shilling to the finances or the commerce of England ; but, on the contrary, has been a heavy burthen upon its finances, and a still heavier burthen upon its commerce.

Unless this system can be *changed*, OUR EMPIRE IN THE EAST MUST BE GIVEN UP. The wealth and the strength of England can no longer be lavished in defence of an interest *hostile* to the interest of the people. Unless the trade of the East can be encreased TENFOLD—unless the revenues of India can be remitted to England, as those of Mexico are transmitted to Spain, our empire in the East *must* be given up. All the energies of the British mind, all our fleets, and all our armies, must be concentrated in Europe, for the defence of the British Isles.

But some members of the Court of Directors have said that the East India Company does now contribute to our finances, because the people of England pay annually to Government a duty of three millions sterling upon teas imported by the Company!

If the absurdity of this assumption is not its own refutation, it is sufficient to remark, that if the Americans, or any private merchants, had imported these teas, instead of the East India Company, the duty would have amounted to FIVE MILLIONS STERLING per annum, instead of THREE, and that without at all encreasing the price of tea!! In proof of this, it is only necessary to observe, that on an average of ten years (I have the documents before me), the American merchants, after allowing for the difference of duties in the two countries, have sold teas in the United States at *eighty-five per cent. lower than the East India Company have sold them in London;* which might, of course, have been *added* to the present duty of ninety-six per cent. without in the smallest degree increasing the selling price.

It has also been said, that it is unjust and cruel to deprive the East India Company of their monopoly, after having suffered them to possess it for two hundred years, and after having suffered them to build palaces, and ships like palaces, for the purposes of their trade.

It is true they have possessed their monopoly for two hundred years, which at first was granted only for *fifteen* years, and that they obtained the early renewals of their Charter by all manner of corruption and bribery. But, Sir, I am not able to comprehend by what possible means they can have obtained the latter renewals.

But whilst I am speaking upon this part of my subject, I will take the liberty, Mr. High Bailiff, to read a few extracts from Dr. Smollett, in order that we may be put well upon our guard against the diabolical weapons with which we may have to contend. Sir, in the year 1693, in the reign of William and Mary, Dr. Smollett reports that—

[Mr. Attwood here read an extract detailing the extreme venality and corruption of many statesmen with reference to the renewal of the East India Company's Charter in 1693.]

Mark, Mr High Bailiff, the conduct of the Duke of Leeds. Mark also the conduct of those Members of the House of Commons whose tongues became mute, and whose patriotism withered away, under the accursed influence of gold. The pen of the historian has unravelled a mystery which might have perplexed the weak heads of the politicians of 1693.

Here, Mr. High Bailiff, is the true use of history. Let us profit by the lessons of our fathers. Let us *mark* the conduct of any individual in England who shall dare to advocate this absurd, this unjust, this odious and ruinous monopoly.

But let these latter renewals have been obtained how they will, it can make no difference in the present instance. It is sufficient for us to know that their lease expires on the FIRST DAY OF MARCH, 1814, and it is our duty to take care that it shall *not* again be renewed. This argument of ships and palaces is by no means new—it is the common argument of lessees, from the East India Company to the lowest tenant of the poorest cottage in England. They have all laid out vast sums of money in erections, or repairs, or improvements of one kind or other, and they can all produce a long string of reasoning why they should have their leases renewed.

If the landlords of England would be guided by their tenants, it would not be long before their tenants would have a much better property in their estates than they would have themselves, and this has been the case with the Court of Directors. They have obtained renewals of their lease for two hundred years, and during all that time there has not been the shadow of advantage to any party but themselves. The reciprocity, as an Irishman would say, has been *all on one side*. They have not paid *any rent*. They have not carried on any trade that is worth naming—they have scarce even paid a moderate dividend to their own proprietors; on the contrary, they have been a perpetual drain upon the wealth of their country, and they are still under the necessity of applying almost every Session to Parliament for pecuniary assistance in order to save them from their creditors.

What have we to do with their ships and palaces? They have built them at their own risk, and not at ours, and yet we have generously granted them in the late Session of Parliament a sum of money more than sufficient to purchase all the ships which they possess.

They impose enormous expences upon the nation, in defending their provinces with British fleets and armies, and in selling their goods at a monopoly price. They *shut out* their countrymen from THREE-FIFTHS OF THE GLOBE; and what little trade they formerly did carry on, has been suffered to fall into decay, and yet under these circumstances, they have the audacity to apply to Parliament for a renewal of their lease!! Fortunately, the eyes of the country are opened—they will never have their lease renewed—they will, in future, be relieved from all care and anxiety respecting their monopoly—and will henceforth be at full liberty to devote all their time, and all their immense abilities, to the improvement of their revenues, and the amelioration of their territories.

Sir, I understand that it is yet contended, that the trade of the East does not admit of extension, because "the experiment has already been tried, and has failed," because by the Act of 1793 a certain quantity of tonnage on board the ships of the Company is allowed to the *private* traders, not more than one-third of which tonnage has ever been occupied. I have heard it said, that we ought to show some argument *why* this tonnage has *not* been occupied. Sir, I tell you, that since the Act of 1793 the Court of Directors have formed a Committee of their number, which they denominate their "*Secret* Committee for the prevention of the growth of *private trade!!*" Is not *this* argument enough? Sir, I tell you that the private trade is subjected to the controul of the East India Company!!! Is not *this* argument enough?

Sir, I tell you that they have succeeded in creating a HOST of *difficulties* and *obstructions*, which nothing but the *fiat* of Omnipotence can overcome!!!

Why should I enter into particulars? Sir, if you would send an agent or go yourself to the East, you must obtain a *license* from the Court of Directors. Sir, if you would ship goods to the East, you must apply to the Court of Directors in *August* for the tonnage which you may want in the *March* following. If you receive goods from the East these goods must be carried in the *Company's ships*, deposited *in the Company's warehouses*, and *sold* just at the *time* that may suit the interests or caprice of the Court of Directors!!! You know yourself, Sir, an instance wherein a private merchant was *compelled* to keep £10,000 worth of East India goods in the warehouses of the Company, full 8 months before he was allowed to sell them!!—But it is ridiculous to enumerate cases of this nature, it is sufficient to assert that the difficulties of entering into the Eastern trade are so great that it is not possible to enter into it at all; and if you should happen to find yourself engaged in it, by any strange concourse of circumstances, it is not possible that you should be able to carry it on.

Sir, I have heard it said, that neither Mr. Pitt nor Mr. Fox, nor the late Lord Melville, ever thought of discontinuing the East India Monopoly, I will not suffer this argument to go unanswered. Why, Sir, an eminent Statesman, illustrious for his character and his talents, and by no means remarkable for the freedom of his political sentiments, assured me himself, that the political weight of the East India Company was so great, that neither Mr. Pitt, nor Mr. Fox, nor any Minister, however strong, could go to the East India Company, and say, "Gentlemen, you must give up your Monopoly," without almost the *certainty of losing his place*. Thus, Mr. High Bailiff, we account, and pretty satisfactorily, for the opinions of Mr. Pitt and of Mr. Fox, and of that *true Scot*, my Lord Melville, of whose memory I will say no more than that this *precious* Act of Parliament ought to be engraven on his tomb, as a *memento* to all *single-hearted* Statesmen.

See here, Mr. High Bailiff, the fatal secret confirmed [Mr. Attwood here read the following extracts, from the *Globe* and the *Courier*]:—

"It would thus appear, that the existence of the present Ministry and the renewal of the East India Charter are incompatible. The settlement of that Charter displaced one Ministry, and from the present temper of the two parties it may possibly displace another."—*Globe*, January 6.

"The Ministers can have no possible interest upon this subject, but that of the general welfare of the country; it is impossible they should have :—but their antagonists, we see, are already warning them of the fate that attended Mr. Fox's Ministry, in 1783. 'Their existence,' says one Paper, 'and the renewal of the Charter, seem to be incompatible with each other.' Another Paper more awfully predicts, 'that the *dissolution* of the East India Company could not take place without bringing with it a *national bankruptcy*, and that must be followed by a *military despotism*?' We make these quotations to shew that attempts are likely to be made to browbeat and intimidate the Government."—*Courier*, January 6.

At this very moment the East India Company are attempting to INTIMIDATE THE MINISTERS OF THE KING! As if the King's Ministers were their Ministers; as if England itself was their property! No sooner do the King's Ministers declare their intention of supporting the rights and interests of the people, than the East India Company presents itself before them with a dagger in one hand and a Charter in the other, and allows to the Ministers no other alternative between the desertion of their public duty and the loss of their places. Is this the boasted patriotism of the Court of Directors? Is it not rather the infernal policy which they imbibe from the slaves over whom they domineer? Let them learn that it is for us to threaten—US THE PEOPLE, by whom they are created, in whom they exist, and FOR whom they only live and move, and have a being.—(*Hear, hear.*)

Let them learn that they are not a Sovereign Power, but merely a creature of the British Legislature, created for limited purposes, and for a limited period; in short, that they are merely the Lieutenants of the King, appointed by Act of Parliament to manage the affairs of India, as those of Ireland are managed by his Lieutenant there.

Sir, I hold in my hands some documents which have been published, apparently, by the Court of Directors, and circulated with considerable assiduity. It is true, the arguments in these documents, which purport to be "Correspondence and Proceedings in the negociation for a renewal of the East India Company's Charter," are not calculated to have much effect upon the public mind; but they are advanced with a degree of confidence strongly indicative of the influence which the human passions have in perverting and depraving the human reason.

In these Documents the Court of Directors affect to take a slight, but very imperfect review of those clear and indubitable arguments, which require the *total* abolition of their commercial usurpations. They then significantly ask, "are these arguments of weight and value sufficient to overturn the present long established system of the Company, and to endanger so large a portion of the public revenue?" as if the first of these objects was a matter of any importance at all, and as if the other could possibly be injured by the enlargement of trade.

Sir, I answer that "the long established system of the Company" is radically wrong, and must be overturned; and so far from injuring the public revenue, I have already shewn by a comparison of the prices of tea in England and America, that the Revenue might be nearly doubled by the opening of the trade, without at all encreasing the prices at which tea is now sold.

The Court of Directors appear to bend their principal exertions against the opening of the out-ports. They contend that smuggling will be carried on at the out-ports, to the injury of the Revenue

Certainly it will to a certain extent, but never to such an extent as it is, and always must be in the port of London, where the long and narrow navigation of the Thames, and the immense and corrupt population, furnish numberless facilities for smuggling, which are not to be found in any other port.

But, Sir, I will answer this objection in the words of a nobleman, whose intellect appears to me to do honour to his rank, I mean my Lord Talbot. "Whether smuggling will be greater at the out-ports or not is no consideration of yours. If the present mode of collecting the Revenue at the out-ports is not efficient, it is the duty of the Commissioners of the Customs to make it so The course of justice and of public interest is not to be impeded because the Custom House may be deficient in the discharge of its duties."

If the Directors should succeed in confining the trade to the port of London, and to their own warehouses and management, they would certainly succeed to a great extent in depressing and destroying the trade, and from thence they would hereafter draw arguments to shew that "the Trade of the East does not admit of extension." Their "secret Committee" for the prevention of the growth of private Trade would here have a grand opening for the exertion of its faculties and utilities, and for the exercise of all those jealous and malignant passions which commercial rivalship never fails to engender when important interests are endangered.

The Directors seem to assume that it is the merchants of the out-ports only who have petitioned against their monopoly They contend that their opponents are "interested persons who are desirous to transfer the present Trade of the Company from London to the out-ports." No, Sir, it is not the merchants of the out-ports, but the manufacturers of the United Kingdom, who refuse to have the trade of the East confined to the Port of London, who demand that all the commercial energies of the empire shall have a free competition in the Eastern Seas. The collision of these energies is vital to the prosperity of commerce. It will *create* a trade in the wildernesses of South America, or New Holland, greater than monopoly can ever discover in the populous Regions of the East Will the Court of Directors say that these millions of manufacturers are interested in the desire to partake of their present trade? Those millions of manufacturers know that if the trade of the East is to be confined to the Port of London it will never reach one half the amount to which it will extend when thrown open to the out-ports, and if it is to be confined to the warehouses, and subjected to the controul of the East India Company, they also know that it will never reach one tenth of that amount.

The Court of Directors complain that it is the single object of the extension of Commerce which is our "governing principle." Sir, I should be glad to learn what other possible principle of public utility there can be in preserving our Empire in the East, unless, indeed, the Revenue of that Empire can be remitted into the British Treasury They have the singular presumption to charge the people of the United Kingdom with "most extravagant expectation and unbounded pretension," because they express a determination to cultivate their own estate! What would be thought of a tenant who should hold to his landlord such language as this?

We only want our own—we want nothing from them—let them keep their trade if they can, but let them not keep a monopoly! Let them have every right and privilege that we have, but let them not have all rights and all privileges, and leave us none. They complain that they have created the Eastern trade at a great risque and expence, and that now we propose to take it from them. No such thing—let them keep their trade—we want it not; if they have created it, let them keep it ; but they have not created their Monopoly—we gave them that, and we will never give it them again ; and are we to be charged with "extravagant expectation and unbounded pretension" because we refuse to give up our own?

We do not even claim to be placed upon an equal footing with the Court of Directors If we embark in the Eastern trade, we are willing that our whole property shall pay the forfeit of our errors, whilst all their private property is protected by the law from injury!

Take this protection away—take away the assistance of the British Government—let the private fortunes of the Proprietors of the East India stock be made responsible for the debts of the Company, and not a single proprietor would be left in six months. The "Ladies and Gentlemen" of the East India Company, who are denominated "Merchants of England trading to the East," would instantly throw up their shares, and gladly save the whole of their fortunes at the expence of their East India Stock! Is it not enough that these mimic "merchants of England" should be protected from those weighty responsibilities to which all their countrymen are liable, and which are so necessary in forming the character of efficient merchants ; and must they also claim to be nursed in swaddling clothes, and fed, like an Eastern idol, at the expence of the rights and interests of their country? The Directors complain that if the trade is opened to the out-ports, they shall be "unable to pay their dividends, and shall be obliged to apply to Parliament for assistance." Why let them apply to Parliament for assistance, and if Parliament is mad, let it grant them assistance. The whole amount of their dividend amounts but to £600,000. What is an additional £600,000 per annum for Parliament to grant them, when we consider the millions and millions that Parliament has already granted them, and is still annually in the habit of granting them? They tell us, too, that there will be no encrease of trade. Why, Sir, there will be more trade to the Western Coast of South America, which is now shut by their Monopoly, than is now carried on to all the countries of the East Is it not true that our exports to the settlements of Buenos Ayres and Rio Janeiro amounted in the last year to four millions sterling? What will our exports amount to when Chili and Peru are opened? —and yet Chili and Peru, and fifty other nations and empires, are now shut by the East India Company!! In the documents to which I have alluded, the Court of Directors ring melancholy changes upon a series of questions, too futile to be noticed. They ask, "Could it be reckoned upon that the Company's goods would be sold as they have hitherto been? How could the currency of the Company's affairs be preserved? How could they pay for exports to India? How could they maintain their ships and transport troops and stores? What must become of their wharfs and warehouses? Where would be the benefit to the nation by the change? Would it be really any accession of benefit to the Empire at large? Would it be possible to prevent (that bugbear) an uncontrouled intercourse with the East?" They then gravely remark, "These questions, to add no more, ought to be very clearly and satisfactorily answered before so great a change is attempted, before an order of things that has subsisted so long, and done so well, is subverted or destroyed." Such are the questions with which the Court of Directors would support their Monopoly. Certainly the cause of truth has but little to fear from ten thousand such questions as these.

They boast of their capital of *sixteen millions* employed in trade, and of the facilities which their experience and power and influence give them What then have they to fear from private merchants, adventuring with caution and anxiety into unknown regions? But, Sir, I will venture to assert, that they have scarce a single million employed in trade. They purchase all their British goods at six, twelve, and eighteen months credit, and they sell all their Eastern produce for ready money, and they even receive the Government duties upon their goods, which too often lie in their hands to a large amount. Where then is the room for this immense capital to be employed in effecting a return of two or three millions per annum? If they have all this capital and all these facilities for trade, what have they to fear? They will still retain their trade. The private merchants will be driven into the deserts of Africa, and will seek there a refuge from such formidable competitors.

But the calculation which the Directors make of their capital is curious, and deserves notice:—They say, "the Company's capital stock of six millions, at the price at which many of the proprietors purchased, will amount to £10,800,000 (which observe is reckoning £4,800,000 too much).

	10,800,000
Capital in warehouses	1,000,000
Capital in ships	3,800,000
Capital in Docks	400,000
	£16,000,000

Thus they have the happy faculty of doubling their capital by merely reckoning it twice over. They reckon it first advanced, and then laid out. These "merchants of England" pay six millions into their trade—they then lay it out in ships and warehouses, and call it Sixteen Millions!! Why the infant at a village school would not be guilty of such a calculation as this, and yet, Sir, I presume that this is by no means an unfair specimen of the general calculations, and general commercial abilities of the East India Company.

Sir, I bear no hostility against the Court of Directors, whom I believe to be highly respectable men, but it is against the system under which they act, that all my hostility is directed. I will never rest until that system is overthrown.

Sir, there are a few other arguments made use of by the Court of Directors, which I will trespass a few moments longer upon your attention to notice. They contend that their empire is an "empire of opinion." In the absence of all rational arguments they conjure up phantoms to alarm us! They tell us that their empire is supported upon such Braminical principles, that it must not be touched by our unhallowed hands, that it is composed of such frail and brittle materials, that if we but touch it, it will shiver to pieces!!

And is it with such nursery stories as these that an enlightened nation is to be insulted? Is it with such a "raw-head and bloody-bones" as this that the merchants of England are to be frightened out of their senses?

Sir, it is not an "empire of opinion"—it is an empire of the bayonet. It is an empire of knowledge, and wealth, and power, over ignorance, and poverty, and weakness It is like the Roman empire, or the Saracen empire. It is like the empire of Aurengzebe, or that of William the Conqueror. It is like the Russian empire, where 7000 slaves govern 40 millions of slaves, or like the French empire, where one man tyrannizes over a hundred millions of souls! The authority which a colonel holds over his regiment, or that of a captain over his ship, is much of the same description. Let justice be done —let severity be tempered with lenity, and there is no danger of mutiny. The combination of individuals against a supreme authority is so exceedingly difficult, and exposed to such certain detection, and to such dreadful punishments, that the human mind shrinks with apprehension, and refuses to harbour the thought. In short, Sir, our empire in the East is built on those eternal and immutable principles, which are the strong foundations of all Governments, and which never fail to support a Government until a Government fails to support itself. Mr. High Bailiff, a lawyer pleading a bad cause should have a good memory. See into what inconsistencies the Court of Directors fall. In one page of this little work, they first tell us that our Empire is an "*Empire of opinion;*" that the number of Europeans in India is so small, that they are every moment in danger of being eaten up by the natives!! In the very next page they tell us of the "danger of colonization." They tell us, that if we but encrease the number of those unfortunate Europeans, our empire in the East *is lost for ever.* And what is the danger of colonization? Why, Sir, there are in India a hundred millions of human beings, who, from the day they leave their mother's breast, to the day they enter into the grave, never taste any other food than rice and salt! Will English labourers emigrate for this? The wages of labour in India are only two-pence per day, equal to about eight-pence per day in England. Will English labourers emigrate for this? Most certainly not. Then how shall India be colonized? It is utterly impossible that the number of the European population can ever reach one-twentieth part of the native population. But "America was colonized, and afterwards deserted us." Sir, there is no analogy at all between the situations of America and of India. When America was colonized, there were a thousand leagues of the best land in the world inhabited only by wild beasts! This fertile land offered *there* to the colonist, without rent, without taxes, almost without labour, all the blessings of life. The earth presented abundantly spontaneous fruits, and there was no hand to gather them. How different was this from the situation of India. There the very Earth is *saturated* with population. There every channel through which labour might support existence, is filled to excess! All the individuals that can ever emigrate to India are merchants, and their agents. It is not in the course of nature that an European population should arise from them sufficiently strong to endanger the British power. If the European population should be encreased in India, it will be much the better for England. Will it not encrease the progress of civilisation and knowledge? Will it not strengthen and confirm the British connexion? Will it not strengthen the British Government itself, surrounded as it is by hosts of native powers, hostile in habits, in laws, and in religion? But, Sir, some of them say that "although it is true we shall not be able to colonize India, yet we shall *sow dissention* amongst the *native powers*, that we shall *stimulate* them to *insurrection* against the British Government, that we shall *turn our unnatural daggers against our country!*" What an *Eastern* notion is this? How little can this man know of the English merchant or the *English heart*. Sir, the very thought is not to be endured.

But, see, again, how the Court of Directors blunder on, like a blind man in a crowd; in one page they *censure* the stupid policy of the Chinese Government, in confining all the trade of Europe to one port in their vast Empire; and in the next they strongly recommend the same policy in England. Nay, Sir, in the year 1793 the Court of Directors put the country to an immense expense, in sending an Embassy to China, in order to induce the Chinese to *open their* ports to *our* trade, and they are now labouring night and day in *patriotic* endeavours to *shut* the ports of England to *their* trade, excepting only the port of London!

They tell us also that we shall *lose* the *China trade*. They tell us that the great Emperor of China is such a wonderful personage, that if we but *look at him he will devour us alive!!* Why, let him devour us alive, what is that to them, we want not their protection. And yet this wonderful personage *admits* the Americans and the Portuguese, and *every nation of Europe* into his Port of Canton, as freely as he admits the East India Company. Does he devour them alive? Does he drive them into the sea? Why should he *devour us?* Is it possible that he can entertain so great a jealousy of feeble, unconnected merchants as he does and *must* entertain against the mighty East India Company, that has conquered Hindostan and *possesses the power of conquering China?*

Sir, it is not possible. There is no shadow of danger of the Chinese refusing to trade with us. There is no possible danger that can arise from colonization, or from the free residence of British merchants in the East. All these are phantoms created to alarm us. But look them in the face, they vanish in an instant.

But the Court of Directors tell us that they "have freeholds in India, which they have the same right to, as to their estates in England." I never heard that there was such a thing as a freehold in India, unless indeed the Directors may mean that *small* freehold which we must all of us come to some time, and which I am sure I am not disposed to dispute with any unfortunate gentleman of the East India Company who may occupy *six feet* of land in Calcutta!

Let the settlements of India be their freeholds, which is utter nonsense to suppose, yet still it can make no difference to *us*. *We* want not their freeholds; *we* only demand permission to breathe the air of heaven, and to walk the public streets, and the king's high roads. Will they call *these* their *freeholds* too? Will they erect barriers of *cobwebs* across the streets and high roads of India, and forbid their countrymen to pass? Suppose Birmingham is *my* freehold, have *I therefore* a right to block up the *public* streets, and to *imprison* every *Englishman* who shall presume to believe that he has a right *to walk along the king's highway?*

But some of these gentlemen tell us that their monopoly was granted by Queen Elizabeth "*in perpetuity.*" Sir, there is no power in England that can grant a Monopoly *in perpetuity*. The power that creates can always destroy. Let it *be* a Monopoly "*in perpetuity;*" let their charter be as immeasurable as are their own desires, let it occupy three fifths of TIME as well as of SPACE, yet still shall the British Parliament *destroy it*. But, Sir, Queen Elizabeth had no more right to grant their Monopoly than *I have*. She *sold* their Monopoly, and a hundred other most infamous monopolies, that, if they had not been destroyed by Parliament, would have *destroyed their country*, or as Mr. Hume most justly expresses it, "*would have reduced England to a desert.*"

But, Sir, I am sick of the *arguments* of the Court of Directors. From *them* we have nothing to fear. Let us look to their *political influence*. That influence presses like a mill-stone upon the neck of the Government. The rooted prejudices of some, and the strong interests of others, bind them to support the Company, and in some instances even to resist the evidence of their senses, and *believe* that the continuance of this ruinous and monstrous system is *beneficial* to the country. There is nothing too absurd for the human mind to believe when strongly biassed by its own interest. But all these rooted prejudices, and all these strong and delusive interests, shall fall before the will of the people. The Ministers of the King are the friends of the people, but if the British Ministers should be overpowered by the weight of the East India Company, the British Parliament shall do us justice. That Parliament emanates from the people. That Parliament will never desert the people.

Sir, I will trespass no longer upon your attention. What are our opponents? Four and twenty individuals, and a few hundreds of *jobbers* and *contractors*. What are we? THE UNIVERSAL BRITISH NATION.

Why should our interests be sacrificed to the East India Company? There is not a single argument which they have brought forward, but was formerly brought forward in defence of all those other infamous Monopolies, which once cursed and disgraced our country! If the East India Company are to have a Monopoly of the *China* trade, why not give them a Monopoly of the *Corn* trade? Why not give them a Monopoly upon *Bread?* and thus expose the *whole of their countrymen to perish under their remorseless cupidity!!* Mr. High Bailiff, it MUST NOT BE. Standing as we do, Sir, on the eternal grounds of justice and of reason, and supported as we are by the whole population of the country, I say, Sir, that if we fail, we OUGHT to fail, we OUGHT to be *trod into the dust*. But, Sir, we shall not fail, seeing our road as *we see it*, and feeling our strength as *we feel it*, what shall resist us?

It is true the Parliament of 1693 did desert the interests of the people. But the Parliament of the present day is not the Parliament of 1693. The necessities of the present day are not the superfluities of 1693. THE PEOPLE might *then* have been trifled with, but WOE UNTO THE MEN THAT SHALL TRIFLE WITH THE PEOPLE NOW!! (*Loud bursts of applause.*)

Woe unto the advocates of the East India Company, if they shall evince themselves the friends of Monopoly and not the friends of the People, for MONOPOLY SHALL COME TO AN END, BUT JUSTICE IS ETERNAL.—(*Loud cheers and thunders of applause.*)

I have copied this speech at length (with the exception of an extract from Smollett), because it appears to me to be not only a fine specimen of eloquence, but also an interesting historical document. Many distinguished authors have written upon Indian affairs, but I very much question whether, amongst all their bulky volumes, there is to be found a clearer and more convincing exposition of the relations between the East India Company and the public, than that which is contained in this comparatively brief utterance. The Monopoly of the East India Company has, with many other abuses, long passed away, and we can scarcely realise the condition of things when it existed, but surely some credit is due to one of its earliest, ablest, and most patriotic opponents. Upon this occasion the Opposition were not successful in preventing the renewal of the Company's Charter, but they were enabled to deprive it of some of its most objectionable features.

CHAPTER V.

Letters from London in 1813—Mr. Attwood is presented with a Silver Cup by the Artisans of Birmingham—Extraordinary Character of the Presentation—Letters to 1815—"The Remedy, or Thoughts on the present Distresses"—Letter to Lord Liverpool—Mr. Brougham presents Petition, drawn up by Attwood, from 17,000 Inhabitants of Birmingham—Cobbett's Remarks—Correspondence with Brougham and Arthur Young.

MR. ATTWOOD went up to London in February, 1813. Here are some extracts from his letters to his wife:—

Bedford Coffee House, 11 Feby., 1813.
. . . I write to inform you, agreeably to your request, that I am arrived here in perfect safety and health, after having a solitary journey nearly the whole of the way. . . .

Bedford Coffee House, Saturday evening.
I am going to dine with my friend the Duke on Monday, and as he has given me a pretty general invitation, I think also to dine with him to-morrow. I meet many members of both Houses there whom I have thus an opportunity of instructing.

Bedford Coffee House, 15th Feby., 1813.
My business is going on, I think, pretty well, although I clearly see that the Opposition members, who were formerly our friends when the Ministers were our enemies, are now seeking reasons and arguments to enable them to turn against the Ministers and the Country. This conduct appears very base in private life, but things are different among public men. I am, however, in strong hopes that our case will be found so clear, as to render it impossible for our friends to desert us without the certainty of losing their characters. This alone it is that binds public men to any principles of political integrity. I think, however, that Wilberforce and Babington and a few others are exceptions to this rule. They seem to act a little from principle or conscience. . . . I afterwards dined with the Duke, and am going to dine with him again to-day. He is generally considered a person of immoral character, but if he ever was so he is not so now, but on the contrary converses as rigidly and religiously as Wilberforce himself. He is a person of a very superior mind and also of a good disposition.

Bedford Coffee House, 17th Feby., 1813
I have seen Woovey and his mother, who are both pretty well, and Woovey reads as well as if he had been at Lancaster's school for 12 months. My father has a bad cold. . . .

E

The "Woovey" here mentioned for the first time, was Matthias Wolverley Attwood, only child of Matthias Attwood, junior, and afterwards M.P. for Greenwich.

Bedford Coffee House, Wednesday.

I rather think to come down for a week or two in a few days in order to arrange my business with Fereday, and there is not just now anything very particular going on in the India business. When we see the plan that the Ministers will propose in opposition to the Company, we shall then know what ground to take. I cannot give you any information respecting the Princess of Wales any more than that I believe that a Bill of Divorce will soon be brought forward.

Bedford Coffee House, 27 Feby., 1813.

I have been to-day to hear Mr. Hunt and Mr. Cobbett plead for themselves in the petition against the Bristol election. Hunt is certainly a clever man, and acts entirely without counsel.

Harborne, Sunday (no date).

Mr. and Mrs. R. Spooner intend to come to the Crescent on Wednesday at 5 o'clock. Your uncle is here. He is very well and says 200 people dined at the Pitt dinner yesterday.

Christ Church, Birmingham, which was erected at a vast expense, but is now generally considered a very ugly building, was consecrated by the Bishop of Lichfield in July, this year. It was, apparently, the first "Free Church" in the town, and matters connected with it are frequently alluded to in Mr. Attwood's letters.

On October the 4th appeared the following advertisement of the artisans:—

"*Birmingham, October* 1, 1813.—We, the undersigned, the Committee of Artizans appointed to carry into effect the resolutions of a meeting held at the Shakespear Tavern, on Wednesday, the 17th of June, 1812, do most respectfully request the Artizans of Birmingham to meet on Wednesday next, at Ten o'clock in the forenoon, at the Shakespear Tavern, for the purpose of receiving the report of our proceedings.

John Steer,	William Wight,	William Hartshorn,
Joseph Wood,	William Cox,	William Stevens,
James Boyce,	George Edmonds,	William Greenway,
John Lane,	Thomas Taylor,	Thomas Hooper,
Charles Kelk,	William Latham,	Joseph Holliman,
John Hinks,	William Bailey,	J. Berresford,
William Jennings,	Jabez Aston,	William Humpage,
Thomas Thorp,	Edward Crowder,	William Dent,
James Connard,	J. Faulkner,	John Sturges.
J. Bower,		

SILVER CUP PRESENTED.

The Committee intend to dine together at the Shakespear Tavern after the Business of the Meeting is over. Such friends as are disposed to honour them with their company may be supplied with tickets at the Bar of the Shakespear. Tickets at three shillings each. Dinner on the Table at Four o'clock."

The meeting was held, says Dr. Langford, and the presentation made on October 6th, and the whole proceedings passed off with great credit to all concerned.

This is the brief report of the ceremony:—

"*October* 9, 1813.—Wednesday, being the anniversary of the birth of our late worthy and public-spirited High Bailiff, Thomas Attwood, Esq., was fixed upon by the Artizans of this town to present that true friend of British Commerce with a Silver Cup, of the value of 200 guineas, as a grateful testimony for the zeal and indefatigable exertions with which he originated, and, in a great measure, assisted in, the destruction of the East India Monopoly, as well as his many other public services. The bells of both churches announced the ceremony with complimentary peals due to so interesting an occurrence."

I am sorry that no better report of this presentation is accessible to me. Mr. Edwards informs us that it took place at Beardsworth's Repository, and that as there was then no modeller in Birmingham capable of carrying out the design of the cup, Mr. Samuel Lines, who had designed it, himself undertook and successfully completed the task. An engraving of the cup was published with a description reprinted from the *Midland Chronicle* of October 9th, 1813, which I copy here:—

"This elegant piece of workmanship is richly adorned with designs in *bas-relief*, indicative of the circumstances which called for the grateful expression.

On the lid is therefore placed an animated personification of *Commerce*, with a joyous and satisfied countenance, seated among bales and packages of merchandize; her raised hand supports the national flag, intimating the necessity of trade to our existence as a people; at her feet is inverted a *cornucopia* pouring forth the riches attendant on successful adventure; close to her crouches the British Lion, his head raised in an attitude of watchfulness and circumspection, prompt to observe and to oppose any attempts to infringe on our commercial rights.

The body of the cup is with great taste formed to represent the prow of a merchant vessel; the head is characteristically adorned with the received personification of the Genius of our Island.

>   Of famed Britannia are the gallant crew,
>   And from that isle, her name the vessel drew.—*Falconer*.

In her hand *Britannia* displays a coronal wreath of laurel, the well-earned meed of those whose exertions extend the commerce of their country.

Favorable *Neptune* in his car drawn by *Hippocampi* rides the waves which wash the vessel's side, vigilant to defend his charge from harm, anxious to promote the advancement of Navigation and Commerce.

Behind the car of *Neptune* is placed a shield emblazoning the arms of Mr. Attwood; above with outstretched wings and elevated head rises an eagle, whose imposing and determined aspect expresses the motto beneath, '*Possunt quia posse videntur.*'

The remaining compartment is occupied by the following inscription, encircled by a wreath of laurel, and enriched with aquatic foliage :—

PRESENTED

By the ARTIZANS of BIRMINGHAM, as a memorial of their Gratitude,

TO

THOMAS ATTWOOD, ESQ.

(*High Bailiff*, A.D. 1812)

For his constant attention to their Interests, and for his well-directed zeal to support and extend the Commerce of the Country.

The stem and foot are also highly embossed; the latter in particular, with an elegant assemblage of Acanthus leaves. W. H. S.

The Designs and Models in wax were furnished by Mr. Lines, except the handles which were produced by Mr. Thornton, who also modelled the foot from Mr. Lines's Design. The execution of the work in silver was entrusted to Mr. Thornton, who has acquitted himself to the entire satisfaction of his employers.

The weight of the whole is 128 ounces. The value is estimated at 200 guineas."

This cup is now in the possession of Mr. Llewellyn Attwood, of Wandsworth, grandson of Thomas Attwood, and makes but an insignificant appearance when compared with showy modern testimonials, but it is not its intrinsic value which makes it an object of interest of almost an unique kind. It is said that by far the greater portion of its value was subscribed in single pennies, and its presentation marks, I think, an epoch in the history of the country. It was the very first occasion (certainly in Birmingham, most probably in England) upon which such a testimonial was originated and carried out by *working men alone*. Not a single gentleman or master manufacturer had anything whatever to do with it. It marks the era (whether for good or evil who shall venture to prophesy in face of the wild theories now being broached?) when the workmen of this country first determined to submit no longer blindly to the guidance of their superiors, but to take their part in the politics of the country. Every one must admit that their first appearance on the political arena was highly honourable to them, and showed that they possessed both intelligence and gratitude. For these reasons Thomas Attwood afterwards marked Wednesday, October 6th, 1813, as one of the four great days of his life, and, as I well remember, when a feeble old man, bowed down by sickness, sorrow, and disappointment, he always regarded the cup with affection as a memento of the brilliant anticipations of his youth.

This was the year of Vittoria and Leipsic, but very slender allusions to the great victories of the day are to be found amongst Mr. Attwood's papers. He never allowed himself to be so dazzled by military glory as to forget the distress of the people, and so long as misery and want existed he could not make himself happy with rejoicings and illuminations.

From October, 1813, to April, 1815, I am again compelled to pass over Mr. Attwood's life without mentioning a single fact. I cannot explain why, after having made his *début* in public life so successfully, he should, in the year 1814, have relapsed entirely into obscurity. Such, however, appears to have been the case, for I have not seen any document, either public or private, relating to that year. Very possibly his expenses during 1812 and 1813 may have necessitated retrenchment and economy, and he certainly appears to have lived closely at home during the whole of the period mentioned. In the spring of 1815 I again meet with his letters to his wife, and make the following extracts from them :—

Piazza Coffee House, Covent Garden, Wednesday.
Our cause seems to wear rather a favourable aspect, and I expect we shall either obtain our own terms or else compel the Committee to leave our land out of their Bill.

Piazza Coffee House, 18th April, 1815.
We are going on well in our business, but what with the mutual restlessness of both parties we get on but slowly. However I expect we shall compel them to agree to our views.

Piazza Coffee House, 23rd April.
I find that we shall certainly succeed in our opposition to the Worcester Bill, and I therefore expect every day that the Canal Company will agree to our terms.

[Was this the time when the canal embankment, which so effectually spoiled the beauties of Shenstone's paradise, was first proposed to be carried across The Leasowes?]

My dear Love, the anniversary of our marriage approaches. Nine short years have changed the fate of nations, but have made no change in us. My heart still swells with the same sentiments to you, with which it was agitated when I first saw you,—those high and romantic principles which used to shake my nerves and confound my senses, when wandering over the fields at Harborne or seated under the cherry tree at Hawn. Your father died when married 9 years. I pray to God that many 9 years may yet pass over our heads before that painful hour arrives, which sooner or later must separate us, I hope, to unite for ever. I am very sorry to hear that Mr. Freeman is ill again. When I saw him last I strongly advised him to make some compromise with his brothers or with the Dudleys in order to enable him to reside frequently at the Sea and to enjoy that change of air and exercise which seem to me absolutely necessary for his health.

Piazza Coffee House, Covent Garden.
14 April, 1815.

I have received my dear Bosco's letter and I want to receive one from my dear Tommy. I love them very much, and I hope they will always be good—Little Angela must be good too. . . .

I called upon John Bradley, but he was not at home; his wife is no better. I have not many opportunities of calling upon any one, being seldom unattended by two or three persons, and not having any time to spare unless in the evenings, when I have also generally many persons dining with me, such as Shirley, &c. I expect to succeed in my object, and in that case shall probably return in a few days, but I will write to you a day or two before. There is no mobbing going on, but everybody is very much dissatisfied at the escape of Buonaparte. I have myself no doubt that he will soon succeed in putting down Europe, unless we put him down whilst we can. . . . Remember me to all my good friends at Brewood.

The next paper is to me more characteristic of Thomas Attwood than any of his famous political utterances. I have no doubt that it was written to amuse his children who accompanied him on the trip alluded to. He was very fond of stocking ponds with fish and of watching their growth, and was never weary of telling stories to children about monster pike. It is—

An account of small pike turned into the pools at Middleton Hall on the 28th June, 1815.

In the Lane Pool, near Hay Green	10	Pike
In the Pool adjoining the above about 4 feet distant, on the other side of the hedge	10	do.
In the small Pool in the same field as the last, being on the left hand of the gate as you go into the field	5	do.

MIDDLETON HALL.

In the very small pit in the lane nearly opposite the Lane Pool, being on the right hand of the gate as you enter into the road up the meadows. Scarce any water in it and full of grass	2	Pike
In the round pool at the bottom of the first meadow, near the gate on the left hand as you enter into the road up the meadows	15	do.
In the Meadow Pool	20	do.
In a small pitt just opposite Wagstaffs, between the Meadow Pool and the round pool, being in the field below the Windmill field. N.B.—Of these 5, 2 were 6 oz. each, and the other 3 of the usual size, viz., 3 or 4 inches long	5	do.
In the Windmill Pool	20	do.
In the Horse Pool	30	do.
In the small pitt on the right hand, about 1 field from the Horse Pool, as you go along the foredraught, being close to the Green Lane and, I think, at the top of the little Lady field	5	do.
In the Lady field Pool	10	do.
In the Stone Pool	20	do.
In the long pitt on the right hand of the Upper Deans, being divided into two small pitts which seem to hold water. In the lower turned 5, and in the upper 4, making 9. This pitt, or these two pitts, are not situate in the field which has the road in it, but in the right hand field and on the right of that	9	do.
In the very long pitt in the Scoring fields, just above where the Reservoir is to extend, and which seems an excellent pitt, being divided, as it were, by grass only into 3 parts, in one of which I turned 6, and in the two other 4 each, say in all 14	14	do.
In the farthermost pool, a good one, at the very end of the farm beyond Green's	6	do.
Total 181, turned up 28 June, 1815	181	Pike

I suppose it was about this time that Matthias Attwood, sen., first acquired possession of Middleton Hall, an estate a few miles from Birmingham. It was one of the Attwood estates which I never saw, but I have heard that the house was ancient and interesting, and I remember seeing at the Priory two cannon balls which had been found in its walls during some repairs, and were supposed to have been shot there in the time of the civil war.

To Mrs. Attwood, Wolstanton Vicarage, near Newcastle, Staffordshire.

Birmingham, 17 *July,* 1815.

Whilst you are at Wolstanton with your uncle, I wish you would take an opportunity of speaking to Mr. Carless about the partition deed of the surface land at Parkfields. That deed still wants his signature, and Gem tells me he has forgotten everything about it. The fact is, however, as your uncle knows, that the partition was finally agreed upon with Mrs. Carless and settled before the granting of Fereday's lease, who now rents 75 acres under a lease from the family, and 25 acres under a lease from me. The mineral property upon the whole 100 acres, however, remains undivided, and I should not much mind about the surface, but that I have let a lease of only 21 years upon my 25 acres, whilst the family have let a lease of 40 years upon the other 75 acres. Now Fereday will have worked out the whole of his mines in 3 or 4 years, and the lower mines, too, if sold, will be worked out before the end of my lease of 21 years, and this shortness of my lease I calculate to be worth perhaps £1,000 to me.

This letter refers to the estate of Parkfields, which was purchased by Edward Sheldon in 1645, or 1652. From him it passed through the Tomkyses to the Carlesses, and at this date Mrs. Thomas Attwood was one of its owners, though I think it must have been sold not long after.

Birmingham, July 22, 1815.

I suppose you have got the newspaper informing us of Buonaparte's surrender. We shall, no doubt, treat him well and give him his liberty as soon as it is safe to do so. Our little children are all well and good. I begin to think I shall submit to your advice in sending them to school, but I am anxious to avoid the contagion of unworthy principles, and to retard the development of those passions which must soon carry agitation and misery into their hearts. Let those passions sleep as long as possible, and when they awake to their work of ruin, let them find matured minds to contend with, let them find prudence and pride and avarice, their strongest opponents, too deeply fixed for the whirlwinds to uproot them.

In after life, Thomas Attwood appears to have changed his opinions respecting Buonaparte, for I remember him saying that the sending of the great man to St. Helena was the only thing the allies could have done with safety to themselves. It was in this year, Mr. Edwards informs us, that he first began to publish upon the currency, and he wrote something upon the same subject every year for the five-and-twenty years following. I am sorry that I understand nothing whatever about the currency question, for it was the central pivot upon which the whole of my grandfather's life turned. Even the great reform of Parliament was to him but a secondary question in comparison, and if he could have prevailed upon any Government to adopt his monetary views he never would have joined the ranks of the reformers. For many years he had deeply studied the question of the national distress, which had become almost unbearable since the conclusion of the war, and he now felt firmly persuaded that he had discovered a remedy for it. No man ever lived who was more keenly sensible to the sufferings of mankind, or more earnest in his attempts to relieve them, and he could not forbear from pressing his views upon every one, whether willing or unwilling to listen. Hence he acquired the reputation of a "currency bore" amongst the ignorant, the selfish, and the careless. In the course of this memoir we shall see that many famous men of both parties agreed with his peculiar ideas on this subject, but his great opponent, Sir Robert Peel, ultimately gained the victory, and in 1819 succeeded in passing, by an unanimous vote of both Houses, what Mr. Attwood considered that atrocious and detestable Bill commonly known as "Peel's Bill," and which he supposed to have been the cause of more misery, suffering, and oppression than any other legislative enactment whatever. Feeling this most deeply, he could not help saying so, and hence he was often betrayed into language most unacceptable to those in high office. The opinions which he adopted at this time he never swerved from, although he knew that they were distasteful to a majority of both Houses and both parties, and that by abandoning or concealing them he might have raised himself to wealth and power.

The earliest currency pamphlet by Thomas Attwood which I have been able to procure is dated July 3rd, 1816, although it is evidently a reprint, and he alludes in it to earlier publications. It is entitled *The Remedy, or Thoughts on the Present Distresses*. In it, after having powerfully set forth the distressed state of the nation, he proposes that Government should proceed to remedy it by the issue of a loan of £20,000,000 in bank-notes. Twenty-seven years afterwards this pamphlet was ably reviewed in a work called *The Gemini Letters*, published in 1844, and written by two authors who were personally unacquainted with Mr. Attwood. From this work I shall make an extract as follows:—

"'*The Government have limited our means of producing and consuming; for by limiting the amount of our money they have limited our means of exchanging commodities, and this gives the limit to consumption, and the limit to consumption gives the limit to production.*' This was the starting point with the Birmingham Economists, and first and foremost of these Economists stands THOMAS ATTWOOD. The first work which Mr. Attwood published was for the purpose of showing the terrible effects of depreciating property by limiting the amount of money, and also for the purpose of showing the 'Remedy' for the great evils which had already been produced. The pamphlet to which we shall first direct the attention of our readers was published seven-and-twenty years ago. At this period the Bank had begun silently to make preparations for the altered state of things which the close of the war, and the expressed determination of the Money Power to fall back upon a high gold standard, seemed to indicate as necessary. The first steps in the way to the depreciation of property caused two hundred and forty banks to stop payment. A cry was raised against country bank paper. The country bankers, who were in reality the victims of the blunders of the Government, were pointed at as the authors of all the mischief, and were thus made the scapegoats of ignorant and designing legislators. It was in the face of this outcry that Mr. Attwood boldly entered the field, and, without faltering, told the Government and the nation that the only proper 'Remedy' for the disasters under which the country was then labouring was the issuing of more paper. That the Government would, notwithstanding the distress and misery which had attended the first restrictions of the currency, permit the Money Power to have their way, he did not contemplate; there was so much absurdity on the face of the thing, that when it was urged by some parties that the 'Remedy' which he proposed would retard the return to the payment in specie, he would not condescend to answer the objection further than by remarking, 'that in the weighty circumstances in which the country was placed, to represent the payment in specie as an object at all, was perfectly drivelling.' In his second edition of the same pamphlet, he adds, that 'the great part of the national debt, and nearly the whole of the private debts of the country, have been contracted in banknotes. They have been contracted in paper currency since the passing of the Bank Restriction Act. To volunteer the repayment of these debts in specie is an act of needless liberality, the absurdity of which is only to be equalled by its difficulty.'"

After giving a long extract from *The Remedy,* "Gemini" conclude thus:—

"The distinguishing characteristic of the economy advocated by Mr. Attwood is this—he regards all other interests as little in comparison with the interests of the producing classes. He would give freedom to industry by adapting the medium of exchange to its wants, and not tie down all trade and commerce to a standard which every day becomes more inefficient, and by this means allow one interest to reap the profit of all our exertions. The absurd and ruinous position the nation is placed in by all prices being regulated by the standard of £3 17s. 10½d. cannot be repeated too often. The mere preparation for returning to this standard broke the fortunes and hearts of thousands. Mr. Attwood, after having summed up the evils of those terrible times, most energetically and feelingly asks, 'Shall we sit down patiently, whilst an apoplexy has struck the circulation of the country, or shall we make an effort to relieve it? Shall we see our palaces desolate, our lands uncultivated, and our labourers unemployed? Shall we see our merchants bankrupt, our manufacturers insolvent, and our mechanics begging their bread? Shall we see hope disappointed, and industry unrewarded? Shall we see the national debt doubled, and the honest debtor compelled to repay twice what he borrowed once? In short, shall we see all the property, and all the active and vital energies of the country laid prostrate at the feet of the Moneyed Interest? Or, shall we use the reason which GOD has given us, and by one slight movement of the nation, one easy, harmless exertion, shake off this ideal pressure, this nightmare of the mind, that paralyses the sinews of our strength, and weighs heavier upon our hearts than all the terrors of Napoleon's sword?'"

I presume that Mr. Attwood forwarded a copy of *The Remedy* with the following letter to Lord Liverpool, then Prime Minister:—

Birmingham, 30 *May,* 1816.

MY LORD,

From the notice which your Lordship has condescended to take of some former communications, I am encouraged to solicit your Lordship's perusal of the enclosed papers.

Placed in the midst of a great mechanical population, and deriving in some degree peculiar means of information from my habits of life, I must rely upon your Lordship's candour and upon the urgent importance of the subject for an apology for my thus intruding upon your Lordship's attention.

I am fully convinced that unless some great public measure is adopted for the purpose of giving temporary employment to the Mechanical and Agricultural population, the system of riot and plunder will inevitably continue and extend; and although it may be arrested for a while by military force, yet I much fear that on the expected rise of the prices of agricultural produce (which your Lordship is aware will naturally take place *before* any great improvement can take place in the employment of the Agricultural or Mechanical labourers), it may encrease to such a degree as may seriously endanger the peace and safety of the Country.

I speak within bounds when I assure your Lordship that the Colliers, Ironworkers, Gun Smiths, and Nailers of this neighbourhood have not one half employment. The Inhabitants of the Town are rapidly falling into the same situation, on account of the total stagnation of the foreign trade which supported them last year. The mind of the whole population is in a state of ferment, and your Lordship must not be surprized to hear of serious commotions breaking out among them, which are the more to be feared in this place on account of the facility of obtaining Fire Arms and other offensive weapons, which might enable the insurgents to get possession of the Arms of the Local Militia, and of the Depôts at Weedon and Derby, before any effectual forces could be brought against them.

An occurrence of this kind, serious at all times, could not be contemplated without grief and alarm at the present period, when the whole of the Agricultural and Mechanical labourers throughout the Country are agitated, gloomy and discontented, and rife for commotion and change.

I am, my Lord,
Your Lordship's humble & obedt. Servant,
THOMAS ATTWOOD.
The Earl of Liverpool.

Edward Marcus, the third son of Thomas Attwood (who inherited no inconsiderable share of his father's ability, but whom constant illness and suffering relegated to a life of obscurity), was born on the 13th of June, 1816, at the old Crescent House, and was baptised by the Rev. John Darwall on the 11th of July following.

Mr. Attwood does not appear to have been much away from home during the year 1816, but he evidently went up to London once, as the following extract shows:—

Grace Church St., Monday (July).
I like the baby very much, but he is, of course, of but little consequence as yet. When he grows big, I have no doubt that he will be as valuable as the others. If you like, you may baptise him by the name of "Edward Marcus," but otherwise, I would have you wait until I return. I will not have him christened "Matthias," it is such a monstrous ugly name.

I have only one other letter for this year, referring solely to domestic matters, dated November 25th, 1816, and addressed to his wife at Corngreaves House.

In the course of the year 1817 he published at London a pamphlet called *Prosperity Restored, or Reflections on the Cause of the Public Distresses and on the only means of relieving them.* This may perhaps have been a second or third edition of the *Remedy.* He also published—*A Letter to the Right Honourable Nicholas Vansittart on the Creation of Money and on its action upon National Prosperity.* Birmingham, May 19th, 1817.

The year was gloomy and turbulent, and the sufferings of the masses almost unbearable. On the 28th of January the Prince

Regent was assailed and grossly insulted by the populace, and riots, treasonable meetings, suspension of the *habeas corpus*, and prosecutions for treason and libel, followed each other in quick succession. Whether rightly or wrongly, Mr. Attwood felt persuaded that he knew how to remedy this deplorable state of affairs, which he considered to arise entirely from monetary causes, and on the 10th of January, 1817, " with about 17,000 of his distressed fellow-townsmen," he forwarded to the House of Commons a petition for its relief, which was presented by Mr. Brougham, afterwards the famous chancellor. I think it worth while to copy this petition, which clearly shows us that whatever distress may exist *now*, it is nothing when compared to that which existed *then*. Mr. Attwood appears to have drawn it up, and the style seems to resemble his. It runs as follows :—

We, the undersigned inhabitants of the town of Birmingham, beg leave to approach your honourable House, and to inform you of our forlorn and miserable situation.

Accustomed from our earliest infancy to habits of continual labour, we have never been forward to obtrude our humble interests upon public attention, but we have always placed confidence in the wisdom and justice of parliament, and of our country ; nor should we now have been induced to prefer our complaints, but that our misery is greater than we can bear, and we are compelled to make known our distresses to your honourable House.

We are in distress, and in our misery we call upon our country for relief.

We ask no more than your honourable House will acknowledge that good citizens have a right to expect. We ask no favour. We only ask to have it placed in our power to earn an honest bread by honest labour. We only ask to be permitted to give to our country the benefit of our labour, and to receive in exchange the scanty comforts necessary for the support of life. Our wants are only food and clothing and shelter from the elements. Never before have we known the time when the labour of an Englishman could not procure him such humble comforts as these ; nor can we now believe that his labour is of less value than formerly. In all former times the labour of an Englishman could produce a sufficient quantity of the good things of life, not only for his own maintenance, but to provide an ample remuneration to his country and to his employers. And we presume to believe, that the labour of an Englishman is still competent to produce a far greater quantity of the good things of life than his humble maintenance requires. But some cause which we cannot understand, has deprived industry of its reward, and has left us without employment and without bread, and almost without hope. We have no longer any demand for our labour, nor any bread for our families. Our life has become useless to our country and burthensome to ourselves. It would be better for us to die than to live, for then we should hear no more the cries of our children. Our hearts would no longer be wounded by the sight of sufferings which we indeed share, but which we cannot relieve.

We implore your honourable House not to misunderstand the expression of those bitter sufferings which we endure. Hunger and poverty and distress have indeed changed all things around us, but they have not changed us. They have not changed that devoted loyalty which as good subjects we feel towards our King, nor that true English spirit which binds us to the constitution, and to your honourable House.

Many of us have not had any kind of employment for many months, and few of us have more than two or three days work per week, at reduced wages. The little property which we possessed in household furniture and effects, and the small hard-earned accumulations of years of industry and care, have been consumed in the purchase of food, and we are now under the necessity of supporting our existence by a miserable dependence on parochial charity, or by soliciting casual relief from persons scarcely less distressed than ourselves.

In the midst of these painful sufferings and privations, our friends and neighbours tell us that we must wait and hope for better times. We beg leave to inform your honourable House that we have waited until our patience is quite exhausted; for whilst we wait, we die.

Upon all former occasions of distress in any branch of trade, it was always found that some other channels of industry existed, through which the honest labourer could obtain his bread; but now we find all other descriptions of labourers equally distressed with ourselves. A general calamity has fallen upon the whole nation and has crushed the happiness of all. We would indeed indulge the hope that our sufferings are peculiar to ourselves, and may have been occasioned by the cessation of the war expenditure among us; but on whatsoever side we turn our eyes, if we look to Manchester or to Glasgow, to the crowded city or the peaceful village, from one extremity of our country to the other, we can perceive nothing but an universal scene of poverty and distress. The sighs and the tears, and the convulsive efforts of suffering millions, too plainly convince us, that some general and universal cause must have operated in producing such general and universal misery.

We implore your honourable House to remove that cause, whatever it may be.

And we cannot but think that your honourable House can remove it. Or if its roots are so deeply hidden that no human wisdom can discover them, or so strongly fixed that no human strength can remove them, we must then consider our sufferings as a visitation from Almighty God, to which we must dutifully bend; but in that case, we entreat that your honourable House will adopt proper measures for the whole nation to humble itself in mortification and prayer, in order to propitiate the Divine justice, and avert those heavy calamities which afflict us.

But we cannot but think that these calamities originate in natural causes, which it is in the power of human wisdom to discover and to remove.

We cannot but think that in a great nation like this, the means of existence must exist for all.

We cannot but think that in a country abounding with every blessing, and with every production of agricultural and mechanical industry, some means may be devised by which the blessings of Providence may be distributed and enjoyed, by which the productive powers of industry may again be brought into action, and the honest laborer may again be enabled to earn an honest bread by the sweat of his brow. We humbly pray that your honorable House will take into consideration our distressed condition, and adopt such measures as in your wisdom may be deemed necessary for the relief of ourselves and of our suffering country, and as in duty bound we shall ever pray, &c., &c.

These representations appear to have had some effect on the Government, for in his *Register* of April 25th, 1835, Cobbett informs us:—

"The year 1818 was a most prosperous year for farmers, the crop was large, the summer fine, and at the suggestion of Matthias Attwood (I believe it was) Vansittart had caused bales of paper-money to be poured out, as a *remedy* (now mark what I say) as a *remedy against the workings of those evil-minded and designing men, who were urging the people on for parliamentary reform.* A pamphlet, in a quarto form, urged the necessity of putting out paper in great quantities, in order to cause the working people to have employment, and to take them out of the hands of designing and evil-minded men who were pushing them on to demand parliamentary reform. A copy of this pamphlet was brought to me in the month of February, 1817, accompanied with an assurance that Mr. Matthias Attwood was the author of it, which I believed at the time, and which I believe still; imputing no blame, but very great error, to the author. . . ."

I have never seen a copy of this pamphlet, and think it possible that Cobbett may have confounded the two brothers Matthias and Thomas, as has been done by Alison and other historians. This, however, is the earliest public mention of Matthias Attwood, junior, that I have met with. The brothers agreed through life upon the currency question, though they unfortunately differed upon so many others. Here is Thomas Attwood's correspondence for 1817:—

"*Thomas Attwood, Esq., Birmingham.*
32, *Sackville St., March* 6, 1817.

"DEAR SIR,—As I think your 'Prosperity Restored' is a Work of much importance to the Public, I was very sorry to hear from my friend Lord Egremont that having sent to the Bookseller to purchase a copy, his messenger was told that the sale was stopped by the Author's order—What can this mean? I beg that you will take your pen, though but for a moment, and explain what appears to be so strange. Excuse this liberty, and believe me to remain with great Regard, Dear Sir, your obliged Humble Servant,

ARTH. YOUNG."

"*T. Attwood, Esq., Birmingham.*

London, Monday (April 14, 1817).

"My dear Sir,—I have received your distressing letter and I do assure you I feel most deeply for the calamitous state of things which it refers to. The admirable conduct of the poor suffering people of Birmingham renders their case still more touching. What can be done for their relief it is difficult to devise—but an immediate attention to their case is indispensable. I shall be present to support their petition to the best of my ability. Be pleased to send it at your convenience. The illness of the Speaker is to prevent us from doing any business for the whole of this week and, it is even supposed, a part of the next. So you may keep the petition for signatures till next Wednesday Sennight. I am, ever yrs. most truly,

H. BROUGHAM."

"*London, April* 22, 1817.

"My dear Sir,—I have received your letter and it is truly afflicting, for much as I feel with you the necessity of something being done, I fear it will be infinitely difficult to devise the means. However, the first step to be taken is to interest the H. of C., and I shall try to do so by following the judicious course of your letters and indeed of the petition itself. I consider politics or party as wholly out of the question, and nothing could more tend towards preventing their interference than your permitting me to cite a part of your letter. Pray tell me by return of post how you feel on this, and

believe me ever yrs.,

H. BROUGHAM."

"*Bradfield Hall, Sepr.* 22, 1817.

"Dear Sir,—It would occupy too much of this paper to detail the causes of my long silence after receiving your most interesting favor, the information of which was to me so very valuable. I had read articles in newspapers—but I know too well the doubtfulness of their authority to place any reliance on it—it is highly satisfactory to me therefore to have your authority for the reviving state of the fabrics at Birmingham and Manchester. I suppose it is not easy to distinguish between the objects of home consumption and foreign export; I take it for granted the great increase is in the former, as the general state of our exports in the papers laid before parliament was extremely deficient; for the year ending the 5th of Jany. 1816, £60,983,000, but for the year ending 5th of Jany. 1817, only £51,260,000, and I should be much obliged to you to explain to me, which I daresay you will be able to do, the cause of this great defalcation, as upon common principles the continent ought to have been better able to pay in the latter than in the former year, at least so far as receding further from the time of war, and consequently having had a year longer to recover from the mischief of war, this is a question which will have no difficulty with you, but I must confess I do not well comprehend it, unless it arose from markets previously glutted; if so the year ending 5th of Jany. 1818 will mark a great encrease above the year preceding; but after all the cause may be owing to the internal demand in a year when corn was at a high price, and this remark suggests another enquiry whether in general your manufactures flourish better with a high price of corn or with a low one. I take it for granted with the former, as the farmers and all dependent on them are so much better able to consume.

There is in your letter an expression of Ministers preserving the currency in an ample and efficient state; what currency? I give them no credit for the coinage either of silver or gold, the old worn-out sixpences and shillings answered all the purposes of the new, which it is said cost the public £700,000, and bank-notes are far more convenient than gold, sure to be sweated and clipt; a cheaper currency could not well be desired than light silver and one pound notes.—Wheat upon the general average of the kingdom has sunk from 116 to 81, and may probably sink somewhat lower; there is no good in this, as high prices are necessary to make manufacturers work six days in a week, and if they do not a greater number of people must be employed, which has a strong tendency to encrease population unnecessarily, and no maxim in political economy can stand on a more secure basis than the certainty that population has always a decisive tendency to encrease too fast; we have been long apt to consider building cottages and small houses as a public benefit, but in general those who pull them down act far more advantageously for the general happiness of the community. I was of a very different opinion for many years, but I must confess I have changed it entirely and wish to see no familys existing but such as are absolutely at their ease, and well supported by constant industry.

I do not admit your reasons for withdrawing from public notice, as I am confident there is not a man in the kingdom more likely to enlighten it than yourself whenever you are disposed to take the pen in hand. Permit me to assure you, my dear Sir, that I shall always be most happy to receive that instruction which your letters are sure to give me.

I remain, With the most perfect esteem,
Your much obliged and devoted Servant,
ARTH: YOUNG."

Mrs. Thomas Attwood, The Leasowes.
Birmingham, 30 June, 1817.

I hope you will take care of my little sons and of yourself. If they catch any pike or other fish, they may put them all in the upper pool in the Shrubbery (Bosco's) until Willm Jones can have mended the two other pools (Tommy's and Angela's), when the fish may be divided as they can agree. All that they do not want had better be turned up again in the Garden Pool. If they catch any young pike they had better keep them in Bosco's pool until my return. If you see my aunt Adams, &c. *. . . Remember not to let any of my little sons go near the deep pools, nor indeed should they play about the Shrubbery pools, without Huxley being with them, because I expect they are deep enough to drown either of them. When children fall into the water they have not the power of getting upon their legs, and therefore a very shallow place will drown them. I hope you will take care not to catch cold, and also how you carry candles, &c., for fear of taking fire.

In the course of this year, Thomas Attwood and his family moved into the new Crescent House.

CHAPTER VI.

Letters during 1818 and 1819—Mr. Peel's Bill for the Resumption of Cash Payments—Matthias Attwood calls a Meeting to oppose it, and is supported by Sir Robert Peel—Correspondence with Lord Liverpool and Sir John Sinclair—Matthias Attwood returned for Callington—Letters during 1820.

THE chronic spirit of riot and disturbance which seems to have flourished during the whole reign of George III. does not appear to have been entirely laid by the prosperous season of 1818. In this year Mr. Attwood published, *Observations on Currency, Population and Pauperism, in two letters to Arthur Young, Esq.*, Birmingham, 1818. He does not appear to have visited London until midsummer of that year. His correspondence from thence runs as follows, and it is amusing to note the uncomplimentary manner in which he speaks of the followers of his future friend, Sir Francis Burdett.

Mrs. Thomas Attwood, Birmingham.
London, 30 June, 1818.

The Election makes great disturbances here. The poor wretches who clamour for Burdett and Liberty, meaning Blood and Anarchy, are far worse in ignorance and stupidity than our Birmingham mobs. But they have got rascals among them who excite them almost to madness just like the Poissardes in Paris. It is the greatest nonsense in the world to attempt to reason with them. They have their opinions because they are told so and because they flatter their hateful passions, and not because they can render a reason for them. Reason has nothing at all to do with their conduct. It is all a mere question of passion, and therefore such creatures ought to have nothing to do with politics. I received Mrs. ———'s letter, but I do not think I can well interfere. It is a wretched business, but I do not know how to mend it. I believe that all men in love are just as great fools as Burdett's gang are in politics. To love and be wise, they say, is impossible. I guess, however, that the proverb is wrong in my case. It is certain, however, that Love was never made for poor men. It is a most expensive passion and ought not to be indulged in by any but rich persons.—I have not yet seen Edward, Charles, or James. Lord Liverpool I have seen, and he treated me in a very friendly way.

London, Thursday.

You can form no idea of the accidents which arise in London to prevent my writing on the days I intend. For instance, I met this evening my old friend Crawford and his son Archibald in the streets. Of course I was detained with them for an hour or two which threw me too late for another appointment, and it is now by an accident that I have it in my power to write to you, for I am 4 miles from my lodgings and am keeping a party waiting for me at dinner, whilst I write. Crawford will dine with me to-morrow. His sons are doing very well in India, rising rapidly. I have scarce found any one at home that I have called upon. They are all in the country. Lord Liverpool tells me he shall endeavour to promote a treaty with France to take Birmingham Hardwares in exchange for wines, which will be a great thing for Birmingham. The India trade here is immense, and so it is in Glasgow, Liverpool, and Manchester. I have seen the British Museum, but the Exhibition at Somerset House is closed. The head of Memnon is arrived at the Museum. . . . The Election grows very warm. It seems that Maxwell will be beat. But I am told this morning that his friends have now decided upon going round and paying up people's poor's rates and taxes for them in order to get them to vote for Maxwell. If this is the case, he will be certain to succeed and it ought to be done. . . . My Brothers are all well. Wovey has got well. Charles is better than he has been for many years. Matthias has been fooled in every respect in his electioneering views. The new parliament seems likely to be changed for the worse. Many of the Jacobins are getting in. Poor wretches! they know not what is good for themselves. ——— is the most complete wretch that ever existed in the world. It is quite a comedy to see and hear him. I expect the mob will be outrageous on Saturday when the poll closes if they are defeated.

London, Saturday (July, 1818).

I went to the Opera a few nights ago to see Figaro. I was much pleased with the dancers, particularly Milanie, Twamley and Ginetti, all very beautiful women, but, I am sorry to say, studying agility more than grace. You will be sorry to learn that Burdett is successful at last. He has a majority of about 400 over Maxwell. The poll is just closed and Burdett and Romilly's parties are making triumphal processions through the streets. They do not seem disposed to any violence, being put into a good humour by success. They would otherwise have been outrageous, I expect. Covent Garden and the streets adjoining were crowded to excess at the end of the poll.

Saturday evening.

Our trial is gained, although it is possible it may come on again some other time.

London, Monday.

I have discovered now what it is that always makes me so languid and unwell in London. It is taking too much exercise. I suppose I have walked 20 miles each day I thought formerly it was drinking too much wine, but that I have avoided, and therefore I find it is the exercise which promotes constant fever in persons not accustomed to it. I had a pleasant party at Colquhoun's yesterday, to whom I was introduced as "the very first political economist of the Age." The old man was quite delighted with me and could hardly be prevailed to part with me. Of course, you will say, I thought him a very clever man. He really is so, a very good and wise and warm-hearted man. His son, too, I found a very decent man. He is our Consul-General in the Hanseatic towns. . . . I hear unbounded praises of my pamphlets among all public men. This rather astonishes me, because it disagrees with the fact of my losing £150 by them Everybody seems to know them, and Colquhoun says there is not a doubt they have saved the country. This is very fine talking, you will say. However, I seriously think they have had great effect upon Ministers in forcing an alteration of system. I don't much care about such things provided I can but see the country happy. You know the happiness of others pleases me and their misery distresses me. That is all I can say for myself.

I have no further information until the spring of 1819, when Mr. Attwood made a short visit to London, apparently for the purpose of attending to a private lawsuit. His letters for the year are as follows:—

Mrs. Thomas Attwood, Birmingham.

London 3rd March, 1819.

You will be glad to learn that Mr. Lamb has succeeded in his election against Hobhouse. They are both bad enough. One is the high road to Hell, and the other is Hell itself. However, as the doctors say, "While there is life there is hope," and therefore we may hope that Lamb and the Whigs will retrace their steps and endeavour to remedy the evil which their drivelling about reform has occasioned. George Barker tells me to-day their proceedings about the Free Church are rather unsettled. I expect it must be given up. Mordaunt has turned his back upon them, for which Spry says he is a shabby fellow, and that he shall tell him so the first time he sees him. If he does, *I guess* Mordaunt will assault the Bishop in rather an uncourteous way. I told I. Spooner before he left Birmingham that Mordaunt would be sure to desert them and that it was his duty to do so. But these High Church people never can believe that anything can happen different from their wishes, and if it does they are sure to reckon there is something shabby or knavish at the bottom of it. Geo. Barker tells me that the Bill would have passed if it had not been for the universal hatred in which ——— is held in Birmingham, but he says it would be more than his life was worth to tell the Bishop so. When I was last at the Square Garden with the children, a poor woman, who lives at the cottage in the garden near our garden, came to me in great distress to get me to interfere with George Barker on her part to let her keep the cottage without any increase of rent from Miss Colmore. Will you be good enough to send William or Charlotte to tell her that I have spoken to Mr. Barker for her and that he says she shall not have her rent raised, at least not until the Canal Company take possession of the land, which may, perhaps, never be. This is all that can be done for her, and it will please her much. She is the grandmother of the pretty children, but who the mother is I know not. I shall remember my dear Tommy's birthday to-morrow, and I shall be sure to come time enough to take you to see Mr. Campbell. I begin to like Lord Byron best.

London, Monday.

I have visited Arthur Young and find him an exceedingly sensible and generous old man. He urges me very much to write more, offering to undertake the printing free of expence, &c., &c., but I believe I must decline it. I shall call upon several of these persons before I come home. I find that the London booksellers object to selling books printed in the country, and if I print again I must employ some one here. Our trial is put off till Wednesday

London, Friday, 5th March, 1819.

I write for the purpose of saying I have sent to the Coach Offices to secure a place for to-morrow evening, and that I have no doubt I shall be with you on Sunday. Our trial came on yesterday and was determined about 4 o'clock by discharging the Jury without any verdict. There were one or two scoundrels upon the Jury who held out and prevented a verdict, and I have no doubt it was the reliance upon these scoundrels which induced ———— to try the cause. The Judge made a speech entirely in our favour from the beginning to the end. The opposite party offered in court to withdraw the action for one half of the sum claimed, and afterwards for one third, but I refused to give a shilling, and so the Jury is discharged, and I suppose I shall never hear any more of the business. . . . I find the *Macaw* will be very troublesome to carry, or else he is such a beauty that I should be much disposed to buy him. The Free Church men have withdrawn their Bill, and to-day they have a grand reconciliation dinner to which I am invited, but I suppose you will believe I can spend my time rather better than that, and therefore I shall not go. They have set on foot a subscription, to which the Bishop (not Spry) has given £500, and the two members £200 each, and therefore I suppose the money will be raised.

"*Thos. Attwood, Esq., Birmingham.*

32, *Sackville St, 26th May,* 1819.

"DEAR SIR,

My health has been of late but indifferent, so that I could not dictate the letters which I wish to send immediately, but had it not been for this obstruction I should much sooner have acknowledged the receipt of your letter, and also of your very valuable publication, which is of such importance that I hope and trust it will have due weight with those who have it in their power to give full efficiency in practice to your highly commendable ideas.

I think there is not much danger at the present moment of attempting those payments which you have so ably explained, but whatever may be the event, you have performed an important duty to the public, and if others who have the power in their hands will be equally patriotic we shall find the beneficial consequences spread throughout the kingdom. The state of the country at present I am afraid is very dubious, for the accounts which we receive from various parts of it mention the bad circumstance that many persons willing to work remain without employment. In answer to your enquiry relative to my son's property in the Crimea, I may inform you that it consists of about 9,600 acres, with a house for a residence and many attached conveniences, that it is within 9 miles of Caffa, the capital of the Crimea, and a small river passes through it turning several mills. I know not what price he fixes upon it at present, but the last that was communicated to me was 80,000 roubles. He could have sold it many times to companies of Armenians who live in the country, but their proposals for payment were by such instalments that unless he had a confidential friend remaining in the country there would have been a difficulty in receiving the money. 80,000 roubles are equal to between 4 and 5 thousand pounds.

I remain, my dear Sir, most truly,
Your obliged and devoted Servant,
ARTH: YOUNG."

This seems to have been the last letter which Thomas Attwood received from the venerable Arthur Young, who died in 1820, and who had evidently formed a high opinion of his abilities. Arthur Young was also an intimate friend of my grandfather, Edward Wakefield, and much of their correspondence has been preserved.

Mr. Peel's famous Bill for the resumption of cash payments by the Bank of England was the great legislative achievement of the year 1819—a Bill which has been considered by his admirers to mark one of the brilliant epochs of his life, but which appeared to the Attwoods to be fraught with injustice, spoliation, and misery. To the last days of their lives both the brothers, Matthias and Thomas, protested against the enactment of this year, which in spite of all their efforts was carried by an *unanimous* vote of both Houses. In the spring of 1819 Matthias Attwood first obtained a seat in Parliament, which had long been the object of his ambition. On the 3rd of April, 1819, he was returned for the old pocket borough of Fowey, in opposition to Lord Valletort, and at once devoted himself to a strenuous resistance to Mr. Peel's measure. Whilst the Bill was in progress he called a meeting of the merchants, bankers, and traders of the city to petition Parliament against the change. No less than from four to five hundred of the most respectable merchants of the metropolis responded to his call, and an important petition was unanimously agreed to at a meeting which was held at the North and South American Coffee House, and subsequently presented by the first Sir Robert Peel on the 24th May, 1819. The day before the meeting was held, Matthias Attwood was astonished to receive a visit from Sir Robert, who he naturally supposed had called to scold him for opposing his son. He was speedily undeceived by the baronet, who not only expressed his approval of the opposition to the Bill, but also promised to attend the meeting and to present the petition against it. Doubleday, in his *Financial History of England*, says that M. Attwood was cajoled into absenting himself from the House on the final division, in order that the vote might be unanimous; but surely Sir Robert Peel and some other members must have followed the same course. The *Sun* of November 13th, 1851, in recording the death of Matthias Attwood, jun., thus speaks of his conduct upon this occasion :—

"Mr. Attwood, however, clearly foresaw and boldly declared the future consequences of the contemplated restoration of cash payments more than forty years since. On the formation of the celebrated 'Bullion Committee' he uplifted his warning voice and implored the people steadfastly to resist a measure, one of the inevitable effects whereof would be the duplication of the value of money, and consequently the proportionate increase of every debt or liability then due and owing. While there was yet a prospect of averting the evil he continued his indefatigable and *disinterested* efforts. We say 'disinterested,' although the term is utterly inadequate to express our meaning,—it was a total disregard, a complete abnegation of self, when placed in the scale opposed to the common weal. He was well aware that his own large fortune would be enormously enhanced, more than doubled by the change, but he knew that the nation would be deeply injured if not ruined, and he looked only to the welfare of the community. Such instances of public spirit are unfortunately but too rare; and the thanks and gratitude of society are due to all who have given such unequivocal proof thereof."

On the 15th May, 1819, Thomas Attwood published a letter to the Earl of Liverpool, then Prime Minister upon the same subject. I do not propose to enter at any length into this intricate question, which I do not understand, but will merely quote the concluding paragraph of the letter :—

My Lord, I will trouble you no more. Our road is clear as the bright Sun in Heaven. It is to accommodate our coinage to man, and not man to the coinage The first duty of the legislature is to provide bread for the people. The second is to secure justice, and peace, and order in society. If we are to neglect these great objects, If we are to forget the warnings of experience, If we are to contract all the transactions of life within the range of an antiquated *maximum*, If we are to force all the wants and modes and means of man into an arbitrary conformity with Gold, we must re-organize our armies and double their pay; for it is only through slaughter and anarchy that we shall succeed

When he saw that the Government were determined to persist in carrying the Bank Reports into law, he addressed a second letter to Lord Liverpool, dated Birmingham, 20th October, 1819, in which he uses still more earnest language and concludes as follows:—

I have now done. This, my Lord, is about the seventh publication which I have issued, in the last three or four years, for the purpose of convincing the public of the necessity of preserving the Circulating System, on the same ample and efficient footing as' existed during the war. I have endeavoured to show that the neglect of this has been the cause of all our sufferings and of all our dangers. That I have not been more regarded is a matter of indifference to me. I only regret it on behalf of my country.

Sedition and disturbances were rife at this time; the so-called Manchester massacre occurred on the 20th August, and the year was closed by Lord Castlereagh's famous Six Acts.

We have seen from Thomas Attwood's letters on the Westminster Election of 1818 that he was still in many respects a Tory, but various facts concur to make me suppose that his opinions were beginning to be shaken. On the 9th November, 1819, the Tories of Birmingham drew up a loyal declaration in which they announced their determination to detect and bring to justice all those who by seditious and inflammatory writings might attempt to create disaffection. Neither the names of Richard Spooner or Thomas Attwood are attached to this document, but amongst many hundreds of others I find the following:—George Attwood, Joseph Grice, Richard Pratchett, Isaac Spooner, and Theodore Price.

I also find from a speech of Mr. Attwood, delivered many years later, that in this year he had contemplated the formation of the famous Political Union, but had been dissuaded by the advice of his friends.

On the 18th November, 1819, he received the following letter from Sir John Sinclair, with whom he became afterwards so intimately acquainted, and who visited him several times at Harborne :—

"DEAR SIR,—I had the pleasure of receiving your valuable letter on the subject of 'Paper Circulation.'—I should be glad to see the Tract you propose to publish on that most interesting subject as soon as possible. If printed in London, it may be sent to my son, who has just gone there to attend the meeting. He resides at 59, South Audley St., and after perusing it (which I am sure he would do) he would send it to me in covers.

I have at last brought into a practical shape the great object of my pursuits for a number of years, namely, 'The Condensing of Human Knowledge and rendering it generally accessible.' The success of the plan, however, must, in a great measure, depend on the formation of a Society, the nature of which I have endeavoured to explain in the enclosed paper. I hope that the plan will meet with your approbation, on account of the extensive benefits which are so likely to result from it. Nothing is wanting to carry it into full effect but the means of rewarding those who assist in its execution. Is it likely that I shall have some friends to the plan from your town and neighbourhood?

I enclose an extract from a very interesting communication sent me by the Persian Ambassador, who speaks English uncommonly well, and even writes it very intelligibly. I am in hopes that we shall derive some useful additions to the Code of Health and Longevity from that quarter. Believe me, with much Esteem,

Your faithful & obedt servant,
JOHN SINCLAIR.

133, *George St., Edinburgh.*"

Algernon, the fourth son of Thomas Attwood, was born at the new Crescent House, Birmingham, on Monday, February 1st, 1819, and baptised by the Rev. J. Darwall on the following Sunday.

On the 27th October in the same year, his sister Susan died at The Leasowes, aged thirty-two, the only one of the ten brothers and sisters who did not attain old age. She appears to have been much beloved by her brothers, particularly by Charles, who, to the last, entertained a most affectionate recollection of her. Thomas also, in a letter, alludes to her literary tastes and intellectual conversation. A brief note from Edward Attwood to his brother, announcing her death, has been preserved amongst the papers of the latter.

It is evident that Thomas Attwood was dangerously ill at

the commencement of the year 1820, but I have no record to show what the nature of his illness was.

I find amongst his papers the following prayer, "composed under the pressure of extreme illness," and dated February 21st, 1820. This seems to be a pretty practical answer to some of the more scurrilous of his opponents, who in later years accused him of Atheism:—

> Almighty and most merciful Father—In the name of Jesus Christ I implore Thee to hear my prayer. Thou hast smitten me with a heavy hand. Blessed be Thy holy name. It has pleased Thee to visit me with Thy Divine Dispensations. Grant, Oh merciful Father, that this heavy affliction may not visit me in vain. The Earthly Body which Thou hast given me to dwell in is filled with weakness and disease and pain. Do Thou, Oh God, fill my Soul with strength and health and joy. Let the grace of Thy Holy Spirit inspire me with the deepest gratitude for all Thy mercies, and above all things let my soul be impressed with a true sense of Thy infinite goodness, in the blessed hope which Thou hast given me in Jesus Christ. The World and all its cares are fast disappearing from my eyes. Open then, Oh God, to my thoughts, that other world, where there will be no more grief, and no more care, but where all tears will be wiped away from all eyes. And if it be Thy will, Oh God, that my days of life should come to an end, do Thou so sanctify and prepare my Soul that I may walk through the valley of the Shadow of Death, upheld by Thy Holy Spirit. It is written in Thy Holy Word, "Death hath no more dominion over us." Do Thou, Oh God, who hast broken the bonds of Death, be a light and a guide to my soul. Thou hast said in the unspeakable goodness of Thy mercy, "Come unto Me all ye that are weary and heavily laden and I will give you rest." Father of mercy, behold me Thy creature. I am indeed "heavily laden," and I fly to Thee my Lord and my God. I, Thy creature, fly to Thee in my hour of need. Be Thou my refuge and my strength. Support and comfort me in my sufferings. Conduct me through all the trials which await me with patience and resignation, and faith and hope. Confirm and establish in me everything that is of Good. Destroy and annihilate in me everything that is of Evil. Finally, Oh most merciful Father, I implore Thee to cleanse and purify my Soul, by the inspiration of Thy Grace, that whenever it may please Thee to call me from this world of trial, I may be found an acceptable vessel in Thy sight, and may enter into Thine Everlasting Kingdom through the merits of my Lord and Saviour, Jesus Christ. Amen.

King George III. died in January, 1820, and a general election followed. Upon this occasion Matthias Attwood, in conjunction with Alderman Thompson, contested the borough of Callington, against the sitting members, Sir Christopher Robinson and the Hon. Edward P. Lygon. The two latter were returned by a majority, but on a petition M. Attwood and Alderman Thompson were seated. At the same election Richard Spooner unsuccessfully contested the representation of Boroughbridge upon Liberal principles.

Thomas Attwood appears to have recovered his strength rapidly, for on the 27th April, 1820, he addressed a long letter to the *Farmers' Journal* on the state of Ireland, which was inserted in that paper on the 15th May following. Ireland was then, as it is now, the great difficulty of all statesmen, and he proceeds to argue that in his opinion the disturbances there arose from monetary causes. He shows at length that the unjust operation of the money laws had raised rents to an amount which it was impossible the farmers could pay, and he states that if the latter had called themselves distressed farmers instead of "Ribbonmen" they would have added an immense moral weight to their cause. Incidentally he mentions that on the very day this letter was written the diabolical Cato Street plot was discovered in London. He concludes by saying, "There will be no peace for Ireland until either the law or the old metallic standard is overturned."

Soon afterwards he went up to London, and from thence addressed the following letters to his wife:—

Bedford Coffee House, May 19, 1820.

R S. has postponed his notice of a motion, at Lord Castlereagh's particular request, until after the holidays, which begin to-day and end on Wednesday next, the 24th inst. It is therefore likely that his speech will not be made until Tuesday, the 30th, when Mr. Holme Sumner brings forward some resolutions for the relief of agriculture, which R. S. will oppose and move an amendment appointing a Committee to enquire into our subject, instead of Webb-Hall's. This man and myself I find are likely to be the great guides of Parliament, but I can perceive that his troops are fast deserting him. F. Lewis said to R S., "We know very well all you are going to say, you will play *Attwood*, and I shall play *Webb-Hall*, and so we shall have the *Farmers' Journal* over again in the house" I send you a *Farmers' Journal* to-day. The editor tells me that the man who signs himself "*Beds*," and praises me so *justly*, is accounted the cleverest man in Bedfordshire, and was my great opponent at first. Ministers are as obstinate as pigs. I do not expect anything will be done *in our way* this session, but I think it will the next. When R. S. speaks upon this subject it will have a great effect, because everybody reads the parliamentary debates and scarce anything else. I have been pressed with different invitations, but accept none if I can help it, in order to come home the sooner. I am obliged, however, to stay after Monday next in order to dispute with Zachy. Macaulay, who wishes much to be *converted* from the error of his opinions as a *bullionist.* I purpose at present to set out home on Tuesday next. In the meanwhile I shall advise with R. S. respecting his speech and conduct. I have not yet had time to call upon Rowcroft, but I will endeavour to do so. Birmingham and Stourbridge are scarcely more separated than his residence and mine. Brogden is altogether with me, but he tells me he dare not say so, and he expects nothing but national ruin.

"*From Edward Attwood to T. Attwood.*
London, June 26th, 1820.

" I corrected the press for your last letter to the *Farmers' Journal,* but the Editor would only admit one half of it into his paper of to-day, reserving the remainder until next Monday. He also took the liberty of leaving out two very important words which I should not have ventured to strike out myself. The words alluded to are these, 'Mr. Editor,' whenever they occurred in the body of the letter. I suppose his modesty and 'diffidence would not allow him to pass them over lest his readers should suppose he had foisted them in himself out of his exorbitant vanity and 'puerile affectation.' The rest was all right."

Amongst Mr. Attwood's papers for 1820 are put up two copies endorsed by him, "Birmingham Currency Resolutions, 11th Augt., 1820," and two other copies endorsed, "Birmingham Currency Petition, 25th August, 1820." The name of Thomas Attwood does not appear in these papers, but he was probably one of the committee mentioned as having been appointed to draw up the Resolutions and Petition, as he alludes frequently to them in his letters. I think it very probable that he did not consider it advisable that his name should appear too prominently upon this occasion, as his opponents were, no doubt, sick of hearing it in connection with the subject. The first paper commences as follows :—

"*Public Office, Birmingham,*
Aug. 25, 1820.

"At a very numerous and respectable Meeting of the Merchants, Manufacturers, and Tradesmen of the Town of Birmingham, held for the purpose of receiving the Report of the Committee appointed to carry into effect the Resolutions of the Town's Meeting of the 4th January last, and of considering the propriety of again petitioning Parliament, and of adopting such other measures as might be deemed expedient,

Joshua Scholefield, Esq., High Bailiff, in the Chair ;
The following Report of the Committee was read from the Chair,
Your Committee were prevented from immediately forwarding your Petition to the Members for the County, by the sudden dissolution of the

late Parliament. They lost no time, however, in having it presented on the assembling of the new Parliament early in the month of May. They also sent a Deputation to London, &c. . . ."

The report then proceeds to detail the extreme distress then existing in Birmingham, and the meeting adopted a strong petition to the House of Commons, praying them to investigate the cause of the general distress and to take measures for its relief. The petition does not specify the kind of relief required, but I presume the petitioners considered that a large issue of inconvertible paper-money would immediately mitigate the sufferings of the people. I do not know what reception the petition met with in the House of Commons, but, no doubt, it was not a favourable one.

Extracts from letters:—

Mrs. Thomas Attwood, Wolstanton.

Bridgewater Arms, Manchester,
Aug. 21 (? 1820).

Mr. Muntz is with me, and he also, like a good husband, is writing to his wife. I wished much to have called as I passed below Wolstanton, but could not.

Birmingham, 24 *August,* 1820.

Yesterday morning, after I parted with you, I endeavoured to console myself by *doctoring* the sick *kite*, but unfortunately I doctored him to death. It appeared, however, that he could not have survived the mortification of his wing, which it was my object to cure, by removing it, as I had done successfully that of the raven. All the other dumb things are well.

Birmingham, 27 *August,* 1820.

We held our grand meeting on Friday, from which day it is to be *hoped* that the restoration of our Country may be dated ; *hoped,* not *expected,* for in truth there is not much reason to expect anything but error and crime from the Aristocratic *Canaille* which governs England. I do not much like the *Democrats* either, and as for Voltaire's favourites, the *Middle Classes,* they are fit for nothing but *dumb sheep* to be shorn at the will of their masters. I wish I was the ruler of these chaps I would make them pay dearly for the *honour* of being *slaves.* However, our meeting went off very harmoniously, and all unanimously. The enemy showed himself on several sides, and even in the midst of our own *camp,* but all our *points* were so well guarded that he durst not venture an attack in any place ; no, nor suggest the improvement of one single word. What a pity it is that so much generalship and discretion should be thrown away !

CHAPTER VII.

Charles Attwood's Letter on the Subject of Queen Caroline—Evidence of Thomas Attwood before Agricultural Committee—Death of Miss Sarah Carless—Harborne Sunday School—Letter from Brougham—Thomas Attwood visits France—Letter from Wilberforce—Debate on the Currency between Huskisson and M. Attwood—Their Speeches highly praised by Alison—Death of Richard Pratchett—Letters to end of 1824—Poem by Thomas Attwood.

UPON the resignation of Sir Charles Mordaunt, Richard Spooner, who had been unseated upon a petition for Boroughbridge, contested the county of Warwick, in opposition to Mr. Lawley, the Tory candidate. On October 24th, 1820, he was nominated at Warwick by no less a personage than the first Sir Robert Peel, but was, nevertheless, unsuccessful. Three copies of Sir Robert's speech are carefully preserved amongst Thomas Attwood's papers, and hence I have no doubt that he took a great interest in the candidature of his friend and partner, although I have found no allusion to it in his letters.

It is in this year that I find the first public mention of Charles Attwood, then aged twenty-nine. Public opinion was greatly excited with reference to the Bill of Divorce then pending between the King and Queen, and people took sides with an earnestness which appears strange to us, who know that neither of the royal parties was deserving of an atom of respect or sympathy. Charles Attwood knew that the Queen was not all she should be, but he thought the King was worse, and that some pity should be felt for her. With this view he had already communicated with Mr. Denman, her solicitor-general, respecting the worthlessness of the evidence tendered by some of the witnesses for the prosecution. It now occurred to him that in the course of the debates on the subject no one had pointed out the disastrous consequences to the Constitution which might possibly ensue if the King were permitted to marry again. He accordingly wrote a powerful letter signed C., and despatched it to the *Times* office by the hands of an Irishman who was then assisting him in chemical experiments. The editor scanned it for a moment and immediately said, "Tell Mr. Attwood it shall appear to-morrow." Next morning not only did the letter appear in leaded type in a prominent part of the paper, but it was accompanied by a leading article homologating and enforcing the opinions expressed in it. The Lords refused to pass the Bill of Pains and Penalties, and Charles Attwood always maintained that his letter had so swayed public opinion as to bring about this result. He may, very probably, in his old age, have exaggerated the effects of his suggestion, but Mr. Holyoake, surely a competent judge, considers it "a remarkable letter, written in the grand style in which Mr. Urquhart has since distinguished himself," and, at any rate, it is interesting to reflect that Queen Victoria *may* possibly owe her throne to this hasty production. Acting upon a hint furnished by Mr. Holyoake in the *Secular Review*, I found the letter, with some trouble, at the British Museum, and made a full copy of it together with the adjacent article.

The great event of the year 1821, so far as Thomas Attwood was concerned, was his examination before a Committee of the House of Commons appointed to devise means for the relief of agricultural distress No full report of his examination is accessible to me, but from a speech delivered in 1836 I take the following :—

I remember, in April, 1821, that I was examined before the Agricultural Committee of the House of Commons. They told me openly and publicly that they had passed a resolution that they would not enquire into the Currency part of the question, and that I must confine my observations to the agricultural part of it. "Good GOD !" said I, "gentlemen, what are you? Are you not a Committee appointed by the House of Commons to enquire into the cause of the distress of agriculture?" "Certainly," said they. "And what is the distress of agriculture? Is it not the low price of agricultural produce?' "Undoubtedly," said they. I rejoined, "Is there any other distress in agriculture, except the low price of agricultural produce?" "Certainly not." "What *is* the low price of agricultural produce? Is it not the small quantity of money or currency which agricultural produce commands in the market?"

"Most certainly it is." "Why then," said I, "do you mean to say that you have passed a resolution declaring that you will not enquire into the very subject which you are expressly appointed to enquire into?" I could get no further answer to this.

This Committee, he says, examined him about "fat cattle and lean, and about plough-lands and grass lands, and about everything else, except the one thing needful, viz, the cause of the low price of agricultural produce." It was this same Committee that refused to insert in their minutes his short "Exposition of the cause and remedy of the Agricultural Distress."

Extracts from letters to Mrs. Attwood:—

Bedford Coffee House, Monday (April, 1821).
I arrived safe and well last night at 9 o'clock. I am to be examined to-morrow, and if they refuse to hear any one else, I purpose to be at home again in a very few days. . . . The men in Parliament are a *sad* specimen of the lords of human kind, but I think I shall make some impression upon their iron heads before I part with them.

House of Commons, 5 o'clock (April 11, 1821).
After being examined four hours to-day and four yesterday, I think I have at last succeeded in making an impression. They have heard me with tolerable patience and have had all their little difficulties removed and some light let in upon their comfortless prospects. I answered all the objections of Ricardo and Huskisson, I believe most completely, and very evidently to their deep mortification. I am obliged to write this letter by intruding upon the clerks, or I should not be able to write to-night, being here two miles from the Bedford, and the post bell ringing now. I believe the Committee will now consent to hear James and Rooke and other lieutenants that I am thinking of bringing forward. I will endeavour to write to you again to-morrow, because I dine with Littleton on Friday.

House of Commons, April 13, 1821.
I believe I shall prevail upon the Committee to hear Rooke and Cruttwell. The former writes me word he is coming to London on Monday or Tuesday next. I rather think I shall be coming home about Thursday next, but I have not yet made a single call upon any one. Nevertheless, I am sufficiently occupied and have scarce a moment to spare. My opinions I find are gaining ground rapidly. Gooch told me this morning that he was quite convinced that Peel's Bill was *intended* to operate a total transfer of the landed rental of the kingdom into the hands of the fundholders. The stupid landholders begin now to see this pretty generally. They are like sheep under the butcher's knife. Their report will, I believe, express a decided opinion upon this subject. But the misfortune is that they are all as dull as beetles, whilst Huskisson and Ricardo are as sharp as *needles* and as active as bees. God

send them a safe deliverance. If they wait another year or two they are lost for ever. They are robbed to a far greater extent, and in a far more infamous way, than even the French Noblesse were. . . . I dine to-morrow with old Peel, and to-day with Littleton. The former I met in the street, and he tells me his son's opinions are *shook*, and that he thinks he repents the part he has taken.

Bedford Hotel, Ap. 16, 1821.

I think to leave here Wednesday or Thursday if I can, but if I happen to see friends it almost "obligates" me to stay longer. I called yesterday upon Colquhoun, and afterwards dined with them at Mrs. C.'s father's, Mr. Deacon, who lives in very good style and seems what is called a highly respectable man. The Colquhouns expressed themselves very much hurt that I had not made their house my home, and pressed me much to do so now. I declined all this kindness, but promised to dine with them to-morrow. They have an excellent house in St. James' Place, No. 13, and seem to keep what is called the best society. A more proper house for you to visit cannot be found, and in the course of the next 10 years I may perhaps bring you. I dined with the beautiful Lady Jane at Sir Rob. Peel's, the same creature who so dazzled and bewildered little Scholefield. Sir Robert told me that his son's opinions are *shook*, and that he believes he repents his conduct. Mrs. Littleton would have taken me to a *grand rout* for the sake of showing me the *female* nobility, but I recollected *one* female that was far from me, and I was very anxious to return to her, and therefore I did not choose to avail myself of an opportunity which I should otherwise have much liked. Whilst I was speaking to this Beauty at the Opera House on Saturday night, the Duke of Wellington came in all his stars to hand her to her carriage, by which I had a close opportunity of observing him. He is certainly not a man of much sense or intellect. Before I knew him I thought very lightly of him. My friend Cruttwell is come to town, and dines with me to-day. He enquires very kindly after you and yours. Hy. James cannot get examined, although we have pressed it in all ways. They will hear no one but me.

Bedford Coffee House, Saturday.

I believe I must begin to allow at last that you are a judge of *Beauty*. I always thought Mrs. Littleton a heavy dull indifferent woman, but I was agreeably surprised yesterday to find her a perfect *Basilisk*. Nevertheless I am not the less anxious to return to *you*, which I hope to do shortly. I purpose to call upon Mrs. Colquhoun to-morrow. The Committee have again positively refused to hear any one else upon the Currency. The landholders are all convinced, and determined to say something upon the subject in their Report. But they say that Huskisson has so contrived to *pre-engage* their time to hear farmers and dealers, that if they hear any others upon the Currency they shall not be able to make their Report this session, which is the very thing Huskisson wants.

Bedford Coffee House, Sunday morn.

I am going to-morrow morning to see the Duke of Sussex, who has been very kind in obtaining for James a letter from Count Lieven to the Govr. of Odessa, which is likely to be of great value to him. I am told the Duke is getting very intimate with the King, and is likely to have great power. He reads all my letters in the Journal, and also all the private ones which I send to Shirley, and which he particularly desires to have.

Rosabel, younger daughter of Thomas Attwood, was born at the new Crescent House on the 24th July, 1821, and was baptised by the Rev. J. Darwall on the 5th August following.

On the 24th February, 1822, died Miss Sarah Carless, sister of Mrs. Thomas Attwood, at the age of thirty-three, and was buried at Edgbaston. Although an invalid for the greater part of her life, she had devoted herself with unremitting diligence to the direction of the Harborne Sunday School, and for several years had even taught the village children during the week, giving up all her friends and amusements, and attending school regularly at eight o'clock. In a paper left by Thomas Attwood, he expresses his great admiration of her piety and charity, and also of the fortitude and resignation with which she bore her long and painful illness, and he expresses his belief in the power of the Christian religion to comfort and alleviate the most terrible sufferings.

The Harborne Sunday Schools were founded in 1794 by Squire Green, with the assistance of Mrs. Carless, who promised to give him her aid in all his plans. He esteemed her co-operation so highly that at his death in 1800 he left her Grove House for life, for fear she should leave the parish and give up the schools. The state of ignorance and depravity at this time in Harborne may be imagined. There was no resident clergyman, and the vicar, a very old man, lived in Newhall Street, Birmingham, and the curate at Halesowen. One of them used to ride over on Sunday when he was able, and when he was not the church was not opened. It was not until 1823, when the vicar died, and Chancellor Law succeeded to the living, that a curate was appointed to live in the parish.

This may be the place to remark that about the same time Mrs Carless opened the first Sunday School at Harborne, Mrs. Attwood of Hawne succeeded in establishing the first at Halesowen.

The first letter which I shall insert for this year is to my mind extremely interesting, for in it Lord Brougham, than whom probably a greater intellect never existed, distinctly and honestly confesses that the unanimous votes of both Houses in 1819 were wrong, and as a necessary consequence acknowledges that the Attwoods were right.

"*T. Attwood, Esq., Birmingham.*

"MY DEAR SIR, *London, Feb.* 23, 1822.

I have to thank you for your kind letter, and perhaps we do not differ so widely as to what ought to have been done in 1819—but rather as to making any change now.

The effects of the change operating since 1816 have been truly distressing, and none but those who are determined to look at one side of the question only can doubt that some other arrangement ought to have been made when we were about it. I am aware of distress not being confined to the agriculturists—but they are certainly suffering most. Any information respecting other branches of employment will be at all times acceptable.

Believe me,
Very faithfully yrs.,
H. BROUGHAM."

Brougham, it should be remembered, was *himself* a Member of the Parliament of 1819.

(*Thomas Attwood to his wife.*)
Betley Hall, Friday morn., Feb. 23, 1822.

I am quite well. I found my boys quite well. I begged them a holiday. . . The Miss Tolletts are very pretty, but not quite so *destructive* as our friend at Mr. Jackson's. Therefore I can discourse politics admirably in their presence without thinking of *love.* I am quite satisfied with *friendship.*

March 18, 1822.

Mr. Graham of Liverpool and my brother George will dine with me at 5 o'clock, and also I expect a Mr. Banks.

Bedford Coffee House, 7 *May,* 1822.

I arrived here safe last night, having been disappointed in one Coach and obtained a seat in another. I had only 2 companions. My pen is very bad. I will get a better at Dover, where I hope to have time to write to you.

MY DEAR LOVE, *Dover, May* 9, 1822, 7 *p.m.*

I am just arrived here quite safe and well. It is however so very cold that I can hardly hold my pen after taking a short walk upon the Beach. The sea is roaring horribly. If it does not get quiet by the morning, I purpose to wait another day, for I have so much regard to you and yours that I do not feel disposed to trust myself upon it in an angry mood. It is like some women that I have seen, whom it is almost pardonable to insult for the purpose of beholding the glorious emanations which their passion exhibits. Pray attribute to this motive any apparently unkind conduct of mine which during all my life may at any time have given you offence. I dined at Canterbury, but had not time to see the tomb of the Black Prince. Kent is indeed a beautiful county. Man and Nature seem to have combined their powers during the whole of my journey of 70 miles through it. It has *women* too. I have seen several that might stand by the side of our lovely Mary. What then does Kent want? It wants a wise and upright Government. I have heard the most bitter curses and lamentations through my whole journey. The thing begins to be understood too. Everybody considers it a question of money, although but few can explain the principles on which it rests. I am got now, you will say, upon my old subjects, *Love* and *money*. And certain it is that, let me begin my letter however I will, I am pretty sure to say something upon both before I close. An odd kind of partnership it is that these two have formed in my mind. The most generous and the most selfish of principles seem to agree very well together. One cultivates the heart and the other the head, and I rather incline to flatter myself that I derive some benefit from each. . . .

Kingston Hotel, Calais, May 12, 1822.

I arrived here very safe and well after a passage of 4 hours. My beautiful mistress proud and fickle. She suddenly changed her smiles into frowns, and I had the pleasure of seeing her in a state of great *irritation* during nearly the whole of my voyage. I was a little sick but not much, and I think I should not have been so at all if the swell of the waters had been moderate. It did not however affect me 10 minutes after I left the ship. We were crowded with passengers, some beautiful and some noble. The former occupied me most according to custom. . . . I have been to drink tea with Mrs. Crawfurd, etc. This is a very pretty little town, and the people in their circumstances evidently much better off than the English. The lower orders of women are far cleaner, better dressed, healthier, happier, and *prettier*. This is beyond a doubt. All the people look happier. But the men seem but poor creatures, little, awkward, ugly old children, that is their character. It seems a pity they should have such nice women. I am going to Paris in the morning by way of *Cambray*. I believe I shall not be there before Sunday night, when I shall expect to get a letter from you. Mr. James met me on the Pier. His contempt of the *Français* is unbounded.

Paris, Tuesday even., May 14, 1822.

I arrived here last night quite well, after a very pleasant journey by the Diligence through Calais, St. Omer, Mountcashel (?), Armentières, *Lille*, Douay, Cambray, and St. Quentin. The whole of the land for this distance of 250 miles was by far the very richest I ever saw, and the country in general by far the most beautiful. I made this *detour* for the purpose of seeing Lille and Cambray, and I was not disappointed.

All the above towns are finer than any in England. . . . I went last night to the Theatre and met Miss Laura Price and Mr. Rollaston. . . .

P.S.—In all the fine towns I have passed through, good houses let for £15 or £20 a year, and other things are equally cheap.

Meurice's Hotel, 17 *May*, 1822.

I avail myself of the opportunity presented by our mutual and beautiful friend Miss Laura Price to inform you that I am quite well, and that I shall probably see you again in a few days after you receive this letter. I could spend, it is true, many weeks at Paris without exhausting the endless amusements which it presents, but I can with truth assure you, &c. . . . I am become a little *serious*, as our friends at St. Mary's call it. I wandered one day in the village of Mountcashel, surveying the glorious prospects around me, and disputing with James upon "fate, fixed fate," "free will, free will immutable," as Milton calls it.

In the midst of our discourse, which had grown rather *sceptical*, we turned suddenly upon a large *crucifix*, with a Latin motto over it, "I tell thee, fond man, Jesus is arisen" I was struck with the coincidence, and confirmed in my opinion that in our English Church we have dispensed with more of the Romish customs than was necessary. I have found Mons. and Madame Gerente exceedingly kind and attentive; the latter is rather an invalid, and their children are but poorly. My time is so much occupied in business and in seeing sights, that I am afraid I shall not have occasion to deliver the letters which Miss Carless was so good as to give me.

. . . The weather here is very warm and pleasant, like England in July. The rye and wheat, in some parts, are nearly ripe.

Paris, May 17, 1822.

You must not give yourself any uneasiness about the *Sea*, which is now brought so much under human subjection, that I doubt if the danger of a Stage Coach passage from Birmingham to London is not greater than that of a voyage from Calais to Dover. . . . My business here is favourable.

Paris, May 21, 1822.

I think to leave Paris for Rouen on Thursday, and shall then return to you by way of Calais, I believe, some time in the middle of next week. I shall probably have to stay a day or two at Rouen and Havre, and also at London. You must not be surprised if you do not hear from me, as the country I am going through is full of cross posts, which may probably delay my letters for many days or weeks. When you get this letter, I shall be obliged if you will write to me a few lines just to inform me how you all are, directed to me at the *Post Office, Dover*, where I will call. Also write another letter to the same purport directed to me at No. 147, *Leadenhall St., London*, in order that I may be quite sure to hear of your welfare. You must excuse my writing more at present, for I have a world of business to attend to, that is to say, the business of seeing sights, respecting which I will inform you when I see you, and which I will some time bring you to see. Everything is prosperous in France. Lord Liverpool and his gang tell nothing but lies.

The following letters refer to the County Election for Warwick in 1822. They are not dated, and were evidently sent by private hand. In order to explain them I shall make the following extract from the *Birmingham Journal* of ——— 26th, 1864:—

"In 1822, Mr. Spooner made a second attempt to enter Parliament. He was chosen by the Reformers as their candidate for the county of Warwick, in opposition to Mr. Francis Lawley. The election caused an excitement which still lives vividly in the memories of those who took part in it. A great number of voters—nearly all of them Reformers—then lived in Birmingham, and Reform principles had developed with such force and rapidity that the Birmingham men were confident of being able to carry the man of their choice against the combination of landlords, who looked upon 'the county' as their own political (as it was their actual) property. Every vehicle in Birmingham was hired to convey voters to Warwick on the day of nomination. Blue ribbons, flags, streamers, bands of music, enlivened the whole length of the road from Birmingham to the county town; and round every man's hat was pinned a blue paper with the inscription—'Spooner for ever!' But unhappily the votes of the enthusiastic Birmingham men failed to secure Mr. Spooner's election. Before he could sit for Warwickshire, it was necessary that he should adjure what then seemed to be his settled political creed."

Warwick, Monday, 2 o'clock.

You take too great an interest in this Election, which is but a twopenny business, whether we succeed or not. You also misjudge the relative strength of the two parties, if you judge by the state of the poll. If we had had room enough in our *one Booth* to exhaust our strength to *the same degree* as our opponents have done theirs in their 3 *Booths*, we should not, I assure you, have cut a *despicable figure*, but quite the contrary. The state of the poll, therefore, is no guide. It ought not to be reckoned a proof of our weakness because we have not been able to overcome a *physical* impossibility which our opponents have not had to contend with. For 7 hours every day we have polled as many votes *as the Poll Clerks could take an account of*, and if we had had 3 Booths as our opponents have had we could, in all human probability, have polled full 3 *times* as many as we have done. Our strength is now all *in reserve*, but our opponents' is gone. *We are certain to succeed in returning Mr. Spooner, provided the Coventry votes are good*, which you know was the grand question upon which we reckoned the Election to depend before we left Birmingham. We have not yet polled *one fifth* of our Birmingham friends. *We want as many as can possibly come to-morrow* at *any expence*, and in any way, provided they are here *before 3 o'clock.* Therefore be so good as to send to your uncle, and let him come to-morrow. *Our opponents have, in fact, made us an offer to let the Election turn upon the Coventry question, but of this please say nothing.* All parties of all sides are agreed that if we had retained 10 or 20 of the principal Lawyers at the time when we issued the first handbill, Lawley would not have had the *shadow* of a chance against us, not even if we gave up the Coventry question. This is what Unett assures me.

This letter has on it an endorsement, apparently in the handwriting of Joshua Scholefield, as follows:—

Mr. Scholefield left Mr. Attwood very well last night, but being midnight before J. S. got home was too late to send this.

Woolpack Inn, Wednesday, ½ past 2 o'clock.

Our adversaries are gaining some advantages over us—from the rascally partiality of the Sheriff, who has kept our votes back almost by hundreds in order to put us to expence, &c. All Lawley's men, however, are in our favour, and they held up their hands for us in the show of hands yesterday. The show of hands was at least 100 to 1 in our favour. The enthusiasm of the populace in our favour is very great, particularly among the women. I expect our opponents will partly have exhausted their strength to-day, and in that case we should soon recover the proper state of the Poll. We have in Warwick now, I believe, full 200 votes, and probably as many as 300. To-morrow we shall bring forward the Coventry men. I have to-day received your kind letter, and am truly glad to find you are all well. Pray send your uncle and Mr. Clarke and Mr. Lycett, and as many more voters as you can prevail upon to come. If you send a note to Mr. Twells he will give you a list of some respectable voters, such as Henry Parker and others, who will probably be prevailed upon to come and vote for Spooner, *if you ask them*. You know the influence of *Beauty* very well, and I also know some little of it.

"*Experientia docet*," which Tommy will interpret for you.

Woolpack Inn, Saturday, 12 o'clock.

I am sorry I have not myself been able to write to you but *once* yet. I assure you I have been totally occupied by day, and almost by night, going to bed at 12 and 1 and 2 o'clock, and getting up at 7, which you know is rather unusual for me. I have sat down several times for the express purpose of writing to you, and before I have written 5 lines I have been interrupted by persons as clamorous as the Messengers of Job. The fact is that we brought with us but 4 members of a Committee for Warwick, and we ought to have brought at least 20, or perhaps 40, which would have given us all a little comfort. You must not be dismayed by the state of the Poll, which is to day at 12 o'clock 870 against us, viz., Lawley 1,465, and Spooner 595. Our opponents have exhausted their strength in these 5 first days, but it was not possible for us to bring ours forward owing to our having but one Booth for polling (Hemlingford) whilst they have 3. If we could have polled our Birmingham friends as fast as they have polled their country friends, we should *now have been even with them*. I am happy to inform you that our *funds* are ample. If we had known their present amount in the first week of our proceedings, our success would have been quite certain, *beyond all doubt*. We should then have had the country lawyers and votes which Lawley now has. . . . If you send to Mr. Twells any letters, he will be sure to forward them much quicker than the post by many opportunities. I thank you for your good spirit in sending Uncle Pratchett and others whom I expect on Monday or Tuesday.

WARWICK ELECTION.

Warwick, Tuesday, 5 o'clock.

The business is now concluded. We have a majority of 300 in our favour including the Coventry voters, but Lawley has a majority of 1,200 without them. This question will therefore go the House of Commons, but how it will decide, God knows. I hope to be able to leave Warwick to-morrow, but having the keeping of the purse, and the paying of all the bills, I cannot come before. Our majority of *good votes* on to-day's poll is 78. I suppose to-morrow and the next day we might increase it to 2 or 300 more. Upon any future occasion we shall be certain. Mr. Spooner will return to-morrow.

To Mrs. Thomas Attwood, Revd. Edwd. Carless's, Wolstanton, Nr. Newcastle, Staffordshire.

Birmingham, Sat., 16 Nov., 1822.

I find that I cannot write *War Poetry* to my satisfaction, and therefore I must content myself with a *Love Ditty* now and then, and you must fancy the whole directed to yourself, for it is certain that they all originate in yourself. But it would not be *classical* to *acknowledge* such a vulgar feeling as this in amatory sonnets. I find, however, that I can write some very pretty *domestic eclogues*, and perhaps I may favour you with one now and then. I can bring in all your Loves in a most *touching* and *pathetic* manner. "Out of the fulness of the heart the mouth speaketh," it is said, and I suppose it is for this reason that I can write about you and your children far readier than upon any other subject. Give my love to my dear Bosco and Tommy, and inform him, &c. . . .

Birmingham, 19 Nov., 1822.

I have partly agreed for you to dine at Elmdon with the Wilberforces some day next week. They are coming there again, and as I knew you were rather disappointed before, I fell in with Lillingston's request to meet him on your return. I am glad Bosco has begun his poetry on Adrastus. It is a noble subject, and I daresay he will produce something good from it. But I am afraid I cannot accomplish anything myself but a *domestic eclogue* now and then. In fact I find out that I am a little what vulgar folks call *uxorious*, and am never truly eloquent upon any subject but my wife and children. Pray ask Bosco how he should like to go into Mr. Price's Counting House. The more I think of it, the more I am disposed to like it. He would be inured early to business in proper hands, and in a good trade, which would probably fall some time into his hands. The Church he would not like, and the *Law* would, I think, be worse *bondage* to him than Trade. *Physic* is good, but very slow. It is what no one can expect to *marry* upon before he is 40 years of age. And I think that would hardly have suited me when I used to be *blind with gazing on you*.

Friday, 22nd Nov.

I write by your uncle to say we are all of us quite well. I have agreed for you to dine with the Wilberforces at Elmdon on *Wednesday* next at 4 o'clock, which will be the day after your return.

90   LIFE OF THOMAS ATTWOOD.

"*From W. Wilberforce to Thos. Attwood.*
Elmdon House, Dec. 7th, 1822.
"MY DEAR SIR,

I return you many thanks for your packet, and I shall read, or rather hear read (my own eyes compel me to that less desirable mode of study), your printed Letter with the deference due to the composition of a man of superior understanding who has thought much on the subject on which he writes. As yet I have not had a vacant ¼ of an hour, nor shall have for 2 or 3 days to come.

I am, my dear Sir,
Your faithful servt.,
Thos. Attwood, Esq.   W. WILBERFORCE.

I forgot to say, I will put ye other copies into ye hands of those whom I may think willing and qualified to understand and consider ye subject."

In the summer of this year there occurred a debate on the Currency, which I notice on account of the high compliment paid by Alison, in describing it, to the talents of Matthias Attwood. He says:—

"The great debate of the session, however, came on on the 11th June, 1822, when Mr. Western moved for the appointment of a Committee to consider the effect of the Act 59 Geo. III, c. 14 (the Bank Cash Payments Bill), on the agriculture, commerce, and manufactures of the United Kingdom. The motion was negatived after a long debate by a majority of 194 to 30. This debate was remarkable for one circumstance. Lord Londonderry spoke against the motion, with the whole Ministers and Mr. Brougham in support of it. It led, as all motions on the same subject have since done, to no practical result, as the House of Commons has constantly refused to entertain any change in the monetary policy adopted in 1819; but it is well worthy of remembrance, for it elicited two speeches, one from Mr. Huskisson in support of that system, and one from Mr. Attwood against it, both of which are models of clear and forcible reasoning, and which contain all that ever has or ever can be said on that all-important subject." [Here Alison gives the speeches of Huskisson and Attwood at length.]

The busy year 1822 appears to have been succeeded by one of absolute retirement from public affairs, except only, I suppose, that my grandfather must have written on the Currency during the year 1823; but the publication, if there was one, has not been preserved. I think it was in this year that he removed with his family from The Crescent, Birmingham, to Grove House, Harborne, the residence of his mother-in-law, and where he resided until the termination of his public career.

I have no private letters for 1823, nothing having been preserved but the accounts of the funeral of Miss Carless.

His letters for 1824 are as follows:—

Mrs. Attwood, Springfield House, Leamington.

Harborne, May 10th, 1824.

I have just heard from Mrs. Waddell that Mrs. Green Simcox died on Saturday night. Pray mention this gently to Mrs Freeman.

Birmingham, 22nd May, 1824.

Mr. Salt came to tell me his tale of sufferings on Thursday evening, and I was of course obliged to decline an invitation from Green Simcox, but I spent last evening with him and found him tolerably comfortable, but we were each of us so confoundedly over-talked by his father, that I had but little opportunity of communication with him. To-night I mean to see Mrs. Jackson, to-morrow I go to Hawn, and on Monday I mean to see Mr. Freeman, unless Mr. R Spooner anticipates my time on his return from Liverpool, which seems likely. . . . Mr. Freeman seems to have made up his mind to fix his residence at Leamington, as soon as he is able to move, and he says he will occupy one of my houses until he wants some other situation.

Birmingham, 23rd June, 1824.

I have agreed with Mr Waddell to bring our whole family from Leamington to Harborne in the coach, and I have partly fixed the day for next Tuesday, on which day I could return with you myself, but I was rather fearful of taking so much upon me as to decide upon the day, &c.

Birmingham, June 27th, 1824.

I am very sorry to inform you that Mr. Freeman was last night taken seriously ill, and Dr. John Johnstone expects he cannot live much longer, perhaps not many hours. I am going over to see him immediately.

Mytchley Abbey, June 29th, 1824.

Mr. Joseph Freeman is come, and everything is done for his brother that can possibly be done. Mrs. Freeman has been exceedingly watchful and attentive, and nothing has been omitted that human art could devise. If therefore it should please God that he should leave a life of trial and of torment for a better state, his wife and children and mother must submit to the Holy Will. I shall see him again in the morning, and shall be glad when you come if you will call at the Bank in order that I may give you and your sister the last report that I can bring.

Richard Pratchett died at his home, Sandpitts, near Birmingham, on July 4th, 1824, aged sixty-seven. His death appears to have been sudden, for I find no allusion to his illness. He was High Bailiff in 1804. I have already alluded to his public services, and it was resolved to acknowledge them with a public monument. The execution of this memorial was entrusted to Mr. Hollins, and in November, 1825, the work was placed in St. Martin's Church bearing a complimentary inscription, but I regret to add that, with the vandalism usual upon such occasions, it appears to have been removed at the last " restoration " of the church.

Mrs. Thomas Attwood, Sandpitts, Birmingham.

New St., July 6th, 1824.

The bearer, Mr. Clark, at the request of Mr. John Clark, Mr. Henry Parker, and several other friends of your deceased uncle, is desirous of being permitted to take a plaster cast from his face, which he informs me he can do in two hours certain. I see no objection to this myself; it is perhaps what your uncle himself would have wished, if he had known the wishes of his friends; it is possible, however, that you may yourself feel an objection to such a proceeding, and if you do I would by no means urge it upon you. It is the only possible relic we can have of him, and I should think myself that such a relic would be as valuable to his family as his friends.

To Mrs. Thos. Attwood, Wolstanton, Staffordshire.

Birmingham, 26 *Oct.,* 1824.

We are all quite well here. Bosco and myself dine with Barker to-day and to-morrow I dine with the Low Bailiff. I expect we shall make Robert Smith High Bailiff. . . . My mother has been very ill, but is better. I went to see her on Sunday, but left Bosco to go to church, agreeably to your and his wishes. When you come on Friday be sure to be very careful to mind that you set off early, by 8 o'clock at the very latest. The nights are very dark, quite so at six o'clock. Make the chaise-boy drive slowly and carefully.

Harborne, Oct. 17, 1824.

Bosco and myself exhibit a picture of domestic happiness, for we discourse, not wrangle, whilst the weighty subjects which we discuss are rather relieved than interrupted by the prattle of Rosabel, serving as a kind of *burthen* to the music of our discussions. We are all very good too. I have been to church with Bosco, and after that I have gathered acorns with Rosabel. So there is nothing among us but love and health and happiness and peace. We often think of you however, and also of Tommy, and our other loves whom you have removed so far from us. . . . Pray give the letter below to Mr. Carless. . . .

DEAR SIR,

The Churchwardens of St. Martin's Church say that an old lost Register of that church was given into Mr. Pratchett's care a few months before his decease. Perhaps you may have noticed it among his papers, or they will be much obliged if you will be kind enough to look for it. It is of much importance.

Birmingham, 28 *Oct.*, 1824.

I hope, however, that you will not delay beyond Monday, and I should be very glad if you could contrive to bring Angela with you. I know not how else to get possession of her before Xmas. Pray remember to set off before 8 o'clock if you come in the chaise. You cannot cross the narrow road at Hockley Brook, but must first ascend the hill towards Key Hill House, and then descend the broad road to Hockley Pool, and then you may get on by the Sandpits and the monument to your happy home. I am sorry that I cannot come for you. It would give me sincere pleasure to see Tommy, and no small satisfaction to have a glimpse of my beautiful cousin. . . . Robt. Smith is made High Bailiff, and John Ryland is made Low Bailiff. . . . You will be delighted to learn that Mr. Jackson has just gained £10,000 by the sale of a Mineral Estate which he bought a year ago. Mr. Robbins has just sent here the plate which belonged to your poor uncle.

To Mrs. Thos. Attwood, Harborne.
Bedford Coffee House, Covent Garden.
21 *Decr.*, 1824.

I have only a few minutes' time to say that I am well, and that I purpose to leave London to-morrow evening, and to be with you on Thursday. Your letter to-day has given me much pleasure. I am glad you have sent Lidy for Angela, and I doubt not that you have given her all proper instructions to take care of Angela. Be sure and pay attention to the *Fires* and take care that none of your clothes or those of the children take fire. Upon this subject I am always anxious as you know, and also upon matters of *health*. I have been very busy or I should have written to you yesterday. We have been obliged to coalesce with the London Co., and now we are threatened with a third Co. of London people, who seem a little animated by *envy* at our success. . . .

It is at the end of this year (1824) that I find the first mention of railroad companies in Thomas Attwood's letters. It seems that railways were then proposed between Birmingham and Liverpool, Birmingham and London, and even London and Bristol. The rage to obtain railroad shares rose to an extraordinary height in Birmingham, and the Bank of Spooner, Attwoods & Co. was thronged by persons desirous of subscribing their names, and such was the eagerness displayed that the number of shares appropriated to the town (2,500) was engaged in less than two hours. Messrs. Spooner, Attwoods & Co. were appointed treasurers, and Mr. Barker solicitor to the new Company.

I omitted to mention at the close of 1823 that on November 24th in that year the Birmingham Eye Infirmary was first established by the energy and persistence of Mr. Hodgson, the first surgeon of the new charity, and that upon its first committee appear the names of Richard Spooner, George and Thomas Attwood, and Joshua Scholefield.

The many deaths amongst his friends and connections during the year 1824 appear to have had a very melancholy effect upon Mr. Attwood, since he found leisure to compose a poem, apparently on the subject of a funeral, of which a few stanzas were written by him from memory twenty years later in his daughter's album. I insert some of these. Their poetical merit may not be great, and several of the lines appear to be borrowed, but, like Cicero's indifferent verses, they possess an interest as the production of a man who took such a prominent part in great events:—

13*th*.

From Dust we come, to Dust we go,
Little we learn and less we know,
We go with groans, we come with tears,
We live with hopes, we die with fears—
Hopes and fears, pleasure and pain,
A few short years and dust again.
This is our life, and from our birth
To the day we go to our mother earth,
Trouble and folly, crime and care,
Sad comrades of our journeyings are;
This is our life, from youth to age
Bubbles and dreams our hearts engage
Till like "*an Idiot's tale*," full fast,
We bring them to an end at last.

16*th*.

The mourners have entered the churchyard gate,
Whilst the straggling villagers round them wait,
They have lifted the dead on their shoulders high,
And moving athwart the evening sky,
They do for another the duty to-day,
They must claim to-morrow when they are clay.
Under their feet, and around them nigh,
The bones of a thousand winters lie,
Above them, below them, death is there,
Before them, around them, death is there,

And moving the churchyard path along,
They hear the bell with its iron tongue,
For a while the notes of death prolong.

18*th*.

The holy priest the service has read,
Soothed the living and blessed the dead :
He has told of a world beyond the grave,
Of a God who died the wretched to save—
He has told of a world where sorrow and fear,
And the bitter sigh and the burning tear,
No more shall trouble the creatures of life,
Nor war, nor crime, nor care, nor strife ;
He has told of that happy and sinless shore,
Where friends that meet shall part no more,
Where all from the tyrant death set free,
The *victor* himself shall a *victim* be.

19*th*

The hungry vault has open'd its door,
And received its prey as heretofore,
That vault never sees the light of the day,
Except when it gapes for its human prey.
A hundred times it has opened wide,
And a hundred victims lie side by side ;
There stretch'd in their silent house they lie,
Unconscious of the scene that's nigh,
Unconscious that a brother shares
Their fate and lays his dust with theirs ;
Nor summer suns, nor winter snows,
Can rouse them from their dread repose,
Nor sabbath chimes, nor midnight bell,
Can wake them with its solemn knell—
No discord there disturbs their rest,
No baleful passions there molest,
But all in peace together sleep,
And in that rest profound and deep,
"Silent and sad communion keep."

20*th*.

I stood in the vault the coffins between
And silently watch'd the solemn scene,
I saw that the dead to the dead were borne,
And I heard the ropes from the coffin drawn,
And the sound of the earth on the coffin head,
Was like the greeting of the dead.
Ashes to ashes, dust to dust,
God is our hope and Christ our trust,

CHAPTER VIII.

Correspondence during 1825—The Great Panic—Important Services rendered by Attwood—Ingratitude of the Government—Commencement of the great case of Small *v.* Attwood—Letters during 1826—Visit to Rouen—Letters of Peel and Liverpool—Caricature by Cruikshank—Correspondence with Sinclair, Finlay, and Gladstone—Death of Lord Liverpool—Letters—John Attwood's Trial—*The Scotch Banker*—Attwood's Estimate of Cobbett—Conduct of Matthias Attwood in Parliament.

MR. ATTWOOD visited London in February 1825, but apparently solely on private business. He writes, Febuary 9th—

I think that William had better not take the Brewery shares. They are not very likely to be good things, although it is possible they may. The best property for him to buy is small freehold houses and lands near Birmingham. These things are sure to answer from the constant improvements going on.

Mrs. T. Attwood, Wolstanton, Staffordshire.

Birmingham, Feb. 23, 1825.

Bosco is gone to London to-day with his aunt Maria, but I expect him back again in a few days. Algernon and Rosabel are quite well and good. The former sings his hymns to me every morning, and the latter tells her pretty tales. . . . I rather think to put Tommy into business at midsummer, which pray be kind enough to mention to his uncle. The railroad goes on heavily The Committee has reported specially that the standing orders have not been complied with in some respects, and therefore we are going to another Committee, called the Committee of Reference, in order to get the said standing orders set aside in our favour if we can, which is doubtful.

Birmingham, Feb. 28, 1825.

I do not like you to come by the Liverpool mail, because I am told that it is frequently overturned. But I wish you to come by whatever coach bears the best character for safety. . . . Miss Jackson has been very ill, rather dangerously so I believe, but she is now better. Her brother is come home to-day, and brings shocking accounts of the conduct of Littleton in the business of the railroad. This gentleman has, I think, raised a little dust which will be troublesome to him at his next election. The railroad question did not come on on Friday, but was deferred until this day, Monday, and now I understand it is likely to be deferred again for a few days. You will be

II

glad to learn that the London Northern Company, after trying all manner of flirtation with us, respecting our London line, have, at last, been unsuccessful at all points, and have decided to go through *Cambridgeshire*, a hundred miles from our line!! So much for the *terror panic* of our friend R. S., who would have had us coalesce with them at all events. It will give you concern to hear that Mrs. Franklyn, the wife of the traveller, has died in 9 days after parting with her husband, upon his setting out on his long and dreary journey. I am sure I should die, if I were to part with you for a tenth of the probable time. But when I am thus candid with you, I hope you will not take advantage of my weakness to play the tyrant on me. "It is excellent to have a giant's strength," says Shakespear, "but it is damnable to use it like a giant." I had rather you would use it like your excellent relation uses her power over her husband, viz., by never appearing to use it at all. Pray give my sincere respects to her and assure her that however generously she may lavish good opinions upon me, I return then sevenfold upon herself. . . .

March 5, 1825.

I have only time to say all are well, and that I shall anxiously expect you by the Eclipse Coach on Monday evening. Therefore do not disappoint me, if you can help it. Bosco is returned much pleased with his visit. Our Rail Road is going on well, but pertinaciously and meanly opposed.

Birmingham, 7 *May*, 1825.

I am really much pleased with your letter. It is always right for good *wives* to write frequently to their husbands, and it is right for *gentlemen* husbands to write frequently to their wives, because they have leisure. But as for us *hewers of wood and drawers of water*, it is pretty well if we can find time to kiss our wives when at home, without writing to them when absent. However, I must say we are all well, mother and all. Alley and Rose very good. Bosco and I rather too good for this world, according to custom. No *spleen, anger* or *hatred*. Neighbours also are all well. Spent a pleasant evening with Mrs. Phipson. Agreed to let Bosco go to Mr. Cook's on Tuesday next. . . . Sister Maria was married on Thursday. Finch called to tell me, and to tell a fine story of how well Mathews is doing. . . . I am very glad to hear such fine stories about the personal beauty of my children. It's all a very fine thing, but if unattended with *virtue*, it only serves to make *mental deformity* more visible. Let my blooming things bear this in mind.

Birmingham, 2 *Septr.*, 1825.

. . . It turns out to be true that John Attwood has sold his works for a large sum, certainly not less than £500,000, as R. S. was assured last night by John Simcox the lawyer. One of the managers of the new company is coming to live at Corngreaves. This purchase raises the value of the Hawn Estate greatly, which ought to bring a good way between 2 and £400,000. . . . I hope I shall be able to go to France in about three weeks, and if you persist in your wish to accompany me, I will certainly take you and Rosebud.

Mrs. Thos. Attwood, Birmingham.

London Coffee House, Ludgate Hill,
Nov. 11, 1825.

I arrived here safe this morning and I lose no time in writing to inform you of such an important event. I expected to find Mr. Salt here, but he is not yet arrived. . . . Pray remind my dear ——— of my desire that he should rise at 7. Perhaps he may summon up resolution to accomplish an object during my absence, which has always been too arduous for him during my presence. If so, I shall be very glad, for I like to see the duties of life *sit easy* upon men. If it costs them too much in the way of sacrifice, the duty is generally, first or last, neglected. It is in this way that vice throws her *cobwebs* round us all. They are things which need but to be *touched* to be snapped asunder, but the mischief is that we have seldom resolution enough to touch them. Now I hope ——— will call up the courage of Hercules in his support, and then he will wonder with what ease the great duty will be accomplished. I hope you will remember to send to my Blossom a large quantity of the best toffy on her birthday. . . . If I can I will see the great elephant before I return and tell her wonders about him. It is a terrible rainy, cold and nasty day. London is much worse than other places in such days. . . .

27, *Gracechurch St.,*
Dec. 17, 1825.

I arrived here safe yesterday morning. . . . I hope Miss Pidcock takes care of you night and day, and in that case I am perfectly satisfied, after having heard how she managed the coachman and other affairs. I am not yet a *minister* quite, although I may perhaps be called a *privy councillor*. Ministers are in a terrible state, and I believe would give their eyes if they could get back one single month. You will see they have issued £1 notes already, so it seems that Mr. Salt's information was correct, and yet it is remarkable that no one in London knew it. All that my brother could learn, until the notes appeared, was that the Bank clerks went to their work at 9 in the evening, as others came from work. You must not be alarmed at the aspect of things. There will be no mobs at present. You may be assured that in whatever I do with the Ministers, I will have no contact with the Radicals, unless things take a strange turn. I know you have an antipathy to those gentlemen, and I am myself not disposed to think very well of them.

London, Decr. 19, 1825.

I write again to say I shall probably be home in a day or two, and that I am quite well. I have no more to say. The emperor Alexander is gone, to heaven, I hope. The king here is well, but his Ministers are in rather a *funeste position* as the French would call it, or as Tommy would perhaps say, *triste position*. It is not unlikely they may be *worse before they are better*.

"*Private.*

"Mr. Robinson presents his Compliments to Mr. Attwood, and begs to inform him, in reply to his note of this morning's date, that altho' he has not felt himself justified in adopting the particular mode suggested in

Mr. Attwood's paper of yesterday, Directions have been given for affording such facilities as may be proper in remitting the Revenue.

Downing St., Saturday, Decr. 17, 1825."

"*T. Attwood, Esq., 27, Grace Church St.*

"SIR,

I think it might be advisable for you again to see the Directors of the Bank of England. I cannot at all presume to say what may be their decision on the suggestion which you made to me this morning—but I have no doubt, from their Disposition to extend under present circumstances as much relief as they can with propriety, that they will give an attentive Consideration to any Proposition which you may have to make.

I am, Sir,
Your obedient Servant,
ROBERT PEEL.

*Whitehall,
Decr. 16, ½ past one p.m."*

We have now reached one of the most interesting epochs in Thomas Attwood's life, when the greatness of the service which he rendered to his country can scarcely be over-estimated. The year 1825 was, for a short time, one of great prosperity, and Mr. Robinson, then Chancellor of the Exchequer, and afterwards Earl of Ripon, discoursed grandiloquently about "the prosperity dispensed from the portals of an ancient monarchy." But in the midst of the sunshine Attwood clearly foresaw the approaching storm, and warned the state pilots of their danger. The nature of the service rendered by him I shall set forth in the words of the *Birmingham Journal* of March 8th, 1856:—

"On the contrary the Government took a diametrically opposite course to that Mr. Attwood recommended, and yet it was through his exertions that the Bank of England and the credit of the country were saved from irretrievable ruin. On the 22nd of November, 1825, Mr. Attwood addressed a note to Lord Liverpool, the then Premier, urging upon him to cause the Bank of England to prepare, without delay, a supply of £1 notes, as there was an extreme probability that their issue would soon be rendered necessary, and the mere signing of a sufficient number of notes would require six weeks' time, even if 200 clerks were employed. This sagacity and foresight were amply confirmed by subsequent events. The exchanges were against this country; speculations in all descriptions of property, in banks and joint-stock companies—to which the mania of 1845, great as it was, scarcely affords the slightest parallel—was at it height, and the nation was in a state of fever. The Bank of England had scarcely a million of gold in its vaults. Huskisson, who was then a member of the Administration, suggested a course which, if it had been adopted, would have ruined half the country. He suggested to the Bank the desperate measure, that if their gold were exhausted they should place a paper against their doors, stating that 'they had not gold to pay with, but might expect to have gold to recommence payment in a short period.' Mr. Attwood, in these circumstances, was called to London at the beginning of December, and was in constant communication with the Government, having been furnished with a special letter of recommendation from the first Sir R. Peel to his illustrious son. Shortly after his arrival, the crash came. The panic began on the 16th of December, 1825, by the stoppage of the house of Sir Peter Pole & Co. Banks failed in all directions, and a run was made upon the Bank of England. The soundness of the advice given by Mr. Attwood nearly a month before was then apparent. It was only by the issue of the £1 notes that the national credit was preserved. How this was done, we shall show by the evidence of Mr. Jeremiah Harman, one of the principal Bank directors, before the secret committee of 1832. The question was asked : ' The Bank issued £1 notes at that period. Was that done to protect its remaining treasure?'

This was the answer: 'Decidedly; and it worked wonders. And it was by *great good luck* that we had the means of doing it; because one box containing a quantity of £1 notes had been overlooked, and they were forthcoming at the lucky moment.'

'Had there been no foresight in the preparation of these notes?' it was asked.

'None whatever, I solemnly declare,' was the reply. It was again asked, 'Do you think that the issue of these £1 notes did avert a complete drain?'

'As far as my judgment goes,' said the director, 'it saved the credit of the country.'

Thus the whole system—debt-dividends, dead weight, half pay, pensions, secret service money, exchequer bills, and altogether, were within a few hours of total destruction and irretrievable ruin, which was averted solely by the advice if not by the influence of Mr. Attwood."

The two letters which I have inserted from Mr. Peel and Mr. Robinson, although cautiously and officially worded, with an evident desire to avoid acknowledging any obligation to Attwood, appear to me to fully prove the truth of the above account, which is also confirmed by the private letters to Mrs. Attwood just quoted. I find also amongst my grandfather's letters the following paper, which shows that *before* the panic he had pressed the remedy upon every one:—

Resolutions for the Bankers of London proposed in first week of December, 1825, by *T.* Attwood, and presented to 6 London Banks by *M.* Attwood and refused by each of them.

We, the undersigned Merchants and Bankers of the City of London, think it our duty to make known to His Majesty's Government:—

First—That the Gold coins and Bank of England notes now in circulation are not sufficient to transact the business of the Country.

Second—That the consequence of this deficiency of the circulation is a general want of confidence, and a general disposition to realise monied engagements to an undue and impracticable extent.

Third—That some legislative interference is necessary, in order to prevent the most serious consequences to the Trade, Commerce and Agriculture of the Country—10 Decr., 1825.

Refused by Jos[a] Walker, Masterman and others.

For his important services on this occasion, Thomas Attwood does not appear to have received the slightest acknowledgment from the Government. I cannot even find amongst his papers a letter of thanks from either Liverpool, Peel, or Robinson, and yet, from the evidence adduced, there seems no possible doubt that the services really were rendered. We shall, however, see that on another and far more memorable occasion, other men in high office reaped all the fruits of his labours and repaid him with nothing but ingratitude and abuse.

This year (although actual litigation did not commence until 1826) may be said to have witnessed the commencement of the famous case of Small *v.* Attwood, a suit which continued until March, 1838, and which—whether we consider the number of years that it lasted, the magnitude of the sum at stake, the eminent counsel employed and the unprecedented fees paid to them, or the celebrated judges before whom it was tried—may fairly be called one of the most extraordinary civil cases ever tried before any tribunal whatever. It was a very El Dorado for the legal profession. Two Lord Chancellors acquired a great part of their fame by its conduct, and men who were juniors at its commencement sat on the Bench at its conclusion. Many tons of paper and parchment were written or printed over, and I have heard my father say that fifteen hackney coaches were employed to carry the papers to the House of Lords.

By an agreement dated June 10th, 1825, John Attwood of Corngreaves (first cousin to Thomas) agreed to sell to John Taylor, James Henry Shears, and Robert Small, the estates and works called Corngreaves Estate, late Banks's Furnaces, Dudley Wood or Netherton Iron Works, and Wolverhampton

Colliery, for £600,000 The plaintiffs took possession of the estates, but soon after, a heavy fall took place in the price of iron, and they found they had made a very bad bargain. They then filed a Bill of Complaint in the Court of Exchequer on the 27th of June, 1826, in which they sought to have the agreement annulled on the ground of fraudulent misrepresentation by John Attwood as to the value of his property. The progress of this great lawsuit is frequently alluded to in Thomas Attwood's letters.

In this year also he published a letter to Sir John Sinclair upon the Currency, but as this was bitterly attacked by Cobbett in 1827, I shall notice it again presently. It appears, however, that Cobbett was mistaken as to the date, as I find Mr. Attwood wrote to Sir John on the 4th January, 1826, "on the future operation of the Metallic Standard, and on the two modes of carrying it into full effect." He appears to have attached considerable importance to this letter, which was reprinted in the *Birmingham Journal* of January 14th, 1832, and he sent a copy to Mr. Peel, then Home Secretary, who replied as follows:—

"*Whitehall, Jany.*, 1826.
"SIR,

I beg leave to return to you the accompanying copy of your Letter to Sir John Sinclair.

I have read it attentively, and it has been seen by Lord Liverpool and Mr. Robinson.

However much I may differ from you as to the expediency of an inconvertible Paper Currency—the vast importance of the subject on which you have addressed me, and my respect for your ability and practical experience, would ensure my best attention to any communications with which you may favour me.

I am, Sir,
Your very faithful Servant,
ROBERT PEEL."

To Mrs. Thomas Attwood, Rev. Edwd. Carless, Wolstanton, near Newcastle under Lyme.

Birmm., 21 *Feby.*, 1826.

I cannot come to Wolstanton at present. I am engaged in the pleasant office of calling in accommodations as Lord Liverpool calls it. I wish I had got him upon my books, and he had nothing but land to pay me with, and no privilege of Parliament. If I did not make a Radical of him in 20 minutes, I would lose my head. Lord Westmoreland says he is *mad*, which is like enough. It is certain that both he and Canning are guided by Cobbett in everything they say or do. I went over to Sir Robert yesterday about the Rail Road. We are going on very well, beating the enemy in every attack. I expect, however, we shall hardly succeed this session, but this you must not mention. Bosco is going to the Concert with Mr. Jackson on Tuesday, or I should send him for you. As it is, I think you will have to come by yourself in the Eclipse. . . .

Birmingham, 27 Feby., 1826.

You have frequently heard me say that the measures of the Ministers wd. renew "*the late panic*," and sure enough I have been correct, according to my custom for 20 years. Seven or eight Banks have stopped payment in different parts, and a considerable demand has been occasioned upon many banks of the very first consequence ; for instance, Smith, Payn & Smith, and Barclays have had last week very sharp runs upon them. In many Country Towns also these pleasant "*panics*" have prevailed. In this town, however, things have been pretty quiet excepting with regard to Moilliett & Co., who have had a very constant and persevering drain upon them. In the meanwhile the positive misery among the lower classes is becoming frightful. Upon the whole, if I were a demon, I shd. take a very sincere pleasure in seeing things taking so rapidly the course which I have prophesied for 10 years. So much for politics.

Mrs. Attwood, at Mrs. Freeman's, 3, North Parade, Weston super Mare.

I have received this morning your melancholy letter of yesterday, which I have immediately forwarded to your dear Mother at Harborne. The news will not be unexpected by her, and therefore I hope she will not be much affected by it. You will, of course, not return until the funeral is over, and I doubt not that you will administer to Mrs. Freeman and to Sarah Eliza all the consolation in your power. Let these things, my dear love, teach us to value our own happiness and to receive with gratitude such blessings as the Almighty God has given us, without repining for others which perhaps He may think proper to refuse.

8 April, 1826.

I am concerned to inform you that our valuable friend Mrs. Price died this morning at ¼ before 9 o'clock. Very few, I fear, have been better prepared to meet their end. When I parted with her I left her with a prayer that the Almighty God would receive her into Paradise, and I doubt not that my prayer will be heard, and that I shall one day have the happiness of seeing her again. Here again, my dear wife, we see cause of gratitude to the beneficent Author of our being. The most awful calamities glare around us on many sides, but, thanks be to God, they never break in upon our peace. My poor sister Susan, whose body reposes side by side with my long lamented Grandfather and Grandmother, if she were alive, would be full of her dismal prognostications upon the frightful changes which, she always contended, awaited me. She treasured up the stores of her learning to produce evidence that all persons whose happiness was great in the beginning of life were exposed to the most dreadful calamities in its end

Polycrates and Crœsus and many other instances were always upon her lips. I have no fear. I will always discharge my duty as a just and upright man. I leave the rest to God, from whom all good and all evil comes.

Mrs. Attwood, 190, *Rue Royale, Boulogne sur Mer.*

3, *Rue Impasse, Route de Caen, Rouen,*
Sept. 4th, 1826.

I arrived here safe yesterday evening at 4 o'clock. The country is beautiful beyond description all the way. If you could have looked down upon Rouen from the hills, you would have thought it the most beautiful city in the world. The dioramic view of it is nothing. The diligence is in my opinion much pleasanter travelling than our stage coach. 28 franks was my whole fare here, a distance of 140 or 150 miles. I came by Neufchatel. I mean to return to Dieppe, which is only 30 miles hence. . . .

Septr. 7, 1826.

I find that my business here will require a good deal of my personal attention. It may perhaps be desirable for me to take a house for 6 months either here or at Dieppe. A few weeks ago I could have bought one here, large, elegant and commodious, with 2 acres of walled garden, for £550 only. I will enquire after one to rent for 6 months, and if I find one will bring you to look at it. Diligences go 5 or 6 times a day in 5 hours from here to Dieppe, and from thence the Steam Packets go twice a week in 10 hours to Brighton. I like the diligences better than our stage coaches because they are more *roomy* and commodious, and far more safe. The people here are excessively ugly. I am sure they never conquered England. And yet Richard Cœur de Lion sleeps in their Cathedral, and William the Conqueror in another of those beautiful and venerable structures at Caen. Here too lies Bedford the Duke Regent of France, close by the spot where he had the cruelty and madness to burn alive the Maid of Orleans. The mountains and the river and the Cathedral remain in their pristine beauty, as they were when they belonged to the Plantagenets. Everything speaks of England. . . .

Hawn, Sept., 18, 1826.

Tommy wrote to you from Dover on Thursday and from Birmingham yesterday. We are all well. I have only time to say that my father is better but still in a precarious state. The probability is that he may survive for a few years, but he may die in a few days. Mr. Hodgson tells me this morning that he saw your mother yesterday and she was walking in the garden as well as usual. Tommy and Bosco went home to her last night, and I intend to see her myself in a day or two.

Hawn, 20 *Septr.,* 1826.

My father is getting gradually but slowly better. I think you have done right in taking the house from Mr. Podevin at 5 guineas per week. . . .

"*Thomas Attwood, Esq., Birmingham.*
Octr , 1826. *Private.*

"SIR,—I beg leave to return to you the accompanying French Promissory note which you were good enough to send for my inspection.

The existence of the facts which you mention as to the number of Dockets which you have struck, and of meetings of Creditors which you have attended, does not appear to me to warrant the inference which you draw from them.

Those who contend against a lavish issue of Paper money consider alternate states of excitement and depression one of the certain consequences of that issue, and would appeal to the facts to which you refer as warranting their conclusions rather than your own.

I confess from what I have myself heard and seen of the state of Birmingham, I should have appealed to it as a Proof that the reduction of Paper by the Country Bankers has not had that fatal effect upon the manufacturing Industry of the Country which some persons anticipated. If since Christmas last you have drawn in £200,000 from the uses of Industry, and if every Banking House in Birmingham has in a degree proportionate to its circulation followed your example—the present state of Birmingham, though perhaps not altogether exactly what we could wish it to be, still is such in my opinion as to warrant a confident belief that the Prosperity of the Country is not quite so dependent on the abundant issue of a Paper Circulation as it appears to you to be.

I am, Sir,
Your obedient servant,
ROBERT PEEL."

"*Fife House*, 2 *Decr.*, 1826

"SIR,—I beg to acknowledge the receipt of your letter to me of the 30th of last Month, with its Inclosure, and to thank you for the present communication as well as for your former one of the 1st Novr.

I am truly sensible of the restless and disaffected spirit which is produced by a period of Distress, and which unfortunately exists in many places at the present moment; but it is to be hoped that the Loyalty of those of better Sense will be sufficient to check and counteract the designs of such as would inflame rather than sooth the minds of the suffering poor at such a moment.

I am, Sir,
Your very obedient humble servant,
LIVERPOOL."

I have an old caricature, etched by George Cruikshank and published in 1826, with which Thomas Attwood amused two generations of children. It represents the Ministers, aided by Cobbett and a number of country squires mounted on asses, busily engaged in slaughtering a flock of rooks who are supposed to typify the country bankers. I remember he used to say that he had himself designed this plate and written the doggrel accompanying it. The engraving itself says, "Designed by an amateur," and the lines, which are as follows, remind me of his style :—

Through the Strand I took my way,
Loitering on a Winter's day,
Soon the place my footsteps tread
Where a tyrant lost his head ;

Onward then my course I try,
Musing on the times gone by,
To where St. Margaret's stands confest
A blister on a Beauty's breast.

There a wild rout invades my ears
Full of strange sounds and stranger fears ;
Loud and more loud the uproar grows
Wilder than aught that Bedlam knows.

"Halloo ! Halloo ! Tally O ! Tally O !
Onward to Heaven or Hell we go,
Down with the Rooks and Down with the Rags,
Up with the Guineas and hard Money bags.

Mercy, Gramercy, I promise to pay,
Promise no more but pay to-day,
"Caw, Caw, Caw, Caw Caw Caw,"
Nothing I hear but " Caw, Caw, Caw."

On February 6th, 1826, the Birmingham Mechanics' Institute was founded, chiefly through the instrumentality of Richard Spooner, who was its first president, Thomas Attwood being the first treasurer. From the letters of the latter just quoted I judge that it was in this year that he established at Rouen some works for the manufacture of cotton-print rollers, which, though never very successful, subsisted for many years and were managed for a short time by his son Edward Marcus. In this year also he seems to have attracted for the first time the notice of Cobbett, who in his *Register* for October 7th, 1826, sneers at the " Little Shilling Project " of Messrs. Attwood and Spooner, and predicts that its adoption would instantly " produce a revolution of the most dreadful character." At the General Election of 1826 A. Baring and Matthias Attwood were returned for Callington, Mr. Badnall being the defeated candidate.

At the end of 1826 and the commencement of 1827, Thomas Attwood engaged in a long correspondence with Sir John Sinclair, Kirkman Finlay of Glasgow, and John Gladstone, father of the present Premier, on the subject of a change of currency. The printed paper containing this is endorsed by Attwood:—"Printed by Sir John Sinclair, and afterwards suppressed by desire of Finlay and Gladstone," and his two long letters on the subject are dated January 10th and February 7th, 1827. At the end of January he visited Mr. Davenport, M.P., at Tarporley, no doubt with reference to Currency matters.

Extracts from letters of 1827:—

Mrs. Thomas Attwood, Wolstanton.

Birmingham, 20 *Feby.*, 1827.

Lord Liverpool seems past all human hope. It is strange, but at the very hour he was struck I was in the very act of cursing him. I do not often use imprecations, but at 10 o'clock on Saturday morning I was plagued with the beggars, the victims of Lord L'pool, and I went back to Mr. Walker calling down curses upon him, and praying to God that I might see him reduced to the misery to which he had reduced others. My heart relented when I heard of his illness, for although the author of so much misery, I can hardly bring myself to think him a villain. The D. of Cumberland is different. Few persons will regret his fate, and none will do so but from the mere impulse of humanity. I forgot to send my remembrances to Mrs. Carless, and her husband and lovely daughter. If I can, I will come to see them shortly, perhaps at Midsr., when we may go to Dovedale, the El Dorado of my family hopes and pleasures. Rosabel has got a small lamb which we brought from Hawn on Sunday. It is a great favourite, as you may think, and when her brothers come home it will be grown into a tame sheep.

Birmingham, 24 *Feb.*, 1827.

I hope Tommy has learnt everything about Mr. K.'s coal and its properties. His grandfather seems to want him very badly. . . .

Birmingham, 26 *Feby.*, 1827.

. . . I am afraid, however, they must have intruded upon Mr. Kinnersley's kindness. Pray thank him in my name and say that he shall have either of them permanently, if he thinks he can make a man of business of him in any of his concerns. I doubt not that he would manage Tommy far better than either I or his grandfather, who both of us rather spoil him. I am glad you have spent a pleasant visit at Clough Hall, and I doubt not that Angela has been delighted. I can hardly make the same offer of her that I do of the others, for I believe I shall want her myself all the days of my life. You do not say anything about my dear Marcus. I hope he has no cough &c. . . . Tommy's grandfather begins to think it a long visit. I hope Tommy will be able to tell him about the North Stafford Coal and Iron, the progress of the Air Castle Tunnel and many other things. I took Rosabel to Hawn yesterday. Our gig quite failed us on our return, and we were obliged to walk from Tennell Hall. Cousin John dined with us, very friendly and good-natured as he always is.

27, *Grace Church Street*, London.
March 19, 1827.

There is no great news going on, only it seems likely that the Marquess Wellesley is forsaking the Catholics and is about to join his brother the D. of Wellington in forming a new Tory administration. This is a good thing, if true, because the Marquess and his brother are no fools, whatever else they may be, and we have suffered so much from fools that I should be glad to see men of some sense in the management of affairs. These people wd. settle the Currency at once ; and follow Pitt's footsteps in heart and soul, and not in mere words. At present Davenport is not making much progress. The bands of conceited drivellers whom he has to deal with, wd. almost prefer ruin to being taught by *him*. Things look bad in Portugal, Spain, Ireland, and France. Beyond a doubt the latter Country is at this moment paying the Portuguese rebels. If the Marquess gets in, he will settle them at once. The very news of the Restriction Act wd. frighten the French out of their senses, but at present they rely on our weakness and absolute inability to support war. As I said in one of my pamphlets, the meanest of our enemies would set us at defiance, and this they wd. certainly do if they were not kept in cheque by the fear of Bank notes. John A. is going on well in his chancery suit. I can make but little of the difference between C. A. & M. A. & B. A., all wrong-headed men. I will perhaps get a swan if I can. . . . Sir John Sinclair says that Charles Jones is a *strong-headed*, but not a *headstrong* man.

27, *Grace Church Street, March* 21*st*, 1827.

. . . The Currency question is certainly making great progress among public men. They almost all acknowledge now that it has done all the mischief, but they say that it is now too late to retreat. However it seems likely that they will adopt some palliatives, such as the allowing of £1 notes to circulate, the making silver a legal tender, &c., &c., and it is barely possible that expedients of this kind may enable them to keep body and soul together. The revenue is falling off in a way which alarms Ministers greatly. They thought the quarter which followed the *late panic* was the very worst that could possibly happen, but the present corresponding quarter has fallen off £500,000 more. Meanwhile their expenses are increasing in Portugal, Ireland and elsewhere. The landowners are much discontented, and it seems they all of them dislike Huskisson and Canning, who are the sons of innkeepers and players, and thought hostile to the aristocracy. I cannot make any impression in the matters of C. A. & B. A. & M. A. . . .

27, *Grace Church Street*, 23 *March*, 1827.

. . . I am afraid I shall not be able to get the Swan, but I will try. I am glad Bosco has got the dibchicks, and perhaps I may get a few teal. Wolverley has a famous raven just like ours. Politics are still unsettled, and it is quite impossible to say who will be Minister. The Spanish king seems to have enough upon his hands. Such horrid wickedness as his ought not to prosper, and, thank God, it seldom does. John A. is returned to Corngreaves for a day or two for some papers. His cause seems perfectly clear and certain. Young Wm. James has at last finished his steam engine, which works beautifully and seems very valuable, but experience only can ensure its success.

Birmingham, 10 *May*, 1827.

My beloved daughter Angela, my most dear sons Marcus and Algernon,—

I have been thinking of you many times. I thought it would have broke my heart to part with you. I said to myself "I will certainly come again," and then I thought "How can little children quarrel with each other whose father never quarrels with them?" and then I began to think of Bradwyll Wood, and of the birdsnests, until the tears came into my eyes. And then I found that it was good to part with children, because by so doing we not only teach them learning but *discipline* and the *habit of obedience*, which are the foundation stones of all happiness, although the laying of them *firmly and well* is generally too difficult a task to be accomplished by parents. They prefer to lay such foundation stones as kisses and caresses and soft indulgences, and you may well think that such foundations as these will bear but very little weight above. Therefore when parents attempt to educate their own children, the whole superstructure generally falls to the ground, and crushes both parents and children in its fall. And so by thinking on these things I consoled my heart.

. And now, my dear children, I do beg and desire, as you value your father's love, that you will be kind to each other, and that you will above all things *bear* and *forbear* with each other. I have seen so much crime and misery arising from discord, that I do dread the slightest appearance of unkindness and disagreement and love of strife among children. The scripture says, "Be kind and affectionate one towards another," and it uses the words "not railing and answering again" to shew that all this is evil, that it comes from evil, and leads to evil. Therefore, my dear children, avoid the use of all unkind or unpleasant words towards each other. Strive carefully in this respect for a little time, and you will find that there is no real difficulty in so doing, but on the contrary, that the words of love and kindness are far more agreeable to all parties, "blessing," as Shakespear says, "both him that gives and him that receives." Why do you not write to me, and tell me all you have to say? I daresay you begin to think of Dovedale and Harborne, and such kind of places; and surely I remember climbing up with Angela into Renaud's cave, when she was a very little girl; and so now, my dear children, I bid you farewell. . . .

(*Mrs. Attwood from G. de B. Attwood.*)

"*Birmingham, Nov.* 12, 1827.

"We are all quite well and transported with joy at the news of the destruction of the Turkish fleet. I stopped till 11 o'clock this morning, firing off the cannons with the little boys and Rosabel, at an old ship which we shattered terribly in honour of Annie's birthday and the great victory gained by Sir Edwd. Codrington. We could hardly restrain ourselves from going out to hurra yesterday when we heard the glorious news As it was we all drank a glass of port to Sir Edwd. and his companions, and we mean one of these days to fit out a ship brimful of gunpowder, and have it blown up on the pool, in imitation of the two Turkish Admiral's ships which have shared that fate."

(*To the same, from Thomas Attwood*)

Birmingham, 13 Novr., 1827.

Bosco is quite in raptures at the destruction of the Turkish fleet. It seems to me rather a more severe measure than was necessary.

Birmingham, 14 Novr., 1827.

You will probably see by the paper that the King's Bench has refused a new trial to the British Iron Co., and consequently the verdict at Stafford stands good, and the Co. is legally saddled with the payment of a rent of £16,000 a year to John Attwood, over and above the money which they have paid him. . . .

Birmm., 17 Novr., 1827.

I am going over to spend the day at Rufford's of Stourbridge on Monday, and to-morrow I am going to Hawn. . . .

Birmm , 16 Nov , 1827.

I have been occupied all day long in the important office of choosing a High Bailiff, and the person fixed upon at last has been Mr. Charles Shaw, who is now sworn in, to general satisfaction. Mr. Ledsam is excused on the ground of ill-health. . . .

In the late application to the King's Bench for a new trial in the business of John Attwood, all the four judges expressed themselves strongly in his favour, declaring the conduct of his opponents to be altogether groundless, and Mr. Scarlett *volunteered* the expression of his opinion that John A. had been most cruelly treated.

(*To the same, from G. de B. Attwood.*)

"*Birmingham, Nov. 21st, 1827.*

"I am therefore going to the concert to-night, either by myself or else with the bold uncle George. My uncle Mathews came down on Saturday, and I went over with him to Hawn, from whence I did not return till late last night, as my father chose me to stay yesterday to look at the Haze. My grandfather is very sanguine now about his Hawn pits, and says he expects to be at the coal in a fortnight. I have little doubt he will before Christmas, and I only hope Angela may be well enough to take some part in the merrymakings upon so joyous an occasion. . . . The other day a skylark fled screaming into the kitchen, and was made prisoner by Elizabeth; it is now in the old lark's cage. I suppose it was driven by some hawk to such an unusual place of refuge. . . .

Wednesday night.—I saw Mr. Grice there as usual, but saw nothing of any of the Barkers. Joe Grice is still at home, where he is likely to remain all winter."

The remainder of Thomas Attwood's letters for 1827 are chiefly taken up with careful inquiries and instructions as to the removal of his daughter Angela, who had recently been seriously ill, from Wolstanton to Harborne.

George Attwood was High Bailiff of Birmingham for the year 1827, and at a public meeting at which he presided held on the 22nd June, he, his brother Thomas, Joshua Scholefield, and a number of others were appointed a committee to forward the objects of the meeting in obtaining parliamentary representation. At this time it was proposed by some to disfranchise East Retford, and to transfer its representation to Birmingham. The grand idea of the Political Union does not appear to have been yet deemed practicable by Thos. Attwood, for on the 25th June, 1827, I find him remarking that as Parliament had held out the hand of favour to Birmingham, he hoped the town would be content to receive the boon and not lose the privilege by contending for minor points. As an acknowledgment of services in connection with this matter, Mr. Charles Tennyson was invited to a public dinner by the committee above alluded to, in the following year. Still Birmingham was not destined to obtain parliamentary representation yet, and few could have foreseen what a bitter struggle had to take place before it was conceded; but she fortunately possessed the man whose rare conduct was soon to procure the much coveted boon for her, in a perfectly legal and peaceful manner, without any violence or bloodshed whatever. In this year the subject of this memoir first fell under the lash of the celebrated Cobbett, who in his *Register* of June 2nd, 1827, assailed him in a remarkably virulent article. Cobbett's ire had been aroused by Attwood's letter to Sir John Sinclair, already mentioned, and, jumping to the conclusion that Attwood was a Birmingham ironmaster most anxious to be made a peer, he treated him to some of his coarsest abuse in consequence. Cobbett was especially furious with Attwood for saying that Lord Castlereagh had "died of a broken heart." In June, 1827, a sharp debate took place in the House of Commons upon Mr. Davenport's Currency motion of the 14th, in which Sir Francis Burdett, Western, Huskisson, and Matthias Attwood took part, when the following passage of arms took place between the two latter:—

Mr. Huskisson replied, that he never had, as the Honourable Member had accused him of doing, treated the Majorities of that House with contempt. He would, however, treat with sovereign contempt the tissue of misrepresentations which made up the speech of the Honourable Member, and would not trouble himself to contradict them.

Mr Attwood explained, and retorted upon the Right Honourable Gentleman (Mr. Huskisson) the expressions which he had applied to his (Mr. Attwood's) observations, desiring to assure the Right Honourable Gentleman that there was no degree of contempt which he had thought proper to express that he (Mr. Attwood) did not equally feel towards the statements of the Right Honourable Gentleman."

Extracts from letters for 1828 :—

Mrs. Thos. Attwood, Harborne, near Birmingham.

Castle & Falcon (London, Feb 21, 1828).

The trial comes on in the morning at 9 o'clock if our opponents have the courage to face it, which I much doubt. I believe it to be totally impossible that any shadow of blame can attach to John A., and if I should be disappointed in this, I am sure that it can only arise from the most frightful knavery among the enemy.

Castle & Falcon, Feb. 22, 1828.

. . . After being in court 2 *whole* days, we have to-night obtained a verdict of *acquittal*, by the interference of the jury, *before we had commenced our defence*. All our counsel, and indeed every individual in court, pronounced it to be the most infamous prosecution they had ever known. If we had began our defence, we should, if possible, have covered our opponents with greater shame. . . .

Castle & Falcon, Feb. 25, 1828.

. . . I have received your letter, and I think you have acted quite right in the matter of Mr. Green Simcox's funeral I had no idea that he was in any danger until a few days ago. If you see his father, I hope you will tell him how I have been occupied in this base and infamous indictment, which has been got up with so much legal fraud and chicanery that no kind of mere innocence, however entire, furnished any kind of protection against it. We were obliged to foresee everything, and to guard against everything in a thousand shapes and ways, and we had the most dreadful villainy to contend against. Added to this, I have been over head and ears engaged, as you know, in the operations between the country bankers and the Bank of England, and in the business of the Birmingham election.

Castle & Falcon, Feb. 27, 1828.

. . . The business of the bankers and of the election has occupied me very much. . . . The political world begins to look serious. The king is unquestionably very ill, and one of his principal underhand council is latterly *missing;* supposed to be on account of some secret plunder in the way of stockjobbing. In the meanwhile nothing is acknowledged respecting the cause of the quarrel between Herries and Huskisson, although the former still asserts that it originated in a *plot*, or rather that its effect in overturning Lord Goderich's administration originated in a *plot*. . . .

Castle & Falcon, Feby. 28, 1828.

I write for the purpose of saying that I have an interview with the Govr. of the Bank at 1 o'clock to-morrow, which will prevent my coming by the Eclipse. I shall, however, in all probability leave town by one of the coaches to-morrow night, or possibly on Saturday morning.

I have not had time to tell you the particulars of our trial, but you will see some of them in the Birmm. paper on Monday next. We had no occasion to enter upon our defence, nor was our Counsel permitted to finish his speech. Our enemies were crushed under the fire of their own guns. The worst thing we had to contend with was the villainy of ———, who absolutely absented himself from the trial, having been bribed, as I believe. Fortunately we had no occasion for him or for any one else. I am going to dine with Mr. Tennyson to-day to meet Lord Althorpe and other important converts to my money views. Mr. Dugdale and Mr. Lawley are very attentive, but I cannot stay in town for the purpose of dining with them. . . . Lord Ferrers desired to be very kindly remembered to you. He acted a very manly part in John A.'s business.

Old Hummums, Covent Garden, May 2, 1828.

. . . The picture and the dress have, no doubt, required attention. The latter, I hope, is made to set off the figure of my beloved. I hope also she will herself study to hold up her head, and walk boldly, easily, and gracefully, which are very charming additions to a fine figure. I am very fond of fine figures as you know. At a distance they do very well without a clear and fine skin, but on a near approach the latter is indispensable. I went last night to see Madlle. Sontag. I do not envy her father, her husband, or her lover. We have 500 better women in Birmm., and more than one in Harborne. She is however rather pretty, and has a tolerable figure—Mrs. Studd is her exact likeness, only not quite so tall. I have seen nothing else in town. We have settled the disputes with the commissioners amicably, and I should now return in a day or two if it were not that I expect to be detained some days with John Attwood and with the bank.

Old Hummums, May 5*th*, 1828.

. . . I am sorry to hear Marcus's foot is bad, and I am glad you have seen Mr. Hodgson respecting it. Sir Francis has put off his motion, and I expect will abandon it. Ministers declare they will persevere, come what will, but I find from Littleton and Lawley that they entertain great fears. I went yesterday to church at the King's Chapel, and heard fine music. . . . I am going down to the House to hear a debate upon £1 notes.

Old Hummums, 7 *May,* 1828.

. . . The picture you say is *standing*, which I like better than *sitting*. I hope Mr. Wyatt will take pains to set off the *waist* properly, and make my Beloved hold up her head boldly for that purpose. . . . But when I am in London I am quite in dread of meeting friends, lest they should lay embargoes on me for dinner, and thereby keep me the longer from home. For this reason I have avoided seeing Davenport and others ; and yet I find myself so busy that I have yet only passed Temple Bar once. John A. is not yet come. If he should not come at all I shall return to you in a few days. The Ministers say they will on no account abandon the Standard of Money, and yet they acknowledge very great dangers attending their proceedings. The Duke is likely to part with Peel, and then I think they will alter. . . .

27, Gracechurch St., June 19, 1828.

. . . We have broken off the negociation with the Iron Co. totally. Their demands were inadmissible. . . . .

To Mrs. Attwood, Wolstanton.
Birmingham, Dec. 18, 1828.

. . . I have succeeded in getting a favourable answer from Mr. Peel respecting the young man unjustly sentenced to transportation for life. I rather think Mr. Peel remembers my services to him and his friends during the *late panic*, and certainly I am of opinion that if the Borough Proprietors were to give me £100,000 a year, they would give no more than strict gratitude would require of them. My *Scotch Banker* is got into great repute, and is particularly praised by the newspapers of Manchester, Liverpool, and Bristol. I believe I gave you one for your Bror. ; if not, let me know, and I will send him one. Marcus attends to his books very well. We are indeed all of us very good, and you would be surprised to find how harmonious we are. We went to Church on Sunday, 2 of us twice, the other once. Miss Judy pays great attention to your mother. When Miss Angela comes home, I have a pretty job for her, which is to make us some of the ancient liquors called Morat, Mead and Pigment, which I have discovered how to make from Dr Henry. . . .

(Same address.)
Birmingham, Sat, Dec. 20, 1828.

. . Bosco and Tommy went to the Ball, and found it very dull. Mr. Vale is leaving his new house, and has taken Mr Villiers's house in Newhall St. He asks £5000 for his house, and Mrs. Redfern has been thinking of it, but she does not like the price, and her sister does not much like the two families being too near together. I intend to go to Hawn to-morrow if I can, and therefore shall not have the pleasure of writing to you again before I see you. . . .

"London, December twenty-seven, 1828.
Thos. Attwood, Esq., Birmingham.

Robert Peel.
Private. <div align="right"><i>Whitehall</i>, 27 <i>Dec.</i>, 1828.</div>
SIR,

I beg leave to acknowledge the receipt of your letter, and to assure you with perfect sincerity, that although I may not arrive at the same conclusions with yourself in reference to the important subject on which you have addressed me, I receive your communications with feelings very different from those which could induce me to characterize them as intrusive or impertinent

I presume the measures adopted some years since for the return to a Metallic Currency have been operating gradually—that they have produced in their progress a considerable portion of that effect which you anticipate from their completion.

Regarding then the general effect supposed to have been produced by those measures upon the manufacturing industry of the Country, how happens it that, according to your own statement, 'every market in the world is glutted already with British manufactures'? and what object could there be, so far as foreign Commerce is concerned, in encouraging (as an abundant Paper circulation would encourage) an increased supply of articles for which there would appear to be no sufficient demand?

What is there in the present state of the Revenue—in the produce of those Taxes which are laid on articles of general consumption, and all fixed in amount—which should lead us to infer, either that the internal consumption of the Country is diminished, or that the Country will be unable to discharge her obligations?

If the manufactured produce of the Country has gradually increased, and if the internal consumption has gradually increased in a ratio equal to that of the increase of population, what are the grounds from which you infer that there is, speaking generally, a deficiency of money? I confess I doubt whether any quantity of grain can be imported from abroad sufficient in amount to derange the circulation.

> I have the honour to be Sir,
> Your obedient Servant,
> ROBERT PEEL."

This letter is endorsed by T. Attwood as follows:—

In reply to T. A.'s letter of 24th Decr., sent by post on 25th Decr. 1828 to Mr. Peel. T. A.'s must have been received by Mr. Peel on Friday morning, 26 Decr., 1828, on which day the *Courier* of the 27th states Mr. Peel had an interview with the Duke of Wellington at the Treasury.

His first letters during the year 1828 allude to an episode in the case of Small *v.* Attwood. The British Iron Company indicted John Attwood for perjury, and the trial took place at the King's Bench on February 21st and 22nd, before Lord Tenterden and a special jury. A full report is given in the *Times* of February 22nd and 23rd. The proceedings excited great interest. The court was crowded during both days of the trial, and Earl Ferrers occupied a seat upon the Bench. Mr. Gurney, Mr. Campbell, Mr. Pollock, Mr. Carter, and Mr. Jardine appeared for the prosecution; Sir James Scarlett, Mr. Brougham, Mr. Serjeant Russell, Mr. Lovat, and Mr. Parke were engaged for the defendant. John Attwood's answer, sworn on the 10th of April, 1827, was produced, and was of amazing length, covering no less than forty-seven large skins of parchment. After occupying two days in bringing forward the case for the prosecution, Mr. Gurney, finding the Judge's opinion against him, said he would not press the case further, and the Jury immediately returned a verdict of *Not Guilty*. John Attwood, who was in court, was at once surrounded by his friends, and warmly congratulated upon the result.

In the *Birmingham Independent* of January 3rd, 1828, there is a complimentary letter addressed to T. Attwood by a Mr. Thos. Lakins, from which it appears that the principles of the former were rapidly becoming more and more Liberal. In this letter the writer proposes that in the event of the Elective Franchise being obtained for Birmingham by Mr. Tennyson's Bill, the voting should take place by ballot, and that the various churches and chapels should be used for polling places!—a little in advance of the times!

On September 27th and October 22nd, 1827, and on April 5th, April 9th, May 22nd, and August 13th, 1828, T. Attwood published in the *Globe* six articles upon Banking and Currency. These, together with three other articles, he afterwards published in a small volume entitled *The Scotch Banker*, a work which became widely known at the time, but of which I possess only a second edition, published in 1832. In this work he gives the following estimate of the character of Cobbett, with whom he was so long and so intimately associated, either as friend or foe, and which, I may remark, forms a striking contrast to the coarse and bitter language which Cobbett often used when speaking of him :—

It is no flattery to Mr. Cobbett to acknowledge that his talents are great and various, and in some respects unrivalled. But his ambition, his inveterate prejudices, his ignorance of the paper system, and his *bitter hatred of existing institutions*, render him but a dangerous guide to those who wish to preserve them. The writer of this paper told Lord Sidmouth, in 1819, that in adopting Mr. Peel's bill, "the Government were falling into the snares of Mr. Cobbett, as completely as ever *bird fell into the fowler's net.*"

Cobbett reviewed the *Scotch Banker* at considerable length in his *Register* of May 24th, 1828, and of course differed very much from Attwood's conclusions. The *Quarterly Review*, No. 78, also notices this book briefly and rather contemptuously. In consulting the few newspapers for 1828 which are accessible to me, I find that during that year Matthias Attwood voted in the minority on Sir Francis Burdett's motion on the Catholic question on May 12th, and that he presented a petition from the Bankers of Cirencester against the suppression of £1 notes, on May 23rd. He also voted in the minority of 49 in favour of Sir James Graham's Motion—" That a Select Committee be appointed to inquire into the state of the circulation in Promissory Notes under the value of £5, in England, and to report their observations and opinion thereupon to the House, with reference to the expediency of making any alteration in the laws now in force relating thereto." Sir Thos. Baring, Sir F. Burdett, Col. Sibthorp, Ald. Thompson, and Mr. E. D. Davenport voted with him in this division. On May 23rd, besides the petition already mentioned, he presented another from the proprietors of lead ore in Wales, and took the opportunity to make various remarks on the state of the Currency, which were protested against by Mr. Peel. On the following June 6th he spoke at length on the "Bank Note (Scotland) Restriction Bill," upon which occasion he was supported by Sir F. Burdett and Sir James Graham, and had another sharp altercation with Huskisson. Generally speaking he neither spoke or voted upon any question save the Currency, but he voted with Mr. Tennyson in a minority of 42 for the postponement of the East Retford Disfranchisement Bill, and he signed a petition in December in favour of a criminal named Hunton, who was then lying under sentence of death for forgery, at the prosecution of Messrs. Curtis & Robarts.

CHAPTER IX.

Commencement of the great period of Attwood's life—Elihu Burritt's opinion of his services.—Birmingham Currency Petition—Great Meeting on May 8th, 1829—Attwood's Speech received with extraordinary enthusiasm—Letter from Cobbett—Contemptuous Rejection of the Currency Petition—Attwood determines to found "The Birmingham Political Union"—Immense sacrifices necessary—First meeting of friends for the purpose on the 14th December, 1829—Cobbett's Remarks—Matthias Attwood.

WITH the year 1829 the great period of Thomas Attwood's life may be said to have commenced. It was then that he emerged from the comparative obscurity in which he had lived since 1813, and commenced that arduous and exhausting political agitation which saved, indeed, his country from anarchy and bloodshed, but broke down his own health and ruined his family. In order, however, that my imperfect statement of the great services rendered by him, at this critical juncture of public affairs, may not rest solely on my own assertions, I propose to commence the narration of this memorable time with a quotation from Elihu Burritt, one of the few writers who have done him justice. In order to attach due weight to this testimony it should be borne in mind that Burritt was an American, and personally unacquainted with Attwood. In his *Walks in the Black Country and its Green Border-Land* he writes as follows:—

"But Birmingham, notwithstanding this outburst of popular violence, is distinguished above any other town in Christendom for organizing a political force which had hitherto acted like the lightning, the tornado, or earthquake, in sudden, wasting, or wasteful explosions. Under the leadership or inspiration of Thomas Attwood, public opinion won the greatest victory it had ever achieved without blood. Under him it was raised from an impulsive brute force to a moral power which the mightiest wrong could not resist. It was a perilous crisis for England. In almost every town or village there was the sharp crack of fiery sparks, showing how the very air the people breathed was charged with the electricity of their passionate sentiment. The approaching tempest gathered blackness, and its thunder-clouds revealed the bolts that were heating and hissing for their work of wrath and ruin. Very few thoughtful men of the nation can now doubt that the storm would have burst upon the country with all the desolation of civil war, if Thomas Attwood and the men of Birmingham had not drawn the lightning out of the impending tempest by the rod of moral force, which was grasped and wielded by his steady hand. From the central hill of the town he lifted up his revolutionary standard, with this new device: 'PEACE, LAW, AND ORDER!' This white flag, and not the bloody banner of brute force and brute passion which had been raised in other times, at home and abroad, to right political wrongs, was the *drapeau* of the Political Union, which he formed and headed in the metropolis of the Black Country. To this rallied men of all ranks and professions and occupations—members of Parliament, peers of the realm, clergy and ministers of all denominations, and the rank and file of the foundries, factories, and workshops of the district. The means were not only worthy the end, but of equal worth in moral value. On that grand march to political right and power, the masses stood shoulder to shoulder with their leaders. It was a great co-partnership and fraternization of the classes. They showed to European Christendom a spectacle it never saw or conceived before, what had never been seen or imagined in England before. That was a mighty mass meeting of the people, which could be counted by ten thousands, and nine in ten belonging to the working classes—a waving sea of faces, with 100,000 eager, listening eyes turned towards the speaker, gazing at principles and resolutions which no human voice could utter in the hearing of the vast multitude, but which were raised in great letters on standard boards, one to each half acre of men. That was about the grandest sight ever witnessed. It is computed that full 100,000 men—and three-fourths of them stalwart men of the hammer and pick, spade and file— were numbered in some of these outdoor meetings, who were swayed with indignant emotion, and listened with wrathful eyes and clenched fists to the story of their political wrongs, till they looked like an army massed for battle. But the small hand of one of their fellow-townsmen waving above the surging host, with the other 'grasping the banner of strange device'—'*Peace, Law, and Order!*'—curbed and kept down the brute force of the mighty sentiment, and held the people back from violence. The white folds of that unstained flag, as it waved over Constitution Hill, seemed to shed outward on the breeze an influence that reached and moved and moulded the common mind of the nation The motto and motive principles of the Birmingham banner of reform were not happy-worded theories which were easy to utter and as costless to practise. At that time the town numbered full 100,000 inhabitants, and no population of equal census in the kingdom was more intelligent and vigorous-minded. Their mechanical industries and occupations, involving and exercising so much science, thought, and skill, tended to quicken and expand the political conceptions and sensibilities of the artisans. No town in the realm could have felt more keenly the aggravated disparities to which it was subjected. Small villages, and even hamlets, in the south and west of England, had each its member of Parliament, and some of them two apiece. There were boroughs possessing thirty seats in the House of Commons, whose whole population put together did not equal that of Birmingham. And what aggravated this disparity, many of these were 'pocket boroughs,' and the pockets that held them belonged to peers of the realm, who had exercised the right to do what they would with their own. Thus, the House of Commons was at the risk if not in the condition of being a mere *apanage* to the House of Lords, and the creature and agent of its will and interest.

These were some of the political wrongs which Thomas Attwood and other orators of the Birmingham Political Union put in fervid and graphic exposition before the swaying, heaving masses of the town and district ; thousands of them being the sons of the rioters of 1791, who burned out Priestley, and mobbed the Liberals for their sympathy with the French revolutionists. It is said that at some of these monster gatherings of strong-willed and strong-handed men, with fierce faces begrimed with the grease and coal-dust of their factories, forges, and mines, Attwood's face would pale at the thought of the deluge that would follow the outburst of all that brute power, should it break the holding of his hand and trample upon his banner of new device— '*Peace, Law, and Order.*' But it held them fast to the end. . . .

If they had burst forth into violence under the pressure, and had been followed by thousands in other towns, the powerful and determined opponents of reform, who had all the military resources of the nation at their command, would have been able and willing to crush the movement by sword, bomb, and bayonet. But here was a force arrayed and engaged in close action, which neither Wellington nor Napoleon ever encountered on the field of battle. The Iron Duke could not withstand it, nor delay its triumph. It carried the Reform Bill of 1832 against all the resistance that could be organised against it.

Thus Birmingham was not merely the accidental scene of one of the greatest political events in English history. It organised the force that produced the event, that has governed the governments and guided the people of the kingdom from that day to this. It erected public opinion into a mighty power and enginery for the public good—a power ever ready to be worked against any evil that legislation could remove, or the enlightened mind and conscience of the people could abolish by moral action. It was worked to a glorious victory against slavery in the British West Indies, and to an illustrious triumph at home against the Corn Laws. From the time, to use the old thread-worn figure, that 'victory perched upon the standard' of the Birmingham Political Union, '*Peace, Law, and Order*,' no other flag has been reared, and no other force that it represented has been contemplated by any party or part of the English people with a view to political or social change. The ends for which the Political Union, the Anti-Slavery Society, and the Anti-Corn Law League laboured, and the triumphs they won, were of immeasurable value in themselves, but the educational means they employed in enlightening the minds of the masses, in teaching them to think, reflect, compare, and observe for themselves, produced results of equal importance. Nor was this organisation of the moral forces of a nation's mind limited in its benefits to England. Like the development and application of some new mechanical or natural force, it extended to other countries, where its operation was even more needed than it was in England

The Birmingham banner, '*Peace, Law, and Order*,' as Lamartine said of the tricolour, will yet make the tour of the world, sweeping away with its white folds all the red flags of brute force, and rallying aggrieved populations to the platform instead of the barricade."

On January 28th Thomas Attwood received the following letter from Mr. Peel, in reply to one of his written the day before:—

"*Private*.   *Whitehall, Jan.* 28, 1829
SIR,
    I beg to assure you that, urgent as the pressure of public business has been, the communication which you made to me on the 8th instant was read by me with the greatest attention.
    I communicated it to the Chancellor of the Exchequer.
                    I have the honour to be, Sir,
                            Your obedient and faithful servt.,
Thomas Attwood, Esq.,   ROBERT PEEL."
    Birmingham.

Thomas Attwood appears to have remained closely at home, and to have been occupied in preparing for the great events which took place later in the year, during the early months of 1829. Before breaking loose from all his previous ties and traditions and openly joining the active party of Reform, he appears to have determined to make one more effort to induce the Duke of Wellington, who was then at the head of the Ministry, to adopt those measures which he deemed essential to relieve the distress of the country. Accordingly on the 25th April, 1829, the following requisition was drawn up at his instigation, and addressed to the High Bailiff of Birmingham:—

"We, the undersigned, request you will call a Meeting of the Merchants, Manufacturers, and Inhabitants of the town of Birmingham, for the purpose of considering the distressed state of the country, and the propriety of petitioning Parliament to adopt such measures as may be necessary for its relief"

Pursuant to this requisition a very crowded and enthusiastic meeting was held at the Public Office on May 8th. In consequence of the very great number of persons present, not one fourth of whom could be accommodated there, it was resolved to adjourn the meeting to Beardsworth's Repository. The chair was taken by the High Bailiff, and about four thousand persons were present. Mr. Attwood addressed the meeting in a speech of nearly three hours' duration, which was listened to with the closest attention, and received with loud applause. At its conclusion thirty-one resolutions were put to the meeting and carried almost unanimously, with only three or four dissentient voices. The resolutions nearly all refer to the favourite Currency doctrines of Attwood and Spooner, and are too long to be reprinted here; but I extract the following:—

"1. That in the opinion of this meeting, the want of employment, the deficiency of wages, and the present general and almost unexampled distress of the country, are mainly to be attributed to the attempt which Government is making to restore the ancient and obsolete Currency of the country, without having previously effected a corresponding reduction in the taxes and monied obligations of the country.

26. That the petition to both Houses of Parliament, now read, be approved and adopted; and that, after lying for signatures at the Public Office, it be forwarded for presentation to Parliament by such Members of both Houses as the Committee hereafter to be appointed shall direct.

29. That the grateful thanks of this meeting be given to T. Attwood, Esq., for his very luminous, convincing, and eloquent address; and that this meeting rejoices to find, after an experience of sixteen years, that the approbation of his conduct, which was expressed by the mechanics of Birmingham in 1812, did equal credit to their heads and to their hearts."

The petition adopted at this meeting was signed by 40,000 persons, and presented to the House of Commons by C. Callis Western, afterwards Lord Western. It was received with distrust and neglect, and Cobbett informs us that scarcely forty members could be got together to listen to it, and several of them expressed their opinion that its statements of distress were much exaggerated, whilst the Duke of Wellington, in his speech on the petition, observed: "The People employed a *fictitious wealth*, and that fictitious wealth having been removed, they cannot immediately come down to those quiet and sober habits which are required from them; and this, in my opinion, is the principal cause of the distress."

But however cavalierly the petition may have been treated by both Houses of Parliament, its effect upon the masses was very different; for from it, as Attwood assures us, sprang the famous Political Union. One of its first results was to convert Cobbett from an enemy into a friend. In his *Register* of May

16th, 1829, he reviewed the petition at length, reprinted many of the resolutions, spoke most favourably of the talents of Thomas Attwood, and bore the following testimony to the moderation of the reforms advocated by him and his brother:—

"Thus it is that we differ. The Attwoods would keep up army, deadweight, sinecures, places and pensions, the Stock Exchange in full swing, and the infamous boroughmongers in the height of prosperity: I would destroy all these except the army, and that I would disband. The Attwoods would not touch the Church: I, on the contrary, would repeal the law by which it was made. The Attwoods, in short, would, if they could, make this system immortal: I would, if I could, put an end to it *this very day.*"

Amongst those who supported Attwood in moving his currency petition I find the names of Scholefield, Salt, Edmonds, and others who were hereafter to be well known in the annals of the Political Union. This, too, was the very last occasion upon which he received the public support and co-operation of his old friend Richard Spooner. Henceforth their political paths diverged, and when Mr. Spooner was solicited soon after to join the ranks of the Union, he excused himself on the ground of his magisterial duties, or, in other words, he had probably made up his mind to join the Tories. He took no part in the stupendous labours of the Political Union, nor did he share in its glorious triumph.

On the 18th May an answer to Attwood's speech was published by W. Redfern, in which the latter sets forth at length the opposition view of the Currency question.

In order to show the high enthusiasm which Attwood's conduct at this time aroused amongst the people of Birmingham, I insert the following lines, not on account of their poetical merit, but for the kindly feeling they display:—

"A Poetical Tribute to Thomas Attwood, Esq., whose bright display of manly energy and eloquence rivetted the attention of five thousand persons for nearly three hours, at the late Town's Meeting.

Addressed to the Artizans of Birmingham.

> For once let Fancy, warm and true,
> Present the Champion to your view;
> Behold him now before you stand,
> Surrounded by a patriot band,

The fire of Freedom in his eye,
That sparkles with a proud defy,
As if some tyrant power withstood
The people's right, the country's good !
Hark ! hear him, with true sterling sense,
Burst forth in strains of eloquence,
Fierce rushing as the tide along,
(Impetuous, bold, resistless, strong)
That each stupendous wave rolls o'er,
And drives the mighty flood before.
And hear him, too, with pride reveal
What Freemen think—what Freemen feel !
Make all your wants and wishes known,
As though your suff'rings were his own,
Nor rank, nor power, nor wealth, nor fame,
Deters him from his godlike aim !
To soothe and succour in distress
The widow and the fatherless ;
The naked clothe, the hungry feed,
And aid the poor in time of need ;
Wipe the salt tear from sorrow's eye,
And hush the supplicating sigh.
These are the cares his mind controul,
These melt with sympathy his soul,
While anguish thrills through every vein,
To hear the starving wretch complain.
Shall he in vain exert his might
To advocate the people's right ?
The thunder of his voice alone
Shall echo to the Monarch's throne !
Make England's King, with fervour feel
The merits of his just appeal !
And proud upon his native isle,
Shall *Attwood's* happy genius smile,
Whose worth shall warble from the lyre,
In strains of true poetic fire ;
Each muse shall tune the vocal shell,
And strive in rapture to excel ;
Chant his loud praise the land around,
While millions catch the mighty sound ;
Nurs'd on the lap of babbling fame,
E'en babes shall learn to lisp his name !
Whose heart no selfish feeling knows—
That vibrates for another's woes ;
Her cheek in tears let sorrow steep,
And ATTWOOD too with her can weep—
The lamb when gentle pity draws—
The lion in a nation's cause !

And when this fleeting life is past,
May Heaven his labours crown at last,
Where perfect joys, to us unknown,
Surround the Great Eternal's Throne.
J. F."

In June Mr. Attwood received the following letter from Cobbett:—

"SIR, *Barn-Elm*, 24 *June*, 1829.

It is quite useless to make *further* inquiries : the distress is like the air itself. I came home on Monday from *East Sussex*.

1. At Sevenoaks in Kent, the Bank shut up for a month past.

2. The inn-keepers, that used (only two months ago) to have, amongst them, 200 farmers, and thus sit down to *dinner*, had not last Saturday one single man. It is a great market.

3. The grocers at this place sell a *third* less than they sold two months back. The drapers next to nothing.

4. Butter (*fresh*) 10*d*. a pound at Tonbridge ; and 8*d*. in the Wealds of Kent and Sussex.

5. Only 2 wheat ricks and 4 bean ricks, and none of any other corn from Barn-Elm to Battle.

6. The *butchers* even selling ¼ less than 2 months ago.

7. The bank at Tonbridge issuing some (?) Lewis & Hastings one pound notes.

8. Change got with *great difficulty* ; and 15*d*. given for changing a 5 pound note of another town.

9. 5 p. notes taken *in payments* at Sevenoaks, and sent off directly to London.

10. The crops, on *the whole*, good, and especially the wheat.

11. The farmers *cursing* the parliament for *separating* and leaving things in this state. Poor devils ! little do they know about the 'parliament.'

12. The hop-grounds *full of weeds* (though so much dry weather) and the people *out of employment!* To be sure , for the planters have *no money* to pay for hoeing and becking.

13. The inn and public-house keepers fairly *frightened*. Even so near to the Wen as Bromley, their receipts have fallen off *two-thirds*. They do not attempt to disguise the fact ; and the discontent is nearly universal. This is, as that old rogue Talleyrand said, *le commencement de la fin;* for I am sure that *the whole* of the country paper will *go*, if these fellows proceed : and that, then, the London fives will go. I remember, that in a time of great scarcity at the close of the American rebellion, my father saying to my uncle one day : 'There, Stephen, I have *lived to see* the *gallon* loaf sold for a shilling !' That is 2 quartern loaves. He thought the Day of Judgment was coming The usual price was 6*d*. the gallon loaf, 4*d*. the pound of fresh butter, real *strong* beer 4*d*. a pot, common beer 2*d*., and green peas 3*d*. a peck in mid-June. And, by God, if they *could* push their scheme along, it would come to this again at last But this they cannot do without reducing the taxes to about 12 or 15 millions a year.

I, in common with many hundreds of thousands, thank you and your towns-men for your excellent petition and equally good speech. I wrote to Lord Blandford and begged him to read the speech, of which I sent him a copy, telling him that that was the *pivot* on which all must turn. You are wrong to say that I have *frightened* the fellows : they have not sense enough to receive fright. Nothing but their impenetrable stupidity prevents one from saying that they are the greatest villains upon earth. The experience of *impunity* makes the fellows careless and bold ; and the country is to perish because they are not to confess their errors, or, in other words, because they are to have our money under pretence of *services* rendered us. *Assignats, Equitable Adjustment,* or a *Blow-up.* One of these they must now choose ; and they must choose pretty soon, or they will have the *last* of the three ; and, if they have *that,* they will have their just reward.

I am, Sir,
Your most obedt. & most hu. servant,
WM. COBBETT."

Unfortunately scarcely anything remains in the writing of Thomas Attwood by which I am able to trace the events which gradually led him to take the decisive step of founding the Birmingham Political Union. But there seems no doubt that the contemptuous rejection of his Currency petition and the sarcasms of Wellington were the last straws which broke the camel's back. For fifteen years, with the greatest sacrifices of himself and his family, he had dinned into the ears of successive administrations, by letters, pamphlets, and petitions, those measures which, rightly or wrongly, he deemed essential to restore the prosperity of the country. All his suggestions had been received with coldness and contempt, and his kind heart could no longer brook the spectacle of the appalling distress around him. He felt that, come what might, something must be done, a grand decision taken. He has himself left it upon record, that had he seen the country happy and prosperous under the rule of the oligarchs, he never would have disturbed their peaceful reign. He cared but little for theoretical perfection in modes of government, provided only that good results were obtained. He may very likely have been mistaken, most people would say that he was mistaken, but he was firmly convinced that he *could* relieve the misery of the nation if he had the power, and he now determined to jeopard everything that man holds most dear, to obtain that power. The grand idea occurred to him that if the House of Commons would not listen to his prayer, he would create a new House which would be more amenable to reason—if the aristocracy would not hear him, he would transfer their power to the middle classes, and see what *they* would do. Actuated by these sentiments he determined to join the party of Reform, and it is a remarkable circumstance, and one which has been most ungratefully passed over by Liberal historians, that, although many great men had pressed for years the question of reform, no substantial progress in obtaining it was made until Attwood took the lead. But in order to obtain his great end, the most terrible sacrifices had to be made, the most serious difficulties surmounted. The public obstacles which he triumphantly overcame, though now forgotten, were sufficiently acknowledged by a grateful people at the time; but I, who know something of the private ones he had to contend with, am astonished at the moral courage he displayed. I can scarcely believe that it was the same kind grandfather, who could never scold a child, reprimand a servant, or send away a beggar, who defied the Iron Duke with all his fame, and organised that formidable and irresistible body of men which Burritt has so graphically described. Nothing but the purest patriotism could have induced him to take this step. Though without any pretensions to aristocratic birth, his social position was just such that he had everything to gain and nothing to lose by allying himself with the boroughmongers, whilst, on the other hand, he was not in the independent position of a man with a large fortune or estate. In those days, peers were very glad to place men of talent in their pocket boroughs, on condition, of course, that they should vote according to the wishes of their patrons. Had Attwood been selfish or ambitious he might have adopted this course, and no doubt have soon risen to a place in the Ministry. His business was that of a banker, and peculiarly dependent upon the support of the respectable classes, who generally regarded the idea of reform with abhorrence. His stern old father, absorbed in business, must have strongly objected to his son mixing in radical politics His wife, belonging to a Tory family, and devoted to Church and

King, must have been horrified at the idea. But it would be an endless task to enumerate the sacrifices which a man in his circumstances had to make before joining the Radical party.

Only two of Attwood's letters for the remainder of 1829 have been preserved. The first, dated September 4th, refers only to domestic and family matters, and is addressed to his wife, who was then staying with Mrs. R. Spooner near Worcester, whilst the second, of October 24th, mentions that he had invited E. D. Davenport, M.P., C. Jones, and B. Hadley to dine with him, and no doubt to discuss his plan of the proposed Union.

All his arrangements being at length matured, on the 14th December, 1829, "when," says Mr. James Jaffray, "hundreds of the inhabitants were shivering by their cold firesides, Mr. Attwood, with Mr. Scholefield and fourteen other gentlemen, met at the Royal Hotel. They were called together by a circular 'signed by six tradesmen.' This little meeting then founded 'The Political Union for the Protection of Public Rights.' They adjourned till the Monday following, when they met at the Globe (now the Clarendon), Temple Street. Mr. Attwood again presided, and he, in conjunction with Mr. Charles Jones and Mr. T. C. Salt, submitted the rules of the Union. They were adopted and signed by twenty-eight persons; and it was resolved that they should be submitted for the approbation of the people."

It is to be regretted that no private memorandum respecting the commencement of the Union has been preserved. The new organisation at once commenced to act upon public opinion, and in the next chapter I shall endeavour to trace its rapid and extraordinary success.

On the 19th December, 1829, Cobbett announced his intention of visiting Birmingham in the following terms:—

"I have chosen Birmingham to begin at, because that town has been distinguished above others by the petition sent from it during the last session of Parliament, and because it is the place of residence of a gentleman who has greatly distinguished himself as a bold accuser of those who have brought the country into its present situation, but who has at the same time expressed opinions with regard to the remedy now to be applied precisely the opposite of mine, who has expressed his opinion that there ought to be a non-convertible paper currency, like that which we had from

1797 to 1817, or a currency regulated by a metallic standard of value, advanced in price in a degree necessary to render it a just and adequate measure of the values and obligations of society; in other, and what I deem plainer, words, a paper currency not convertible into gold, and permanently depreciated; or, a gold and silver money of less intrinsic value than the current coin of the realm. Either of these measures Mr. Attwood thinks would be just for the present, and safe for the future; whereas I think that either of them would be unjust towards individuals, ruinous and disgraceful to the nation, and that, after inflicting this injustice, ruin, and disgrace, would prove insufficient to preserve the country from that violent convulsion that all men so justly dread. The talents of Mr. Attwood, aided by his high character, and the weight which he must otherwise have in the community amongst whom he moves, make it desirable that those which I deem to be his errors should be frankly combatted in the face of that community; and I cannot give a better proof of my sincerity and of my confidence in the soundness of my own principles, than by venturing whatsoever I may possess of reputation for knowledge upon that spot where of all others I may reasonably expect the greatest difficulty to contend with. This, therefore, I shall do, and I shall do it with unfeigned respect for Mr. Attwood, not only on account of his great talents, but on account of the bold and honest manner in which he has expressed his indignation, &c. . . ."

Matthias Attwood appears to have attended frequently during the parliamentary session of 1829. On March 18th he voted with the minority against the second reading of the Roman Catholic Relief Bill, and again on March 27th he voted against bringing up the report of the same Bill. In the debate of May 2nd, on the Silk Trade Bill, he spoke at great length, and was complimented by Mr. Baring and Mr. Maberly on the ability displayed in his speech. On May 7th he was again in the minority on Mr. Tennyson's motion for giving members to the town of Birmingham, and on the 9th he spoke at length in the debate on the Budget, and was again warmly opposed by Huskisson. In the *Times* of June 13 I find him mentioned as Vice-President and Treasurer of the East London Pension Society, and the same paper of that date devotes part of a leading article to an attack upon his Currency views, whilst in the debate of June 12th on the "State of the Country" he was again considered a worthy antagonist of Huskisson.

CHAPTER X.

Establishment of the Political Union on January 25th, 1830—Extraordinary success of the movement—Objects, Rules, and Duties of the Union—Its first Declaration signed by Attwood, Scholefield, Muntz, and thirty-three others—Lord Blandford joins the Union—First meeting of the Union on May 17th—Grandeur of the spectacle—Thomas Attwood is presented with a Gold Medal by the Members—Speeches of Attwood, Scholefield Hadley, and others, and unqualified success of the first meeting—Attwood's Letters from London—Sir Francis Burdett visits Harborne and presides at the first Annual Meeting of the Union—Alison on the Parliamentary Proceedings of M Attwood—Deaths of George IV and Huskisson—Grand Dinner at Birmingham on October 11th, 1830, to celebrate French Revolution—Unprecedented magnitude of the entertainment—Town's Meeting of December 13th in support of Earl Grey—Triumphant Speech of Attwood—Spread of Political Unions throughout Britain—Petition of Rights—Charles Attwood founds the Northern Political Union.

THE year 1830 opened gloomily. The distress was fearful, and even the Duke of Wellington, says Martineau, was obliged to take emphatic notice of it in the Royal Speech. In consequence, the efforts of Attwood and the other promoters of the Political Union were welcomed with extraordinary enthusiasm in Birmingham, and the Town's Meeting held at Beardsworth's Repository on January 25th, 1830, for the purpose of establishing it, was admitted by every one, alike by friends and foes, to have been an unprecedented success. A full report of this meeting has been fortunately preserved, but as it is too long to insert entire, I shall abridge it to the best of my ability as follows :—

"This morning the largest meeting ever assembled in this kingdom within the walls of a building took place at Mr. Beardsworth's Horse and Carriage Repository, for the purposes set forth in the requisition published in the newspapers, and signed by 200 respectable inhabitants of the town There were at least from 12,000 to 15,000 persons present, and although the chair was taken at half-past ten in the morning, and the meeting did not separate until near five in the evening, the mass of spectators was so immense that

K 2

hundreds were compelled to retire in consequence of not being able to get sufficiently near to hear the proceedings.

The High Bailiff, Mr. W. Chance, having refused to convene the meeting, Thomas Attwood, Josh. Scholefield, G. F. Muntz, and nine other gentlemen summoned it upon their own responsibility, and G. F. Muntz was called to the chair.

After the reading of two requisitions by the Chairman, Josh. Scholefield proposed the first resolution and spoke as follows :—

'The resolution which I hold in my hand is almost simply declaratory, and as I defy any man to deny that the deepest distress imaginable pervades the town, there will be the less occasion for argument to support the resolution. It is fortunate for myself, too, that the next resolution will be brought forward by my friend Mr. Attwood, who will fully explain the objects we all have in view, and who, happily, is as capable of convincing his friends as he is powerful in silencing his calumniators. But why should I describe Mr. A. as my friend?—he is your friend and the friend of all men ; unceasingly labouring to do good to his fellow men, and to his townsmen in particular.'—Mr. S. then proceeded to produce proofs of the deplorable state of trade in Birmingham and the country generally, and concluded by moving the following resolution :—

'1. That the ruinous depression of the trade of the town of Birmingham has been progressively increasing for the last four years, and has now arrived at an extent never before equalled ; and when we look around us, and see that all the great productive interests of the nation are suffering, and have been suffering equally with ourselves, we are convinced that the hopes of amelioration, which have been so long and so frequently held out, are altogether fallacious and delusive.'

Previous to the motion being put, Mr. W. Redfern rose and stated that he suspected the sincerity of the principal promoters of the meeting, on the ground that they had hitherto talked of nothing but currency, and opposed all reform. After considerable confusion the meeting decided that Mr. Redfern should not be heard, and the first motion was then put and carried unanimously.

Mr. Attwood then rose. They had met to discuss a subject, important not only to themselves and to their children, but to the country generally, and to generations yet unborn; he should not, therefore, trespass much upon their time in discussing trifles. (After some remarks upon the conduct of the High Bailiff, Mr. A. proceeded). It was well known that the meeting in May last produced a very important effect throughout the country. He had heard it spoken of in at least 100 companies, in all of which he never heard one word of censure on its objects or resolutions dropped. In fifteen or twenty newspapers their resolutions had been advertised gratuitously ; and it was satisfactory to reflect that no document, in the recollection of any man, produced a stronger impression upon the public mind than the one which was issued by them on that occasion. He must, however, say that, although it produced so beneficial an effect upon the country, it did not produce the same upon the Legislature. Lord Carnarvon, in introducing their petition to the House of Lords, acted a manly and consistent part.

Mr. Brougham, although he could not support one part of our plan, undertook its presentation to the House of Commons. He told us that he did not agree with us that it would be advisable to lift up our means to the level of our burthens, but he would fight to bring down our burthens to the level of our means. He (Mr Attwood), however, was sorry to say that Mr. Brougham never fought at all, and the petitioners were much disappointed.

The Duke of Wellington, of whom he (Mr. A.) wished to speak with respect, when the petition was presented to the Lords, had made one or two curious observations. He said, 'You have been accustomed to a fictitious wealth—your habits are above what they ought to be—you must go back to the ancient modes of thinking and acting.' . . . No nobleman was, however, found to tell the noble Duke that his £700,000 was granted in fictitious money. (Cheers). No nobleman was present to tell him, that if the middle and lower classes were to return to the ancient level, that it was just that his salaries and grants, and the emoluments of his family, amounting to about £60,000 per annum, should be reduced to the same standard. No nobleman was found to ask, whether it was not equally just that salaries, grants, and places should be reduced with the wages of labour. (Cheers.) . . . He (Mr A.) had always been an advocate for reform, and he would defy any one to deny it. (Cheers.) When in a state of national prosperity—when there was abundance of trade for the manufacturer, and abundance of labour for the workman—when humble wages were the reward of humble labour, he did not come publicly forward as its advocate, he did not run his head against a wall, nor like Don Quixote charge windmills He had, however, always expressed a wish for reform. Gentlemen, however, argued, that because twenty years ago they were not public reformers they were inconsistent in being its advocates now. Was he (Mr. A.), now he had with him nine-tenths of all the respectability of the kingdom, and 99 out of every 100 of the assembly around him, not to come forward? He (Mr A.) should not sleep sound in his bed if, at the present crisis of national affairs, he did not lend his assistance to avert the awful consequences which he anticipated. (Cheering.)"

After Mr. Attwood had spoken for a considerable time, chiefly upon the panic of 1825, and Peel's Bill of 1819, the plan of the Union was read, the reading of which occupied a full hour, and was listened to throughout with the most profound attention.

I give the following extracts:—

"BIRMINGHAM POLITICAL UNION
FOR THE
PROTECTION OF PUBLIC RIGHTS.

"The experience of the last 15 years must certainly have convinced the most incredulous that the rights and interests of the middle and lower classes of the people are not efficiently represented in the Commons House of Parliament. . .

. . On whatsoever side we turn our eyes, we thus find subjects of the highest public importance everywhere demanding the public attention, and everywhere requiring the legal interference of the industrious classes. The vindication of the NATIONAL JUSTICE, the equalization and reduction of the NATIONAL TAXES, the protection of public rights, THE REDRESS OF PUBLIC WRONGS, the necessity of REFORM IN PARLIAMENT, and the relief of the NATIONAL DISTRESS, *all require that the* NATIONAL MIND *should slumber no more.*

Under these views and impressions it is therefore that we propose to form in BIRMINGHAM a GENERAL POLITICAL UNION of the INDUSTRIOUS CLASSES, for the PROTECTION of PUBLIC RIGHTS. We are forbidden to exercise the constitutional privilege of electing MEMBERS OF PARLIAMENT. But we are not forbidden to appoint *Councils of our own*, under whose guidance we may act. . . .

The following then are the objects of the POLITICAL UNION :—

1st. To obtain by every just and legal means such a Reform in the Commons House of Parliament as may ensure a real and effectual Representation of the Lower and Middle Classes of the People in that House.

2nd. To enquire, consult, consider, and determine, respecting the rights and liberties of the industrious classes, and respecting the legal means of securing those which remain and recovering those which are lost.

3rd To prepare Petitions, Addresses, and Remonstrances to the Crown and the Legislative Bodies, respecting the preservation and restoration of Public Rights, and respecting the repeal of bad laws, and the enactment of good laws.

4th. To prevent and redress, as far as practicable, all local public wrongs and oppressions, and all local encroachments upon the rights, interests, and privileges of the community.

5th. To obtain the repeal of the Malt and the Beer Taxes, and in general, to obtain an alteration in the system of Taxation, so as to cause it to press less severely upon the industrious classes of the community, and more equally upon the wealthy classes.

6th. To obtain the reduction of each separate Tax and expense of the Government in the same degree as the legislative increase in the value of money has increased their respective values, and has reduced and is reducing the general prices of labour throughout the country.

7th. To promote peace, union, and concord among all classes of His Majesty's subjects, and to guide and direct the public mind into uniform, peaceful, and legitimate operations; instead of leaving it to waste its strength in loose, desultory, and unconnected exertions, or to carve a way to its own objects, unguided, unassisted, and uncontrouled.

8th. To collect and organize the peaceful expression of the Public Opinion, so as to bring it to act upon the legislative functions in a just, legal, and effectual way.

9th. To influence by every legal means the elections of Members of Parliament, so as to promote the return of upright and capable representatives of the People.

10th. To adopt such measures as may be legal and necessary for the purpose of obtaining an effectual Parliamentary investigation into the situation of the country, and into the cause of its embarrassments and difficulties; with a view of relieving the National Distress, of rendering justice to the injured as far as practicable, and of bringing to trial any members of either House of Parliament who may be found to have acted from criminal or corrupt motives."

[Here follow the 16 Rules and Regulations of the Political Union.]

"The following are the Duties of the Members of the Political Union:—

1st. To be good, faithful, and loyal subjects of the King.

2nd. To obey the Laws of the Land; and when they cease to protect the Rights, Liberties, and Interests of the Community, to endeavour to get them changed by just, legal, and peaceful means only.

3rd. To present themselves at all general meetings of the Political Union, as far as they conveniently can; to conduct themselves peaceably and legally at such meetings, and to depart to their respective homes as soon as the Chairman shall leave the Chair.

4th. To choose only just, upright, and able men as members of the Political Council, and to dismiss them, and elect others in their stead, whenever they shall cease to watch over and defend the Rights, Liberties, and Interests of the Lower and Middle Classes of the People.

5th. To obey strictly all the just and legal directions of the Political Council, so soon as they shall be made public, and so far as they can legally and conveniently be obeyed.

6th. To bear in mind that the strength of our Society consists in the Peace, Order, Unity, and Legality of our proceedings; and to consider all persons as enemies who shall in any way invite or promote violence, discord, or division, or any illegal or doubtful measures.

7th. Never to forget that by the exercise of the above qualities we shall produce the peaceful display of an immense organized moral power which cannot be despised or disregarded; but that, if we do not keep clear of the innumerable and intricate Laws which surround us, the Lawyer and the Soldier will probably break in upon us, and render all our exertions vain."

Then follow the Duties of Members of the Political Council, and the plan concludes with further remarks on the general excellence of the British Constitution, the patriotism of the King, and the absolute necessity for a union between the lower and middle classes of society in order to obtain their just rights. The following thirty-six names were attached to the first declaration of the Birmingham Political Union:—

Thomas Attwood,	Joseph Russell,
Joshua Scholefield,	Urban Luckcock,
G. F. Muntz,	Thomas Shorthouse,
Edward Hobson,	George Edmonds,
John Laurence,	Josiah Emes,

Charles Jones,	C. W. Firchild,
John Slater,	James Claridge,
Benjamin Hadley,	T. W. Evans,
Thomas Todd,	William Beach,
Felix Luckcock,	J. B. Oram,
John Betts,	John Allday,
Charles Grafton,	Samuel Allen, sen.
Matthew Dixon,	Robert Cottrill,
Joseph Bodington,	William Birken,
Henry Knight,	D. B. Smith,
John Dyer,	John Wingfield,
William Pare,	T. C. Salt,
Joseph Hadley,	Thomas Parsons, jun.

Birmingham, Jan. 25, 1830.

Mr. Attwood resumed: "I feel it my duty to declare to you, that I know the country to be on the verge of dreadful calamities. It may be thought because I come forward now, that I shall be ready, 'come weal come woe,' to lead you through thick and thin—through the dark and dreary scenes which are approaching. As far as law will justify me, I will go with you. (Tremendous cheers.) When I say I will go with you as far as law will allow, I declare to you most solemnly, I will not go further one inch. (Cheers.) I know that a great crisis is approaching. I will do all I can to avoid that crisis; but if the nation is to go through the ordeal of political convulsions I will not interfere in those convulsions, and I wish you to bear this in mind when those dreadful circumstances arise. I know you will come to me and say, 'Lead us.' My friends, I will not lead you. I will go with you as far as law will justify; but if the elements of law and order are disorganized, I will go with you no further.'—Mr. Attwood retired amidst loud and vehement cheers.

The following motion, previously read by Mr. Attwood, was seconded by Mr. Betts:—

"2. That in the opinion of this meeting the general distress which now afflicts the country, and which has been so severely felt at different periods during the last fifteen years, is entirely to be ascribed to the gross mismanagement of public affairs; and that such mismanagement can only be effectually and permanently remedied by an effectual Reform in the Commons House of Parliament; and this meeting is also of opinion that for the legal accomplishment of this great object, and for the further redress of public wrongs and grievances, it is expedient to form a general Political Union between the lower and middle classes of the people in this town."

Mr. Joseph Parkes, although a Reformer, opposed the resolution at considerable length, objecting strongly to the Currency doctrines of the chief promoters of the Union, and concluded by moving a long amendment, which was seconded by Mr. W. Redfern; but the meeting having decided to hear them no longer, Attwood made a reply in which occurs the following passage:—

"The God of nature had not provided that mass of gold which was required to pay off the national engagements. Eight thousand tons of solid gold were equal to 800 millions of pounds sterling ; such an amount was not within the bowels of the earth. He would make one other remark, to show that he was no enemy to the Fund-holder. Consols had arisen from 60 to 93, while the value of land had been reduced from 60 to 30. During the war the two interests were upon a footing of equality. Now one was three times larger than the other. . . ." After some further remarks Mr. Attwood sat down amid loud and continued cheering. Mr. Edmonds warned the assembly against voting for the amendment, and the motion was then put and carried 1,000 to 1, amidst the most deafening cheers.

Such an exhibition of public feeling, or one which has excited so intense an interest throughout the whole neighbourhood, is not in the recollection of man.

Some other resolutions were also passed, one of which was that the 36 gentlemen who had brought forward the plan should be appointed the Political Council for the year ending the 1st Monday in July, 1830, and that after that date the Council should be elected agreeably to the rules. A petition to the House of Commons was also agreed to and signed by 30,000 men.

Thus was established what was probably the most successful, the most powerful, and the most peaceful and orderly organisation ever known in England. The Birmingham Political Union instantly attracted attention throughout the country, and on the 6th February, 1830, Cobbett reprinted its rules and regulations, and accompanied them with a very favourable notice. He said :—

"This is a very important matter. We see, at last, then, the middle class uniting with the working classes. Everywhere, where I have been, I have endeavoured to show the necessity of such union. The boroughmongers have long contrived to divide these two classes for purposes much too obvious to mention. At last the middle class begins to perceive that it must be totally sacrificed, unless it make a stand, and a stand it cannot make unsupported by the lower class. The declaration, or address, put forth by the leaders in this Union, is evidently from the pen of Mr. Thomas Attwood, and, like everything else that comes from his pen, exhibits a great deal of knowledge and a great deal of talent. . . ."

On January 29th, 1830, the Marquis of Blandford announced his adhesion to the Political Union in the following letter.—

"*To Thomas Attwood, Esq.*

"SIR,—Though I have not the honour of your personal acquaintance, I feel assured that I may use the name of our mutual friend, Mr. Scott, to justify the step I take in addressing you But on public grounds I feel I may also take this liberty.

Without further digression I therefore proceed to declare to you the intense interest and satisfaction I have received at perusing the account of your late town's meeting. I beg, by all means, that my name may be enrolled amongst you.

I wish, with all my heart, it were in my power to contribute in the shape of subscription in the proportion in which it might be expected of one whose misfortune it is to possess so high a rank, and still be so crippled in his circumstances as to find it inconvenient to do what might be looked for.

But I will hope to be considered a worthy member of your Union under a different point of view If I cannot pay in purse I will endeavour to do so in *kind;* and I have the pleasure to assure you that I am now prepared to introduce a Bill into the House—falsely called the Commons House—which is so constructed as to meet every single point you dwell on in the report of your speech

I am sensible that all such attempts may be styled '*delusions*'—and so they have ever proved, and have, I believe, been intended to be in the hands of their former advocates , but it is my firm conviction that *regeneration* is fated to proceed from another quarter.

Be it as it may, we must all do our utmost in our respective spheres.

I have the honour to be, Sir, &c.,

Harling, Norfolk." BLANDFORD."

On the 3rd February Thomas Attwood addressed a kind letter to his daughter Angela, who was then with her uncle Edward Carless, at Wolstanton, urging her to be very careful to avoid the extreme cold, but I can find no further mention of him, either in print or MS., until the 17th of May, when the first meeting of the Birmingham Political Union was held at Beardsworth's Repository. The report shows clearly that he had been fully occupied during the interval, and also how astonishingly successful the movement had been. I give an abstract of the proceedings as follows:—

" It having been resolved that a band of music should precede the procession, at nine o'clock on Monday morning, May 17, 1830, a large crowd assembled in Temple-street, and by half-past ten o'clock that and the adjoining streets were choked by thousands. The excitement intended by the display and exhibition of a procession was certainly most fully answered, as hundreds pressed into the Council rooms to enrol their names in the lists of the Union and receive the medal, the acknowledged and authorised badge of Membership. Among the names entered was that of Sir Charles Wolseley, who, in a letter to Mr. Creswick, of New-street, containing his subscription, expressed himself a warm supporter of the objects and plans of the Union. It may be safely asserted that since the year 1818, the time of the celebrated election of the legislatorial attorney, the town never presented so extraordinary a scene of commotion. Soon after 10 o'clock, the members were ordered to form two deep in St. Philip's Churchyard, where they were informed the members of the Council would join and head them. Mr. Edmonds's known influence over the populace was never more conspicuously displayed than on this occasion With a beck of the hand he succeeded, in the course of a few minutes, in marshalling the dense thousands, occupying every avenue in the neighbourhood of the place of rendezvous. During these preparations, the band, situated in front of the Globe Tavern, struck up 'God save the King!' and other of our most popular national airs.

On proceeding from Temple-street, down New-street, the Bull-ring, and Digbeth, the sight was one of the most imposing that can be conceived. The shops were almost entirely closed, the upper windows of the houses throughout the whole line of procession were crowded with gaily dressed spectators, and the streets themselves so densely thronged that it was found almost impossible for the members to make their way. A gentleman who witnessed the procession from a balcony in New-street declared that he was made giddy and unwell by the prodigious mass of human beings which crowded that spacious street, and passed beneath him, like a floating pavement of human heads Long before its arrival at Mr. Beardsworth's Repository, the place of meeting, the building was more than half filled, and before the Council had taken their places in the gallery every corner of this magnificent erection was occupied. Not less than from 18,000 to 20,000 persons must have been assembled within its walls ; while according to the calculation of competent persons, not fewer than from 80,000 to 100,000 must have witnessed the promenade.

We had the good fortune, through the politeness of Mr. Beardsworth, to see the procession as it moved from the end of Moat-Row to the Repository, from the site of the famed White Horse. From this elevation we commanded a complete view of the immense concourse from the place of meeting to the end of New-street ; and a more animating spectacle was never presented to the human eye. The most remarkable feature in the conduct of the populace was the great attention paid to Messrs. Attwood, Scholefield, and Muntz, who headed the procession. Several sturdy fellows formed a sort of body guard, and by dint of hard labour and great exertion succeeded in keeping off the pressure of the multitude from these gentlemen.

On the Council entering the Repository, they proceeded to the end gallery, the middle of which was partitioned off for their accommodation, and the convenience of the reporters. Immediately over this space the Royal Arms were placed, the opposite auction-rooms and galleries being occupied by ladies and gentlemen as spectators. G. F. Muntz, Esq., was immediately called to the chair, and after a few remarks proceeded to read the Report of the Council of the Birmingham Political Union, which was dated May 19th, 1830, and signed by Thomas Attwood as Chairman and T. C. Salt as Secretary. The report stated that when the Union was first commenced the Council thought it prudent to have recourse to no excitement of the public mind in the enrolment of members of the Union. They thought that if a sufficient number of members did not come forward spontaneously it would not be practicable to effect any great or salutary purpose. They had then, however, the satisfaction of reporting that 2,200 individuals, subscribing each from £2 2s. to 4s. per annum, had joined the Union, and they thought the time had come for personally soliciting their fellow townsmen to join their ranks. The Council then proceed to state, at great length, that after mature consideration, they had decided not to claim universal suffrage, vote by ballot, or annual parliaments, but to confine themselves to the ancient and well-tried lines of the Constitution, which experience had proved to be fully capable of bestowing happiness and prosperity upon the people.

After a long discussion the report was adopted almost unanimously, and Mr. Attwood then rose and said When last he had the honour of addressing them he had occasion to congratulate them on the effect produced by the meeting in the month of May last year ; now he had the pleasure of congratulating them on the success of the great meeting held in that place on the 25th of January last. To him it was a great satisfaction that the effect produced had not been confined to this neighbourhood, but that it resounded throughout England, and throughout Europe. . . . In accomplishing their object, the Council had had to struggle with innumerable difficulties, surrounded on every side by such a confused mass of inexplicable laws, that it was scarcely possible for human wisdom to escape these numerous *deviltraps.* (Laughter and cheers.) He could assure them that but for their great prudence they would have been destroyed like the reformers of old, and he (Mr. A.) picked out from amongst them, and in all probability lodged in a dungeon.

Mr. Attwood then proceeded to argue at length in favour of prudence and moderation in their demands, pointing out that by these means they had secured the support of a considerable section of the aristocracy and middle classes,—that universal suffrage was unknown to the English Constitution, and that the French, with all their violence and bloodshed, had only succeeded in obtaining a very limited amount of freedom. He then proceeded to read the declaration of the Political Council on the Marquis of Blandford's Bill of Reform, which was drawn up at a meeting held at the Globe Tavern in Temple-street, on the 16th March, 1830. (The Marquis's Bill was far too drastic to please the majority of either Whigs or Tories, but it met with the cordial approval of the Birmingham Political Union, who tendered him their grateful thanks.)

Mr. Hadley, in proposing the third resolution, said it became his duty to submit for their consideration a resolution respecting the medal and ribbon which the Council had thought ought to be worn by the members of the Union on all public occasions, when they were called together. The obverse of the medal was the British lion, rousing himself from slumber · the legend above, '*The safety of the King and of the people.*' The legend below, '*The Constitution, nothing less, and nothing more.*' The reverse of the medal : the royal crown of England irradiated ; immediately beneath the crown, on a scroll, the words, '*Unity, Liberty, Prosperity.*' The legend above, '*God save the King.*' The legend below, '*Birmingham Political Union, 25th January, 1830*' On the ribbon was inwoven the red cross of St. George, quartered with that of St. Andrew, commonly called the British Union Jack. He could not help thinking with the Council, that the members of the Union ought to have some appropriate badge, which would at once show their loyalty and patriotism, and distinguish them as men who were willing to make some sacrifice, and lend a helping hand in order to purify their corrupt political system, and to secure their political privileges. He should, therefore, beg to propose that the medal described in the advertisement in the public papers be adopted as the badge of the Union. (Cheers.) The motion was seconded by Mr. Betts, and carried unanimously.

Mr. Hadley, in proposing the fourth resolution, said he held in his hand a resolution which, if he were capable of doing justice to the subject of it, he should feel nothing but unmingled pleasure in proposing. On this account, and on this alone, did he regret that it had not fallen into abler hands. They were all aware of the gentleman who was the originator, and who was the principal supporter of the Birmingham Political Council, which had for its objects their happiness and their prosperity. The virtue, talent, and public spirit which that gentleman had shown in stemming the tide of a powerful opposition, arising alike from his friends and his enemies, in his judgment, entitled him to their gratitude, and as they had adopted a Medal to be worn by the Union, he should before he sat down propose that a Gold Medal, with the badge of the Union attached to it, be presented to the talented and patriotic Chairman of their Council (T. Attwood, Esq.). If he were not fearful of being accused of that adulation which his heart abhorred, he should dwell on his humanity to the poor, his inflexible integrity, his disinterested friendship, his single-eyed patriotism, and entire devotedness to those pursuits whose objects were to ameliorate the condition of the labouring population of this country. Really it was a cheering sight to behold a man like him, in these days of prostituted talent and low subserviency, stepping forward to advocate the cause of the people. With him, then, for a Leader, backed by his talent and influence, they might confidently look for success. Let them then show him that they were not insensible of his worth, and present him with a Token of their Gratitude for those exertions which he had made for them, and was still willing to make. [During the delivery of this speech Mr Hadley was frequently interrupted by tremendous cheering.]

Mr. Weston cordially seconded the resolution. Mr. Attwood was eminently entitled to the mark of respect and esteem they were about to evince towards him. The goodness of his heart was only exceeded by the wisdom of his head. (Cheering.) There was not a man, he was sure, who heard him, but would join with him in wishing Mr. Attwood many years of health to wear that small testimony of their gratitude and esteem. (Loud cheers) It would be the proudest moment of his life when they were enabled or could present consistently the same token of approbation to each of the 658 gentlemen who now sat in Parliament as their law-givers and rulers. (Laughter and cheers.)

Mr. Scholefield : Mr. Chairman, I cannot give a silent vote on this question. While Mr. Hadley was speaking, I was forcibly reminded of the will of the immortal Franklin, in which was the following bequest :—' I give to my friend General Washington my gold-headed cane ; if it were a sceptre he has deserved it, and would do honour to it.' (Cheers.) The same words might truly be applied to my friend Mr. Attwood, on the presentation of this medal (Cheers.)

Mr. Edmonds said that it would be in the recollection of many who heard him, that in 1813 Mr. Attwood received a similar token of regard from the Artizans of Birmingham. This second testimonial proved that time had now only rendered his patriotism a habit; and he was sure it would with Mr. Attwood continue so until he lost his habits and life together. (Cheers.)

The resolution was then put, amidst cheers which lasted for some minutes. On the excitement occasioned by this vote subsiding, Mr Hadley said that, anticipating the vote they had just passed, a few members of the Union had prepared themselves with the Medal and Chain, which he begged to produce. Their appearance occasioned a renewal of cheering, at the end of which, ornamented with his gift,

Mr. Attwood rose, and spoke as follows :—Gentlemen, I feel covered with confusion, at finding myself decked with this beautiful testimonial of your approbation. And yet I know not why an honest man should feel confused upon such an occasion The sweetest reward a good citizen can receive is the approbation of his countrymen. But, in truth, gentlemen, I want no honours and no distinctions. I only want to see my country flourish, happy, and free; and I can truly declare that it would have been more pleasing to *me* if you had selected my excellent and noble-minded friend in the chair, or that sound, sterling, upright, and patriotic man, Mr. Scholefield, a man never to be sufficiently estimated in these *backsliding* days, for it may be said of him that he has been *tried in the furnace*, but never has been found wanting in his country's cause. But, however, gentlemen, as you have indulgently thought proper to bestow this honour upon *me*, all that I have to say is, that I accept it with gratitude, and only regret that my humble services are not better deserving of it.

After some further discussion several other resolutions were passed, and the meeting quietly dispersed with the greatest decorum. At its close, when the band struck up the national anthem of 'God save the King,' every head was instantly uncovered, and the sight from the galleries was magnificent in the extreme. Every face was turned upwards, looking towards the gallery, and the dense mass of perhaps 20,000 faces thus exhibited had an extraordinary effect. The voices of this immense mass, joining cordially in the anthem, produced also a great effect.

The day was remarkably fine, and not the slightest accident or unpleasant circumstance occurred. We observed some of our veteran reformers of the ancient days come forth upon the occasion, forgetting their years and their infirmities.

Amongst others the following resolutions were passed unanimously :—

'IV. That a gold medal, with the Badge of the Birmingham Political Union, be presented to our patriotic and highly talented Chairman of the Council of the Union, as a token of our esteem and gratitude for his invaluable services to this Union, to the town of Birmingham in particular, and to the whole British nation.

'V That only one medal shall be delivered to each member of the Union, and that it shall on no account be delivered to any person whatever whose name is not enrolled as a member of the Union, with this exception, that each member shall have the liberty of purchasing one silver medal in addition.'"

The gold medal and chain mentioned above are now in the possession of Mr. T. A. Carless Attwood, of Malvern Wells. I have one of the ordinary medals in white metal, of which a great number must have been preserved.

On June 2nd, 1830, Thomas Attwood's name appears on a committee appointed at a public meeting for the purpose of opposing the Birmingham Free Grammar School Bill, then in progress through the House of Lords, and shortly afterwards he went up to London for the purpose of advancing the cause of reform. I give the following extracts from his letters:—

To Mrs. Thos. Attwood, Birmingham.
Wood's Hotel, Furnival's Inn,
June 19, 1830.

. . . I arrived here safe at 7 o'clock by a most safe and pleasant coach. My companions were two old women, a child, and Watson the Bible Society man, who converted me one way, whilst I converted him the other.

Wood's Hotel, June 21, 1830.

My hotel is really about the best I ever occupied, everything being new and clean, and well-appointed in all respects. I hope to be with you again by Friday or Saturday, but I have a host of occupations. I went on Saturday to see the harpy eagle, and a most grand and beautiful creature he is. To-day I dine with Lord Radnor, and to-morrow with Burdett. The latter, I have no doubt, will attend our meeting. These are the two noblest men in England. I have not yet seen Lord Blandford, or any other of my noble friends, but I must call upon them and also upon Western, if possible. I think I was of service at the dinner on Saturday. It was got up by Hume and O'Connell, and neither Burdett, Hobhouse, or Davenport were invited. Hume is certain to be Member for Middlesex next election. Mark the signs of the times. It is the old *Tories* of Middlesex who have invited him, and, of course, he stands well with the others.

I was delighted with the Zoological Gardens. I am sorry to hear so bad an account from Wolstanton, and also of your dear mother. . . . I went yesterday to the Park, and Westminster Abbey, which is a place I am never tired of.

Wood's Hotel, June 23, 1830

I am very glad to find by your letter that the boys are safe, and that you are all well, except my dear little Rosabel, to whom pray deliver many kisses from me. On Monday I dined with a large party of ladies and gentlemen at Lord Radnor's, and I contrived to make myself agreeable to both parties, particularly "*la fumeuse moitié.*" One of them, a Miss Brummell, would have made Miss Angela jealous. The dinner was very splendid, and Lord Radnor assures me that luxuries have increased quite as much among the aristocracy as they have among us middle classes. Yesterday I dined at Sir F. Burdett's with Davenport, Lord John Russell, Hobhouse, and Jones Burdett. Lady B. and her 3 daughters are evidently admirable and estimable women, and you would call them beautiful. I met 3 or 4 beauties at Lord Radnor's. Lady R., a fine woman but 50 yrs. old, gave me a ticket to the Zoological Gardens, for which I stole 3 hours from more important business. Davenport brought me a message from Lord Dillon saying that he much wished to see me and would call upon me. But I, being too polite, called yesterday upon him. He earnestly invited me never to go to London without spending a day or two with him in Oxfordshire on my road. He professes great intimacy with Lord Grey, and said he wanted to learn from me how to extricate the country, in the event of Lord G. coming into power. I promised to see him again, but fear I shall not be able. However, I made him understand things pretty well. I was much pleased with Lord Blandford, whom I found a very handsome, manly, and gentlemanly man. I am going now to see Burdett again, and so I must conclude.

P.S.—I have not yet quite settled with Burdett to come down to Birmm. The day is too early. I was disappointed with O'Connell's party on Saturday.

Mrs. Attwood, Wolstanton, Newcastle under Lyme.

Wood's Hotel, June 24, 1830.

. . . I have taken my place in the Tally Ho safety coach for Saturday morning, and I expect to be in Birmingham by 6 o'clock on that day at the Castle Inn. I have settled everything to my satisfaction with Burdett, who has promised to take the chair at our meeting, and I have agreed to postpone it for a week or two for his convenience. . . . I have not had time to call upon Western or Cullen, or many other of my political friends. A month is soon occupied in making calls in this large town, or rather collection of towns. . . . Wolverley says he can give me some storks, which I am sure Bosco will like.

Wood's Hotel, June 25, 1830.

. . . I am much concerned, but not surprised, to find from your letter to-day that the sufferings of your poor relation are terminated. I think you have done quite right in going to see your brother and sister. I should have much pleasure if I thought it in my power to render them any comfort or consolation. But I know that there is in these things a sacredness which belongs to grief, and which renders all expressions of sympathy almost intrusive. I shall therefore say nothing. Indeed I deeply feel that I can render but poor comfort upon such occasions, for God knows I should be without any comfort myself.

I hope you will have taken care of yourself, and I doubt not that you have left proper instructions at home, where I am happy to inform you I intend to be to-morrow evening. I have taken my place in the safety coach and shall stay at home with our dear children on Sunday. If you should think that I can be useful in any way, I can come to you on Wednesday or Thursday. But

I know that in all situations of this kind you can be far more beneficial than myself, and I trust that you will conduct yourself with fortitude and discretion.

The death of Maria Carless, only child of the Rev. Edward Carless, at the age of twenty, appears to have been the only sad event in this brilliant and successful year of Thomas Attwood's life, though, doubtless, the illness of his son Marcus was beginning to cause him grave anxiety. The first annual meeting of the Birmingham Political Union took place at Beardsworth's Repository on Monday, July 26th, 1830, and was presided over by Sir Francis Burdett with great *éclat*. Sir Francis, in company with Mr. E. Davenport, arrived at Grove House, Harborne, on Sunday afternoon about five o'clock, and was afterwards met at dinner by a party of gentlemen from Birmingham.

On Monday morning, says the *Journal* report, the day set in extremely fine and propitious. By half-past nine o'clock the members of the Union began to collect in Temple Row and Waterloo Street; and by half-past ten all was prepared for moving forward. Sir Francis and Mr. Davenport joined the Council about ten, and were present during a great part of the preparatory deliberations. The Union band, for the first time, wore their own uniform, their caps and arms being ornamented with the Union Jack. The procession on starting moved down Upper Temple Street, Sir Francis walking arm-in-arm with Mr. Attwood, at the head of the Council. The crowds in the streets were scarcely as dense as on the last occasion, owing, doubtless, to the extreme heat of the weather; but every window along the streets through which the procession passed was crowded with spectators.

Sir Francis Burdett, having taken the chair, addressed the meeting at length, alluding to his past services in the cause of reform, the corrupt state of the representation, and defending himself against the charge of lukewarmness.

Mr. Attwood then rose and said that the Council surrendered into the hands of the Union the honourable trust confided to them. He discoursed upon the distress of the country, the weight of taxation, the corn laws, &c., and strongly insisted on a dogma which many thought, and still think, most dangerous and injudicious, viz., that the Government should be held responsible for the prevailing depression and misery. He concluded by reading the Report of the Council, which stated that the number of members of the Union now amounted to 5,000, and its annual income to about £1,100 per annum. The formation of Political Unions was going on rapidly in all parts of the kingdom, and the Council fully expected them to become general. The Council invited their fellow-townsmen to join the Union without delay, strongly censured Sir Robert Peel, and after some further remarks concluded by offering themselves for re-election. This report is signed by Thomas Attwood, Chairman, Joshua Scholefield, Deputy-Chairman, T. C. Salt, Secretary, and thirty-four others, amongst whom I find, on his first appearance in public, George De Bosco, eldest son of Thomas Attwood. He was then twenty-two years old, and might reasonably have looked forward to a brilliant future, but ill-health and misfortunes prevented the anticipations of his friends from being realised.

The Council were unanimously re-appointed, and after the presentation of a service of plate to Mr. Beardsworth, for having generously allowed the Union the use of his vast building, and some further speeches, the popular Baronet took his leave of the meeting of 20,000 persons amidst the most deafening cheers. At half-past six on the evening of the same day a public dinner was given to Sir Francis at the Royal Hotel, in Temple Row, to which all parties had free access. About 120 persons sat down, Thomas Attwood in the chair, with Sir Francis on his right and Mr. Davenport on his left, whilst the vice-chairs were filled by Joshua Scholefield and Benjamin Hadley. A curious mixture of parties attended, including Mr. Hanford, a dissenting magistrate of Worcester, Mr. M'Donnell, a Catholic priest, and Mr. Richard Spooner. The latter defended himself from the charge of inconsistency in attending the dinner whilst refusing to join the Union, stating that he appeared to show his esteem for Sir Francis Burdett's conduct as a Reformer. The healths of O'Connell, Sir Francis Burdett, Thomas Attwood, Hanford,

Sir J. C. Hobhouse, and Richard Spooner were drank with enthusiasm, and the Chairman quitted the table about midnight.

Sir Francis Burdett left the Stork Hotel, for London, on Tuesday morning, and Mr. Davenport for Cheshire.

Matthias Attwood of course differed widely from his brother with respect to the foundation of the Political Union, but he still continued to advocate, with great ability, those views on the Currency which were common to both. Sir Archibald Alison, in the following passage (vol. iv, p. 231), thus does justice to his talents:—

"But there were not wanting those who took a nobler as well as a juster view of the general distress, and boldly pointed out its cause in the policy regarding monetary matters—so profitable to realised capital, so ruinous to laborious industry—which had for ten years been pursued by the Government. The subject was brought before the House of Commons by *the two men in the kingdom most competent to master it*, Mr. Attwood and Mr. Baring, who moved that a gold and silver standard should be substituted for the gold one, and that the act for prohibiting the issue of bank notes below £5 in England and Ireland should be repealed. Nothing could be more convincing than the arguments and facts by which these very eminent men supported the motion, or more sophistical than those by which it was resisted; but it was all in vain The House was resolved not to be convinced: the interests of realised wealth had become so powerful in the legislature that those of industry were overpowered: and the debate—the last which took place on the subject before the irrevocable change the existing system had brought about was introduced—remains a memorable and instructive monument for all future times of the manner in which the plainest truths can be disregarded when they run adverse to the interests of a powerful section of society, and a course of policy can be persisted in fraught with consequences which those who originated it are to be the first to regret."

In the course of this year Matthias Attwood also spoke on the "Issue of Gold," "State of Currency," and "Exports and Imports," and on the 7th June, 1830, he voted with the majority of 151 for abolishing the punishment of death in all cases of forgery except the forgery of wills, remaining, however, a staunch Tory. The King, George IV., died on 26th June, and in the election which followed, Matthias Attwood was returned for Boroughbridge in conjunction with that famous Conservative, Sir Charles Wetherell, who was a near connection of Richard Spooner. His patron was that Duke of Newcastle whose well-known utterance, "May I not do what I will with mine own?"

in reference to his borough property, did so much to pass the Reform Bill.

The first great English railway, that from Liverpool to Manchester, was opened on the 15th of September, and the celebrated Huskisson, who had had so many bitter altercations with Matthias Attwood, met with his death upon the occasion. It was Huskisson, too, who first made mention of Thomas Attwood and the Political Union within the walls of Parliament. He there stated, in a debate on Reform, that admiring, as he did, the talents of Mr. Attwood, he would much sooner have him for an opponent in Parliament than out of it.

The French Revolution of July caused intense excitement in England, where it was hailed as an omen of success by the Reformers. Extraordinary preparations for celebrating the event were made in Birmingham, and on Monday, October 11th, 1830, a grand dinner was held at Beardsworth's Repository, from the *Journal* report of which I give an abstract as follows:—

"This day the long-promised dinner of the Political Union, to commemorate the recent glorious Revolution in France, took place in Mr. Beardsworth's Repository. To those unacquainted with the extent and remarkably apt accommodation of these magnificent premises it will appear more as a tale of extravagant fiction than reality when we assert that not fewer than 3,700 persons sat down to dinner under one roof. Such, however, was the case on this day. The Repository, used by Mr. Beardsworth (the winner of the late St. Leger) for the show and sale of horses and carriages, is formed of three sections of an oblong, the fourth section consisting of his private residence and out-houses. The longest part of the building, the whole of which is galleried round, is 108 yards. On this occasion there were six tables running parallel the whole length, besides fourteen tables filling the broad area of the Repository. The preparatory arrangements for a dinner of such immense magnitude were admirable. The party was divided into *sets*, a steward being appointed to every twenty individuals, and these officers distinguished by a neat flag, on the one side of which was the British Jack, and on the other the French Tricolor. The duty of each steward was to carve for the persons under his immediate superintendence, to attend to their convenience, to assist in keeping order, and communicate with the Political Council, if required.

The quantity of provisions, all of which we can pronounce to have been of the very best description and quality, will afford some idea of the amazing extent of the dinner. Not less than 3,500 lbs. of butcher's meat was placed upon the table, consisting of rounds and loins of beef, fillets of veal, hams, legs of pork, legs of mutton, &c., &c. Each man was allowed a pint of beer to dinner, and a quart of ale afterwards.

GREAT DINNER OF OCTOBER 11, 1830.

It is impossible to give an adequate description of the interior of the building previous to or at the commencement of the dinner. The best view was from the harness gallery, above Mr. Beardsworth's auction-chair. From this elevation the spectator commanded a complete view of every part of the edifice. The scene, before the party took their seats, was the most picturesque that can be imagined, and strongly reminded the cursory observer, at the first glance, of the Mosaic pavements, as given in some of our old pictures. The whole area of the building, together with all the galleries, was completely set apart and aptly laid out for the entertainment of the company. The stewards, 200 in number, entered the Repository at 12 o'clock, and immediately took their seats at the table. Soon afterwards the band took its place in the orchestra, having in the front about 50 glee and chorus singers. The band was dressed in the uniform of the Union, and occupied a temporary orchestra, erected in the southern gallery. Thomas Attwood, Esq., entered the building about the same time, accompanied by many members of the Political Council. On his appearance he was loudly greeted by the enthusiastic plaudits of the company assembled.

. . . At half-past one, Mr. Attwood, as Chairman of the Union, took the chair. The trumpets immediately sounded attention. The Chairman, after briefly recapitulating the regulations adopted by the Council, requested the company to implicitly obey them. It was highly desirable that all should keep their seats, and not upon any occasion deviate from this prudent recommendation. The trumpets again sounded, when the whole assembly being uncovered, the Chairman asked a blessing in the following words :—
' God, we thank Thee for the good things which are set before us, and we implore Thy blessing upon us and our righteous cause.' *Amens* resounded from every corner, and the whole party sat down to dinner. Accustomed as we have been for many years to witness the proceedings of public bodies— familiar as we have been with all scenes, either convivial or political, for many years past, we have never seen one of so grand or imposing a description as that presented upon this occasion. Almost as far as the eye could, without straining or inconvenience, reach, it rested upon one orderly, organised mass of people. A considerable number of ladies occupied the upper galleries above Mr. Beardsworth's sale rooms, and appeared highly amused and gratified by the spectacle. At the close of the dinner the Chairman, hitherto situated in the long gallery, moved by invitation into the lower of these galleries, where it was considered he would be much better heard.

The tables being cleared, *Non nobis Domine* was sung by 50 professional singers.

The Chairman then rose and gave the following toasts, each accompanied by a speech of some length.

Our Gracious Sovereign William IV., may God prolong his reign for the liberty and happiness of his people.

Louis Phillippe, King of the French.

Honour, gratitude, and prosperity to the noble people of France.

The people of England, may they speedily recover their lost Rights, and be fully and fairly represented in their own House of Parliament.

G. F. Muntz, Esq., then proposed the health of General La Fayette, and dwelt on the career of that extraordinary man (who, as we shall presently see, was an intimate and affectionate correspondent of Thos. Attwood).

A number of other liberal toasts were then drank, and Mr. Beardsworth finally proposed the health of their worthy Chairman, Thomas Attwood, Esq. (*The cheering on the announcement of this toast lasted for some minutes.*)

Mr. Attwood : Gentlemen, I feel as a man and an Englishman ought to feel, on having my health received in this extraordinary manner. Placed by your favour at the head of this great association, my constant study has been to endeavour to direct it well. I have neglected no possible means which I thought calculated to give security, system, order, and success to your operations. (*Cheers.*) That my humble labours have given you satisfaction the honourable badge which I wear and your conduct upon this occasion are to me very gratifying proofs. (*Tremendous cheers.*) I have made many friends, it seems—(*cheers*)—perhaps some enemies. (*Loud cries of 'No, no.'*) Certainly I have had a good deal to contend with, and have had occasion for some little nerve. Many of my friends attempted to alarm me with all manner of terrible representations. They told me that I should set in motion a tremendous principle, which no human power could control—that I should, like a Frankenstein, create a monster of gigantic strength, endued with life, but not with reason, that would hunt me about the earth to my own destruction. Look around now, upon this peaceful and magnificent assemblage—are we not all met here the friends of the law?—('*Yes, yes*')—and of the peace and order of society? What possible mischief can arise from men animated with the same motives which animate you? (*Cheers*) And as for me, what possible danger do I incur? ('*None, none,*' *great cheering.*) I am like a father in the midst of a pretty numerous family—(*laughter and great cheering*)—or like a General surrounded by his faithful soldiers (*Cheers.*) Where is the man among you who would injure me? ('*None.*') Where is the man among you who would not follow me to death in a righteous cause? (*The cheering was immense on the delivery of this passage, and lasted for some minutes, accompanied by cries,* '*All, all.*') I see, gentlemen, your hearts are mine, and mine is yours ; we will go on in our peaceful and legal career, and by God's grace we will recover the liberties of our country—not by violence, anarchy, or brute force, but by the peaceful, organised, and magnificent display of the will of the people. When the barons of Runnymede recovered the liberties of England from the tyrant John, they took up the bow, and the spear, and the battle-axe, and the sword ; and they were justified in so doing. Thank God, we have no occasion now to take up murderous and destructive weapons like these : the progress of education and knowledge has changed this state of things—our weapons are union, truth, justice, and reason ; our sword is 'the sword of the spirit,' which is *the will of the people;*—(*cheers*)—and let no one doubt that this great moral sword is not efficient for every just and useful purpose. (*Cheers.*) Look round again upon this assembly, and I will say, show me twenty such dinners as this, and I will show you the governors of England—not the governors by violence, anarchy, or brute force, but by the moral agency of public opinion, peacefully and legally influencing the conduct and the opinions of the Government.

(*Great cheers.*) I am now about to propose the last toast, and I must request that after it is drank you will all retire to your respective homes. Your good conduct is our strength, and I beseech you to bear this great truth in mind, upon this and every other occasion. We will now part with the concluding toast, 'Peace and goodwill to all mankind.' This toast was received with great enthusiasm, in the midst of which Mr. Attwood and the rest of the immense company retired, the band again playing, 'God save the King. The Union Hymn, the Marseillaise, The Gathering of the Birmingham Union, and other songs, were sung in the course of the proceedings."

After reading the above report one is not surprised to find by a subsequent letter that Thomas Attwood considered the 11th October, 1830, one of the great days of his life. The dinner had been preceded by a town's meeting "for the purpose of expressing the sense of the inhabitants on the recent events in France," at which he assisted; but the mass of printed matter relating to him during these eventful years is so great that I am compelled to omit or greatly abridge a considerable part of it. About the same time an address to the King, pressing upon His Majesty the necessity of Reform, was drawn up by the " Political Council." The members much wished to present it to the King personally by a deputation, but after some correspondence between Mr. Attwood, Sir Herbert Taylor, and Sir Robert Peel, the project had to be abandoned as unconstitutional, and Mr. Attwood, Mr. Scholefield, and Mr. C. Jones waited upon Sir Robert at Drayton, and delivered the address to him for presentation. Shortly afterwards the Minister, in a curt note to Mr. Attwood, intimated that he had laid the address before the King. The stiffness and brevity of Sir Robert Peel's note is not surprising when we consider that the address amounted practically to a request to the King to turn out himself and his colleagues. A few weeks afterwards the Tory Ministers resigned, and their places were taken by that famous Ministry, who gained, indeed, no little glory for themselves by their carriage of the Reform Bill, but who never could have passed that great measure without the assistance of Thomas Attwood, whom they treated with extraordinary ingratitude. On the 13th December, 1830, a town's meeting was held at the Repository in support of the Grey Ministry, which, though convened by the Union, was not confined to its members, but was attended also by many influential inhabitants who had not joined its ranks.

About twelve o'clock, Mr. Thomas Attwood, accompanied by friends, entered the building, and was, on being recognised, vehemently cheered by the assembly. From ten to twelve thousand persons were present, and on the motion of Mr. Edmonds, seconded by Mr. Weston, Mr. Attwood was called to the chair. The Chairman then proceeded to give the history of the petition to the King to which I have already alluded, stating that it was printed in London four days before the vote of the House of Commons which compelled the Wellington Ministry to resign, and that he trusted it had had some effect in bringing about that result. He next went on to remark that he had watched the conduct of Lord Grey for twenty-five years, and that he felt sure that that nobleman would do his duty to the people, if properly supported Messrs. Scholefield, Hadley, Muntz, Jones, and others then addressed the meeting, and Mr. Parkes, at great length, entered into the question of the desirability of the ballot. Some further discussion ensued, and the chair having been taken by Joshua Scholefield, Esq., Mr. Richard Hipkiss moved the thanks of the meeting to Thomas Attwood for his conduct in the chair, and expressed a hope that ere long he would be returned as one of the Representatives for the town of Birmingham. (*Great cheering.*) Mr. J. Parkes seconded the resolution, and Mr. Attwood replied :—

Gentlemen, I thank you most sincerely for this renewed expression of your kindness and approbation. With regard to what has been said respecting Members of Parliament for this town, I have only to observe that I have never yet, in any shape or way, attempted or desired to become a Member of the House of Commons. It has always appeared to me that I could not possibly do any good in that House, constituted as it has hitherto been. I have always thought that I might just as well have reasoned with the waves of the sea, as with the individuals there. But, if we are to have a Reform, and that Reform is to be efficient, I have not the weakness to pretend that I think I could not be of service in that House. (*Cheers.*) And undoubtedly, when the frame and fabric of society is giving way over our heads, and its foundations trembling under our feet, it is the duty of every good subject of the King to come forward and offer his services at this momentous period. (*Cheers*) I do hope that I may possibly be able to serve the country upon this occasion. (*Cheers*) I have studied the circumstances of this country, and ought to understand them. I see approaching famine, national bankruptcy, and revolution These things I have foretold for fifteen years, and possibly I might assist in arresting the progress of these devastating and destructive contingencies. If, therefore, a Reform in Parliament should take place to any real extent, I might, perhaps, be proud of the honour of representing this great and important community. (*Cheers*.) With regard to the establishment of Political Unions, which have been alluded to, I have to observe that it gives me great satisfaction to perceive that they are spreading everywhere. From Devonshire to Caithness they are studded throughout the country. In the extremities of Fifeshire and Forfar, for instance, in Glasgow and Paisley, in Leeds, Manchester, and Liverpool, in Sheffield, Newark, Nottingham, Norwich, Stockport, Bolton, Coventry, Bilston, Walsall, Kidderminster, and many other places, they have taken deep root, and I trust they will flourish for the benefit of the people. The principle of these Unions is, in fact, a mere shifting of the burden of national errors and mismanagement upon the Government, instead of leaving it to fall with unbroken force upon the people. (*Cheers*) The interests of masters and men are, in fact, one. If the masters flourish, the men are certain to flourish with them; and if the masters suffer difficulties, their difficulties must shortly affect the workmen in a threefold degree. The masters, therefore, ought not to say to the workmen, "Give us your wages," but take their workmen by the hand and knock at the gates of the Government and demand the redress of their common grievances. In this way the Government is made answerable for its own acts at its own doors: and in this way only can the rights and interests of the middle and lower classes be supported. (*Cheers*.) I have known some men with a hundred thousand pounds in their pockets, and ten thousand pounds in their trades, who are the deadliest enemies of the industry of the country. They have climbed the ladder themselves, and their sole study is to kick it down, in order to prevent their neighbours and competitors from climbing it These are not the men to be trusted. The only men to be trusted are the men who are engaged in the anxious concerns of life, and whose interests mainly depend upon the success and prosperity of the respective occupations in which their capital and industry are embarked. Return this kind of men to Parliament, and you are safe. (*Cheers*.) If you trust any other you will be deceived. (*Cheers*.) I will trouble you no further than by remarking, that I have had the greatest satisfaction in observing the progress of Political Unions. I have displeased many friends, and made a few enemies; but I trust where I have made one enemy I have made a thousand friends. I rejoice in the course of conduct which I have pursued, more and more under the awful circumstances which I see approaching, and I have now only to say that whenever I die I wish no other inscription to be placed upon my tomb than, " Here lies the founder of Political Unions." (*Immense cheering*.)

Amongst the resolutions passed at this meeting were the following:—

"1st.—That this Meeting cordially congratulates the people of the United Kingdom upon the dismissal of His Majesty's late Ministers, rejoicing most sincerely that ignorant, incapable, and, as Ministers of the Crown, unfeeling, as they have proved themselves, they have at last been driven from power, and have now no longer the opportunity of insulting the nation by denying the necessity of Parliamentary Reform, and proclaiming the existence of '*social happiness*,' and '*commercial prosperity*,' whilst general distress and discontent prevail everywhere, and whilst the fires of discord and revenge are blazing throughout half of England."

"8th.—That with the view of strengthening the hands of Government, and of humbly assisting in carrying into effect His Majesty's gracious and paternal designs, it is expedient that a PETITION of RIGHTS should be forthwith presented to both Houses of Parliament from the inhabitants of the town of Birmingham."

The "Petition of Rights" above mentioned claimed as follows :—

"1st.—The right of having all *Placemen* dismissed from the House of Commons, agreeably to the great Constitutional Act of Settlement, which places the present illustrious family on the Throne.

2nd.—The right of having '*Triennial or more frequent Parliaments*,' as recognised and secured by the great Constitutional Act, the 6th of William and Mary, cap. 2.

3rd.—The right of sitting and voting in the Commons House of Parliament, *when lawfully chosen*, without the *qualification of property* which was fixed unconstitutionally by the Act of 9th of Queen Anne.

4th.—The right of having all the Knights, Citizens, and Burgesses of the House of Commons paid the reasonable '*wages of attendance*' by a rate upon their Constituents, in order to enable the common people to have the benefit of the services of persons living under the same circumstances, and having the same knowledge and the same wants and interests as themselves.

5th.—The right of having the large towns and populous districts of the country represented in the House of Commons, in the place of those decayed boroughs which return Members to Parliament, although now containing but few inhabitants.

6th.—The right of every man to have a vote in the election of Members of the House of Commons who is in any way called upon to contribute to either National or Local Taxation, direct or indirect, by which your Petitioners understand that, either all the taxes ought to be taken off from those articles necessary for the subsistence and comfort of working men, or that all working men, who are compelled to pay such taxes, should have a vote in the election of Members of your Honourable House.

7th.—The right to have elections for Members of the House of Commons, *free and unbiassed*, and with this view to have such arrangements made in the conducting of elections as may effectually prevent all force, fear, or intimidation, and all bribery or undue influence of any kind, from acting upon the minds of the electors."

The petition concludes by representing the desirability of the ballot.

I think it must have been in this year that Charles Attwood founded, at Newcastle-on-Tyne, the Northern Political Union of which he was afterwards Chairman. His opinions were at this time more radical than those of his brother Thomas, and as he did not share, or, at any rate, did not bring prominently forward, the Currency views of the latter, his conduct met with the unqualified approval of Cobbett in his *Register* of January 1st, 1831.

A number of agricultural labourers in the South had been convicted of various acts of incendiarism and riotous violence, and it was believed to be the intention of the Government to inflict capital punishment upon some of them. Acting upon this supposition, Charles Attwood drew up a powerful petition for mercy to the King, which was inserted in the Tyne *Mercury* of December 28th, 1830, and which was signed with extraordinary rapidity by a great number of persons at Newcastle. The punishment of the condemned men was ultimately commuted to that of transportation, and the Newcastle petition was generally supposed to have contributed materially to this result.

CHAPTER XI.

Influence of Attwood felt everywhere—Lord John Russell introduces the Reform Bill—Meeting of March 7th, 1831, to support Ministers—The King dissolves Parliament—Excitement in Birmingham—Letters—Lord Radnor and Sir Francis Burdett—Proceedings of Charles Attwood at Newcastle—Letter from James to Benjamin Attwood on Russian and Polish affairs—Matthias Attwood—Earl Grey—Extraordinary Petition from the Union presented by O'Connell—Letters of Thomas Attwood to October, 1831.

THE general political excitement which had been so great during 1830 continued to increase throughout the whole of 1831. A gloomy apprehension of impending change seemed to spread over all classes of society. Men, says Martineau, feared to wish each other a happy new year, and yet the vast majority agreed that a great change of some kind in existing institutions must take place. It is not too much to say that during the whole of this eventful period the influence of Thomas Attwood was felt throughout the kingdom, and yet, strangely enough, the very scantiest mention of him is made by the Liberal historians. Martineau and Molesworth both admit that the country was saved from anarchy by the power of the Political Unions; they dwell upon the admirable patience, firmness, and forbearance exhibited by those bodies; and yet, with singular injustice, they omit to give any credit to the man who founded them.

The political year opened with a visit from "Orator Hunt" to Birmingham in the early part of January. The Radical Member for Preston had a long conference with Thomas Attwood, attended a meeting of the Union, and was entertained at dinner by a portion of its members; but his views, at this time, appear to have been too extreme to coincide with those of the Chairman.

From my grandfather's private letters I find that Mrs. Attwood spent the early part of this year with her brother at Barlaston, and that she and her husband were beginning to suffer great anxiety on account of the health of their son Marcus, who was then under the care of Mr. Hodgson.

On the 25th of January, 1831, the anniversary of the Political Union was celebrated in Birmingham by various public dinners. Mr. Attwood took the chair at the Globe, and in the course of his remarks said, "It was not too much for him to say, that if the King required it, they could produce him, in this district, at his orders, within a month, two armies, each of them as numerous and as brave as that which conquered at Waterloo."

In February, says Dr. Langford, a petition from those of the inhabitants who did not generally co-operate with the Union was presented to Parliament on the subject of the representation of the country, and, later in the month, another attempt was made to give Birmingham a Member by disfranchising Evesham.

On the 1st of March the great Reform Bill was brought into the House of Commons by Lord John Russell, and most protracted and animated debates ensued, in the course of which Matthias Attwood always appeared as an unflinching Tory and a worthy colleague of the famous Sir Charles Wetherell.

The Birmingham Political Union at once took measures for supporting the Ministers, and on Monday, March 7th, 1831, a meeting of 15,000 persons was held at the Repository for the purpose, and Thomas Attwood called to the chair. The Government proposal was not all that he could wish, but with rare prudence and discretion he considered that it would be better to support it in its entirety than to run the risk of alienating many of the middle class by bringing forward a more radical measure. Upon taking the chair he congratulated his audience upon the close union which now existed between the King and the people. He eulogised Lord Grey, and stated that even Mr. Cobbett had avowed his intention of waiting patiently to observe the results of the Bill, and concluded, amidst cheers, by declaring his conviction that it was admirably calculated to restore the liberty and the happiness of the people.

Mr. Scholefield followed, and moved a resolution expressing the gratitude of the meeting to the King for the Bill of Reform which his Ministers were bringing forward. Messrs. Muntz,

M'Donnell, Salt, and others then spoke at length, and the meeting adopted an address to the King and a petition to both Houses of Parliament, in which they expressed their approval of the proposed Bill of Reform in the strongest language. It was then carried unanimously—

"That a deputation, consisting of Thomas Attwood, Joshua Scholefield, and G. F. Muntz, Esqrs., be appointed to convey the address and petition to London, and that they be directed to request Earl Grey to lay the humble address of the Meeting before His Majesty, and to beg of his lordship to present the petition to the House of Lords, and to request Sir James Graham to present the petition to the House of Commons."

The deputation proceeded to London next day, and late in the evening Mr. Attwood wrote to his wife from Radley's Hotel as follows :—

I am arrived safe, and have no more to say. Everything is comfortable about me. You must not depend upon hearing from me often, because I shall be occupied and disappointed in a hundred ways. The debate was again adjourned last night, and is likely to go on in the same way. The City of London has petitioned manfully, and the thing is working just as it ought. The Duke of Sussex declared last night that he cordially approved the whole of Lord Grey's Bill. Every one approves it but those who are called upon to give up their illegal and ill-used power by it. The Duke of Norfolk made a noble declaration. When I informed our meeting of it I asked them if they would injure men like these, and some one cried out, "Not a hair of their heads shall be touched," and you would have been delighted to hear the shouts which followed. Pray attend to my dear family and to all my instructions respecting them. Above all things attend to the fires.

Great events soon after occurred. Ministers being unsuccessful in passing the Bill of Reform through the House of Commons, the King dissolved Parliament with great suddenness on the 22nd April, and announced his intention of proceeding to Westminster in a hackney coach, if his state carriage could not be got ready in time. This step procured him immense popularity, and was, of course, very gratifying to the Reformers of Birmingham. Thomas Attwood and the other members of the Political Council at once called a meeting to express their approval of the royal conduct. This meeting was held at Beardsworth's Repository on the 2nd May, 1831, and was said to have been attended by nearly 20,000 persons. The proceedings were reported at length, but I can only notice them briefly,—

" Mr. Attwood, on taking the chair amidst the most enthusiastic cheering, stated that he had never been the flatterer of Kings, nor the sycophant of men in power ; and although his fellow-townsmen had frequently honoured him with the most gratifying testimonials of their favour, yet he trusted that no one could justly say that he had ever sought to obtain their approbation by any unjust or unworthy means. (*Cheers.*) But although it was wrong to flatter, it did not therefore follow that we ought not to do justice to each other ; still less ought they to refrain from doing justice to a Patriot Monarch, whose conduct in support of his people touched a pulse in the very bottom of their hearts, and compelled them to break out in one general spontaneous and universal cry of God save the King.

Mr. Scholefield followed, and concluded by moving the adoption of an address to His Majesty setting forth their gratitude and admiration of his conduct

Mr. Attwood was about to read the address when a great pressure was visible at one of the outer doors. Mr. Hutton and others forced their way in and informed the meeting that many applications had been made to the magistrates to induce them to prevent the ringing of the bells, but that they had refused to interfere. He (Mr. H.) had been to the magistrates at the public office, where he found a secret conclave sitting in deliberation. He told the disaffected persons openly that he thought it wrong that the joy of the people should be interrupted—(*cheers*)—upon such a glorious occasion. (*Cheers.*) The voice of the people ought to prevail. He was happy to repeat that the magistrates refused to interfere. He had come down to announce to the meeting that the bells were now ringing, and he hoped they would continue to ring till twelve o'clock at night. (*Loud cheering.*)

Mr. Attwood then proceeded to state that he much regretted that the ringing of bells, or any other demonstration of joy, should be put forward in any irregular way. He could assure the meeting that the gentlemen who had called it had in no respect sanctioned any irregular interference. They had not, in any way, proposed the ringing of the bells, nor even the illumination which it was intended should take place this evening—leaving things of this kind to be decided only by the free will of the parties concerned. And here he thought it his duty to urge upon the meeting the absolute necessity of their exhibiting no violence or dislike of any kind towards any individuals who might have the misfortune to differ from them in opinion. (*Cheers.*) They should consider that one man's rights were as good as another's ; and therefore he urged them, by the sacred cause they were met to support, to allow to every individual the same liberty and freedom of expression which they claimed themselves. The inhabitants of Birmingham had acquired immense power and influence over the minds of their countrymen, by the combined prudence, justice, moderation, forbearance, and strict legality of all their proceedings. Here was their strength, and they must take care that they did not abuse it—(*cheers*)—for if they did it was most sure that they would lose it.

The address was then read and supported at length by G. F. Muntz, B Hadley, and the Rev. T. M. M'Donnell, a Roman Catholic priest, after which a stranger made it known to the meeting that in consequence of a refusal being made to permit the ringing of the church bells of St. Martin's, the ringers had made an entry through the belfry window. He recommended, therefore, that a subscription should be entered into by the meeting to reward the spirited conduct of the ringers. He also informed them that a placard had been exhibited upon the walls of the town, in some measure prohibitory of the intended illumination.

Mr. Attwood recommended every one to illuminate or not, just as they thought proper He afterwards remarked that a clergyman at Warwick had gone so far as to attribute the late burnings in Kent to his influence. He certainly did not relish the idea of the burnings being placed to his account, but it made him proud to hear that the excitation throughout the country was owing to his endeavours. He had told the meeting at which he was present at Warwick that if he had roused the British Lion he was indeed proud of it. He could say that his heart and thoughts had been at work for 30 years to promote the happiness of the great mass of the people.

The immediate business of the meeting having been concluded, Mr. Attwood left the chair, and it was moved and seconded that Mr. Scholefield should succeed him in that office. A vote of thanks was then passed to Mr. Attwood, and Mr. Salt, in moving it, termed him 'a man who had bought golden opinions from all sorts of people'"

Whilst Thomas Attwood was so closely occupied in carrying out his gigantic scheme of political agitation, private and domestic affairs of no mean magnitude pressed upon him unceasingly. The great case of Small *v.* Attwood dragged its slow length along, and although it does not appear that he was to gain anything by its successful issue, he took as much interest in the proceedings as if he had been a principal defendant. On the 30th of April he wrote to his son Bosco—

I understand that it is the intention of the British Iron Co. to cross-examine you shortly respecting some points of John Attwood's case. If so, it will be proper for you to be upon your guard, and not to answer any questions respecting which you are not positive in your knowledge.

The ill-health of Marcus Attwood appears to have induced his mother to take her four younger children to Ramsgate in this spring. A visit to the seaside was not then the simple matter it has since become, and must have been a formidable undertaking for middle-class persons residing near Birmingham. I insert here some extracts from Mr. Attwood's letters:—

Mrs. Attwood, Albion Hotel, Ramsgate.
Birmingham, 4*th May,* 1831.

The post is just going, and I have only time to send you a cheque and to say that your dear mother, myself, and Aurelius are quite well. Mrs Tibbatts kindly calls every day to sit with your mother. Sir Gray Skipwith and Lawley come in for the county without opposition. Sir C. Greville is beaten at Warwick.

Mrs. Attwood, 28, Wellington Crescent, Ramsgate.

Birmingham, 11 *May,* 1831.

My friends had nothing to do with the bell-ringing. It was done spontaneously by the ringers themselves. Mr. Moseley the rector outraged the people, and a few children and loose women outraged him. But during the night not a single outrage of any kind was committed except the breaking of the windows of Pountney the churchwarden.

Lawley and Skipwith were elected yesterday without opposition. Spencer is in advance of Lygon, and all things are working well.

Birmingham, 13 *May,* 1831.

All things seem to go on properly, both *domestically* and *nationally*. Mr. Lygon has resigned. There are now 66 county members returned, only 3 of which are against the Reform Bill. We have, therefore, gained a great victory. If we could not change the *measures* of these great criminals, it seems that we can change *themselves*. I have wanted only justice for the poor and the oppressed, and if I should not succeed in getting this, I shall at least obtain judgment upon their oppressors.

I go to Hawn every Sunday, and see your dear mother almost every day. The east wind is cold, but the flowers bloom beautifully. The ravens and eagles are my morning and evening companions.

Birmingham, 16 *May,* 1831.

To-day I send you a *Birmm. Journal* in which you will see Mr Winfield's account of the ridiculous outrage upon the Rector. At the worst it was a mere *farce*, but if Winfield had told the crowd that he had called the King a "*catspaw*," it would have probably been converted into a *tragedy*. The elections are now nearly over, and I believe all the counties have returned friends to Government, excepting only Buckinghamshire and Salop, where a few disaffected men have, unhappily, obtained a temporary advantage. Bosco has returned quite well, and his uncle writes me word that he has been exceedingly useful to him.

27, *Gracechurch St., London.*

May 19, 1831.

I arrived here yesterday and intend to go to Ramsgate by the Packet on Saturday. I left your dear mother quite well yesterday morning, and also Bosco and Aurelius. I am afraid I must leave you again on Monday and shall be glad if you can get Mr. Snowden to meet me on Saturday evening in order that I may learn from him how my dear Marcus is going on.

(*From the Earl of Radnor.*)

"*Salisbury, June* 2, 1831.

"DEAR SIR,—Your letter of the 28th ult. only reached me while sitting on the Special Commission here yesterday.

I have no objection to your shewing my letter to any friends of your own, if you think any good can be effected by your so doing—and I see no possible objection to your stating the sentiments as mine ; but I should be very sorry that it should appear in print : therefore, however reluctantly, I must refuse your request.

I hear of a packet having been found at my house in town, which I presume is your letter on the Currency. I shall, I hope, see it in a few days, and will attend to it as I ought to all that comes from you to me, but on that point I fear we differ. Excuse haste and believe me,

Dear Sir, faithfully yours,

RADNOR."

(*From Sir Francis Burdett.*)

"DEAR ATTWOOD,

You are quite right, in my opinion, and your Brother quite wrong upon every subject but the one you mention. I shall strive to get a Repeal of the Corn Laws, which I am perswaded are bad for the landed interest instead of being advantageous to it.

Indeed I am certain the landlords have no interest distinct from that of the community excepting the Public Annuitants.

I enclose the money for my medal, and wish you had mentioned to me any sum you had thought proper for a subscription, as I am so much at a loss that I know not what to send.

I am very sorry I miss'd seeing you when in London. Kind regards to Mrs. Attwood and family, and remembrances and congratulations to all friends.   Yours &c.,

F. BURDETT.

I have written to Davenport to Paris saying he should return without delay."

It need hardly be said that the Tories of Birmingham took a very different view of the bell-ringing incident mentioned in Thomas Attwood's letters, and *Aris's Gazette* of May 9th, 1831, contains a long article denouncing the persons who insulted the rector and those who got up the illumination. Meanwhile, at the general election just concluded, Sir Charles Wetherell and Matthias Attwood were returned to Parliament without opposition, and were the last Members who sat for Boroughbridge. At Newcastle-on-Tyne, Charles Attwood was actively engaged in supporting the cause of Reform, and in May or June, 1831, he took the chair at a public dinner given at the Black Bull Inn, Gateshead, to Sir Hedworth Williamson, Bart., and Mr. William Russell. the Members for the county of Durham.

I shall next insert part of a letter from James Attwood, then a merchant at Odessa, to his brother Benjamin, as it throws an interesting light upon the then state of the Polish war, in which all the Attwoods took so deep an interest.

"*Odessa, May* 31/12 *June*, 1831.

"MY DEAR BENJAMIN,

I wrote you under date of May 22/3 June by post advising my draft on you and mentioned my intention of sending you a duplicate, as the last Brody post had not arrived here. I now consider it unnecessary, as the said post has subsequently come to hand, having taken the route from Austria through Bessarabia to avoid interception by the Poles.

The contingency I referred to in my last was, as I presume you would easily conjecture, the probability of the arrival of the Polish insurgents which increases with the news of every day.

As this goes by a safe hand over the frontiers, I shall take the opportunity of giving you a little on local politics, which interest me now, as importantly connected with my affairs.

In the first place, I must tell you that there is nothing more erroneous than the statements which the English and French journals have been accustomed to give out, and continue to re-echo, of the enormous military power of Russia. They always speak as if the forces which Russia had the means of bringing into the field were sufficient to overrun and desolate the half of Europe arrayed against her; the very reverse is the fact in the present day.

Russia never had anything like the forces which the papers of France and England attributed to her.

When this Government counted her forces at 800,000, which was just before the Turkish war, the amount was made up by counting regiments as complete that had only, for the most part, from one to two thirds of their complement, and comprising what might be called in England the Civil Power, or Constabulary Force, viz., Police, Custom House, Quarantine and Civil department officers and soldiers of all sorts. The real fact is that Russia took into the Turkish war, not only the entire of her disposable force, but nearly all that the nobility would allow to be extracted of new recruits or conscripts from their peasantry. All was but barely enough to vanquish the feeble power of the undisciplined Turks, who, during eight years of war, had not succeeded in subjugating a handful of rebellious Greeks.

The losses which Russia sustained during that war, in the field, before the fortresses, by the plague, and still more by disease and sickness, occasioned by want of sufficient and wholesome food (through the mismanagement of their commissariat, which is, and must be, under the present system of Russia, the worst in Europe),—these losses left her at the close almost without an army, certainly with less than 100,000 disposable troops in her vast empire. This, during the peace, was probably increased to the amount of 220,000 men, all of which have been brought into the Polish war, and now it appears she is obliged to retreat before the Poles at all points, with the probable loss of nearly one-half of it already, whilst the power of the Poles is rapidly increasing every day. The new Russian recruits which are now calling out will amount to 80,000 or 100,000 men at most, instead of 150,000 as the Petersburg journals have it, and they are raised with the greatest difficulty and creating exceeding discontent among the Nobility as well as Peasantry. The accounts of their battles in the Petersburg papers, as well as in the little bulletins issued here, are so absurdly false and contradictory, for the most part, that they cease to mislead even the ignorant Russians themselves at present. Our friends the Sabanowskies, who have been wounded and killed, in three successive bulletins published here, we know were alive and well some days after the dates referred to in the last. At the same time that they keep telling us week after week that they have cleared and recleared Podolia and Wolhynia of insurgents, we find the post several times taken by these same Poles.

The direct post road from St. Petersburg which met our Brody post at Gitornir, in Wolhynia, is obliged to be changed and carried on the eastern side of the Dniester, and the Austrian obliged to take the west of the Dneister.

We hear on the authority of many travellers, notwithstanding the prohibition of telling any news but what the Government publishes, that the insurgent forces in Wolhynia and Podolia amount to 60,000, and the Russian authorities here admit that the whole of the proprietors without exception in those provinces are engaged in the rebellion, on which ground all their houses and property, which are immense here, are laid under sequestration, and we know well that if there were only half that number, whilst Diebitch is obliged to retreat from Schzynicky, whilst Lithuania, Samogitia, and all the intermediate provinces are in open revolt, that Russia can bring no force into these parts capable of contending much longer with them. On this ground it is that I calculate on seeing the Poles in possession of this place, possibly in three weeks, very probably in a month or five weeks; but will they stay? That is the question interesting to me and all the traders of this place whose interest it is that Odessa should form part of Poland instead of Russia. If the stupid Turks saw but their own interest it would cost them nothing now to recover their lost provinces and noble line of fortresses on the Danube, and then by ceding their right to this district to the Poles, to establish a permanent Polish barrier against their natural enemies, who otherwise will certainly not fail to take an early opportunity of recovering the glory lost in Poland by another crusade against the feeble Turk, who will then be obliged at least to yield up his European provinces and capital, as an indemnity for the pecuniary expenses of justifiable war.

In my opinion three line of battle ships and two or three frigates, English or French, or double the number of Turkish, would be sufficient to clear the Black Sea of the Russian fleet, consisting of about 15 sail of the line and 6 or 7 frigates.

In the Turkish war the fleet was not half manned for want of sailors, one third of the complement were landsmen who had never been to sea. They lost about 2,000 by the plague and other diseases at Varna, Sisopoli, and Sevastopol, they banished as many more on account of the mutiny, and to crown the matter they made marine corps of nearly all their remaining sailors at Sevastopol and sent them to join Diebitch in April last, so that I am of opinion that it would not be possible for them to man properly above two line of battle ships At present Admiral Greig has been detained nearly 10 months at St. Petersburg, and, it is generally thought, is not likely to return to this command.

The system of Russia is to conquer by bribery and espionage, and it is well known that immense sums have been paid to the principal journalists of the different capitals in Europe to extol Russia, its emperor and power, and that to an enormous extent in the time of Alexander when the foundations of her false fame were laid.

A few weeks ago a very high order was given to the editor of the *Berlin State Gazette*, no doubt for its great assistance lent to the cause of misleading Russia and Europe on Polish affairs. She got Varna by bribery at last, though she might have had it with a tithe of her loss by one vigorous effort at the commencement of the siege. She has even bribed the treacherous Pashaws to revolt, to keep the Turk occupied at home, at the same time that she coaxes the Grand Signor by relinquishing the instalment for a season of the Turkish compensation for justifiable war debt, and Russian money prevented the Polish agents from having an interview with the Grand Signor.

As Matthias seems latterly paying much attention to politics generally, it might be interesting to him to see this letter, as literally nothing is written from hence by other merchants through the post as to what is going on in this quarter. In this town the Russians, with few exceptions, are in favour of the Poles, and the foreigners almost to a man that are not employed or interested in the Russian service. It ought to be the policy of England to excite the Turks to support the Poles, and if they do not there is little doubt that European Turkey will make part of Russia in a very few years, and the invaluable Turkey trade will become of no more value to England than the valueless Russian trade, which has no reciprocity in it Great interests are at stake on the Polish question, and a very little would secure them now. But if the Turks cannot be excited without assistance to support the Poles, surely it would not be a great task for England to find an excuse, perhaps on the score of the projected infringement of the treaty of Vienna by annexing Poland to Russia, for meddling in the affair and dispatching a secret expedition of two or three large class line of battle ships and two or three frigates (of which there are perhaps sufficient on the Malta Station) to this place, well and fully manned, so that they might have enough to make the Russian ships they took available to fight the rest, and I am persuaded they would not only ensure the success of the Poles, by affording them supplies of arms and ammunition through this port, and guarantee them the frontier of the Dniester and Dwina necessary to the maintenance of their future independence, but would also be recompensed by sufficient prizes in line of battle ships and frigates to well compensate any losses which a war with Russia might occasion to some parties, and the war in this quarter would be made much shorter than if the Poles and Russians are left to fight it out alone. The Polish and Turkish Empires, thenceforward united in alliance, would be more than a match for dismembered Russia, the land of real slavery in civilised Europe, and where the slaves (whose average value is from £20 to £25), according to the accounts of the enlightened Russian nobles, are incomparably worse treated than the negroes of the West Indies. Here each petty noble knouts or flogs his slaves as his passions or caprice excite him. No laws protect his victim, and no press publishes his crimes; only in case of death from severe punishment does the fragile and uncertain law even authorise an enquiry, and accord a small penalty in case of conviction, which circumstances render almost impossible in the worst of cases.

Since writing the above, I learn that our Government has received the intelligence of an insurrection in Wallachia and Moldavia, which took place in consequence of those provinces being called upon to raise recruits or militia. The Russian authorities have been expelled from Bucharest and are arrived at Yassy."

It is impossible to read this letter without reflecting upon the immense advantages which would have been gained by England had she adopted the policy recommended in it. A strong Poland stretching from the Baltic to the Black Sea would have effectually protected Turkey against Russian aggression, we should have had no Crimean War, and the ever-recurring scare of the Eastern question would have been finally set at rest.

The new Parliament met on June the 14th, and on the 24th the Reform Bill was again introduced. Matthias Attwood continued to oppose it as strenuously as his brother supported it. He lost no opportunity of attacking the Grey Ministry, occasionally with success, and was in consequence furiously assailed by the *Times*, which termed him one of the Duke of Newcastle's Members. On the 19th of March, upon the occasion of a debate on the Timber Duties in which he spoke at considerable length, he carried a motion for adjournment against the Government by a majority of 46, the numbers being—for Mr. Attwood's motion, 236; against it, 190. About the same time he was mainly instrumental in getting up an anti-Reform declaration by the merchants and bankers of the City, and was coarsely abused in a leading article in the *Times* of March 21st. On the 30th March, Mr. G. R. Dawson wrote to the *Times* complaining of the gross partiality with which "the masterly speeches of Mr. W. Bankes, Mr. Attwood, and Sir R. Peel were curtailed and disfigured," and one of the reporters replied stating that Mr. Attwood was generally inaudible in the gallery. It appears, indeed, that his voice was weak and his utterance indistinct, but he nevertheless proved himself a formidable champion of the losing cause, and evidently possessed considerable weight and influence in the City. On the 30th March he made some stinging allusions to the conduct of the Attorney-General during Queen Caroline's trial, and a sharp altercation ensued in which Lord Palmerston, Mr. Spring Rice, and Sir John Sebright took part. As a general rule he confined himself entirely in his speeches to the Currency or to mercantile matters, but the threatened extinction of his borough of Boroughbridge seems to have roused him to strike a blow in its defence.

I now revert to Thomas Attwood's letters :—

Mrs. Attwood, 29, Wellington Crescent, Ramsgate.

. . . I am glad the porpoises are abroad, and should much like to watch them with Marcus. These strange beasts of the sea seem hardly to belong to our earth. I begin to fear that Capt. Ross and his crew are lost. They have been gone now 3 years on their dreary voyage and not a word has been heard of them since they left the North Cape of Norway. The colliers of Wales are showing symptoms of that great catastrophe which awaits the Government, and whenever it comes I think it will come justly. With regard to myself, my dear, my motto is " Be *just* and fear not " With this I left the cradle, and with this I mean to enter the grave. Cardinal Wolsey could hardly say as much.

Birmingham, 17 June, 1831.

I have taken 2 places for Algernon and Miss Grice on Tuesday morning next by the Tally Ho, and one outside place for Wm. Evans. Mrs. Barker wishes me to add Eliza Barker, but I doubt the propriety of filling Mrs. M. A.'s house in this way. However you may expect the other two by the steam packet on Wednesday evening. . . . Numerous great failures are taking place everywhere, just as they did in 1825, and it is certain that the mischief will go on. It is by no means unlikely that it may arrest Lord Grey in his career, and suddenly blow his Reform to the winds.

Birmingham, 1 July, 1831.

I shall send you to-morrow a Birmingham paper by which you will see that we are not asleep in the matter of Reform, and that some degree of watchfulness is necessary. When we have settled this point we shall look up Sir Robert Peel. . . . Pray remember me kindly to Miss Grice and Mrs. Taylor, and do not forget to give Rosabel some kisses for me. She will be pleased when she sees the spoonbills. But I am almost afraid lest they should swallow *Tiny*, for I saw them swallow a big fish. We have parted with both the eagles.

On July 4th, 1831, the second annual meeting of the Birmingham Political Union was held at Beardsworth's Repository. Mr. Muntz was called to the chair, and in his opening speech advocated an alteration of the money laws in accordance with the views held by the Attwoods. Thomas Attwood then read the annual report, and also a memorial which had been forwarded to Earl Grey, with the following reply :—

"*Downing Street, June* 30*th*, 1831.

"SIR,—I have had the honour of receiving your Letter, enclosing a Memorial of the Council of the Birmingham Political Union, in which objections are stated to limiting the £10 franchise to persons paying their rents half-yearly.

It is with great satisfaction that I have to inform you, that the words so limiting the franchise were inadvertently inserted, and will be altered in Committee, the only object in contemplation being that of insuring a *bonâ fide* holding of £10 per annum.

The Memorial also refers to another supposed alteration as to the division of Counties.

You will find by referring to the Bill of last Session, that on this point no alteration whatever has been made.

I have the honour to be, Sir,
Your obedient Servant,
Thos. Attwood, Esq." GREY.

The above letter shows clearly what power and influence the Birmingham Political Union had already obtained. In the course of his speech Mr. Attwood remarked :

The Union would recollect that at the great meeting at which the Union was formed, eighteen months ago, he had made them five promises. The day was very cold, the snow very deep, and he recollected they had seven Babylonish fires among them. He then told them that, by their assistance, he would certainly recover the rights and liberties of the country ; but if they were disappointed of this, the public mind should shortly be brought into such a state of excitement that the dying father should call his children to his bedside, and taking the Holy Scriptures in his hand, he should make them swear eternal hatred to the borough system. At that period the national mind was asleep ; no one spoke of Reform.

The remainder of Attwood's speech, as well as the Report itself, was of a triumphant and congratulatory nature, for no one then foresaw the severe struggle which had still to be gone through, owing to the obstinacy of the Lords, before the Reform Bill was finally passed. After the adoption of the Report the meeting proceeded to elect the Council for the ensuing year, and then George De Bosco, the eldest son of Thomas Attwood, proceeded to make his first public speech. He was then twenty-three years old, and the subject which he selected, and upon which he felt most deeply throughout life, was well calculated to inspire an amiable and enthusiastic young man. In a speech of considerable length, which was very well received, he moved the following resolution :—

"That in the opinion of this Union the Polish Nation has been driven into the present contest by the atrocious violation of the rights and liberties guaranteed to them by the Treaty of 1814 ; and that, therefore, it is both the interest and the duty of every civilised country, and more particularly of England, to interfere by arms, if necessary, in the efficient protection of their righteous cause."

On the 2nd of August, Daniel O'Connell presented to the House of Commons a petition from the Council of the Birmingham Political Union, setting forth "that the petitioners had observed with disgust and indignation the factious and puerile opposition made to a majority of that honourable House, and to the demands of an oppressed and insulted people; and, with feelings of a nearly similar character, they contrasted the rapidity with which measures of penalty and spoliation had been enacted by former Parliaments, with the extraordinary tardiness at present displayed in completing a wholesome and healing measure of wisdom, justice, and conciliation." This objectionable language naturally occasioned a scene in the House, and the Speaker having justly characterised it as "grossly disrespectful and directly tending to violate the privileges of Parliament," O'Connell withdrew the petition. The Speaker's view of the matter was no doubt correct, but the truth was that Thomas Attwood knew the state of men's minds far better than he did. Attwood knew that the country trembled on the verge of revolution, and that the time was past for using strictly polite and constitutional terms.

I now insert a few more extracts from his letters :—

Mrs. Attwood, 29, Wellington Crescent, Ramsgate.

We are all quite well. Your dear mother was never better. She has made many improvements during your absence. With one of them, I am sure, Rosabel will be pleased, but I will not say what it is. Poor old Towler has died, and after a week his body was found in Mr. Firchild's land, where he had contrived to wander, and where he is now buried. The pretty goose has become quite tame again, and more impudent than ever. Bosco and I have discovered that it is not a *goose*, but a *familiar*, like that which attended Socrates and Friar Bacon. We expect to make some great discoveries from it, of which we shall give you the benefit at the proper time.

Birmingham, 8 *Augt.*, 1831.

I now trouble you with a portrait of your dear husband, which is certainly sufficiently flattering, but not much of a likeness. I am afraid he was at no time half so captivating a person. The quotation at the bottom, however, is genuine, and I am sure you will approve it, because it claims no abstract or dubious rights, but merely makes the Ministers answerable for the distress which afflicts the country. If the people will follow my advice, we will allow no Minister to rule in England unless he can make the people prosperous and contented. By acting in this way, I trust we shall relieve more distress in one year than all the charity in the world would relieve in a hundred years. I send you also my two old letters on Irish Distress, but I am afraid you will not read them. If you do, you will consider them prophetic, when you recollect the proceedings in England during the last winter.

. . . I have no news to tell you except that Sir Robert Peel is now dealing rather severely with his victims. Poor creatures! they die without seeing the hand that destroys them. Three Bank Directors have stopped during the last 6 months. Three great houses have stopped at Bristol, and all the very richest houses there, and three of a similar kind have stopped at Kidderminster. Among the *Buttons* too some mischief has happened, but not very extensive.

A good many copies of the lithographed portrait referred to in the above letter are still preserved. The quotation at the foot of it is as follows :—

Let not the masters oppress their workmen. Let not the workmen be unreasonable with their employers. Let them unite cordially together. Let the masters take the workmen by the hand, and let them knock at the gates of the Government and let them say to the Ministers, " This is our situation, this is the situation of our misgoverned country. Where are the just and rightful profits of our honourable industry? Where are the just and necessary wages of our honest workmen? If you cannot preserve the reward of industry upon which the foundations of society rest, you are not competent to govern this country. If you cannot secure an honest bread for honest labour in a nation like this, you ought not to stand where you do ; you must retire and give place to better men."—*Vide* speech of Mr. Attwood, July, 1830.

Amongst the numerous portraits of Thomas Attwood which were published during the years of his fame, the earliest seem to have appeared in 1830, but, owing to the date being wanting on many, it is difficult to determine their relative age. Several of them represent him in his then famous fox-skin collar, which he wore to protect himself from the cold, but which some of his baser adversaries accused him of wearing to render himself conspicuous.

Birmingham, 10 August, 1831.

You must not think I have no respectable men on my side in politics; you should call upon Sir Peter Payne and his daughter, who will give you a very different account. All landowners are with me, although few have the courage to own it. P.S.—Mr. Cobbett says in his Last *Register* that it is our rejected petition which has caused the amazing dispatch now visible in the honourable House. The ironmasters are beginning to give way, ——— is the first, who six years ago laid out £20,000 in a house, and £3,000 in furnishing a drawing-room

Birmingham, 13 August, 1831.

I am quite well again. We are all well Bosco thinks of going to London on Thursday or Friday next, and to be with you on Saturday evening. I am glad you have seen the grand fleet, and I hope the Russians will also see it before long.

Fendall's Hotel, Palace Yard, London,
Sept. 19, 1831.

I left all well at Harborne yesterday, and I hope to be able to come to you some day by the end of this week. If I should then find Marcus well enough, I should like to bring you all home in the beginning of the following week. I am quite tired with the solitary comforts of an old bachelor, and begin to be of opinion with Saml. Johnson, that if "marriage has many cares, celibacy has no pleasures."

. . . Things go on in their usual state in Buttonland Sir R. Peel is gradually breaking down the master buttons, and they likewise, fools as they are, are venting all their anger upon each other, and upon the poor. I am sitting here in a very nice room, which looks right upon the Abbey " where St. Margaret's stands confest, A blister on a Beauty's Breast " One of these days we will tear off the blister, but you may be assured we will never touch the venerable and sublime structure behind it.

What shocking news from Warsaw ! I must not talk politics, or I should say, that although *we*, the tame kitten-hearted slaves of England, may submit to this, yet I am convinced that the noble and generous French people will not bear it. Therefore I say with Lafayette, " Poland will yet be saved."

Harborne, Octr. 2nd, 1831.

We are all quite well, and I will be sure to write to you on Tuesday next. Do not have any fear of our meeting. You know how well we always manage things, and you know also that now we have the King and the Government on our side.

CHAPTER XII.

Progress of the Reform Bill—First grand open-air meeting of the Political Union on October 3rd, 1831—100,000 persons present—Extraordinary order, magnificence, and regularity of the proceedings—Speech of Attwood—Gratitude of Ministers—Lord John Russell's famous letter—Letters from Lord Althorp and Sir T. G Skipwith—Stormy discussion in the House of Lords—Fame of Attwood—Abandonment of Organisation of the Union—Mr. Attwood's letters—Mr. Thornton's account of meeting at Studley—Gloomy aspect of affairs—" Small *v.* Attwood"—Matthias Attwood.

THE new Parliament assembled on June the 14th, and on the 24th the Reform Bill was again introduced. On July 7th the second reading was carried by 367 against 231. The final debate occupied the evenings of the 19th, 20th, and 21st of September; and at its close the Bill passed the Commons by a majority of 109; the numbers for and against being, according to Martineau and Langford, 345 to 236, but according to the *Times* of September 23rd, 347 to 238. Matthias Attwood was, of course, in the minority, and paired against W. Brougham. "The House," says Martineau, "was surrounded by crowds, who caught up the cheers within on the announcement of the majority —cheers which were renewed so perseveringly that it seemed as if the members had no thoughts of going home. There was little sleep in London that night. The cheering ran along the streets, and was caught up again and again till morning. Such of the peers as were in town, awaiting their share of the business which was now immediately to begin, must have heard the shouting the whole night through. It is certain that it was the deliberate intention of the greater number of them to throw out the Bill very speedily. . . . Before daylight the news was on its way into the country, and wherever it spread it floated the flags, and woke up the bells, and filled the air with shouts and music. In the midst of this, however, the older and graver men turned to each other with the question, 'What will the Lords do?'"

In Birmingham the rejoicings were very great, but Attwood and the Union well knew that the most serious part of the struggle was yet to come, and they took measures accordingly. The House of Lords was not then the mere ornamental appendage to the Constitution which it has since become; it possessed a real power, and was determined to exercise it. The problem which Attwood and his compeers had to solve was, how to make the Lords give way, peacefully and legally, and without violating an iota of the Constitution. The coronation of the King took place on the 8th September. The ceremony was quiet and unpretending, suitable both to the advanced age of the monarch and the distressed state of the country. The event was celebrated in Birmingham by various public dinners, and Thomas Attwood took the chair at the Globe, presiding over the Union party. Soon after, preparations were made for the great contest which was now visibly approaching. The second reading of the Bill in the House of Lords was fixed for the 3rd of October, 1831, and on the same day there was held upon Newhall Hill that extraordinary meeting which was one of the most famous of the many at which Thomas Attwood presided, and which, perhaps, on account of its priority, caused more excitement throughout the kingdom than any other. The meetings which had been hitherto held, though probably the largest that had been known, were confined to the interior of Beardsworth's Repository, and their numbers could never have exceeded from 15,000 to 20,000 persons. But now, in order to demonstrate to the House of Lords that the public enthusiasm in favour of the Bill had not abated, Attwood determined to astonish the world with the unprecedented spectacle of 100,000 undisciplined men assembled together, firmly determined to assert their rights, but equally resolved to remember his strange motto of "Peace, Law, and Order." Hitherto no one had supposed it possible to bring together so huge a mass of men without the inevitable result of riot and bloodshed, but Attwood knew his power, he knew the men he had to deal with; he decided to make the magnificent experiment, and complete success fully justified his boldness. I give the following abstract of the proceedings from the report of the *Birmingham Journal*:—

"There never was, we may safely assert, any previous occasion upon which such a deep and universal excitement pervaded the public mind of Birmingham and its neighbourhood. Notwithstanding the numerous and highly respectable meeting which took place for a similar purpose under the auspices of the High Bailiff so late as Friday last, the inhabitants looked up to the meeting of Monday as the one which would most effectively develope the state of public feeling; and in this they were not mistaken. The day was ushered in like a day of triumph by the ringing of the church bells, and by ten o'clock the inhabitants were upon a general move to the place of meeting. The spot fixed upon for the scene of this amazing spectacle was Newhall Hill—a large vacant spot of ground situated in the northern suburbs of the town, and peculiarly well formed for such a purpose. It consists of about twelve acres of rising ground, in the form of an amphitheatre. In the valley a number of waggons were ranged in half-circle; the centre one being appropriated to the Chairman and the various speakers who addressed the meeting. About half-past eleven o'clock the Birmingham Union, headed by Messrs. Attwood, Scholefield, Muntz, Jones, &c., and preceded by the band, began to arrive on the ground; but such were their numbers that a considerable time elapsed before all had taken their stations. The scene at this moment was peculiarly animated and picturesque. At different points of the procession various splendid banners were carried, on which were as varied devices and mottoes; among the latter we noticed 'William the Fourth, the People's hope.' 'Earl Grey. The just rights of our order secured, we will then stand by his order.' The device of a dove with an olive bough, and the rising sun, with the motto, 'Attwood, Union, Liberty and Peace.' 'Taxation without representation is tyranny.' 'Lawley and Skipwith, and the independent Representatives who voted for Reform.' 'Let it be impressed upon your minds, let it be instilled into your children, that the liberty of the Press is the palladium of all your Civil, Political, and Religious Rights.' 'Union, until England is regenerated, Scotland renovated, and Ireland redressed.' 'The best security for the throne of Kings is the People's love.' It is utterly impossible adequately to describe the appearance of this most magnificent assembly when the Council had taken their stations on the platform. Upon the lowest computation, not less than 80,000 persons were within the range of vision; and in about half-an-hour afterwards, when the Staffordshire Unions arrived upon the ground, the number present was calculated by some at considerably above 100,000. In our opinion, moderately speaking, the numbers could not possibly fall much short of that amount. The spectacle was the most splendid of the kind we ever remember to have witnessed. On the ridge of the hill which crowned the amphitheatre, the banners, in number about 20, were placed at equal distances, and gave a beautiful finish to the perspective. Among other distinguished persons present on the occasion, drawn to the spot by motives of curiosity, but who took no part in the proceedings, were Prince Hohenlohe (the brother of the celebrated prophet of that name) and the Chamberlain to the King of Prussia. They accompanied Mr Attwood, to whom they had been introduced by Mr. Rothschild for the purpose of witnessing the progress and perfection of Birmingham manufactures—they had likewise the fortune of witnessing an unparalleled exhibition of Birmingham public spirit. After waiting a considerable time for the arrival of the Staffordshire Unions, Mr. Edmonds at length rose, and after a few introductory observations proposed, 'That Thomas Attwood, Esq., take the Chair.' The proposal was received with three times three.

The Chairman, Thomas Attwood, Esq., then rose and presented himself to the immense assemblage amidst the most vehement cheering. He commenced by thanking the meeting for the high honour they had conferred upon him in appointing him to take the chair upon that great and glorious occasion. It gave him great pleasure to witness the countless thousands which there presented themselves, developing the moral energies of a great nation, and it gave him more pleasure to know that they came at the call of the Birmingham Political Union, of that formidable and patriotic body whose influence was felt not only throughout all the towns of that district, but throughout every part of England. (*Cheers.*) He trusted he might say throughout every part of the world where English hearts and English feelings dwelt. He (Mr. A) would now ask how had they acquired that strength? By the peace, the order, and the strict legality of all their proceedings. To use the words of the Political Council, it was by 'courage, patriotism, and public spirit, tempered by prudence, caution, and discretion ; submission to the law, mingled with determination to correct the law.' These were the qualities by which they had gathered up their giant strength, and these were the qualities by means of which they would use that strength for the recovery of the rights, liberties, and happiness of the people. (*Cheers*) When the Union was first formed, they were told by his friends that they would have no power—that the oligarchy were too strong for them—and that all their efforts would be in vain. [At this period of Mr. Attwood's speech he was interrupted by the arrival of an immense assemblage from some of the Staffordshire Political Unions, with their bands, banners, &c , the number which then arrived on the ground was computed at 20,000 They were received with three times three tremendous cheers. After the applause and commotion arising from this accession of numbers had subsided, Mr. Attwood proceeded] He resumed by congratulating his hearers upon the truly English reception which they had given their distant friends from the neighbouring towns. He was about to say when he was so agreeably interrupted by the arrival of these Staffordshire friends, that when he had been informed that the Union would not be able to controul the oligarchy, he had said, ' We will get two millions of strings, and we will place each string in the hands of a brave and strong man, and we will twist those strings into a thousand large ropes, and we will twist those ropes into one immense cable, and by means of that cable we will put a hook in the nose of *Leviathan*, and guide and govern him at our pleasure.' (*Cheers.*) ' Now,' said Mr. A., 'have we not put a hook in the nose of Leviathan, and have we not twisted the strings and the ropes and the cable well—have we not thwarted that atrocious influence behind the throne, which Lord Chatham said was stronger than the throne itself?' (*Cheers.*) He would explain that atrocious influence of the oligarchy which had governed the King, the Lords, and the People. He did not say it was the House of Lords,—that honourable and illustrious House, composed of an Aristocracy associated with so many great and glorious recollections,—but it was a *junta* of about 150 individuals, and some of whom were members of that right honourable House, and who had secretly and fraudulently usurped the powers of King, Lords, and Commons, and had in fact governed everything in England with despotic sway. (*Cheers.*) These were the men who were rightly called 'OLIGARCHS,' and whose dominion was now coming to an end. In accomplishing this great work no violence was required ; 'by obeying the law,' said Mr. A , ' we become powerful to controul the law.' (*Cheers.*) They had united two millions of men peaceably and legally in one grand and determined association to recover the liberty, the happiness, and the prosperity of the country, and he should like to know what power there was in England that could resist a power like this. (*Cheers.*) He would explain what he meant by *prosperity*. He did not mean to say that men could live without labour, and hard labour too. This was the will of God. But he meant to say that every honest labourer in England had as good a right to a reasonable maintenance for his family in exchange for his labour, as the King had to the crown upon his head : and this was the right that he (Mr. A.) was determined to enforce. (*Cheers.*) If he had seen this right secured—if he had seen every honest man in England possessing an undoubted security for an honest bread for his family —if he had seen every honest labourer possessing abundant wages for himself, and at the same time leaving reasonable profit to his employer, he (Mr. A.) should never have assisted in the formation of the Political Union. But when he found beyond doubt that the oligarchy had either no knowledge of the wrongs of the people, or no disposition to redress them, he felt compelled to come forward to assist in bringing the political influence of the people to relieve their miseries and redress their wrongs. There was no difficulty in this operation. The most illustrious man in Europe, La Fayette, had told them 40 years ago that 'for a nation to be free it was sufficient that she wills it.' (*Cheers.*) Look around at this immense and magnificent assemblage in the very heart of England, where the English blood was pure and uncontaminated with foreign alloy, see this prodigious mass of brave and upright men assembled together to support their good, and gracious, and patriotic King,—and who with such a spectacle before them could possibly doubt that the British nation *willed* that the Bill of Reform should pass, and therefore that it must pass. (*Cheers*) And did they not see at this moment that the British nation was lifting up its mighty shoulders, and peacefully and legally shaking off the oppressive burden with which the productive energies and happiness of her people have been weighed down. (*Loud cheers.*) Now if the oligarchs had done their duty, if they had fed the hungry and clothed the naked, and rendered justice to the poor and oppressed, he (Mr. A.) for one would never have disturbed their peaceful reign, for he deemed all power good that was used for the happiness of the people ; but inasmuch as they had been bad shepherds, who had fed themselves and neglected their flock,

he had thought it his duty to endeavour to pull them down. The Holy Scriptures had said, 'Woe unto the shepherds of Israel that do feed themselves and neglect the flock. Therefore I am against the shepherds, and I will require the flock at their hands.' It was therefore, said Mr. A., that we removed the people of England from the care of the Oligarchy, and that we placed them in the hands of eleven hundred thousand of their next door neighbours and friends. Mr. Attwood concluded in the following words :—
'It is to the King personally that we owe more in this great work of reform than to any other human being in existence. An ancient philosopher has said that to see an honest man struggling with adversity and preserving his integrity was a sight which the gods themselves might contemplate with satisfaction. I will now call upon you to exhibit a spectacle, and that spectacle shall be one of loyalty and devotion. I am about to ask you to cry out the words, "*God bless the King !*" I therefore desire that you will all of you take off your hats, and that you will look up to the heaven where the just God rules both heaven and earth, and that you will cry out with one heart and one voice, "God bless the King !"' [The spectacle which here presented itself was beautiful and magnificently sublime. Every head was uncovered, every face was turned up to heaven, and at one moment a hundred thousand voices responded to the cry, 'God bless the King !' Mr. A. resumed his seat amidst the most deafening cheers.]

Mr. Scholefield followed and moved the adoption of a petition to the House of Lords, praying them to forthwith pass the great Bill of Reform.

Mr. Edmonds seconded the motion at great length, and concluded by declaring that should all constitutional modes fail to obtain the success of the Reform Bill, he would be the first man to refuse payment of taxes except by a levy on his goods. This announcement was received by the vast multitude with tremendous cheers, and the motion having been carried unanimously, Mr. Muntz moved the adoption of an address to the King praying him to create, if necessary, a sufficient number of new peers to pass the Bill.

The meeting then adopted a memorial to Earl Grey, praying him on no account to resign his station, and this was seconded by Mr. P. Haynes, in what was probably the most violent and revolutionary speech delivered on the occasion.

Mr. B. Hadley next moved the fourth resolution as follows :—

'That the cordial and grateful thanks of this Meeting be presented to Lord John Russell and to Lord Althorp, for the patriotism, ability, and unwearied industry, and the admirable temper and firmness, with which they have conducted the great Bill of Reform, through all its stages, to a triumphant issue in the House of Commons.'

Resolutions of thanks to the county members, &c., were also passed, and the Rev. Dr. Wade, rector of St. Nicholas, Warwick, and others having spoken, Mr. Attwood, in acknowledging the flattering approbation with which he had been received, took occasion to explain his conduct in consenting to assist at the formidable meetings which he had the honour to promote. He had been much censured for exciting the mass of the people upon subjects vital to their interests. He was aware of the responsibility he had thus incurred, and he could assure the meeting that it was not lightly or inconsiderately. For fifteen years together he had laboured incessantly in all other kinds of exertions to arrest the merciless and remorseless course of the oligarchy. All his efforts had been in vain. He saw the ship, as it were, running upon the rocks—he saw the captain dead drunk (he meant by the captain the Duke of Wellington)—he saw the officers all playing at cards, &c.—in this dreadful position he had determined upon appealing to the crew! Had he not done right in so doing? (*Cheers.*) Remember the *Rothsay Castle!* If the passengers there had called upon the crew, the vessel might have been secured, and a hundred valuable lives preserved to their families. He (Mr. A.) would do the best in his power to prevent the good ship Britannia from coming to the same fate as the *Rothsay Castle*. It was with this good object that he had been induced to assist in these great and formidable combinations, but he had not moved until the last extremity. He had called to mind again and again the words of the Holy Scriptures, 'This is a nation robbed and spoiled—they are all of them snared in holes—they are hid in prison houses—they are for a prey and none to deliver—they are for a spoil and none to say *restore*.' He (Mr. Attwood) for one had felt it his duty to cry out 'restore,' and by their aid he had been enabled to cry out in a voice which had echoed through the land; their gracious King cried out 'restore;' the House of Commons had cried out 'restore;' the whole people of England had cried out 'restore;' and where was the power upon earth that should resist a voice like this? Mr. A. concluded by thanking the different Unions who had attended from so many distant parts of the country, and requested them to disperse to their respective homes—too many of them, he feared, melancholy homes; and he assured them it should be the study of his life to give plenty, peace, and happiness to them and to their families. (*Cheers.*) 'I now take my leave,' said Mr. A. 'and I pray that the Almighty God will shower down His blessings upon you and your families for ever.' (*Loud cheers.*)

At the conclusion of Mr. Attwood's speech, three cheers were given for the King, three for the Reform Bill, a farewell cheer for the country visitors of the meeting, three cheers for Mr. G. Edmonds, and a long discordant groan for the expiring Boroughmongers. The meeting then, in a peaceful and orderly manner, quietly dispersed."

Extraordinary was the excitement which this great meeting created throughout the country. Nothing of the sort had been witnessed in England before. Friends and foes were alike astonished at the peaceful, orderly, and unanimous conduct of its proceedings. The *Times* gave a very full report of the meeting, and in a leading article solemnly warned the aristocracy not to oppose so formidable a combination. Ministers felt themselves under the greatest obligations to Attwood, and, upon this occasion, they did not hesitate to acknowledge it openly and honourably. I regret that the original of Lord John

Russell's famous letter has been lost, and that I can only give that portion of it which was printed everywhere, and which has become historical; but I am fortunately able to copy the whole of Lord Althorp's, including a portion never before printed.

"*Lord John Russell to Mr. Thomas Attwood.*

I beg to acknowledge with heartfelt gratitude the undeserved honour done me by 150,000 of my countrymen.

Our prospects are now obscured for a moment, and I trust only for a moment. It is impossible that the whisper of a faction should prevail against the voice of a nation."

(*Lord Althorp to the same.*)
"DEAR SIR,

I beg to acknowledge the receipt of your letter, containing a vote of thanks to me from the great meeting at which you presided. The unanimous approbation of 150,000 of my Fellow Countrymen is no trifling honor; I feel sincerely thankful for it, and I beg to assure you that it gives me the highest gratification.

The Large Majority by which the Bill has been lost in the House of Lords is, I fear, a very serious calamity. It can only however postpone the success of our cause; but I beseech you to use all your influence not merely to prevent any acts of open violence but any such resistance to the law as is threatened by the refusal to pay taxes. Such a course as this is the one least likely to promote our success. Depend upon it, if the people continue peaceable but firm and united, no power on earth can prevent a full and efficient Reform being carried, whether we are able consistently with our Characters to remain Ministers or not. Whether in administration or not we are as determined to carry such a measure as any one man in the United Kingdom; the only possible doubt I have of success is from the imprudence of those who agree with us.

I have the honor to be, Dear Sir,
Your most faithful humble Servant,
Downing Street, Oct. 8th, 1831."   ALTHORP.

(Endorsed by T. A. as follows:—Oct. 8, 1831. From Lord Althorp, *in re* thanks of the Union, and about preserving ye peace.)

(*Sir G. Skipwith, M.P., to the same.*)

"6, *Pall Mall East, Oct.* 8, 1831.

"MY DEAR SIR,

I beg through you, in such a manner as may be most convenient to yourself, to offer to the Inhabitants of the Town and Neighbourhood of Birmingham, my sincere and heartfelt thanks for the honor which they did my colleague and me on the occasion of the late Meeting.

The approbation of my Constituents is the great reward which I am ambitious of receiving for my humble, but zealous and honest endeavours to promote the cause of Reform—a cause on the success of which, at this moment, depend the tranquillity and happiness of our Country.

It is with the deepest sorrow I confirm, what you will have already learned from other sources, that the second reading of the Reform Bill was rejected in the House of Lords this morning by a majority of 41.

It would not be true to say that the rejection came unexpectedly on the friends of the measure, but so large a majority against it was not contemplated, I believe, by anybody.

I am just returned from a Meeting at Willis's Rooms. It was attended by all or nearly all the Members of the House of Commons now in London who are Friends of Reform, and Supporters of the Government, and it was unanimously resolved to adhere to the Bill, and to the Ministers, and to give them every support in our power towards accomplishing the great measure of carrying it into law.

There is to be a Call of the House on Monday, and Lord Ebrington will submit a motion to it on the present state of Public Affairs.

God grant that, in the anguish of disappointment, the people may not forget that the observance of tranquillity and order is the surest, safest, and best way of effecting the great purpose which we seek and will have.

Let them also remember, that the Lords in what they have done have only exercised a right confided to them by the Constitution of the Country.

If the Ministers do their duty, and who can doubt but they will do it, it is folly to suppose that a measure sanctioned by the King, the People, and a majority of their Representatives in Parliament, will not be carried.

Mr. Lawley is at this moment at Brighton.

I have the honor to be, my dear Sir,

Yours very faithfully,

To Thomas Attwood, Esq." G. SKIPWITH.

These letters were immediately circulated everywhere, and created a great sensation in both Houses of Parliament. The Duke of Buckingham, Lord Wharncliffe, Sir Henry Hardinge, and others commented strongly upon the language employed at the Birmingham Meeting, and denounced the subserviency of Ministers to Attwood and the Unions. In particular the word "faction" in Lord John Russell's letter, which was supposed to apply to the House of Lords, gave great offence. Lord John defended himself rather lamely by saying that he had corresponded with Attwood, not as the head of the Political Unions, but as the chairman of a meeting of 150,000 men. All this discussion greatly increased the fame of Attwood, who was everywhere regarded as the great champion of Reform, whilst the Tories trembled at his name.

Fearful consequences followed the rejection of the Bill of Reform by the Lords. Windows were broken, peers insulted in the streets, and Lord Londonderry struck senseless from his horse. Then followed the riots and burnings at Derby and Nottingham, and the still more terrible outbreak at Bristol, which last, combined with the persuasions of his female relatives, is said to have made the King waver in the cause of Reform. But before this he had prorogued Parliament on the 20th October, and Ministers announced their intention of speedily bringing forward the Reform Bill again. In Birmingham the excitement was tremendous, but owing to the influence of Attwood and the Union, very slight breaches of the peace took place. On the 20th of October an important meeting of the inhabitants was held at Dee's Royal Hotel, to express their regret and disappointment at the rejection of the Bill, and very strong and almost revolutionary language was used by men not accustomed to it. The Council of the Political Union issued an address to their fellow-countrymen exhorting them to stand firmly by the King and Lord Grey. This address was signed by Thomas Attwood and concluded as follows :—

"Without blood, without anarchy, without violation of the law, we will accomplish the most glorious reformation recorded in the history of the world."

In the early part of November a large Reform Meeting was in the Market Square, Warwick, under the presidency of the High Sheriff. Thomas Attwood attended this meeting in company with Lord Hood, Sir J. Chetwynd, Sir G. Phillips, and other local magnates, who were beginning at last to see that it was necessary to adopt the principles which he had long professed, if they wished to save the country from revolution. Shortly afterwards the weekly meeting of the Council of the Union took place, and Mr. Attwood, in opening the proceedings, took occasion to deny that he had ever stated that he would be exposed to personal danger in the event of a Tory Administration succeeding to power. He had violated no law, and therefore had no fear. He had not been actuated by any low fear for his own life, but he feared the universal ruin and distress which must result from any civil commotion in England. He also denied that the Council had ever entertained the idea of arming the Union, a desperate measure about which sinister rumours had been afloat. Mr. Jones then submitted a plan for the organisation of the Union, with gradation of rank, offices, and titles, but this was voluntarily abandoned a very few days afterwards. The Whig Ministers had at first smiled on the Unions, upon whose shoulders they had been carried into power, but they soon became alarmed at the formidable power so rapidly acquired by these bodies, and terrified by some recent turbulent proceedings of the Metropolitan Unions, they issued a proclamation against all Political Unions on the 22nd of November. The boroughmongers no doubt hoped that this measure would cause a breach between the Government and Attwood, but in this they were wofully disappointed, for, says the *Times*, "on the very day on which the proclamation appeared in the *Gazette* did the grand Political Union of Birmingham relinquish the only part of its composition which affected its legality—namely, organisation." In opening the meeting of the 22nd Mr Attwood noticed the "atrocious lies" propagated by the Tory newspapers. It seems they had stated that the Birmingham Union had sent emissaries to Bristol, and 10,000 organised men to London, for the purpose of promoting a revolution. He then denounced the Bristol riots, which had disgraced the cause of Reform. Those shameful proceedings, I may notice, must have been brought nearly home to his consideration by the fact that Sir Charles Wetherell, whose entry into Bristol occasioned them, was the brother of Mrs. Richard Spooner, and the colleague of Matthias Attwood in the representation of Boroughbridge. Mr. Parkes then made a long speech upon the legality of the Union, in the course of which he stated that at Christmas, 1829, Mr. Attwood had told him that the days of the boroughmongers were numbered and fast drawing to a close; he then differed from Mr. Attwood, and predicted they would prove too strong for his grasp, but Mr. Attwood had been right.

Mr. de Bosco Attwood then moved that the plan for the organisation of the Union be abandoned, and his motion was carried. Further explanations respecting this matter were made a week later, and were reported at length in the *Times* of December 2nd, 1831.

I shall now return to Mr. Attwood's letters for the remainder of this eventful year:—

(*From G. de B. Attwood to Mrs. Thos. Attwood.*)
"*Birmingham, Monday, Oct.* 3, 1831.

". . . My father is so much engaged just now that he has deputed me to write in his stead to say that the meeting is over, that all has gone off peacefully, and that we are all very well. The meeting consisted of upwards of 100,000 grown men, and nearly as many women and children. It is reckoned that more than 20,000 came from the collieries, from Bilston, Darlaston, and Dudley. . . . My grandmother Carless seems unusually well, and my grandmother Attwood came on Thursday last to the fair with my grandfather. She said she had not been to a Birmingham fair for more than 30 years She had a narrow escape of being burned to death the other day. . . . There was an Ourang Outang exhibited at this fair, which was the greatest curiosity I have ever seen . . ."

(*From T. Attwood to the same.*)

I write these few words just to assure you that I am quite well, after seeing my 150,000 friends all disperse to their homes as quietly as a few children from a village school. The day was very fine, and the whole of this immense assembly stood patiently for 5 hours, and would have staid all night if I had desired them to do so.

Mrs. Attwood, 29, Wellington Crescent, Ramsgate.
Harborne, Octr. 9th, 1831.

We are all quite well. I prefer your coming by the Safety Tally ho, because it puts up at the most convenient inn, the Belle Savage in Ludgate Hill, and because I think it is the safest. Before you set out you should write to the Landlady to engage the rooms and the coach, a day or two before. If you like, Bosco shall meet you at the inn, or at the Steam Packet wharf, on Wednesday evening, the 29th inst. . . .

The news of the Reform Bill being thrown out arrived here last night. All the churches and chapels of Birmingham had their bells muffled, and each bell complained to the others in solemn melancholy all night long. It was the dirge of the oligarchs re-echoing in the heart of England. Everything is perfectly peaceful and will be so. Do not you have any kind of uneasiness, for you may depend upon my prudence and discretion. The firmness of the King, of his Ministers, and of the House of Commons, is undoubted.

Birmingham, 13 *October*, 1831.

. . . Aurelius will go to London on Sunday and come to you on Monday, for the purpose of returning home with you on Wednesday. *Everything is quiet here*, and will be so. You know I always told you there would be no disturbances in places where our Unions exist. Unhappily they have not got them at Derby and Nottingham.

Mrs. Attwood, Harborne, Birmingham.
London, Decr. 1st, 1831.

I am quite well and hope to return to you in a few days. Pray take care of yourself and of Angela and Rosabel. Bosco is discreet, and I know he will do what is right. I hope he will stop the proceedings of McDonnell, if I should not have returned.

London, Decr. 3rd, 1831.

Perhaps I may come home on Tuesday or Wednesday evening. I have been treated very kindly, and trust I have done some good. All parties agree in praising my political conduct, whether friends or foes. To-day I have been to see the 3 murderers, and I could not help being sorry for the poor creatures. Upon my taking leave of Bishop, he burst into tears. Williams has confessed to three murders. They are dreadful villains certainly. But if it is a crime to *burk* one or two men, what is it to *burk* a nation?

It would be quite impossible, without extending this memoir to a tedious extent, to give any account of all the numerous meetings at which Thomas Attwood or his sons assisted in the course of the years 1831 and 1832. Some idea, however, of the extraordinary political excitement which pervaded the neighbourhood of Birmingham at the time may be gathered from the following recollections of Mr. Edwin Thornton, printed in the *Birmingham Weekly Post* of June 2nd, 1883. Mr. Thornton says :—

"A year or two before the passing of the great Reform Bill in 1832, a branch of the Political Union Association was established at Astwood Bank, the meetings being usually held at the White Lion Inn, kept by Thomas Richards, who was also a painter and glazier by trade. Weekly meetings were held in the 'big room' of the inn to advocate Reform principles, and assist in preparing the Government to pass the Reform Bill. The inhabitants of Astwood at that time could not have been more than about six or seven hundred ; but a goodly number of those read the weekly papers, and took great interest in Liberal politics. A Tory at Astwood was then a *rara avis*. The *Birmingham Journal*, *Worcester Herald*, *Worcester Chronicle*, and the London *Weekly Dispatch* were the papers chiefly read. The local 'dailies' had not made their appearance. Among those members of the Union who regularly attended the meeting at the White Lion, and who were expected to be always prepared to make a speech, were J. B. Smith, Thomas Willmore, Thomas Hemming, Charles Hiam, J. Willmore, Thomas Thornton (the writer's father), and a few others. Of those mentioned, only one is now alive. Branch Unions were established at Feckenham, Studley, Redditch, Crabb's Cross, &c , the members of each branch attending occasionally the meetings of the respective localities. The country was thoroughly aroused to the necessity of political reform, an extension of the franchise, and the abolition of a number of old rotten boroughs. There was great and almost universal distress, as a natural consequence of Tory misrule ; and the people were on the verge of open revolt. Old Duke Wellington wanted to bring thirty thousand soldiers to Birmingham to calm the political excitement ! I have a vivid recollection of a great Political Union gathering and public banquet at Studley, Warwickshire, at which Mr. Thomas Attwood, of Birmingham, was expected to address the assembled Unionists of the district. Both Mr. Scholefield and Mr. Attwood were announced to be present on the occasion. For the local Reformers it was a most enthusiastic field day. I do not remember the date, but on the morning of the day there was a strong muster at Astwood. All the leading men on horseback, wearing blue sashes over their shoulders, and rosettes of blue ribbon upon the collar of their coats in front, formed the advanced guard of the procession. Each section of the Unionists forming the procession had at least one large flag and several banners. There were, therefore, several large flags in the procession requiring two or three men to carry them, extending the entire width of the road, and banners, with mottoes innumerable. One of the flags bore, I believe, the date of the establishment of the 'Union.' Thus accoutred, the cavalcade started to Crabb's Cross to meet other branches of the Union. A band of music accompanied each branch. From Crabb's Cross the multitudinous procession proceeded down the 'Slough' (locally pronounced *Sluff*) on its way to Studley, four or five bands playing simultaneously. At Studley great preparations were made for their reception at the Golden Fleece Inn, kept by John London. In the extensive yard at the back of the inn, temporary wooden booths had been erected, in which to hold the banquet and address the people. Tickets were issued at five shillings each. Messrs. Attwood and Scholefield were to arrive in Studley at a stated time. A cannon, charged with powder, was stationed nearly opposite the Barley Mow Inn, the muzzle pointing to the avenue leading to the Priory. The arrival of the two gentlemen from Birmingham was to be announced by the discharge of the cannon. Something at Birmingham occurred to prevent Mr. T. Attwood coming; but he did the next best thing he could, by sending his son. And about the time stated, young Mr. Attwood and Mr. Scholefield made their appearance, arm in arm, round the corner of the Barley Mow Inn; the cannon was duly discharged, making a tremendous report and shaking the glass out of the windows of the houses in the immediate vicinity. A short distance from the cannon was a glass and china shop, where considerable damage to goods and windows occurred from the report. Some thousands of persons were congregated in Studley. The public dinner came off at the Golden Fleece, and numerous speeches were made. I remember listening attentively to young Mr. Attwood's address, and noted a sort of impediment in his speech and considerable hesitancy in his delivery. He apologised for his father's absence, and told us how it happened, but I have forgotten what it was. I well remember Mr. Scholefield; he had on a black coat and trousers, and a dark crimson velvet waistcoat, with a gold watch-chain about it. I particularly noted him and his attire, but do not remember his address to the people. Mr. Attwood is associated in my mind with a suit of light grey tweed, or something of that sort

No such exciting times have been experienced in politics as were experienced from about 1830 to 1832, when the Reform Bill was passed. No such extensive petitions to the House of Commons were ever presented before or since. Many of the events of that important period are more vividly impressed on my memory to-day than many things which occurred only a few years ago. Although then merely a boy about twelve years old, I attended many of the political meetings at Astwood and elsewhere. At most of the public houses 'Union' cups and jugs for ale were used, and 'Union' clay pipes, upon which were 'Union' emblems, for smoking tobacco. Upon the pint jugs (which didn't hold a pint) was a head and shoulders portrait of Thomas Attwood, underneath which, in a semicircle, were the words, 'Attwood and the people;' and upon the rim, on each side, the motto, 'Union is strength.' One of these jugs is before me as I write. It belonged to my father, who carefully kept it so long as he lived. . . . I have not one of the Union pipes, and do not suppose there is one in the neighbourhood."

Martineau gives a graphic description of the gloom and terror which overspread men's minds at the close of 1831. People could talk of nothing but the disputed Bill, the cholera, the distress, and the riots. Even so moderate and scholarly a man as Dr. Arnold wrote in terms of despair as to the fearful times which his children would probably live to see. But Attwood was calm, confident, and happy. He felt certain that he had gained the mastery over the oligarchy, and that the assembling of a reformed Parliament was now only a question of time, and equally sure did he feel of his ability to persuade such a Parliament to adopt his favourite policy. Parliament was opened by the King on the 6th of December, and on the 12th Lord John Russell moved to bring in a new Reform Bill, very similar to the last. The debate on the second reading began on Friday, the 16th, and was continued to the morning of Sunday, the 18th, when the majority was 162 in a House of 486, and the House then adjourned for the Christmas recess.

The case of Small *v.* Attwood came on for hearing in the Court of Exchequer, before Lord Chief Baron Lyndhurst, in the early part of November, and was argued for twenty-one days. Sir Edward Sugden was John Attwood's leading counsel, and received for his services the enormous fee of 6,000 guineas, which, with the exception of a similar one afterwards paid to Sir Thomas Wilde, was, I believe, the largest ever received by any barrister for a single case, either before or since. Lord Lyndhurst took nearly a year to consider his judgment, which was not given till November, 1832.

I shall now close my account of this important year with a lighter incident. In June, 1831, Matthias Attwood dined at the annual dinner of the Merchant Taylors' Company, with the Duke of Wellington, the Marquis of Salisbury, the Earl of Eldon, Sir Henry Hardinge, Sir Charles Wetherell, and about 200 of the Tory leaders, from which I assume that the Merchant Taylors were strongly opposed to Reform. On December 23rd Alderman Garratt invited his friends of Bridge Ward, without regard to politics, to dine with him at the London Coffee House, Ludgate Hill, upon the occasion of his resigning his gown. Matthias Attwood proposed the health of the Alderman, and in the course of the evening several songs were sung, one of which, coming immediately after a speech of his, excited great merriment at his expense. The song was supposed to be sung by the old London Bridge, then just about to be demolished.

> "Oh, now, in spite of all my cares,
> I'm placed in schedule A ;
> The reason Y as all may C,
> I've long been in DK.
>
> I'm sure in A, I should not B,
> Unless, as some allege,
> They've for a borough taken me,
> And called me Borough Bridge."

Boroughbridge, it will be remembered, was one of the unfortunate boroughs set down in Schedule A of the Reform Bill for total disfranchisement.

From an Engraving published in Birmingham, July 11th 1832.

CHAPTER XIII.

The year 1832 the most important in Attwood's life—Letter from Lafayette—27,000 men solemnly pledge their obedience to Attwood—Mr. de Bosco Attwood's narrative of the Crisis—Great meeting of May 7th—Enormous assemblage of the people—Mr. de B. Attwood's "Call of the Unions" sung by 200,000 persons—Speech of Thomas Attwood setting forth the solemnity of the occasion—Resignation of Earl Grey—Indignation of the people—500 men of substance join the Union—Great spontaneous meeting of May 10th—Gloomy and serious aspect of affairs—"Solemn Declaration" against the Duke of Wellington—The Duke resigns—Earl Grey reinstated—Excessive joy of the populace—Mr. Parkes's letter—10,000 men assemble at Grove House and escort Mr. Attwood to Birmingham, where a third great meeting is held on May 16th amidst the most extraordinary demonstrations of popular gratitude.

WE have now reached the great year in Thomas Attwood's life, the great year in Birmingham history, and certainly one of the greatest years in the history of England. For in 1832 there was consummated that great, though bloodless, revolution which transferred the power of the aristocracy to the middle classes, and I think that no one, who will take the trouble to read carefully the contemporary history of the time, will deny that that grand change, whether for good or evil, was chiefly brought about by Thomas Attwood.

"Old Birmingham men," says Mr. Langford, "who took part in the Reform victory, look back to it with not unnatural pride, and encourage their degenerate and apathetic sons by telling them to read of 1832 and the Political Union. The year opened with the new Reform Bill being sent into Committee. On January 20th, Daniel O'Connell, accompanied by his son, visited the town, and addressed the people. On the 19th of March the Bill was read a third time in the House of Commons. It was sent to the House of Lords on the 26th. On April 9th the second reading came on, and was carried on the 14th of the same month. Still the Bill was not considered safe. The Political Union was more active than ever."

Upon turning to Attwood's private correspondence, I find that the year commences appropriately with a letter from Lafayette. The "hero of two worlds" condescended to acknowledge in Thomas Attwood a kindred spirit, and during the short remainder of his life addressed to him a number of friendly and flattering communications. His attention had probably been first turned to Attwood by the exertions of the latter in the cause of Poland, though I am unable to ascertain the date at which the Birmingham Polish Association was founded., He now wrote as follows :—

"*Paris, January 3rd*, 1832.
"MY DEAR SIR,

While I have the honor to offer to you the tribute of a double and most heartily felt gratitude for the patriotic Birmingham Association and its respectable president, permit me to consider myself as a personal friend and sympathising correspondent. You have heard of a sort of Alien Bill, with respect to foreign Refugees in France, which our . . . . could not procure the House of Deputies to adopt. This disposition has been lately, to my great regret, applied, not so far as to exile from the Country, but in an exile from Paris, to the signers of an address to the Russian people, which gave offence to the Autocrat, and was by the despotic cabinets assimilated to the publications of the Carlists, whose exterior intrigues had been complained of by the cabinet of the Tuileries. Under these deplorable circumstances one of the gentlemen of the Polish Committee, Mr. Erasmi Rickacrewski, has determined to go to England, and applies to me for letters of introduction. I cannot better serve his wishes than by directing these lines to you, at the same time that I am happy in every opportunity to offer the high regards and the best wishes of
Your sincere obliged friend,
LAFAYETTE."

The *Birmingham Journal* of January 14th, 1832, republished Thomas Attwood's letter to Sir John Sinclair of January 4th, 1826, with the following remarks :—

"We think it proper in another column to republish a letter from Mr. Thomas Attwood to Sir John Sinclair, which, when the date is considered, will, we think, exhibit a remarkable foresight into the present condition of the monetary and political affairs of the country. At the expiration of the last quarter the bank-note circulation was reduced agreeably to Mr. Attwood's prediction, as low as 17 millions sterling, and at the same time the country has been deprived of the £1 note circulation. Have the taxes, tithes, rents, debts, contracts, and obligations of the country been reduced correspondingly? If they have not, there seems no occasion to search further into the cause of the very general difficulty, embarrassment, and distress which prevail. Men have the same burthens to bear, and about half the means to bear them. It is true the political discontents which Mr. Attwood has foretold have not quite taken the course of those of 1816 and 1819. Instead of the '*Blanketeers*' of Manchester, and the '*Northern Cloud*' from Glasgow, and the *Cato Street Plot*, and the Staffordshire colliers dragging loads of Coal to London, we have now the terrible '*burnings*' which alarm half of England, the reduction of profits, employment, and wages ; and the '*Political Unions*,' which we apprehend are equally significant of the grand catastrophe which awaits us, *unless arrested by the timely interference of a wise, upright, and powerful Government.*"

The 21st March, 1832, was appointed by proclamation for a general fast and humiliation to avert the progress of the cholera. A copy of the form of prayer is preserved amongst Mr. Attwood's papers, and gives a vivid idea of the apprehension which the spread of the disease was then inspiring. On the 22nd of February Mr. Attwood wrote to his wife at the Albion Hotel, Ramsgate, as follows :—

. . . You may be assured that I will come to you as soon as possible, and it is not improbable that I may come by the steamer on Saturday next. But I am oppressed with business and cannot be certain of my movements. You do not say how you bore the travelling. I was in hopes our dear Marcus would have had no swelling left by this time Perhaps it might assist in reducing it to bring him home again. Pray, my dear, do not trust too much to the open windows. All of you require much care in this respect. You may see in the *Sun* paper of to-day an account of the prudence and forbearance with which we managed the reception of our grand address. Afterwards we invited the Deputation of 15 gentlemen to dinner with the Council, at which Bosco and Aurelius distinguished themselves as usual. This is about the 4th great event in my life. The cup, 20 years ago, was important, so was the dinner at Beardsworth's, and so was the presiding at the Newhall Meeting. But I think a solemn pledge of obedience volunteered by 27,000 men is more so. Few subjects have received an honour of this kind. In our prudence we *cut out the pledge of obedience*, and received only the testimony of confidence and esteem. . . .

I regret that, owing to my inability to obtain the Birmingham papers for 1832, I am unable to enlarge upon the important event alluded to in this letter.

The final struggle for Reform, so far at least as Birmingham was concerned—and it is admitted that what took place there at this time determined the fate of the kingdom—may be said to have commenced on the 27th April, 1832. On that day the Council of the Political Union met at their rooms in Great

Charles Street, Thomas Attwood in the chair, and transacted the following business:—

"This Council considering that the enemies of Reform, and of the peace and order of Society, have held out the most unfounded representations respecting a reaction, an indifference, and an apathy in the public mind, in the great cause of Parliamentary Reform, and considering that a grand exhibition of public feeling and determination is thereby rendered absolutely necessary, in order to contradict and refute such false and unfounded representations, and in order to assist in enabling our most excellent King and his patriotic Ministers to accomplish their great designs for the happiness of the people, and to carry the great measure of Reform into a law, uninjured and unimpaired in all its great parts and provisions, *it was resolved unanimously—*

1st That a General Meeting of the Inhabitants of Birmingham and its neighbourhood be held in the open space at the foot of Newhall Hill, on Monday, the 7th day of May next, at eleven o'clock in the forenoon. The Chair to be taken at twelve o'clock precisely.

2nd. That this Council, having heretofore declared that they will '*cease to labour in the great work of exciting the public mind to political objects when the Bill of Reform shall have become law, and when the prosperity of the lower and middle classes of the people shall have been restored*,' do now think it their duty to recommend to their fellow-countrymen to declare most positively, that if the Bill of Reform should be rejected or in any way injured or impaired in its great parts and provisions, they will never cease to use every possible legal exertion in their power to obtain a more complete and effectual restoration of the rights of the people than the Bill of Reform is calculated to give.

3rd. That this Council, feeling deeply grateful to the inhabitants of the town and neighbourhood of Birmingham for their uniform, peaceful, legal, and loyal conduct upon so many occasions, do earnestly urge and enjoin all persons attending the meeting, as they value the great objects which they meet to promote, strictly to respect the law, since nothing can tend so much to endanger the cause of the Reform and the happiness of the people as any disorderly or illegal act upon this occasion of unprecedented importance.

4th. That the Council do walk in procession from the Rooms of the Union, in Great Charles Street, to Newhall Hill, at eleven o'clock in the morning of the intended meeting, and that the members and friends of the Union be invited to join in the procession.

By order of the Council,
THOMAS ATTWOOD, Chairman.
BENJAMIN HADLEY, Secretary."

And now ensued that memorable period, during several days of which England was without a Government, and it is no exaggeration to say that the peace of the kingdom rested with Thomas Attwood. The main events of this momentous time have been fully narrated by Harriet Martineau, though that well-known authoress has strangely omitted to give to Attwood the credit that was justly his due.

Fortunately there has been preserved an account of the events in Birmingham which succeeded Earl Grey's resignation, written by Mr. G. De B. Attwood, and sent by him, at the editor's request, to the *Birmingham Journal* on February 11th, 1853, at which date they seem to have been nearly forgotten in the town. As Mr. G. De B. Attwood was a principal actor in the scenes which he describes, his account is most valuable; but in reading it, it must be borne in mind that, through modesty, he omits to treat of the important services rendered by his father at sufficient length. I shall first give his account *verbatim* as follows, and then supplement it from other sources:—

"The services rendered by the Political Union consisted—1st, in creating Public Opinion in favour of Reform; 2nd, in producing the strongest possible proof and manifestation of such Public Opinion without any infraction of the law; and 3rd, in keeping up public spirit, maintaining enthusiasm at boiling point, and preventing any reaction or appearance of reaction, such as in most cases follows after great efforts and sacrifices.

The power of the Union in the above three respects was never so perceptible as in the crisis of May, 1832.

At the commencement of that month, the Reform Bill was once more to be entrusted to the tender mercies of the House of Lords. The Tory papers had been falsely boasting that a change in Public Opinion had taken place, that the reaction had set in, and that the people were becoming indifferent to the fate of the Bill.

The Union felt it necessary to move in order to prove the falsehood of these assertions, and for this purpose held the great Meeting on Monday, the 7th May, 1832. Of the meeting a very fair and faithful report is given in the paper printed at the *Birmm. Journal* Office.

A Petition was passed praying the House of Lords to pass the Bill unmutilated, and the petition was entrusted to the Lord Chancellor.

On the morning of Thursday, May 10th, it was known that Lord Grey found it impossible to pass the Bill and had tendered his resignation. The excitement produced was tremendous. Business seemed everywhere at a standstill. All the respectable young men of Liberal opinions of all classes, who had not yet joined the Union, hastened to enroll themselves as members. The Council met immediately at their rooms in Gt. Charles St. The space allotted to the audience was crammed, and an immense crowd assembled in the streets demanding an immediate adjournment to Newhall Hill The demand was complied with, and, as if by magic, the same ground which had been occupied on Monday was again covered, though this time only by residents in the town. Symbols of anger and desperation everywhere met the eye. The flags and trophies which had been borne in triumph on the Monday again made their appearance, but either *covered in black drapery* or furled and reversed. The speeches made were violent and angry, and various recommendations were made. Some proposed a general league to refuse payment of all kinds of taxes. Mr. Muntz recommended to run the Savings' Banks, which advice was to some extent followed, and, no doubt, had its effect. In the midst of the storm my father remained calm and imperturbable. He reminded the excited populace that the hour of despair and vengeance had not yet arrived. He begged them to wait till they could see how the House of Commons would act, as if that House would still rally firm around Lord Grey all might yet be safe, and he *pledged himself* that if the Union would still stand by him, and *keep within the bounds of the law*, they should soon see Lord Grey carried back into power '*on the shoulders of the people*.' This promise and my father's influence calmed the agitated mass; the plan for refusing to pay taxes was withdrawn, and the meeting broke up peaceably after deputing Mr. Scholefield to wait upon and consult with Lord Grey.

From that time the sittings of the Political Council were held permanently from day to day. Blue ribands had been adopted generally as a badge of Liberal opinions upon the arrival of the bad news; and the Union members all wore permanently a Union Jack riband as a badge. The first step taken by the Council was the adoption of a 'Declaration against the Duke of Wellington' drawn up by my father. It contained a pledge to use all legal means to prevent the Duke's accepting office, or to drive him from office if he accepted it, and it stated briefly, but very forcibly, some 12 *reasons* for giving this pledge. I am very sorry that I have no copy of this declaration to refer to. When the ground on which the Duke had quitted office in December, 1830, is recollected, and his known opinions and qualifications are borne in mind, it is evident that there were the strongest reasons possible for keeping him out of power by all means available. One reason was 'Because he can only govern by the sword, a power to which the English people have never submitted and never will submit'—or nearly in these words. The Declaration was circulated very widely and produced a very great effect. The town, however, remained in the greatest anxiety and alarm. A deputation waited upon some of the members of the Political Council to offer a guard of 1,500 men armed with muskets, &c., to protect the meetings of the Council. All such offers were, of course, respectfully declined, and the people encouraged to keep within the law and look to the law only for protection. Still the feeling grew that if once the Government were established in office some desperate measure would be had recourse to, the most probable being the summary arrest of my father and the other leading members of the Council.

To meet such an emergency it was proposed that every member of the Council should authorise a deputy to act in his absence, so that in the event of a sudden disappearance of the leaders, their deputies might step into their places, the people might still have leaders to look to, and measures might yet be taken to obtain justice and redress.

MR. DE B. ATTWOOD'S ACCOUNT OF THE CRISIS.

Once, late at night, when the excitement was at its highest, we heard voices in the lane at Harborne, and on enquiring into the cause it was found that a party of villagers had taken alarm and expected that my father would be arrested that night; they had accordingly come down with firearms to line the hedges and drive back the expected soldiers or police, whoever they might be. The men were, of course, pacified and sent home.

Count Czapski, the Pole, made his first appearance at the meeting of the 7th May, and he spent most of the remaining anxious days with us. A braver or truer spirit never tenanted a mortal body, and he was as courteous and humane as he was brave and true. He was then fresh from the glorious death struggle of his own unfortunate and deserted country, and we gathered strength and confidence from his presence and advice. Poor fellow! he finished his mortal career not many months ago, a life spent in vain in the cause of European liberty, although terminated unexpectedly by sickness. He was a zealous and useful member of the Birmingham Political Union, and deserves that his name should be perpetuated in its records.

On Sunday, the 13th of May, 1832, Mr. Scholefield returned and reported to my father that he had seen Lord Grey, who had, with tears in his eyes, assured him that '*all was over*,' that his return to power then was impossible, that there was nothing to be done but to keep the people quiet, and that, doubtless, the Duke of Wellington would before long bring in a Bill of of Reform nearly as good as that of Lord John Russell.

This advice seemed to be palatable to some of the more lukewarm, but it did not at all suit my father. He saw that if, after all that had passed and been done and suffered, the House of Lords should be allowed to throw out the Bill and the Ministry, and make new Ministers of its own, there would, for the present, be an end to popular power in England and the spirit of the people would be utterly broken, but he also felt confident that this would be found to be impossible.

The Council continued its daily labours, and on Wednesday, the 16th of May, the good news arrived and the spontaneous meeting was held which is faithfully described in the *Birmingham Journal* Report.

It is evident that this meeting was, in some measure, the result of a ruse of that very clever and shrewd reformer Mr. Jos. Parkes.

All that was certain at the time was that some difficulty had been experienced by the Duke of Wellington, and that some communications had been made to Lord Grey as to his resuming office. But the news which Mr. Parkes had brought down express was understood to be that Lord Grey was actually again in power. He travelled from London express by night (no railways) with printed slips of the good news which he distributed on his road to tried, good men, so as to ensure a general outburst of enthusiasm at a dozen places the next morning. The plan succeeded, numerous enthusiastic meetings were held next day (besides the Birmingham Meeting), and the reports of them tended more than anything else to weaken the position of the Duke and strengthen that of Lord Grey

When, however, the Birmingham Deputation arrived in London, on the morning of the 17th of May, we found the victory not only not won, but quite hanging in the balance. This state of suspense lasted some days, during which my father was in constant communication with the leading London reformers. The London Political Unions adopted the badge of the Birmm. Union, and the Union Jack riband began to appear pretty generally in the streets. Arrangements were in progress for holding a monster Reform Meeting on Hampstead Heath when the Duke, at the last, really took fright and gave way. Lord Grey returned to power '*on the shoulders of the people*' with a carte blanche to make peers *as might be necessary*, and to prevent the exercise of this power the Duke of Wellington persuaded the Tory peers to stay away from the House and leave the Whig lords to pass the Bill unopposed.

At one of the first meetings of the House of Lords, after this arrangement was made, I had the great pleasure of being present in the gallery, from whence I looked down on a house full on one side, empty on the other, and heard the then Lord Caernarvon denouncing Lord Grey in the most furious manner, intimating that his head ought to be brought to the block, and that, for his own part, he should by no means regret to see him meet his fate.

The account of the triumphal return of the Deputation to Birmingham on Monday, the 28th of May, 1832, is given very well in the report of the *Birmingham Journal*.

I need scarcely say that I never saw anything nearly so grand or so touching. The utter impossibility of the carriage and horses, in which my father was, to make their way up to the Bullring, until the horses were taken out, and the carriage wheeled or *rather carried* by the crowd, and the final arrival in New Street, cannot be described ; but to me the most affecting sight was to see my aged grandfather (then about 90 years old) and grandmother standing at a window to welcome my father on his return.

I believe that through the whole of the exciting period of which I have above given a brief sketch, the police reports at Birmingham, and indeed throughout the country, were no heavier than usual. Certainly, no political outbreak of any kind took place The people were wild, almost mad, with excitement. The object for which they had striven so hard was snatched from them when, as it were, within their grasp, and held before them as if to tantalise them. Under the guidance of my father and the Union they never forgot themselves. They won as great a prize as nation ever struggled for, and they won it by their own perseverance and the display of their own irresistible power ; but in doing so they broke no law and shed no blood.

It will be recollected that during the period noticed above, the enthusiasm which prevailed throughout the populace gradually spread to the army, and was manifested among the troops. Occasionally soldiers from the barracks appeared among the audience at the meetings of the Council. Somerville was one of these, and there seems little doubt that when flogged ostensibly for some blunder in horsemanship, he was really flogged for having made a display of Liberal opinions. I believe that when the Duke was about returning to office he caused enquiries to be made from the War Office as to the spirit of the troops, and as to how far they could be depended on in case of need.

The replies he received were said to have been far from satisfactory to him, and from Birmingham the answer is said to have been that the troops were not numerous enough to defend their own barracks, and that if they were more numerous they could not be relied on to act against the people. Soon after the arrival in Birmingham of the news that Lord Grey had tendered his resignation, and that the Duke of Wellington was engaged in forming a Ministry, my father wrote confidentially to two of his fellow labourers only, viz , to Mr. Wallace, Chairman of the Glasgow and Greenock Political Unions, and to my uncle, Mr. Charles Attwood, then Chairman of the Northern Political Union at Newcastle-on-Tyne. My father requested the presence of both these gentlemen in Birmingham, stating that Birmingham was by circumstances placed in the front of the battle, and that on the formation of the new Ministry the first blow would probably be struck there ; that being so situated he felt the want of their presence and advice as to the proper course to be taken, and as to how far he might depend upon Birmingham being supported in any course it might take by the other great towns. Mr. Wallace replied cheeringly and cordially, but declined leaving home saying, that in the midst of so much excitement and anxiety, his proper post was in the midst of his own Political Union. Mr Charles Attwood hurried to Birmingham as fast as horses could carry him, but before his arrival my father had left Birmingham with the Deputation for London on the 16th May."

The following is an account of the great meeting held at Birmingham on May 7th, 1832, for the purpose of petitioning the House of Lords to pass the Reform Bill, abridged from the *Journal* report :—

"So early as Saturday the population of the town and its immediate districts began to evidence symptoms of great excitement, and on Sunday the roads leading to Birmingham, but more especially the northern roads, showed that the attendance from distant parts of the country would be immense. Some thousands arrived in the course of that day, many of whom came from the extremities of the counties of Worcester, Stafford, and Gloucester. Before daybreak yesterday morning all was bustle and preparation The previous arrangements made by the Council were in themselves admirable, and executed with precision and punctuality by the various gentlemen to whom they were entrusted. By 8, the persons appointed to conduct the Unions of the various towns in the neighbourhood that intended visiting the meeting repaired to their respective stations on the different roads, each mounted on horseback, and decorated, or distinguished, by a broad sash of office, embroidered with the Union Jack. As all the Unions round the country had resolved either to attend in a body, or to send deputations to the Meeting, a superintendent was appointed by the Council of the Birmingham Union to meet them on the different roads, and to lead them, with other bodies, into the town. Between 9 and 12 these various bodies began to enter Birmingham, all being preceded by bands of music, and exhibiting flags upon which were inscribed various patriotic devices and mottos. At 10 o'clock the Council, with numerous gentlemen of consequence unconnected with the Association, assembled at the Union Rooms in

Great Charles Street, and, all arrangements being completed, the procession, consisting of countless thousands, proceeded to Newhall-hill, the place appointed for the Meeting. The spot fixed upon is a large waste piece of ground, situated on the north side of the town, containing in size about six acres, and capable of accommodating, according to the most accurate calculation, the immense number of 150,000 persons. The ground rises on the front and on each side in the form of an amphitheatre, and taking into consideration the numbers who occupied the roofs of houses and various contiguous elevations, we should say that not less than 200,000 persons were present. Shortly before 12 o'clock, the programme being all arranged, the immense multitude, headed by Thomas Attwood, Esq., the Chairman of the Birmingham Political Union, and the Founder of that and all other Unions, in company with the Council carrying white wands, and followed by an immense procession, preceded by the Birmingham Union Band in their superb uniform, proceeded to the place of Meeting. We were favoured with a seat in the first carriage, but, admirably situated as we were for viewing the whole of this most splendid cortège, we are unable to give anything like a description of the scene which it presented. Looking from the top of Mount-street up Newhall-street, to the end of Great Charles-street, the spectacle, from the countless myriads of which it was composed, and the splendid devices and colours which it exhibited, was truly magnificent. On the arrival of the members of the Union at Newhall-hill the ground was found to be almost completely pre-occupied. With difficulty the cavalcade approached the waggons allotted for the accommodation of the speakers. The whole of the ground and the tops of houses, as far as the eye could discover, appeared to be completely covered with human beings.

At appropriate distance, on the ridge of the hill opposite the speakers, were various banners, amongst which, in the centre, waved the Royal Standard, the same which was exhibited at Somerset House when the King went to open the New London Bridge. Among the almost innumerable flags we noticed the banners of the Coventry, Warwick, Wolverhampton, Darlaston, Wednesbury, Walsall, Alcester, Bromsgrove, Studley, Stratford-upon-Avon, Redditch, and Shirley Unions. Our attention was necessarily in a great measure confined to one spot, but a gentleman who visited the several divisions gives us the following particulars from personal observation. He estimates the Grand Northern Division, including Wolverhampton, Bilston, Sedgeley, Willenhall, Wednesbury, Walsall, Darlaston, and West Bromwich at 100,000 persons. The procession was four miles in length, the whole of the road for that distance being literally crowded. In this Division there were 150 banners and 11 bands of music. The Grand Western Division, including Stourbridge, Dudley, Harborne, Cradley, Lye Waste, Oldbury, Rowley, Hales Owen, &c., was two miles in length, in numbers about 25,000, and exhibited 70 banners. The Eastern Division, including Coventry, Warwick, Bedworth, Kenilworth, Leamington, and Stratford-upon-Avon, consisted of about 5,000, and exhibited 30 banners. The Southern Division, including Bromsgrove, Redditch, Studley, Worcester, Droitwich, and Alcester, had 12 banners, 6 bands of music, and consisted of about 10,000 persons. The above estimates are exclusive of the immense numbers who attended the Meeting from Birmingham and its vicinity, which include a population of about 150,000.

By twelve o'clock the vast cavalcade had reached the hustings. On Mr. Attwood's appearance he was greeted with loud and continued cheering Among the company present, and by whom he was more immediately surrounded, we noticed—J. R West, Esq. ; A. F Gregory, Esq., R Knight, Esq., M.P. ; General Count Czapski, — Acland, Esq. (brother of Sir T. Acland) ; Joshua Scholefield, Esq ; H. Boultbee, Esq. ; Stubbs Wightwick, Esq., R. Fryer, Esq., G. Osborne, Esq (nephew of the Duke of Leeds) ; Joseph Parkes, Esq ; W. Collins, Esq. ; G. F. Muntz, Esq. ; James Webb, Esq ; and several County Magistrates. The business of the Meeting was delayed for a considerable time, owing to the perpetual arrival of subsidiary Unions. At length—

Mr. Thomas Attwood (the Chairman) rose, amidst *loud cheering*, and addressed the Meeting as follows :—' Men of Warwickshire, Staffordshire, and Worcestershire—My dear friends and fellow-countrymen,—I thank you most sincerely for the immense, glorious, and magnificent assemblage which you now present in the hour of your country's need. To see the call of the Council of the Political Union answered in such an effectual way—not only by the inhabitants of Birmingham, but as it were spontaneously by the inhabitants of twenty towns and districts around them—is to me a subject of the deepest and sincerest gratification. (*Cheers.*) The enemies of the liberties of their country have spoken of reaction and of indifference in the public mind towards the great cause of Reform—how are they answered by the people of the midland counties ? We have had but to stamp upon the earth, as it were, and instantly from above the ground and from beneath the ground a hundred thousand brave men, besides the thousands of beautiful women I see before me, determined to see their country righted, present themselves at our call.' (*Great cheering.*)

Mr. A. was here interrupted by the arrival of several Unions on the ground. After having first cheered their arrivals, the assembly, under the leadership of Mr. Edmonds, proceeded to sing the following Union Hymn, written by Mr. De Bosco Attwood :—

'THE CALL OF THE UNIONS.

Over mountain, over plain,
Echoing wide from sea to sea,
Peals, and shall not peal in vain,
The trumpet call of Liberty.
Britain's guardian spirit cries,
Britons ! Awake ! Awake ! Arise !

Sleep no more the sleep of shame,
Arouse and break Oppression's chain !
Lull'd by Freedom's empty name,
Worse than slaves no more remain :
Freedom's rights, not Freedom's name,
Learn to know and dare to claim.

Lo ! we answer, see we come,
　Quick at Freedom's holy call,
We come ! we come ! we come ! we come !
　To do the glorious work of all ;
　　And now we raise from sea to sea,
　　Our sacred watchword, Liberty !

Shall honest labour toil in vain,
　While plunder battens on the land ?
Still shall a tyrant faction's reign
　People and King at once command ?
　　No ! it may not, shall not be,
　　For we must, we will be free.

You will not sleep while, one by one,
　Each sacred, dear-bought right is lost ?
Rights which your father's broad-swords won,
　Rights which your father's life-blood cost.
　　No ! it may not, shall not be,
　　For we must, we will be free.

See ! we come ! God our Guide.
See ! we come ! from field, from wave,
　From plough, from anvil and the loom,
We come our country's rights to save,
　And speak a tyrant faction's doom !
　　And now we raise, from sea to sea,
　　Our sacred watchword, Liberty !

See ! rises from his bed of fame,
　Each chief of glorious Runnymede,
With Hampden, history's noblest name,
　They call us to our country's need.
　　They call, and can we heedless be ?
　　No ! for we must, we will be free !

But not to war and blood they call,
　They bid us lift nor sword nor gun :
Peaceful but firm, join one and all
　To claim your rights,—and they are won.
　　The British people's voice alone
　　Shall gain for Britain all her own.

See ! we come ! Heav'n our aid.
See ! we come ! no swords we draw,
　We kindle not war's battle fires ;
By union, justice, reason, law,
　We'll gain the birthright of our sires.
　　And thus we raise from sea to sea,
　　Our sacred watchword, Liberty !'"

MR. ATTWOOD'S SPEECH.

I presume that the choruses only of this hymn were sung at the meeting, but as it was Mr. G. De B. Attwood's composition I have inserted the whole of it from another source.

"After this spirit-stirring composition had been thundered forth by many thousand voices, silence was obtained by the sound of the trumpet ; and the mighty murmurs of the multitude being immediately stilled, Mr. Attwood continued :—

'We had determined never again to petition the House of Lords, but feeling, as we do, the greatest respect and veneration for the ancient and honourable aristocracy of the land—for such men as Lords Westminster, Cleveland, Shrewsbury, and Radnor, those ornaments of English History— we have not hesitated to call this Meeting, for the purpose of petitioning their Lordships, as soon as ever we saw that the calumnies and misrepresentations of the enemies of the people as to the state of public feeling and opinion rendered such an exhibition necessary. (*Cheers.*) The enemies of the people have told their Lordships that the country is indifferent in this great cause. If we hold no meetings they say that we are indifferent ; if we hold small meetings they say we are insignificant ; and if we hold large meetings they say that we are rebellious and wish to intimidate them. (*Laughter.*) Do what we will we cannot do right it seems. Now, God forbid that I should wish to intimidate them—I only wish to speak the plain and simple truth, which my duty compels me to speak, and which is this :— I would rather die than see the great Bill of Reform rejected or mutilated in any of its great parts or provisions. (*Immense cheering*, which lasted for a considerable time) I had rather hide my head under the earth than live to witness the misery, the degradation, and the slavery of my country. I see that you are all of one mind upon this great subject. (*Cheers*). Answer me then, had not you all rather die than live the slaves of the boroughmongers? ("*All, all !*") We are told, indeed, of apathy and indifference in the public mind ; now, I have some means of understanding what public feeling is, and I say that the People of England stand at this very moment "like greyhounds on the slip ," and that if our beloved King should give the word, or if the Council should give the word in his name, and *under his authority*, the grandest scene would be instantly exhibited that ever was witnessed on this earth before. (*Loud cheers.*) Now I beg, my fellow-countrymen, that you will not think the House of Lords are your enemies because they do not happen to understand your interests, and your wants, and your wishes. The House of Lords are, in my opinion, taken as a body, kind-hearted and humane men ; but I am sorry to say that they are excessively ignorant of the state of this unfortunate country. They were cradled in those clouds which are now passing over our heads : in the clouds were they cradled—in the clouds will they die. (*Cheers.*) Not many days ago a Noble Lord of the highest character assured me that there were not ten individuals in the Right Honourable House who knew that the country was in a state of distress. Amazing as this ignorance is, it is the natural result of their position in society. They come into no contact with you and your wants and interests

——they are surrounded by a few Lawyers and Clergymen, and bands of flatterers and sycophants, whose interest it is "to prophecy smooth things" to the very last, and thus the Lords are shut out from any knowledge of the real state of the country. It was but the other day that another Noble Lord assured a friend of mine that the demand for Reform arose from the riches and prosperity of the middle classes, who had become jealous of the Aristocracy. Never upon this earth was there a greater error. The middle classes had been literally scourged with whips—they had been scourged with scorpions—and they had been scourged with red-hot iron, before they had ventured to interfere in any powerful and effectual manner. Here, then, is a proof of the absolute necessity of Parliamentary Reform. Give us a House of Commons who are identified with the Commons, and with the feelings and interests of the Commons, and everything will be right in England. . . . Now, my friends, I must beg leave to explain to you the absolute necessity of the peace, the order, and the strict legality which you have always exhibited. But for these great qualities our cause would have been lost. Within the law the People are strong as a giant; beyond the law they are weak as an infant. See now the prodigious strength which this meeting has peacefully and legally accumulated, and compare it with the failures which, for want of due attention to these great principles, have been exhibited in other quarters. On the late Fast Day about 30,000 worthy and well-meaning men met together in London, for the purpose of holding a harmless procession. A few individuals began to hiss, and to hoot, and to throw stones, and thus the meeting was made illegal, and the leaders of an innocent procession were brought to punishment and sentenced to different periods of imprisonment. So also in the town of Manchester lately a considerable meeting was held, which, it is probable, had not any illegal views or objects; but a few individuals among them having made use of violent, inflammatory, and illegal observations, the whole meeting was thereby rendered illegal, and the leaders of it are now imprisoned in Lancaster Castle for different periods. The different meetings had no power to prevent the punishment of their leaders, because they were guilty of violations of the law. . . . See now the prodigious power which this association has obtained. Under the sanction of the law we have here produced probably 200,000 human beings in one great assembly, not half of whom I am afraid can come within the hearing of my voice. Hitherto our exertions have been confined in direct operation to this town and neighbourhood. Suppose now we should erect the standard of the Birmingham Union in London—that glorious standard which acts so terrifically upon the mind of his Grace the Duke of Buckingham. I can tell you, and I can tell his Grace, that if we should so act, nine-tenths of the whole population of that immense city would instantly rally round the sacred emblem of their country's freedom. (*Cheers.*) The same would be the case in Newcastle, Manchester, Glasgow, and Dublin. The whole of the British people would answer to the call wherever the standard of the Birmingham Union should be unfurled under the sanction of the King and of the law. (*Cheers.*) This is the power which we have gathered up under a strict and dutiful obedience of the law, and therefore I do strictly urge and enjoin you to continue still the same dutiful and legal conduct which you have hitherto exhibited, and never to suffer any circumstance whatever to seduce you into any illegal or violent proceedings. When I had the pleasure of meeting you here in October last, I asserted that every honest workman in England had as good a right to a reasonable maintenance, in exchange for his labour, as the King had to the crown upon his head A noble lord, Lord Wharncliffe, is reported to have contradicted this assertion in a high quarter. I therefore beg leave to repeat it most positively, and to state most distinctly, that every honest workman in England does, in fact, when in full employment, produce more than four times the comforts and necessaries of life which he and his family can possibly consume. If, then, the giving to his country of more than four times the quantity of comforts and necessaries which he himself requires is not sufficient to constitute a right, I know not what is. The laws of God and of nature have ordained that man shall live by the sweat of his brow,—the labour of man's hands produce in England four times as much as his humble wants require, and therefore I insist upon it, that of all the rights in civilised life, the oldest, and the strongest, and the most righteous is the right of living by honest labour. (*Cheers.*) If the great Reform which we are now about to obtain does not have the effect of establishing this great right, and of confirming it for ever, it will never satisfy me. My friends, I will trouble you no more Your destinies, and the destiny of our country, are at this moment in the hands of the House of Lords. We have met this day for the purpose of discharging our duty to them. If that august body should neglect to discharge their duty towards us and our country, upon their heads alone will rest the awful responsibility of the tremendous consequences which may ensue. A nation may advance in the career of liberty, but to go back is not possible. (*Cheers.*) When the immortal Hampden hoisted the standard of Liberty in England, he adopted as his motto the words "*Vestigia nulla retrorsum,*" or in English, the words "*No retreat.*" (*Cheers*) Now this is *our* motto in the peaceful and legal contest in which we are engaged, and I will tell the boroughmongers that they will find it as easy to turn the sun from its course as to make the English people now be content with less than the Bill of Reform. . . . We have not called this Meeting from any distrust of Lord Grey, but in order to contradict the falsehoods of the enemies of Reform, and to place a weapon in the hands of his Lordship. When the enemies of Reform speak of indifference in the public mind, Lord Grey will answer, "*Look at Birmingham,*" and no other answer will be necessary. It was our anxious wish not to have been under the necessity of calling this great Meeting, and I do assure you that we should not have required at your hands so great a sacrifice if the falsehoods and misrepresentations of the enemies of Reform had not rendered this great exhibition necessary to the safety and liberty of the country. (*Loud cheering.*) Remember, my friends, *our* weapons are PEACE, LAW, ORDER, LOYALTY, and UNION. Let us hold fast to these weapons, and I tell you that the day is not distant when the liberty and prosperity of our country will be restored'—Mr. Attwood resumed his seat amidst long and enthusiastic cheering.

R. Fryer, Esq., next presented an address from 3,000 householders of Wolverhampton, approving of the conduct of the Birmingham Union.

Joshua Scholefield, Esq., then addressed the meeting, severely commenting on the conduct of the Duke of Wellington and upon the enormous pensions granted to him and other members of the aristocracy.

Messrs. Muntz, Edmonds, Hadley, Parkes, and Dr. Wade then spoke at length, after which Count Czapski said a few words, and then Mr. De Bosco Attwood rose and said he felt the cause of Poland the cause of Europe and of liberty ; he felt the liberty, and he would say the independence, of England to be essentially connected with the independence of Poland. He had that day seen a flag bearing the motto 'a tear for Poland.'—No one could more deeply feel than himself for the wrongs of the Poles ; but he had often heard it said, that when a mighty nation spoke, it might not be a word and a blow, but the blow before the word. He felt that if it was a disgrace to the English nation that when the cause of justice, of humanity, and of England too, was at stake, they had not sent a blow before a word, it was also a burning disgrace then that they did not proffer a sword to Poland, as well as a tear. *(Loud cheers.)* He trusted the day was near at hand when the English People, in possession of their own liberty, would be able to assert their own honour and the principles of justice abroad. He trusted then that England would at once step forward manfully in defence of betrayed and oppressed, but heroic Poland ; that nation which, in the midst of its calamities, had earned for itself a glory never possessed by any nation before, and he trusted then that England would speak in her behalf in a voice of thunder, and that when once the arm of England was raised, and her sword unsheathed, that arm would never be lowered, and that sword never sheathed, till Polanders were fully and entirely free. *(Loud cheers.)* He should call for three cheers for the revival of Polish Liberty, and the end of Polish calamity.

Mr. T. Aurelius Attwood commenced by lamenting the weakness of his voice, which had been exhausted by the fatigue of marching at the head of the Union over which he had the honour to preside, from Hales Owen, and giving orders during the march. But he assured the meeting of his readiness, when called upon, to undertake any march, however distant, if such a step should be ever thought requisite for the insuring of the liberties of the People. *(Cheers.)* Notwithstanding the fatigue (said Mr. A) it is with the greatest pride and satisfaction that I now rise to address you ; and strange would it be if I did not feel proud when I consider that I joined in its infancy the Birmingham Political Union, which Association has now gained such vast strength that at its call the thousands, and I may say tens of thousands of my countrymen, who now present so grand a spectacle to my eyes, are gathered together ;—when I call to mind that I assisted at the planting of that acorn of the British oak which now, verifying the eloquent prophecy of our Chairman, after having escaped unhurt the designs of its enemies when first shooting from the ground and when but a tender plant,— rears its gigantic trunk on high, spreads its wide-branching arms from one end of England to the other, affording shelter and protection to the People, —and, confident of its strength, laughs to scorn the attacks of its foes. *(Loud cheers.)* It is under the shadow of this oak that the British People have been enabled to carry on that contest for their rights and liberties which I now trust will speedily be brought to a happy termination. *(Cheers.)*

Opposition and contumely have but increased our strength. The haughty rejection of the Bill by an infatuated majority of the House of Lords has but had the effect of an ineffectual barrier thrown across a mighty river ;—it has delayed the stream until it has gained irresistible strength, when, sweeping away the feeble opposition to its course, it rushes foaming along so powerful and impetuous as to threaten immediate destruction to anything that dares to attempt to check its career. (*Cheers.*) The Commons of England, for once nobly advocating the cause of the people, passed the Bill a second time by a larger majority, and have sent it up again to the Lords. Soon shall we see who are to be the victors,—the people of England, headed by the most noble and most ancient of our Aristocracy, or a few misguided Oligarchs, whose hearts, one would almost suppose, had been, like Pharaoh's, hardened for their destruction. (*Cheers.*) Can there be any doubt as to the result? No. But our victory must be bloodless ; and as there are the means to render it so, God forbid that our oppressors should be allowed, by again scorning the demands of the people, to expose themselves to punishment for their temerity. (*Loud cheers.*) Without alluding to the power possessed by the House of Commons to pass the Bill without the consent of the House of Lords, or without inquiring into the right of the Lords to legislate upon a subject which *ought* only to concern the representatives of the people, our gracious King possesses the means by constitutionally creating any number of peers—

'A breath can make them as a breath has made ;'

and if no one ought to be elevated to the peerage without having done some service to his country, I should like to know what greater service can be rendered than the restoring liberty and happiness to the people, and preserving the country from anarchy and bloodshed. (*Loud cheers.*) Now I feel confident that His Majesty will not allow the people, already goaded by distress, to be driven to despair by a second rejection of the Bill, or the whisper of a faction to prevail against the voice of the nation ; and, placing confident reliance on His Majesty, I feel satisfied that he is the best judge of the time when it is necessary to exert his high prerogative. (*Loud cheers.*) Mr. Aurelius Attwood concluded by seconding the fifth resolution, which requested the King to create a sufficient number of peers to pass the Bill.

Mr. De Bosco Attwood then spoke again at length, and concluded by proposing the sixth resolution, which strongly denied that the distress of the country was to be attributed to the introduction of the Reform Bill.

Mr. T. C. Salt, in seconding the seventh resolution, which expressed the thanks of the Meeting to those bodies of men who had attended from a great distance, concluded by requesting every one to repeat after him ' In unbroken faith, through every peril, and trial, and privation, we devote ourselves and our children to our country's cause.' (The scene which ensued was most solemn and impressive, and is particularly noticed by Harriet Martineau in her 'History of the Peace.')

A vote of thanks was afterwards passed to Mr. Attwood amidst the most enthusiastic cheering, and in the course of his speech returning thanks he said :—' When I first assisted in the formation of the Political Union, it was not without long and anxious deliberation that I embarked in it. I solemnly declare to you that the night before I decided I sat up all night in serious and anxious meditation ; and after I had made up my mind, I went down upon my knees in the grey of the morning and prayed to Almighty God that if this great Association was not calculated to promote the liberty and the happiness of the mass of the people *it might not prosper*. This was the spirit with which I embarked in the Political Union ; and this is the spirit with which I will continue in it, until I see my country prosperous and free. . . .'

The business of the day having been gone through, three discordant groans were given for the bishops who had voted against the Bill upon its memorable second reading. The vast assemblage then began to leave the ground ; the Unions of the neighbouring towns gathering their scattered members together, and arranging them beneath their banners ; the bands belonging to each company playing lively and patriotic airs ; and the whole crowd marshalling into procession and joining, as the various bodies quitted the ground, the long line of the retiring multitude, that, extending itself in beautiful array, at length melted into distance far beyond the extremest point that could be reached even by the strongest vision. No murmur of disapprobation was spoken, nor a single attempt to break the peace made. All was equanimity and order. The night was quiet. The number of intoxicated persons few. And the morning dawned upon the town of Birmingham without a single appearance to be found in its streets indicative of the fact that one of the largest and most important Meetings ever held in England upon any occasion had concentrated the united attention of nearly 200,000 persons upon the previous day."

At eleven o'clock on the morning of May 8th an express arrived in Birmingham with the news that Lord Lyndhurst's motion, practically amounting to a rejection of the Reform Bill, had been carried by a majority of 35 on the previous night. Tremendous excitement at once prevailed throughout the town, and early on the morning of May 9th numerous placards appeared in the windows announcing that no taxes would be paid until the Reform Bill was passed. When the London evening newspapers arrived by the mail an extraordinary development of public feeling took place, and a very singular and remarkable compliment was paid to the talents and foresight of Thomas Attwood. Hitherto the majority of the respectable inhabitants of Birmingham had held aloof from what they considered the noise and vulgarity of the Union. But now, on the receipt of the unwelcome news, a great change took place, and men of all creeds and opinions who had previously taken no part in politics suddenly perceived that the only way by which they could avert a revolution was to join the Political Union, and strengthen by all possible means the party of Reform. On Tuesday four Catholic priests enrolled themselves, and on Wednesday twenty Quakers became members. Finally, on the morning of Thursday, the 10th, 500 merchants, bankers, solicitors, surgeons, master manufacturers, and other influential men accepted the following declaration :—

"We, the undersigned, Inhabitants of the Town and Neighbourhood of Birmingham, who have hitherto refrained from joining the Birmingham Political Union, deem it our duty to our country at this awful crisis to come forward and join that body for the purpose of promoting the further union, order, and determination of all classes in support of the common cause of Parliamentary Reform."

A spontaneous meeting of the Council, under the presidency of Thomas Attwood, was held in the morning, and after an animated discussion on the fearful aspect of political affairs it was decided to meet the inhabitants upon Newhall Hill, at three o'clock on the same day, in order to determine what measures should be taken at such an eventful crisis. The people accordingly assembled to the number of 100,000, and one of their first steps was to receive by acclamation the 500 gentlemen just mentioned. Mr. Attwood having taken the chair, Mr. Edmonds read the following resolution which had been passed by the Council :—

"1st. That the Members of the Political Union be invited to wear on their breasts the ribbon of the Union Jack, until the Bill of Reform is become law; and that the friends of their country and of the cause of liberty throughout the kingdom be invited to do the same; and that all persons be requested to provide themselves with a piece of blue ribbon to wear on the breast until the Union Jack can be obtained."

The meeting then adopted a strong petition to the House of Commons praying them to refuse supplies, and to adopt other extreme measures to secure the passage of the Bill, and the continuance of Earl Grey in office This petition contained the following ominous clause :—

"That your Petitioners find it declared in the Bill of Rights that the people of England '*may have arms for their defence*—(*tremendous cheering, which lasted for some minutes*)—*suitable to their condition, and as allowed by law;*' and your Petitioners apprehend that this great right will be put in force generally, and that the whole of the people of England will think it necessary to have arms for their defence, in order that they may be prepared for any circumstances which may arise." (*Renewed cheering.*)

As this great spontaneous meeting has already been noticed in Mr. De Bosco Attwood's account, it will be sufficient to add here, that soon after its termination, Messrs. Scholefield, Parkes, and Green, who had been appointed a deputation to proceed to London, left Birmingham in a carriage and four, and were loudly cheered as they passed along New Street.

Those gloomy days then succeeded which have been well described in Mr. De B. Attwood's narration. It seems worth while, however, to give that important document, the "Declaration against the Duke of Wellington," in full, as it created a great sensation in its day, and was actually translated into French, and extensively circulated throughout France. It ran as follows:—

"*Birmingham, May* 14, 1832

"We, the undersigned, think it necessary, in this awful Crisis of our Country's Fate, to make known to our Fellow Countrymen the alarm and horror with which we are impressed by the Report of the Duke of Wellington having been placed at the head of His Majesty's Councils. We entertain this alarm and horror on the following grounds :—

First.

The Duke of Wellington's general avowal of Arbitrary Principles.

Second.

His speech against all Reform, made only about a year and a half ago.

Third.

His protest against the Reform Bill, as entered on the Journals of the House of Lords, on the 17th of April last.

Fourth.

His reported expressions in the late Parliament, amounting to those of regret, that the Irish People 'would not' break the Law.

Fifth.

His being a Pensioner of Foreign Despots ; and as such exposed to their influence, and unfit to govern a Free People.

Sixth.

His conduct to Marshal Ney, who was murdered by the Bourbon Government, in violation of the Convention of Paris, notwithstanding his appeal to the Duke of Wellington, who had signed that Convention.

Seventh.

His general support of Arbitrary Power on the Continent of Europe, and the certainty that his policy, if he be true to his principles, will necessarily involve the Nation in unjust and ruinous Wars against the Liberties of Europe.

Eighth.

His utter incompetency to govern England by any other means than by the Sword, which has never yet been, and never will be, submitted to by the British People.

For these and various other reasons we hereby solemnly declare our fixed determination to use all the means which the Constitution and the Law have placed at our disposal, to induce His Majesty to reject from his Council that Faction, at the head of which is the Duke of Wellington, who have by their arbitrary principles excited the distrust and abhorrence of the whole Population of the United Kingdom, and we declare our firm conviction that the public excitement and agitation can never be allayed until the great Bill of Reform shall be carried into law by that Administration by whose wisdom and virtue it was first introduced.

These are our fixed and unalterable sentiments, and we hereby appeal to all our fellow countrymen, throughout England, Scotland, and Ireland, and we confidently call on them to unite with us and sign this our solemn Declaration, in support of the liberty and happiness of our Country."

This Declaration was signed by forty-five members of the Council, including Thomas Attwood, Josh. Scholefield, G. F. Muntz, Charles Jones, Benjamin Hadley, Arthur Wade, D.D., G. De B. Attwood, T. C. Salt, and T. Aurelius Attwood. An engraving, of which a few copies are still extant, was afterwards published in Birmingham, representing Thomas Attwood holding the "Solemn Declaration" in his hand.

The Council met again with Mr. Attwood in the chair on the morning of May 15th, and it was resolved unanimously that copies of the Solemn Declaration should be sent off express to all the great towns of the kingdom, and that every effort should be made to obtain signatures thereto.

Early on the morning of the 16th, however, Mr. Parkes arrived in Birmingham with the joyful news of Lord Grey's reinstatement, and in a letter to Mrs. Grote, wife of the historian, which has been published in her husband's memoirs, he thus describes his arrival at Harborne :—

"*Wyndham Club, London, 18th May,* 1832.

. . . You say right—that a more glorious gratification than my arrival at Attwood's house, on Monday morning, could never fall to my lot. I arrived at my own door at six. In one hour I sent letters and expresses to all the towns within fifteen miles, directing meetings to be instantly held by beat of drum and bells, and their addresses to be expressed back to me by four that afternoon In that hour, between six and seven, the inhabitants of the whole town of Birmingham were tumbling into the streets, and the bells clamming. At seven I started in a chaise and four (the horses decorated with blue ribbons to Attwood's cottage. The sun never shone brighter or more smilingly in an English spring. The meadows were embroidered with every colour and blossom of the May flowers; the blackthorn pushing into bloom, and the birds singing sweetly. On my arrival at the village—a retired country hamlet buried in trees in full leaf—Attwood was in bed, his whole family really expecting warrants for high treason or sedition. I need not tell you what were the grateful sensations of the whole family, or the tears of the women. The country villagers, ardently attached to him, had closely watched his house, and lay all night, with arms, in the shrubberies! After an hour's breakfast and purification, Attwood and I adjourned into his study to prepare the resolutions and addresses. In an hour afterwards, half-a-dozen members of the Council came up in cars, and I had to wage an hour's war with these ultra, but honest, men to agree to *prudent* documents. By half-past nine, upwards of 10,000 persons, with bands and banners, were in Attwood's pleasure grounds, playing cheering national airs. At half-past ten or eleven, we moved off towards Birmingham in the carriage, and half-way, a mile and a half from Birmingham, the whole body of inhabitants met us and the procession paraded through the town. The scene was animated beyond description—Canaletti only could paint it, Sir Walter Scott only describe it in the English language. The proceedings of the meeting you know tolerably accurately from the public papers. The deputation leaving the town reminded me of the old scriptural descriptions of public meetings of the children of Israel; and our entrance into Coventry was of a similar triumphal description. . . . Lord Durham told us last night, at a meeting of good men at Ellice's, that 'the country owed Reform to Birmingham, and its salvation from revolution to the *last* stroke.'"

The following is an account of the proceedings at the meeting of May 16th, abridged from the *Journal* report:—

"The intelligence of Earl Grey having been recalled to His Majesty's Councils arrived in this town by express yesterday morning at six o'clock. Mr. Joseph Parkes and other gentlemen, some of whom formed part of the express deputation, immediately on their arrival in this town started for Harborne, the residence of T. Attwood, Esq. By 8 o'clock the news became generally known in Birmingham, and in the course of a short time the whole population was in a state of the most extraordinary excitement. The chief point of attraction were the rooms of the Political Union, in Great Charles Street, from whence it was speedily ascertained that, in order to give *éclat* to the victory which had been achieved, it was determined to give an immediate and triumphant reception into town to Mr. Attwood. Harborne, the village in which Mr. Attwood resides, is four miles distant from Birmingham; but so early as 9 o'clock the roads leading to his place of residence were filled with carriage company and pedestrians.

Anxious as we were to obtain the best and speediest intelligence, we arrived at Harborne at half-past nine; at that hour the great body of the inhabitants of that neighbourhood were assembled and marching towards Mr. Attwood's residence, and by eleven o'clock all the roads leading from that village to Birmingham were completely choked with the population of Birmingham and its vicinity.

The whole neighbourhood of the Five-ways Turnpike-gate, at which it was arranged that Mr. Attwood should be met, presented a most animated appearance. The whole town seemed, from the number of persons present, to have entirely emptied itself. Not only was the main Turnpike-road crowded with thousands walking in procession, but the broad footpaths on each side were covered with people. The great place of meeting was the wide open space immediately beyond the Five-ways Gate. At this point countless thousands were collected, and with several cars, containing members of the Council, and an immense assemblage of members of the Union on foot, awaited the approach of Mr. Attwood. The vehicles and the most part of the crowd afterwards went to meet the procession from Harborne. At length the music of the band gave the welcome intelligence that the cavalcade was approaching, and upon its arrival at the Turnpike joined the numerous bodies that were in waiting, proceeded down Islington, along Holloway-head road, to Smallbrook Street, at which place a heavy shower of rain, accompanied with tremendous peals of thunder, and the most vivid flashes of lightning, saluted it. This was deemed to be a heavenly rejoicing over the discomfiture of the Duke of Wellington, and was also hailed as a happy omen of the eventual success of the Reform Bill. From thence the whole multitude marched forward through High-street, New-street, Bennett's-hill, Newhall-street, and Mount-street, to Newhall-hill, where a temporary hustings was erected for the speakers. The assemblage of people upon the ground must have exceeded 40,000, and at one time during the latter part of the meeting it was calculated that not less than 50,000 were present.

Mr. Edmonds: 'Fellow-countrymen, I have the honour to propose that our noble Chairman (Thos. Attwood, Esq.), who is this day crowned with eternal glory, do take the Chair' (*Cheers.*)

The motion being seconded—

Mr Attwood advanced to the front of the hustings amidst the most enthusiastic cheering.—' My dear friends, I feel so much gratitude to Almighty God for the escape which the nation has had from a most tremendous revolution, that I cannot help wishing that our Reverend Friend near me would publicly return thanks to our wise and beneficent Creator for the success of our righteous cause.' (*No sooner was this intimation made by the Chairman, than all hats were doffed, and the most death-like silence pervaded the immense assembly.*)

The Rev. Hugh Hutton, in a most impressive manner, offered up the following extemporaneous thanksgiving:—'Oh Lord God Almighty! who orderest the affairs of all men, behold Thy people before Thee with grateful and rejoicing hearts, looking up to Thee as the Author of every blessing. We thank Thee for the great deliverance Thou hast wrought out for us, and the great and bloodless victory which Thou hast conferred. We thank Thee, the God of all blessings, for delivering us from the bonds of our oppressors, and the designs of designing and bloody-minded men. Imbue, we beseech Thee the hearts of all now assembled with a spirit of Christian benevolence, so that in the hour of our triumph we may cheerfully forgive all our enemies and oppressors. Grant that we may so use and improve the great privileges Thou hast conferred upon us, that we may secure them to us and to our children, for Thy glory and for the universal benefit of the family of man.

. . May Thy blessing rest on the proceedings of this day, and more especially on him called to preside at this glorious meeting of emancipated and exulting freemen. May the feeling of all hearts be more united in the glorious cause in which we have engaged, and through Thy blessing enjoy a more abundant victory. Amen, Amen.' (*Thousands of voices re-echoed Amen, Amen.*)

Thomas Attwood, Esq.: 'My dear friends, I thank you most sincerely for the honour you have conferred upon me in appointing me your Chairman. With me you cannot but be moved by the very affecting address to Almighty God just made by my rev. friend. . . . When called to congratulate you upon the glorious victory we have achieved, I cannot but express the great delight I feel in Birmingham having been mainly instrumental in the accomplishment of this glorious consummation. I congratulate you from my heart for the unparalleled promptitude, courage, and strictly legal courage, which you have at all times exhibited. (*Cheers.*) Surrounded by temptations of a hundred kinds, the powers of hell have not been able to prevail, or succeed in diverting you from the strict path of justice or of law. (*Loud cheers.*)
. . . Let the great Bill pass—let Lord Grey have a little time to look around him—and I am quite sure the hopes of the nation will not be disappointed. The prosperity and happiness of the people will be restored—not, indeed, the happiness or prosperity of the cloud-born part of the community—but the happiness and prosperity of the industrious, the laborious, and kind-hearted part of the People. (*Cheers.*) That is the great boon to which I am ever looking forward. Prosperity to the millions is what I want —I look for liberty first, and through liberty, prosperity. (*Loud cheers.*) I shall never be content until I see the happiness and comforts of the poor settled upon a sure basis—until I see all interests of society—but more especially the labouring classes—receiving that remuneration to which, both by the laws of God and of nature, they are entitled.' (*Loud cheers.*)

Messrs. Muntz and Scholefield then spoke amidst great applause, proposing and seconding the first resolution as follows:—' That this Meeting will hail with heartfelt gratitude the complete emancipation of His Majesty from the snares and wicked devices of base, evil-minded, and desperate councillors.'

Mr. Edmonds then said:—'Although I am appointed to move a vote of thanks to the House of Commons, and to the Minority who voted for the Reform Bill in the House of Lords, I cannot help but say that in my opinion —and in that opinion I am sure you will concur—to our noble Chairman the thanks of the country, more than any other, are most eminently due. (*Loud cheers.*) He it is who at this great crisis has preserved entire the institutions of this great country; and I am sure, were His Majesty present, and not incapable of feeling and expressing kingly gratitude, he would at once extend his Royal hand and thank Mr. Attwood for having, by the concentration and force of public opinion, driven the bloody Duke from his post, and by this measure secured the safety of the Crown to himself and his posterity. (*Cheers.*) It ought never to be forgotten that, however we may reverence ancient institutions, however sacred antiquity may have rendered them in our eyes—if once found hostile to the liberties and interests of the nation, we are in duty bound, by the duty we owe to mankind—by the duty we owe to posterity—to raze them to the ground—to banish them from our country. (*Cheers.*) The House of Lords ought to be, and no doubt are, obliged to the Union of Birmingham, under the able and discreet controul of our Chairman, at the present moment for the preservation of their lives, their estates, and their order. (*Cheers.*) I certainly am disposed to premonish their Lordships, but have little doubt but the events of these three days will teach them and their posterity that it is neither wise nor safe to despise the united voice of a brave and determined people. (*Cheers.*) If the Bishops were present they, doubtless, would be ready to acknowledge their obligations to the Birmingham Union for the preservation of themselves and their mitres. The fact was, and it could not be concealed from any, even inattentive observers, that by the means of our most powerful Association the country has been mainly preserved from all the horrors of a bloody revolution. (*Cheers.*) Before I was aware this morning of the great news which had arrived, two gentlemen called upon me and stated that not fewer than 1,500 men were already under arms in this town, for the purpose of enforcing the rights of the people. This is but an intimation of the attitude assumed by the people throughout the whole nation. The disposition to employ force if required is not wanting. (*Cheers.*) It is delightful to find that this alternative is not now to be dreaded. I remember that Sterne, in one of his works, represents that a certain Noble Marquis of France from poverty was unable to wear his sword. Afterwards, after having become possessed of property by commerce, he was overjoyed in being able to resume this emblem of war. If such were his feelings, if such was his joy at being able again to wield a sword, how much more ecstatic ought to be the joy of Mr. Attwood when he found he had no occasion to buckle on the sword he would have been compelled to use in his country's cause, had public affairs taken the turn which we all dreaded. (*Cheers.*) I recollect the imaginary traveller in the work to which I have alluded, after stating, with honour, the redemption of the Marquis's sword, exclaimed, "Oh! how I envy his feelings." Taking from envy all its ill-will and all its baseness, any man may well envy the feelings of our Chairman, when he considers how his exertions have terminated without the shedding of a single drop of human blood, or the shedding of one solitary sorrowful tear. (*Loud cheers.*) A certain Grecian General, after the obtainment of a victory, was heard to say, "What will my father say when he hears of this?" Might not Mr. Attwood, in the same spirit of self-congratulation—at once creditable to the patriot and the man—exclaim, "What will my father, my wife, and my children say to this?" (*Loud cheers.*) Knowing as I do the nobleness of his disposition—the warm and generous affections with which he is endowed—I can have no hesitation in declaring that he is equally the admiration of his family and the whole People of

England.' (*Cheers.*) Mr. Edmonds concluded by proposing a vote of thanks to the House of Commons.—Mr. Parkes and Mr. De Bosco Attwood then spoke, after which Mr. Aurelius Attwood observed that his mind was actuated by so many feelings, arising out of the occasion, that if he failed in eloquence, he trusted it would be referred to the proper reason, and that he should stand excused. The feeling, however, which was at the present moment uppermost in his breast, was thanksgiving to God; by the goodness of that omnipotent and all-seeing Being their hands had been rescued from being imbrued in blood. For his own part he had made up his mind to whatever might have come. He had nailed the colours to the mast, and they should not have been suffered patiently to have been torn down. They might have had, instead of peace, if certain personages had been placed in power, their requests answered by the roar of cannon, the thrusts of lances, and the cuts of sabres. . . .

After speeches by Messrs. Hadley, Jones, Salt, and Lewis, the proceedings terminated, amidst great enthusiasm, by the adoption of a memorial to Earl Grey, congratulating him upon his restoration to power, and suggesting the propriety of a further extension of Reform.

Messrs. Thomas Attwood, Josh. Scholefield, De Bosco Attwood, Jos. Parkes, G. F. Muntz, B. Hadley, W. G. Lewis, and W. Boultbee were appointed a deputation to proceed to London forthwith and present the memorial to Earl Grey."

CHAPTER XIV.

Mr. Attwood arrives in London—His interview with Earl Grey—He declines to accept any reward for his services—His final threat of calling together a million of men upon Hampstead Heath—Magnificent reception at the Guildhall—He is presented with the Freedom of the City—His eloquent speech on returning thanks—Banquet at the Mansion House—Testimony of Grote, Campbell, and others to his vast services—Letters to his wife—Return to Birmingham on the 28th of May—His public entry into the town and extraordinary reception by the people—Flags, banners, and decorations in Birmingham.

THOMAS ATTWOOD and the deputation arrived in London on the 17th or 18th May, 1832. On the 19th they had a memorable interview with Earl Grey and Lord Holland at the Treasury. Lord Grey expressed in his own name, and in that of his colleagues, his sense of the important services which Mr. Attwood had rendered by his excellent management of the enormous power of the Political Unions. "We feel deeply indebted to you," said Lord Grey, "and shall be happy to do anything in our power to mark our sense of the obligation." "My Lord," was Mr. Attwood's answer, "I supported your Administration on public grounds alone, I never expected to receive any reward, and I must beg to decline any." And none he ever did receive, either for himself, his family, or friends. This brief account is taken from the *Gentleman's Magazine*, and I regret that I have not been able to find a more detailed account of this extraordinary conversation, of the truth of which, however, there can be no possible doubt, as it occurred in the presence of the other members of the deputation and is corroborated by several expressions in Mr. Attwood's letters. It is impossible to say what particular reward Earl Grey contemplated when he made the above-mentioned offer, but considering the vast services which had been rendered by Attwood to the Whig Ministry, it may reasonably be supposed that a peerage, or at least a baronetcy, must have been the lowest form of recognition thought of. This supposition is strengthened by the recollection that Lords Western, Hatherton, and others were ennobled about the same time for services which were insignificant indeed when compared to Thomas Attwood's. Thus grandly did the great Reformer falsify the assertions of his baser adversaries, who had insinuated that he had only striven to acquire popularity with the masses in order to raise himself to rank and wealth. Had he, indeed, been disposed to sell himself, no man had ever had a more dazzling opportunity presented to him.

Previous to this, of course, the great struggle for Reform was practically over, though various technicalities remained to be gone through before the Bill received the Royal assent. Attwood's magnificent threat of holding upon Hampstead Heath a colossal meeting of 1,000,000 men was the final measure which compelled the Duke to give way. Notwithstanding the extraordinary power of managing vast masses of men which Mr. Attwood possessed, it may be doubted whether the preservation of order amongst so huge and heterogeneous an assemblage would not have been too great a task for even his abilities, and that riot and bloodshed must not inevitably have ensued. When all was over, the Tories, of course, denied that the Duke of Wellington had ever had any intention of resorting to the sword, but Martineau has collected sufficient evidence to show that, for a time at least, he really did contemplate the employment of force. On the Sunday following the great Birmingham meeting of May 7th, the Scots Greys were strictly confined to barracks and engaged in rough-sharpening their swords. They were kept supplied with ball cartridge and booted and saddled day and night. It is said also, that before the Duke resigned he caused warrants to be prepared for the arrest of Attwood, Scholefield, Salt, and other leaders of the Union, but that when Earl Grey succeeded to his office he found them still unsigned. If this story be true, it furnishes, I suppose, a solitary instance of irresolution on the part of the great warrior.

And now to the days of gloom, uncertainty, and dread of impending revolution there succeeded a fortnight of the most enthusiastic and triumphant festivities. These are sufficiently alluded to in Mr. Attwood's letters, which I shall presently insert; but the great day of Wednesday, May 23rd, upon which he, the first private individual, was, contrary to all precedent, presented with the Freedom of the City of London, demands a fuller account, which I have abstracted from the *Birmingham Journal* report of May 26th, 1832, as follows :—

"It is really impossible to describe the respect and enthusiasm with which the deputation has been received by all classes of the people in London, excepting the Boroughmongers. They have been everywhere hailed as the representatives of the men who, by their display of patriotism, promptitude, and courage, insured the recall of Earl Grey to office, and in all probability saved the nation from falling into a state of anarchy and confusion. We do not say this for the purpose of flattering the people of the Midland Districts, but because it is a fact universally acknowledged. The members of the deputation, since their arrival in town, have had invitations to dine with several of the most distinguished members of both Houses, and other patriotic and wealthy individuals, amongst whom we may mention Earl Radnor, Lord Durham, Sir Francis Burdett, Mr Secretary Ellice, Mr. Hume, and Mr. George Grote. They have either met at dinners or had interviews with the *élite* of the members of the Upper and Lower Houses. This day His Royal Highness the Duke of Sussex has appointed to receive them at Kensington Palace. On Thursday they dined with the Polish Association, where they met Prince Czartoriski, several noblemen, and some of the most distinguished literary characters of the day. This day week they presented the memorial to Earl Grey, and had an interview with his Lordship and Lord Holland, by whom they were received with every mark of attention and respect. They afterwards presented at the Home Office memorials and petitions from Wolverhampton, Dudley, Warwick, Oldbury, West Bromwich, Brierley Hill, and other places.

On the arrival of the deputation in London, they ordered the vote of thanks to the Corporation of London, which had been passed at the meeting on Newhall Hill, to be written on vellum, and a request was forwarded to the Lord Mayor that he would name a time for receiving the deputation.

His Lordship immediately ordered summonses to be issued to the members of the Corporation, calling a Special Court for that purpose, and on Wednesday Mr. Attwood and the deputation, accompanied by Mr. T. C. Salt, Mr. Jones, Mr. G. Edmonds, the Rev. Dr. Wade, and other Birmingham gentlemen, with many Members of Parliament, attended the Court, and were received in form by several of the Common Council, who conducted them to the seats provided for their accommodation.

There was an unusual attendance of the members of the Corporation, and the place allotted to strangers below the bar was crowded beyond all precedent, to witness the interesting ceremony. In consequence of a requisition presented to the Lord Mayor by Mr. Charles Pearson, and several of the staunch Reformers in the Corporation, his Lordship placed upon the paper of business, the requisite notice of motion for presenting the freedom of the City to T. Attwood, Esq., in a box of heart of oak.

This distinguished honour, thus proposed to be conferred on our renowned townsman, has been hitherto exclusively confined to Kings, Princes, and distinguished Statesmen, and great military and naval commanders. We hail it, therefore, as one of the important signs of the times, that the Corporation of the first city in the world should enroll the name of a private gentleman in the long list of England's worthies, solely on account of his distinguished and patriotic services in the cause of the people.

Mr. Charles Pearson said he had no doubt but that the members of the Court had learnt with great satisfaction, from the summons which called them together, that they were about to be attended that day by a highly respectable deputation from the patriotic town of Birmingham, to communicate a vote of thanks, passed by the loud acclaim of assembled thousands, who had been engaged, like themselves, in the active and ardent pursuit of the object nearest to their heart—Parliamentary Reform. (*Hear, hear.*) Before he did himself the honour of introducing those gentlemen, he should trouble the Court with a few observations in support of the propriety of their greeting the deputation with a most grateful and respectful reception, as well as of their presenting to Thomas Attwood, Esq., the freedom of the city, in token of the admiration in which they held his virtues, his talents, and his services, and as a testimony of the high respect they bore to the people of Birmingham, for their peaceable, but firm and manly conduct during what he might happily call the *late* crisis of their country's fate. (*Cheers.*) It had been whispered abroad that the little remnant of the Tory faction which still lingered in that Court, stung to the heart by the defeat of the Wellington set, intended to raise the standard of opposition, and that, by one plausible pretext or another, they had contrived to create a division of opinion upon the subject of the proposed measures amongst some of the best and staunchest Reformers the Court could boast of. (*Hear, hear.*) He (Mr. Pearson) would unmask the enemy, expose their artifices, and refute their statements; and whatever might have been the impression they had produced upon the minds of some good Reformers, he felt convinced, that when he had explained all, they would speedily return to the party with whom they had so long and so honourably acted, and that the measure would receive the hearty concurrence of the whole Court—(*hear*)—except, always, the undesired support of the little faction to which he had adverted. (*Hear, hear.*) The first argument against the measure was, that Mr. Attwood did not hold any official situation, and that however respectable and honourable might be his character and station (as they were on all hands admitted to be) he could only be considered as a private English gentleman. (*Hear.*) He would ask the Court of what prouder distinction an Englishman could boast? (*Cheers.*) Around the hall in which he was then speaking were the portraits of distinguished warriors, upon whom that Court had conferred the freedom of the city, in honour of great naval and military achievements (*Cheers.*) Upon their list of freemen were enrolled the names of patriots, princes, public-spirited tradesmen, and constitutional lawyers, in testimony of the estimation in which the citizens of London held their talents and their virtues. (*Hear.*) And if the Court would bestow its honours upon those who, in the discharge of duties—many of them emolumentary—which their public situations imposed upon them, how much more did it become that Court to award this mark of their esteem to one who had gratuitously and largely contributed to confer the greatest blessing upon his country—the blessing of peace and tranquility—at a time when it was threatened with riot and bloodshed, and all the calamities of civil commotion, which had been almost rendered unavoidable by the mad proceedings of a wicked and desperate faction. (*Great cheers.*) . . . In order to catch some of the easy, good-natured members of the Court, the Tories had argued, that although it was very proper to give the freedom to a gentleman so respectable as Mr. Attwood, yet that was not the precise time for doing it—they should wait a month or so. Aye (said Mr. Pearson) wait till the Reform Bill shall have passed; and when Birmingham shall have been enfranchised, and can confer a corporate honour the same as themselves, then indeed would these fastidious gentlemen bestow it upon the great Birmingham Reformer and thus resemble Dr. Johnson's definition of a patron. . . . The public-spirited members of that Court would spurn such contemptible and degrading advice. (*Hear, hear.*) They would not put off to another period what could be done at once. They would that day receive, with suitable honours, the respectable Deputation; and by conferring the freedom of the city upon Mr. Attwood, as the representative of all that was great and good in his native town—(*cheers*)—they would show that a spirit of liberality governed their proceedings, and that they were prepared to hold out the hand of friendship and of brotherly love to the representatives of those great towns which would shortly take their place in the political institutions of the country—to which their wealth, their industry, and their intelligence had so long entitled them. (*Great cheering.*) Mr. Pearson then entered into a long detail respecting the proceedings of the Birmingham Union, and in a very animated manner vindicated that body from all censure and shewed that its proceedings had met with the approval of Earl Grey, Lord Althorp, and Lord John Russell. He highly eulogised Mr. Attwood and his friends for their support of the Bible Society, Sunday Schools, Lancastrian and National Schools, and Mechanics' Institutes, and for the manner in which they had thereby raised the character of the people of Birmingham. He enlarged upon the mental and moral, the political and personal qualifications of Mr Attwood, and finally concluded amidst much cheering by moving that the freedom of the city, in a box made of the heart of British Oak, be presented to Thomas Attwood, Esq., in testimony of the high esteem in which the Citizens of London hold his distinguished services in the cause of Parliamentary Reform, and also of the ability displayed by him in uniting the intelligent and industrious artizans, and the inhabitants generally of the Midland Districts, in their firm but peaceable pursuits of that great national object

Some slight opposition was raised by Mr. Under-Sheriff Wood and a few others, but this only served to bring out more clearly the great admiration with which Mr. Attwood's conduct was generally regarded by the Common Council. Mr. Figgins considered that Mr. Attwood's interference at Newhall-hill meeting alone was sufficient to entitle him to the best thanks the Court could bestow. Had he not acted with firmness and good sense at that critical period, the probability was that the country would have been plunged into revolution and blood. On that ground alone the Court, nay the whole empire, were indebted immeasurably to Mr. Attwood.

Mr. Jupp, Mr. Ridley, Mr. Pewtress, Mr. Galloway, and Mr. Thornhill spoke enthusiastically of Mr. Attwood's conduct, and Mr. Pearson, in replying to the objectors, stated that he had only known Mr. Attwood by reputation till his last visit to London, and he knew that no other man in England was better qualified, morally or mentally, at such a time, to direct the people, and it was the proudest day in his life to have been the means of introducing such a citizen amongst them. If they found no precedent for admitting such a man as Mr. Attwood in such a cause, then he urged them, by all means, to make one.

The motion was then put and carried by a majority of upwards of 200, not more than a dozen hands being held up against it.

Mr. Pearson and Mr. Stephens then accompanied Mr. Attwood to the Chamberlain, Sir James Shaw, who, after the various forms were gone through, presented Mr. Attwood with the freedom in a highly complimentary speech, and added his own warm congratulations upon the high honour to which his talents and virtues and vast services to his country had raised the great Reformer. Mr. Attwood bowed, and then returned thanks in the following eloquent and memorable speech, which created the greatest enthusiasm, and has been printed and reprinted in every variety of type and colour :—

My Lord Mayor, and Gentlemen of this Right Honourable Court—

It is not possible that I, on this great occasion, should not feel as a man of true sensibility and honour should feel; it is not possible that the true spirit of a Briton should not be kindled within me. I am here this day crowned with a great and lasting glory. You have conferred upon me an honour which Kings and Emperors have coveted, and deemed it an honour to obtain. It is, too, an honour which Warriors and Statesmen have looked to as an accumulation of their glory. Why, then, should not I, a plain and humble citizen, plodding my calm but steady way, through a weary and dangerous course of politics, feel more than usual exultation and gratitude at the conferring of such an honour? I have, however, one consolation, one cheering hope, one buoyant principle to uphold me, that I have never swerved from the duty which my own conscience and the good confidence of my Fellow-Countrymen are calculated to inspire. I feel that I have done my duty, and it is to me a great source of gratification that an honourable and upright line of conduct has secured for me this lofty and permanent reward. I have for some time adopted a decided, perhaps bold, line of politics,—I have, perhaps, made myself obnoxious to many, whose experience, wisdom, and intellect are far superior to my own; but I acted on my knowledge of the exigencies of the times, and the wants and wishes of the People. I never resorted myself to measures, nor countenanced their adoption by others, which would trench on the Law, until I saw that great, terrible, and general emergencies arose. I have ever respected the prerogatives of the Crown, the rights and privileges of both House of Parliament, when fairly and constitutionally exercised. But when I saw the foundations of society loosening and breaking under our feet,—when I saw storms and tempests gathering and blackening in the distance,—when I felt the incipient heavings of a political earthquake that I knew would disorganise and crush all the institutions of this powerful Empire,—then I thought it right to step forward and stand between the People and Rebellion. I saw there was still a door left open for reconciliation. I did not wish to close it. My efforts and those of my colleagues were incessantly and vigorously directed to inculcate the necessity of obedience to the Laws, and the preservation of public order and respect for public property. Thanks, first to GOD and next to the PEOPLE, we have succeeded. But while we did this, we strove to lift the People to the proper standard of moral energy. For this useful and well-designed work we have had already a noble portion of our temporal reward. We have been honoured with the approbation of this mighty Corporation—boundless in influence and wealth, as it is great in character, in talent, and independence. From the remotest period of our history this body has been the bold and able asserter of personal worth, of popular rights, and national glory. It has ever stood in the van of the people in their fight for liberty, and how proud shall we of Birmingham be to adopt so great a precedent, and be tutored by such masters! It might be said that the men of Birmingham and all the populous districts that surrounded it were guilty of indiscretion. But let their position and circumstances be considered. They were in some degree cut off from all communion with the State—their ignorance was not instructed, and no anodyne of good legislation was applied to heal the burning sores of their political wrongs. They were left unrepresented, unheeded. They were consigned to themselves—to those of a superior station whom accident had placed and choice kept amongst them—to accident and the dispensations of Providence. When the news of the rejection of the Reform Bill reached Birmingham, they assembled at a moment's notice in tens of thousands—despair and sullen rage painted in every face I then strove to calm them. Well, another meeting full of the same terrible resolution was held. I saw it. I was collected, though appalled. Then came the news that Lord Grey was reinstated, and I witnessed a scene that I never saw equalled, and could scarcely think on:— resolute and gigantic men shedding tears of joy, true tears of gladsome emotion. My nerves never failed me till then. You cannot believe me until you see the men of Birmingham. I have read of the tears of valiant men—I never saw them until then, and it was a sight to shake a man to the heart. I have only again to say that I am devoted to the constitutional privileges of the Throne, the Altar, the Lords, and the Commons; and because I am so devoted, would resist the usurpation of either order. And for the great and lasting honour conferred on me by the Corporation of London I will only say that all my life and efforts shall be directed to merit it.

Mr. Attwood, on receiving the freedom, and on concluding his address, was welcomed with shouts of applause by the whole Court After he had received the congratulations of his friends, the Court adjourned

After the business of the Common Council had been concluded, the Lord Mayor invited a large party of the most distinguished Reformers connected with the Corporation of the City of London to meet Mr. Thomas Attwood and a number of gentlemen composing the Deputation from Birmingham, and to partake of the splendid hospitalities of the Mansion House. Such was the eagerness to obtain cards of invitation to this memorable dinner, that it was found necessary at a late hour to enlarge the arrangements which had been made, and to add side tables to receive the additional guests. More than one hundred persons of high character, Members of Parliament, and others, personally applied to the Lord Mayor for cards, to meet the Birmingham Deputation, not one of whom could be admitted, the invitations having been principally confined to the most influential civic Reformers. The banquet was laid out in the Egyptian Hall, in a style of magnificence and profusion which did honour to the munificent hospitality of the highest civic dignitary in this country. Perhaps on no previous occasion has there been assembled together at any festive board so large a number of the leading Reformers of the kingdom. Among those present we noticed Lord Ebrington, Sir F. Burdett, G. Byng, Esq., M.P., Jos. Hume, Esq., M.P., Colonel Torrens, M.P., Alderman Wood, M.P., Count Czapski, Dr. Bowring, Thos. Campbell, Esq., Rev. Mr. Fox, and many other distinguished metropolitan Reformers. T. Attwood, J. Scholefield, W. G. Lewis, and G. De B. Attwood, Esqrs., and the Rev. Dr. Wade, with other gentlemen from Birmingham, R. Potter, Esq., from Manchester, and several gentleman from Bristol, Liverpool, Stroud, &c., were present.

The Lord Mayor was seated in the State Chair, a little elevated above the seats of the company. His Lordship was supported on his right by Lord Ebrington, Mr. Potter, Alderman Wood, &c., and on his left were Mr. Attwood, Sir F. Burdett, Mr. Parkes, and Mr. Hume.

The Lord Mayor having pledged the company in the loving cup, gave the following toasts :—

'The King, with four times four.'

'The Queen.'

'His Royal Highness the Duke of Sussex.'

'Earl Grey, and His Majesty's Ministers.'

The Lord Mayor rose again, and said he had recently had the pleasure of proposing the healths of individuals eminent for their rank as public men, and he had now the honour to introduce the health of a gentleman who, though he did not occupy any important public situation, was yet entitled to the cordial thanks of the whole kingdom. When he announced his name he was convinced further eulogium would prove superfluous, for the toast would be received with spontaneous enthusiasm. He proposed 'the health of Thomas Attwood, Esq.' (*Tremendous applause.*) The manner in which the toast had been received convinced him he had not formed a wrong estimate of the sentiments of his fellow-citizens towards that distinguished individual. (*Cheers.*) The freedom of the city had often been conferred on those who had excited their sympathy by performing feats of valour, as military commanders in the cause of the liberty of other and their own countries. But Mr. Attwood had far higher claims than such individuals could have, for their victories had been obtained with effusion of blood, while he (Mr. A.) had achieved a glorious triumph in support of the liberties of the people, without shedding one drop of that people's blood. (*Immense cheering.*) This glorious achievement had been accompanied solely by the influence of his character. By that influence he had been enabled to controul and direct that important and influential body of which he was so able and so efficient a representative. (*Cheers.*) He should be glad of the opportunity of dilating further on that gentleman's merits, but the company had shown it was entirely superfluous, therefore he should conclude by proposing 'the health of T. Attwood, Esq., Chairman of the Birmingham Political Union and Citizen of London.' The toast was drank amidst loud and long-continued cheering.

Mr. Attwood then rose and said: I feel deeply indebted to your Lordship and this respectable company for the high honour you have just conferred upon me. To-day it has been my fortunate lot to be admitted a citizen of the first city in the world,—to be received among strangers as a friend and as a brother. It is gratifying to an upright mind to find that my humble exertions in the country, in the cause of popular rights, have been estimated more highly than my utmost ambition ventured to expect. Few men have, under such circumstances, been honoured as I have been this day; and when I attended the Court of Common Council, and was called on suddenly to receive and to acknowledge such an unexpected honour—though my life has ever been chequered with great hopes or great fears—I confess that never before were my nerves so shaken. I felt then as if the principles which, as a public man, I had publicly advocated, had received the protecting shelter of the oldest and most illustrious Corporation in this empire. I could not but feel that in my humble person the seal had been put on the great League and Covenant with the people of England,—that, with a free people like this nation, come what will, the Reform Bill must and shall become the law of the land. (*Cheers.*) I had for a short time been fearful of the reception I should meet with from the citizens of this metropolis; for after trenching almost on the boundaries of the law, I fancied the uprightness and integrity of my purpose might have been misinterpreted; but I am rejoiced that those whom I will call my fellow-citizens have thrown their shield over me, and have awarded me that token which I most earnestly covet—their approbation. But this city has always been foremost in the fight of liberty. I will recall to your minds its history, its noble stand against the tyrant John, and that time when its Train-bands marched to defend the persons of a Hampden and a Pym. (*Cheers.*) I have been watching with anxiety the conduct of this great and illustrious Corporation in the present crisis, and I have gathered strength from every movement it has made, for if I had not seen the citizens tread in the steps of their glorious predecessors, I should have thought that I had been treading in the path of guilt and crime. . . . I have this day received the most distinguished honour which one citizen can bestow upon another; and it shall be the study of my future life to conduct myself peaceably, loyally, and yet determinedly, in support of the people's liberties. But should the time come when the laws of England are sought to be violated by despotic tyranny, most unquestionably I will not be the last to repel force by force. (*Shouts of applause.*) Mr. Attwood concluded by proposing the health of the Lord Mayor, Sir John Key. The healths of Sir F. Burdett and Messrs. Byng, Hume, Potter, and Parkes were afterwards drank, and the Lord Mayor then gave 'Count Napoleon Czapski,' who returned thanks as follows:—' I rise to speak of unfortunate Poland, but I know not how to return thanks for a dead country. The

Spoiler of the North has spread over her his black wings—her funeral dirge has been sung amidst the smoking ruins of her temples—the groans of her dying victims forming an accompaniment   Poland fell—her name is erased from the list of nations. . . .   Poland is dead!   But no, no, she is not dead, she sleepeth only.   She will awake—one day she will awake and break her chains upon the heads of her oppressors.   This hope alone keeps up the beatings of my heart.   I return thanks, but I cannot drink to you. (Here the speaker held his glass inverted.)   But I will when Poland awakes!'

Mr. Attwood then rose and addressed the company with energy. Poland, he observed, as truly stated by the gallant nobleman, only slept—it was not crushed. Had England sent but a single fleet to the Baltic or Black Sea, the northern autocrat had not been enabled to crush the rising spirit of that gallant nation. But there was a spirit abroad which would spread and make the upholders of tyranny tremble; and when that hour arrived, he felt confident that the gallant Poles would be rescued from their present degradation.

George Grote, Esq. (afterwards the famous historian of Greece), in returning thanks said:—'But if, Gentlemen, I were required to name the person whose services I appreciate highest, and whose feelings I envy most, throughout this momentous period, I should not hesitate to pronounce the name of Thomas Attwood. It is to him, more than to other individuals, that we owe the success of this great measure. He has taught the people to combine for a great public purpose, without breaking any of the salutary restraints of law, and without violating any of their obligations as private citizens. He has divested the physical force of the country of its terrors and its lawlessness, and has made it conducive to ends of the highest public benefits.'

The poet Campbell next took occasion to say:—

'It is additionally gratifying to my pride, that my health is given by that patriotic individual (Mr. Attwood), who has pre-eminently, even among eminent patriots, distinguished himself on the present occasion in the cause of Reform . . . Gentlemen, I have the honour, like many more of you, to wear a Reform medal at my breast, presented to us by the dauntless patriots of Birmingham. That token is to me a treasure. It is the custom of that hapless, but high-minded race of men, the Poles—(*immense cheering*)—when they leave their native land, to take with them some handfuls of their native soil, in order that in case they should die abroad, the dust of their mother country may be buried with them in their coffins   My friends, if ever I go abroad I shall not take a handful of British earth, but I shall take this Reform medal, to be buried with me in my coffin; and if I should sleep in death on the farthest shores of the earth, I shall have with me a true token and type of the spirit of England.'

Shortly afterwards, Mr. Attwood gave as a toast Campbell's lines—

'Prone to the earth, oppression shall be hurled,
Its name, its nature, withered from the world.'

The effect of this apposite quotation was quite electrical, and the sentiment was hailed and drank with the utmost enthusiasm.

The festivities and conviviality were protracted to a very late hour, and the company separated, highly delighted with the harmony which had prevailed, and the hospitality they had experienced

As a curious fact, we may mention that Lord Ebrington, Sir F. Burdett with the Reforming Members of Parliament and other distinguished individuals, contrary to the usual custom, did not quit the table until the company formally broke up, which was about one o'clock in the morning."

Thus ended the proceedings of this memorable day, and illustrious as the roll of London's Honorary Freemen undoubtedly is, it may be questioned whether the much coveted honour has ever been conferred upon any one else upon such an extraordinary occasion, or amidst such an outburst of popular excitement.

The box, of the then customary value of one hundred guineas, which was presented with the Freedom, is made of the oak of old London Bridge, heavily lined and sculptured with gold, and the resolution is emblazoned on vellum, with the arms of the City of London at the top and those of Thomas Attwood at the foot. Both are now in the possession of Mr. T. A. C. Attwood, of Malvern Wells.

The receipt of the intelligence of the proceedings at the Guildhall created a *furore* of excitement in Birmingham of which several anecdotes have been preserved. Upon the arrival of the news at the Coach and Horses, Worcester Street, the company present at once subscribed a sum to purchase a portrait of Mr. Attwood, together with his speech printed in letters of gold, to be hung in the coffee-room. The metropolitan vestries, wards, and boroughs followed the example of the City, and showered their thanks upon the great Reformer. At a meeting of the householders of St. Leonard's, Shoreditch, it was unanimously resolved that the Solemn Declaration of the Birmingham Political Union should be engrossed and signed by the inhabitants of the parish, and a deputation, headed by the chairman and churchwardens, was appointed to wait on Mr. Attwood and present to him the resolution of thanks passed at a late meeting of the parish

The following are the short and simple letters written by Mr. Attwood during this great crisis:—

Mrs. Thomas Attwood, Birmingham
Bedford Hotel, May 18, 1832.
. . . We are all quite well, and I believe everything is now going on right. Our declaration against the Duke has done the business.

Bedford Hotel, May 19, 1832.
MY BELOVED WIFE,
We are quite well. We have gained a great victory and everything is safe. One of the Ministers said to me, "*We owe our situations entirely to you,*" and others have made use of similar remarks. This *entre nous*. We are troubled with morning calls and invitations from all classes; and if we do not leave London shortly we shall have more to fear from the dinners than from the barricades and cannon balls. To-morrow we dine with Lord Radnor and Josh. Hume, on Monday with Burdett, on Tuesday with Ellice and Lord Durham, on Wednesday with the Lord Mayor of London, and on Thursday with the Polish chief Czartoriski. We will come back to you then, for we much prefer your society to that of generals, lords, and politicians.

Our meetings in Birmingham have been like claps of thunder bursting over the heads of our enemies, and our declaration against the Duke of Wellington has sealed the doom of his party for ever. It is felt here as a victory for *Europe* more than for England. I am afraid some of us men from Buttonland will get proud and puffed up with worldly pride. I am sure I shall want myself the friendly cautions of my old friend Geo. Simcox, and therefore I hope that you, my dear wife, will redouble your cares for me and keep me still in the right path of virtue and humility.

We had arranged partly for a great meeting of 1 *million of persons* to meet me here on Hampstead Heath in a few days, but the happy settlement of affairs renders such a grand exhibition unnecessary. You know, my love, that I never exhibit myself from low motives. . . .

Bedford Hotel, Covent Garden,
May 23, 1832.
MY BELOVED WIFE,
I write for the purpose of informing you that I have to-day received the distinguished honour of being admitted a Freeman of the City of London, by the Lord Mayor, Aldermen, and the Common Council. There were, I believe, 200 persons present, and only 10 hands were held up against me. This we consider a great victory. To see these ancient and powerful corporations thus fraternizing, as it were, with our new political societies may well be supposed to cut off all hope from our opponents.

I hope to return home in a few days "bearing my blushing honours thick upon me." My election is said to be the only instance of a similar kind in the history of the Corporation, all other Freemen thus elected having been either Kings, Emperors, Generals, Ministers, or Statesmen.

Bosco and myself are quite well. We dine to-day with the Lord Mayor, to-morrow with Prince Czartoriski, and on Friday we go to the Duke of Sussex and other great men.

Bedford Hotel, May 26, 1832.

MY DEAR LOVE,—We come home on Monday, and shall be at Harborne by 9 or 10 o'clock in the evening of that day. We shall be at Small Heath Turnpike at 6 o'clock, and shall make a grand entry into town, which I am sure you would like to witness. I shall then have to address a few words to the people in the Market Place. If you like to go to Mr. Sumner's, you may see the show pretty well.

We are tired to death with honours and dinners, but both of us are quite well. I shall have to return to London in a few days in order to be examined before the Banking Committee, and then I will bring you with me, and we will send for Marcus and see Lawrence or Brodie. . . .

P.S.—The £10 clause is passed, and the Bill will become law, I believe next week.

Mr. Turner, Mr. Stothard, and other painters plague me to death.

The Banking Comm[ee.] seems likely to fall into my hands. In this case you will see, my dear, that I shall have been a great instrument in giving Liberty, Prosperity, and *Virtue* to a distressed and oppressed people.

Few men, indeed, if any, have experienced such extraordinary popular ovations as fell to the lot of Thomas Attwood during the year 1832. But of all these perhaps the greatest was that of May 28th, upon which day he made his public entry into Birmingham amidst the most unexampled enthusiasm. I have copied, therefore, nearly *verbatim*, the *Journal* report of the proceedings of that memorable day :—

"TRIUMPHAL ENTRY OF MR. ATTWOOD INTO BIRMINGHAM.

The inhabitants of Birmingham did Mr. Attwood and themselves immortal honour by the splendid reception which they gave our distinguished townsman on the 28th May. It having been made known on that day that he and the rest of the Deputation would return from London, immediate steps were taken to give them a public entry. The Council of the Political Union issued a placard, in which the public were informed of the whole particulars of the intended procession. The Members of the Union were directed to meet opposite the office in Great Charles Street, under the direction of Messrs. Haynes and Pierce, and proceed from thence by way of Bull-street, High-street, Deritend, &c, to Small Heath Turnpike Gate, where it was appointed to meet Mr. Attwood at 6 o'clock in the evening. Accordingly, at 4 o'clock, the procession, consisting of several carriages filled with the most influential Members of the Council, headed by their band of music, and exhibiting numerous banners (hereafter enumerated), proceeded along the streets named in the placard of instructions. Along the whole line in which it proceeded, it was evident that the occupiers of houses had been industriously employed during the short time allowed for preparation.

While all was bustle and stir in Birmingham, Mr. Attwood was not less busily engaged in receiving the hearty congratulations of his friends in Coventry and its neighbourhood. Information having been received in that City that the Birmingham Deputation would pass through on Monday, the members of the Political Union, joined by the great body of the inhabitants, determined to form a public procession to meet and accompany them through the City. About the middle of the day a procession was formed in Little Park-street, and after proceeding through several streets headed by a band of music, went on the London road about a mile, where they met Mr. Attwood, who arrived by the Wonder coach Mr. Attwood and Mr. W. G. Lewis having been literally forced out of the coach, the procession, consisting of several thousand persons, mostly wearing the Attwood medal, suspended to the Union Jack, immediately returned to Coventry.

On reaching the City Hotel, Mr. Attwood ascended the balcony, accompanied by Messrs. Hadley, Boultbee, W. G. Lewis, De Bosco Attwood, and Jones, and addressed the assembled multitude. We only give an abstract of this address, as the main points upon which it touched will be found in Mr. Attwood's speech delivered in this town the same evening, and reported below.

He commenced by expressing the high gratification he felt at the mark of respect which had that day been shown him and the other gentlemen who formed the Deputation from Birmingham, by the inhabitants of the City of Coventry ; the same kind feeling had also been expressed towards them by the inhabitants of every place they had gone to. In London they had not only received the commendations of the Citizens, but Deputations of Poles, of Spaniards, and of Portuguese had waited upon them to thank them for their exertions in the great cause of Liberty and Freedom. Ten days ago, when he passed through that City, on his road to London, the Duke of Wellington was endeavouring to form a Government, under the idea that a complete reaction had taken place in the public mind, and that the people were become indifferent to reform ; but the Noble Duke, whom he respected for no one thing but his martial fame, must have been ignorant and blind to the great meetings that were taking place throughout the country, decidedly expressing their determination, though in a peaceable manner, to continue the slaves of a corrupt oligarchy no longer. He knew that that great, that good man at the head of His Majesty's Government, Earl Grey, was at that moment employed in concerting measures for the benefit of the trade and commercial affairs of the country, which would place it in the highest state of prosperity ; and, as was beautifully expressed in the words of Scripture, ' Every man would sit under his own vine and his own fig-tree, none making him afraid.' He had no doubt that in twelve months, instead of a man having low wages, or no employment, if he should be turned off from one master, two would come after him to solicit his labour That this happy state of things might come to pass was his sincere wish. As the time for meeting his friends in Birmingham was drawing nigh, he would not detain them longer, but would conclude by praying the Almighty to bestow every blessing upon them.

At the conclusion of Mr. A.'s speech, which was frequently interrupted by loud cheers, he and the other gentlemen of the Deputation got into an open coach, which was waiting for them, and proceeded towards Birmingham, the procession accompanying them to the New Allesley Road, where three hearty cheers were given them.

After leaving Coventry, the Deputation proceeded at a rapid rate to the delightful village of Meriden, where they were unexpectedly but agreeably interrupted in their journey by the appearance of a number of young ladies, headed by Mr. Allbut, their tutor. The ladies, beautifully attired in white, and decorated with blue ribbons, stood in the elevated garden adjoining Mr. Allbut's house, where that gentlemen presented Mr. Attwood with the following address :—

'TO THOMAS ATTWOOD, ESQ,

President of the Council of the Birmingham Political Union.

SIR,—In behalf of myself and numerous family, I beg most respectfully and gratefully to address you, as having through your personal exertions, and the influence of your character, been the happy means, in the hour of peril, of preserving the peace of an extensive and most populous district—and as an honoured instrument in the hand of Divine Providence for the destruction of an usurping Oligarchy, which has for many years ground down and cruelly oppressed a loyal and industrious people.

May you live, Sir, many years to enjoy the fruits of your labours—may Heaven's best gifts be your portion—and may the grateful recollections of generations yet unborn embalm your memory, when the names of all tyrants and every willing tool of despotism shall have perished, or be remembered only with detestation.

May those gentlemen who have participated in your arduous labours enjoy their due share in the reward.

May Birmingham ever stand pre-eminent for religion, sound morality, good order, commercial prosperity, and devoted patriotism. And should Britain's liberties ever again be put in jeopardy, may she never want a Grey, a Russell, and an Attwood to plead her cause and defend her rights.

I am, Sir,
Your Debtor Insolvent,
And truly obliged humble servant,

Meriden, May 28th, 1832.' JOHN ALLBUT.

Mr. Attwood acknowledged this flattering Address in a short, neat, and appropriate reply; and having taken leave of his fair attendants again set forward to Birmingham. After leaving Meriden the numbers of carriages and horses they met on the road gave palpable evidence of the excitement of which they would shortly be witnesses. Labourers, decorated with emblematic blue ribbons, were seen hastening across the fields to add their congratulations to the general outpouring of exultation exhibited by the inhabitants of the several villages through which they passed; while even the stone-breakers on the roadside erected on their various heaps the standard of 'Attwood and Liberty.' Between Stonebridge and Yardley Mr. A. was joined by some hundreds of horsemen, besides numerous carriages and gigs filled with company. The scene between these two places

HIS PUBLIC ENTRY INTO BIRMINGHAM.

was of the most exciting nature; the journey being performed at full gallop, the wonder with us, considering the number of horses and vehicles, and the rapid pace at which they travelled, is that no accident occurred. As the immense cavalcade, not less than two miles in length, proceeded, the crowd from Birmingham thickened upon it, and about a quarter of a mile on this side of Yardley it was found impossible to proceed at faster than a walking pace. The population of the surrounding country appeared to be collected in the roads and adjoining fields, and every cottage exhibited a flag or some other sign denoting the cordial feeling of its inmates. The Deputation thus passed on, amid the cheering of the multitude, to the house of Mrs. Kendall, at Small Heath, opposite which a triumphal banner was extended across the road, having emblazoned on one side the words, 'Welcome, Attwood, the Friend of the People!' and on the other 'Earl Grey and Reform.' A large handsome tricolour flag was likewise exhibited from the window, on which was inscribed, 'Three cheers for Attwood, Earl Grey, and Reform.' Mr. Attwood having proceeded under the triumphal banner to which we have referred, he alighted, according to arrangements, at the house of Thomas Potts, Esq. Here he was joined by Joshua Scholefield, Esq., G. F. Muntz, Esq., William Broomhead, Esq., and numerous other gentlemen of influence in the town of Birmingham. After partaking of a lunch, the party, joined by other friends, re-ascended their carriages, and amidst the most enthusiastic cheering formed a junction with the Union procession at the Small Heath Gate. It was here intended to have presented a congratulatory Address to Mr. Attwood, but this was rendered completely impossible owing to the immense crowd which had assembled, and the great confusion arising in executing the order of procession. After a short pause, the cavalcade moved forward, the pedestrians and horsemen taking the precedence, while the carriages and other vehicles followed Mr. Attwood. The following is a list of the banners connected with the procession, and the order in which they were borne :—

Grand Standard of the Birmingham Political Union.
The Union Jack.
Bundle of Sticks—motto, Union is strength.
Banner, 1st. Attwood; an honest man, the noblest work of God.
2nd. Political Unions have nailed their colours to the mast, and will carry the ship Britannia through, or go down with her cannon pealing their knell.
3rd. The sovereignty of the People.
4th. A Home of Freedom or a Grave of Glory.
5th. Cheap Government, Cheap Religion, and Cheap Bread.
6th. Like unto Pharaoh's, their hearts were hardened against the Liberties of the People, and the Plagues have come upon them.
7th. Prone to the earth, oppression shall be hurled,
Its name, its nature, withered from the world.
8th. The Rose, the Thistle, and the Shamrock will not flourish in a land of slavery.
9th. Representation of the Devil shaking hands with the Duke; motto, *Should old acquaintance be forgot*, on one side; on the other,

representation of Earl Grey holding an extinguisher in each hand over the Duke and Sir Robert Peel, both kneeling down.

10th. May Wellington's sword be useless when drawn against Reformers, And Attwood's tongue prove a dagger in the hearts of Boroughmongers

11th. The honour of Wellington was buried in the Tomb of Marshal Ney.

12th. Success to the Yeomanry Cavalry who have thrown away their swords rather than serve under a Boroughmonger.

13th. A garland, fourteen feet wide and sixteen feet high, carried by eight men.

It is impossible for words to do adequate justice to the remainder of this splendid scene—this extraordinary exhibition of enthusiastic public feeling. On descending the hill from the Gate to the top of Bordesley, the lofty trees which overshadow a great part of the road appeared almost as thickly populated as the very ground on which the multitude walked. At this point, a sailor, situated in one of the trees, presented a fearful object of attraction. Standing on the extremity of a high and slender bough, only holding with one hand by a mere switch, he fearlessly undulated over the heads of the cavalcade, as it passed under him. Fortunately, this daring act of presumption was not followed by any fatal consequence. On reaching the junction of the Coventry and Oxford roads, the scene presented down Bordesley was truly magnificent, and such was its amazing vastness that it suggested to the mind, like one of Martin's splendid pictures, a faint idea of infinity. Through the whole of this long and commodious street, and indeed in every street through which the procession moved, the houses were decorated with every species of gorgeous exhibition.

'———— all the walls
With painted imagery.'

The characteristic feature of the day was the universality of the attendance. Persons of all ranks, from the highest to the poorest classes, were to be seen participating in all the delirium of ecstatic joy. The windows of the houses presented a gay appearance, being chiefly filled with the ladies of the town and neighbourhood. We never before witnessed so profuse a display of the beauties of Birmingham.

'You would have thought the very windows spake,
So many greedy looks of young and old
Through casements darted their desiring eyes.'

On the procession reaching Digbeth, a splendid tri-coloured balloon, under the management of Mr. Sprason, ascended from the Unicorn Inn, while the arrival of the cortège within the immediate confines of the town, was otherwise announced by the firing of musketry and the clamorous ringing of the church bells. During the whole of this overpowering expression of popular feeling and public approbation, Mr. Attwood was, as might be expected, pleasantly though fatiguingly engaged in acknowledging with his native gallantry and courtesy, the happy and cheerful congratulations of lovely woman—

'The last but best of God's creation.'

In the Bull-ring and Market-place the procession was to be seen to the greatest advantage; and from this spot we understand that an eminent artist, who had come from London for the express purpose, took a descriptive sketch of this most extraordinary and splendid scene—a plate of which will be published, containing likenesses of the principal Reformers in the procession. It was remarkable that, in passing Deritend Chapel, where the street is comparatively narrow, the clamming of the bells belonging to that chapel was occasionally heard during the slight intervals which occurred in the shoutings and rejoicings of the multitude; but when the procession reached St. Martin's Church, and the spacious market-place developed its thousands, or rather tens of thousands, the clamming of the bells of the parish church, although a peal of twelve, and considered one of the finest in England, and immediately over our heads, was entirely drowned by the shouts, songs, and huzzas of the people—the bells were altogether inaudible. The greatest pressure was visible when the dense crowd, which had choked the market-place, issued round the corner of High-street into New-street. So great, indeed, was this pressure, that the pole of the carriage in which Mr. Attwood rode was broken, the harness torn in pieces, and the carriage itself almost demolished. The kicking and plunging of the horses, under these circumstances, rendered it absolutely necessary to disengage them from the carriage; and the people then drew it, or rather carried it, to the front of the Hen and Chickens Hotel. While passing the bank of Messrs. Attwood and Spooner we noticed, at one of the windows, Mr. and Mrs. Attwood, the venerable parents of the hero of the day. They appeared much affected, and no wonder, at the extraordinary public homage done to the patriotic exertions of their son. It was now after nine o'clock; and as darkness was rapidly approaching, it was thought better, by the gentlemen of the Deputation, that Mr. Attwood should address the immense assembly from the balcony of the Hen and Chickens, and thus terminate the glorious proceedings of this memorable day, and thereby release the many thousands of patriotic men who had travelled ten or fifteen miles, from Dudley, Wolverhampton, and other distant towns, for the purpose of expressing their feelings, and of giving that cordial and triumphant reception to their political chief, which his firm, manly, patriotic, but conciliatory conduct entitled him to. It will be seen from our report of the proceedings at the Political Council the following evening that Mr. Attwood expressed his regret at not having been able to reach the Five Ways Gate in procession, according to the previous arrangements. The immensity of the crowd, and the extreme slowness at which it was possible to move, would have rendered it impossible for him to reach that point in less than three hours more; and he felt the greatest reluctance to intrude, to such an extent, upon the generous enthusiasm of his countrymen. Indeed, one might readily have conceived, from the enormous multitude present, that the whole of the population of Birmingham, and also of the neighbouring towns, had been condensed in

New-street, High-street, and the market-place. Mr Attwood accordingly, in accordance with his own wishes and the advice of his friends, ascended the balcony of the Hen and Chickens Hotel, accompanied by Messrs. Edmonds and W. G. Lewis, and addressed the people to the following effect :—

'My kind, generous, and brave friends, I thank you from the bottom of my heart for this extraordinary testimony of your confidence and esteem I feel it deeply on my own account, but more on account of the crowning effect which it is calculated to have upon the public cause. Who, that has witnessed what I have witnessed to-day, can possibly imagine that it is possible for any human power to govern England by force? The Duke of Wellington is a great man—great, perhaps, I ought not to call him, except as a soldier—but be he what he will, he could not have witnessed what I have seen to-day without acknowledging that this great and glorious nation is only to be governed upon principles of liberty, justice, and humanity. (*Cheers.*) The Duke of Wellington has been bred up in camps, and nurtured, as it were, with the milk of foreign despots, and probably thought, a little while ago, that it was possible to extend the same principles to England. The proceedings of this great day have crushed, for ever, the hopes of despotism in this patriotic, heroic, but long misgoverned and oppressed nation. (*Cheers.*) The final knell of despotism has tolled—the night of our misery is passing away—the bright day of our liberty and our happiness is beginning to dawn ; and I trust that in a very short period the liberty and happiness of England will be restored, never to be lost again. (*Cheers.*) I have the gratification to assure you that, in all human probability, the Bill of Reform will receive the Royal Assent next week, uninjured and unimpaired in every one of its great parts and provisions. (*Cheers*) I have the further gratification of assuring you, that I have good reason to know that the great and good man now again at the head of His Majesty's Government is at this moment engaged in plans to relieve the distress and produce the amelioration and happiness of the people. I am sure that he understands these things well ; and I entertain an entire confidence that, in a very short time, he will bring England round into such a state of prosperity and happiness that the oldest man amongst us will not remember a period of greater felicity, and the youngest individual among us will not live long enough to witness its coming to an end. (*Cheers.*) This has been the great end and object of all my humble labours in the cause of liberty. I have not been seeking for shadows, but the substance of benefit to my fellow-countrymen. I know that they are entitled to a just and reasonable reward for their capital and industry, and to a state of full employment, and of full wages in exchange for their labour ; and I will never cease my exertions until these great and righteous objects are secured. (*Cheers.*) If anything could have tended to confirm me in this course it would have been the glorious reception with which you have honoured the Deputation and myself this day, it would have been the reception which I have experienced from all descriptions of my fellow-countrymen, and, above all things, from the City of London. (*Loud cheers.*) That illustrious Corporation has been pleased to honour me with the freedom of their city—a high and distinguished honour, which has hitherto been conferred only upon kings and emperors, and heroes and statesmen, but which in the present instance has been conferred upon me, as your representative and personation. It was to me a subject of the deepest interest and gratification to see this ancient and venerable Corporation—the richest and most illustrious in the world, holding, as it were, divided empire with the King himself in the jurisdiction of the city—casting its mantle over me, a private gentleman, representing a new town, and standing at the head of new and important political associations. This exhibition must have been a proof of harmony and mutual co-operation among the people of England, which, of itself, must strike despair into the hearts of the oligarchs. I received the same generous confidence and friendly treatment from all other descriptions of His Majesty's subjects in the metropolis, whether Princes of the Blood, or the ancient Aristocracy of the country, or the numerous and patriotic body of men denominated the middle classes of society. Among all classes, in fact, I have found the same generous and cordial treatment, which was more gratifying to me as bestowed upon your representative than as in any way due to myself. I found no jealousy or distrust of any kind; but my generous and brave countrymen seemed all to unite in one spontaneous exhibition of friendship and confidence towards the people of Birmingham, as humbly represented in my person. When our Deputation left Birmingham we were all rejoicing most cordially in the restoration of Earl Grey; but when we reached London we found the political horizon blackening; and, with the view of giving undoubted evidence of the real state of the public mind, we were proceeding to get up an immense exhibition of public feeling and determination upon Hampstead Heath, about two miles from Regent's Park; and I cannot doubt that, if the Duke of Wellington had taken office, we should have produced a meeting of seven or eight hundred thousand persons upon Hampstead Heath, within a week. This meeting, I have not the shadow of a doubt, would have been conducted in a strictly legal and peaceful manner, and would for ever have put an end to the misrepresentation of the borough faction respecting the indifference of the public mind in the cause of Reform. I rejoice, however, that this great exhibition was fortunately rendered unnecessary by the happy reconstruction of His Majesty's Government; and I trust that all our labours in the cause of Reform are now rapidly drawing to an end. My dear friends, I know that many thousands of you have come many miles upon this occasion, and as it is now dark I am anxious to trouble you no longer. I will, therefore, conclude by again thanking you, most sincerely, for the high, and distinguished, and undeserved honours which you have been pleased to confer upon me. I shall retain a most grateful sense of them to the last moment of my life; and I now most respectfully take my leave of you, most fervently praying to Almighty God that He will grant all manner of liberty, prosperity, and happiness to you and your children for ever.'

Mr. A. retired amidst loud cheering.

Mr. W. G Lewis then came forward and said he would not detain the immense assembly before him more than a few minutes. In the joyous conclusion of the proceedings of the day they should not forget the miseries of those brave men, though foreigners, now suffering under the yoke of despotism—and suffering, too, principally in consequence of the vile, the dastardly, the un-British conduct of the Tory Oligarchy. He should only mention the name of unhappy Poland—(*loud cheers*)—and call upon them to give three groans for the three allies of the Duke of Wellington : the bloodstained barbarian of the north, the Muscovite tyrant—the wretch, Ferdinand of Spain—and the half monkey and half tyger, Miguel of Portugal. (*This address was followed by three tremendous groans.*)

The cavalcade, then assembled in New-street, for the most part separated. It must be confessed that its not proceeding further was a subject of deep mortification and regret to the thousands who lined the streets and road for two miles farther—to the Five Ways ; and to the numerous and highly respectable company which crowded the windows of the houses in those spacious streets through which the procession was expected to pass. At the Five Ways a gallery had been erected for the accommodation of ladies, and the whole line of road in this direction, even as far as Harborne (four miles from Birmingham), the place of Mr. Attwood's residence, exhibited proofs that no small pains and industry had been used in preparation. Mr. Attwood left Birmingham in a car soon after ten o'clock. The crowd recognised him and gave him three cheers as he entered it. In the course of a short time afterwards the streets were perfectly quiet, and presented their usual appearance. We are happy to state that we have heard of no serious accidents having occurred. It is true, we believe, that part of a new building gave way in Digbeth or its neighbourhood, and that an old lady was in some degree, though not dangerously, injured. Many carriages were broken down, but none of the passengers were in any instance injured. The only violence of which we have heard was a few panes of glass broken in the office of *Aris's Gazette*, High Street ; but it is satisfactory, even upon the admission of the gentlemen who were the sufferers, that the act was not committed by any person connected with the procession.

Thus ended the proceedings of this extraordinary day, which presented altogether, we should imagine, a scene which has seldom been witnessed in the world before. Whether considering the immense masses which were assembled—or the high excitement of their minds—or the universal expression of their feelings, among all classes, from the highest to the lowest—or the thousands of flags, banners, and devices exhibited from every window—the waving of flags, handkerchiefs, and the gratulations of so many thousands of beautiful women—or the loud, and joyous, and never-ceasing shouts of tens of thousands of exulting men—the whole presented a *tout ensemble* which literally defies description.

The following are some of the banners, with their devices and mottoes, exhibited from houses in the several streets through which the procession passed :—

Small Heath.

Kendall—Tri-coloured flag—motto, Three cheers for Attwood, Earl Grey and Reform.

Potts—Tri-coloured silk flag.

Harvey—Ditto—motto, Attwood, Union, Liberty, Peace.

Garter, Lord Nelson Inn—Blue colours.

Coventry Road.

Jenkins—Banner—motto, No Duke, no despotism.
Betford—Blue colours.
Hill—Blue colours.
Webb—Blue flag.
Cave—Blue colours.
Miles, Bordesley Park Tavern—Tri-coloured flag.
Page—Blue colours.
Bordell—Ditto, ditto.

Deritend and Bordesley.

Cochrane—Banner, with two Union Jacks.
Harson—Blue banner—motto, Earl Grey and Attwood for ever.
Baylis—White flag—motto, The Bill and nothing but the Bill.
Rice—Blue banner—motto, Let Attwood live in memory dear.
Wareham—Blue banner—motto, Reform; Attwood, the man of the People.
Harris—Blue flag with Union Jack.
Wood—Banner—motto, Attwood, the Saviour of his country.
Jelp—Blue flag.
Brough—Ditto.
Chillingworth—Blue banner—motto, Thomas Attwood, the patriotic restorer of our rights and liberties.
Burna—Blue banner—motto, T. Attwood, Esq, the Friend of the People.
Fletcher—Blue flag.
Lakins—Banner—motto, Liberty, the birthright of man, is a nation's safeguard.
Davis—Blue flag with Union Jack.
Moore—Ditto with two ditto.
Jackson—Ditto with one ditto.
Averill—Blue and white ribbons on a gilded bough.
Allday—Blue silk flags, decorated with ribbons, three Union Jacks and a medal of Mr. Attwood.
Felton—Blue flag with Union Jack.
Hinchley—Blue banner—motto, Union is strength—we will have our rights.
Key—Blue flag, with Union Jack—motto, May the friends of liberty never want supporters.
Hooper—Blue flag.
Tomkins—Oak bough, decorated with Union Jacks, ribbons, &c.
Jackson—Blue flag, with Union Jack.
Low—Blue banner—motto, Reform—liberty well understood, and zealously defended.
Horn—Banner, with a bundle of sticks—motto, Union is strength.
Barrow—Blue flag—motto, Attwood and union will gain our rights.
Howlette—Blue flag with Union Jack—motto, May Attwood and the Union triumph over our oppressors.
Bevins—Blue flag.

Parkes—Blue flag—motto, Attwood for ever.
Hildick—Blue banner—motto on one side, The Constitution in its purity On the reverse—Unity, Peace, and Prosperity.
Michael—Blue banner—motto, May the late emblem of our Patriot ever entwine round the British Oak.
Davis—Blue silk flag, with Union Jack.
Edkins—Blue flag, with Union Jack.
Taylor—Ditto, ditto.
Sargent—Ditto, ditto—motto, Attwood, the people's pride.
Carr—Blue flag.
Brown—Ditto with Union Jack
Richardson—Blue flag, with a splendid Lion in the centre—motto, Attwood and the Unions
Hulse—Two flags, with Union Jacks.
Daws—Banner—motto, Attwood for ever, the Friend of the People.

Digbeth.

Bradley—A figure above the shop window, decorated with a blue scarf wearing the Union Jack suspended from a tri-coloured rose. A tri-coloured banner waved over the device with the following motto :—
  O'er the vine-covered hills and gay regions of France
  See the day-star of liberty rise, &c. (four verses).
George Inn—Blue colours.
James—Blue flag.
White Hart—Blue colours.
Thomas—Blue flag with Union Jack.
Parry—ditto
Smith—Blue flag.
Linnard—Tri-coloured flag
Beale—Two flags, with Union Jack.
Matthison. Blue banner—motto—Union, liberty, and prosperity.
Robins—Blue flag, with Union Jack.
Ingall—Ditto, ditto.
Marston—Ditto, ditto.
Greensil—Blue banner, edged with white.
Allen—Blue banner—motto, Success to Mr. Attwood and the Members of the Political Council.
Davis—Blue banner—motto, May we obtain our liberties with peace.
Sheldon—Blue banner—motto, Attwood, Union, Peace, and Reform.
Bullerin—Blue ribbons and wreath of flowers.
Allday—Blue flag.
Gooch—Blue ribbons and wreaths of flowers.
Haywood—Ditto, ditto.
Hill—Blue flag.
Smallwood—Ditto.
Trow—Blue flag—motto, God bless the King.
Cooper—Tri-coloured flag.
Fox—Three colours.

Rider—Blue flag.
Goostry—Ditto.
Duckey—Ditto.
Scarrott—Blue flag—motto, Attwood for ever.
Jenkins—Blue flag.
Selby—Blue and pink flag.
Kyte—Blue silk flag.
Twigg—Talbot Inn—Blue flag.
Parkes—Blue flag.
Pugh—White and red flag.
Assinder—Blue colours.
Whittingham—Tri-coloured flags.
Turner—Blue flag.
Dunn—Ditto.
Mountain, Three Tuns—Blue flag.
Lyndon—Blue colours.
Pegley—Four blue flags.
Portway—Blue flag edged with white.
Richards—Union Jack—motto, Attwood for ever.
Varney—Blue colours.
Crompton—Blue banner—motto—

> 'Prone to the earth, oppression shall be hurl'd,
> Its name, its nature, withered from the world.'

Clarke—Two grotesque figures, made of wicker work, male and female—motto over the man—

> 'God speed the plough,
> I'm for Reform or else a row.'

Motto over the woman—

> 'Attwood and the Union we have no doubt,
> In time will rout the rascals out,
> I hope you'll copy my husband and me,
> In cheering up Attwood with three times three.'

Ludlow—Blue colours.
Lees—Ditto.
Bodington—Ditto with Union Jack.
Fluitt, Unicorn Inn—Blue flag—motto, Attwood and Union will gain our rights.
Onions—The Royal Oak, surmounted with a Cap of Liberty, and the Union Jack.
Amos—Garland of Oak, with blue colours.
Underhill—Blue colours.
Biggs—Banner—motto, Attwood, Union, Peace, and Reform.
Turner—Blue colours.
Johnson—Blue flag.
Beech, Old Guy Inn—Blue flag—motto, Attwood and Union.
Palmer—Blue colours.

Bull Ring

Ethell—blue flag.   Pritchard—blue silk flag.
Tidmarsh—tri-coloured flag.
Taylor—blue and white flag.
Smith—tri-coloured flag.
Renault—three blue flags.
Kendrick—two blue flags
Whittall—large blue flag.
Harris—blue and white flag

Spiceal Street

Spread Eagle—Blue colours
Perkins—Blue flag.
Brinton—Blue flag.

High Street.

Peters' Wine Vaults—Blue banner with Union Jack—motto, on one side, Attwood, the unassuming friend of the people ; reverse, What power can resist a mighty nation's will?
Bourne—Blue flag.
Tooting—Three tri-coloured and two blue flags.
Sumner—Blue flag.
Flint—Tri-coloured flag.
Phillips and Palmer's Wine Vaults—A white and blue flag with Union Jack.
Leggett—Five small blue flags.
Partridge—Blue flag.
Maxwell—Blue flag—motto, God armeth the patriot.
Perry—Tri-coloured flag.
Butterworth—Tri-coloured flag.
Whittle—Blue flag with Union Jack.
Price—Large blue flag.
Savage—Blue flag.
Poole—Tri-coloured flag.
Ford—Eight small flags
Birch—Two large flags, with Union Jacks—motto, Reform ; Cannister ornamented with laurel, blue ribbons, &c.
Banks—Blue colours.

New Street.

Hancock—Three blue silk flags.
Jones—Blue flag, with Union Jack.
Hen and Chickens Hotel—Wreaths of flowers.
Goode—Blue flag.
Hensman—Blue flag.
Reynolds—Tri-coloured silk flag, with a splendid King's Arms.
Creswick—Blue flag.
Jones, Pantechnetheca—Four blue flags.

Selby—Blue colours.
Mitton—Blue flag.
Johnson—Blue colours
Lomax—Blue colours
Iliffe—Blue flag.
Drake—Tri-coloured flag.
Hickman—Tri-coloured flag.
Henderson—Two flags—mottoes, Attwood for ever and Reform.
Taylor—Blue colours. Tiplady—Blue banner.
Brookes—Two blue flags.
Radenhurst, Royal Hotel—Union Jack.
Taylor—Blue silk flag Lane—Blue silk flag.
Brown—Two blue silk flags. Dewson—Blue flag.
Carpenter—Blue flag Reynolds—Two small flags.
Hayden—Blue colours.
Pugh, Wheat Sheaf—Blue flag.

Ann Street.

Suffield—Large blue flag, with Union Jack.
Lucas—Blue colours.

Paradise Street.

Brindley—Two large blue flags, with rosettes.
Lyon and Calisher—Union Jack.
Groove—Blue flag—motto, Attwood, huzza!
Hall—Blue colours.

Easy Row.

Perrins, Woodman—blue flag.
Wood—Blue flag.

Broad Street.

Brookes—Blue flag. Crowthers—Blue flag.
Foster—Blue colours.
Stephens and Harris—Blue flag, with four Union Jacks.
Owen, Crown Inn—Tri-coloured flag.
Stole—Blue colours. Abbott—Blue flag.
Castle—Tri-coloured flag. Lodge—Tri-coloured flag.
Howes—Tri-coloured flag. Timmins—Three Union Jacks.
Inions, Compasses—Tri-coloured flag.
Bridge—Union Jack. Lewis—Blue colours.

Five Ways.

At the turnpike there was a large banner across the road, with a Union Jack at each end; motto, Attwood for ever, Britons be firm and true. Over the house waved a British pennant, with a white flag—motto, Victory, Attwood for ever, the Champion of Reform.

Lichfield Street.

Parsons—Banner, carried on two poles—motto, Attwood for ever, Liberator of his Country.

Banner attached to the third carriage from Mr. Attwood's.

T. Attwood, Esq., and an honest, undaunted People for ever. On the reverse, Be united to obtain your just Rights and Privileges.

CHAPTER XV.

Passing of the Reform Bill—Attwood and the Secret Committee on the Bank Charter—G. De B. Attwood's Candidature for Walsall—Thos. Attwood's Address to the Electors of Birmingham, June 29th, 1832—Third Annual Meeting of the Political Union—Famous Discussion between Cobbett and Attwood on the Currency—Matthias Attwood, sen., and East Worcester Election—Birmingham Polish Association—Defeat of G. De B. Attwood at Walsall—Attwood and Scholefield are returned without opposition as the first Members for Birmingham—The chairing on December 17th—Lord Lyndhurst's Decree in Small v. Attwood—M. Attwood returned for Whitehaven, and Chas. Attwood defeated at Newcastle-on-Tyne—Letters of Campbell and Lafayette.

THE Reform Bill passed the Lords on the 4th of June, 1832, and on the 7th received the royal assent, and "thus," says Mr. Langford, "triumphantly closed one of the most splendid moral spectacles which the world has ever seen." I have already quoted the distinct and decided opinions of Thomas Campbell, George Grote, and Elihu Burritt to the effect that the chief glory of peacefully passing that great measure was unquestionably due to Thomas Attwood, and there is therefore no necessity to say anything more upon the subject.

It is to be very much regretted that the three great meetings on Newhall Hill, and the public entry into Birmingham, were never adequately represented pictorially. Haydon the painter fully intended to paint a large picture of the meeting of May 16th, at the moment when the Rev. Hugh Hutton was engaged in offering up prayer, but want of means prevented him from carrying out his intention. The only picture of the great meetings existing is a lithograph twenty inches by twelve, drawn and published by Henry Harris of Birmingham. I have heard several eye-witnesses, notably the late Mr. T. C. Salt, say that this lithograph gives a good idea of the extraordinary scene depicted, but, of course, it is not in a style of art worthy of the subject, which ought to have been commemorated by several oil paintings and steel engravings of the largest size.

Whilst these stirring events were in progress, a secret committee, the operations of which were in no way understood or regarded by the general public, was quietly pursuing its labours; and by influencing that committee Thomas Attwood fondly hoped that he would be shortly able to effect more towards the restoration of prosperity than by passing the showy Reform Bill. This was the Secret Committee on the Bank Charter, which was also empowered to deal with the question of £1 notes, and the Currency generally. It was appointed on the 22nd of May, 1832, and numbered amongst its members Lord Viscount Althorp, Sir Robert Peel, Lord John Russell, Matthias Attwood, Lord Ebrington, and many others. Frequent allusions to this Committee will be found in Mr. Attwood's letters, though his sanguine hopes were doomed to disappointment.

No sooner was it certain that the Reform Bill would pass, than the country began to be greatly excited with regard to the general election which would shortly take place under it. George De Bosco Attwood, the eldest son of Thomas, then twenty-four years old, who had inherited his father's poetic temperament, and unselfish enthusiasm for the public good, determined to offer himself as a candidate for the new borough of Walsall.

On the 4th of June father and son visited the town, and were received with great enthusiasm by an immense crowd of the inhabitants with twenty banners. Upon their arrival in the market place Mr. Attwood introduced his son in an affectionate speech, stating how much he had been indebted to his assistance during the late arduous conflict with the boroughmongers. He then proceeded to say that although he had himself been always ready to face exile, the scaffold, or the felon's gaol, yet he had at first thought that one victim out of one family was sufficient. But "when new circumstances arose—when he saw that the Union had taken a firm hold of the public mind—when he saw that it had taken deep root in the hearts of the British people— when he saw the sword and the bayonet glistening in the vistas of the barricades—when he saw that, if he fell, he should fall like Hampden, covered with the blessings of his country—when he saw that danger was attended with immortal honour—(*loud cheers*)—he then consented that his son should come forward and share with him whatever fate might await them." Mr. Attwood proceeded to say that his son's opinions were identical with his own, and should the electors of Walsall think fit to return him they might rely upon his enthusiastic devotion to the cause of the people.

Mr. Edmonds and Mr. W. G. Lewis then warmly eulogised the young aspirant to parliamentary honours. The latter said that, for want of any other objections, the Tories might possibly find fault with Mr. De Bosco Attwood's youth, but let them remember that William Pitt, the prince of Tories, was Prime Minister at an earlier age. He concluded by stating that the day would come when every man would be proud of having given Mr. De Bosco Attwood a vote.

Mr. Attwood, junior, then addressed the people amidst great applause. He dwelt at length upon the misery of the masses, and stated that it would be the first duty of the new Parliament to investigate the causes of the national distress. He thanked them for their kind reception and said that, on a future day, he should be happy to answer any questions. When the meeting dispersed, the prospect of Mr. Attwood's return seemed highly probable, though it afterwards appeared that his popularity lay chiefly amongst the non-electors of the borough.

On the 12th of June the Council of the Birmingham Union issued an address to their fellow-countrymen commencing as follows:—

"The judgments of God are righteous."
"Blessed be His Holy name."

"It has pleased Almighty God to grant to this nation a great, a glorious, and a bloodless victory—a victory unparalleled in its character, inestimable in its value to us and our posterity. That sordid and remorseless oligarchy which had hardened its heart against the prayers and the tears of the people —which had closed its eyes *that it saw not*, and its ears *that it heard not*— which so long has been fattening on the plunder of industry, and drinking, as it were, the life-blood of the poor—that cruel and obdurate oligarchy has at length fallen under the justice of an outraged and insulted nation. Its usurped power is taken away, and delivered into the hands of the great bulk of the middle classes of the people."

The address then goes on to declare that the national work was but half done, and to implore the people not to return to Parliament any one who would not pledge himself to support an honest investigation into the cause of the national distress. This address, which is signed by Thomas Attwood, was evidently drawn up by him, and aims at a reversal of the monetary policy of 1819.

On the 29th of June, 1832, Thomas Attwood issued his address to the Electors of the Borough of Birmingham. He naturally preferred to represent the town with which he had been so long identified, and for which he had done and suffered so much ; but he was by no means obliged to seek a seat there, for the late Mr. Wm. Mathews has recorded that he saw, at this time, lying on the patriot's table, twenty letters from twenty different boroughs, each offering to return him to Parliament. His address ran thus:—

MY DEAR FRIENDS AND FELLOW-COUNTRYMEN,—Upon the great occasion of the approaching assemblage of the Reformed Parliament I think it my duty to offer you my services. The long and anxious attention which I have paid to the general Distress of the Industrious Classes, and to the wrongs of which they have been made the victims, induces me to believe that I can be of service upon this great and vital crisis of our country's fate. To stay the march of Anarchy—to relieve the general Distress—to rectify the general wrongs—to secure a full measure of Justice, Liberty, and Prosperity to all, and to unite all classes and all sects of my countrymen in peace, happiness, and contentment, under the shadow of the King's Throne,—*these* are the objects which I have in view, and which I trust I can assist in accomplishing.

But, gentlemen, I beg to be understood that I solicit no favours. The day of favours, of influence, and of patronage has passed away. Men must now act from sterner motives, if the happiness of our country is to be restored. If any man is *my* friend, and thinks that I am not competent to serve my country, the best proof he can give me of his friendship is to *vote against me*. I have no desire that anyone should gratify his friendship to me at the expense of his duty to his country. And if any one should be my enemy, but should think that I possess the knowledge and the virtue which may be useful to the people, the best proof that he can give of his own virtue is to *vote for me*. It is not right that private friendships and private animosities should enter into our consideration in the discharge of great public duties.

These, gentlemen, are my views. I wish every one to vote according to his conscience, without favour or affection, enmity or fear; and *then*, if the majority of your votes should determine in my favour, I am prepared to do my duty.

With sincere wishes for your health, prosperity, and happiness, I am, My dear Friends and Fellow-townsmen,

Your faithful friend and servant,
THOMAS ATTWOOD.

This address, though very well received in Birmingham, drew down upon its author the wrath of Cobbett, who, in his *Register* of July 7th, sharply criticised its vagueness and want of specific pledges. The subject of pledges to be exacted from parliamentary candidates caused several stormy discussions at the meetings of the Political Council, some members of which seemed to think that Mr. Attwood had been too great a Tory in past years to be altogether trusted without them. At one of these meetings he certainly seems to have forgotten himself, and to have reproved the proposers of pledges with considerable asperity. For this he was severely taken to task by Cobbett in a bitter article in the *Register* of July 21st, entitled "Puddle in a storm, or King Tom in his tantrums;" but soon recovered his influence and popularity. Some of the expressions, however, which he used on this occasion, were never forgotten, and were often quoted against him in later years.

Mr. Attwood visited London again in July, and wrote from thence to his wife as follows:—

London, 12 July, 1832.

. . We had upwards of 400 M P.'s and Lords at our dinner yesterday, and I, of course, as a "distinguished visitor," had a seat upon the hustings among them. I did not speak much, but the people cried out, "*Go on all night*," when I did speak.

London, 14 July, 1832

. . . The Banking Committee have so many engagements before them, that I expect they will not be able to hear me before the week after next.

I have called upon Davenport, Czapski, and Minusewitz, but found none of them at home.

(This letter is endorsed by T. A.—"+ *a great day*," but there is nothing to indicate for what reason, save the following: —P.S. Tell Bosco that his uncle has quite demolished Tooke as well as Horsley Palmer.)

MY DEAR SIR, "*To Thos. Attwood, Esq.*,

It is my intention most certainly to propose to the Committee on the Bank Charter that you should be examined as a witness, but I cannot just now state the time when I shall ask you to attend.

Believe me, my dear Sir,
Yours most sincerely,
ALTHORP.

Downing Street,
July 15, 1832."

To Mrs. Thos. Attwood, Birmingham.

London, July 17, 1832.

I shall return home by the safety Tally ho, if I can get a place in it, to-morrow morning, and sincerely hope to find you all well. In a few days I will try to go with my dear family to the Comers, and before the summer is over I purpose not to forget Clent Hill, &c. . .

London, August 2nd, 1832.

. . . I have been examined to-day, and hope I have made some impression. I expect I may return to you on Saturday evening, but of this I am not sure. I found my brother Matthias exceedingly unwell and confined to his bed. I had, therefore, no friend upon the Committee, and in my examination was obliged in a great degree to trust to my means of converting the questions of an enemy into the answers of a friend. The impression upon my mind was that Lord Althorp had come round to my opinions.

To Mrs. Attwood, Richd Spooner, Esqr's., near Worcester.

Harborne, 2 *Sept.,* 1832.

. . Aurelius is here, and quite well. I am glad you are so happy in your parties, and hope you will be careful. I send you a newspaper which I daresay you will like containing a discussion between the Conservatory and Destructive principles. Now, if I succeed in getting the Currency rectified, I am afraid it will make you proud. Only think what a fine thing it will be to have assisted, first in obtaining *Liberty*, second in preventing *Anarchy*, third in restoring *Prosperity!* . . . Bosco and Aurelius go to the Comers to-morrow.

The third annual general meeting of the Birmingham Political Union was held at Newhall Hill on Monday, July 30th, 1832, to "consider the extreme distress of the times, and the wretched condition of Poland." The Union met under altered circumstances. When the Reform Bill passed, many men of high rank and station pressed Thomas Attwood to dissolve the Union, urging upon him that by so doing he would "fix upon his shoulders for ever the glory of having carried the Reform Bill." Had he cared anything for rank, wealth, or posthumous fame he would undoubtedly have taken this course, but his one thought was to alleviate the distress of his fellow-countrymen, and no other consideration had the slightest weight with him. Nevertheless, Mr. Joshua Scholefield and other influential members of the Union thought differently, and resigned their membership. Mr. G. F. Muntz was called to the chair, and announced his intention of continuing firmly to support the Union. Thomas Attwood made a long speech and moved the adoption of the report, the substance of which was that it was imperatively necessary to continue their agitation until some effectual measures for the relief of distress were adopted by the Government. It was evident that his confidence in Earl Grey was beginning to be shaken. Mr. De Bosco Attwood, in a long and enthusiastic speech, then moved the adoption of a petition to the House of Commons praying them to compel Russia to restore the independence of Poland. A new Council was elected, and the thanks of the Union voted to Thomas Attwood "for his able and patriotic conduct on all occasions, particularly during the important and trying crisis in which during the past year he has been placed."

On the 28th and 29th of August great public interest was excited by a famous discussion between Thomas Attwood, Charles Jones, and William Cobbett, held at Beardsworth's Repository, upon the subject of the Currency. They met before an audience of 1,300 persons, although all paid for admission, and only three days' notice had been given. Persons attended from Worcester, Warwick, Coventry, Leamington, and other distant towns. The question was, "Whether it is best for the safety and welfare of the nation to attempt to relieve the existing distress by an action on the Currency, or by an equitable adjustment of the taxes, rents, debts, contracts, and obligations which now strangle the industry of the country?" The *Journal* says: "Mr. Attwood and Mr. Jones maintained the first proposition of the question; Mr. Cobbett took the alternative. It was a very interesting debate, and excited much attention throughout the country. Mr. Cobbett cleverly supported his view of the subject, and made a powerful impression upon the vast assembly. Mr. Attwood, however, in a masterly reply, without artifice, but closely reasoned upon broad principles, carried the meeting with him, and had a decision in his favour of at least three to one." Considering that Cobbett was then, and still is, thought to be one of the greatest masters of the English language, this was no mean triumph for Attwood; but in fairness it must be remembered that the discussion would probably have had a different result had it taken place anywhere else but in Birmingham.

Mr. Attwood sent a copy of this discussion to Earl Grey, and received the following reply:—

"*Private.* *Howick, Septr.* 5, 1832.

SIR,—I have this morning been favoured with your letter of the 1st, with the accompanying Birmingham Paper.

Being very much occupied at this moment, I have been unwilling to delay thanking you for this mark of your attention, till I should have time to read the report of the controversy between you and Mr. Cobbett.

I have no doubt that I shall find the question treated with great ability on both sides, but I much fear that your opinions and mine will not agree as to the nature of the remedy to which you look for the relief of the existing distress.

I remain, Sir,
Your most obedt. servt.,
GREY."

In October, 1832, Sir John Sinclair published a long letter to Thomas Attwood on the Currency, which Cobbett reprinted in his *Register* of October 20th, with the following characteristic comment:—

"I am loath to say anything disrespectful of the author of this letter: but, good God! how *wild* is this!"

About the same time Mr. Attwood received the following letter from his father with reference to the election for East Worcestershire:—

(*Enclosure.*)
"*Hawne House,* 25*th Octr.*, 1832.

"MY DEAR SIR,—In reply to your note relating to Mr. Pakington's canvass, I regret to say that, having long since made up my mind not to interfere in any electioneering concerns, I declined registering my vote for any place or county whatever, and having also declined using my vote or interest to others of my friends before, I cannot consistently interfere in the way you desire. I wish, however, not to be considered as in any way opposed to your friend Mr. Pakington, who, from all I am able to judge

may be a very proper person to represent this division of the County of Worcester. My grandson is not now in the neighbourhood, but, should he be here before Saturday, I will recommend him to attend at the New Inn, for the purpose of using any influence he may possess to procure Mr. Pakington a fair hearing With much respect, I remain, my Dear Sir, your most obedt. servant,
MATTHIAS ATTWOOD."

"DEAR TOM,—This evening I received the enclosures from Mr. Brettell. You will see my answer above, and that I decline attending the meeting. However, I should think Mr Pakington to be a more likely person to meet your views on the currency and other questions than either of the other two candidates, who, I believe, have declared no opinion on those points. You will use your own discretion as to sending Tommy over or not, as I conceive his appearing there may tend (in some measure) to keep the people quiet. I hear that warrants have been issued this week against several of his Union friends in Hales Owen, for breaking Bloxham's windows.
Your affectionate Father,
MATTHIAS ATTWOOD."

Mr. (afterwards Sir J. S.) Pakington lost the election for East Worcester in 1832, and two Liberals, Messrs. Russell and Cookes, were returned.

In this autumn the Birmingham Polish Association was founded, chiefly through the influence of Thomas Attwood and his son, for the purpose of supporting the cause of Polish liberty and independence. Shortly after, its directors determined to celebrate the anniversary of the revolution of Poland by a public dinner on the 29th of November. A splendid commemoration accordingly took place at Dee's Royal Hotel, and for the first time in Birmingham ladies were invited to witness the festivities. Thomas Attwood took the chair, and presided at the centre table, supported by Count Ladislas de Plater, and Mr. Dempster Heming ; W. Boultbee, G. F. Muntz, T. W. Hill, W. G. Lewis, and G. De B. Attwood presided at the other tables. The Chairman, in proposing "The King, God bless him! May he never forget the principles which placed his family on the throne," said :—

It was true that the illustrious individual at the head of the nation might not, in every respect, have given satisfaction to his people ; yet still they were under a debt of everlasting gratitude to him, and great allowance should be made for the extremely difficult circumstances under which he had been placed. The whisperings of the oligarchs poisoning his royal mind, and insinuating all manner of infamous calumnies against his people, might well be supposed to have some effect.

The Chairman next proposed the health of Earl Grey, and said it had been his lot to know that there was no man in England who had incurred so much personal danger as he had.

During many months the axe of the oligarchs had, in fact, been suspended over his head by a single thread. He (Mr. A.) could assure them that if it had not been for the courage and spirit which the people had exhibited, and more particularly for the wisdom and virtue which the men of Birmingham had shown, that venerated head would long ere now have slept under the ground. The House of Commons would have impeached him—the House of Lords would have condemned him, and the influence behind the throne, stronger than the throne itself, would most certainly have executed judgment upon him.

In a long speech, amidst great applause, the Chairman afterwards gave the toast of the evening, "The ancient and heroic Polish nation; may their cause never be abandoned by the British people." When the applause had subsided, the following Polish war-song, translated by G De Bosco Attwood was sung with great effect by Mr. Barker, and encored:—

"Skrenetski leads on!
Leads on! leads on!
Each battle blade shall be
   Speedily gory:
On! On! to victory,
   Freedom and glory!
Come where the musket's flashing,
Come where the sabre's clashing,
Fast shall the Muscovite
   Vanish before us;
God will defend the right,—
   God watches o'er us.

Skrenetski! We come!
We come! We come!
Fear is for craven slaves,
   No freeman falters!
Strike for your father's graves!
   Strike for your altars!
On, where the storm is thickest!
On, where death comes the quickest!
   Fast shall, &c.

> On, brothers ! Hurrah !
> Hurrah ! Hurrah !
> Soon shall our woes be o'er,
> Our chains be broken !
> Hark ! in our cannons' roar
> Triumph is spoken !
> Charge ! Charge ! the trumpet's calling !
> Charge ! Charge ! the brave are falling !
> Fast shall, &c. . . ."

Many other songs were sung, and speeches were made by Count Plater, the Chairman, and Mr. Muntz, the latter of whom proposed Mr. G. De Bosco Attwood's health, which was enthusiastically received. Mr. Attwood, junior, in returning thanks, protested his devotion to the cause of liberty and Poland, and concluded by expressing his conviction that "Poland should wake again."

The proceedings terminated, amidst great applause, by the presentation of the banners of Poland and England to Count Plater by the Chairman.

It is impossible to read the account of these proceedings without a feeling of melancholy regret that so much generous and unselfish enthusiasm should have led to no result. Had the advice of the Attwoods been followed, Russia would now be permanently enchained within her hereditary dominions. She is now more powerful than ever; Poland is still enslaved, and, one of these days England will probably have to fight the Bear of the North for her existence in India!

Meanwhile the Walsall election was being fought out with a coarseness and bitterness astonishing to us at the present day. The Tories had brought forward as their candidate Mr. Chas. S. Forster, a local banker, who was greatly superior to Mr. G. De B. Attwood in the important qualifications of age and fortune. The latter, however, had the support of the masses, and for some time his friends felt confident of success. A considerable number of handbills, squibs, and placards relating to this election have been preserved, and show how much men have improved in courtesy and politeness during the last fifty years. Charges of corruption, bribery, intimidation, and malicious injury were freely exchanged between the opposing parties, but it is remarkable that the Tory publications far exceed those of the other side in rudeness and vulgarity. The Tories of that day considered that it was very proper that a young lord of twenty-four, brought up in idleness, luxury, and self-indulgence, should aspire to represent his county or borough in Parliament; but that a young banker of the same age, of irreproachable character, who had devoted his scanty leisure to the study of history, poetry, and politics, should dare to wish to occupy the same position, was, in their eyes, an unheard-of piece of audacity. There was published at this time in Birmingham, and for some years before and after, a very coarse and abusive little print called *The Argus*. This publication indulged in the most violent and personal abuse of the Attwoods, but it is significant to note that the worst nicknames it could invent for Thomas Attwood were those of "Sultan Attwood," "King Tom," and especially "Pompey the Great." We are thus indebted to the scribbling of an enemy for a grander idea of the power and popularity of Thomas Attwood at this period than anything furnished by the most studied panegyrics of his friends. The parallel between the last-named personages was closer than could have been foreseen at the time, for just as Juvenal says that Pompey would have been happy had he died of his Campanian fever before Pharsalia, so it might be said of Thomas Attwood that he would have been one of the most fortunate of men had he died at the close of 1832. If the father fared thus at the hands of the Tories, it may be imagined that the son experienced no better treatment, and "Boy Bosco," as they delighted to call him, came in for a full share of their choicest abuse. The very unreasonableness and persistency of their attacks, however, show how much they dreaded his talents, and it must ever be a subject of regret to his family that feeble health and want of means prevented him from pursuing a public career. The election came off at Walsall on the 12th of December, and Thomas Attwood, who had just been returned for Birmingham without opposition, hastened thither to assist his son. The show of hands was in Mr. G. De B. Attwood's favour, but when the candidates came to the poll the numbers were—Forster 304, and Attwood 231. A troop of cavalry having presented themselves before the hustings with drawn swords, and a body of infantry with loaded muskets and fixed bayonets within a few yards of Mr. Attwood's committee-room, no tumult or riot having taken place during the day, Mr. Attwood protested against any further proceedings in the Poll, and requested the Mayor to make a special return to his precept. Also several of Mr. Attwood's committee, on behalf of themselves and other unpolled voters, protested against any further proceedings in the election; notwithstanding which the Mayor continued the Poll the next day, and Mr. Forster was declared duly elected. There seems no doubt, however, that Mr. Attwood's supporters had been guilty of several acts of violence. Considering G. De B. Attwood's youth at this period, he had no reason whatever to feel disheartened at the untoward result of his first candidature, but the coarseness and scurrility with which an election was conducted in those days sank deep into his sensitive nature. He declared himself "sick of politics," and never again attempted to enter Parliament. He possessed many amiable and excellent qualities, but was not made of that stern stuff from which practical politicians and statesmen are manufactured.

On the 4th of December, 1832, Thomas Attwood appears to have received his last friendly communication from the Whig Government, from which he was soon to dissever himself. It ran thus.—

"*Private*

MY DEAR SIR,—Parliament was dissolved by H M. in Council to-day, and the writs go down by this Post I hope you will get your election over on Saturday. If not till Monday, and I get off easily at Coventry, I will go over and see the writing of the new Bill in your favour.

I wish to see you and talk over many things with you. In the meantime I must thank you for your kindness in writing to your unmanageable fellow-unionists at Coventry—altho' I wish you had not alluded so pointedly to Ld. Durham or myself. Howr. on this and many other points when we meet.

In haste, ever faithfully yours,
Monday, 3 Decr, 1832." EDWD. ELLICE.

Upon the extraordinary occasion of the first parliamentary election ever held in Birmingham, some feeble attempts were made by the Tories to bring forward a candidate. Several names were mentioned, the most prominent being that of Mr. Horsley Palmer, Governor of the Bank of England, a man of great wealth and considerable reputation. But upon inquiring into the state of affairs he prudently abstained from entering the lists with the great champion of Reform. It soon therefore became evident that, as was most justly their due, Thomas Attwood and Joshua Scholefield would be returned without opposition as the first members for the great and important town for which they had done so much towards obtaining the right to send members to Parliament at all.

"The nomination took place on the 12th of December, 1832, when Mr. Attwood, having been proposed by Mr. Thomas Wright Hill (father of Sir Rowland Hill), and seconded by Mr. John Betts (two old and tried Reformers), was elected by an unanimous vote of the crowded assembly who had met for the purpose; and Mr. Joshua Scholefield, the respected Vice-Chairman of the Union, was at the same time elected as Mr. Attwood's colleague on the nomination of Mr. G. F. Muntz, seconded by Mr. Thomas Clark."

"The chairing of the two members," says an account published in 1840, "took place on the 17th of the same month, and a memorable day it was for Birmingham.

"Under the direction of the Committee of Management, a magnificent car was constructed for the occasion, and the populous district of which Birmingham forms the centre poured forth its tens of thousands to do them honour. It is described as being a spectacle of surpassing interest; not only was every window and roof thronged with admiring spectators, but every street through which it passed presented a dense mass of human beings, all seeming to be animated by one common feeling—that of joy and congratulation."

An engraving of the car in which Attwood and Scholefield were chaired was published by the *Birmingham Journal*, which considered that its cost and beauty ought to have saved it from the usual fate of being broken up, but I am not sure whether it was preserved or not.

Thus, amidst almost every concomitant of the most complete

and triumphant success, appropriately terminated this great and glorious year. The life of Thomas Attwood, to have attained dramatic completeness, should have closed in 1832. He was then the idol of the populace, his portraits were in every shop window, ballads in his praise were hawked through every street, great painters contended for the honour of taking his likeness, and twenty boroughs solicited him to represent them in Parliament. Whenever he appeared in the streets he was followed by admiring crowds of young and old, anxious to shake his hand as a thing to be remembered. To use his own language, he had " prevented anarchy," he had " recovered liberty," and he fondly hoped that it would shortly be granted him to "restore prosperity." Politically, in the midst of so many victories, he had received but a single check, in the failure to secure his son's return for Walsall. In his domestic relations, Mr. Attwood's only trouble during the year 1832 was the increasing illness of his third son Marcus. In other respects he was singularly fortunate. His own age was forty-nine, not so very long past his prime. Both his father and mother were present in New Street to witness his grand entry His two elder sons already gave brilliant promise and were exceedingly popular, whilst his other children were old enough to appreciate and admire the magnitude of his triumph. In the *Argus*, to which I have before alluded, there is a satirical piece representing Bosco and Aurelius Attwood at Harborne, indulging in visions of future greatness, the one proposing to commence his career as Member for Walsall, and the other for Dudley. This at least shows that there were many who considered the young men fit for such posts.

On the 1st of November, 1832, Lord Lyndhurst delivered his judgment in the case of Small *v.* Attwood, which had been tried nearly a year before. That judgment, says Lord Campbell, was " by all accounts the most wonderful ever heard in Westminster Hall. It was entirely oral, and without even referring to any notes he employed a long day in stating complicated facts, in entering into complex calculations, and in correcting the misrepresentations of the counsel on both sides. Never once did he falter or hesitate and never once was he mistaken in a name, a figure, or a date." The result of the judgment was apparently disastrous to John Attwood, for by it the agreement of 1825 was annulled, and he was condemned to pay the enormous costs of the proceedings. Party spirit then ran so high that although the case was a purely business one, in no way connected with politics, some of the lower Tory prints indulged in a scream of indecent exultation upon what they supposed to be the total ruin of an Attwood. But "he laughs best who laughs last" is a proverb peculiarly applicable to legal matters, and so thought John Attwood when, six years later, the House of Lords reversed the decision of Lord Lyndhurst.

During the whole of the year 1832 Charles Attwood, as Chairman of the Northern Political Union at Newcastle-upon-Tyne, strenuously assisted his brother in forwarding the cause of Reform. As we have seen, Mr. Wallace of Glasgow and he were the only two persons to whom Thomas Attwood applied for advice and assistance during the great crisis in May. He had, however, no intention of offering himself as a candidate for Parliament, not being possessed of sufficient fortune, and being closely engaged in business. Nevertheless, at the very last moment, in compliance with the earnest solicitations of his party, he permitted himself to be put forward in opposition to Mr. John Hodgson Hinde, the Conservative candidate. He only issued his address on the Saturday night, and the election was to take place on the Tuesday following. He found also that every attorney in Newcastle, except one, was retained by the other two candidates. At the nomination on Monday Charles Attwood obtained the show of hands in his favour, but at the poll the numbers were—Sir M. W. Ridley, 2112; John Hodgson Hinde, 1686; Charles Attwood, 1092. This was the only occasion during the course of his long life upon which Mr. Charles Attwood attempted to enter the House of Commons, although he always took an active part in public affairs.

Not even the extinction of his favourite borough of Boroughbridge, or the discredit into which his party fell at the passing of the Reform Bill, could prevent a man possessing the talents of Matthias Attwood from obtaining a seat in the new Parliament. At the election of December, 1832, he was returned for the new borough of Whitehaven by a majority of thirty-four over the Liberal candidate, Mr. Isaac Littledale.

Towards the end of the year 1832 Mr. Attwood received the following letters from Campbell and Lafayette:—

"*Nov* 12, 1832.
*Sussex Chambers, Duke St, St. James's,
London.*

"DEAR SIR,—I beg leave through you to present my respects to the Polish Association of Birmingham, and to thank you for the honour which you have done me in inviting me to your approaching Festival. I regret to say, however, that from peculiar circumstances I am not able to be absent a single day from London, and must therefore decline the invitation.

I remain with much respect,
Yours very truly,
T. CAMPBELL."

"*Paris, Xbre* 31, 1832.

"MY DEAR SIR,—I have received from Ladislas Plater the very honourable and gratifying dispatches you were pleased to entrust to him. As I was going most gratefully and respectfully to acknowledge them, I am called upon for Letters of Introduction in behalf of Mr. — Menotti, brother to the celebrated victim of the petty tyrant of Modena, himself a sufferer in the cause of liberty. Permit me to avail myself of the friendship, most cordially reciprocated, which you have so kindly expressed, to give this special line of presentation to you, reserving for another day the tender of a double and highly felt gratitude.

Your sincere friend,
LAFAYETTE."

CHAPTER XVI.

Parliamentary failure of Thomas Attwood—His Irish policy—His motion for a Select Committee to inquire into distress of the country—Letters of Campbell, Niemcewicz, Plater, Western, Lafayette, Dwernicky, and Barrot—Death of Rev. Edward Carless—Letters—Great Meeting of May 20, 1833—Cobbett's motion against Peel—Charles Attwood and Lord Durham—Cobbett's account.

WITH the year 1833 we enter upon a new epoch of Thomas Attwood's life. We have seen him struggling for twenty-five years to influence the Government by means of letters, pamphlets, and petitions. We have seen him, baffled in these modes of procedure, form the famous Birmingham Political Union, which not only carried him triumphantly into Parliament, but rendered him, for a time, the most popular man in England. We have now to enter upon what must be considered, from a worldly and party point of view, the period of his decadence. There can be no doubt that, had he retired into private life at this time, his fame would have stood far higher, and the extraordinary services rendered by him in 1832 would have been far more gratefully remembered. In allusion to his parliamentary career, the *Birmingham Journal*, writing in 1856, says:—

"He entered the House of Commons in December, 1832, the hero of the Reform Bill, the most popular and powerful man in England; he retired from Parliament in 1839, weary and disappointed. His Parliamentary failure may have been somewhat owing to excessive vehemence of manner, and unrestrained violence of expression, and to his incessant and not always seasonable or skilful advocacy of his monetary views. But it was still more emphatically owing to the nobleness of his nature, to the disinterestedness of his patriotism, to his intense abhorrence of party selfishness, to his utter disdain for mere party interests, to his entire incapacity for, and hearty detestation of the not very exalted manœuvres, and the not very creditable intrigues, of which too much of parliamentary life is made up."

Mr. Edwards, writing in 1879, says also:—

"His greatest admirers must admit that his parliamentary career was comparatively a failure. The great popular leader did not make a good legislator. The man's life work was done before he entered the House of Commons, and he made no headway there."

It is most difficult to account for the fact that a man possessed of so much power *outside* the House should have exercised so little influence *within* it. Such a state of affairs could not happen in these days. Public opinion now bears upon the House of Commons with a force and directness quite unknown in Attwood's time, and hence it is that his successors, Bright and Chamberlain, occupy a very different parliamentary position.

He commenced the year by a proceeding which was tantamount to a declaration that he had severed himself from the Whigs, and that the loaves and fishes which Ministers had to offer should not tempt him to swerve, in the slightest degree, from what he believed to be his duty. On January 1st a meeting of the Council of the Union was held, and it was resolved to keep "firmly united." On January 26th Daniel O'Connell was entertained at a dinner in Birmingham, and on February 25th a meeting of the Union was held at Beardsworth's Repository, at which the "atrocious conduct of the Ministry" was condemned with reference to the measures contemplated for Ireland, and for "their neglect in regard to the distressed condition of the working classes."

The first reformed Parliament met, amidst extraordinary excitement and expectation, upon January 29th, 1833. The Tories feared and the Radicals hoped that it would prove a very revolutionary assembly, and that great and startling changes would be immediately attempted. To the astonishment of every one, however, the new House of Commons proved to be uncommonly like the old one. There was an increased tendency to Liberalism, no doubt; but it was evident that things in general would go on pretty much as they had done. This state of affairs in no way met with the approval of Thomas Attwood, and he soon had an opportunity of giving expression to his feelings. He does not appear to have been present at the choice of the Speaker, Manners Sutton, but he made his maiden speech on

February 12th, in the debate on the Address in answer to the King's Speech. Oratorically considered, it does not seem to have been a success. It certainly did not meet with the approval of the House, however much it may have gratified his constituents. Ireland was then, as it is now, and has ever been, the grand difficulty of the English Government, and Earl Grey proposed to meet the state of the case by severe measures of coercion. This part of the royal speech was strongly opposed by Thomas Attwood, and he moved an amendment, which was at once negatived, that "As soon as we shall have adopted means for relieving the distress of the Irish people, &c., then it will be time to think of coercion," and so forth. He at once took part with Cobbett and O'Connell, and showed himself, in most respects, a decided Radical. I by no means intend to express any approval of Attwood's Irish policy, but it certainly is very strange that it should not have secured for him the eternal gratitude of the Irish Liberals. O'Connell was an Irishman and a Catholic by birth, and might reasonably have been expected to pursue the course which he did. Attwood was an Englishman and a Protestant, and by coalescing with O'Connell he incurred the greatest obloquy amongst his friends and relations. Yet the name of O'Connell is still regarded with gratitude by the great majority of Irishmen, whilst their historians have never mentioned the name of his unselfish and disinterested supporter!

On February 27th Mr. Attwood presented a petition complaining of the conduct of the military at Walsall, and was answered by Mr. Forster to the effect that his son's supporters had originated the disturbances.

On March 21st Thomas Attwood moved, in a long speech, "that a Select Committee be appointed to inquire into the causes of the general distress existing among the industrious classes of the United Kingdom, and into the most effectual means of its relief." In this speech he draws an appalling—his enemies said an exaggerated—picture of the distress which prevailed everywhere. I quote one or two extracts which seem to throw some light upon his ordinary life :—

This very morning I was told—for I did not count them—that fifty

Staffordshire colliers came to my door. The poor fellows had been wandering all over England; they were totally unable to get employment, and they came to me to ask my advice and assistance. . . .

I recollect once, when I was a boy, and out fishing, I saw a hat in the middle of the water—it was a large pond—I got the boat and went up to it, and I found that under the hat there was a man quite dead. He had walked deliberately, being drunk at the time, a hundred yards into the middle of the pond, and he went blundering on until the water got over his nose, and he died. He might have retreated with perfect ease, but he was so bigoted, so blind, and so obstinate in his drunkenness, that he would not turn back even when he could. Is it the disposition of this House to allow the Government of this country to come to the same end by an obstinate perseverance in a similar rash, drunken, and headlong course? . . .

Sir, I have been an agitator, but, God knows, I never found it a very "profitable trade." When I became an agitator I expected and experienced many certainly not very advantageous or pleasing results. I had to face the suspicion of the weak—the alarm of the timid—the jealousy of all—the alienation of friends—the bitter hatred of enemies; with the bayonet, the scaffold, and the gaol continually before my eyes.

It is almost needless to say that the motion was lost, because every one knew that its mover aimed at a rectification of the Currency; but the Attwoods appear to have been more nearly successful with respect to their favourite Currency doctrines upon this than upon any other occasion. The numbers were—for the Committee, 160; against it, with the Ministers, 194. Shortly afterwards, Matthias Attwood brought forward another motion to much the same effect. He was treated with great courtesy by Lord Althorp, and his long and thoughtful speech, combined with his great financial experience, evidently made a deep impression; but he was equally unable to carry his favourite proposition against the whole weight of the Government. I shall next insert some of Thomas Attwood's correspondence up to the time of the great meeting in May, 1833.

"*Sussex Chambers, Duke St., St. James's, London,*
Jany. 20, 1833.

"DEAR SIR,—Knowing your attachment to the cause of Poland, I take the liberty of introducing to you Mr. Stanislaus Kosmian, a Polish gentleman who has fought and been exiled in the cause of his ill-used country.

Trusting that this will find you in good health,

I remain, Dear Sir,
Yours very truly,
Thos. Attwood, Esq." THOS. CAMPBELL.

To G. De B. Attwood.

London, 9 Feby., 1833.

MY DEAR BOSCO,—I have written to Mr. Cotterill saying that he should forward the Petition to Mr. Hume at once, who is probably too much occupied to be able to answer his letters for the present. The Petition should be sent by coach, carriage paid, to Josh. Hume, Esq., Bryanstone Sqre., London.

I am quite disgusted with the King's Speech. I fully intended to speak upon it, but the crowds of other speakers prevented me. I voted both with O'Connell's amendment and with Tennyson's. The divisions would have been much larger if it had not been that O'Connell proposed to withdraw his amendment at the last, which was refused by the House.

I have postponed my motion for the select committee until 5 Mch., when I think I shall succeed. If I do not, you may be assured that nothing is intended to be done, and that the Whigs must follow the fate of the Tories I told Charles Wood last night, that if the Ministers persevered in obtaining a suspension of the constitution against Ireland, their doom was sealed.

I shall be glad to receive the petition against military interference.

Your affectionate father,
T. ATTWOOD.

(To Thomas Attwood)

"*Feb.* 14, 1833.

"MY DEAR SIR,—I do myself the pleasure to transmit to you different pamphlets respecting the unhappy Poland. In the Constitutional Charter you will see all the violations of it, &c., p. 47, and what passed at the Congress of Vienna. Subsequent events and cruelties will be found in *Polonia*, a monthly publication. I shall likewise give you information, when favourable opportunity offers to introduce it in the House. Present my respects to Mrs. and Miss Attwood, and believe me, dear Sir,

With gratitude and devotion,
Sincerely yours,
NIEMCEWICZ."

"*Paris,* 1 *Febr.,* 1833.

"SIR,—I have received with very great pleasure your letter, in which you do me the honour to invite me for the Honorary Member of your Association. I am always ready to participate in any favourable way to the cause of Poland. We are proud to have in you so influential a friend of our country ; your noble conduct in promoting the cause of Polish liberty and independence inspires a general admiration, and your name will be associated with the names of the liberators of oppressed Nations.

I hope you will do me the honour to accept the title of Honorary Member of the Lithuanian Association, whose presidency I have accepted. This Association is particularly devoted to the publications relative to the ancient Polish provinces which constitute the heart of Poland. My brother, who is one of your best friends, presents to you his compliments.

I have the honour to be yours,
COUNT . . . PLATER,
President of the Lithuanian Association."

"*Paris*, 2 *Febr*., 1833.

"SIR,—I cannot but regret that some unknown to me circumstances presented new difficulties in sending the flags to Paris. I am so much more anxious to have them as I am obliged to go shortly to London. My countrymen are waiting with very great anxiety, and the delay is beyond their expectation. However, I believe that you will be kind enough to send these flags to Paris without any delay, so that I could be able to present this proof of British sympathy to my countrymen. I have not received any letters from you since I left London; please to favour me with your correspondence, and believe me that you have in every Pole the best friend. I wrote to you a few days ago, and I mentioned in my letter the establishment of a new Polish institution in Paris for the education of the young Poles who have not the means to continue their studies. I join to this letter the prospectus of this excellent institution, which can prepare in a very eminent degree the future regeneration of Poland. This prospectus, translated into English, may be inserted in your papers (it is a very important measure). Perhaps your Association will make an appeal to the people to contribute to the establishment of this useful institution; an appeal of this kind published in the papers may be very effective, and may produce a large subscription. My brother was one of the principal founders of this institute. I have just received a copy of the petition of Hull in favour of Poland, addressed to the new Parliament: it is full of patriotism and energy. Birmingham, I have no doubt, will follow the example of Hull, and will present a petition to the reformed Parliament. Pray, what is the prospect of your Parliament? How many Radicals, Whigs, and Torys? The circumstances begin to be very favourable for the cause of Poland, and the intrigues in the Levant are more visible to-day than ever. Have you heard anything about a new congress in Franckfurt for the general settlement of Europe? Is the result known of the mission of the diplomatic agent from Persia? The news from Poland are the most deplorable, the ruin of families, of fortunes, of churches, the destruction of religion, the transportation of children. Are the Polish songs published? My compliments to your family.

I have the honour to be yours,
COUNT L. PLATER."

"*Felix Hall*,
Jany. 21, 1833.

"DEAR SIR,—Ministers have not given a thought to the subject of the Currency, I am pretty sure. They have had nothing to encourage them and the light has not broken in upon them. They are in the perfect belief that *all* the powers of the country are against an alteration of the system *now*, though 1819 was a grand mistake.

Ireland, a thiefism in the Church, Slave Trade—and they are too important to admit another subject, to say nothing of the East India and Bank Charters. *I* should still take the Currency *first* as bearing upon *all*, and the only directly *tranquilizing, antiradical measure*, the only, or if not the *only*, the *indispensable* one, for the preservation of our *Institutions*, and internal peace, prosperity, and happiness.

I think the *Session* may in its progress bring forth a different opinion in the public, *but* great care will be necessary in choosing the *moment* to moot it, and the man to do it. There are some men generally there who are most forward and unpopular, who will damn the best motions in the world, and as to time, there is a time to drive a nail, and if that is not waited for and seized when it presents itself, in vain all reasoning and argument. You have a great deal to learn of the House of Commons, I mean all you who have not tried it and mean to mix in the war of words. The good humour and favourable opinion of the House must be cultivated in order to get any fair play for your argument.

As to Sutton, why not Speaker? He was complimented *highly* by all parties and *sincerely* by a *great majority* of the last Parliament. I believe if Ministers had proposed another, and Sutton had been nominated by the Tories, they would have been hard run. . . . I know Jos. Hume and some others are out of humour upon it, but he would rather keep Ministers down, to make himself and his assistance more necessary. *He* and Co. would be *most inimical* to *our* object, for they know, as does Cobbett, that *their* occupation would be pretty well at an end.

I am, Dr. Sir, yours truly,
WESTERN."

"*Paris, February 24th,* 1833.

"MY DEAR SIR,—The friends of freedom and progress in France are more feelingly attentive to your reformed parliamentary transactions, and more than ever acknowledge the importance of a sympathetic popular union of good hearts and good wishes on both sides of the Channel. These general sentiments cannot but be peculiarly enhanced by the grateful remembrance of the honour which the Birmingham Association and their respectable president did formerly confer upon me, and by my late adoption in your Polish Society. It is in this last capacity that I beg leave to send you some additional facts relative to the abominable conduct of the monarchs of Russia and Prussia. I hope something will be done by your House and Government in behalf of heroic Poland and her unhappy sons Permit me also to suggest the propriety of private subscriptions which in this country have been of great assistance to them. One of the most urging measures to be obtained would be to relieve about —— thousand soldiers now detained in Prussian fortresses and victims of a most cruel treatment.

Be pleased to accept the respectful regards and sympathies of your sincere friend,

LAFAYETTE."

"*Paris, ce* 25 *Fevrier,* 1833.

"MONSIEUR LE PRÉSIDENT,

Le Comité National de l'Emigration Polonaise, considerant les services qu'a rendus à la cause Polonaise, l'Association qui travaille sons votre direction, en entretenant dans l'esprit public une vive et profonde sympathie pour la Pologne, m'a autorisé de vous envoyer, Monsieur le Président, son addresse aux Associations Polonaises en Angleterre, que vous aurez la bonté de communiquer aux Membres de votre Societé. Vous y trouverez un sentiment d'admiration et de reconnaissance qu'anime tous les cœurs Polonais, et l'espoir bien fondé que les brillans efforts des amis de la cause Polonaise en Angleterre, apporteront des fruits dignes de leur dévouement genereux et patriotique.

Agréez, Monsieur le President, l'assurance de la consideration distinguée, avec laquelle

J'ai l'honneur d'être,
votre très humble serviteur,
Le Président du Comité National de l'Emigration,
GENERAL DWERNICKY.

Rue Rivoli, Hotel de la Terrasse"

"*Paris, April 6th*, 1833.

"MY DEAR SIR,—I have been requested by my friend Mr. Sarran to give him a letter of introduction to you. He was one of the first on the Revolutionary breach of July, 1830. He remained in my national military family until I have resigned my command, not willing to stand a screen between the people and the new system of Louis Philipp. He has since published a book, on which it does not behove me to give an opinion, partial as it is to me, severe upon others. Mr. Sarran has been a distinguished officer, honourably wounded in the imperial wars He is a distinguished literary man and a distinguished friend of liberty. I am doubly gratified to procure him the pleasure of your acquaintance, and to find an opportunity to repeat that I have the honour to be,

Your sincere and obliged friend,
LAFAYETTE."

"*Paris*, 21 *Mars*, 1833.

"MONSIEUR LE PRÉSIDENT,

J'ai reçu votre lettre de 14 Décembre. J'y trouve des temoignages d'estime d'autant plus precieux pour moi qu'ils me sont donnés par des hommes qui ont fait leur preuves de patriotisme et de devouement pour la liberté. Je suis très honoré du choix que l'association Polonaise de Birmingham a bien voulu faire de moi pour m'associer a ses travaux. J'accepte cette affiliation avec reconnaissance, et je ferai tous mes efforts pour en accomplir les devoirs. Veuillez faire agréer à l'honorable association l'hommage de ma vive gratitude et de mon respect, et recevoir pour vous personellement l'expression bien franche de ma haute estime.

ODILON BARROT."

The Rev. Edward Carless, brother of Mrs. Thomas Attwood, died on the 21st March, 1833. "He was vicar of Wanaston, having read himself in on the Sunday preceding his death. He was on a visit to his patron, Sir William Pilkington, who afterwards spoke with great admiration of the various acquirements he had displayed during their conversation on the morning which was to be his last. What then must have been the shock which Sir William received on being informed by the servant whom he had sent to call his guest to dinner, that Mr. Carless was dead. He was educated at Wadham College, Oxford, where he took the degree of M.A., and on his marriage removed to Wolstanton, in Staffordshire, of which parish he continued curate for twenty years during which period he devoted himself ardently to the duties of his profession. He possessed an excellent and highly cultivated understanding, maintaining through life the highest character for integrity, virtue, and the most exalted Christian piety."

Mr. Carless was born on May 23rd, 1780, and married (August 1st, 1805) his first cousin, Anna Maria, daughter of the Rev. Mark Noble, M.A., F.S.A., Rector of Barming, who survived him till April 15th, 1861. Both he and his wife were buried at Wolstanton. He educated his four nephews and also Richard Spooner, son of the Member for North Warwickshire. He was a Tory and high churchman of the old school, and consequently strongly opposed to the radical proceedings of his brother-in-law. He possessed, for a man of moderate means, a fine library, of which his widow retained 3,000 volumes, a few of which are now in my possession.

To Mrs. Thomas Attwood, 13, Abingdon Street, Westminster.
Birmingham, 9th April, 1833.

. . . I found your mother very comfortable, and to-day I have seen her again, looking better than usual, and saying what a good night she has had, &c. My father and mother are both breaking up rapidly. All others are quite well. I quite approve of Marcus going to Ramsgate, and I think Algernon should go with him, and that he may be allowed to row. I shall return to you on Monday next, when I will fix with you the manner of sending them. If possible, I will go with them myself, and indeed I do not see why we should not all of us take a trip there, and return to London in two or three days.

(To the same, 22, Wellington Crescent, Ramsgate.)
Abingdon St., May 15, 1833.

. . . I shall go to Button Land on Friday and return about Wednesday or Friday. O'Connell will follow me.

(To the same from T. Aurelius Attwood.)
"Hawne House, May 14, 1833.

". . . I left Harborne last Friday, when your mother was pretty well, as was Mrs. Cresswell whilst she was at Grove House—she left, I think, on Wednesday for Mr. Chattock's.

My grandmother Attwood returned from West Bromwich some days ago, and is pretty well, but still very weak and lazy, and I am inclined to think that she is approaching her latter end.

I was at W. Bromwich on Sunday, where I met G. de B. A., who was pretty well, but still rather feeble and indolent, which is however (you will say) nothing very unusual or surprising. Mr. and Mrs. Mathews and the boy were well, and they begin to move their furniture to Corbyn's Hall next week.

I have no doubt you are looking forward with anxiety to the meeting next Monday. The Hales Owen Political Union is going to march in procession, as it did twelve months ago, as are the Dudley, Stourbridge, and Lye Waste Radicals, and the Worcester men are coming by canal. Some think that we shall have a larger meeting than ever—some that it will be a failure, but should it be a fine day, there will be no danger of that. Should we not kick the Ministers out, I really don't know what we must do. The Northern Political Union were to meet at the Guildhall, Newcastle, yesterday, in order to obtain Universal Suffrage! Annual Parliaments!! and vote by Ballot!!!—Poor Bosco, who is heartily sick of politics, says in his elegant phraseology, that he will 'cut his stick,' but I do not fancy he will be able. I think he will have to stand or fall with the people. For my own part, I think the prospects of poor England are now more gloomy and discouraging than they have been for a long time—much more so than when Boney threatened to invade her. It really looks now as if the Revolution would come to the door."

(*To the same from Thomas Attwood.*)

London, May 16, 1833.

To-morrow I go to Birmingham, where I have fixed for O'Connell to meet me. Lord ——— is under a cloud at present, but he assures me, and I hope correctly, that it will shortly disappear. Sir Wm. Brabazon says that he has only borrowed money at 10 p. cent. and that his political enemies have taken advantage of this little fact to trump up a conspiracy, &c. The landowners are all put about, and poverty, it is said, makes us acquainted with strange bedfellows. . . . I shall be sure to take proper care of No. 1, be you assured, and I doubt not that my great meeting will go off beautifully like all the others.

Birmingham, 18 *May,* 1833.

. . . I shall go to Hawn to-morrow and shall return to London, I expect, on Wednesday next. You may be assured that everything will be strictly quiet and orderly at our meeting. The meeting in London was clearly illegal, and was forbidden by the Secretary of State as such. . . .

I thought it better not to speak on Cobbett's motion against Peel on account of the general feeling of the House, but I could not refuse to vote for the motion without incurring a charge of subserviency or timidity to the Tory party, at the very moment when I am attacking the Whigs.

I find all our friends in distant towns have passed resolutions to join us on Monday, when we shall certainly present a grand and beautiful sight.

Birmingham, 20 *May*, 1833.

I have only a moment to say that everything has gone off well at our Meeting. I expect to be in London on Wednesday evening, and Bosco will come with me.

On May 10th, 1833, Thomas Attwood attended the King's levée at St. James's Palace, and was presented by Lord ———. The fact of his never having been presented before shows, in a striking manner, his contempt for the vanities of courts. Lord ——— was then under "a cloud," on account of circumstances just alluded to, and the Tory papers, of course, made the most of the fact and sneeringly inquired whether his lordship was the most respectable acquaintance whom Mr. Attwood could find to present him. The selection certainly does not appear to have been a happy one on his part.

The great meeting, to which allusion has already been made, for the purpose of petitioning the King to dismiss his Ministers, was held at Newhall Hill on Monday, May 20th, 1833. So far as mere members were concerned it was a wonderful success, and 20,000 more persons attended than even at the meeting of May 7th, 1832. The display of flags, banners, and bands was extraordinary, the unanimity and order of the proceedings were as striking as ever, and Attwood received, as usual, his more than royal reception from the people. Still I cannot help regarding this great assemblage of 200,000 men as a comparative failure. The more respectable classes, who had suddenly made so formidable an addition to the ranks of the Union in the previous year, appear to have been wanting, and the alliance of Attwood with O'Connell had evidently disgusted many Conservatives and Protestants. The opinion which some people formed of the meeting may be inferred from a coarse caricature in the *Argus*, wherein Attwood and O'Connell are represented as embracing each other whilst the devil is throwing his arms round both!

Mr. Muntz was called to the chair, and he, O'Connell, Attwood, Hadley, Edmonds, Fryer, and G. De B. Attwood, then secretary to the Union, were the principal speakers. In a long speech, Thomas Attwood acknowledged that he had been deceived in Earl Grey, and that he was now obliged to petition the King to dismiss the very man whom he had borne into the Royal councils on the shoulders of the people in the preceding year.

Cobbett, in his *Register* of May 25th, 1833, thus commented on the great Birmingham meeting :—

"This meeting was held on Monday last, and it appears to have consisted of more than a hundred thousand persons ; and the first thing to observe with regard to it is, that not the smallest disturbance arose, nothing indicating a riot, or riotous disposition, and that all passed off as quietly as if it had been the meeting of a religious congregation. No police, no breaking of heads, no sending of inoffensive people home with skulls cracked and arms broken. The object of the meeting was principally *to address the King to turn out his Ministers*. Such an address, coming from those very people who had put these Ministers in place, and kept them in place ; such an address, coming from such a quarter, would make an impression upon any body in the world, except a band of pelf-loving Whigs. Mr Thomas Attwood, who was the guide of this great mass of people upon this occasion, has more right to complain of these Ministers than any other man in the Kingdom · all along his conduct has been marked by the greatest degree of disinterestedness, and of every good quality of the heart : he has erred only in thinking and talking too well of these men, who have treated him with ingratitude, quite unexampled within my experience of the acts of mankind. They have not had the courage to hoot at him and bawl at him themselves ; but they have set their curs to bark at him, and to calumniate him in the vilest and most base and cowardly manner. If he were to pursue them in a manner much more bitter than that in which he does now pursue them, he would be fully excusable. However, the main thing to be considered is, where all this is to *end*. Mr. Attwood is the representative of ninety-nine hundredths of the people of England ; that is to say, the state of his mind with regard to these Ministers is a fair specimen of that of the minds of the whole of the people."

Notwithstanding the confident tone of these remarks the petition does not appear to have had any immediate effect, though it may very likely have contributed to bring about the downfall of the Whigs in the following year. Earl Fitzwilliam having declined presenting it to the King, it was determined to try Lord Melbourne, but I cannot ascertain whether it was ever actually presented or not. The petition to the Commons from the same meeting, against all restrictions on the importation of animal and vegetable food, was presented by Mr. Attwood ; as was one also from the Council of the Union against the conduct of the police at the late Coldbath Fields meeting.

Thomas Attwood does not appear to have been separated

from his family during the remainder of the year 1833, as no letters have been preserved, but I insert three more from the illustrious Lafayette :—

"*Paris, June* 16, 1833.

"MY DEAR SIR,—This letter will be delivered by a French gentleman of high merit. *M. Charles Combes, ingenieur des mines et professeur de mecanique et d'exploitation des mines à cette école Française*, is going to visit England for scientific purposes. Permit me to present him to you, and to entreat the services you can render him to forward his views. I wish I might give you satisfactory accounts of the system adopted by this government. What I think of it, I have had opportunities to proclaim. Yes, the sense of liberty is not by far extinct.

Most sincerely, your obliged friend,
LAFAYETTE."

"*La Grange, July 1st*, 1833.

"MY DEAR SIR,—Permit me to introduce to you a gentleman whose name is German, Mr. Meyer, but whose birth and whose heart are perfectly Italian. It is probable that was he still in his country he would be exposed to a share in the persecution which the patriots are now suffering. Duty to a late countryman of yours carries him to England. He has requested a line of presentation to you, and I give it with the greater pleasure as you will find in his conversation correct information on the present state of his fair, native, but unfortunate land. Be pleased to accept the best wishes and regards of your sincere friend,

LAFAYETTE.

Mr. Meyer is not a refugee, and can return home when he pleases. His country had hitherto been in a better situation than the rest of Italy, but it appears they are sharing the same fate."

"*La Grange, July* 14, 1833.

"Permit me, my dear Sir, to present to you, Mr. Theophile Zakrewski, who has been formally introduced to me by one of his most respectable countrymen. He is obliged to leave France, and I hope he will find some support on your side of the channel.

Most truly and affectionately yours,
LAFAYETTE."

In November, 1833, Cobbett moved that the King should be petitioned to dismiss Sir Robert Peel from his councils for his conduct in bringing in the Cash Payments Bill of 1819. The motion occasioned extraordinary excitement in the House, being regarded by the great majority of members as a personal insult offered to so respectable a statesman as Peel by a low Radical like Cobbett. Nevertheless, Thomas Attwood deemed it to be his duty to vote in the minority with only five other Radicals—Cobbett, Fielden, Patrick Lalor, James Roe, and John O'Connell—whilst 298 members voted against the motion. To show the feeling of the House it was immediately afterwards carried by 295 to 6, "that the proceedings on this resolution be *expunged from the minutes.*" Thomas Attwood does not seem to have taken this marked course without some qualms, for he had long known and most highly esteemed the first Sir Robert Peel, and although strongly opposed to the politics of his famous son, he always personally respected him.

The fourth annual meeting of the Union was held at Beardsworth's Repository on September 16th of this year. Mr. Muntz was called to the chair, and Mr. Attwood spoke at length. G. De B. Attwood, as hon. secretary, read the report and prefaced it by a speech.

The report, which was unanimously adopted, mingled expressions of gratification and regret. It pointed out the shortcomings of the Reform Bill and of the Whig Ministers, and asserted that, in order to remedy the evils under which the people were suffering, it was necessary to obtain triennial Parliaments, household suffrage, and, perhaps, vote by ballot. The report was signed by Thomas Attwood, his two elder sons, and many others.

In the *Pioneer or Trades Union Magazine* of October 5th, 1833, I find a letter addressed to "Thomas Attwood, Esq., M.P., the friend of the industrious classes," in which the writer begs him to guard carefully against any legislative interference with Trades Unions or combinations of workmen.

On the 12th of December, the anniversary of the first return of members for Birmingham, Messrs. Attwood and Scholefield were entertained at dinner by the electors of Deritend and Bordesley. Mr. W. G. Lewis and Mr. James Thornton were the Presidents, and Mr. Aaron and Mr. Ellis the Vice-Presidents. In returning thanks Thomas Attwood commented on the evil influences by which the King was surrounded, and stated that of the brilliant assemblage of 1,800 persons whom he had seen at court, none were competent to advise the sovereign as to the

T

real condition of the people. The speeches of both members generally went over the same ground that I have already treated of. At the conclusion the Chairman said he had another toast to propose, which would require but a short preface to insure it a hearty reception. They had four sons in the room, belonging to their two members. (*Loud cheers.*) More able and patriotic young men did not exist. Their whole course of life had been honourable to themselves and those who brought them up. They were noble scions of a noble stock. Without naming any of them, he should propose—" The four sons of their two members." (*Loud applause.*) Mr. De Bosco Attwood and Mr. C. Scholefield severally returned thanks. At half-past ten o'clock Messrs. Attwood and Scholefield retired amidst loud cheering.

On the next day the annual general meeting of the Birmingham Polish Association was held, Thomas Attwood in the chair.

During the course of this year Charles Attwood took an active part at Newcastle-on-Tyne in opposing the measures of the Whig Ministry. His conduct met with the unqualified approval of Cobbett, who has narrated his proceedings at length, with laudatory comments, in the *Register*. On the 29th of March he took a prominent part in a meeting held at the Guildhall, Newcastle, to consider the provisions of the Factory Bill. At the end of May a public meeting was held on the Town Moor to consider the conduct of His Majesty's Ministers, and Charles Attwood was called to the chair, Messrs. Doubleday, Fife, and Larkin taking part in the proceedings. Resolutions similar to those passed at the Birmingham meeting were unanimously agreed to, and a petition embodying them was entrusted for presentation to Thomas Attwood. On the 23rd of October a very amusing scene took place. The Whigs of Newcastle and its neighbourhood gave a grand dinner to Lord Durham for the purpose of congratulating him upon the success of the Whig administration. The Radicals determined to take the opportunity of presenting to him an address showing what they thought of the matter, and Charles Attwood was deputed to present it. In a courteous note, dated October 22nd, he informed Lord Durham of his intention and received an acknowledgment. Mr. Attwood, surrounded by his friends accordingly awaited the arrival of his lordship at Calvert's Half-Moon Inn, High Street, and, bowing politely, at once attempted to read the address. The Earl, however, without taking any notice, pushed past him, and what followed shall be narrated in the words of Cobbett :—

"Mr. Attwood now appealed to his friends to know how to act, when the cry of 'Follow, follow,' arose. Mr. Attwood and his friends were pushed onward, and found his lordship in an ante-room. Mr. Attwood here again addressed himself to his lordship, who strutted up to the former gentleman, and rearing himself as loftily as possible, throwing his body haughtily back, and casting his eyes on the ground, then raising them gradually up with a look of great disdain, pride, and contempt, said, 'Are you Mr. Attwood?' 'I am, my lord,' Mr. Attwood replied, and fixed his keen eye upon the Earl, which rather changed his manner and look. The Earl proceeded in a more subdued tone. 'Sir, I think I ought to have the choosing of the time and place for receiving an address. I do not think the present a proper time. I do not refuse your address, but at present there is no time. I did not deserve this from you, Sir.' Mr. Attwood said, 'My Lord, allow me to explain.' His lordship paced up and down the room, fuming, fretting, and agitated. His agent came and asked Mr. Attwood to go out—Mr. Attwood still attempting to speak. His lordship, still pacing up and down, at last called out, 'Mr. Brockett.' Sancho appeared at the call, and his lordship seizing his arm they rushed past Mr. Attwood and his party, and pushing through the crowd, gained the large room Mr. Attwood instantly appealed again to his friends, who cried 'Forward.' Mr. Attwood and a few friends gained the large room, where the dinner party was, and followed his lordship to the foot of the room. To describe the scene now would be impossible. . . . Mr Attwood and his friends left the street immediately, and also the bands of music. The people, however, would not leave for some time, which detained the dinner party. The calling in of the Scots Greys and the reading of the Riot Act were severally discussed. To each dish of puddings, soups, tarts, game, &c., two of the dinner party acted as guards across the street, and the people assembled amused themselves by knocking the luxuries out of their hands, which greatly tended to lessen the splendour and plenty of the repast, whilst they passed their jibes and jokes on the 'guinea collops,' 'guinea men,' 'guinea fowls,' and 'guinea-pigs.'

The Earl was escorted across by a body guard of between twenty and thirty of the party to the dinner-room, amidst shouts of derision and disapprobation."

CHAPTER XVII.

Last letters from Lafayette—Grand Dinner to Attwood and Scholefield on September 15th, 1834—Attwood's speech—Death of Mrs. Ann Attwood—Letters—Address to Electors—Election of 1835—Attwood and Scholefield returned by immense majorities—Last letter from Cobbett—Correspondence to close of 1835.

THE materials which I have been able to collect for narrating the public proceedings of Mr. Attwood during the year 1834 are somewhat scanty, but fortunately his political actions are sufficiently referred to in a speech delivered by him in the autumn of that year, from which I shall presently make some extracts. In March he voted in the minority of fifty-nine, with Cobbett, upon the motion of the latter for the abolition of the malt tax, and spoke at considerable length upon the occasion, and in June he again strongly supported, in his opposition to the Poor Law Bill, the member for Oldham, who, upon this subject, had also the support of his brother Matthias. Three letters only have been preserved for the early part of this year, which run as follows:—

"*War Office, 6th Jany.*, 1834.
"*Private.*

MY DEAR SIR,—All I can say, in answer to your letters, is that they are invariably sent to the proper quarter, and, I hope, produce a proper effect. We do not disagree much in the main question in them. However, we can talk over this when we meet.
Always yours faithfully,
EDW. ELLICE."

"*Paris, January 14th*, 1834.

"MY DEAR SIR,—I am requested to give a letter of recommendation to a very interesting young Pole, Lieutenant Frederic Fischer, who is going to London with the hope to find some employment. I am sure that if you can assist him to the success of his pursuit you will do it with pleasure, and beg you to receive the high regard of
Your sincere friend,
LAFAYETTE."

"*Paris, February 22nd,* 1834.

"MY DEAR SIR,—I have been happy to hear that your name is one of the Committee who have taken under the protection of British philanthropy the fate of the Polish soldiers sent from Prussia to the other side of the Atlantic. A hundred and fifty are fortunately stopped at Havre. We shall take care of them, but the remainder will, I trust, be taken care of by English patriots. I hasten to dictate these lines from my bed, where I am still kept by an indisposition, and beg you to accept the best regards of

Your sincere friend,
LAFAYETTE."

This seems to have been the last letter which Thomas Attwood received from the great Lafayette, who died on the 20th May following, aged seventy-five.

Earl Grey resigned in July, and a period of political confusion and uncertainty followed, which is frequently alluded to in Mr. Attwood's correspondence.

In September the Liberals of Birmingham determined to show their appreciation of the conduct of Messrs. Attwood and Scholefield by inviting them to a grand dinner, which was accordingly given on the 15th of the month at Beardsworth's Repository, and seems to have been an extraordinary success. Nearly 3,000 tickets were sold, and the number might have been doubled had the accommodation permitted. Galleries were fitted up for 1,000 ladies, and from 4,000 to 5,000 persons were present within the building. W. Medley of Iver, George Attwood, and T. Aurelius Attwood were present on the platform, with many others. The then attitude of the Church of England was significantly shown by the fact that grace was said by a Catholic priest. The report says:

"There were twenty-three tables in the body of this immense building, and an entire double range in the south gallery, being in the whole nearly eight hundred yards of tabling, which was covered with a profusion of solid food, consisting of beef, roasted pigs, tongues, veal and ham, bread, cheese, &c.; and ale in the proportion of one bottle to each man."

After the usual toasts, Mr. Joshua Scholefield, by desire of his colleague, addressed the assembly, and Thomas Attwood then rose and was received with enthusiastic cheering. He said:

My dear friends and fellow-townsmen,—I thank you from the bottom of my heart for this renewed testimony of your confidence and esteem. I come from Parliament among you with much pleasure, but I cannot say that I bring with me the information which a reformed Parliament ought to have enabled me to give. The last time I had the honour to meet you here at dinner, four years ago, the Duke of Wellington was then in power; we met in celebration of the glorious French Revolution, and I then said to you, 'Show me twenty such dinners as these, and I will show you the governors of England.' We have not been able to exhibit twenty such dinners, but nevertheless we have been able to make exhibitions, originating in the spontaneous patriotism of the English people, which have had the effect of shaking the late oppressors of their country from their unhallowed seats. I think I do no more than justice to you, as men of Birmingham, when I say that you were mainly instrumental in creating the general demand for Reform among the people of England, and when that Reform was endangered it was you that placed yourselves at the head of the public mind, and, speaking the voice of the nation, commanded its success. (*Cheers.*) I will not congratulate you too much on the Bill of Reform, because I know it has disappointed your expectations and mine. (*Loud cheers.*) It has given us a House of Commons but little better, I am sorry to acknowledge, than the old concern. Some few good men it is most true there are in Parliament, but it is with deep and bitter regret that I acknowledge that the majorities have generally been as servile and selfish as in former Houses. (*Hear, hear.*) When I entered Parliament I expected to meet bands of patriots animated with the same interests as the people, feeling for their wrongs and oppressions, and determined to redress and relieve them. I almost regretted that I had had a hand in the Reform when I saw troops of sycophants and time-servers, who seemed only anxious to regard their own selfish interests, and to destroy the very system of liberty and Reform from which they themselves had drawn their existence. (*Shame, shame*) These gentlemen, you may well believe, were not very partial to me; they looked upon me in the same light as a cow looks upon another cow's calf—as a stranger out of my place—a mere Birmingham tradesman, very disagreeable in their eyes. You must not be surprised that I received this kind of treatment. The House of Commons is divided into two great parties, the Whig and the Tory. To the former I had been mainly instrumental in assisting to do a favour too great for proud men ever to acknowledge; and to the latter I had been instrumental in assisting to do an injury which *interested* men could never forgive. (*Hear, hear, and laughter.*)

Mr. Attwood then narrated at length his opposition to the Irish Coercion Bill, and the "atrocious" Poor Law Bill for England He then said:

For four days in one week I was present in the House of Commons, with slight intermissions for food, from 11 o'clock in the morning until 3 o'clock the next morning. I could not leave my post for a moment without the danger of being absent in some great division affecting the liberty and welfare of the people. (*Loud cheers, and cries of "Hear, hear."*) It is certain the House of Commons is not what it ought to be: one half consists of lawyers, Jews of 'Change Alley, and monks of Oxford—(*laughter*),—the other half consists of lords and country gentlemen, too rich and too far removed from the wants and interests of the mass of the people to have any clear views respecting them, or any common feeling with them. . . . We ought to have household suffrage, triennial Parliaments, wages of attendance for representatives, and vote by ballot.

Mr. Attwood then proceeded to state his abhorrence of impressment, flogging in the army, the new police, and all centralisation. He called attention to the impossibility of getting the House to listen to his Currency views, and then said:

I must now close with a few words respecting myself. You all know that I entered Parliament with reluctance, I had studied the situation of the country for twenty years—I had foreseen and foretold every fluctuation of national prosperity or adversity which had occurred during that period; and I thought it my duty to obey your orders, and have done everything in my power, without fear or affection, favour or reward, during two years. I have incessantly dinned the truth into the ears of the House of Commons, and in my conscience I believe that three-fourths of that House, if the truth could be known, entertain opinions very nearly analogous to my own upon the great question of the national prosperity and adversity. (*Cheers.*) In the meanwhile I have incurred much expense and much injury from the loss of time, and I think I should do wrong if I did not inform you that I entertain serious thoughts of resigning the situation which I hold. (*Loud cries of " No, no."*)

Mr. Attwood concluded amidst loud and long-continued applause, and the band struck up an entirely new piece, composed for the occasion by the leader, entitled "Attwood's March." After some further proceedings the large company quietly dispersed.

Ann, the mother of Thomas Attwood, died at Hawne House on the 28th of October, 1834, in the eighty-third year of her age, and was buried in the Attwood vault at Hales Owen Church on the 7th November.

I now give some extracts from Mr. Attwood's letters for the remainder of this year:—

(*Thomas to Edward Attwood*)
Birmingham, 6 *Octr* , 1834.

MY DEAR EDWARD,—I do not think that my mother can possibly last many weeks, if she does days. Her appetite is now gone, and she has recovered greatly the use of her faculties, which I think a bad sign My father is broken down, as you may suppose, but I hope he may last a few months longer, unless his old complaint should attack him. All the rest of us are well, but of course entering rapidly into the vale of years. I am 51 to-day. James is not much altered in the last 14 years. His daughter is a sweet girl, and I much doubt if ever I saw one more beautiful.

I am quite tired with politics, but I think yet to make a grand out-of-door assault upon Peel's Bill, in which case I shall confine my operations to what are called, *par excellence*, "respectable men," and shall shut out all *politics*. I hope you got an account of our dinner I generally send you these things, but sometimes both I and George may possibly forget to do so. If ever you can pick me up a tale of misery, injustice, and ruin, I shall be glad. I am like Mrs. Radcliffe, always looking out for horrors, and a pretty lot of them I have collected. Pray give my respects and kind wishes to your wife, and believe me,

Your ever affectionate brother,
T. ATTWOOD.

Mrs. Thos. Attwood, Birmingham.

London, Nov. 4, 1834.

I hope to be with you to-morrow by the Safety Tally Ho, and shall probably bring Marcus and Algernon with me. . . . I find myself very much occupied, and I believe I must return to London in a day or two after the funeral. I have not been able to call upon Mr. Medley.

London, Nov. 5, 1834.

. . . I shall go to Birmingham by one of the day coaches to-morrow. Algernon will go with his uncle and Wolverley. He has some new black clothes with him. I forgot to say that Mr. Wakefield's letter informs me that Miss Wakefield is very ill. I have been so much occupied with John A.'s affairs that I have scarce had a moment's leisure. When I return to you I must come back to London in a few days. By ignorance, neglect, and crime, on the part of his advisers, his affairs have become very complicated and difficult, but I fully rely upon the practicability of restoring them. There has never been the shade of a misrepresentation, and yet the judgment has been given against him! So much for Courts of Equity, which are in fact mere courts of trickery, chicanery, and robbery and murder.

"*T. Attwood, Esq., M.P., Birmingham.*

Warwick Castle, Novr. 10th, 1834.

SIR,—Some short time since you did me the favour to forward me your speech in Parliament printed—which I put by intending to read with attention, and to have returned you my thanks for the same—since which I have been touring during the autumn and have mislaid the speech—it may be in my house in town. But should you have any copies by you and would forward me one here I shall feel obliged.

I remain, Sir, your obt. Hle. St.,
WARWICK."

(*G. De B. Attwood, Birmingham, from T. Attwood*)

Nov. 14th, 1832.

. . . I am sorry to say that old Mr. Wakefield tells me there is no hope of his niece. She is gone to Southsea with Lady Charlotte Bacon in a state of nervous debility of extreme character. Pray write a note for me to old Mr. Boultbee, saying that I have mislaid my tickets for the Philosophical

Society, but that you are authorised to write to Mr. Haycock in my name, requesting him to admit Mr. Boultbee and his daughter.

To Mrs. Thomas Attwood, Birmingham.
London, 15 *Novr.,* 1834.

. . . The Duke of Wellington is said to be forming a new Ministry. People think it will be a medley, and that Brougham will contrive to be one of them. I am concerned to hear so bad an account of your dear and good mother. Tell the young ladies that I have seen Mr. Medley, and that he is quite well. I shall dine with him to-morrow, and Algernon will dine with John A.

London, 19 *Novr.,* 1834.

. . . I am much concerned but not surprised to hear of the attack of your dear mother. She cannot last much longer, I fear, but it is gratifying to know that the pain has left her. Pray remember me to her very kindly, and renew to her the expression of my deep and sincere gratitude for the long and uninterrupted kindness and affection which I have always experienced from her. I pray God to bless her last moments, and to grant her eternal happiness in Paradise. You must not think me unkind, my Dear, in not writing oftener. The truth is that I am constantly occupied, and generally in lawyers' offices and other places where I cannot attend to anything but the subject in hand. I have dined twice with Mr. Medley, and have seen him to-day. Mr. Dudley Fereday left London a few days ago for Bilston, and Mr. Medley says he expects when Mr. D. F. returns to London he will bring our two friends at Harborne with him. I have no news to tell. I do not purpose to interfere at all in the matter of the Duke and the Whigs. The latter, I perceive, are very low, and they seem to want me to do something for them But I remind them that the King, in turning them out, has *merely complied with my petition presented to him last year.* Lord Wharncliffe is said to have been at the bottom of the change. I expect the Duke will succeed in forming a Ministry, and perhaps his very unpopularity may induce him to act liberally and kindly by the country, as affording him the only chance of keeping his place. . . .

27, *Gracechurch St., Nov.* 21, 1834.

. . . Mr. D. Wakefield gives me no hope of the recovery of his niece. I have sent your letter to Mr. E. G. Wakefield. . . . I think the Duke will succeed in forming a Ministry. Lady Jersey gives out that he will certainly rectify the Currency.

London, Nov. 24, 1834.

. . . It gives me much concern to hear of the state of your dear and good mother You must certainly be prepared for the worst, which, I doubt not, under the mercy of God, will to her be the best. I would come down for the purpose of assisting you at this anxious period, but I am compelled to stay here at present by imperative circumstances I have taken no part whatever in politics, nor do I mean to do so. I might make a great movement and perhaps force in Lord Durham, but it must be attended with danger and injury, and possibly with no good to the country. Certainly, if necessary, I shall act upon Charles's advice; but I do not mean to act at all, and therefore you may be quite easy upon this head.

London, Nov. 24, 1834.

. . . I am glad that your kind relations from Barlaston and Northampton are arrived. Algernon is very well and happy and busy. I do not purpose to trouble myself in the matter between the Duke and Durham, unless, as Charles says, I have the latter first in black and white. I have been deceived once, but I shall not be so again. . . . It is said that we shall have a dissolution immediately that Peel arrives. This is doubtful. I have reason to think that my speech at Beardsworth's has had something to do in breaking up the late concern. Give my love to Edward Freeman, and congratulate him on the dismissal of the false, perjured, and cruel Whigs.

London, Novr. 25th.

. . . I find the Whig Ministers have been setting on their retainers throughout the country, and I daresay we shall have a dissolution and a trial of strength. The Duke only counts upon 140 members in the present House, and in my opinion he will not count upon many more in the new House, unless he takes a large, liberal, and just ground of policy. I am pestered with letters from all parts of the country, but I do not answer many of them.

London, Novr. 27th.

. . . I could not come down to the meeting (which, by the bye, hardly includes me in its call), but I have written a letter to my constituents and sent it to Edmonds to read to the meeting, and to publish in the *Journal*. This letter, I doubt not, will please you.

London, Novr. 28th, 1834.

I shall probably come home to you on Sunday by the Safety Tally Ho. I doubt not that my letter to my constituents will have given them satisfaction to-day. You know that I have always acted on the principle of public good, without regarding my own interest. If I had been willing to sell my country, I could have done so much to my interest, but I have never considered interest if it is to be bought by a sacrifice of principle and duty. It is much to be doubted whether the Duke and Peel will be able to form any kind of Administration. In this case Lord Durham will come in. I expect, however, that the Duke will contrive to get on, either with or without Peel, and in this case we shall have a speedy dissolution. I have left this question open, whether to act again as a member or not. It requires much consideration and the watching of times and circumstances.

Towards the end of 1834 both parties commenced to make preparations in view of the impending dissolution. The Conservatives of Birmingham met at Dee's Royal Hotel on December 17th, and founded the "Birmingham Loyal and Constitutional Association," in opposition to the Political Union. Theodore Price, Esq., a gentleman of great local influence, and first cousin to William Carless of Harborne, was in the chair. The Earl of Dartmouth was chosen President of the new Association, and the Vice-Presidents were the Earl of Bradford, Lord Calthorpe, the Hon. F. Calthorpe, W. P. Dugdale, M.P., and Mr. Gough. Mr. R Spooner was appointed Chairman, and it was unanimously resolved to request him to contest the borough against the sitting members. Nothing could show more clearly the extraordinary confidence which the people of Birmingham then reposed in the firm of Attwood & Spooner, and nothing could make one feel more regret at the present day that the failure of 1865 should ever have been permitted to take place, than the fact that the only person whom the Tories could venture to bring forward in opposition to Thomas Attwood, with the slightest prospect of success, was—his own partner! Mr. Spooner acceded to the requisition, and funds for the approaching contest were lavishly subscribed by his aristocratic supporters. The election excited great interest, not only in Birmingham, but throughout the country, and Cobbett, in his *Register*, very fully narrated the proceedings. On the 19th December Mr. Attwood issued his address as follows :—

GENTLEMEN,—Mr. Richard Spooner, seduced by a knot of Tories, has thought proper to offer you his services.

It is singular that these gentlemen, in their repugnance to me and my political conduct, should be so pressed for an advocate of their principles, that, after tendering the honor of their support in many quarters, they should at last be compelled to have recourse to my own partner and intimate friend.

This clique of Tories had no hand in making the Reform. Through our labours they have obtained "a share in the commonwealth." A little more modesty or gratitude in the use of it might perhaps have become them.

In the year 1832 similar manœuvres were at work, but they were baffled by your firmness and patriotism. A large and liberal party in this town were then combined with the Tories against us, and yet they could not produce more than 600 votes to tender to Mr. Horsley Palmer, a liberal Tory, of the Canning school, a man of great commercial rank and experience, and of much political knowledge. That party have now thrown their weight into *our* scale. What then can the Tories expect ! You, gentlemen, will quickly teach them their true position; and my worthy friend, Mr. Spooner, estimable as I know him to be in many points, will, I doubt not, as quickly discover that his High Church notions and Tory politics are out of date, and that, however prevalent they may be at Oxford and Cambridge, they are not suited to the meridian of Birmingham. They are just forty-three years too late.

Gentlemen,—*I will not desert you on this occasion, I will give you all an opportunity of expressing your opinions;* and if those opinions should be against my political conduct, I shall regret it only as a symptom of the decay of principle and public spirit in the nation.

My friends! *this little fight is yours.* We, the men of Birmingham, mainly assisted in making the Reform. If gentlemen who are the enemies of Reform can beat us now in our own camp, we shall merit and receive the contempt of our country. I am, gentlemen,

Your faithful Representative,
THOMAS ATTWOOD.

The nomination took place on January 7th, amidst a scene of indescribable excitement, and seems to have been the first occasion upon which the present Birmingham Town Hall was used for an important public meeting. The High Bailiff, Mr. Paul Moon James, having congratulated the electors upon their meeting upon such an occasion for the first time in the history of the town, called upon any elector to nominate a candidate to represent the borough in Parliament. Mr. Benjamin Hadley, amidst loud cheers, proposed Thomas Attwood, and in the course of his speech made the following remarks:—

"It should never be forgotten by Birmingham men, that Mr. Attwood established the Political Union on the 25th of January, 1830—at a time, be it remembered, when that heartless and profligate Monarch George IV. sat on the throne of these realms, and that unrelenting despot the Duke of Wellington was Prime Minister of England. (*Cheers.*) It required no common courage at that time for a man in his station to show himself in the front of the battle which was to be fought for the liberties of his countrymen, at a time, too, when not only Europe generally, but England in particular, was sunk into a state of mental bondage and apathy to which there appeared no prospect of a termination. A man of less nerve and foresight would have shrunk from so arduous a task, and nothing but his undaunted spirit, and his unconquerable love of freedom, could have upheld him in those times of difficulty and danger. But, gentlemen, he *was* upheld in spite of the sneers of friends and the hatred of enemies, thanks to his own firm heart and the patriotic spirit of the people of Birmingham; and not only did he succeed in rolling up in this town the most formidable engine of political power that ever existed in the world, but he had the satisfaction of seeing established, in every considerable town throughout Great Britain, similar associations for the peaceful redress of our common grievances. (*Loud cheers.*) The truth of the principles which he held, and the righteousness of the cause which he espoused, became all but universal; and not only Great Britain caught the patriotic flame, but all Europe felt and acknowledged the blow which he had struck against despots and despotism." (*Cheers.*)

Mr. George Edmonds seconded the nomination of Thomas Attwood amidst tremendous cheering, after which Mr. W. Phipson proposed and Mr. Muntz seconded Mr. Joshua Scholefield. Mr. Richard Spooner was then, in the midst of groans, hisses, and confusion, proposed by Mr. James Taylor, and seconded by Mr. John Simcox. Mr. Attwood next presented himself, and was received with an extraordinary expression of public approbation. After a long speech, in the course of which he called Sir Robert Peel "the scourge of God, a name first given to the barbarian Attila," he sat down amidst loud, long, and continued cheering. Mr. Scholefield and Mr. Spooner then addressed the electors, the former amidst great applause, and the latter amongst hooting, hisses, and confusion. Whilst Mr. Spooner was speaking the front gallery gave way, and great consternation ensued; but such was the excitement that the building was immediately filled again after the wounded persons had been removed to the hospital. The scene at the show of hands is said to have been very striking. The hall was packed with more than 7,000 persons, and when a forest of arms were held up for Attwood and Scholefield, many were bare to the shoulder, coat and shirt sleeves having been torn off by the excessive pressure. On Friday, the 9th of January, the polling commenced at eight different parts of the town, and was kept up with spirit during the day. It was evident from the first that the Tories had no chance, but they determined to poll their last man, and, as a start, polled their committee without being able to gain the ascendancy for a minute. At the close of the day the numbers stood as follows:—

Attwood	1,295
Scholefield	1,268
Spooner	658

After the announcement Messrs. Attwood and Scholefield addressed at least 5,000 persons from the portico of Radenhurst's Hotel, and congratulated them on the prospects of the Liberals. The polling was resumed on Saturday, but without the slightest hope of success for the Tories. The numbers as first announced were:—

Attwood	...	...	...	1,729
Scholefield	...	...	1,664
Spooner	...	...	...	907

The announcement was received with tremendous shouts, and Messrs. Attwood and Scholefield again addressed their supporters at Radenhurst's Hotel. In the course of his speech Mr. Attwood made the following remarks :—

> The man did not live who could say that his vote had been either directly or indirectly bought by him or his friend (*Cheers.*)
> With regard to his friend Mr Spooner, whom, he must say, he respected, he regretted that he should have suffered himself to be seduced by a knot of Tories. He regretted that he had not courage to resist their solicitations. He had spent a long and honourable life, and he (Mr. A.) now lamented that his friend had tarnished it. (*Hear, hear.*) He regretted much the conduct which he had pursued. He (Mr. A.) advised him against it, but he persisted, and the consequence was he was now humbled and mortified, and he must say he could not but rejoice in his humiliation. . . .
> One remark more. He was determined not to be chaired : he could not fall in with the old practices of the Tory oligarchy. The honour consisted in being really and honourably elected by the people, and not in being dragged about the streets like a puppet show. He consented on the last occasion to be chaired because he was willing to afford the people every possible opportunity of celebrating the great triumph which they had achieved in carrying the Reform Bill. The Tories, who were the public robbers of the people, had introduced the system of chairing : it was one of their tricks to render the expenses of electioneering so heavy that no man unless possessed of great property could contend against them. Another of their plans was canvassing by well paid lawyers, not such as had been engaged in the present election—(*cheers*)—and then followed treating in public houses, wearing of ribbons, and all other means of expense. What a contrast the expense of his victory and that of his colleague exhibited to that of the Tory candidates wherever they succeeded in getting returned. There was a population of 150,000 in Birmingham, and a constituency of between 3,000 and 4,000, and yet the whole expense would not amount to more than £200. (*Loud and continued cheering*)

On Monday morning the High and Low Bailiffs attended at the Town Hall, for the purpose of announcing the final state of the poll. The doors were opened at ten o'clock, and in a short time the entire of the hall was as full as on the day of nomination. About eleven, Messrs. Attwood and Scholefield arrived, upon which a tremendous burst of applause resounded from all parts, and the High Bailiff soon after officially declared the state of the poll to be as follows:—

Attwood	1,718
Scholefield	1,660
Spooner	915

The successful candidates returned their thanks in long speeches amidst the greatest enthusiasm, and thus terminated the first contested election which Birmingham ever witnessed.

At this general election Matthias Attwood was returned for Whitehaven without opposition. His son Wolverley also made his first essay in the political arena, in which he would doubtless have distinguished himself had his health equalled his talents, by contesting unsuccessfully the borough of Greenwich in the Conservative interest. The numbers were:—

John Angerstein, L.	1,826
Edward Geo. Barnard, L.	1,102
M. Wolverley Attwood, C.	1,063

It was either during the progress of this election in Birmingham, or of the subsequent one of 1837, that the Tories published a funny caricature representing G. F. Muntz as a huge and shaggy bear, with Thomas Attwood as his showman. In the background the Dissenters are endeavouring to destroy St. Philip's Church, and at the side is a chest labelled "Brass buttons without shanks for the new currency."

Here is the last letter which Thomas Attwood received from the famous, or, as his enemies would have said, notorious, Cobbett, with whom he had been so long associated either as friend or foe, and who has devoted so much space in his *Register* to the political actions of the Attwoods:—

"*Wolseley*, 15 *January*, 1835.

"MY DEAR SIR,

1. I leave this place on Tuesday morning next to go to Birmingham. I shall go to the Swan.

2. I wish very much to see you, and Mr. Scholefield also, if possible, in order that I may communicate with you, in the freest possible manner, my opinions, and my intentions, as to public matters.

3. I have written to Wm. Martin to meet me at the Swan; and I shall possibly stay a couple of days at his farm at King's Norton.

4. I have requested Mr. Oldfield to send you a copy of my *Legacy to Labourers;* and, as it will not cost you above three hours to read it, I request you to do me the honour to read it between this and Tuesday next; and

I remain,
Your most faithful and obedient servant,
WM. COBBETT.

P.S.—We drank your healths at Oldham with great glee."

Mrs. Thomas Attwood, Bank, Birmingham.

London, Jany 28th, 1835.

I am concerned to learn by your letter of to-day that you are so unwell. If you continue so, pray send for Mr. Hodgson or John Ledsam, or go to the former with my dear Sarah Eliza.

I think with you that probably we had better accept Mrs. Latty's offer, but there is no hurry. If you should decide to come and live in London permanently, I expect you would be pleased with the house which I looked over yesterday.

I have seen no politicians, but I shall dine with Medley on Friday. John Attwood's affairs look now very well, and I expect they will detain me here until about the 10th or 12th Feby.

London, Jany 31, 1835.

. . . I will come down in a day or two if I do not hear that you are better. But I expect a great point in John A.'s case will come on about the 6th or 8th Feby., and I must try to be back again by that time. This morning I saw Marcus safe on board the Eclipse steamer on his route to Ramsgate.

London, Feby. 5th, 1835.

. . . I am glad to receive Angela's letter this morning informing me that she and Rosabel are safely landed with you. . . . On Monday, the 16th, I have engaged to dine with our good friends the politicians of Deritend. I am in hopes of being able to make an arrangement which will be satisfactory to Bosco. If not, I think he should join his uncle Charles, in which object I doubt not that Medley could assist him. . . . I have engaged to dine with the Medleys on the 12th inst., if my law affairs will permit, in order to meet Dr. and Mrs. Spurgin. You have heard, I daresay, that Sir C. Wetherell is about to be made a Peer and Speaker of the House of Lords. This is greatly in John A.'s favour. On the 12th inst. we have some important measures of his coming on before Scarlett, who shews himself just and impartial. I believe we shall certainly succeed in getting Abercrombie made Speaker of the Lower House.

London, 6 *Feby,* 1835.

. . . I think that Bosco should consult Hodgson or Ledsam. If he has a cold, he should have a fire in his bedroom, and spend a day or two, or thereabouts, in bed, and if he has no cold he should take a little ginger and rhubarb and drink three glasses of port wine in the day, and some good ale. If he has a little low fever, the doctor would probably give him a dose or two of James's powder, which may be right, but I think a little medicine with port wine and ale will quickly set him right. All this debility is either fever or indigestion, or both, and it should not be neglected, or it may lead to the same complaint as Benjamin had, who, you will recollect, was primarily low and weak and ill all the summer. I shall leave the affair of our residence here to you, only I must insist on its being moderate and cheap.

London, 10 *Feby.,* 1835.

. . . Scarlett heard a part of John A.'s cause to-day, but postponed giving judgment until a future day.

Hawne, May 20*th,* 1835.

My father is, I think, a little better to-day, but in a very dubious state. I should think it not correct that Ministers contemplate a dissolution.

Mrs. Attwood, 13, *Abingdon Street, London.*

Birmingham, 14*th August,* 1835.

Yesterday we placed our poor old friend my aunt in her place of long rest John and his sisters were much distressed. The latter did not attend the funeral. We left a place for my father by the side of my mother, and close to my grandfather. Very peacefully they sleep. No discord, but a silent and dread concord prevails there. Certainly we ought so to live as to be always ready when our hour comes. I think, also, that we ought in life to rest as peacefully by each other's side as we do in the grave. This has always been my study, and if I have not succeeded with others, I have at least succeeded with you and my own family. Your dear mother I saw yesterday and to-day. She sits up and spins, and seems better than I have seen her for many years. My father also is quite well. Aurelius and myself equally so. . . . I am very anxious about my dear Angela. The step she thinks of is very important. Pray consult with her You know my wishes, which are solely for her happiness, and whether that is promoted by her continuing in her present state, or by marriage, is much the same to me I should not like her to go to Australia, and I take it for granted that Mr. Wakefield will not go. With his talents and connection, I hope he may do well in England.

Hales Owen, 16 *August,* 1835.

. . . I have decided to go London on Tuesday night, and therefore I hope to be with you by 8 or 9 o'clock on Wednesday morning, in time for me to attend the meeting at Fendall's by 11 o'clock. I have not failed to see your dear mother this morning. She is in good health and spirits. The dogs also are well—Dash and Beau and Zephyr, and a tribe of Gad and Naphtali whose names are to me unknown. The flowers are beautiful We hold our meeting on Tuesday, and we consider nothing but the Corporation Bill. I do not take quite so gloomy a view as you and Mr. Wakefield take. I daresay the Lords will not venture to do much damage. We have got a hook in the nose of Leviathan, as you know I always promised, and let him kick and struggle as he please, he cannot escape the righteous judgment which approaches. I have come over here and attended church this morning. You know I was always seriously disposed, and although in my youth the black eyes and blue eyes might sometimes call off my attention, yet now, in the autumn of my years, I find all these tender fascinations gone, and I am left to indulge at leisure in the deep and solemn sentiments which the death of friends, and churches and churchyards, and the bones of a thousand winters are calculated to inspire. I begin to think that I could form a prayer, and adapt words and sentiments, which the creature might humbly and awfully address to the Creator. This is the sublimest effort of man's mind. I always shrink from the attempt. I was disgusted when I was at the funeral, at again seeing the church doors closed against the poor, and I was more disgusted at the use of the whip of the beadle upon the backs of the little children. If ever you survive me, let nothing of the kind be done. I should much prefer being carried naked in the arms of the poor, with no other mourners around me but ragged and barefooted children, reading a lesson of mortality and humanity over my grave. Very fine and sentimental this, you will say. But I am sure you will agree with me in opinion, that youth and age, riches and poverty, should lose their distinctions in death.

Angela, elder daughter of Thomas Attwood, was married to Daniel Bell Wakefield, Barrister, at St. Margaret's, Westminster, on September 1st, 1835.

(*Mrs. Thos. Attwood from James Henry Attwood.*)
"*Hawne House, Sept* 10*th*, 1835.

"MY DEAR ELIZA,—Although rather late, I am not the less sincere, in offering you my cordial congratulations on the marriage of dear Angela to Mr. Daniel Wakefield. I most heartily wish her all the felicity she so well deserves, and of which, from the short acquaintance I have had with Mr. Wakefield, I think she has a well-founded prospect. The Mathewses, after christening little Benny at Hales Owen Church on Monday, proceeded on Tuesday morning on their journey to London and Hastings, intending to sleep on Tuesday night at St. Albans, but the weather has been so bad that I doubt if they have yet reached London. . . . My sister Mary Ann talks of going to Hastings in about a week, but as I hear Miss Phipson cannot accompany her, I rather doubt if she will put her project into execution. . . ."

"*Thomas Attwood, Esq., M.P.*
House of Lords, Decr. 15*th*, 1834.

"SIR,—I have read your letter and the accompanying paper with the attention that whatever comes from you on the subject of the Currency requires. I am convinced that you must either raise the prices to the Currency or lower the Currency to the prices. I do not know *yet*, for until lately I have not had time to consider the subject, which course is the best. I incline to think that both should be attempted, that the Currency should be lowered and the prices raised, so that both may meet at that point which will enable the debtor to pay, deranging as little as possible the spirit of the contract with the creditor. I am sorry that enquiry was not granted to some extent. I desire those who thought my motion unsuitable, to propose some other remedy. No, not the answer, 'We cannot go as far as you propose, and therefore we will do nothing.' I shall devote my mind to this subject, and shall feel much obliged to you if you will give me any of your valuable information.

I have the honour to be,
very faithfully yours,
WYNFORD."

"*Hawne*, 14 *April*, 1835.

"DEAR TOM,—You cannot be insensible to what is going on in this division of the country, and you ought to have some ideas of what may be the results of it. You may easily conceive in what way my own mineral property may thereby be ultimately affected, and you are likely enough to have many applications to promote the interests of others which may be found injurious to my own. I wish therefore to give you my sentiments and to put you and your brother (to whom I have not written) on your guard, and in the first place to enquire how things now doing are likely to answer, my own opinion being decidedly against the new projects now going on. I think that they, or most of them, cannot be supported, and to let them alone will be your best policy. The Joint Stocks must be found insufficient, neither, in my judgment, can the Bank of England, if willing (a thing unlikely), support them. Let them alone and no longer interfere either with Joint Stocks or Railroad Shares. Things as they are cannot be carried on, I conceive. Matthias, if it be true, is joining a nest of new-fangled squires and the like in an extensive plate glass and window glass concern of great extent in this part of the country, and, if he does, I will not be a shareholder therein, nor will I pay the piper. Let every tub stand on its own bottom. Nothing in my family ought to be taken up against the interests of poor Charles. I wish to hear how his health goes on. They ought not to forget he is my son.

Your affectionate Father,
M. ATTWOOD."

I have not been able to obtain much information respecting the political proceedings of Charles Attwood during the years 1834 and 1835, but on the 7th August, 1834, he addressed to the *Newcastle Press* a trenchant letter in opposition to the Poor Law, which was reprinted, with approving comments, by Cobbett in his *Register* of the 16th.

George De Bosco, eldest son of Thomas Attwood, married, on the 31st of December, 1835, Mary, eldest daughter of William Medley, of Westminster and Mansfield, near Uxbridge, J.P. for Middlesex and Bucks.

CHAPTER XVIII.

Address and Petition drawn up by the Political Union, January 18th, 1836—Benjamin Disraeli's letter to Thomas Attwood—Great Reform Dinner at Birmingham, January 28th—Dinner of non-electors, February 1st—Letters—Death of Matthias Attwood, senior.

THE first number of the *Agriculturist*, which appeared on the 2nd of January, 1836, contains a very full account of the proceedings at the formation of "The Central Agricultural Society of Great Britain and Ireland." Thomas Attwood was present at a dinner given on the occasion, and upon his health being drank with much enthusiasm, he made a speech which is too long for insertion here, but in which occurs the following noteworthy passage:—

> You will therefore allow me to say, that I have always been a Reformer from my earliest youth; but it is certainly true that I never had recourse to extreme measures for obtaining reform until I found, by long years of painful experience, that all other means of obtaining justice for the people were in vain. (*Loud cheers.*)

On the 5th of January a meeting of the Council of the Birmingham Political Union was held, Thomas Attwood in the chair, when a petition and address to the King and House of Commons, praying for various extensive reforms, and drawn up by Thomas Attwood, were adopted.

This was followed by an important town's meeting, convened by the Political Union, and held at the Birmingham Town Hall on Monday, January 18th, 1836. This meeting was, like every other in which Mr. Attwood took part, a grand success. The hall was crowded, and his petition and address were adopted amidst the greatest enthusiasm, without a single person suggesting the amendment of a line. Mr. Muntz took the chair, and explained that the boasting of the Tories in connection with their recently formed Constitutional Association, had compelled him to come forward and assist at the revival of the Political Union. Mr. Attwood then addressed the meeting amidst the usual acclamations; but it will be sufficient, I think, to give a couple of extracts from the address and petition to show that Radical opinion fifty years ago had advanced as far as it has at present. The address concludes as follows :—

"And we more particularly pray, that your Majesty will be graciously pleased to afford your royal sanction to the following measures :—

1st.—The carrying into full and complete effect of the great measures of Corporation Reform as originally brought forward, &c.

2nd.—A substantial, but judicious and safe, Reform of the House of Lords.

3rd.—A correction of the acknowledged abuses in the Irish Church, &c. . . ."

The petition commences in this way :—

"That your petitioners are of opinion, that it is necessary to the peace and well-being of the country, and to the efficient discharge of the legislative functions, that the House of Lords should undergo some organic change, which may bring it forward into a conformity of views and interests with your Honourable House, and into a state of harmony and mutual advance and co-operation with the spirit of the age, and the interests of the people."

The following passage from Thomas Attwood's speech on this occasion seems also to be worthy of preservation :—

Mr. O'Connell knew no more of the formation or getting up of the Birmingham Political Union than Sir Charles Wetherell did. Both of those eminent men were consulted after the Union had been formed, and after all the rules and regulations had been printed. They were consulted professionally, regarding the legality of such rules and regulations. Mr. O'Connell gave us his opinion gratuitously, and I am bound to say that Sir Charles Wetherell acted a very honourable part by us. (*Hear, hear.*) The truth is, I had meditated the Union for ten years, from 1819 up to 1829, but my friend Mr. Scholefield, and others around me in the year 1819, persuaded me not to attempt to carry the Union into effect, because, as they alleged, the distress was not great enough amongst the industrious classes to enable the Union to be carried into successful effect. They told me that such were the rooted and fixed habits of respect and deference of the English people towards the aristocracy, that it would be impossible to promote any efficient union amongst them until long years of sufferings, and injuries, and privations should have exasperated their minds. Fortunately for our country the sufferings of the years 1826, 1827, and 1828 did prepare the means of creating the Birmingham Political Union — (*cheers*) — that formidable association whose every movement but a few years ago made the earth rock under the feet of the Government, but which afterwards sunk to rest like an infant on the mother's breast.

The proceedings at this meeting drew from Benjamin Disraeli the third of his "Letters of Runnymede," which is addressed to Thomas Attwood, and dated January 21st, 1836. I have copied it at length, partly on account of the celebrity to which its author subsequently attained, and partly because I wish to give a fair view of Thomas Attwood's politics, and to show what his enemies, as well as his friends, thought of him. It is needless to point out the sharp contrast which necessarily existed between the fawning courtier and the unselfish patriot:—

"SIR,—You may be surprised at this letter being addressed to you; you may be more surprised when I inform you that this address is not occasioned by any conviction of your political importance. I deem you a harmless, and I do not believe you to be an ill-meaning, individual. You are a provincial banker labouring under a financial monomania. But amidst the seditious fanfaronade which your unhappy distemper occasions you periodically to vomit forth, there are fragments of good old feelings which show you are not utterly denationalized, in spite of being 'the friend of all mankind,' and contrast with the philanthropic verbiage of your revolutionary rhetoric, like the odds and ends of ancient art which occasionally jut forth from the modern rubbish of an edifice in a classic land—symptoms of better days, and evidences of happier intellect.

The reason that I have inscribed this letter to your consideration is, that you are a fair representative of a considerable class of your countrymen— the class who talk political nonsense; and it is these with whom, through your medium, I would now communicate.

I met recently with an observation which rather amused me. It was a distinction drawn in some journal between high nonsense and low nonsense. I thought that distinction was rather happily illustrated at the recent meeting of your Union, which, by the bye, differs from its old state as the drivellings of idiotism from the frenzy of insanity. When your chairman, who, like yourself, is 'the friend of all mankind,' called Sir Robert Peel 'an ass,' I thought that Spartan description might fairly range under the head of low nonsense; but when you yourself, as if in contemptuous and triumphant rivalry with his plebeian folly, announced to us that at the sound of your blatant voice 100,000 armed men would instantly arise in Birmingham, it occurred to me that Nat Lee himself could scarcely compete with you in your claim to the more patrician privilege of uttering high nonsense If indeed you produce such marvels, the name of Attwood will be handed down to posterity in heroic emulation with that of Cadmus; he produced armed men by a process almost as simple, but the teeth of the Theban king must yield to the jaw of the Birmingham delegate; though I doubt not the same destiny would await both batches of warriors.

But these 100,000 armed men are only the advanced guard, the imperial guard of Brummagem, the heralds of a mightier host. Nay, compared with the impending legions, they can only count as pioneers, or humble sappers at the best. Twenty millions of men are to annihilate the Tories. By the last census, I believe, the adult population of Great Britain was computed at less than 4,000,000. Whence the subsidiary levies are to be obtained, we may perhaps be informed the next time some brainless Cleon, at the pitch of his voice, bawls forth his rampant folly at the top of Newhall Hill.

Superficial critics have sometimes viewed, in a spirit of narrow-minded scepticism, those traditionary accounts of armed hosts which startle us in the credulous or the glowing page of rude or ancient annals. But what was the great King on the heights of Salamis or in the straits of Issus, what was Gengis Khan, what Tamerlane, compared with Mr. Thomas Attwood of Birmingham? The leader of such an army may well be 'the friend of all mankind,' if only to recruit his forces from his extensive connexions.

The truth is, Xerxes and Darius, and the valiant leaders of the Tartars and the Mongols, were ignorant of the mystical yet expeditious means by which 20,000,000 men are brought into the field by a modern demagogue, to change a constitution or to subvert an empire. When they hoisted their standard their chieftains rallied round it, bringing to the array all that population of the country who were not required to remain at home to maintain its order or civilisation. The peasant quitted his plough and the pastor his flock, and the artisan without employ hurried from the pauperism of Babylon, or the idleness of Samarcand. But these great leaders, with their diminutive forces which astounded the Lilliputian experience of our ancestors, had no conception, with their limited imaginations, of the inexhaustible source whence the ranks of a popular leader may be swollen; they had no idea of 'THE PEOPLE.' It is 'the people' that is to supply their great successor with his millions.

As in private life we are accustomed to associate the circle of our acquaintance with the phrase 'THE WORLD,' so in public I have invariably observed that 'THE PEOPLE' of the politician is the circle of his interests. The 'people' of the Whigs are the ten-pounders who vote in their favour. At present the municipal constituencies are almost considered by Lords Melbourne and John Russell as, in some instances, to have afforded legitimate claims of being deemed part and parcel of the nation; but I very much fear that the course of events will degrade these bodies from any lengthened participation in this ennobling quality. It is quite clear that the electors of Northamptonshire have forfeited all right to be held portion of 'the people' since their return of Mr. Maunsell. The people of Birmingham are doubtless those of the inhabitants who huzza the grandiloquence of Mr. Attwood; and the people of England, perchance, those discerning individuals who, if he were to make a provincial tour of oratory, might club together in the different towns to give him a dinner. I hardly think that, altogether, these quite amount to 20,000,000.

Yourself, and the school to which you belong, are apt to describe the

-present struggle as one between the Conservatives and the people—these Conservatives consisting merely of 300 or 400 Peers, and their retainers. You tell us in the same breath, with admirable consistency, that you possess the name, but not the heart, of the King ; that the Court is secretly, and the Peerage openly, opposed to you : the Church you announce as even beholding you with pious terror. The Universities, and all chartered bodies, come under your ban. The Bar is so hostile that you have been obliged to put the Great Seal in commission for a year, and have finally, and from sheer necessity, entrusted it to the custody of an individual whom by that very tripartite trusteeship you had previously declared unfit for its sole guardianship. The gentlemen of England are against you to a man because of their corn-monopoly ; the yeomanry from sheer bigotry, the cultivators of the soil because they are the slaves of the owners, and the peasantry because they are the slaves of the cultivators. The freemen of the towns are against you because they are corrupt ; the inhabitants of rural towns because they are compelled ; and the press is against you because it is not free. It must be confessed that you and your party can give excellent reasons for any chance opposition which you may happen to experience. You are equally felicitous in accounting for the suspicious glance which the fundholder shoots at you ; nor can I sufficiently admire the admirable candour with which the prime organ of your faction has recently confessed that every man who possesses £500 per annum is necessarily your opponent. After this, it is superfluous to remark that the merchants, bankers, and shipowners of this great commercial and financial country are not to be found in your ranks ; and the sneers at our national glory and imperial sway, which ever play on the patriotic lips of Whigs, both high and low, only retaliate the undisguised scorn with which their anti-national machinations are viewed by the heroes of Waterloo and the conquerors of Trafalgar. Deduct these elements of a nation, deduct all this power, all this authority, all this skill, and all this courage, all this learning, all this wealth, and all these numbers, and all the proud and noble and national feelings which are their consequence, and what becomes of your 'people'? It subsides into an empty phrase, a juggle as pernicious and as ridiculous as your paper currency !

But if you and your friends, 'the friends of all mankind,' have, as indeed I believe you have not, the brute force and the numerical superiority of the population of this realm marshalled under your banners, do not delude yourselves into believing for a moment that you are in any degree entitled from that circumstance to count yourselves the leaders of the English people. A nation is not a mere mass of bipeds with no strength but their animal vigour, and no collective grandeur but that of their numbers. There is required to constitute that great creation, a people, some higher endowments and some rarer qualities—honour, and faith, and justice ; a national spirit fostered by national exploits ; a solemn creed expounded by a pure and learned priesthood ; a jurisprudence which is the aggregate wisdom of ages ; the spirit of chivalry, the inspiration of religion, the supremacy of law ; that free order and that natural gradation of ranks, which are but a type and image of the economy of the universe ; a love of home and country, fostered by traditionary manners, and consecrated by customs that embalm ancestral deeds; learned establishments, the institutions of charity, a skill in refined and useful arts, the discipline of fleets and armies; and above all, a national character, serious and yet free; a character neither selfish nor conceited, but which is conscious that as it owes much to its ancestors, so also it will not stand acquitted if it neglect its posterity:—these are some of the incidents and qualities of a great nation like the people of England Whether these are to be found in 'the people' who assemble at the meetings of your Union, or whether they may be more successfully sought for amongst their 20,000,000 of brethren at hand, I leave you, Sir, to decide. I shall only observe, that if I be correct in my estimate of the constituent elements of the English people, I am persuaded that, in spite of all the arts of plundering factions and mercenary demagogues, they will recognise, with a grateful loyalty, the venerable cause of their welfare in the august fabric of their ancient constitution."

The Birmingham Liberals followed up the meeting of the 18th by a grand Reform dinner at the Town Hall on January 28th. Nearly 900 persons attended, and the chair was taken by G. F. Muntz. A single clergyman, the Rev. W. B. Collis of Norton, my wife's grandfather, showed his moral courage by attending this great meeting of Whigs, Radicals, Catholics, and Dissenters, at a time when the Liberal cause was most unpopular amongst the bishops and clergy of the Established Church. Amongst the gentlemen who sat on the right and left of the chairman were the following:—

JOSEPH HUME, M.P.	MESSRS. G. ATTWOOD.
SIR WM. MOLESWORTH, BART., M.P.	„ C. SCHOLEFIELD.
DANIEL O'CONNELL, M.P.	„ R. FRYER, JUN.
T. THORNLEY, M.P.	„ D. WAKEFIELD.
E. P. VILLIERS, M.P.	„ B. HADLEY.
THOMAS ATTWOOD, M.P.	THE MAYOR OF WARWICK.
J. SCHOLEFIELD, M P.	„ WORCESTER.
SIR G. CHETWYND, BART.	„ LEICESTER.
SIR PETER PAYNE, BART.	„ WALSALL.
SIR C. WOLSELEY, BART.	„ DROITWICH.
REV. W. B. COLLIS.	REV. HUGH HUTTON.

Thomas Attwood, in responding to the toast of "The Members for the Borough," gave his reasons for cordially supporting Lord Melbourne, and strongly condemned the foreign and domestic policy of the Duke of Wellington and Sir Robert Peel. In particular, he dwelt upon their base conduct in truckling to Russia, and in permitting her to declare war against Turkey, and concluded by pointing out the falseness of the assertion that the Tories possessed all the respectability and wealth of Birmingham. Whilst he was speaking, O'Connell arrived, and upon taking his stand close to Attwood was received with enthusiastic applause.

The Liberal demonstrations did not end here, for on February 1st the non-electors of Birmingham invited the borough members to another grand dinner, also in the Town Hall, where 996 persons sat down. Amongst the company were the following staunch Reformers:—Messrs. Daniel, Morgan, and John O'Connell, Attwood, Scholefield, Wakefield, T. A. Attwood, C. C. Scholefield, W. Scholefield, P. H. Muntz, &c., and Mr. Geo. Edmonds, who took the chair. In the course of the evening Mr. Attwood spoke at length upon his usual topics, and concluded by proposing the health of O'Connell, who was again received with vehement applause.

Mr. Attwood appears to have resided with his family during nearly the whole of 1836, as I find only the following letters preserved:—

"*Paris*, 3 *Feby.*, 1836.

"DEAR SIR,—I cannot let depart from here your excellent son, Mr. De Bosco Attwood, without giving him a word for you, my dear Sir. He and his lady will tell you how many enquiries I made of them about you. I am an old grateful animal. I shall never forget the friendly attentions shown me by you, as well in Birmingham as in London, and more so the constant zeal nesiz you have so many times evinced in behalf of my unfortunate country. I am confident that in the present session you'll raise your great voice for this sacred cause. I beg you to read the *Morning Chronicle* of 26th December, it will inform you of what we have endured from the mad Constantine and the cruel Nicholas. In the address from the House depict in the strongest words that Poland is necessary to the balance of Europe, tell that it is not only a political cause, but also that of humanity and of safety for Europe, which otherwise will prove an easy prey to Russian barbarity and slavery. I send you a medal of General La Fayette: it cannot be in more worthy hands. . . .   Faithfully yours,

J. URSIN NIEMCEWICZ."

"*May* 13*th*, 1836.

"SIR,—I take the liberty of again requesting you to do me the favor of franking a letter to the Editor of the *Brighton Patriot*, Brighton; and remain, Sir, your obliged obedient servant,

WM. COBBETT.

P.S.—May I request you, Sir, also to be so kind as to frank the letter to Mr. Whitehouse, and to allow both letters to go to the post with your own?"

SECOND MEDAL OF POLITICAL UNION REORGANIZED 1837.

CHAPTER XIX.

Anxieties of Mr. Attwood during 1837—He presents Address to the Princess Victoria—Second movement of the Birmingham Political Union—Death of the King—Correspondence with Sir H. Taylor—Proclamation of the Queen and extraordinary compliment paid by the people to Attwood—Address to Electors—Attwood and Scholefield again returned—M. and M. W. Attwood returned for Whitehaven and Greenwich—Letters of Thomas Attwood to the close of 1837.

I FEEL it utterly beyond my power to present anything approaching to an intelligible abstract of the numerous and important public events in which Thomas Attwood took part during the year 1837. In previous years I have often experienced difficulty from the lack of materials; now I am appalled by their superabundance. I do not mean that the politics of this year can compare for magnitude and importance with those of 1832, but there was about the main events of that great year an unity and grandeur which render them comparatively easy to narrate, whilst the complexity of those of 1837 makes the task a most difficult one. In this year occurred the death of the King, and the accession of the Queen, the dissolution of Parliament, and the ensuing general election, the revival of the Birmingham Political Union, and last, though not least, it was then that Mr. Attwood "placed himself at the head of the greatest movement for Political Reform which had been made in England since 1689." I propose to postpone an account of the connection of Mr. Attwood with the Chartist movement until 1840, when I shall have occasion to quote largely from his own narrative,— to give a very brief account of some of the public events of the year with which he was more immediately connected,—and to leave his letters to tell the rest.

The domestic anxieties with which my poor grandfather had to contend at this period were sufficient to have unnerved a selfish politician, or, indeed, any one to whom the public good was not paramount to all other considerations.

His income had never been sufficient to enable him to maintain the position of a Member of Parliament without great sacrifices, his son-in-law had proved unsuccessful, and in consequence two of his grandchildren were born under his kind and generous roof, whilst the severe and increasing illness of his son Marcus was a source of constant anxiety and expense. The stagnation and distress in Birmingham was fearful, and he was penetrated with grief at his inability to relieve it, and he was mortified at what he considered the unreasonable and useless opposition of the Tories. Nevertheless he manfully faced the accumulated difficulties of his position; never was he more active, both with tongue and pen, than during this eventful year, and before its close he was cheered by some extraordinary testimonies of popular gratitude and affection.

The Princess Victoria attained her majority on the 24th of May, 1837, and the evidently nearly approaching event of her accession to the throne invested the event with great interest and importance. As a protest against any imputations of disloyalty, the Birmingham Political Union determined to present addresses both to her Royal Highness and to the Duchess of Kent. These addresses, which were probably drawn up by Thomas Attwood, were accordingly presented by him and Joshua Scholefield at Kensington Palace, and I subjoin the *Journal* report of the proceedings:—

"These Addresses were presented to Her Royal Highness the Princess Victoria, and to Her Royal Highness the Duchess of Kent, on Thursday, by

Mr. Attwood and Mr. Scholefield. Our representatives were honoured with an audience of Her Royal Highness at Kensington Palace for that purpose. On presenting the address to Her Royal Highness the Princess Victoria, Mr. Attwood spoke as follows :—

May it please Your Royal Highness—I have here an humble and affectionate address from a body of men calling themselves the Birmingham Political Union—a body of men than whom His Majesty has not more loyal subjects in his dominions—who have not intruded on public attention for some years, but who now come forward for the purpose of mingling their tribute of loyalty and affectionate respect with that of all their countrymen, in congratulating Your Royal Highness upon this happy occasion.

Mr. Attwood then read the Address :—

'Unto Her Royal Highness the Princess Alexandrina Victoria, the respectful and dutiful Address of the Birmingham Political Union.

The Members of the Birmingham Political Union, in common with their fellow-countrymen, take the liberty of approaching your royal presence, to offer to you their congratulations on the auspicious advent of your eighteenth birthday.

The destined Sovereign of our beloved country could, under no circumstances, be regarded with indifference; but Your Royal Highness has peculiar claims to our respect and affection.

We are told that by the judicious care of your illustrious and excellent mother, you have been trained up to know and to cherish those great principles of civil liberty which it is the birthright of Englishmen to enjoy, and the first and highest privilege of their Sovereign to maintain. We believe, and sincerely rejoice in the belief, that Your Royal Highness's education and sentiments have, in this respect, been truly reported.

The Throne of Great Britain and Ireland, which in the ordinary course of nature you will be called on to fill, demands from its occupant, at all times, and more especially in ours, the entire resources of an enlightened patriotism.

On ascending it, you may expect to find many public grievances to be redressed, and many public wants to be supplied ; nor will the difficulties opposed to your most zealous endeavours be few or small. You will have to suffer numerous anxieties, and to brook not a few disappointments. But as the obstacles to a faithful discharge of the high duties which Providence has imposed upon you are great, so great will be your praise and your glory in overcoming them. And the path to victory in such a cause is known and certain.

If, as Queen of this mighty nation, you steadfastly resolve that your royal affections shall be circumscribed by no other limits than the hearts of the entire of your subjects ; if you determine to study the happiness of the universal people, without respect to creed or opinion ; the march of your reign will be ever onward, assured, and joyful. Faction may flatter you for its selfish ends, and abandon you when they are served ; the most powerful party will, in the day of trial, prove a broken reed ; but the People will never forsake you, in good report or in evil, unless, unhappily, you shall have first forsaken or deceived them.

Hoping and trusting that the confidence of Your Royal Highness in the People will be as fixed and permanent as their affection towards your person and character is hearty and sincere, the Radical Reformers of this great town, whose voice we speak, respectfully tender to Your Royal Highness the willing tribute of their loving and dutiful wishes. May length of days be in your right hand, and in your left hand riches and honour! May your ways be ways of pleasantness, and all your paths be peace!

In the name and on behalf of the Union,

P. H. MUNTZ, Chairman.
B. HADLEY, Secretary.
R. K. DOUGLAS, Treasurer'

The honourable gentleman afterwards read the Address of the same body to Her Royal Highness the Duchess of Kent :—

'To Her Royal Highness the Duchess of Kent, the respectful and dutiful Address of the Birmingham Political Union

May it please Your Royal Highness—The members of the Birmingham Political Union respectfully offer to Your Royal Highness the tribute of their affectionate congratulations, on the happy event of your illustrious daughter's eighteenth birthday.

Whilst they warmly sympathise in the honest exultation of a mother's heart, at the mighty prospect that Providence has seen fit to open to her beloved child, they would most earnestly thank Your Royal Highness for the successful pains that Your Royal Highness has taken to fit that child for the worthy fulfilment of her high destinies.

It is their hope and prayer that Your Royal Highness may be spared for many years to reap the fruits of your enlightened care, and to trace the wisdom and honour of your illustrious daughter's reign, in the peace and prosperity of a grateful people.' (Signed as before.)

The communication which announces the presentation of the Addresses adds :

'On Mr. Attwood's reading the Address of the Birmingham Political Union to the Princess Victoria, both Her Royal Highness and her royal mother the Duchess of Kent were greatly affected. Mr. Attwood then read the Address of the same body to Her Royal Highness the Duchess of Kent, who was unable to repress her emotions, and expressed her high gratification at the sentiments of gratitude and respect towards herself contained in the Address, and at finding that her anxious labours in forming the character of her royal daughter were so highly appreciated by all classes of His Majesty's subjects.'

A letter from Mr. Scholefield says :

'I should not rest satisfied if I did not acquaint you with the truly gracious (and to my colleague and myself, most flattering) reception which we met with at the Palace of Kensington to-day. . . . The Duchess of Kent was actually moved to the shedding of tears on the mention of her own valuable direction of the education of her royal daughter, and her reply was in terms so touching, and evidently so sincere, as to impress Mr. Attwood's mind and my own with feelings of the most ardent hope from the rule of the future Queen of England.'

We should be sorry to weaken the effect of these communications by one word of comment"

In the course of this year three separate memorials on the Currency question were presented to Lord Melbourne by the inhabitants of Birmingham Whigs, Tories, and Radicals of the town all agreed in recommending the changes in the monetary system advocated by Thomas Attwood, and the third memorial, presented in the autumn, was read to the Premier by him.

Meanwhile active steps were in progress for initiating the "Second Movement of the Birmingham Political Union," and the first great meeting was held on Newhall Hill on the 19th of June, when Mr. Attwood was, as usual, received with the most vehement cheering. The King was then at the last extremity, and when the popular member, in a most solemn and impressive manner, called upon the meeting to implore the blessing of God upon him, the vast multitude instantly uncovered, and repeated with one voice, "God bless the King!" The effect is said to have been extremely awful and sublime.

A long petition was unanimously agreed to by the meeting, but the radical nature of its demands may be sufficiently gathered from Mr. Attwood's address to the electors which I shall presently quote.

The news of the King's death, which had occurred very early in the morning of the 20th, reached Birmingham on the same day, when the following correspondence took place:—

(From Mr. Attwood to Sir Herbert Taylor.)
Birmingham, June 20, 1870.

SIR,—To-day the melancholy news has reached us of the death of our good King. We are all impressed with real grief. But yesterday I had the honour of presiding at a great meeting of the inhabitants of Birmingham, at which we all of us offered up a spontaneous prayer to Almighty God for his safety. I assure you, Sir, that it was a grand and sublime sight to see, as I did, a hundred thousand of the late King's subjects, all taking off their hats in solemn silence, and all lifting up their faces to Heaven, and all crying out with one heart and one voice, "*God bless the king !*"

We fondly flattered ourselves that our good King would have lived to

X

hear the prayers of his people in his behalf. And we thought that the knowledge of those spontaneous and heartfelt prayers would have been a comfort and consolation to him in his last hour. It has pleased Almighty God to remove him suddenly from this world. I request the favour of you, Sir, to make known to our present young and interesting Queen the new proof which I now present to you, that her Royal Uncle descends into the grave covered with the blessings and the prayers of a grateful and devoted people.

I have the honour to be, Sir,
Your obedient humble servant,
THOMAS ATTWOOD.

"*Windsor Castle, June* 22, 1837.

"SIR,—I do not delay in acknowledging the receipt of your letter of the 20th inst., and assuring you of the heartfelt satisfaction with which I have read so just and so well merited a tribute to the memory and worth of my late revered and lamented Royal Master. I have not failed to take the earliest opportunity of submitting it to Queen Adelaide, whose feelings have, in this period of affliction, been gratified in the highest degree by the expression of the loyal and affectionate sentiments of the assembled inhabitants of Birmingham, when they offered up their prayers to the Almighty for their excellent King, as also by the terms in which you have conveyed them.

As I am not in communication with any person in immediate attendance upon our present Queen, I have transmitted your letter to Lord Melbourne, with a view to the accomplishment of the wish expressed in the concluding part of it.

I have the honour to be, Sir,
Your most obedient humble servant,
H. TAYLOR.

Thomas Attwood, Esq."

The Queen was solemnly proclaimed in Birmingham on the 26th of June, when a most extraordinary and unprecedented compliment was paid by the people to Thomas Attwood. As soon as they caught sight of him walking in the procession, the young and interesting Queen was entirely forgotten, and the whole affair was turned into a gigantic demonstration in honour of him, to the infinite disgust of the Tories, who were compelled to walk about for three hours listening to deafening shouts of "Attwood for ever." This remarkable event is briefly but graphically described in Mr. Attwood's letters from which I shall presently quote.

A meeting of the Council of the Union was held on June 27th, when an address to the Queen on her accession, drawn up by

Attwood, was unanimously adopted. I am compelled to omit this for the sake of brevity, but in moving its adoption he said :—

. . . The Address should also be made a petition praying Her Majesty's serious attention to the distressed condition of her subjects. He recollected that the Union had agreed to an Address of that description to His late Majesty, in which they prayed him to dismiss the Peel and Wellington faction from his councils. The Address was forwarded to Sir Herbert Taylor, and that gentleman returned it, stating that it must be conveyed to His Majesty by his Prime Minister. He, Mr. Attwood, accordingly went over to Drayton, and handed it to Sir Robert Peel, and requested him to present the Address which prayed for his own removal. (*Laughter.*)

On the same day Thomas Attwood issued his address to the electors of Birmingham as follows:—

To the Electors and Inhabitants of the Borough of Birmingham.
FRIENDS AND FELLOW-TOWNSMEN !
On the dissolution of Parliament, consequent on the death of our good King, I think it my duty again to offer you my services. The accession of our young and interesting Queen to the most powerful and most glorious throne in the world, may possibly give me the opportunity of assisting in the relief of the general distress of the industrial classes, and in the prevention of those terrible calamities which threaten all. There is not a fluctuation of adversity or prosperity among the industrious classes, which has occurred in England for the last twenty-two years, which I have not *foretold*, and *foreproved* in print, as the inevitable result of the *monetary policy* which the Government was at each period adopting. It is no vanity in me to believe, therefore, that the circumstances of my life have given me a knowledge of this vital and all-important subject, which enables me to act with confidence and decision, in recommending the measures which are necessary to the relief of industry and to the safety of the country. I assert, confidently, that by the adoption of a just, upright, and judicious system of *monetary policy*, the general distress in the manufacturing districts may be relieved in one single month, and that within three months a general and permanent state of prosperity and contentment may be established in agriculture, manufactures, and commerce, without injustice or material injury to any class of the community.

Friends and Fellow-Townsmen !
In these days of change and of backsliding from the public cause, it is, perhaps, proper for me to inform you that I have myself experienced *no change*. I still support the great principles of Reform which I claimed in 1830 as the undeniable constitutional rights of the People, under the advice of a sound and eminent constitutional lawyer, viz :—

1st.—Household Suffrage, or Representation co-extensive with Taxation.
2nd.—Triennial or more frequent Parliaments.

3rd.—Freedom of Election, secured by Vote by Ballot.
4th.—Wages of Attendance for Members of the House of Commons
5th.—Abolition of Property Qualification in Members of the House of Commons
6th.—Dismissal of all Placemen from the House of Commons.

These are the rights of the People, consecrated by the blood of their fathers, and which, I trust, will be shortly restored and secured to them and their posterity for ever.

Friends and Fellow-Townsmen!

The more I reflect upon the history and character of my countrymen, the more I am convinced that, under a wise and just administration of public affairs, there is in England no hostile feeling towards the Aristocracy, or towards the just and rightful prerogatives of the Crown. Misgovernment and ill-usage may sometimes draw the People astray; but when the misgovernment is removed, and justice is done, their hearts always rally round the ancient Constitution, which gave shelter to their fathers, and made England the admiration of the world. Therefore, the Constitution shall receive no injury from me. As far as my humble efforts go, the wrongs of the people shall be redressed, the rights and interests of the industrious classes shall be restored, and the Crown, the Aristocracy, and the people, shall flourish together in mutual harmony, prosperity, and happiness, for ages yet to come

My Friends,

I will not support a low and niggardly economy in any department of the State. I will not consent to cut down the Navy. The honour and safety of England demand that the Navy should be largely and speedily increased. I will not consent to cut down the Army more rapidly than is perfectly consistent with the honour and safety of the country. I will never consent that England shall not be in a condition suddenly to BREAK THE HEAD of any enemy that may insult her. I have no fear of the Army proving hostile to liberty. So long as the Army consists of Englishmen, their English hearts are always with the people. Nor will I consent to any niggardly economy to the Crown. The Crown is the unity of the people. So long as the Crown protects the rights, and liberties, and interests of the People, it shall receive a large, and liberal, and generous consideration from me. These low and niggardly economies are beneath the dignity of a great nation; and as to the burden which they remove from the people, it is ridiculous to speak of it. It is not the burden of taxes which crushes the nation, but the arbitrary, cruel, and unjust laws which paralyse industry on the one hand, and quadruple the burdens of industry on the other. Let the industry of the nation be set free; and let the taxes be imposed upon wealth, and not upon poverty, and there will be no burden in taxes. The nation will scarcely know that they exist. The rich will expend their superfluities in the maintenance of line-of-battle ships; and they will possess more dignity and more honourable gratification in the national power which they will thus exhibit than any which the selfish and paltry distinctions of individual expenditure can bestow.

These, my friends, are my principles—principles which I have acted upon from my youth upwards, and which I will carry with me to my grave.

But all these principles are subsidiary, in my mind, to the great and crowning principle—LET INDUSTRY FLOURISH. I consider the right of living by honest labour, comfortably and securely, to be the first and most sacred of all rights, in civilised life. "The ox must not be muzzled, that treadeth out the corn." The workmen and labourers must have full employment, and a fair and just share of the fruits of their own labour; and after this, the surplus must go to their employers and the nation. Unless this great primeval right, the right of living by honest labour, is made secure, all other rights are a mere delusion. Under the pretence of liberty, they give to a nation the worst of slavery. There can be no liberty in a nation which merely gives to the industrious classes a melancholy choice between the gaol, the workhouse, and the grave.

My Friends,

If these sentiments meet with your approbation, I am ready to serve you in the ensuing Parliament. If not, I am content; satisfied with the reflection that, both in Parliament and out of Parliament, I have done everything in my power to restore the liberty, the prosperity, and the glory of my country.

I am, my friends,
Your faithful Representative,
THOMAS ATTWOOD.

This address shows very clearly the difference between the Radicalism of Thomas Attwood and that of the gentleman who has succeeded to his influence and popularity in Birmingham. He was a Radical, indeed, but he was as anxious to uphold the honour of the British flag as any Tory. He knew that fleets and armies were necessary in the present state of humanity. John Bright thought the Crimean war "wicked" and unnecessary; Attwood, on the contrary, would have prosecuted it until he had brought the Russian despot to his knees, and curbed him for ever by the re-establishment of the Kingdom of Poland.

On the 4th of July an address of condolence to Queen Adelaide was drawn up by Mr. Attwood, and unanimously adopted by the Political Union. It was graciously received and acknowledged by Lord Howe in a letter dated August 28th. The election of 1837 created the greatest excitement in Birmingham, and for some time a serious riot was anticipated. As, however, it is pretty fully described in Mr. Attwood's letters, I shall only allude briefly to it here. The Tories brought forward the Hon. A. G. Stapleton to oppose the popular members. The

Royal Hotel, where his committee met, was attacked by the mob, and the windows broken. The Riot Act was read, and a troop of the 5th Dragoons brought in from West Bromwich, and drawn up in front of the hotel. Before proceeding to extremities, Colonel Sir Maxwell Wallace waited on Mr. Attwood and requested him to induce the people to disperse. He, accordingly, at considerable personal risk, and subjected to many gross insults by the hangers-on of the opposite party, accompanied the colonel to the Royal Hotel, where by his great influence over the people he soon induced the majority of the rioters to disperse, with the exception of a small number who insisted on remaining to protect him. "On the following morning," says Mr. Langford, "the disturbance was renewed. The Riot Act was again read, and, to crown all, a troop of the Worcestershire Yeomanry were brought to the town, and their presence produced the utmost indignation." To avoid a collision Colonel Wallace requested them to leave the town, and Mr. Attwood assisted him by drawing off the populace to the front of the Town Hall, where he addressed them. The unfortunate troop then left the town amidst a storm of yells, groans, and stones.

The nomination, which took place at the Town Hall on July 24th, afforded another grand scene and memorable triumph for Thomas Attwood. He was proposed by Mr. B. Hadley, and seconded by Mr. Geo Edmonds. His appearance upon the platform was the signal for a tremendous outburst of applause, and eye-witnesses state that, although they had beheld the scenes of '32, they had hardly ever been present at its equal. In the course of a long and powerful speech he administered a severe castigation to the Tories, for having, in a season of great want and distress, insulted the townsmen by daring to bring amongst them a perfect stranger, utterly ignorant of industrial matters, as a candidate: he sternly warned the Duke of Wellington of the fate which awaited him, should he, as rashly advised in '32, attempt to restrain the people by force, and concluded amidst vociferous cheers by calling upon all those who thought with him—all those who were ready to follow him

ELECTION OF 1837.

to the last extremity—to hold up their right hands. In reply six thousand hands were upheld with loud shouts. Mr. Attwood then requested any one present who really believed him to be a dangerous politician, to hold up his hand, when only *four* hands were raised by members of Mr. Stapleton's committee. "My friends," said Mr. Attwood, "I sit down content."

In the course of this speech he made the following remarks:—

I know that it has been represented that I am not a religious man. They say that I swear and curse. The worst curse that I ever uttered against mortal man was a blessing. It is true I sometimes use the phrase, "I don't care a damn," or "I don't care a rush," but that is merely my mode of expressing unmeasured contempt for the subject. I do not mean, nor ever did mean, to expose any human being or any living thing to the condemnation or censure of Almighty God A man must be a demon incarnate who, in his heart, can wish that the censure of the Almighty should follow a fellow-creature beyond the grave I attend church every Sunday, except when I am called away by far more painful duties. Does that look like irreligion? For the last thirty years I have attended family prayers every night in my own house. Does that look like irreligion? No, my friends, it is not the want of religion, but the absence of a base hypocrisy, which my Tory opponents lament in me. I was born in the Church of England, I have always lived in the Church of England, and I shall die in the Church of England. In a few years I shall sleep in the churchyard at Harborne and there, I trust, that many a brave man, and not a few beautiful women, will shed a tear over my grave.

The result of the election was, of course, a foregone conclusion, though the Tories contrived to make a better show at the polling booths than they had done at the hustings. The numbers at the close of the poll were, according to McCalmont, as follows:—

Attwood	2,145
Scholefield	2,114
Stapleton	1,046

At this election Matthias Attwood was returned, without opposition, for Whitehaven, in the Conservative interest, and his son Wolverley headed the poll at Greenwich as a supporter of the same politics, defeating Captain (afterwards Sir Charles) Napier. At the latter borough the numbers were—

Attwood, M. W.	1,368
Barnard, Ed. Geo.	1,194
Napier, Capt. C.	1,158

There were thus three Attwoods, all closely related, in the House of Commons at the same time, but, owing to their opposition to each other, this rare circumstance, out of which many selfish politicians would have carved their way to fame and fortune, rather diminished than increased the influence of the family as a whole.

On the 7th of June, a medal was struck by Mr. Davis, of Birmingham, to commemorate the reorganization of the Political Union. It bears upon the obverse, Attwood's favourite emblems of the lion, the serpent, and the lamb, together with a figure of Justice and a banner inscribed "Peace, Law, Order," and upon the reverse, the crown and Magna Charta, with the inscriptions, "Birmingham Political Union, established 25th January, 1830. Reorganized 7th June, 1837 " "Unity, Liberty, Prosperity."

I am not sure whether Thomas Attwood was present at the Queen's coronation on the 28th of June, but Mr. Ll. Attwood has given me the order for his admission to Westminster Abbey signed by the Speaker.

I have alluded to the domestic trials of my grandfather during this year. These culminated soon after the coronation, when his son Marcus, after much suffering, was compelled to have his leg amputated by Sir Benjamin Brodie. I can only notice very briefly the public events for the remainder of this year. Mr. Attwood's labours, both in and out of Parliament, were incessant. In order to facilitate intercourse between the members and their constituents, Birmingham had been divided into sixteen district committees, and all these bodies appear to have expected Messrs. Attwood and Scholefield to dine with them occasionally. I find noted amongst Mr. Attwood's papers an account of a dinner at The Swan, in Harford Street, which he attended in August, and on the 21st of the same month Mr. Scholefield and he were entertained by the thirteenth district committee at the Golden Lion, Aston Street. About a week later he was present at a dinner given by the ninth district committee at the Crown, Broad Street. Meanwhile the meetings of the Council of the Union were incessant, and there was a formidable agitation, in which Tories, Whigs, and Radicals joined, to compel the Government to adopt the monetary policy so long advocated by Attwood, Spooner, and their followers. A great meeting was held at the Town Hall on October 4th with this object in view, when a long memorial was drawn up, and the two members, the High and Low Bailiffs, and Messrs. R. Spooner, W. Chance, C. Shaw, G. Edmonds, T. C. Salt, Baker, Corbet, Watson, Sutton, and P. H. Muntz, were appointed to present it to Lord Melbourne. In Parliament Thomas Attwood does not appear to have gained any ground during the course of this year, though he was treated with great courtesy by the Premier upon the occasion of his presenting the memorial referred to above. I shall now give some extracts from his letters for the year 1837:—

Mrs. Attwood, Grove House, Harborne.
13, *Upper Seymour St. West, Jan.* 30, 1837.

. . . I arrived here last night quite well at 9 o'clock. It snowed all day. I am pleased with Bosco's house, and with Mary's management and everything I see about it. It is prudent, careful, and respectable.

Jan. 31, 1837.
. . . Nothing is said about Russia in the King's Speech. . . . I have just walked two miles in a hurry to hear the Speech, but was too late. I am now going to deliver your letters to Marcus and Algernon, and then I come back to the House of Commons, to hear the course decided upon, at 4 o'clock, and afterwards I am going to dine with John Attwood.

London, Feby. 1st, 1837.
. I was concerned to see Marcus, and could not look at him without the tears gushing into my eyes—of course, not for him to see. I think to go to Ramsgate with him on Saturday, and to return on Monday. He seems in good spirits, and says that Scott says he is doing well. . . . I would send you a paper with the King's Speech, but I cannot get one here in Seymour St. Fortunately it contains nothing at all. The base Jews and Boroughmongers are all trying to palliate and explain away the conduct of Russia.

(*Mr. Attwood to the Right Hon. Sir Robert Peel, Bart.*)
6, *York Road, Upper Stamford St.*,
Feby. 7, 1837

SIR,—In the debate in the House of Commons last night upon Joint Stock Banks, Honourable Members were so eager to address the House that I found it quite impossible to obtain an opportunity myself. Much was said by Honourable Members which I was desirous of obtaining an opportunity of refuting; but there were three representations made by yourself, which I deem totally erroneous, and calculated, if not contradicted, to do much injury to the public cause. I am therefore induced to take this means of endeavouring to counteract their effect on the public mind.

I understand you to make the three following representations :—

First,—That *Cash notes* are *Money*, and that to allow to the public the right of making and issuing them is to allow them the privilege of *coining money*, and is a virtual interference with the King's Prerogative.

Secondly,—That workmen and labourers generally have been benefited by the Bill of 1819, which made all the *paper* debts, taxes and all the obligations of the nation payable in *standard gold*, without making any allowance or reduction whatever for the increase of burthens thus effected.

Thirdly,—That the fluctuations of the last twenty years are occasioned by the Metallic Standard of Value, and would have been occasioned under any other Metallic Standard of Value which could have been adopted. . . .

[After combating these propositions at great length, and refuting them to his own satisfaction, Mr. Attwood concludes :—]

It is true, Sir, as you stated, that the *original cause* of all this misery, fraud, and danger may be traced up to the Bank Restriction Act of 1797. Without giving my opinion on the subject of that Act of Parliament, or of the war out of which it arose, and which it was the means of bringing to a successful issue, I may be permitted to observe, that the Act of 1797 furnishes no excuse or palliation whatever for that of 1819. The one might be perfectly sound, just, and beneficial, whilst the other is wild, unjust, cruel, and destructive in its operation. If a man is murdered in the highway by a robber, we must not therefore charge the blame upon such unhappy man's father, although casuists might possibly trace a remote connection between the father and the son, without which the latter could never have been murdered. But the Act of 1797 was thought by the Government, and by the people, at the time, to be wise, just, and necessary. It was agreed on all hands that we could not borrow another one thousand millions sterling of *private* debts and obligations without the aid of the Paper System ! It was reserved for you, Sir, and the bands of Jews and lawyers, Whigs, Tories, and Radicals, among whom you have the misfortune to act, to discover in 1819 a *truth*, as you deem it, unheard of in the history of the world before, viz., *that it is easier to repay debts than to contract them !!!*

Wishing most sincerely, Sir, both to *you* and to *them*, a safe deliverance from the tremendous issues into which you have brought our unhappy country,

I remain, with respect, Sir,
Your faithful and humble servant,
THOMAS ATTWOOD.

To Mrs. Attwood, Harborne.

London, Feb. 11, 1837.

. . . You wonder, my love, that I do not write more fully. But London is an immense place, and engagements of many kinds press upon me. See how I was engaged yesterday. At 9, I rose, and half read a dozen letters, thought of Harborne, &c., and at 11 went with Marcus 3 miles to Scott. At 12, went in an omnibus 4 miles to Baker St. At 2, went to 13, Seymour St. ;

at 3, went to the Cab Repository in Baker St.; at 4, went 3 miles to the House of Commons, stopping a moment for a little comfort at Mrs. Fendall's. Then went to meet D. Wakefield in York Road, at ½ past 6, and being disappointed in that object, I spent the evening with Marcus and Algernon in friendly communion; and so, my dear love, this is the way in which my days pass, and if I should omit to write to you, you must not think that I forget you, but that I am probably 4 or 5 miles from the Post Office. . . .

London, Feb. 14, 1837.

. . . The times are very gloomy. I think to come to Harborne shortly. My letter to Peel, I find, pleases the M.P.'s. It was not possible for human contrivance to get an opportunity of answering him in any other way.

London, Feb. 17, 1837.

. . . Since I wrote to you yesterday, I find that a grand Irish division on municipal affairs comes on, on Monday and Tuesday next, and I must therefore continue here for a few days longer. I fear also that I shall be obliged to wait here until Saturday or Sunday, the 26th inst., because on Friday the new Poor Law comes on, and I am always strongly against it.

. . . I am going to-morrow to dine with old Mr. Wakefield to meet Daniel and the two Edwards, and *Arthur*, the last just returned from the Mediterranean after 11 years' absence.

London, Feb. 23, 1837.

The Tories, I am informed confidentially, are terrified at the aspect of the money affair, and *dare not take office at present.* They wish to leave the responsibility of the crisis on the shoulders of the Whigs. Therefore the Lords will probably pass the Irish Corporation Bill.

To Master E. A. Freeman (now D.C.L., LL.D., Historian of the Norman Conquest, &c).

Birmingham, 10 *Mch.*, 1837.

MY DEAR NEPHEW,

I have much pleasure in sending you some franks agreeably to your wish. I congratulate you on the state of Spain and Portugal Not a single murder or robbery appears to have been committed by your old friends the Liberals; and now I think the career of Don Carlos is drawing to an end. It would have terminated, I believe, 4 years ago, if the Queen had not given secret orders to her Generals to thicken the mess, in order to force French interference.

I expect we shall be at war with the Russians shortly, and then the poor Poles will have a chance. Your sister and all your friends are well here. I am myself going to London to-morrow. With sincerest wishes for your health and happiness, I remain, my dear nephew, yours affectionately,

T. ATTWOOD.

Mrs. Attwood, Grove House, Harborne.

London, Mch. 14, 1837.

. . . I merely write to repeat my last letter, and to say that I shall dine with Bosco to-morrow, and shall be most happy to meet you and Angela on Thursday evening at Mr. Humphrey's Hotel.

I find our Birmingham Deputation has had a great effect, but I have not yet seen any of yesterday's papers which give a copy of it, such as the *Globe*, *Morning Chronicle*, &c. Division on the Church Rate is expected to-night.

. . . D. W. and Alley and Jno. Barnes dine with us to-morrow.

Mrs. Attwood, 15, Wellington Crescent, Ramsgate.

Birmingham, Mch. 31, 1837

. . . Things here are much as usual, but getting rapidly worse. "The tender mercies of the wicked are cruel;" and so our poor Buttons find Sir Robert Peel.

Birmingham, April 4th, 1837.

. . . Your mother never was better. My motion will not come on on the 12th, but shortly after. The Kinnersleys left the Priory on Saturday last, first calling to see your mother. The parrot and the canary are well, and also the dogs, cat, pigeons, little bantam, &c. I found a blackbird's nest this morning, and a little nest with blue eggs. Do not part with Rosabel until you see me again.

London, April 12th, 1837.

. . . I send you the *Times* of yesterday and to-day, by which you will see our division of last night (55 majority), and also Greenacre's trial and conviction. The times grow rapidly worse. Notwithstanding the many millions just lent to the American Houses, a deputation from L'pool came yesterday, to ask more assistance from the Govt., and was referred to the Bank of England, and to-day Pattison tells me the assistance will be refused, contrary to his wish. A deputation from Manchester went also to the Govt. for assistance, and was refused yesterday. The weather is still odious. I am sorry to find Marcus continues so weak. . . .

London, May 10th, 1837.

. . . I saw D Wakefield, and attended Leader's committee yesterday, but the *Times* gives a rascally report of my speech.

London, May 11th, 1837.

. . . Burdett has gained the election by a majority of 3 or 400. I told you that the Poor Law Bill would destroy Leader's cause. . . .

The election alluded to above was that for Westminster, in May, 1837, when Sir Francis Burdett turned Conservative, and Attwood was obliged to side against his old friend. The numbers were:—Burdett, 3,567; Leader, 3,052 Mr. Leader, however, obtained the seat at the ensuing general election.

London, May 26, 1837.

. . . I had quite a scene in presenting addresses from the Birmingham Union yesterday. The Duchess of Kent exhibited the finest qualities of the heart and head. . . I am happy to say that there is still a just God in heaven, and that General Jackson is ruined by his own measures, combined with those of Sir Robert Peel. . . .

London, June 3, 1837.

. . . The three great houses are the mere rumbling of the social earthquake. And our wise fools in the House of Commons look upon their ruin as the mere consequence of speculation and overtrading. The truth is, my Love, as I have often told you, that Oxford and Cambridge are the ruin of England. It takes every man 20 years to *unlearn* all the nonsense which he learns there; and most persons die under the trial, like Liverpool, Canning, and Castlereagh. I think probably to go to Birmingham in a few days; but, as the time is favourable, I shall try to force on my motion first. Terrible news about the *Vixen*. Poor John Bull has still his bitter cup to drain, *internal misery* and *foreign shame*. . . . See the fruits of a good character. You know I always boast that whenever I die, the tears of the people shall water my grave.

London, June 6, 1837.

. . . I send you some papers to amuse you, with accounts of my 3 hours' speech, which was heard with very creditable patience and attention.

London, June 7.

. . . I sent you lots of papers yesterday, and I send you a *Standard* to-day, which gives a tolerably fair abstract. The *Morning Post* also does the same. The *Times* and *Chronicle* are a mass of wilful lies. The truth is, however, coming out, and although some 50 members left the House, I find that a great impression was made. . .

Sad work about the *Vixen*. What a horrible shame that we who crushed Napoleon should tamely submit to be insulted by Nicholas! These are among the hoarded injuries which cry out for judgment against the Govt. and the Parliament.

The "Vixen" was an English vessel which had been seized by the Russians on the Circassian coast. Alison, in his *History of Europe*, notices, with approval, the patriotic conduct of Attwood in reference to the seizure.

London, June 8, 1837.

. . . I find my speech has had a great effect. Muntz had a long interview with Lord Melbourne yesterday, who highly praised it. One of these days I expect that they will coolly turn a corner and retreat, and then gravely declare that they are not in any way following my advice. This would break their hearts outright.

Kozmian writes to me that he shall certainly go to Ramsgate on Saturday, unless something particular should happen. Dwernicki and Zaba called upon me this morning, and they also partly promised to go.

London, June 9, 1837.

. . . The trial of my friend Muntz comes on to-morrow morning at 10 o'clock, and I have occasion to speak to his character, &c., and therefore I shall not be able to come to you in the boat to-morrow, but I will be sure to come on Sunday. Perhaps Marcus may stay for me.

I am sorry to say that the King cannot possibly live, and his death is expected to-day. The House may then sit 6 months longer, under a late Act of Parliament.

Salt writes me word that 8,000 men have now re-enrolled their names and paid up their subscriptions to the Union, and that the Council is better and stronger than ever Sir Richard Nagle tells me that the mail could not force itself through the crowds assembled at the new election of the Council on Wednesday evening. All this is spontaneous, and has received no further encouragement than the prophetic warnings which I gave them 6 or 12 months ago.

Birmingham, June 23, 1837.

. . . Sir Herbert Taylor writes to me that Queen Adelaide is delighted with my letter, and I much regret, as I told you, that I omitted to name her, who ought to have been named first

Birmingham, June 24, 1837.

. . . I send you two *Journals* in which you may see how kindly Queen Adelaide received my letter; although I quite forgot to allude to her, as I should have done if I had had time to read over my letter. Our deputation goes to London to-morrow to offer the *Olive Branch* or the *Moral Sword* to Lord Melbourne.

Birmingham, June 26, 1837.

. . . To-day we have had a grand proclamation of the Queen. I thought it my duty to attend, but I did not intend the result which followed. The young and interesting Queen was quite forgotten ; and I, a simple citizen of Birmingham, without flag or banner, or distinction of any kind, and walking alone *immediately behind the Clergy and Magistrates*, was received with ten times ten thousand shouts of "Attwood for ever," throughout every street, during a 3 hours' progress. At the end of this triumphant procession I addressed 30,000 *men* in New Street ; I comforted them with the hopes of the future, and at my call they gave 3 unanimous cheers for the Queen, 3 tremendous groans for her enemies, and 3 universal shouts for Old England.

My dear love, you would have been delighted with the wild frenzy of the people. The old men burst through the soldiers to shake me by the hand, and the young women acted in a still more gratifying and tender way. I am pretty well flattery proof, you know, or I fear that I should become vain, and lifted up with a base pride. But all my pride, as you know, is the liberty and happiness of the people ; and if I know my own heart, the disappointment of *all my* means of producing those great ends would be no disappointment to *me*, provided only those great ends were obtained and secured.

I hope shortly to be able to come to Ramsgate. To-morrow I shall offer myself again as Member for Birmingham.

Birmingham, 27*th June,* 1837.

We are all quite well. I read your letters to your mother this morning, who was delighted with them. I went to church on Sunday afternoon alone, which you know is not often the case with me. Then I took the dogs a walk in high glee, and afterwards I spent an hour or two in churchyard meditations. This is a favourite occupation of mine. Twenty years after her death, I shed a tear over the grave of our beautiful Helen. How pleased the poor thing would have been if she could have been sensible of it. Then I thought of Rosy, Anny, you and Marcus, and crowds of tender thoughts. I thought my dear Anny was with you, or I should certainly have sent her a *Journal* to Barming. Now, I cannot get one for love or money. I say no more of *my* Proclamation yesterday, only I must tell you that, by a curious coincidence, Theodore Price was condemned to walk next to me during the whole day. I daresay that he frequently thought of his dirty trick in taking down my humble head from Saml. Pritchett's house, and he perhaps recollected what he wrote to me, 2 years ago, about Scholefield's election being sure, and about mine being a dream

Birmingham, June 30, 1837.

. . . Melbourne has acted most handsomely to our ambassadors, asking them for their plan of relief, and promising either to act upon it, or to meet them again and discuss his grounds for refusing. P.S.—Rosy would have been quite jealous if she had seen the kissing which I was compelled to submit to,—hard fate!!

Birmingham, July 2, 1837.

. . . I am just come from church, sadly regretting that I have neither wife, or mother, or child to accompany me. Whenever I die, I think I shall be buried in the new burial ground of Harborne Church, unless, perhaps, I may prefer Newhall Hill. Both will be near enough for my faithful *Buttons*, with their wives and daughters to make a little *Beckett* of me. . . . I cannot give you much account of our embassy to Melbourne. It is sufficient to say that, in effect, our ambassadors are virtually admitted into the Queen's Cabinet ; and I trust their advice and counsel will prove useful to the nation. . . . As you are so much pleased with my address, I send you a small edition of it. I sent you yesterday a *Journal* with an address to the Queen, which I know you will like. My friends did not alter a single word, nor would they have altered one word of my petition to the House of Commons if I had been present to explain it.

July 5, 1837.

. . . Parliament will be dissolved on the 20th inst. I look on Stapleton as a mere tool to serve the spite and jealousy of our unworthy neighbours. He cannot possibly poll so many votes as R. Spooner did.

London, July 14, 1837.

. . We shall come to you to-morrow by the "Fame." I must return on Tuesday and attend the Levée on Wednesday, to present the address of the Birmm. Union, and after that I must go to Birmm., where I expect the election will take place on Monday week, the 24th inst.

London, July 19, 1837

. . . To-day I have attended the Levée and given my petition to the Queen, who looked quite pretty. I thought of Rosabel. I go to Birmm. in the morning by the Tally Ho.

Birmingham, July 21, 1837.

We have a nightingale sings every night on the poplar in our garden. Three little ducks have found their way to the ground without injury. D. W.

could not leave London, or I should have brought him with me. Our nomination takes place on Monday, and the election on Tuesday. Our majority will be 2 to 1. The Tories merely act to put us to expense. They have subscribed £600 for Stapleton, but I have reason to think that he has already spent £3,000, supposed to come from the Carlton Club. He keeps a kind of open house at the Public Houses.

Birmm., Tuesday Evg.
MY DEAR LOVE,—The Poll has closed with 1,000 majority in our favour, as follows :—

Attwood	...	.	. .	2,160
Scholefield	..	...		2,132
Stapleton	...	...	...	1,045

Everything is peaceful and we are all well. To-morrow I shall write to you again in a frank. I send love and kisses to all. Of the latter I have had ten thousand to-day, principally from old women, but some of them from the most beautiful women in the world. I often thought of you and Rosabel.

Birmm., July 26, 1837.
. . . The election is over and no mischief done. Our majority is more than 2 to 1. Aurelius is here. I have not time to tell you about the election. I have only time to tell Rosabel that my lips are quite *sore* with the kisses of yesterday. . . .

Mrs. Attwood, Hotel du Nord, Boulogne.

Birmingham, Aug. 1, 1837.
. . . Stapleton certainly polled 150 more than R. Spooner, but I polled 350 more than at last election. Stapleton's friends had been canvassing for 5 weeks, my friends only one week, and in this way feeble spirits are talked over. I believe that the contest was got up with the object of making a disturbance on which to ground a petition to the H. of C., and I expressly warned my Buttons against this object when I first came from London, urging them to bear and forbear, &c. I cannot see how any petition can now be grounded, but if one should be presented, I shall have no other expense but a new election.

Birmm., August 3, 1837.
The elections look blank, but, as I always told you, I trust the weakness of the Ministers will prove to be the strength of the people.

August 4, 1837.
. . . Benny Mathews is much improved since he went to Leamington. I dined with Aurelius at Firchild's last Sunday, after church. The elections turn against the Ministers, which is caused by their wretched Poor Law Bill and by their stupid measures about the Church. . . .

Harborne, Aug. 6, 1837.
. . . It is all a lie about my violent language at Dee's. It was all what the *Philanthropist* calls "mental melody," but the more beautiful, the more criminal, in base and unworthy eyes. I send you a handbill which I

have found absolutely necessary to prevent 10,000 applications per day for relief.

(*Copy of enclosed handbill.*)

To the *Unemployed Workmen* and others who apply to me for Relief.

MY FRIENDS,

I am exhausted with incessant labour in your cause. I cannot find time to speak with you ; I cannot find money to relieve you. Let me alone, and I hope that I shall be able shortly to restore to you a GOOD TRADE, which will secure to you permanent comfort and independence. In the meanwhile, all that I can do for you is to recommend you to apply to your respective Parishes. The Parishes ought to relieve you *generously*, and I trust that they will do so, during the present wretched state of the country. If not, I think that you have a claim upon the gentlemen who oppose me in everything which I do for your relief. *They* have no *Political Unions* to attend to—they have no *Parliamentary Duties* to attend to—they have leisure to listen to your distresses and complaints I cannot doubt that they have also the disposition to relieve them. They can find *time* and *money* to obstruct *me;* undoubtedly they can find *time* and *money* to serve *you*. Go then to those gentlemen ; let them give to you the time and money which they have wasted in opposing the *Political Union*, and in fruitless exertions to prevent my election in Parliament. At any rate, let them know your distresses, and take the measures which *they* may deem necessary for your relief. For myself, I feel for your wrongs and sufferings ; but I *can* do no more than I *am* doing for their redress

Harborne, July 31, 1837.　　　　　　　　THOMAS ATTWOOD.

Harborne, August 13, 1837.

. . . My Buttons are all faithful and true ; but their 16 district committees occupy me pretty well with dinners, &c. Sarah Eliza is not yet come.

Birmm., Sept. 8, 1837.

. . . Ask Algernon to get you a *Weekly Dispatch* to-morrow. Our old friend Ewart has made them publish my speech at the Golden Lion.

Harborne, Sept. 12, 1837.

. . . Yesterday we dined at the Priory, and found my brother Edward and his wife, who is really a handsome and very interesting woman. . . I had a letter to-day from my brother James, saying that he is comfortably settled with his son and daughter, in a farm near Whitehaven, and is working some ironstone mines.

To Mrs. Attwood, Mrs. Carless's, Barming, Maidstone.

Birmm , Sept. 13, 1837.

. . . I believe our great meeting will be put off for another week, until the 3rd of Octr , on account of the Town Hall not being at liberty, and the High Bailiff objecting to calling the meeting in the open air. . . . I hope you have found Rosy well and good. Sarah Eliza makes a very good deputy for her, in taking care of me ; but I fear she has half converted me into a Tory. My election dinners are not quite ended, but they are drawing to a close. In the meanwhile, my prophecies are coming true about Jackson and Van Buren. . . .

Sept. 14, 1837.

You may be assured of my usual discretion in the matter of the meeting. We shall hold it in the Town Hall, and then, if the crowds press, we shall adjourn into Paradise Street. All this is peace and conciliation.

Harborne, Sept. 16, 1837.

. . . I begin to think that it is possible that our great meeting may be so frittered away, that it may probably be *infra dig.* for me to form one of the deputation. I have received the new pansies, but they are not like those of my dear Rosy. Her garden blossoms like the mind of its mistress, with a hundred beauties. I am anxious to see my dear Marcus. Perhaps you may bring him here when he has seen Scott again, and perhaps it would be better for you all to come by the Oxford day coach, and sleep at Oxford.

Birpnm., Sept. 21, 1837.

. . . I have told you before, I think, that our great meeting is put off until Tuesday, the 3rd of Octr., then to be held in the Town Hall, for the sake of peace and conciliation; but I doubt not that we shall be obliged to adjourn into Paradise Street. I send you a *Philanthropist*, containing a short letter from myself in reply to Mr. Lloyd Williams, and also Mr. Ll. W.'s answer to Mr. Webster.

Sept. 22, 1837.

My brother George will accept Wm. Newey's offer of managing the Colmers, &c. . . . During the winter I must be in London principally. I rather think that I shall not come to London on the deputation to be appointed on the 3rd of Octr. The thing will probably not suit me. . . . Parliament will not meet, I believe, until the 13th of Novr. . . . Aurelius and Uncle George and Augustus Tulk are going to the Fancy Ball to-night, and I am going to my two young friends, who have almost converted me into a Tory.

Harborne, Sept. 24, 1837.

Parliament does not meet until the 15th of Novr., and, of course, will adjourn before Christmas, and will probably not meet again before March. I told you that George will accept Wm. Newey's offer to manage the Colmers for a year upon trial, but I am sure the trial will give satisfaction. A total change is necessary there. I am not sure what I shall do myself. If I succeed in John A.'s business, I may possibly go to Corngreaves; but if not, I shall make an agreement with my partners, and leave Birmingham for a year or two, perhaps permanently. . . . I think that Melbourne has been acting on my advice, for I see the bullion arrives daily on acct. of Govt., and the Bank has now more than 7 millions.

Birmingham, Octr. 3rd, 1837.

. . . I am busy with my meeting to-morrow, which is sure to go off well, although I think to take no part myself in the proceedings. I give them the Resolutions, which is enough, and perhaps I may do good by keeping in the quiet

To Mrs. Attwood, Harborne, Birmingham.
London, Novr. 3rd, 1837.

. . . I expect to be at home on Sunday evening, when I will tell you all about our Deputation. In the meanwhile, I can only say that each member made a speech, and that every one of them spoke very properly and effectually except ———, who committed great blunders, which luckily were not much observed. . . . We shall hold the Town's Meeting on Tuesday next to receive our Deputation.

House of Commons, Novr. 15, 1837.

. . . To-day we are going to dine with Bosco, if possible, it being Violet's birthday. The H. of C. meets to-day at 2 o'clock in order to choose a Speaker, and to-morrow we shall be sworn in. The Speech, it is thought, will not be delivered until Monday, but I will take care to hear it according to your orders. Sir W. Molesworth, I see by his speech, relies upon *Ballot* to save the Ministers, but the great Whigs will not allow this, and I think that nothing can save them long but *Currency*, in the way pointed out in my letter to Lord M.

London, Novr. 17, 1837

. . . We are now most of us sworn in, and on Monday we shall have the Speech. No dispute occurred about the Speaker. Our Corporation affair is going on well.

London, Novr. 20, 1837.

Marcus seemed better and stronger, and went yesterday to Boulogne. I crushed into the H of Lords, but could not see or hear the Queen. I enclose her Speech, which is just worth a rush. Wakley is now moving three amendments to the Address, and I think I must vote with him. They relate to Suffrage, Ballot, and duration of Parliament. I cannot go to dine with Bosco, but Algernon is gone.

Nov. 21, 1837.

Bosco and his wife are going to the Polish Ball to-night. Zaba tells me that all the tickets are gone, and that they shall realize £1,000. Lord John Russell declared last night that he would never consent to any improvement in the Reform Bill, which he said was passed as a *final measure.* Thus, my dear, we have Ld. Melborne telling us that the House of Commons will not change the Currency, and Lord John R. telling us that he will not change the House of Commons. *Time will shew.* You remember the Duke of Wellington's declaration in 1830, and its consequences. . . . We hear nothing yet of John A.'s affair. . . . I crushed into the H. of Lords, *one of the first*, but could neither see nor hear the little Queen, except a few words. The crowd was dangerous. T. Hawkes and others cried out like women. . . . P.S.—I see no symptoms as yet of a permanent alteration of the Currency, and yet the Ministers will do nothing. Pray see if you cannot find a Birmingham Journal containing my speech at the Political Council about a month or six weeks ago, in which I pointed out the certain fate of Lord Melborne, unless he jumps into our Birmingham boat. Send one of those Journals to me and inform me how many you have of them. Send me also a London *Dispatch*, and a *Journal* of about the 8th or 9th of

October last, containing my memorial. Love to Anny and Rosy, and my kindest remembrances and best wishes for the restoration to comfort of our dear and kind mother, the last link which connects us with the past.

London, Nov. 23, 1837.

I think Wakley's amendment was imprudent, but I thought right to vote with him. When you have read Lord John Russell's statements of Monday and Tuesday last, you will see that the Ministers have, as I told them, no safety but to jump into our Birmingham boat. I cannot yet be quite sure that they will do so, but I am quite sure that they are lost if they do not. Read my speech to the Council of the Union in the paper of Oct. 14th, which you have sent me.

Novr. 25, 1837.

. . . Scholefield and I saw Lord Lansdown (Lord President of the Council) last night, and he assured us that all was right about our Corporation. You see also that Ministers have granted an enquiry into the Pension List. It seems, therefore, that they will rely upon these kinds of *Little Goes*, and upon the weakness of the Tories, to keep them in place. I can make nothing out respecting the Currency. I find the M P.'s as ignorant as asses and as obstinate as hogs. They have no fear of either God or devil before their eyes. They only fear the Political Unions. I have seen no one from the Polish Ball, but I understand there were 2,500 persons present. I have promised to attend the celebration of the Polish Revolution on the 29th inst.

London, Novr. 27, 1837.

You know, my love, that I have always so lived with every living thing that the death of no one can ever afflict me with remorse. The lacerations of nature are quite enough for me. You are right about Brougham and Durham. They begin to see that great changes *must* come.

London, Novr. 30, 1837.

. . . I enclose some letters and a programme of Harvey's dinner. I attended it and also the Polish meeting, and gave much pleasure to the natives, if I may judge from Mrs. Birkbeck and her lovely daughter. . . . The Corporation affair is all right. The thing cannot be hurried. It is certain to come on, and to be granted as soon as Parliament meets in Feby. next.

London, Dec. 1, 1837.

Scholefield and I have had an important interview with Melbourne to-day, but I fear he has not the *power* to act as we wish. I am sure that his opinions are much the same as my own, and that he takes very nearly the same gloomy view of things. I always told you that this was a *doomed* and a *God abandoned land*.

London, Dec. 5, 1837.

To-day I have been with Marcus to Gravesend, and left him at the Falcon Inn there, very comfortable, and in a very pleasant room The passage is only 2 hours, and I purpose to go to him again to-morrow. I cannot tell you how much I feel on his account. I took leave of him cheerfully, but in the bitterness of my heart I prayed to God that He would take my life for his. Nevertheless, I think he is doing well. His knee diminishes in size and his appetite is good. He does not know that I am coming to him tomorrow; but he will go to the Royal Oak at Ramsgate in a day or two, unless he feels improving at Gravesend. I look back upon *my* youth, and I compare it with *his,* pleasure and pain, happiness and misery, hope and despair, the wild enjoyments of love and the melancholy anticipations of death—form a solemn and most painful contrast. And yet I think he will recover.

London, Decr. 7, 1837.

In America, my dear, it is clear that Van Buren is breaking down rapidly In the last New York legislature (his stronghold) he had a majority of 91 to 32. The new election has cast him in a minority of 27 to 103!!! This (as I told the House last session) is the power of the democracy breaking in upon the Government without being opposed by a breakwater like our House of Lords. I told them that the Americans would quickly cashier Van Buren or bowstring him. Trade mends a little, but very slowly. I have given a notice to the House about Russia, which will come on, on Thursday, the 14th inst., unless the sordid and stupid M.P.'s count me out. To-day we have delivered the Householders' Petition for a Corporation to Lord Lansdowne, and he has promised us that that it shall be laid before the Privy Council next week, and that the business shall be disposed of early in February, unless some opposition petition should be presented, which I do not anticipate, although I hear threats to that effect, much like those against the late election. To-night we have a great fight upon a little subject. I am therefore pressed for time, as, indeed, I always am.

Falcon Inn, Gravesend, Dec. 9, 1837.

. . . We had sharp debates last night and the night before, dividing at 2 and 3 o'clock in the morning. The Ministers are evidently trying to make up in some degree for Lord John Russell's declaration against Reform. Last night we carried the enquiry into the pension list by a majority of 62, 500 men in the House! I daresay I shall not have 100 on Thursday next, when I shall bring on the Russian aggressions, a subject of a hundred times the importance. The M.P.'s care little for domestic misery or foreign shame, but they care much for the gratifications of spleen and the paltry interests of party.

London, Decr. 11, 1837.

. . . I did vote on Thursday in favour of O'Brien's motion, and *also* in favour of Harvey's amendment upon it. I voted for *both*, as I expect you will see on referring to the lists. . . . I suppose you have the *Journal* of Saturday last. . . . It contains a long declaration against Ld. John Russell, but was very properly printed and published before I heard of it.

London, Decr. 15, 1837.

. . . Marcus and I propose to take our places in the Rail Road coach for Monday morning next, and we expect to be at the Nelson Hotel by $\frac{1}{2}$ past 9 or 10 o'clock on that evening, when, perhaps, you will send for us. The M.P.'s heard me with marked silence for $1\frac{1}{2}$ hours, except my friends the *Radicals*, for which I trimmed them properly. I am now going to support the Queen.

CHAPTER XX.

Attwood and the Chartists—Visit to Scotland and grand reception at Glasgow
—Great Meeting at Holloway Head, August 6, 1838—Death of Mrs. Mary
Carless—Her exemplary life—Small *v.* Attwood—Decision of the Lords
in John Attwood's favour—Letters for the year 1838.

DURING the course of the year 1838 Thomas Attwood became more and more democratic in his political opinions. Hitherto we have seen him working cordially with men who, although advanced Liberals, were nevertheless persons of ancient birth, rank, or wealth. But all such individuals gradually disappeared from the ranks of his intimate allies. They had been shrewd enough to see that the passing of the great Reform Bill was the only means by which they could hope to preserve their titles and estates; but, naturally, they could not bring themselves to support such extreme measures as were now advocated by the Chartist leaders, of whom, by this time, Attwood may be considered to have been one. Deferring my account of his connection with the Chartist movement for the present, I shall only observe here that the great event of the year was his visit to Glasgow and enthusiastic reception by the Scotch Radicals in the month of May. Unfortunately no newspapers containing full accounts of his proceedings in Scotland have been preserved, but the events of his journey are sufficiently described for the purposes of this memoir in various letters. The Scotch demonstrations were followed by a great meeting held at Holloway Head, Birmingham, on the 6th of August. It was computed by those friendly to the movement that 200,000 persons were present, and Thomas Attwood took the chair amidst the usual enthusiastic applause. The chief business of this important meeting, which was attended by delegates from Glasgow and many other parts of the kingdom, was to approve and adopt " THE NATIONAL PETITION," and to appoint delegates to attend the *General Convention* of the industrious classes which was shortly proposed to be held in London. The once famous, though now almost forgotten, national petition is too long for insertion here, but its great demands were—Universal Suffrage, The Ballot, Annual Parliaments, Abolition of the Property Qualification, and Payment of Members of the House of Commons.

At the conclusion of this grand meeting Mr. Attwood spoke as follows :—

I thank you, my kind friends, from the bottom of my heart. Much as I rejoice in the sight of this great and magnificent meeting, I rejoice more in the great objects for which it was assembled. Many persons will tell you that these great meetings are dangerous, if not illegal. Mark what the best of the Queen's Ministers has lately said in open Parliament. I mean Lord Holland, the nephew of Charles Fox. That illustrious nobleman, but a few weeks ago, stated to the House of Lords that "these great meetings of the people are as much a part of the constitution of England as the meetings of the House of Lords itself." Undoubtedly they are so. They have existed from the earliest ages of our Saxon ancestors, and I trust they will exist to the end of time. They enable the people, by the peaceful but overwhelming expression of public opinion, to command those great and necessary changes in society which, without them, could only be effected by years of anarchy and blood. My friends, there shall be no blood in any measures in which I am concerned. (Cheers.) I will never act the part of Robespierre in England ; nor shall there be any violence or injustice towards any class of society. The Lords and the Crown shall each keep their own safe and untouched ; but I will take care, as far as my means enable me, that they shall no longer keep the people's own. (Cheers.) They shall give up the House of Commons into the hands of the Commons of England, and then I trust that measures will be adopted there which will give security, happiness, and contentment to all. But, my friends, I find myself in a painful position ; you all know my opinions respecting the Currency. I believe that no human wisdom and no human power can make the industrious classes flourish permanently in England under the present monetary system. See, then, my painful position. The day is coming in which these words may appear like a prophecy. You have placed me at your head ; if I should succeed in giving you the liberty, and not succeed in rectifying the Currency, and consequently in giving you the prosperity, the liberty will but precipitate anarchy, and your misery will be greater than even it now is. I must dare this great contingency ; and I must trust to the confidence of the industrious classes, and to the wisdom and virtue of the forty-nine delegates whom they will elect, to enable me to insure the prosperity and the liberty at the same time. Without this, my prospect is but gloomy. If I fail in the great work of liberty, I shall fall under the vengeance of the boroughmongers ; and if I fail in the great work of prosperity, I shall fall under the fury of a disappointed and exasperated people. (Loud shouts of No, no, never.) Now, my friends, many hours have elapsed since you met, and you are wearied, but there is still left in the meeting fifty thousand brave men before me, and I will call upon them to exhibit a spectacle. A year ago I met six or seven thousand of you in the Town Hall, in the presence of some friends of the Duke of Wellington, and on that occasion I requested of the meeting, as a personal favour to myself, that every man of them who deemed me a dangerous politician should hold up his hand. Not more than seven hands were raised in the whole meeting. I then requested that every one of them who was ready to hold the power of his right arm at my disposal, would hold up his hand. The sight was sublime. I now call upon you, my friends, and request you, that every one who considers me a just and upright man, and is willing to stand by me, "come weal, come woe," and to hold the strength of his right arm at my disposal, will hold up his hand.

(The whole meeting, apparently without a single exception, held up their hands with vehement shouts of applause.)

Due consideration for brevity prevents me from giving a fuller description of this great meeting, which, according to all accounts, presented a spectacle fully equal, for magnitude and imposing numbers, to those of 1832, although the more respectable classes appear to have been absent.

In *The News* of September 2nd, September 9th, and September 23rd, three very long letters from Thomas Attwood on the Currency were published.

In the autumn of this year Mr. Attwood visited Ryde with his family, and from thence, on the 15th of November, he addressed to the Birmingham Political Union a long letter, congratulating them upon the progress of their cause, but emphatically warning them against violence. In this letter occurs the following grand and noteworthy passage:—

Friends and fellow-townsmen! I am not superstitious; but I believe that there is a God in Heaven who blesses a righteous cause. My opportunities of serving the people have been but few. But I have lived to see some changes. I began the war against the East India monopoly. I saw its downfall. I began the war against the American Orders in Council. I saw their abolition. I began the late war against the boroughmongering Parliament. I saw its REFORM.

He was still at Ryde on December 15th, when he published in *The News* another long letter upon the state of Ireland, advocating his usual remedies. Domestic afflictions continued to press heavily upon Mr. Attwood during this year, and the critical state of his son Marcus's health was an unceasing source of anxiety. In March, his wife's mother, Mary Carless, ended her long and exemplary life at the age of seventy-nine. She was the daughter of Thomas Pratchett of Bilston, and since the death of her husband, William Carless, in 1787, had resided at Grove House, Harborne, devoting herself with the utmost self-sacrifice to the spiritual and temporal requirements of the parish. In 1794, in conjunction with Squire Green, she established the first Sunday School in Harborne, and to the last day of their lives both she and her daughters watched over its interests with the most affectionate solicitude. When Squire Green died, in 1800, he left to her Grove House for life, in order to secure her residence in the parish; but ever afterwards she devoted the whole of the rent to charitable purposes. It need hardly be added that she was greatly beloved and respected in the village, where she was always known as "Madam Carless." Possessed of a comfortable income, she might easily have mingled in the pleasures of the world, had she chosen; but such a thought seems never to have occurred to her. Similar lives were led by Thomas Attwood's aunt, Mary Adams of Cakemore, who passed her long life of nearly ninety-two years in the same house in which she was born, and by his wife's cousin, Mrs. Carless of Barming and Wolstanton, who spent her seventy years between the two parishes of her father and husband. These excellent women belonged to a type which, unfortunately for the country, has almost entirely disappeared from modern society, and it has often occurred to me that a number of similar women scattered throughout England must have formed a grand antidote to the bad example set by the Court, aristocracy, and squirearchy during the evil period of the regency. For, surely, if the masses had then no better examples than the majority of those who held rank and office, they must have sunk to a still lower depth of vice, misery, and degradation than we know to have been the case.

The same month witnessed the close of the famous, costly, and interminable suit of Small v. Attwood. By this I mean that the great question of it was decided, for litigation respecting the payment of costs was continued for some years longer. After the most tedious and innumerable delays, the case at length came on for hearing before the House of Lords, and was argued for no less than forty-six days. Lord Lyndhurst adhered to his opinion, and again displayed his extraordinary power of memory, making a speech "which," says Lord Campbell, "again astounded all who heard it;" but numbers were against him, and on the motion of Lord Chancellor Cottenham, supported by Lord Brougham and the Earl of Devon, the House reversed his decree. Mr. John Attwood was so delighted with this result that he immediately purchased the finest brougham and pair he could procure in London, and sent them as a present to Sir Thomas Wilde, his leading counsel, to whom he had already paid the enormous and unprecedented fee of six thousand guineas, and the horses were long afterwards known, when conveying their master to Westminster Hall, the one by the name of "Small," and the other by that of "Attwood." Amongst the numerous witnesses examined in this case were— John William, Earl of Dudley, George Attwood, George De Bosco, Attwood, William Mathews, Jeremiah Mathews, and Alexander B. Cochrane. To give some idea of the appalling magnitude of the suit, I take the following extract from a work published by Mr. H. James in 1834:—

"In the Appeal to the House of Lords, the Appendix to the Respondent's case fills three large folio volumes of full-sized demi paper, containing upwards of 1,500 pages. The Appendix to the Appellant's case is not quite so bulky, but contains about the same quantity of matter, being printed somewhat closer. The weight of the two cases and the two Appendices is 27 lbs., and as 500 copies of each are printed, the total weight will be 6 tons, enough to fill two large waggons, if all sent down to the House of Lords. The expenses attending the printing, to both parties, cannot be less than £3,000, and perhaps much more ; there are nearly 700 reams of paper used. A very large proportion of the documents in the cause are not printed, namely : the Interrogatories, many thousand folios. The Decree, which recites all the pleadings, some thousand folios, not printed. The long Cross Bill and three long answers, and two amended answers, many thousand folios, not printed. Many orders, affidavits, notices, &c., &c., and two subsequent Bills and the pleadings, and answers thereto. Altogether more not printed than printed, and this suit now going on for eight years, merely to ascertain a few plain and simple facts, which common-sense men of business, as referees, or a Jury, would have decided in a few days, and at a few hundred pounds cost."

During the session of 1838 Thomas Attwood resided at 4, Connaught Square, Paddington, and there I was born, on the 1st of May, and immediately became an object of his far-reaching affection and benevolence, which were continued to me until my seventeenth year.

Some extracts from Mr. Attwood's letters will sufficiently illustrate the remaining events of this year:—

To Mrs. Attwood, Harborne.

London, Jany. 28, 1838.

. . . I am arrived quite safe and well, and find Algernon the same. Marcus has not been able to come on account of the ice, which quite obstructs the river

I find that Lord Lansdowne was anxious to get an answer to his letter, and therefore it is well that I wrote to him this morning. Douglas and 4 or 5 others are come up on the deputation, and I suppose we shall succeed in nipping the opposition in its bud.

(*To the same from E. Marcus Attwood.*)

"*London, Jany.* 31, 1838.

. . . I started from Ramsgate on Monday, but I was obliged to go to Margate as the "Princess Victoria" would not go out. We had upon the whole a pleasant passage, and I never saw anything so curious as the ice. There were large fields of it floating about as low as the Nore, and by the time we got to Woolwich the river was quite filled from shore to shore; it was with the greatest difficulty we got as far as Blackwall. It was very lucky I got up on Monday, as it enabled me to keep term. I shall dine there to-day, which is the last day of term, and thus be barely enabled to keep it."

(*To the same from G. De B Attwood.*)

"7, *St. Helen's Place, Jan* 29, 1838.

. . . The ice has been very remarkable on the Thames. You would see that, at Hammersmith, a sheep was roasted on the middle of the river, and on one day people could walk across below the Tower. During the whole frost the river has been covered with ice, but generally it has been broken in pieces by the rising and falling of the tide. . . ."

(*To the same from Thomas Attwood.*)

London, Feb. 1, 1838.

. . . I went to-day with my dear Marcus to Blackwall, and left him safe there, on board the "Dart," Capt. Large, for Margate. Scott says his knee is doing well. . . . No vessel of any kind can yet come up the river above Blackwall, which is 4 miles below London Bridge. The river is still beautiful, with a thousand little icebergs floating up and down with the changing tides.

The Lords of the Privy Council decided yesterday to refuse to hear our opponents by counsel, and they fixed to give us their final answer on Tuesday, the 13th Feby., when I have no doubt that they will grant us the Corporation. This is as I told you. The beef is come and is very good, but Algernon and his friend Wm. Scholefield, the High Bailiff, are, I fear, too busy to eat it. . . . D. W. dined with me and three of the Deputation at Parkes's.

London, Feby. 3, 1838.

. . . Sir Robert Peel has now petitioned against our Corporation as owner of the Manor of Tamworth, with which the Manor of Birmingham is, in some way or other, connected. It may possibly put us to the expense of employing counsel. . . .

London, Feby. 5, 1838.

. . . I am anxious that you should not attempt to leave Harborne until you get stronger, and the weather gets milder. I am sorry to hear of my old friend Rabone's death. I told Mary Jackson that the frost would kill him. You must not, my dear love, be surprised, or even distressed, if it should carry off your dear mother. That cough, which troubles her, always attends old age, and it generally destroys by suffocation. This is the nature of things and the will of God, and we must bear it as we can.

The Canada business is, I think, now over. The adventurers from Canada had just the same right to seize the steamboat in the American harbour, as the adventurers from America had to seize the Canadian island. It will come to nothing.

Nothing more is known of John A.'s affairs, nor will be before the judgment on the 22nd inst. I expect no mischief from Peel's opposition to the Corporation. . . .

London, Feby 9, 1838.

. . . I shall see Bosco to-day. On Tuesday we shall get the answer to our Corporation. I see by the papers that Col. Wakefield has again distinguished himself. D. W. took a cold dinner with me and a few of our Birmingham friends on Tuesday last.

8, St. George's Terrace, March 9, 1838.

. . . To-day we have received the letter of Aurelius informing us of the melancholy termination which we all expected. I trust that you were fully prepared for it, and that you bear it with resignation and fortitude. I am sorry to say that Marcus is worse to-day, complaining of great pain in his knee, and of extreme debility and restlessness. . . E. G. Wakefield called this morning.

March 10, 1838.

. . . I will come down any day you please for the funeral if Marcus should get better, but I cannot leave him in his present state. He has been obliged to go to bed to-day for the last 2 hours, which I hope may do him good. I shall be sure to pay close attention to him, and I shall take care that he knows not how much I feel on his account.

Sunday, 2 o'clock, March 11, 1838.

. . . I am happy to inform you that Marcus is much better to-day. . . . I shall go with him to-morrow to Scott, and if he continues comfortable I shall not fail to come to you and attend the funeral of your dear mother. I suppose you will fix on Friday or Thursday. . . . I trust that Angela and Rosabel take good care of you. I hope also that they will support and comfort you in the loss you have sustained. It is to me a source of gratification to reflect that I never in my life used any harsh or unkind conduct or expression towards one who, for 38 years, has always acted with undeviating kindness towards me. . . .

London, March 13, 1838.

. . . Marcus has had a good night. . . . If he should not get worse I shall be sure to come to you and attend the funeral of your dear mother on Saturday. But if he should get worse I certainly cannot come. The cruelty of leaving the dying, without the hope of serving the dead, would be evident, I am sure, to you, as well as to me. Algernon stays with us now, and is a great comfort to Marcus. Mary is all kindness and attention to us, as are also the Miss Kinnersleys. I hope Rosy and Anny are well, and I shall be happy if I find your cold in a fair way. Death, come when it will, is an unwelcome visitor, but when it comes in an honourable old age, and after a well-spent life, we can face it with fortitude and resignation. . . .

London, March 14, 1838

. . . On Friday morning I shall go to you with Bosco, leaving Marcus in the care of Algernon, Mary, Mr. Cox, and I. Spooner, who have all been very kind to him. . . . At some periods his sufferings have been extreme ; and then, although little can be done for him, it is cruelty to leave him. His spirit still keeps up, for which I thank God. When I told him that I did not like to leave him on this melancholy occasion, he declared that he would, in that case, go with me to Harborne himself, which I think would be certain death to him. . . .

Mrs. Attwood, 8, *St. George's Terrace, London.*

Warwick, March 30, 1838.

. . . The trial of Muntz and others has lasted from 9 o'clock this morning to half-past 6, and it is now postponed until to-morrow. The Judge takes a stupid view of the case, and it is therefore of consequence that I should not leave Warwick until to-morrow evening, but you may rely upon it that I will be with you early on Sunday morning. . . .

" *To Thomas Attwood, Esq.*

Glasgow, 25*th April,* 1838.

" SIR,—In accordance with enclosed minute of committee, I am desired to request that you and such other friends as you may think most favourable to the cause, or most willing to aid and assist in the glorious struggle for the freedom of the masses, would be so kind as to favour us with your presence on the 21st inst I am likewise desired to return our heartfelt thanks to the men of Birmingham for their noble and patriotic conduct in rousing the country from that apathetic slumber which we feared was the emblem of political death; and for deputing Mr. Collins for that purpose, whose cool, cautious, yet firm and determined adherence to principle, has gained him both our confidence and esteem. We have many difficulties to encounter—many obstacles to overcome—many prejudices to dissipate; but the masses are with us, and we therefore feel confident that you will be more cordially received, more heartily responded to, and by a larger assemblage, than ever congregated on the Green of Glasgow for a similar purpose

I have the honour, &c.,
A. PURDIE, Secretary."

The resolution alluded to runs thus :—

"Compeared the delegates from the various districts, factories, trades, shops, and associations, when it was unanimously resolved :—'That a demonstration be made in favour of universal suffrage, annual Parliaments, and vote by ballot, on Monday, the 21st of May, and that T Attwood, Esq., and other friends from Birmingham, should be invited to attend, and that a committee be appointed to correspond with that gentleman, and to carry this resolution into effect.'"

The following is a copy of Mr. Attwood's answer :—

London, May 5, 1838.

SIR,—Before I returned a reply to your letter of the 25th ult., I was desirous of consulting my friends at Birmingham. This has occasioned some delay, which I trust you and the men of Glasgow will excuse Sir, I accept, with pleasure, the invitation which you have done me the honour to send me; and I will not fail to attend the great meeting at Glasgow, on Monday, the 21st inst., accompanied by four or five of my Birmingham friends, who will be appointed at a town's meeting which will be held in a few days. Pray have the goodness to inform me, as early as you can, at what hour of the day of the 21st inst., and at what place, it will be convenient to the men of Glasgow to receive us. It is of high importance that the meeting should be a day memorable in the history of Scotland and of England. We come to you with no base pride to gratify; but we come as the representatives of millions of our countrymen, determined to unite in the great work of restoring the prosperity, and vindicating the liberty of our country—our long-oppressed, misgoverned, and exasperated country. It is this great and holy cause, therefore, which we shall represent; and in our humble persons I doubt not that the men of Glasgow will take care that this glorious cause shall be gloriously vindicated.

Remember—PEACE, LAW, ORDER, LOYALTY, and UNION—*these* are our *motto*. Under these *banners* we will gather up the strength of the people. Under these *banners* the people possess a giant's strength. But if they once abandon them, they become but as an infant in a giant's hand.

I am, with respect, Sir, your faithful servant,
THOMAS ATTWOOD.

Mr. A. Purdie.

LETTERS.

To Mrs. Attwood, 8, St. George's Terrace, London, from Thomas Attwood.
Wigton, May 18, 1838.

. . . I am arrived here quite safe and well, and shall be at Carlisle in an hour. It is so very cold that I can scarcely write, and the horses are waiting. . . .

Carlisle, 4 o'clock.

The post was gone, and so I finish my letter here. I hope I shall find a letter from you to-morrow at the Post Office, Hamilton, near Glasgow, and on Monday at the Post Office, Glasgow. I hope Angela is comfortable. Algernon will, I doubt not, attend to Marcus as much as possible. I will write to you as often as I can, and will not forget to tell you on Monday the result of our great meeting. When I got to Birmingham I found that Salt had been for the last few days at Dr Clutton's funeral, and that, in consequence of my not arriving, my friends had issued handbills putting off the procession, and that they had proceeded to Manchester by the morning train. Salt and I overtook them at Manchester by ½ past 10 o'clock The wind has been so boisterous to-day that I begin to think I should not have reached Glasgow in time if I had gone by the steamboat from Liverpool. . . .

P.S.—Have no fear for our great meeting.

Hamilton, May 20, 1838.

. . . I have received your gratifying letter and hope to have another at Glasgow to-morrow. I find all is enthusiasm in Scotland, having received already invitations from all the chief towns. But you need not fear that I shall be led astray into visiting other towns. Many gentlemen from Glasgow are come over here to meet us, 11 miles, and they give us a grand account of our reception to-morrow. . . .

Glasgow, May 21, 1838.

. . . Our great meeting has gone off well, attended by at least 200,000 persons in the midst of cold and constant rain. Our procession reached more than 2 miles in one continued stream from beyond Parkhead to Glasgow, and thence for a mile more to Glasgow Green, which is the finest place I ever saw, consisting of 100 acres of land in an amphitheatre surrounded by good houses. Near the end of the meeting I counted 150 large banners in the field, and I think there must have been 300 in the whole. Forty-three bands of music, all in uniform, met us at Parkhead. The whole of our resolutions were passed unanimously; and the whole meeting pledged themselves to support us. Last night and to-day I have had at least 20 deputations from different towns to request that I will visit them; and under all the circumstances of my position I have thought it my duty to go to the Renfrewshire county meeting to-morrow at Paisley, a few miles hence; and then I shall return to London by the Glasgow steamer on Wednesday, leaving Kilmarnock, Edinburgh, Dundee, &c., to be attended by Salt, Hy. Muntz, and Douglas. I shall therefore, with God's blessing, certainly reach London either on Thursday night or Friday. . . . I wish my dear Marcus could have been with me to-day. I am sure he would have been delighted with the high enthusiasm of the people.

Glasgow, May 22, 1838.

. . . I shall leave Glasgow by the steamer at 11 o'clock to-morrow morning, reach Birmingham by 5 in the morning, and certainly be with you on Thursday evening. I am quite well, and this moment setting off for the Renfrewshire County Meeting at Paisley. The rest of the deputation will visit Edinburgh, Perth, and other towns where the enthusiasm is the same as in Glasgow. . . .

Copy of card enclosed in foregoing letter:—

BANQUET.

On Monday Evening, the 21st. *May,* 1838.
In the Arena, Hope Street.

JAMES MOIR, ESQ., Chairman.
ALEXANDER PURDIE, ESQ. } Croupiers.
ROBERT M'GAVIN, ESQ.

LIST OF TOASTS.

Chair.—" The Majesty of the People—the true source of all Political Power."

Chair.—" The Queen!—May she never forget that the Happiness of the People is the safety of the Throne."

Chair.—" Her Majesty's Ministers—may they see the propriety of adopting those practical measures necessary to the Peace and Prosperity of the Kingdom."

Chair.—" The Magistrates of Glasgow, and all in authority throughout the Kingdom—may Justice, Mercy, and Integrity be their distinguishing characteristics."

Chair.—" THOMAS ATTWOOD, ESQ., M.P., and the Deputation from Birmingham—may the cause in which they are engaged be eminently successful."

Mr. Attwood.—" Universal Suffrage, Annual Parliaments, and Vote by Ballot."

Mr. Salt.—" Woman—the Companion and Comforter, not the slave, of Man."

Mr. Scholefield.—" Free Trade—a speedy Repeal of the Corn Laws and all Commercial Restrictions."

Rev. Mr. Wade.—" The Rights of the People—infamy to all who dare invade them."

Mr. Muntz.—" Justice! or Emancipation to the Colonies of Great Britain."

Mr. Edmunds.—" Freedom to the Bondman, and an Adequate Reward for Labour."

Mr. Douglas.—" The Liberty of the Press—may its powerful influence be ever exerted for the good of man."

Mr. Hadley —" Ireland—Equal Rights administered by equal Laws."

Mr. Edwards.—" Civil and Religious Liberty all over the World."

Mr. Purdie—" Mr. Collins, and the Men of Birmingham."

Glasgow, May 23, 1838.

. . . Mr. Edmonds and I are just setting off by the steamboat for Liverpool, 11 o'clock; and I may probably reach you before you get this letter; but I write to you to prevent mistake.

We had a grand Renfrewshire county meeting yesterday at Paisley, and all went off well. The people met us with 20 bands of music 4 miles from the ground, which was the sacred field of *Ellerslie* (Wm. Wallace), and I suppose 50,000 of them, after waiting an hour for us in the rain, escorted us for the 4 miles, and most of them continued with us in the rain during the whole day. All is enthusiasm and devotion to the cause. My friends are gone to Kilmarnock, Edinburgh, Perth, &c., but I cannot stay from you and Marcus, and therefore I am returning to-day.

All men tell me that my reception in Scotland has far exceeded that of Lord Durham, or of O'Connell, which last is now sadly faded in public opinion.

Birmingham, Thursday,
24 *May,* 1838.

. . . I arrived here safe and well to-day at 5 o'clock; but I found that the London train at 5 o'clock has ceased to run, and therefore I am obliged to come to you by the 9 *o'clock train to-morrow morning.*

Bm, Monday, July 9*th,* 1838.

. . . I forgot to save you a frank, and therefore I write without one, to say that I arrived very safe, and found everything comfortable at the Acorn. We came from Coventry to Birmingham, 18 miles, in 35 minutes.

Birmingham, 10 *July,* 1838.

. . Pray have the goodness to inform Mr. Baker that no house will suit me if it is more than 2 miles from our kind sister Carless, who has always been a second mother to my family. Within 2 miles of her, with two sitting rooms, and 5 bedrooms, I should be happy to spend a few months, if my dear Marcus can be moved. I am glad to hear the account which Mr. Good gives, and also that you and Angela are well. Pray give my love to her, and give a kiss to little Betsey from her dear grandpapa. I will be bound she will understand what it means. I am myself very careful respecting diet, &c., and I expect to return to London much improved. To-day our kind friend Mr. Hodgson called to say that he is coming to London *this day* by the Rail Road, and that he will be sure to see Marcus. This will give you pleasure. Pray let him examine the *knee* and give his opinion, whether Mr. Good happens to be present or not. No offence will be given, and it is important that Hodgson should see the knee.

Birmingham, 13 *July,* 1838.

. . . I hope to see Hodgson shortly. On Wednesday next I shall go to Stafford by Rail Road, and return the same evening. (John A.'s trial.)

Birmingham, 14 *July,* 1838

. . . I sent your letter to Mathews, but did not see him. I am going to the Leasowes to-morrow with Salt, and I shall return in the evening. I hope to get a letter from you before I go. . . . I send you a *Journal*, by which you will see the usual discretion of my proceedings. You would have been delighted if you had seen the reception of my faithful "*Buttons*." They were like 500 *Rosabels* clinging around me. We think to hold a Grand Central Meeting on the 6*th of Augt.*, at which I must of course be present for 2 or 3 days.

Birmingham, July 17*th*, 1838.

. . . I walked to the Leasowes with Salt and returned in a car. I am going to-morrow to Stafford, and shall return in the evening. . . .

P.S.—To-night we issue our *Grand Call* upon the neighbourhood—a *Call* which, I trust, will shake the Temple of *Baal* to its foundations. But all is " Peace, Law, Order, Loyalty, and Union."

Birmingham, 18 *July*, 1838.

. . . I am just returned from Stafford, where we have lost our cause for £15,000 of *interest upon interest*, owing to the *dog-headed* partiality of Lord Abinger to Lord Lyndhurst, the stupidity of the Jury, &c. However, it is no great damage, and John A. can well afford the loss, which idea mainly acted on the Jury.

Birmingham, 20 *July*, 1838.

. . . I shall certainly be with you by the Rail Road early on Sunday evening. I am glad to find that Benjamin continues so kind and friendly. It does him much credit, and is never forgotten by me. I have a letter from your sister Carless saying how happy Rosabel is.

Birmingham, 3 *Augt.*, 1838.

. . . Immersed in business, I have only a moment's time to say that I am well, and that I shall hope to hear from you in the morning. I did not arrive until 11 o'clock last night at the Acorn, where I found my rooms very comfortable and much improved.

Everything is going on well for our great meeting, and I expect we shall muster 200,000 men, all bold as lions, but innocent as lambs.

I hope my dear Marcus continues comfortable, and that little Betsey improves. Give her a kiss from her dear grandpa. . . .

P.S.—I travelled with a very clever, but conceited gentleman, who told me that "everybody within 20 miles of Birmingham was bit by Attwood, and that there was no doubt that he was mad"!! Quite a novelty to me, as you may imagine.

Birmingham, 5 *Augt.*, 1838.

. . . I never forget your letters, and generally I contrive to obey your orders But to-morrow will be a busy day, and I almost fear that I shall not have left the ground until the post is gone, and I know you would not like me to write to-day the letter intended for to-morrow. We have delegates from Glasgow, London, and many other towns, who will be crowding around me after the meeting. . . .

I send you a *Birmingham Journal* for you to see the order of the meeting. I doubt not that it will be grand, orderly, and very imposing, but I shall not at present uncover the mysterious "*Serpent Banner*," because I have not got it!

I am careful of my health, and am well, as you may judge from my handwriting.

(*To same address from T. Aurelius Attwood.*)

"*Birmingham, Aug.* 6, 1838.

"DEAR MOTHER,—We have had a very fine meeting indeed, and the day for the principal part of the meeting very fine. I have left it some time and since then it has been wet I am going to dine with my father, &c., at the Bell in Philip St., and will write to you again to-morrow. Lots of reporters were there, and must have been astonished at the numbers. The *Morning Advertiser* had four reporters. . . "

(*To same address from Thomas Attwood.*)

Birmingham, Aug 7, 1838.

Our meeting was a grand affair, and everything went off well. The best report in the London papers at present is, I think, that in the *Morning Advertiser* of this day. Cutler can get you one, if you send him. I could not possibly write to you myself, but I knew that Aurelius would do so. First and last there could not have been less than 200,000 persons on the ground, all of whom conducted themselves as well as a meeting of 20 gentlemen could do. I took the chair myself, and during the 5 or 6 hours that the meeting lasted, I had not once occasion to make the trumpets sound to order "*Silence.*" In the very thick of the meeting a man was arrested for having killed a girl in the morning by a rash blow, and he was carried out without the slightest interference or enquiry. I opened the meeting with a short prayer to Almighty God, and I assure you that the effect was magnificently sublime. We had deputations from many distant towns, such as Liverpool, Manchester, &c, but we had not time to allow them to speak. . . . I shall be certain to return to you early on Friday evening, if it please God. I am quite well, although the labour of three great meetings in one day was great.

Enclosed with this letter is a cheap ballad, with a rough portrait of Thomas Attwood engraved on it, entitled "A new song on the Great Demonstration Meeting to demand the People's Rights! Held at Holloway Head, Birmingham, August 6th, 1838." The poetry is such sad doggrel that it is not worth copying, but it is interesting as showing that Attwood fully retained his great popularity at this date, and also to what extremely radical opinions he had then descended or "advanced."

Birmingham, Aug. 8, 1838.

. . I am much concerned to hear that you are yourself unwell, but I am not surprised. Pray be careful, and cool and tranquil. We cannot avoid the decrees of Providence, but we may by patience and resignation submit cheerfully to those decrees. I am glad to find that you expect to move

Marcus comfortably; and that Angela and her little charges are already removed. I am sure to be with you early on Friday evening. I receive every day many proofs of attachment and fidelity from all parts of the country, but I assure you, my dear love, that none are so dear to me as those that I receive from you. . . .

Mrs. Attwood, Mrs. Carless's, Barming.

London, Sept. 6, 1838.

. . . Anny requests me to write. She is well, and I am happy to say that Marcus is comfortable, and, I hope, improving. I am concerned to hear that you continue so unwell. I hope to see you again on Monday. I send love to Rosey, who sends none to me, and, I fear, feels none. She is a sad pet of mine . . .

Mrs. Attwood, Ryde, Isle of Wight.

London, Novr. 10, 1838.

. . . Sir B. Brodie and Mr. Keate have seen Marcus to-day, and they both agree that he may go safely and properly to the Isle of Wight on Monday. We shall therefore be at the George Inn at Portsmouth on Monday evening, by about 4 or 5 o'clock, and shall join you at Ryde on Tuesday morning; but if we should happen to get to Portsmouth, in time for the steamboat, we shall join you at Ryde on Monday evening. Of this you can judge better than I can. . .

Mrs. Attwood, Beechlands, Ryde.

Blenheim Hotel, London,

Decr. 26, 1838.

. . . I am arrived here quite safe after a pleasant journey. I forgot to give the old rosy coachman anything. When you come on Friday, pray give him 2s. 6d. for me if you see him. The cab called the "Tot" shakes terribly. I think you had better come here in a coach. I send love to all of you, and many injunctions to take care of fire.

In order to avoid a possible confusion in the future, it may be noted here, that in the year 1838 died Mr. Thomas Attwood, organist of St. Paul's, a pupil of Mozart, and a well-known musician and composer. Mr. T. A. C. Attwood informs me that this gentleman was related to his namesake of Birmingham, though I do not know in what degree.

CHAPTER XXI.

Return of Mr. Attwood to Birmingham—Address of the Female Political Union—Discord in the Political Union—He presents the Great National Petition, June 14, 1839—He is heard at length in support of it, contrary to the rules of the House—His motion rejected, July 12th—Lord Palmerston and Russia—Mr. Attwood's address announcing his resignation—His private letters during 1839—Letters from Lords Melbourne and Western.

IT would be easy to fill a volume with an account of the last eventful year of Thomas Attwood's parliamentary career, but for reasons already given a very brief sketch must suffice. On the 1st of January, 1839, the Council of the Political Union held its weekly meeting, and it being known that Mr. Attwood had arrived in Birmingham the room was crowded to excess. Shortly after 7 o'clock he joined the meeting and was received with enthusiastic cheering. In the course of a long speech he observed that the indisposition of himself and his family had lately prevented him from attending the Council meetings, but that he approved of everything that had been done in his absence.

He congratulated his hearers upon the progress of their cause, and assured them that if they persevered in just, legal, and peaceful means their victory was certain. But he emphatically warned them against the consequences if, misled by evil advisers, they should attempt to obtain their objects by physical force.

On January 8th the Female Political Union of Birmingham, with their friends, to the number of about 1,000 persons, took tea in the Town Hall. Thomas Attwood attended, in company with J. Scholefield and other friends, and made another long speech of similar purport. At its conclusion he was presented with the following address by Mrs. Ann Henley, which was read by the Chairman amidst great applause:—

"HONOURED SIR,—We, the members of the Birmingham Female Political Union, beg most respectfully to congratulate you upon your restoration to health, and also to welcome you upon your return to that town and people who esteem you as the firm and zealous friend of freedom and humanity whose unceasing exertions and integrity of conduct in their cause have rendered you so worthy of their regard. We likewise express our gratitude to that good and gracious Being who, in His mercy, has spared your life and renewed your strength—a life which has hitherto been spent to obtain for the industrious classes an amelioration of their sufferings, and to secure to them their just rights and privileges. Sir, we trust you will still pursue the same course, until the great principles which you have so long, so nobly, and with so much energetic zeal contended for, become the law of the land. Sir, we hail your presence among us this day as an earnest that you will—as on all past occasions, and with the same perseverance—aid and assist us in the forthcoming struggle for universal liberty. Then, Sir, having faithfully discharged your duty, you shall wear the laurels you have so gloriously won, which will be to you, as to all true patriots, that balmy consolation which will make your sun set, after a stormy and boisterous day, beautifully calm and serene; and when your strength fails you, and your voice is no longer heard in the cause of liberty, will shed a halo over your name, which will be gratefully cherished by every British heart."

At the Council meeting of January 15th, held at the Public Office, Mr. Attwood attended and again urged upon his hearers the necessity of abstaining from all thoughts of violence, pointing out to them that if the 2,000,000 persons who, he trusted, had by this time signed the National Petition would only subscribe one shilling each the victory of their cause would be certain.

Feeling it to be his duty to make every possible exertion at this great crisis, he was again present at the Council meeting of January 22nd, and, after speaking at length upon the proposed religious service for the people and the great delegation of the industrious classes which was to meet in London upon the 4th of February, concluded as follows:—

In the year 1831 he had the honour of an interview with Lord Grey, before the passing of the Reform Bill. Lord Grey said to him—"Mr. Attwood, pray tell me your real opinion. When the Reform Bill is carried, will it lead to a revolution, or will it not?" He (Mr. A.) answered in exactly the following words:—"Lord Grey, as you put to me an honest question, I will give you an honest answer. My firm opinion is, that if you give the liberty, and give the prosperity at the same time, the liberty and the prosperity will walk hand in hand together; the child in the cradle will never live to hear the voice of discontent in England; and you will leave the greatest name in English history behind you. But, if you give the liberty, without giving the prosperity at the same time, the liberty will but precipitate anarchy; and you will be deemed the *Neckar* of England, instead of its saviour." Was this the part of a dangerous man, to give the Minister a fair warning of this kind? He (Mr. A.) had never been dangerous He had always studied, to the best of his power, to restore the prosperity of the people, and to give security to the rich, by giving happiness and contentment to the poor

I cannot find any account of the meeting of the General Convention of the Industrious Classes, which was advertised to be held at Brown's Hotel, Palace Yard, London, on the 4th of February, 1839.

In the early part of March, Mr. Attwood brought under the notice of the House of Commons the state of the Russian fleet in the Baltic, and warned the House not to risk ten or twelve badly-manned British sail-of-the-line against twenty-seven well-manned Russians; but he met with little or no support. Towards the end of the month he again spoke with great earnestness upon the miserably weak condition of the British Navy, but met with no better success. Finally, on the 25th of March, he made a last effort in the same direction, and descanted at great length upon the arrogant and iniquitous encroachments of Russia; but his speech was received with derision, and he could not even find a seconder to the motion which he founded upon it.

At a public meeting held in Birmingham in the early part of April, Mr. Salt read a letter, from which I take some extracts, addressed to him by Mr. Attwood, with reference to the violent and shameful proceedings of the physical force party of the Chartists:—

London, March 28, 1839.

MY DEAR SALT,—I have received your letter of yesterday, informing me of the unhappy discords which have broken out between the Council and the members of the Political Union. Those discords are much to be regretted. They threaten more injury to the cause of the people than all other mischiefs combined. So long as Birmingham remains firm, true, and united, acting *under the law and in defence of the law*, but permanently and inflexibly determined to use every possible legal effort to obtain from the justice of Parliament the objects of the National Petition, the cause of the people can never be said to be lost. . . . Undoubtedly the wild nonsense about *physical force* has done much mischief. . . . I assert with confidence, that if the bitterest enemies of the people had sat down in an infernal conclave to devise the means of injuring the people's cause, they could not, by any possibility, have devised more efficient means than by recommending the people to have recourse to *physical force*. . . . You know, my dear Salt, that I have never been a man of blood—never animated by a guilty ambition. My sole object has been to assist in obtaining liberty, prosperity, contentment, and glory for our country. In endeavouring to obtain these great objects I have shrunk from no danger; but I shrink from crime and from madness. The miseries of the people shall never be increased through me. If I am to die a premature death, I will face it in a good cause; but will not die the death of a fool, or of a scoundrel. I will leave an unstained name behind me. . . .

The reading of this letter was received with laughter and dissatisfaction, and some persons wanted to know whether Mr. Attwood himself had not threatened to march to London with 200,000 men in 1832, although he had repeatedly explained that he only offered to do this "*if the King should command it.*"

On the 1st of May Mr. Attwood addressed a letter to the General Convention in reply to their application to Mr. Fielden and himself to present the National Petition, stating that before doing so he must require from them a distinct disavowal of all intention of employing physical force or of creating discord between masters and men. He also drafted some stringent resolutions upon the subject, which he recommended them to adopt. The Convention appear to have rather shirked a distinct reply to Attwood's question, but they seem to have satisfied him, for on Tuesday, the 8th of May, the Petition was formally conveyed to him for presentation, with considerable ceremony. Previous to this, however, a sharp debate had taken place at the rooms of the General Convention, in which he was treated with considerable insult and contumely for standing fast to his old motto of "Peace, Law, and Order." I give, from an MS. note in his own handwriting, what he thought of these proceedings:—

I insert this Debate from the *News* of May 5, 1839, as a small specimen of the brutal stupidity of the members of the General Convention. I had been the means of *creating* them. I had been a principal means of giving more power and unity to the industrious classes, within a few years, than Cobbett, and Major Cartwright, and Horne Tooke, and a host of Whigs, Radicals, and *Patriots*, had been enabled to give them for a century before; and yet their representatives *here* treat me with insolence, calumny, and suspicion, merely because I resisted their brutal passions, and pointed out to them that they were ruining the public cause. From the very first they had always exhibited this feeling towards me. They had, more or less of them, attended hundreds of public meetings throughout the country, and not one single vote of thanks at any such meeting had ever been voted to me, or to the Birmingham Council, who had set the whole machinery in motion !!

The Petition was conveyed on a van, accompanied by fifty-two delegates, to the residence of Mr. Fielden, in Panton Street, where Mr. Attwood appeared and informed the delegates that he had seen the Speaker and arranged all preliminaries, but requested them to keep the Petition in their own hands until the evening for its presentation arrived.

Meanwhile, on the 31st of May, Mr. Attwood made a long speech on the Exportation of Gold, but his resolutions were negatived without a division.

The last great public act of Thomas Attwood's life was the presentation of the monster National Petition on Friday, June 14, 1839; and whatever may be thought of the justice or expediency of the Chartist demands, all must admit that the closing scene was worthy, in its imposing grandeur, of him who had originated the extraordinary meetings upon Newhall Hill. No such petition had ever before been presented to the House of Commons, nor has there been one since. The ponderous document, nine or ten feet in circumference, and bearing 1,286,000 signatures, was carried, or rather rolled, by twelve men to the Speaker's table. The great majority of the House were, of course, hostile to its demands, but they "wisely resolved," says Mr. Molesworth, " to treat the petitioners with every courtesy and consideration." The Standing Orders of the House were suspended to allow Mr. Attwood to state the case of his clients, and, amidst great excitement, he spoke as follows:—

Sir,—I rise to present this extraordinary petition, no less important than extraordinary. (Hear, hear) I am aware that the rules of the House will not allow me to trespass upon their attention by going into any argument in defence of the great principles which the petition lays down, therefore I shall not attempt to go beyond what the rules of the House allow. (Hear, hear) I shall confine myself to stating briefly the contents of the petition, and the circumstances under which it originated, and perhaps the House will indulge me with a few words of explanation of the peculiar circumstances in which I am situated with regard to it. The petition originated in Birmingham; it was adopted at a large meeting there on the 6th of August last, immediately after that, it was sent to Glasgow and adopted there in a similar manner, where it received upwards of 90,000 signatures, having received a nearly equal number in Birmingham and the surrounding districts. It was then handed round the country generally; and 214 towns, counties, and districts have adopted the petition nearly universally. The signatures amount to 1,280,000 and upwards. The principle has been affirmed by not less than 500 meetings, at all of which those who had signed it had stated that they were suffering great distress, which had been too long disregarded by this House. I attribute the whole of the recent discussions to the sufferings of the people—sufferings which they have long endured with admirable patience, and which have been too long disregarded by this House. I hope the House will give its serious attention to the contents of this petition, and not think that, because the humbler classes of workmen are the sufferers, it is not entitled to the consideration of this House. (Cheers.) It will be most painful to the honest men who have signed this petition if their delegates, who, by the favour of the House, have been permitted to witness its presentation, should carry back a report that the petition has been treated with disrespect by the House. (Hear, hear.) Many who have signed it are at present suffering under extreme distress—distress of such a nature that gentlemen born in the lap of affluence and luxury, whose wants are all supplied by the property they have derived from their forefathers, can form but a very feeble idea of the agony which an honest man suffers, whose hands are able, and whose heart is willing to work, but who yet is, with all that, unable to get a living. At all the meetings which have been held, the persons attending them have confined themselves strictly to the lawful pursuit of their constitutional rights; and they have been induced to do so on account of the injuries and sufferings which they have endured for so many years, without finding any efficient relief. The handloom weavers, the artisans, the agricultural labourers—all these classes find themselves aggrieved; they find that they receive no sympathy from this House, and they consider themselves bound to use every just and legal exertion to recover the whole of their constitutional rights. I hope hon. members will not be prejudiced against this demand by thinking there is any slight or any improper reflection upon themselves. All the petitioners say is, that the members of this House, in consequence of their birth, parentage, education, wealth, and habits of life, have not felt that anxiety for the sufferings of the lower classes which they think is absolutely necessary to the enjoyment of their rights as British subjects. They have, therefore, adopted this measure for the purpose of recovering their ancient rights. They and their fathers and grandfathers had trusted to the noblemen of England to protect them, but no protection having been given to them for years past, they have been obliged to have recourse to this petition, in order to obtain their just rights. They say they only ask for a fair day's wages for a fair day's work, and that if you cannot give them that, and food and clothing for their families, then they say they will put forth every power the law allows them to change the representation of this House, that they will use all means to act upon the electors, by which they hope ultimately to produce such a change of opinion as finally to lead to success. (Hear, hear.) I have no doubt that they will succeed ultimately, but I trust in God they will shortly succeed in obtaining all the objects of the petition. (Hear, hear.) The first object of these honest men, who every one of them produce four times more than they want, and yet their country refuses them one fourth of the value of their labour, not only that, but some of them are put at three-days-a-week work—the first object of these honest men who are pressed down by the hand of oppression—and I am sure that such being the case, the House will not be surprised at their using stronger language than they otherwise would have used—(Hear, hear)—the first part of the petition claims universal suffrage; it claims representation co-equal with taxation, which was the ancient law of England; it says that they have been bowed down to the earth; and then it goes on to describe the suffering they have endured, and that they come before this House to tell them that the capital of the master must not be deprived of its due profit; and the labourer must not be prevented from having the reward of his labour, and that the laws that make labour cheap should be abolished. They then demand universal suffrage in the language used by our forefathers in the celebrated Bill of Rights. They next go on to show that when the Constitution grants a right, it must be understood to guarantee the means of exercising it. The Constitution guarantees the right of election, and these petitioners contend that vote by ballot is absolutely necessary to secure freedom of election, and, therefore, they contend that they have a constitutional right to vote by ballot. (Cheers.) They go on further, and claim annual Parliaments, agreeably to the Constitution. The Act of Settlement, orders that the Parliaments shall be triennial; and under the old practice of the Constitution they were annual. Then they go on to demand that the labour of representatives shall be rewarded. (Loud laughter.) That was the ancient practice of the Constitution, as exemplified by Andrew Marvel; and I could to-morrow apply to my constituents, at Birmingham, the Constitution authorising members of this House to be paid the wages of attendance by a rate on their constitutents. (Much laughter.) They consider, unless this right is restored, that they cannot have members of this House properly feeling and understanding the wants and sufferings and distresses of the people. The fifth demand is, that the property qualification of members of this House should be abolished. Now, in all these five points of the petition I most cordially agree, and I do sincerely hope that, by the progress of public opinion, the day may not be distant when the whole of these five points will be granted to the people; that they will have them in full measure, full weight and pureness, and no mistake about the matter. (Cheers and laughter.)

Sir G. H. Smyth rose to order. He contended that the hon. member was transgressing the rules of the House. He himself had been prevented from speaking on the presentation of a petition the other night, and he could not conceive how any hon. member, with that ridiculous piece of machinery, could be allowed to transgress the rules of the House. (Loud cries of "Chair" and "Order.")

The Speaker said if the hon. member appealed to him as to what was the strict rule of the House, he must, unquestionably, say that no hon. member had a right to speak at any length in presenting a petition. But when the House considered the peculiar circumstances under which the petition was brought forward—(loud cheers)—and the position in which the hon. member stood, they would, perhaps, be inclined to grant him some indulgence. (Cheers.)

Sir G. H. Smyth, as an individual, would enter his protest against it. (Cries of "Oh.")

Mr. Attwood resumed: Sir, I thank you for the indulgence you have extended to me, and I shall not trespass long upon the attention of the House. (Hear, hear.) But I beg leave to say a few words with regard to my own peculiar position. Although I most cordially support every part of the petition, and am ready to support and verify every word of it, and although I am determined to use every legal means in my power to carry it into law, I must say that many reports have gone abroad of arguments that have been used, or that are said to have been used, in various parts of the country, which I disavow. (Hear.) I never, at any period of my life, recommended any principles except those of peace, law, order, loyalty, and union, and that, Sir, in good faith, not holding one face here, and another out of doors. (Cheers) The face which you now see, I have always held out of doors and within doors; my determination is to do all that lies in my power, as a man, a Christian, and as a gentleman, to work out the wishes of the petitioners. (Cheers.) Having stated so much, I wash my hands of any talk of physical force—(loud cheers)—or arms. I want no arms but the will of the people, legally, firmly, and constitutionally expressed—(cheers)—and if the people will only send to this House a similar petition from every parish in England, and if they will go on using every argument which justice, reason, and wisdom dictate, they will create such an action upon the public mind, which will again act upon the members of this House, that when the people shall ask for a remedy of their grievances, in the manner dictated by the Constitution of the country—when they only ask for that which belongs to them by the Constitution of the country—I hope, that though hon. gentlemen here differ from me in opinion—I will not insinuate that they differ from me in feeling—I say, if the people go on, washing their hands from all threats and insolence, but go on firmly, honestly, and constitutionally, I am sure their demands will meet with respectful attention. Having said so much, I will now read the prayer of the petition :—

"May it, therefore, please your honourable House to take this our petition into your most serious consideration, and to use your utmost endeavours, by all constitutional means, to have a law passed granting to every male of lawful age, sane mind, and unconvicted of crime, the right of voting for Members of Parliament; and directing all future elections of Members of Parliament to be in the way of secret ballot; and ordaining that the duration of Parliament shall in no case exceed one year; and abolishing all property qualifications in the members; and providing for their due remuneration while in attendance on their parliamentary duties." (Cheers.) I thank the House for the patient hearing they have given me upon this occasion. I will trespass no further, but move that the petition be brought up. (Laughter.) The hon. member had unrolled a considerable portion of the petition, and took its heading up to the table amidst loud laughter and cheers.

Mr. Fielden : I beg to support the prayer of the petition.

Mr. Attwood then moved that the petition be printed.—Ordered.

The Speaker : Does the hon. member mean to found any motion on the petition?

Mr. Attwood : Yes, Sir; I beg to give notice, that on the first supply day next week, I shall move that the House do resolve itself into a committee of the whole House, to take the petition into consideration.

The *Birmingham Journal*, commenting upon the above scene, says :—

"All accounts concur in describing the presentation of the National Petition by Mr. Attwood as distinguished by the most correct taste and feeling, on the part of the hon. member; and his speech on the occasion as marked by great dignity, as well as sound sense and moderation. An ear and eye witness of the whole says, in a private letter addressed to a friend here, 'I wish you could have seen our excellent friend Attwood, when he presented the petition on Friday. It was done to admiration, and, except the single interruption from the Essex baronet, the member for Colchester, not a whisper of dissatisfaction was breathed during the whole delivery of his sensible speech. On the whole, it was, I assure you, a successful exhibition.'"

On the next day (June 15th) an interesting meeting of the friends of Poland took place at Freemasons' Hall. The Duke of Sussex presided, and the attendance was numerous and most respectable. Mr. Attwood was present and spoke with great energy upon his favourite topics—the iniquities of Russia, the servility of England, and the misfortunes of Poland.

The great motion came on before the House of Commons on Friday, July 12th, 1839, when Lord John Russell, having moved the order of the day, in order to allow Mr. Attwood to proceed with his motion, the latter thanked him for his courtesy and proceeded to move the adoption of the National Petition in a speech which occupies two-and-a-half columns of the *Birmingham Journal*. He enlarged upon the misery and destitution which everywhere prevailed amongst the industrious classes, and warned the aristocracy against incurring the fate of the French noblesse. Towards the conclusion he gave the following interesting anecdote:—

When political unions were first formed in this country, he had sent a case to a very eminent counsel for the purpose of having his opinion as to the legality of those societies. The able man whom he had consulted returned the case, with an intimation that, if he said political unions were illegal he should be saying what he did not think ; and if he gave his opinion that they were legal, he feared he might lead many honest men astray, for it would be difficult, if not morally impossible, to join those associations without trenching upon the law. He therefore returned the fee, and expressed no opinion upon the subject. (Hear, hear.) This was the way in which Sir Charles Wetherell acted upon that occasion. He (Mr. Attwood) had profited by the opinion which he had thus obtained without a fee, and had avoided the danger of overstepping the *flammantia mœnia* of the law.

Mr. Fielden and other Radical members supported the motion, but the result was, of course, foreseen, for nobody ever expected such a revolutionary proposal to be as well received by the House as it actually was. In the course of the debate Mr. Attwood experienced bitter mortification, which he thus describes in a letter dated July 17th :—

Lord John Russell, as his main answer to my arguments, produced to the House a placard, unheard of by me before, and signed apparently by every member of the General Convention of the Industrious Classes, openly rejecting these my known and proved doctrines and opinions, denouncing what the placard calls *the power and corrupting influence of paper money*, and declaring that the industrious classes have been " *defrauded by the fraudulent bits of paper, which our state tricksters dignify with the name of money*, and are at this moment being *robbed by that system of three-fourths of their labour ! ! !*"

Here was an argument which I could not answer. When Lord John Russell, holding the placard in his hand, and reading its contents, triumphantly enquired, "of what use would my reform be when my own friends rejected its most important objects?" I was paralysed. I had created the General Convention. It was the offspring of my own brain. I was surrounded by enemies on every side, *many of them interested against me*, and all contending against me. At this very moment, *out of my own camp*, a mortal weapon was directed against my heart !

I leave you, my friends, to judge of my feelings. For twenty-five years I have wasted my life in incessant labours.

The House divided, and the numbers were—

For the motion	46
Against it	235
Majority	189

The events which followed the rejection of the National Petition almost broke the heart of Thomas Attwood ; but all

Conservatives must be thankful that they happened, for there cannot be a doubt that, had the Chartists loyally accepted him as their leader and persevered in the course of firm, persistent, and peaceable agitation recommended by him, the famous five points would have been conceded many years ago. The country has made great advances towards democracy during the last forty-five years, but only two of the least important of the five demands have been obtained. All sorts of disorders soon took place. Some of the Chartists resolved to carry out the scheme of a "sacred month's" abstention from labour, but others made several abortive and absurd attempts to employ physical force. These were easily suppressed by the military and police, and they served the purpose of disgusting the respectable classes with the movement. Birmingham was in a fearful state during July, and the riots culminated on the 15th, when lamp-posts and pavements were torn up, houses sacked and pillaged, furniture burnt, and at length houses set fire to. Order was at last restored by the Rifles and Dragoons, with some bloodshed. The masses had, for once, escaped from the firm and steady guidance of Attwood, and the consequences were deplorable. His melancholy letter of July 17th, to which I have already referred, concludes as follows:—

> My Friends,—In final reply to your kind and gratifying invitation to me to attend a great meeting in Birmingham, for the purpose of restoring harmony and reconciliation amongst the different classes of our townsmen, I have to say that I do not think it prudent to do so in the present excited state of men's minds. The enemies of the people, always on the watch to injure the people's cause, with spies, traitors, enthusiasts, and fools, would undoubtedly be at work. Mischief of some kind would probably be produced, and that mischief, whatever it might be, *would most certainly be laid at my door.*

On the 6th of August Mr. Attwood made his last, despairing, effort in the House of Commons to arrest the progress of Russian ambition in the East. He spoke thus:—

> There is one subject of my recent lucubrations which will be anything but gratifying to the noble Secretary for Foreign Affairs, and on which I must ask him a few questions. I was indeed truly glad to hear the noble lord express this evening such interest in, and such desire to extend the commercial relations of this country, but if the noble lord is really in earnest,

how is it he has allowed British trade to be excluded from the Black Sea? How is it that he has allowed the Circassians, a gallant people, who alone brave the whole power of Russia, to be cut off from all intercourse with England? Why does he not enter into commercial treaties with the Circassian chiefs, who have an extent of 300 miles of coast? He knows the importance of that country as a barrier to India, as the only means of arresting the designs, and effectually opposing the aggressions, of Russia in that direction. The noble lord surely cannot now sanction the Treaty of Adrianople, by which Russia claims the Circassian territory, as he has that of Unkiar Skelessi, by which the British flag is dishonoured by its exclusion from the Black Sea. I have heard the noble lord say in this House that he did not recognise any claim of Russia to the possession of Circassia—that Russia had no right to receive Circassia—that Turkey had no right to give it, as it was never subject to her—that Russia had not actual possession, and therefore could not establish custom-house regulations in a country which she did not hold; indeed, in the disgraceful affair of the "Vixen"—that burning shame to England—he only justified the capture of that vessel under the pretext that Russia had a fort in the Bay of Soudjoukkale—a pretence by which he attempted to throw dust in the eyes of the country. Why, then, I ask the noble lord, why does he not extend British commerce by opening communications with the Circassian chiefs, who look to England with hope and for protection? Where could he find better or more important allies? If Circassia falls, the supremacy of Russia is thus established at once in the East: how long then will he guarantee to this country the continuance of her trade with Turkey and Trebizonde? If the noble lord would imitate in the West the energy displayed by the Indian Government in the East, matters would soon be brought to an issue. Why, indeed, is not the British fleet in the Black Sea to protect our commerce with Circassia? The noble lord has said Russia possesses Anapa and a few other places or forts on the coast; but the Circassians have 300 miles of coast; and, supposing Russia to hold 50 miles of it, is it any reason why we should allow her to possess the remainder, and thus forward the views of Russia, who has that obstacle to remove before she seizes the Dardanelles, and eventually drives us out of India? I again call to the noble lord to know why he does not recognise the independence of Circassia? It has been thought and said that Russian gold has found its way into this House. I do not mean to accuse the noble lord of having received Russian gold, but the idea has gone abroad that Russian gold has found its way into this House. The noble lord cannot but be aware that charges involving criminality of a serious nature have been put forth against him—in print too—not alone in the daily and weekly press, but in pamphlets and works, some of which I now hold in my hand—not the productions of obscure and unknown individuals, but respectable gentlemen, having filled high offices—secretaries of embassy—employés and protegés of the noble lord himself. Mr. Urquhart and Mr. Parish have brought forward these accusations, and supported them by documentary evidence. God forbid that I should say that they are true; but they are uncontradicted —they have gone forth to the country, and why is it that the noble lord has not instituted legal proceedings against these gentlemen? I think it right to state to the noble lord that the country expected that he would have taken such a course as a means of self-justification. Why have not the parties who bring forward such charges been prosecuted for libel? I have not brought this forward to the notice of the House from any unpleasant feeling to the noble lord, but in fulfilment of a duty; I have a right to call attention to this subject."

Strange to say, this remarkable and temperate speech elicited no reply whatever from Lord Palmerston, and the House was too servile to insist that he should give one. Stranger still, the speech was suppressed by all the London newspapers except the *Era*, which printed it in full, with an article of indignant comment upon the unworthy cowardice displayed by all the members present.

The numerous disappointments and mortifications which Mr. Attwood underwent this year, combined with the illness of his relatives, seem to have brought home to him the necessity of seeking a decided change of scene. Accordingly, in the course of October, he removed to St. Heliers, Jersey, with all his family. In this retirement, however, he still continued to take a warm interest in public affairs, and frequently corresponded with his friends in Birmingham. On the 24th of October he wrote to Mr. Thos. Mackay a desponding letter concluding thus :—

"If I had seven lives, I would give them all to see the people of England as happy as those of this happy island."

In the *Journal* of November 30th there appeared from him the following interesting letter, which I wish I had seen when writing the earlier portion of this memoir :—

The editor has been imposed upon grossly by some one respecting my having been a Tory. During the last forty years, ever since I was a boy, I have been the foremost amongst the middle classes of Birmingham in supporting every possible measure of reform. In the year 1819, twenty years ago, I projected the Political Union, and was only prevented from forming it then by the counsels of several friends who all now recollect it. In 1811 I originated the great delegation, which I formed in defiance of the Corresponding Act, the Tory Ministers, and the East India Company. In 1812 I did the same with respect to the Orders in Council, and in that year 20,000 men of Birmingham gave me a silver cup for my conduct in attacking and controlling the Tory Ministers; and this conduct gained me also the friendship of the late Duke of Norfolk and other Whig leaders. This was thirty years ago, and it was not the conduct of a Tory. But before that time

I had gained the warm applause of Dr. Parr, by proposing, at a public dinner, the toast of—"The cause of liberty all over the world." I never uttered one word in opposition to reform all my life, although I have always (since 1810, when the bullion report passed) expressed the same opinion that I expressed at Holloway Head on the 6th of August, viz., that no reform of Parliament would be worth a rush to the people if it left the present metallic standard to execute its murderous operation upon them. In 1820 I refused to support the nonsense about legislatorial attorneys; and during my whole life that is all that can be said against me as a Reformer. And even then my heart was so much in the cause, that I befriended both Edmonds and Ragg when they came out of prison, as you have often heard me say to their credit. In those days only think how —— and —— would have stared, if they had been told I was a Tory, or even a Whig! I was intimate with —— and —— at a time when both of them were in nearly as much danger as John Frost now is; but I never in my life had a political friend amongst the Tories.

To this he adds in MS.—

I might also have added, that between the years 1810 and 1820, I subscribed to 3 different efforts to establish, or support, a Reform Paper in Birmingham, and lost my money in each.

In face of the above facts it is very strange that a notion should have been widely prevalent in Birmingham that Thomas Attwood had been a Tory in his youth. This probably arose from the circumstance that his opinions on the Currency were those which had been considered characteristic of many of the Tory leaders. They were held by the great Pitt, and have since received the hearty approval of Sir Archibald Alison.

Another cruel disappointment was in store for Mr. Attwood during the course of the autumn of 1839. The disgraceful riots of July gave his opponents a cogent and irresistible argument for the establishment of a police force in Birmingham. He fruitlessly opposed the Bill in all its stages, but in one instance was even unable to find a seconder. This is one of those cases in which even his warmest admirers of the present day must admit him to have been mistaken. All respectable people have long become accustomed to consider the new police indispensable, and every one would now laugh at the idea of their being hostile to liberty. In justice to his memory, however, it should be remembered that his opinions on this subject were shared by many other politicians, both Tory and Radical.

Borne down at length by public mortifications, domestic anxieties, and failing health, and penetrated with grief at his inability to relieve the distress of the nation, he determined to retire into private life. I do not know when he first made known his intention of resigning his seat, but his retirement seems to have been expected in Birmingham for some time before its formal announcement. He issued his farewell address to his constituents on the 9th of December, 1839. It is a lengthy document, but its importance, in explaining his political conduct and his reasons for resignation, demands that it should be reprinted here in full :—

To the Electors and Inhabitants of the Borough o Birmingham.

MY DEAR FRIENDS AND FELLOW-TOWNSMEN—

After having served you faithfully in Parliament for seven years, I now resign into your hands the honourable trust which you have three times confided to me. I rejoice much in these repeated testimonies of your confidence and esteem, and I rejoice more in the reflection that no part of my conduct has ever given you occasion to regret them. For myself, my only regret is that I have been enabled to do so little service to you, or to your country.

For seven years I have toiled on under the influence of the righteous hope that I might probably be of service in assisting to restore real and permanent prosperity to the industrious classes, and real and solid liberty to the people. All my hopes have been disappointed. I have found it utterly impossible to do any good to my country by honest means, either *within* the walls of Parliament, or *without* the walls of Parliament.

This latter failure has been to me a bitter mortification. When I found that all hope was vain, *within Parliament*, I turned to the people *out of doors* I had done everything in my power to give the Reform Bill a fair trial. I had waited for year after year, in the hope of its producing fruit *meet for the people*. It was not until all hope was abandoned that I cried out to the people, "Cut down the tree. Why cumbereth it the ground?"

You will recollect, my friends, that in 1832, when the Reform Bill was carried, I cordially united with you in suspending all further political agitation The immense movements of the public mind ceased; and the nation, to use my old phrase, sunk to rest as peacefully and tranquilly as the infant on its mother's breast. If wisdom and virtue had presided in Parliament, never was there a finer opportunity of restoring the prosperity, the happiness, the contentment, the power, the glory, and the dominion of England For year after year this grand opportunity was totally neglected. In the years 1834, 1835, and 1836, some little relaxation of the national misery was effected. But in the year 1837 the fatal "*screw upon the currency*" was turned upon the people as severely as before.

But in 1837 I again united with all parties among you in suspending political agitation. Three times in that disastrous year we appealed to the Ministers of the Crown. We implored the Government *to let the people live.* We represented their miseries and their distresses, and we pointed out the just and effectual means of relieving them. Lord Melbourne did not appear to be *against* us; but he openly told us, in the November of that year, that "*Birmingham was not England*," and that "*the House of Commons was against us.*" I ventured to assure his lordship that we would prove to him that "Birmingham *was* England, and that we would change the House of Commons;" and on taking leave of him, in the presence of the deputation of fifteen masters and workmen, I made use of the following words :—" My lord, I think it my duty to express to you my conviction that, in neglecting the prayers of the people, upon this great occasion, you will raise a *moral tempest* round your head, which no *moral means* can by any possibility resist; and if you attempt to apply physical means, it will be an act of madness and suicide."

It was not until *then* that I thought it my duty, after long and painful reflection, to appeal to the people, and to unite with many of my most intimate friends in the last grand movement to obtain a further political reform.

I did not look upon such reform as absolutely certain to be obtained; nor, if obtained, in any degree, however extensive, did I reckon it *absolutely certain* that it would produce either *prosperity* or *liberty* for the people. But under the dire circumstances of our country, I thought, and I still believe, that in the present state of the House of Commons, there is but little hope of recovering either the domestic prosperity or the foreign honour or safety of the nation; and, therefore, I considered that it was necessary to accomplish a radical change.

In attempting this great work, seven times greater than that of 1832, I was sensible of the difficulties which surrounded it. I had to move in darkness and danger through uncertain means to an uncertain object, and that object, *when obtained*, doubtful in its results of *ultimate weal* or *woe* for the people. *This* I explained to you at Holloway Head. But I *knew* that if wisdom and justice presided in the councils of the people, their *will* would be omnipotent. I *knew* that the interests of both masters and men, among the industrious classes, are *one* and *the same*, no possible mischief reaching the workman without first coming, as it were, through the very heart of the master; and I *knew* that, in *reality*, the masters had suffered more wrongs and oppression, from the state of the law and the conduct of the Government, than even their unhappy workmen themselves had endured. Above all things I *knew* that the *masters* among the industrious classes, *suffering at least equal wrongs and injuries with their workmen, possess the votes which command the elections of the House of Commons;* and judging from that community of feeling and opinion which common injuries and common sufferings promote, and from that *electrical* effect which *mind* has upon *mind*, and which *masses of minds* have upon *individual minds;* judging by these things, and also by the experience of 1832, I thought it practicable, by *just* and *legal* means, so to *gather up* and *unite* the mind of the industrious classes, as ultimately to secure either liberty or prosperity, or perhaps both, for our country. The dangers of the attempt were great; but, in my humble judgment, the necessities of our country were greater. I saw the industrious classes crushed and broken down, no hope to cheer them, no friend to protect them I saw the best hearts in England breaking; some perishing by an untimely death, some flying to the extremities of the earth, and others

"Whispering low,
Unhallow'd vows to *Guilt*, the child of *Woe*."

It was under these circumstances that I resolved, in conjunction with my friends, to make the last great effort, by just, legal, and peaceful means, to establish a system which should give hope to the wretched and protection to the poor and the oppressed; and at the same time restore the prosperity, the power, and the violated honour of England. That effort has been made, and has totally failed.

Opposed on every side by guilt or folly, supported nowhere but in Birmingham, and almost unknown in my motives and objects in every other part of the country, all my labours became worse than useless. My humble warnings were unheard and unseen. The public press, whether Whig, Tory, or *Radical*, throughout the whole nation, concealed them from the public eye. All things went wrong. Whilst I was *building up* in the *day*, others were *pulling down* in the *night*. Whilst I was recommending unions between masters and workmen *against their common oppressors*, others were recommending unions of workmen *against their masters*. Whilst I was pointing out the just and righteous and effectual means of giving victory to the people, others were recommending *arms* and *physical force*. Whilst I was recommending PEACE, LAW, ORDER, LOYALTY, and UNION, and harmony and friendship between masters and workmen, and mutual and legal co-operation between all the industrious classes generally, others were promoting violence, discord, jealousy, suspicion and division, separation of interests and of feelings between masters and workmen, and general hatred, distrust, and alarm among all classes of the community. The deluders of the people succeeded in leading the people astray. The irresistible *moral tempest* which I had foreseen, was converted into hopeless and feeble exhibitions of *physical force*. The people had no hope whatever, *except in moral force;* and *there* their triumph was comparatively certain. *This* they were taught to despise and *throw away*. They did not possess the means of availing themselves of *physical force*, and if they had possessed them, it would certainly have done them more *harm* than *good;* and yet upon this broken reed they were taught to rely. Their *poverty* was the grand oppression which rendered reform necessary. They had not the *money* to *buy bread* for themselves and their families, and yet they were gravely recommended to *buy arms* for their country. Their *disease* was *poverty*, and the remedy which *rich men only* can make use of, was recommended to them. They were omnipotent *under the law*. They were weaker than infants *against the law*. They were seduced to set the law at defiance And now what is the result? The people are delivered up into the hands of their oppressors

Yes, my friends, *this* is the melancholy state of our country. The deluders of the people, by guilt or by folly, have delivered them into the hands of their oppressors. They have rendered it *now* almost impossible to form large combinations, or to hold assemblages of the people They have recommended measures *notoriously illegal;* urging the people to *provide arms for the purpose of either attacking, controlling, or intimidating the Government.* They have thus set *the law* against them. They have set every *jury* in England against them, they have set every *rich* man, every *humane man*, and almost every *rational man* against them. By unjust calumnies they have set the middle classes against them. By sanguinary threats they have set the upper classes against them. The master has been set against the workman, and the workman against the master. My friends in Birmingham, who for ten years have been the very *life and soul* of the Reform interest, have been rudely thrown aside as leaders of the people for merely standing on their known RULES AND REGULATIONS, and refusing to lead the people astray; in fact, for refusing to lead the people into that very line of conduct which has now enabled "*the lawyer and the soldier to break in upon them, and render all their exertions vain.*" Discord, suspicion, hatred, and alarm have been scattered everywhere. The peaceful, legal, and sublime *moral movement* of the nation which I was contemplating, has been shattered and broken up into a thousand fragments; and I have not the means of restoring the *public confidence*, the *unity*, the *morality*, and *strict legality* which are absolutely necessary to give it a chance of success.

The people have thus become a *rope of sand*. Their strength is withered, and their hopes are blighted. If they had "*held fast to the law*," the middle classes would, by this time, have been gained over to their side; and the strength of their enemies would have been paralysed. But they have been taught to rely upon *illegal weapons* which they have not the *means of obtaining*, nor the means *of using beneficially if obtained;* and to neglect, despise, and *throw away* that tremendous *moral power* which was *in their own hands*, and which the experience of 1830, 1831, and 1832 ought to have taught them was *omnipotent*. But *within the walls of Parliament* my humble labours have been equally disappointed in their result. Again and again I have pointed out and foretold in Parliament the calamities of 1837, and those of the present year, and I have shown how those calamities were, in a great degree, necessarily producing or increasing similar calamities in America. I have pointed out again and again the certain, just, and safe means of preventing them, and of relieving them permanently. I might just as well have preached to the winds of heaven.

Here has been my severest mortification. Twenty-five years of incessant labour have been thrown away. From 1815 to 1829 I had laboured incessantly *out of Parliament*, in unavailing efforts to prevent and relieve the miseries and the dangers which the unjust and insane attempts *to restore the value of the currency were producing.* I had reminded the Government, that no nation upon the face of the earth had ever accomplished such an object. I had stated to them, that it was an "object which even Jengis Khan, in the height of his power, and of his madness, would never have had the audacity or the cruelty to attempt." I had proved, in every possible shape, that *if persevered in*, it would ultimately produce "the wildest anarchy and revolution" I had proved that "the miseries of the people would become so great under its pressure that no taxes could be endured, and that the nation would become so weak and powerless that, in less that twenty years, the meanest of her enemies would *sweep her navies from the sea.*" I had even pointed out the *fluctuations*, the alternations of *real adversity* and of *apparent prosperity*, with which it would necessarily be attended. I had proved upon a hundred occasions, that "in attempting to restore the *ancient standard of value*, the Government, instead of adding only "*four per cent.*" to the value of money, as was pretended, were literally *doubling the* burdens of the people, and at the same time halving their means!!" In these facts and representations I had been supported and confirmed by many of the ablest men in the country, and *contradicted by none.*

In the year 1829 I had made this *monster grievance* of the nation the main basis of the Political Union. I considered that the first work of a reformed Parliament would necessarily have been its rectification. By your assistance, I had then rendered some service in promoting the Reform Bill, and I had indulged the hope that, although the *measure of liberty was niggardly*, the measure of *prosperity might yet be full for the people.* Seven years of bitter experience in the reformed Parliament have now convinced me that all my anticipations of national benefit were vain.

In 1832 I went into Parliament, as you well know, with the main object of rectifying this terrible oppression, and thereby of relieving the distress of the industrious classes, and restoring *the full employment of well-paid labour* and the full prosperity of the manufacturers, commerce, and agriculture. I lost no opportunity of attempting this, whenever I could break through the innumerable forms and entrenchments of a reluctant House of Commons. My facts and representations were never denied. My arguments and proofs were not contradicted. The House of Commons would listen to me with patience. None would answer me; few would support me; but many would give me privately the most solemn assurances that all my representations were correct. If I ever received any slights or contumelies, they were always, I believe, where they ought not to have been, from among the *Radical* members of the House. It was in vain for me to prove to the House, as I had so often proved before to the country, that the discontent of the people originated *mainly* in their *poverty;* that their *poverty* was occasioned by the want of full employment and of *well-paid labour;* and that these terrible calamities were occasioned *mainly* by the attempts of the rich classes to convert their *paper* rents, taxes, debts, and dividends into *standard gold*—attempts which tended to *strangle industry*, reducing the industrious classes occasionally to *one-half employment*, at the same time extorting from them *double* the quantity of the products of their labour, and thus in reality *quadrupling* all their public and private burdens, instead of increasing them "*only four per cent*" as was pretended. It was in vain for me to prove to the House, as I had so often proved to the country, that this terrible state of things could not permanently be endured, and that, if allowed to continue, it would ultimately terminate in the convulsive agonies of a fearful revolution. My arguments were incontrovertible. If I had been a Minister, they would perhaps have been irresistible, but as a plain tradesman of Birmingham they produced but little effect.

In the year 1833 they gained me a *minority* of 158 in the House, but in the year 1839 that *minority* dwindled down to 48! How could I contend with such a state of things as this? The members of the House of Commons, whether Whigs, Tories, or Radicals, have neglected all my warnings, and have persevered in supporting measures which have covered England with poverty, misery, discontent, and shame, and which are certain ultimately to produce its ruin

But, opposed and strangled as I was *within the walls of Parliament*, ought I not to have been supported *out of doors?* There was not a man in the GENERAL CONVENTION OF THE INDUSTRIOUS CLASSES who did not know my opinions upon this great subject. *They were altogether ignorant of it themselves.* They had selected *me* as their organ in presenting the national petition That petition expressed my opinions. At the very moment that I was *justifying the petition and defending their cause and their country's*, they joined the ranks of my opponents against me!! The men chosen by universal suffrage, and the men chosen by the £10 Franchise, were all equally hostile to *me.* How could I stand up against *friends and foes combined?* And how could I benefit a country which sends me such *friends* for my support?

> " So falls the land to sure and swift decay,
> When folly guides, and madness points the way ;
> So perish all the remnants of their line,
> When *love* and *hate* to work their *doom* combine."

I know, my friends, that you agree with me in opinion, that these unjust and insane attempts to convert the *paper* rents, debts, taxes, and obligations of England into *gold of the ancient standard,* have been and are the fatal source of nine-tenths of the fluctuations, difficulties, miseries, and distresses which afflict, degrade, debilitate, and endanger our unhappy country. Undoubtedly there are many other laws of a cruel and oppressive character, but the most oppressive of these, as you well know, are either *founded upon* or intimately *connected with* this *monster grievance* of the nation. The *corn laws* and the *new poor laws* are in reality *one and the same* with the *money laws.* They are all three like the *Siamese twins.* If you destroy one of them, the other two die a natural death. And the *new police laws* are much of the same character. I have often told you, as I have told the House of Commons, that "the *landlord* and the *money lord* have entered into an unholy league together. They first passed *corn laws* to make scarce the food which *supports man's life.* They then passed *money laws* to make scarce the *money which purchases the food.* When the people of England, ground between these *twin iniquities* like wheat between the upper and the nether millstone, seek refuge in the *workhouse,* the melancholy patrimony of their fathers, their oppressors then pass *new poor laws,* to close the gates of the workhouse against them, and to open *bastiles* in its stead ; and foreseeing that oppressions like these would drive the people to despair they are now preparing *rural police laws* to nip sedition in the bud. If you repeal the *corn laws*, you compel the landlords to repeal the *money laws* in their own defence. If you repeal the *money laws*, you render the *corn laws a dead letter;* and if you repeal the *new poor law*, you take the ground from under both the others! In this latter case, the usual burdens of the *owners of land* and of the *owners of money* will soon compel justice to the unhappy *owners of labour*.

With these my known views and opinions, expressed upon a hundred occasions, you cannot doubt, my friends, that I have done everything in my power to prevent the passing, and to obtain the repeal, of *all and each* of these oppressive laws. From the very first I have been their constant, bitter, and unflinching opponent. All my labours have been fruitless.

Nearly the same fate, *but not quite so inefficient*, has attended my constant and repeated warnings upon *foreign affairs*. I have proved, upon many occasions, in the House of Commons, the absolute necessity of humbling the barbarians of the north. I have pointed out their violations of the faith of treaties, their immense preparations for war, and their repeated encroachments upon English honour, interest, and safety in Poland, in Turkey, and in Circassia. I have shown repeatedly, that these barbarians have *literally menaced the shores of England with twenty-seven line-of-battle ships, assembled in one fleet, within a week's sail of the Thames, and that, too, at a time* (1837) *when England could not possibly have produced ten line-of-battle ships to meet them.* Animated apparently, *as David Hume foretold*, by one favourite object, by the *auri sacra fames*, "*the cursed thirst of gold*," by some wild anxiety to realise their own *claims upon industry in standard gold*, the members of the House of Commons appeared to me to have but little disposition to give serious attention to any other subject, unless occasionally, perhaps, when the sordid squabbles of party faction might excite them. The prosperity and happiness of the people, the glory and dominion of England, the honour and safety of the nation, appeared to me to have but little attraction for them. As I told you last winter, the very earth might have been rocking under their feet, and the Russians might have been thundering at their gates—all would have been unseen, unheard, unfelt, unknown.

How different would have been the situation of England if this "*cursed thirst of gold*," this "*beggar's vice*," had never prevailed! The people would have been happy at home, and omnipotent abroad. Poland, Turkey, and Circassia would have been safe *as Affghanistan is*. The Russians would have been humbled in the very dust; or, at least, they would never have dared to build the fleets which now threaten the dominion of the sea.

These barbarous Russians, for the last twenty-five years, have had no *legal money* whatever, except *paper money*, and yet they have recovered from the devastations of Napoleon, and have suddenly become the most flourishing, the most prosperous, and the most powerful nation of Europe. England has been engaged for the last twenty-five years, through all manner of miseries and dangers, in establishing her *gold money*, and in thus *quadrupling the burdens of industry;* and what has *she* become? This glorious England, but late the mistress of the world, now miserable and distracted *at home*, and feeble and contemptible *abroad*, has become the *football* of the barbarians *to-day*, and not improbably will become their plunder and their conquest *to-morrow*.

Strange it is to reflect, that whilst despotic Russia, despotic Austria, and despotic Prussia have each been acting upon a wise, benevolent, and patriotic policy, and have thereby made their people prosperous, happy, and contented, constitutional England and constitutional America have each been acting upon a policy directly opposite, producing directly opposite effects. In these latter countries, no *Hardenbergs*, no *Nesselrodes*, no Metternichs, are now produced. In both of them *industry is hunted down*, under the name of *speculation*. The *democracy* in America are at this moment *cutting their own throats as madly*, and working the very same wild havoc among the industrious classes *there*, as the *Jewish aristocracy* are working *here*. In their wild efforts *to convert a fiction of the law into a reality*, they are abolishing *credit and paper money*, which have been to *them* more valuable than the land which they occupy, and more vital, if possible, than the very air which they breathe. *Credit and paper money* have been to *them* the very life and soul of their industry; and yet they *virtually* insist that no man shall, in future, be permitted to plough the ground, or to cut down the forests, *excepting only the few lucky individuals who happen to be born with* golden ploughs or golden axes at their command! And this is Democratic America! *She* has universal suffrage, *she* has no national debt and no taxes; but she has raised the rate of interest to fifty per cent per annum; and her people, like ours, *except the Jews among them*, are *steeped* in poverty, misery, and distress. Greediness, malice, pride, envy, and hypocrisy appear equally to have animated the councils of both nations; for, strange to say, all this wild havoc is being effected in America, as in England, under the extraordinary pretext of *benefiting the industrious classes!*

Under the pretence of restoring "a sound and healthy currency," the legislators of both countries have *taken away the paper money without taking away the debts and obligations contracted in it*, leaving just sufficient gold and silver money in circulation to pay their own *legal claims* upon industry, but not sufficient to give more than half employment, or half food to the people. In both countries the people have been told that the *monied interest* was too powerful under a *paper system;* and under the pretence of reducing this power, the two legislatures have strangely contrived to *double* and *treble* it, by *doubling* and *trebling* the value of the money which measures it, thus grinding and crushing the industrious classes in both countries, and delivering them up "like sheep in the butchers' shambles," or, at the best, converting them, as I have always foretold, into mere "hewers of wood and drawers of water for the Jews!" What is this madness in the two foremost nations of the earth? Is it the mere effect of human passion blinding the human judgment? Or is it the effect of some mysterious Providence working its awful dispensations among us? My mind is in the dark.

But does it follow, because the Russians, the Prussians, and the Austrians are happy, and the English and the Americans are distressed, that therefore despotism is better than liberty? God forbid! Nations are made unhappy by despotism much oftener than they are made unhappy by liberty. But all human systems are liable to error. It is undoubtedly true, as I have often observed to you, that the happiness of nations depends more upon *wisdom and virtue* in Governments than upon any *forms* under which Governments are *created* or *administered;* but it is equally true, that the best security for wisdom and virtue in Governments is *the representative principle, fairly, honestly, and efficiently carried out.* That glorious principle, delivered down to us by our Saxon ancestors, may occasionally fail, under the pressure of human passions, or under the inscrutable decrees of a mysterious providence, but it has been the light of the world for a thousand years; and I trust in God that it will never permanently fade.

My dear friends and fellow-townsmen,—Injured in my health, and mortified to the very heart at the state of things which I have described, both *domestic* and *foreign,* and both *in Parliament* and *out of Parliament,* I now retire from political labour. Standing on the rocks of Jersey, or wandering over its beautiful and most happy valleys, I have had leisure to reflect upon the course which duty requires, and I am satisfied that no further sacrifices can justly or beneficially be required of me. If I had been supported by the industrious classes throughout England as I have been supported by *you* I should not have despaired of the safety of our country; nor, indeed, if I had received any sufficient support *within the walls of Parliament.* But I have received no support whatever, *except in Birmingham,* from either Whigs, Tories, or *Radicals,* either *out of Parliament* or *in Parliament,* and therefore I *entertain no hope.* With my rooted opinions, *confirmed by the facts of twenty-five years,* I should deceive you if I pretended otherwise. If the prosperity or the liberty of our country is to be restored, it must be done by other hands than mine. *Nothing will please me more than to see others succeed where I have failed.*

But in closing my political labours, I must beg the favour of your attention to one further remark. I foresee that, in the course of the winter, the necessities of the Government will probably compel them to have recourse to a Bank Restriction Act, or to a *paper system* of some kind. If this should be done *honestly, efficiently, judiciously, and in good faith,* it will yet give prosperity and contentment to the people, and rescue our country *permanently* from domestic misery and foreign shame. But if it should be done, *as I fear it will be done,* with the guilty determination of preserving the *paper money at a value equal to that of the present gold money,* it would do no good whatever. It will only complicate and increase the difficulties of the nation, without long averting the terrible catastrophe which awaits her It will, in fact, close the *gates of retreat,* by rendering *paper money* as noxious and as odious as the *gold.* If this *new curse* should be inflicted upon our country, viz., *paper money of equal value with our present gold money,* there is in that case, in my humble but decided judgment, only one possible contingency which can long prevent either revolution *at home,* or conquest *from abroad* That contingency is the possible depreciation of *gold itself, as compared with commodities and labour,* occasioned by other nations also adopting a *paper system,* or by the discovery of *new mines of gold* producing the same effect. Respecting this contingency, I forbear to give an opinion. *I am only sure that money of the present value, whether paper or gold, cannot be endured in England, I am equally sure that money of a cheaper character, judiciously issued, with open ports, would give high wages, high profits, and general full employment and contentment to the people, without raising the retail prices of food materially beyond their present level*

But this brings me to the consideration of another analogous danger, which ought to be guarded against. In reverting to such a *paper system* as may be absolutely necessary to prevent anarchy, and to restore and secure the full employment of *well-paid labour* throughout the country, at a time when a *real scarcity of food* is known to exist, it is probable, unless caution is used, that the *abundance of money*, co-operating with the *scarcity of food*, may give rise to *speculations* which, *for a time*, may raise the price of food to an *extreme level*, in defiance of all foreign importations, and this *temporary* rise of prices is rendered the more probable from the immense increase of the consumption of food which would be consequent upon the restoration of general prosperity. In this case the whole discredit of such extreme high prices of food may possibly be laid upon the *paper money;* and under impressions of this nature, confirmed by the calumnies of the last twenty-five years, it is not improbable that the very soldiers and the labourers may reject the paper money, and throw it back in the face of the Government. In 1797, this very evil was partially met and counteracted by forthwith raising the pay of the soldiers and the sailors, and soon after, of the labourers generally. It is possible, however, that we may thus be brought into a very serious predicament, which I have always described as a *false position*, in which "*it will be ruin to advance, ruin to retreat, and ruin to stand still.*"

If the Government should persevere in enforcing the *present gold money*, they may have to face *panic*, bankruptcy, and the universal discharge of workmen throughout the country, and if they should fly to a *paper system* for refuge, that refuge may fail them. *To persevere in the present gold system is impossible, without ruin. To restore paper money of equal value with the gold would be worse than useless. To restore safely an efficient paper system, under the present circumstances of the nation, and of the public mind, will require knowledge, judgment, caution, and decision.*

My dear friends and fellow-townsmen,—I thank you, from the very bottom of my heart, for your long-continued and well-tried confidence in me. I have never solicited the vote of any one of you, and I know not that I have ever thanked any one of you, individually, *for* his vote. Your own virtue and public spirit, and your own, too friendly, I fear, appreciation of me, and of my character and disposition, have been my only passports into Parliament. You have selected me with a noble and high-minded patriotism. I have had no honours and no emoluments to offer you, and no hopes to allure you. The seat which you gave me, I have always held at your command—"at the command of the *electors* or of the *non-electors* of Birmingham." I now retire from your service, exhausted, disappointed, and mortified, but rejoicing in the reflection that I have never *sold* you, nor *betrayed* you, nor *deceived* you. I do most sincerely hope, that in the choice which now devolves upon you, you will succeed in finding a representative who, with equal honesty of purpose, will be more successful than I have been, in relieving the distress of the people, and averting the *doom* which overhangs our country.

My dear friends and fellow-townsmen, I remain, under all circumstances, ever and most sincerely,

Your faithful friend and servant,
THOMAS ATTWOOD.

St. Heliers, Jersey,
9th Dec., 1839.

Reviewing this address by the light of forty-five years' experience it cannot be denied that many of its gloomy predictions appear exaggerated, and to have been falsified by subsequent events But it does not follow that Attwood's arguments were unsound; for no man, whatever his power of foresight, could possibly have foreseen the extraordinary development of the world during the last half-century. Being, as I have said, utterly ignorant of the Currency I have merely given Mr. Attwood's opinions on that subject without comment; but I think I may venture to remark that it is *possible* that the enormous and utterly unexpected discoveries of gold in California and Australia *may* have saved his opponents from the necessity of acknowledging that his views on the matter were correct.

Mr. Attwood's appointment to the Chiltern Hundreds is dated December 18th, 1839, and signed by Mr. F. T. Baring, then Chancellor of the Exchequer.

I have found it impossible to compress the events of this memorable year into a shorter space, but I now close my account of it with extracts from Mr. Attwood's private letters:—

To Mrs. Attwood, Beechlands, Ryde.

Fendall's Hotel, Palace Yard,
Feb. 4, 1839.

. . . I arrived safe and well here at 6 o'clock this morning, and went to bed for a few hours. I then went with my friend Scott to look up my *Shepherds*, and I found about 100 or 150 of them assembled at the British Hotel in Cockspur Street The Birmingham men came out and told me that everything was going on well; and they anticipate no mischief from the madcaps, who appear to be a good deal tamed. I then went to John A., and recommended him to close his litigation finally, lest his contract should be overhauled by an *Equitable Adjustment*, agreeably to the Tamworth Petition, which is probably drawn up by Sir R. Peel.

I am now sitting down to dinner, and expect shortly to see Bosco and Ally, who will find me alone. I hope you got home safe. I send much love to you and Bessy and to everybody. . . .

London, Feb. 6, 1839.

. . . The division last night will surprise you We poor Reformers had only 86 against 426!!

London, Feb. 7, 1839.

. . . My "shepherds" are working admirably, all prudent and good men. They will not appeal to the country as yet, until they have first canvassed every member of the bad House. John A. called yesterday and behaved very properly and kindly. . . .

London, Feb. 8, 1839

. . . John A.'s cause is expected to come on in the Vice-Chancellor's office on Tuesday morning next. The Compy. offer him £300,000 in long dated debentures, but the directors refuse to guarantee the debentures, and therefore this offer would not put an end to the prospect of future litigation He tells me that he has now £500,000 in his pocket, exclusive of the above £300,000. John A. strongly advises G. A. and me to get Lord Lyttelton's land at the Hayes, and build furnaces and mills there. . . . Love to Bessy, and Marcus, Rosy, Anny, and Patty and little Mark, and though last, not least, to Sarah Eliza and my dear Algernon . . My friends do not read newspapers, but, like Shakespeare's blacksmith, they "stand on their hammers thus," and listen. . . .

Feb. 16, 1839.

. . . Old Wakefield has distinguished himself very much to-day in John A.'s cause, which will come on again on Monday and during next week. . . .

Feb. 18, 1839

. . . To-morrow night we shall have a discussion on the Corn Laws, and again on Thursday. The Vice-Chancellor said to-day that he should take a few days to consider his decision in John A.'s cause. It involves the question of whether or not the directors of the Iron Co. are to be as personally liable for the payment of the remainder of the purchase money, £325,000, as it is acknowledged that Small, Shears, and Taylor are. The Compy. have offered to pay him £280,000 for the £325,000.

My "shepherds" continue to conduct themselves very well; but they have not yet obtained more than 700,000 signatures, and will have to produce 1,300,000.

Feb. 20, 1839.

. . . The Corn Law agitators had a sad defeat last night in the H. of C., viz., 173 to 363. To-day they bluster much and threaten to join the Radicals. To-morrow the battle comes on again in a new shape, led on by that redoubtable champion, H. G. Ward. In the meanwhile my faithful "shepherds" are coolly and prudently collecting their flocks into the fold. They are not yet as numerous as the sands of the sea, but they are enough. . . .

London, May 1, 1839.

. . . Kiss little Mark for me, and be sure to kiss Bessy. I shall come to her before she goes away from Ryde. . . . My rugged battalions are a little restive, but I shall bring them into strict order, or have nothing to do with them. I do not mean to be made either a fool or a scoundrel, and therefore I mean to have my own way. Peel again shows what is called a *white feather*. I believe he will drop his little Jamaica affair, which is now again postponed until Monday next. . . .

P S.—Bosco, Mary, and I dine with John A. and Richard Spooner on Friday, and to-morrow Mr. Martin dines with us.

Mrs. Attwood, Arabin Cottage, Ryde.
London, May 4, 1839.

. . . You will see in the *News* my proceedings with the Convention.

The Jamaica affair is adjourned until Monday, when I think the Ministers will have a majority of 40. I declined Dwernicki's application. I am almost daily compelled to do things which are nearly as painful as the cutting off of my hand. . .

London, May 6, 1839.

. . . We had a pleasant trip to Windsor yesterday, and wished much that you had been with us. Marcus would have admired the oaks in the little park, and also Virginia Water. . . . I shall not let the *mad-caps* go to Birmingham; and if they do, I will have nothing to do with them. It is well that I sent my letter to the *News*, as I perceive all the Radical papers wilfully omit it. Be assured that I shall not commit myself in any way.

The Jamaica Bill comes on again to-night, and I think it my duty to vote with the Ministers, who seem disposed *not* to allow in Jamaica the very game which they themselves are practising here, viz., striving by underhand means to overturn and neutralise the benefits of the Reform Bill. It is now currently said that the Ministers have resolved to fortify Shooter's Hill as a protection to London!! This a pretty commentary upon my Russian alarms. Besides, they are now surveying the coasts for fortifications!!

Numbers of M.P.'s have assured me how much good I have done although none had the virtue to support me. . . .

London, May 7, 1839.

. . . I have only time to say that the Ministers have all resigned to-night, and that the House is adjourned until Monday next. I had just fixed with the Speaker to give notice of the National Petition to-morrow; but all is now abroad for a few days. Be assured that I shall do nothing imprudent. It is said that Lord Normanby will be the new Premier, and that Lord Durham will be also in office. I will inform you more to-morrow.

The Jamaica Debate, which gave us last night only a majority of 5, out of 590, is the ostensible cause of the resignation; but I suspect the real cause is deeper. In the Jamaica affair almost all the Radicals deserted the Whigs, but I was true to my principles, which are *the known hatred of oppression all over the world*. In this way we had a majority of 5. . . .

London, May 8, 1839.

. . . I hear no news of the formation of a Ministry to-day, but it is certain that the old ones are gone. I think that Durham and Normanby will be consulted, or that the Duke of Wellington (if consulted) will give a large measure of reform It is indeed said that the D. of Wellington has recommended the Queen to send for Durham

I cannot tell now when I shall present the Grand Petition, but I think it will probably be after Whitsuntide.

. . . It is well that I have taken care to have my letter and resolutions printed in the *News* and the *Chartist*, for the other Radical papers have burked them, except the *Sun* and the *Champion*, which only insert the letter, complaining that my resolutions had been *somehow taken out of the hands of the secretary.*

P.S.—I hope to spend Whit-Sunday with you at Ryde.

London, May 9, 1839.

. . . I have no more to tell you than you will find in the *Morning Chronicle*. I expect Peel will succeed in getting up a Tory Ministry, but unless he repeals his Bill, he cannot rule six months. R. S was lately quite confident that in case of Ld. Melbourne's resignation, the Queen would first send for Peel, and that Peel, after consideration, would advise her to send for Durham. Time will show.

Czapski is coming down to you on Sunday or Monday, and I hope myself to come on Wednesday or Thursday next. I cannot leave London just at present, lest among all the "odd bedfellows" which it is said "Poverty brings us to sleep with," her little Majesty should possibly think of *me!*

Joking apart, I am really anxious to come to you, and shall do so some day next week. I do not like the nonsense of the Portsmouth Ball. There is too much danger, trouble, and expense attending it. The launch is quite another thing, and I will come to see it if possible. . . .

H. of C., Monday Evg.

. . . Whatever you do will be agreeable to me, but, if possible, I should wish Marcus to wait at Ryde until I come to you, which is pretty certain to be on Thursday or Friday next. . . . Sir Robert Peel has just given his explanation to the H. of C., and read the correspondence between the Queen and himself, laying all the difficulty upon the court ladies Lord John R. is now replying, and then the House will adjourn till Wednesday, when Lord John will make some further communication, and then the House will adjourn again for ten days.

At Molesworth's dinner yesterday, 15 of us Radical M.P.'s signed and sent in an intimation to Lord Melbourne that we shall withhold our support from any Government composed of the same persons, and following the same policy, as his late Government. This intimation will either drive Melbourne out again, or compel him to liberalize largely. We found out that he was thinking merely of toddling on in the same way.

London, May 14, 1839.

. . . I have no more to tell you to-day. Only I think Melbourne will *liberalize*, as he walked down to the H. of Lords yesterday, in the middle of the street, accompanied by Durham and Normanby. Our representation to him is certain to compel him either to liberalize or to retire again from office.

Do not trouble yourself about the Chartists. It is all stuff that is said about them.

I do not think that I shall be able to come to you before Saturday or Sunday next, and then I must certainly return to London on the Thursday following, as the Speaker will be chosen on the Friday. . . .

London, May 16, 1839.

. . . I have no letter from you to-day, which I suppose is owing to the launch. I am afraid I shall not be able to come to you before Sunday as I am engaged with my brother George and John A. We got no important information from Ministers last night; but it is expected by us Radicals that Melbourne will largely liberalize, without which he cannot continue in office a month. He told the deputation from our Molesworth clique that he would consider seriously upon the subject To-day I have answered the application of Stanley to promise to support Shaw-Lefevre as Speaker, that everything depends upon Melbourne's conduct in this respect.

When I come to you on Sunday I hope to stay with you until the Sunday following, as the House will not meet to choose the Speaker until the Monday. . . . You will see by the *Chronicle* that the Convention has left Birmingham, and dissolved itself until the 1st of July, when they purpose to assemble in Birmingham again. . . .

London, May 17, 1884.

. . . I can hear no more of the Ministers, but many things lead me to expect that Melbourne will liberalize largely; if not, he cannot hold office for a month, unless, perhaps, he acts upon the Currency. This I have told Stanley, and I believe our redoubtable 15 Radicals have given much the same answer in reply to Stanley's request to them to support Shaw-Lefevre as Speaker. So you see, my dear, rather an odd state of things. Here are 3 ladies and 15 Radicals playing at shuttlecocks together, and the shuttlecocks are called Peel and Melbourne. The 3 ladies strike back Peel, and the 15 Radicals strike back Melbourne, and thus the interests of a great nation are played with. I guess the ladies will gain the victory.

It is possible that I may bring Miss Charlotte Medley with me on Sunday, on which day I fully purpose to come to you. I am now busy with G. A. and John A. Love to Anny, Marcus, and little Bessy. . .

London, May 18, 1839.

. . . I called upon the young ladies at the Belle Savage last night, and found that they were gone with Ally to the Lyceum, where I followed them with Charlotte Medley and found them very well and happy. To-day they are gone to Kent. . . . I have no news to tell you, only to say that everything is quiet at Birmingham and everywhere else. . . .

H. of C., May 27, 1839.

. . . The division for Speaker has just taken place, and Mr. Shaw-Lefevre has 317 to 299, being a majority for Ministers of 18, one of which I thought it my duty to form. I left Patty safe with her father. Mary will have written to you to-day about a house, No. 27, Connaught Terrace, Edgware Road, which will do very well for Marcus, Angela, and the rest;

Mary proposing for you and me to stay with her for a fortnight. The rent will be £4 4s. per week, the same as R. Spooner's, which is at No. 30 . . .

London, May 31st, 1839.

. . . The House heard me with great patience from ½ past 9 to ½ past 11, but I did not think it right to divide. The report is short, owing to the Jamaica affair preceding mine, and filling up the papers. . . . Come safely and carefully on Monday . . I have written to-day to Mr Lefevre. Lord John has just declared for the Penny Postage. . . .

The above is the last letter from Thomas Attwood to his first wife which I have been able to find, but there is one addressed by her to her daughter and franked by him, dated August 29th, 1839.

(*Lord Melbourne to Thomas Attwood.*)

"*Windsor Castle, October* 1, 1839

"SIR,—I beg leave to acknowledge your letter of the 20th inst., which I received here yesterday. I thank you for it.

You know very well well that I differ from you. I differ from your opinions, from your views, and . . . , and still more from the measures you have taken to accomplish them. I always considered those measures certain to lead to the consequences to which they have led—danger to others whom you encouraged, danger to the State, and their own failure.

I trust now that your anticipations will not be realised, but I shall be happy to receive and to consider any suggestions which you may think of importance.

Believe me, Sir, Yours faithfully,

MELBOURNE."

(*Lord Western to Thos. Attwood.*)

"*Bath, Decr. 28th,* 1839.

"DEAR SIR,—I have received the copy of your address which announces your intended resignation of your seat in Parliament, and have read it with great interest I am not surprized at your determination, considering all the circumstances to which you feelingly allude.

I see the Chamber of Commerce at Manchester is at work in a way that shews that the light is breaking upon them, and symptoms of proceeding to act upon it in a different way than heretofore. I suppose the Report will be printed and published. I should like very much to have a copy, but know none of the parties who have taken the lead. Can you help me to a copy? —When all our Commercial and Manufacturing difficulties are seen by Commercial and Manufacturing Capitalists to be owing to *our Currency*, statesmen, however ignorant, must follow. I have never doubted that our gold idolaters have been the *Disturbers* of the *World*, and whether we shall *right* again without a storm of tremendous character is problematical

I am, Dr. Sir,

Your faithful and obt. st.,

WESTERN."

CHAPTER XXII.

Mr. Attwood's resignation—Proposed monument in his honour—Death of Mrs Attwood—Birmingham Loyal and Constitutional Association—Mr. Attwood returns from Jersey and proposes Mr. Scholefield at the election of 1841—Correspondence with Sir Robert Peel.

THE resignation of Thomas Attwood created intense excitement in Birmingham, and the *Birmingham Journal* of December 21st, 1839, which announces it, is half filled with the address itself, a leading article commenting upon the retiring member and his probable successor, and with letters and advertisements relating to the ensuing election. Speaking of Mr. Attwood, the editor said :—

"Mr. Attwood came to the representation of Birmingham neither unknown nor untried. He had been an earnest and honest advocate of economic reform for many years. As a politician, he was the first who, in modern times, organised victory in the ranks of the people of England. Birmingham carried the Reform Bill through the means of that great instrument, which was planned and framed by Thomas Attwood, and which, while subject to his management, was so powerful for all good purposes—the Political Union. On every consideration of justice and of gratitude, he is entitled, not only to our thanks, but to the thanks of every liberal man in the empire. He carries with him into his retirement a name without stain, without reproach, without suspicion. Of honour unquestioned, of intentions pure and disinterested, of temper and deportment mild, benevolent, and conciliatory, Thomas Attwood has contrived, during a long life, in and out of Parliament, to attract more of the kindness and goodwill of all parties than perhaps ever fell to the share of one whose opinions harmonised so indifferently with those of the men by whom he was commonly surrounded. We believe that there is not an individual in this large town whose hearty good wishes do not accompany our own—that as his public life has been one course of uprightness, so may the private life on which he is now entering be crowned with comfort and peace."

The great body of Birmingham Liberals at once determined that Attwood's tried old friend and coadjutor, George Frederick Muntz, should succeed to his seat in Parliament. A small section proposed Mr. Joseph Sturge, but these gave way, and at the election in January, 1840, Mr. Muntz was returned by a large majority over the Tory candidate, Sir Charles Wetherell.

Upon this occasion Mr. Joshua Scholefield paid the most generous tribute to the character of his late colleague, concluding thus :—

"It was not in his power to express his feelings respecting their late representative, Mr. Attwood There did not exist many men of greater powers of mind, and most certainly there did not exist a man of a more tender heart, of more generous disposition, or purer patriotism. (*Cheers.*) He was, in his estimation, positively one of the most perfect creatures ever known. He therefore proposed, with infinite pleaure, the following resolution :—

'That this meeting entertains the most grateful recollection of the talent and virtues of their late faithful and beloved member, Thomas Attwood, Esq ; and that it is the bounden duty of the Burgesses and inhabitants of Birmingham to express, by some permanent memorial, their gratitude for his disinterested, laborious, and patriotic services, both in and out of Parliament.'"

Mr. Edmonds seconded the resolution, saying in the course of his speech :—

"With respect to Mr Attwood's merits, he would not then pretend to go into them. He could not do anything like justice to them ; and nothing less than a town's meeting would satisfy him (Mr. E.), where everyone would have an opportunity of giving vent to his feelings in reference to one of the best of living men—(*loud cheering*)—a man who had served them with a desperate fidelity for many years, and who came before them with hands as pure as ever. Had they ever found Mr. Attwood the slave of any Ministry, whether Whig, Tory, or Radical?—(*No, no*)—No ; he had well and nobly done his duty, and carried with him the hearts and best wishes of his countrymen."

On the 26th April, 1840, Elizabeth, wife of Thomas Attwood died at Samares Manor House, Jersey, aged fifty-five, and was buried in St. Clement's Churchyard. Henceforth, the regular series of his letters ceases, and for the remainder of his life I must trust to my own childish recollections and to the few public letters and documents which he cared to preserve. And of these last, it should be noted that he only kept those which bore upon the question of the public welfare, never preserving anything as a testimony of his great popularity, or even to gratify the legitimate curiosity of his children and descendants. I have already given some particulars respecting the family of Mrs. Attwood, and need only add here that she possessed a fortune of £20,000, which, with a generous, though imprudent, magnanimity, she had refused to have settled upon herself, and which was never inherited by her children, a fact which I think should have been made known to the public at the time of the failure of Attwood, Spooner & Co., in 1865. Belonging to a Tory family, proud of their supposed relationship to Colonel William Carless, of Boscobel fame, the Radical politics of her husband were naturally distasteful to her, and although, I suppose, dazzled by his brilliant success, she always regretted the friends she had lost through his espousal of the popular cause; for party spirit, at that time, extended itself to the private relations of life, in a way of which we have no conception in these days. Like her mother she was a devoted churchwoman, and her liberality to the poor was boundless. Mr. Edwards, writing in 1879, thus describes the pleasant memories which still lingered around her name in the village of Harborne:—

"The older inhabitants of Harborne still speak of 'the Attwoods' as the best people that ever lived in the village. Their old coachman, William Newey, is never tired of telling of their many acts of kindliness to their poorer neighbours. Mrs. Attwood was the 'good angel' of the place —the Lady Bountiful. Every day—winter and summer—at the hour when her children and servants dined, came troops of messengers to the hospitable doors of the Grove, and none went away without carrying to their sick or aged friends dishes—designed and manufactured purposely, with three compartments to each—filled with the best cuts of the meat, ample supplies of vegetables, and huge slices of delicious pudding, all carefully covered with clean napkins, and tied in flannel to keep it hot. The coachman tells how he has often seen a joint, prepared for Mrs. Attwood's children, stripped almost to the bone to supply the wants of the poor and the needy outside."

On the 22nd of November, 1840, Mr. John Allday, of Birmingham, wrote to Mr. Attwood, informing him that the inhabitants of Deritend and Bordesley had held a preliminary meeting for the purpose of presenting him with a testimonial of their esteem and attachment. In reply to this letter Mr. Attwood sent a long and grateful reply, published in the *Journal*, and commencing as follows:—

St. Heliers, Jersey, 25th Novr., 1840.

MY DEAR SIR,—I thank you most sincerely for the kind and friendly sentiments which you always exhibit towards me, but I do beg that you will do me the favour to discourage, at least for the present, any efforts on the part of my kind and excellent friends to present me with any testimonial whatever. In the present state of trade, it would be too heavy a tax upon their friendship and generosity, and this reflection would be painful to my feelings Let them wait until my measures for the relief of the nation shall have been acted upon by the Government, and shall have produced the permanent fruit of justice, prosperity, and contentment for all classes of the people, and *then* either I or my family will receive with gratitude and *without pain* any token of their friendship and esteem which they may think proper to grant.

I cannot but painfully feel that I have failed entirely in my honest efforts to obtain UNIVERSAL SUFFRAGE for the people, but I much fear that I have succeeded too well in proving, *through the conduct of the late* GENERAL CONVENTION, that UNIVERSAL SUFFRAGE, if obtained, would give but a poor guarantee for the wisdom and virtue which are necessary in A HOUSE OF COMMONS . . .

Notwithstanding this discouragement, the admirers of Thomas Attwood held a meeting on Thursday, January 7th, 1841, at the Public Office, Birmingham, to consider the propriety of testifying the gratitude of the town towards him, by some fitting monument. Joshua Scholefield, Esq., M.P., took the chair, and the following resolutions were unanimously agreed to :—

"Moved by the Low Bailiff, and seconded by Alderman Betts—

'1. That the exemplary devotion of Thomas Attwood, Esq., to the welfare of the commercial and trading classes of the community during the long course of thirty years; his eminent political services during the struggle for Parliamentary reform, so successfully crowned by the great Act of 1832 ; and his zeal and integrity as a member of the Reformed House of Commons for seven successive sessions, entitle him to the warm and lasting gratitude of the country at large, and in a special manner to that of his fellow-townsmen the inhabitants of Birmingham'

Moved by Thomas Bolton, Esq., and seconded by R. K. Douglas, Esq.—

'2. That, in the opinion of this meeting, such gratitude ought to be recorded by some public and permanent monument which shall be at once worthy of the merits of Mr Attwood, and of the high character for liberality and intelligence of this great and populous town.'

Moved by G. Edmonds, Esq., and seconded by Alderman Jenkins—

'3. That a committee be now formed for the purpose of bringing the object of this meeting effectively before the public, with a view to the raising, by subscription, such a sum as shall be adequate to the carrying of it into execution with as little delay as possible ; and that the following gentlemen, with power to add to their number, do form such committee, namely :— Joshua Scholefield, Esq., M.P., The Low Bailiff, Messrs W. Scholefield, John Betts, T. Bolton, D. Barnett, J. H. Cutler, T. Clark, jun., H. Knight, W. Jenkins, T. Phillips, R. K. Douglas, T. C. Salt, J. Webster, T. Sturland,

S. Bray, G. Edmonds, R Ryley, T. Sutton, T. Mackay, R. C. Mason, J. Allday, W. Sandiland, J Ellis, W. Jennings, E. Mitton, G V. Blunt, Cutts, Lander, White, Hobbis, Sansum, Allen, W. Mincher, jun , Maddocks, Wilkes, Ault, J. Hawkes, J Rawlings, J Hardwick, J. Feild, C. Truman, J. Hampton, S. Thomas, T. Steel, E. Banks, G. Richards, J. Rodway, Reuben Wigley, Whitworth.'

Moved by Alderman Cutler, and seconded by Mr. Knight—

'4 That Alderman Phillips be requested to act as treasurer, and Mr. Douglas and Mr. Whitworth as secretaries to the committee'"

The *Birmingham Journal* of January 9th, 1841, adds the following —

"There was a good deal of animated conversation on the subject of Mr Attwood's great deservings, moral, commercial, and political, in which the honourable chairman, the low bailiff, Mr. Edmonds, Mr. Salt, Mr H. Knight, Alderman Jenkins, Aldermen Philips, Cutler, and Betts, and other gentlemen present, joined ; and the greatest enthusiasm was exhibited by the auditors. A recommendation was given, which we have no doubt will be very soon acted upon, to call a public meeting in the Town Hall on the subject. In the course of the evening Mr. Salt read some extracts from a letter recently received from Mr Attwood, which our readers will not deem uninteresting. They respect the most false and cowardly attack upon Mr. Attwood's character, made in the report of the Loyal and Constitutional Association, under the leading of Lord Dartmouth, Mr George Barker, Mr Richard Spooner, and the rest :—

'These men have the cool audacity to say that I had "*but little respect in the Senate and but little in my own town apart from the mob*" There is not a man among them who does not *know* that I was three times returned to Parliament by immense majorities, in *my own town*, without ever *soliciting* or *thanking* one single elector for his vote ' Can they find another man in England who can make this assertion ? They know also that the franchise in Birmingham is quite of an aristocratical character, being confined by the Reform Act, and by our local Acts, to householders paying £20 a year rent, and upwards. And yet these honourable and excellent men, the £20 householders of Birmingham, supported *me*, with immense majorities, upon each occasion.

But the Conservatives speak of "THE MOB" too ; by which unworthy term they are pleased to designate my innumerable friends among the workmen of Birmingham I rejoice in the reflection that I always *had* the confidence of the workmen of Birmingham, and I am determined that so long as I live, no conduct of mine shall ever forfeit it Twenty times over I made to them the pledge, which I was always ready to fulfil, that "although chosen to Parliament by the *electors* of Birmingham under an aristocratical franchise, yet I would never condescend to hold my seat one single day against the wishes of the workmen, or even of the women of Birmingham, whenever such wishes should be generally expressed." It cannot be doubted, then, that I had for seven years the unlimited confidence, alike of the working classes and of the more wealthy classes of Birmingham ; and yet my ungenerous and ungrateful friends among the Conservatives gravely pretend that I had "*but little respect in my own town !!*"

But my Conservative friends travel still further, and appear to think that I had "*but little respect in the Senate.*" It is very certain that I took all the three factions "*in the Senate*" by the *throat* and *grappled* with them in defence of the people, more vigorously and more constantly than any other man in the House of Commons. But it is equally certain that each of these factions always treated me with kindness, indulgence, and respect I was assured by all parties, and from all quarters, that no other man in the House would have been treated so respectfully as I was, both in presenting and in supporting the NATIONAL PETITION.'

In the course of the meeting, Alderman Phillips reported on behalf of the committee for Deritend and Bordesley, which is now embodied in the general committee formed on Thursday, that the subscriptions already received by him from a very limited circle of subscribers, amounted to nearly £200. Amongst these, the first received from a distance, we have peculiar pleasure in specifying a subscription of two pounds, by that able, honest, and patriotic individual, the author of the "Corn-law Rhymes." The announcement of Mr. Elliot's subscription, in his own characteristic handwriting, bold and rugged and free, is now before us."

The promoters of the testimonial to Attwood endeavoured to induce the lately formed Town Council of Birmingham to take the lead in the matter, but the majority of that body, with some reason, declined to introduce party politics into it, and the movement appears to have fallen into abeyance soon after. I cannot ascertain the precise causes which led to this result, but, whatever they were, there can be no doubt that the result itself was highly discreditable to the liberality and gratitude of the Whigs and Radicals, not only of Birmingham but of all England. Attwood's own sincere discouragement of the proposal does not excuse their want of common gratitude. It is certain that from this time to his death no public monument in his honour was ever erected in Birmingham, nor was any testimonial presented to him, although every man of his party admitted that the want of such recognition reflected anything but credit on the town.

Inured as he was to party abuse, the untrue and ungrateful reflections of the Birmingham Constitutional Association, already alluded to, appear to have caused much pain to Mr. Attwood, perhaps the more so as coming so soon after his own domestic affliction, for in the course of January, 1841, he published two long letters to Lord Dartmouth in which he called upon that nobleman either to prove or retract some of his assertions, but, as usually happens in such cases, his lordship adhered to his original opinions.

Attwood's old friend, Mr T. C. Salt, wrote to him on January 17th, enclosing the first bank-note issued in New Zealand, which is now in my possession. It was sent to him by Mr. John Pierce, a former active member of the Birmingham Political Union, who emigrated to Wellington, New Zealand, and was drowned there a few weeks afterwards The following extract from Mr. Salt's letter is interesting, when we think of the present state of New Zealand, and bears strong testimony to the courage and foresight of Edward Gibbon Wakefield in undertaking the colonisation of those distant islands :—

"I enclose you the first New Zealand note issued; it is sent you by John Pierce, who seems making a fortune; but, as far as I can judge, the New Zealand Company is a *greater* swindle than any joint stock bubble yet brought forward There is no timber, no river worthy the name, no land but an impenetrable forest of scrub."

Mr. Attwood resided in Jersey for more than a year after his wife's death, spending part of the time at Samares Manor House, and part at St. Heliers. During this period he drew up, and wrote in a large scrapbook, an account of "The Second Movement of the Birmingham Political Union between the Lower and Middle Classes of the People in the years 1837, 1838, and 1839." This was printed in the *Birmingham Journal* of June 19th, June 26th, and July 17th, 1841. The narrative naturally covers much of the same ground as his farewell address to the electors, but I select two passages, the one because it illustrates in a striking manner his fondness for the brute creation, and his habit of drawing similes therefrom, and the other because the language which he used in 1832 has been the subject of misapprehension from that time to this:—

In the spring of 1838, I then cordially united with my friends in this great *moral campaign*. I did *hope*, but I will scarcely say *expect*, that the patriotism of my countrymen would have rallied round the SERPENT BANNER of the POLITICAL UNION which I was raising in the HEART OF ENGLAND; and that, under that glorious banner, the SERPENT, the LION, and the LAMB, the industrious classes of the people might have been gathered up into one grand, peaceful, and legal combination Everything went wrong; the SERPENT, the LION, and the LAMB, and all the great principles which they involve were forgotten Instead of being wise as the Serpent, courageous as the Lion, and harmless as the Lamb, the people were taught to rally round new and unknown principles, which partook more of the nature of the ASS, the WOLF, and the TIGER. The doctrines of PEACE, LAW, ORDER, LOYALTY, and UNION passed away, and those of VIOLENCE, ARMS, PHYSICAL FORCE, and DISCORD sncceeded them. . . .

Some of the Tory papers have asserted also, that in the first movement of the Political Union, in 1830, and 1831, and 1832, I used violent and extreme language, and "*threatened to march* 100,000 *armed men upon London.*" *That assertion is also false,* IF TAKEN WITHOUT THE CONTEXT. In the year 1831, when we had the KING with us, and the Ministers with us, and the great WHIG ARISTOCRACY with us, and the HOUSE OF COMMONS with us; and when the King's Minister described the opposition to our views as the "*whisper of a faction,*" I merely asserted, at such a time, "*that if the* BOROUGHMONGERS *should be determined to drive things to extremities, and to have recourse to* ARMS, *I was myself ready,* AT THE KING'S COMMAND, *to produce, within a month, two armies, each of them as numerous and as brave as that which conquered at Waterloo.*" Can *this* be thought violent and extreme language *under such extreme circumstances?* If so, I can only say, that I intended it in defence of SOCIAL ORDER, in defence of the CROWN, of the ARISTOCRACY, of the LAW, and of the CONSTITUTION.

I do not know when Thomas Attwood left Jersey with his family, but I remember that his voyage home was a very tedious and almost dangerous one, owing to a breakdown of the machinery of the steamer. He was in Birmingham at the election of 1841, and made his appearance in the Town Hall on June 30th, amidst rapturous applause, for the purpose of nominating his late colleague, Joshua Scholefield. Mr. G. F Muntz found a mover and seconder in Mr. S. Beale and Mr. W. Mathews; while Mr. Spooner was recommended to the electors by Mr. W. C. Alston and Mr E Armfield.

Mr. Attwood commenced his speech thus.

My dear Friends and Fellow-Townsmen,—Since I last met you here in this temple of liberty, I have suffered much—domestic afflictions and public anxieties have pressed heavily upon me; but I thank God that I have yet strength to come among you, and to see the prospect of better days dawning upon our country. It is to me a subject of no little mortification that I should find it my duty to come forward on this occasion, because I know that I must come in opposition to an old and intimate friend—the friend of my youth and the friend of my age, and than whom I know very few better men in existence. I have no fault to find with him as a man or a gentleman—a friend or a patriot: it is his politics only that I disapprove. I do not believe that his politics are suitable to support the interests of the nation at this great crisis. It is therefore that I am compelled to go against him; and if he were my own brother or my own son, I should go equally against him on this great occasion. The ties of friendship have no effect on me when great public duties are at issue. . . .

He then spoke at length upon his favourite topics of the Currency, Corn Laws, &c., and in the course of his remarks he acknowledged, with characteristic candour and unselfishness, that the foreign relations of the country had greatly improved since he resigned his seat, and that England had recovered her honour abroad. He modestly reminded his hearers that he had always done his best to bring about this great result by maintaining the British navy at its proper strength.

The poll closed as follows:—for Mr. Muntz, 2,176; Mr. Scholefield, 1,963; Mr. Spooner, 1,825.

At this election, Mr. John Attwood, first cousin to Thomas, and defendant in the case of Small *v.* Attwood, was returned as a Conservative for Harwich, making the fourth Attwood elected to Parliament within the space of ten years, and Matthias Wolverley Attwood retired from the representation of Greenwich, whilst his father was returned without opposition for Whitehaven.

At the close of this year Mr. Attwood received the following letters from Sir Robert Peel:—

"*Whitehall, Dec* 7, 1841.

"SIR,—I beg leave to acknowledge the Receiving the Letter which you have addressed to me, and the report of a Speech delivered by you which accompanied it.

The attention which you have devoted to the important subject to which your communication refers, and my respect for the disinterested motives which have actuated your conduct in public life, have ensured for that communication an attentive and respectful perusal.

If I limit myself to this assurance, you will not, I am sure, attribute my reserve to any other Cause than a sense of public Duty.

I have the honour to be, Sir,
Your obedient servant,
ROBERT PEEL"

"*Whitehall, Dec.* 14, 1841.

"SIR,—I beg leave to acquaint you that I have duly received the Second Letter which you addressed to me, dated the 10 Decr

I have &c.,

ROBERT PEEL."

At the commencement of the year 1842 Mr. Attwood appears to have had an idea, soon abandoned, of emigrating to Canada. I can only find the following two letters preserved for that year; but it is evident, from the numbers, that many of Sir R. Peel's letters have been lost:—

(*Sir Robert Peel to Thomas Attwood.*)

"*Whitehall, March* 31, 1842.

"SIR,—I have great pleasure in complying with your Request and inclose a note of Introduction to Lord Stanley. In that note I state to him, what is perfectly Consistent with the fact, that amid the turmoil and excitement of Politics—I have always heard your name mentioned (so far as private Character and Conduct are concerned) even by your strenuous political opponents, with sentiments of esteem and personal goodwill.

I thank you for your good wishes for the successful issue of the arduous Labours, in which a sense of public Duty has engaged me.

I am, Sir,

Your faithful and obedient servant,

ROBERT PEEL."

"*Whitehall, August* 18, 1842.

"SIR,—I beg leave to acknowledge the Receipt of your Letter of the 18 August.

The report of my observations with respect to the issue of one pound notes which you have seen must have been a very erroneous one.

I deprecated any such issue as calculated to give possibly a temporary stimulus to Trade, but to ensure a subsequent aggravation of present distress.

I am, Sir,

Your obedient servant,

ROBERT PEEL."

On the 14th of July, 1842, Mr. Attwood drew up a long petition to the House of Commons on his favourite subject of the Currency. This was presented by Mr. Scholefield on the 18th, but probably met with no greater attention than his previous efforts with reference to the same matter.

CHAPTER XXIII.

Recollections of Thomas Attwood—Grove House, Harborne—16,000 inhabitants of Birmingham implore him to return to public life, September 29th, 1843—His reply—The "National Union"—Its failure—Letter to Sir Robert Peel—Letters from Lord Palmerston—Letters to the *Times* and *Morning Post*.

MY first clear recollections of Thomas Attwood commence about the year 1843 (although I seem to remember him vaguely at Jersey), and Mrs. Attwood has been kind enough to assist me with a few notes as to his personal appearance. Mr. Edwards, writing in 1879, says:

"The old women of the place still speak enthusiastically of his handsome face and noble figure, and of his cordial, courteous, and friendly manner."

That he was a man of striking appearance, every one admitted, though I have heard it said that he was never regularly handsome.

He had a grave, intellectual face, a grand forehead and massive head. His expression was thoughtful and benevolent, but often with a far-away, dreamy look. His hair turned grey early, but seems to have been dark brown in youth, and his eyes were hazel. The nose was rather large and aquiline, but not Jewish, and the retreating chin took away from the force of the face. In stature, he was just six feet, broad shouldered, but always thin. A caricaturist of the great meeting of 1833 takes care to contrast his spare frame with the portly person of O'Connell. He always wore black during the later period of his life, and out of doors a great-coat with fur collar and cuffs, which was very famous at the time of the Reform Bill. Owing to the strong objection which he had to sit for his portrait, it is to be regretted that no satisfactory likeness of him has been preserved, though of few public men were so many engravings published. Probably these were all taken from hasty and indifferent sketches. I have already pointed out some of the principal traits of his character, but may note here that a great fondness for children was one of the chief, and that even when oppressed by the heaviest cares of business and politics, he was seldom provoked into losing his temper by their naughtiest pranks. Many of his early Currency pamphlets were written with a child on each knee. He was profuse in his charity to the poor, and never admitted for a moment the modern doctrines of political economy with regard to the distribution of alms. No doubt he was mistaken on this point, and his indiscriminate generosity was grossly abused. Grove House was always beset by troops of beggars, who were never sent away empty-handed. He persevered to the last in the amiable, though dangerous, delusion, if delusion it was, that it was the fault of the Government that so many persons were wretched and starving. Charity was his only extravagance, and I should doubt whether any one, of his fame and reputation, ever lived in so poorly furnished a house or dispensed with so many luxuries, which other Members of Parliament would have considered necessaries. I can only remember two paintings in his house, and these had been acquired in a characteristic manner. One had been purchased to relieve a needy artist, and the other, a portrait of his elder daughter, had been painted by another, who had vainly importuned him for permission to take his own gratuitously. To rank he was utterly indifferent. He neither courted it, like the majority of Englishmen, nor did he affect to hate and despise it as many extreme Radicals do. He treated a duke and a labourer with the same kindly courtesy; but whilst giving to the former his legal titles, never showed the slightest subserviency to his rank. This, it should be remembered, was an exceedingly rare characteristic fifty years ago. He was utterly fearless for his own person, but nervously apprehensive of the slighest danger to those near and dear to him, and his letters are filled with minute directions for the avoidance of danger from boats, carriages, fire, cold, damp, &c.

At this time he was residing at Grove House in great

economy and retirement, with his two daughters and the children of the elder. Grove House was a plain building, of moderate size, which had been formed by the addition of a thin front of three stories to an old farmhouse. The grounds, however, were pretty, owing to their supply of water. In front of the lawn there was a good-sized pond with an island in the middle to which access was obtained by means of a wooden bridge. At the outlet of this piece of water, Mr. Attwood had constructed a little pond for the amusement of his children, and placed there a small water-wheel and hammer. The stream afterwards filled a sunk fence, and then found its way across a field to the "Bell" pool. Here lay a pretty coppice called "The Grove," where Mr. Attwood allowed the public to walk, though it has since been closed. Beyond this, a rough road led to some fields and to Harborne Reservoir, a sheet of water twenty acres in extent, round which, in the decline of life, he used to take his favourite evening walk. Harborne Brook, the water of which ultimately finds its way to the Trent, rises within a mile or so of The Leasowes springs, which flow to the Severn. Judging from a naturalist's point of view, there were some interesting differences between the two localities. Thus, the rose beetle (*Cetonia aurata*) occurred rarely at The Leasowes, but was never seen at Harborne, where the streams, scantily supplied with trout, nourished several kinds of coarse fish, whilst the beautiful rivulets of Shenstone produced trout only. One of the earliest facts which I can remember in connection with Thomas Attwood, is being taken by him to Harborne Brook, where I was delighted to catch two large bull-heads in some water left by a flood. At certain seasons, the lampern, or "nine-eye," used to ascend this stream in such dense shoals that it was easy for a child to catch them by the handful. In these childish amusements the large, benevolent mind of Thomas Attwood took a warm interest, whilst he viewed, with a contempt worthy of him, the costly and frivolous entertainments of the fashionable world. He still retained his love for animals, which, next to his affection to all mankind, was his most distinguishing characteristic He had long parted with his horses, but I well remember the three dogs—a large water spaniel named

"Beau," a liver-coloured retriever called "Myrtle," and a Scotch terrier named "Muff." Besides these, there were a grand old macaw, which survived both him and his son Aurelius for many years, and a cockatoo. His bear and eagles had disappeared before my time. Up to the time of his leaving Harborne, he generally spent part of the season in London, occupying modest lodgings in Connaught Terrace or the Edgware Road, and still taking a keen interest in the parliamentary debates. Of his four sons, none had fulfilled the brilliant anticipations which had been generally entertained in the neighbourhood with regard to them. The two elder had emerged into manhood with a reasonable probability of representing important constituencies in Parliament, but after his defeat at Walsall, want of means and a feeble constitution had compelled G. de B. Attwood to relinquish all ambitious views, and he was now cheerfully devoting himself to city drudgery, as Secretary to the Bank of British North America. Aurelius was leading a bachelor life at Hawne, managing the estates of his uncle, George Attwood. Edward Marcus was a barrister residing at No. 3, South Square, Gray's Inn, but the loss of his leg, and the sufferings connected therewith, rendered him incapable of professional work, whilst Algernon was in the house of Spooner & Attwoods, of Gracechurch Street, with the hope of ultimately being admitted to a partnership in that well-known firm. In the north, his brother Charles was busied with his scheme for opening gigantic ironworks at Tow Law, and had just energetically conducted an anti-Palmerston campaign in conjunction with David Urquhart.

Owing to various unfortunate circumstances, all my early recollections of Thomas Attwood seem tinged with melancholy. The recent death of his wife at the age of fifty-five; the paralytic disorder which, I suppose, was then beginning to undermine his strong constitution; the long and painful illness of his son Marcus; his daughter's unsuccessful marriage; and, above all, the failure of his unwearied and unselfish endeavours to induce any Government to adopt those measures which he deemed essential to the relief of distress, and to restore the prosperity of the country; all these sad events contributed to overshadow with clouds the setting of a brilliant sun. Although no politician in history ever obtained less of substantial emolument for his services, it may be questioned whether any one ever received more striking and extraordinary testimonies of popular confidence and affection. The last and crowning compliment (and I cannot call to mind that any other retired politician ever received a similar one) was paid to him in the course of this year. Forty inhabitants of Birmingham, bearing a petition signed by 16,000 of them, and appointed at a public meeting held in the Town Hall, waited upon him at Grove House and implored him to again take part in public life! This occurred on the 29th of September, and previously, upon the 8th of August, a large meeting of Chartists had agreed to accept his leadership, provided he would make the five points of the Charter the basis of his new scheme. To this flattering request Thomas Attwood returned the following reply:—

> My kind, generous friends,—It is very gratifying to me to receive from sixteen thousand of my fellow-townsmen this flattering but unexpected testimony of their long-continued confidence and esteem. It was never my intention to interfere again in any public movement of the people. For many years I have anxiously watched the slow but certain progress of the national ruin. A great change now comes over the prosperity of our country. I now think that the time has come in which I should be criminal if I did not co-operate with you in making one other effort to relieve the distress of the people, and to rescue the nation from the fearful anarchy which threatens it. The late great changes in the corn and provision laws, by removing in a great degree the buttresses which propped the powerful landed interest, have given a prodigious accession of strength to the public cause. Those changes are now forcing the owners of land into a community of suffering and feeling with the owners of labour. This I stated would be their effect, in my petition to the House of Commons in the month of July last year. Those great measures have already produced the disturbances in Wales, and the Repeal proceedings in Ireland; and they are at this moment rendering the payment of the rent of land literally impossible much longer in England. under the present monetary laws. Holding these opinions, and having your confidence to assure me, I do not hesitate to say that I will immediately consult the able and estimable friends upon whose assistance I must rely, and by whose counsel I must mainly be guided; and with their concurrence I will very shortly submit to your approbation the best plan which my humble reason can devise, for restoring safety, prosperity, harmony, and contentment to all classes of the people.

In conformity with this promise, Mr. Attwood consulted his

friends, and having invited the inhabitants of Birmingham to meet him at the Public Office on the 26th of October, he there submitted to them his plan for a " National Union." A large number attended, and many gave in their adhesion to his proposals, but the more respectable Liberals appear to have held aloof, and amongst the names of his proposed " Council " I see none of political reputation, save his own and that of T. C. Salt. In brief, the scheme was a failure. Attwood's great work was done, and it was too much to expect that in his declining years, borne down by sorrow and disappointment, he should a second time lead the people to victory. The details of the " National Union " occupy nearly three columns of close newspaper print, but the whole may be compressed into a single idea, that of " holding the Ministers of the Crown legally responsible for the welfare of the people." This scheme appears to have been too radical even for the borough members, neither of whose names appear in connection with it; yet, for a while, it seemed likely to meet with success. The *Times*, usually so hostile to anything novel or extreme, not only published Attwood's letter in full, but devoted several leaders to combat his arguments. His letters for this year, from which I shall now give some extracts, throw some further light upon the scheme of the " National Union."

On the 23rd of January, 1843, Mr. Attwood published a very long letter of 5¼ columns of close print, entitled, " Observations on the Letters of the Rt. Hon. Sir Robt. Peel, Bart., to the Birmingham Chamber of Commerce," which concludes thus :—

The labours, anxieties, and difficulties which the Right Honourable Baronet has to endure, and, I hope, to overcome, are certainly immense, and such as require the warm sympathy and support of the country. Fortunately for him, the period of his difficulties is short. He must either change his policy or he must retire. If the country should be suffered to continue in its present state for only three months longer, it is exceedingly probable that the *malt tax* will be *wrenched* out of his hands. In the present distressed state of agriculture and of trade, both the county members and the borough members will co-operate in *this;* and thus the falling revenue will sustain an additional loss of five millions per annum.

The Minister will then be driven upon an increased *Property Tax*. But here again both the *landed interest* and the *moneyed interest* will be combined against him.

Universal distress, a falling revenue, dangers latent and apparent, crowding around him. No hope to cheer him. I cannot therefore perceive how the Right Honourable Baronet can possibly hold the helm of public affairs much longer without relieving the national distress, and increasing the national revenue, by the adoption either of a just, fit, and practicable metallic standard of value, or of a non-convertible paper currency. In either of these cases, it would be advisable, in the first place, to have recourse to a temporary Order in Council to restrict and protect the Bank of England.

The course before us would then be safe and clear, but a measure of this kind requires extreme caution and discretion.

Mr. Pitt thought the danger so imminent in 1797 that he literally passed the Order in Council to restrict the Bank of England *on a Sunday*. . . . In the present state of monetary obligations in England, it is only this elevation in the prices of property and labour, *effected through an action upon the Currency*, which can set free the great processes of production and consumption throughout the country, which can effect a just and equitable distribution of the values of society among the people, which can restore the reward of industry and the beneficial employment of labour among the productive classes, and, at the same time, give equal justice, protection, and security to the monetary classes of the community.

(*Lord Palmerston to Thomas Attwood.*)

"*C. T.*, 18 *Ap.*, 1843.

"DEAR SIR,—I have to make you many apologies for not having sooner answered your Letter of the 1st inst , for which I am much obliged to you. Upon the Subject to which it relates, I fear, however, that we are not likely to come to identity of opinion; as my opinion is strongly formed one way, and yours, as I well know, is deeply rooted the other way. I am at present on my Road from Hampshire to Hertfordshire, where I shall remain for a week or Ten days, but if anything should bring you to Town after Parliament meets I should be very happy to discuss the matter with you, as you propose, at any Time that might suit you.

I fear, however, that the Result of our Conversation might perhaps be, as sometimes happens in such Cases, that we might each of us remain more deeply impressed by the Force of our own arguments.

I am,
Dear Sir, yrs. Faithfully,
PALMERSTON.'

"*C. T.*, 13 *June*, 1843.

"MY DEAR SIR,—I am sorry that a hurried Excursion to the Country has hitherto prevented me from thanking you for your Two recent Communications, but I shall not fail to read with attention the Paper you have sent me.

My dear Sir, yrs. Faithfully,
PALMERSTON."

(*Sir Robert Peel to Thomas Attwood.*)

"SIR,—I beg leave to acknowledge the Receipt of your Letter of the 1 of August, and to thank you for your intentions in offering the Suggestions which it conveys.

I am, Sir, your obedient Servant,
ROBERT PEEL.

Whitehall,
Aug. 3, 1843."

(*Thomas Attwood to Sir Robert Peel.*)
Birmingham, 4 *Novr.*, 1843.

SIR,—I have taken the liberty of forwarding to you a *Birmingham Journal*, reporting some late proceedings of mine in this Town. I should be much concerned if I thought that you could suppose them to be, in any way, dictated by any personal disrespect or ill-feeling towards yourself. If they should produce any effect, it is my sincere wish that they may assist in strengthening your hands, and in enabling you to overcome the sinister influences which have brought the country into its present fearful state, a state in which to retreat is difficult, to stand still is impossible, and to advance is certain ruin.

I have the honour to be, Sir,
Your obedt. humble Servant,
THOMAS ATTWOOD.

"*Whitehall, Novr.* 8, 1843.
"Sir Robert Peel presents Compliments to Mr. Attwood, and begs leave to acknowledge the Receipt of his Communication of the 4th Instant."

(*Thos. Attwood to the Editor of the "Times."*)
Birmingham, Novr. 10, 1843.

SIR,—In your paper of the 7th inst. you have done me the honour to publish my letter to the sixteen thousand inhabitants of Birmingham who have lately requested from me some plan for the relief of the general distress of the industrious classes, and for the common safety and protection of all classes. In your paper of the 8th inst. you are pleased to make some observations upon the plan which I accordingly presented to them, and you appear to assume that it involved exclusively a question of currency, a question which it was my object to avoid thrusting upon the public mind. I think, therefore, that you will oblige me by publishing the plan itself, in order that your readers may have an opportunity of deciding how far your criticisms upon my humble labours are correct. Certainly, there is no part of my plan which can in any way be twisted into a disposition to render the Ministers of the Crown responsible *personally* for any unhappy "condition of the labour market," or for "the number of bankruptcies" in the country. I only insist upon the facts that, in such a country as this, the industrious classes *ought* to flourish ; that nothing can prevent their flourishing but the mismanagement of public affairs ; that the Ministers of the Crown have the supreme government of public affairs ; and that no Ministers ought to be allowed to govern England who are not both able and willing to restore general and permanent prosperity and contentment to all.

By the term *Productive Classes*, I certainly mean both masters and men in every branch of Agriculture, Manufactures, Commerce, and Trade But I have always contended that the interests of these two most important classes of men are inseparable ; and that no possible good or evil can happen to the workmen, without first being experienced by their employers

You are quite right in your views, that in my opinion the increased pressure of the National Debt "is mere dust in the balance," when compared with the vast, subtle, poisonous, and deadening consequences which I attribute to the present currency system. I have proved upon a hundred occasions that nearly the whole of our "*fluctuations*," distresses, and discontents have been produced by it ; that its tendency is to place the workmen upon half employment and half wages at the same time ; to estrange the hearts of the people from the Government ; to strangle the industry of the country ; to make the yoke of *accumulated wealth* too heavy to be borne, and, if *persevered in too long*, to produce the certain destruction of our present social system.

You appear to assume that it is quite impossible that there can be any real connexion between the Provision Tariff of 1842 and the Repeal agitation in Ireland, and the Rebecca agitation in Wales, in 1843. Reflect for a moment, and you will perceive that the two latter movements are created entirely by the former. The Tariff of 1842 removed in a great degree the *uttresses* which propped the agricultural interest, broke down agricultural prices, and rendered it impossible, under our present system, that those prices should again assume a permanently remunerating level. From this great cause, from the pressure of the Metallic Standard of Value, being thus at last brought to bear with nearly unbroken force upon the agricultural classes, proceeds the unmeasured ruin amongst the innumerable little farmers of Ireland and of Wales. If no fall of agricultural prices had taken place during the last 15 months, the movements *ostensibly* against Turnpike Gates in Wales, and *ostensibly* against the Legislative Union in Ireland, could never have been heard of The distresses of Ireland, of Wales, of Scotland, and of England, were almost insupportable a year ago. By the Tariff of 1842 they are rendered absolutely so. "This last drop," in the cup of Agricultural Distress, "has made the waters of bitterness overflow."

Undoubtedly the proceedings in Ireland and in Wales are mere symptoms of a great organic disease. They are the mere mutterings of the thunder of the public wrath, directed against Legislative Unions and Turnpike Gates to-day, but which, under our present system, may probably be exhibited in one deadly and universal war against Rents, Custom Houses, and Excise Officers *to-morrow*.

Louis the 16th was dancing in a Ball at Versailles at the very moment when the Towers of the *Bastile* were trembling over his throne. Charles the 10th was hunting in the woods of Fontainebleau when Marshal Marmont galloped up to him with the terrible words, "Sire, it is not a Riot, but a Revolution." Our own James the 2nd was dining in the camp at Hounslow when the shouts of his soldiers for the release of the Bishops shook the crown from off his head. These great changes in the History of Nations never occur without the public mind being previously prepared for them by hoarded injuries and oppressions, nor without their being attended by premonitory symptoms which it is of the highest importance that Statesmen should regard. These *premonitory symptoms* are now visible in every quarter of the British Empire. Woe unto the Statesmen who may disregard them.

I am, Sir,
Your obedient humble Servant,
THOMAS ATTWOOD.

Three long letters from Mr. Attwood on the Currency appeared in the *Times* during the course of November and December, 1843; but, as my plan requires brevity, I take from them only the following extracts, which appear to me to possess an interest apart from the special subject of which they treat :—

A few years ago, in one of the Committees of the House of Commons, the extraordinary evidence of Dr. Franklin, given before the Privy Council of England, soon after the Peace of 1783, was brought to light The Privy Council enquired of him, "What, in his opinion, was the real cause of the discontents of the American Colonies and of their separation from England?" That illustrious statesman, the more than Washington in originating and conducting the American Revolution, answered, to the best of my recollection of the evidence, in nearly the following words .—" It has been generally represented in England," said he, "that the American Stamp Acts and the Boston Tea Duties were the cause of the Declaration of Independence in 1776. *That* is a great mistake. *Those* were mere symptoms of a great organic disease. That organic disease was an Act of the Imperial Parliament of England, passed 13 years before, in the year 1763, tyrannically abolishing, without knowledge or enquiry, all the Paper Money issued by the Colonial Legislatures of America. That arbitrary and injudicious Act created one general mass of poverty, difficulty, and distress throughout the colonies, which rankled in men's minds for 13 years, until at last the American Stamp Acts and the Boston Tea Duties came like sparks to ignite a magazine of gunpowder, and then the Declaration of Independence was issued."

Amongst the very few papers preserved by Thomas Attwood there is put up a copy of the Act of 1763, showing the importance which he attached to that measure.

In my letter in your Journal of the 7th December, I had no desire whatever to disparage the character of the late Mr. Cobbett, or to hurt the feelings of his family, which I appear, unintentionally, to have done, by your Journal of the 12th inst. He and I always agreed in opinion respecting the monetary *disease* of the country But we differed *wholly* as to the *remedy*. His remedy was to restore payments in specie, under the old standard of value, giving an "equitable adjustment" at the same time. My remedy was either to continue a regulated paper system, or to regulate the standard of value in conformity with the state of prices, rents, debts, and taxes then existing in the nation. I believe that he sincerely wished to lift up the condition of the labouring classes, but he never disguised the fact that he wished also to humble the Aristocracy, the Church, and the richer classes. This latter feeling certainly rendered him not a very proper guide for these latter classes; and this is all that I intended to express in my letter. I always made a point of reading his *Register* from its commencement to its close. He was a man of very strong prejudices. He always vituperated the paper system without measure and without reason; calling the bankers "Rag Rooks" and the paper system "worthless rags." He also always deprecated any depreciation in the metallic standard of value, which he designated as "the little shilling" policy, and he facetiously nicknamed Mr. Henry James under the title of "Lord Little Shilling." For very many years, perhaps 10 or 20, he invariably urged the restoration of payment in specie, on the ancient metallic standard of value; but it is due to his memory to say that, at the same time, he always urged the absolute necessity of an "equitable adjustment," which I deemed then, and still deem to be, literally and absolutely impossible. The Ministers at last adopted Mr. Cobbett's hatred of paper money. They adopted also his hatred of "little shillings." But they neglected to adopt his admiration of an "equitable adjustment." . . .

(*Thos. Attwood to G De Bosco Attwood, 7, St. Helen's Place, London*)

Harborne, *Novr.* 7, 1843

. . . In the meanwhile, you may see my *introductory letter* published in the *Times* of this day; and I think also you may see the whole plan published in the *Morning Advertiser* of yesterday This latter paper I have not seen, but the *Morning Advertiser* of to-day speaks of it as having been published yesterday

The publication of my letter in the *Times* seems ominous of some great change going on. . . .

(*Thos. Attwood to Algernon Attwooa, 27, Grace Church St.*)

Harborne, *January* 27, 1843.

. . It is possible that Salt may write to you to ask you to apply at the *Times* office for a manuscript of mine, on the subject of Sir R. Peel's letters on the Currency. In this case I shall be obliged if you will get the manuscript from the *Times* office, and take it directly to the *Morning Herald* office, saying that they were kind enough to insert my petition on the Currency in the month of August last, and that I hope they will now do me the favour to insert my present *Observations* on the same subject. In this way, it is possible that my *Observations* may be printed before the Queen's Speech is finally decided upon, which in the present state of things, and of Sir R. Peel's mind, I think is very important. . . .

Halesowen, Decr. 29, 1843.

. I have a letter in the *Times* of yesterday, and expect to have another or two, in a few days. As a matter of course, the *Times* must sneer and complain; but they appear to me not to touch my argument. Angela gets better very slowly; but the children are getting about again.

I was much pleased by the *Morning Post* which Marcus sent me, containing the letter of Muntz, but I could not find the quotation from Alison. . . .

Dransfield, the accountant, told me yesterday that the Iron Co. have given John A. notice that they are prepared to pay him the last £150,000 in May next. But I had understood that the money was due on the 4th April next . . .

This is the last mention that I find of the famous case of Small *v.* Attwood, which thus appears to have endured, from first to last, for nineteen years! I suppose that no other case on record ever put so much money into the pockets of the legal profession.

I have already noted the interest which Thomas Attwood took in this suit, and his readiness to assist his cousin in every possible way, although I cannot ascertain that he ever derived any benefit whatever from the large fortune which thus accrued to his relative. I have heard it said, though I know not with how much truth, that, but for his unflinching firmness, the case would never have been fought out to the bitter end.

(*Thos. Attwood to the Editor of the "Morning Post."*)

April 4th, 1844.

SIR,—Your remarks on my letter in your Journal of yesterday are calculated to excite the most profound reflections. Into these it is not my object to enter. But respecting "Jews and Lawyers," I beg your permission to state that when I speak of them, it must not be thought that I mean to speak disrespectfully of the most ancient and venerable nation in the world; nor that I mean any slight to the profession of the law, which I know has produced, and still produces, many of the most able, upright, and benevolent men that ever existed. By the term *Jews*, I only mean such men as Lord Chatham called *muckworms*, and as David Hume foretold would ultimately be the ruin of England—those bands of sordid and greedy men who are so blinded by the *auri sacra fames*, by avarice and jealousy, by the eager desire to aggrandise their own wealth, and to humble that of their rivals, that if it were proposed to them to restore the standard of William the Conqueror, or even to coin a quarter of a *ton* of gold into a pound of sterling, instead of a quarter of an *ounce*,—would, many of them, verily believe that it is both just and right and safe and practicable to do so. The late Mr. Rothschild was a *Jew*, and a most able and upright man. Whilst the late Mr. Ricardo, and the late Lord Grenville, the two "*oracles*" in both Houses of Parliament, were prattling their nonsense about "*Three per cent*," and urging the restoration of the ancient standard of value, Mr. Rothschild solemnly deprecated such restoration, and fearlessly told the House of Lords that they did not seem to know what they were about. . . .

April 15*th*, 1844.

SIR,—In your Journal of the 5th inst. I partially explained the fatal delusions under which the terrible Bill of 1819 was made the law of the land. Well might M. Say exclaim, "*Voila l'Angleterre, elle se coupe la gorge.*" There is no public man alive now, I believe, who does not readily acknowledge that, in 1819, the *unanimous votes* of both Houses were "*a gigantic error;*" but, wonderful to say, the very same men now commit a still greater error by asserting that "*it is too late to retreat!*" I believe that this last error is more terrible than the former. If it is not an error, I have only to observe, that in my humble judgment the doom of our country is sealed . . . I was once conversing with a nobleman of the highest rank, and distinguished for his virtues, and his well-deserved influence in the nation. He said to me, "I do acknowledge that we committed a *gigantic error* in 1819, but it is now too late to retreat." Upon which I remarked, "My Lord, I told you in 1819 that you were committing a *gigantic error*, did I not?" "Yes," said he, "I must honestly acknowledge that you *did*, but I must repeat my opinion, that it is now *too late to retreat.*" "Then," said I, "my Lord, mark! I, that told you in 1819 that you were committing a *gigantic error*, which error you now acknowledge, *and which error was then remediable*, I tell you that in saying that it is *now too late to retreat*, you commit another error, *which error is fatal.*" "Well," said he, "I can't help it; to the *Devil* we must all go, I suppose." And thus our melancholy conversation ended. . . .

[I am not sure to what nobleman this anecdote refers, probably to Earl Grey or Lord Althorp, although the strong language seems characteristic of Lord Melbourne.—C. M W.]

. . . No! The Bill of 1819 is not yet a *thing done*. It is at this moment, under the mask of returning prosperity, just *commencing* "*the beginning of the end.*"

When the payment of *monetary rent* shall have ceased, when the taxes which support the *national debt* shall have been abolished, and when *social order* shall have been reduced to the wildest anarchy in England, *then* the Bill of 1819 will be "*a thing done*," but not till then.

Birmingham, May 24, 1845.

. . . The Government and the Parliament cannot, I *believe*, produce one single petition that was ever presented to Parliament against the free circulation of "*worthless rags*" Why then is mortal war declared against them? If it is not the busy interference of *Lawyers*, some deeper and more criminal cause remains at the bottom. The late Sir Robert Peel told me that "the whole was a *Conspiracy*, and that Huskisson was at the bottom of it." And the late Sir John Sinclair urged me to move in Parliament for *a list of the persons largely interested in Funded Property* in 1815 and 1819, assuring me that I should find names of great authority, to which I forbear to make further allusion, but which might possibly tend to throw a light upon the deadly secrecy with which this whole subject has been attended.

I made the motion accordingly in the Reformed House of Commons. It was received with marks of general disapprobation on all sides of the House If I had thrown a *Serpent* down upon the floor, the *Representatives of the People* could not have been more alarmed.

It need scarcely be mentioned that the doleful predictions contained in these letters, and other similar ones, exposed Mr. Attwood to a great deal of ridicule from his opponents. Whether it was deserved or not I leave to those who understand the Currency question to say. But to show that his opinions were not singular, I note that there was published in London, in 1844, a book called the *Gemini Letters*, from which I have already quoted, which reviews the Currency question at length, and exhaustively examines the principles of Attwood and Cobbett, "who have long been considered as the leaders of the opposing Currency parties;" and that this work distinctly decides in favour of Attwood, from whose *Remedy* and other pamphlets it reprints long quotations. The authors who wrote under the name of "Gemini" were Birmingham men, but Mr. Attwood states that they were personally unknown to him.

Thomas Attwood.
Aged 62 - from a Daguerreotype
taken at Scarborough in 1845.

CHAPTER XXIV.

First appearance of Mr. Attwood's fatal illness—His second marriage, June 30, 1845—Visit to Germany—He leaves Harborne—Residence at Scarborough—Corn Law Agitation—Removes to York and Harrogate—Residence at Handsworth—Last appearance in public at the election of 1847—Removes to Allesley—Deaths of Peel, Wellington, and Matthias Attwood, jun.—Deaths of George and G. De B. Attwood—Thomas Attwood removes to Ellerslie, Great Malvern, and dies there, March 6th, 1856—The *Birmingham Journal* on his death—Mrs. Attwood's lines.

AFTER the failure of his projected great movement in 1843 Thomas Attwood appears to have finally decided to again retire into private life, a course to which many reasons, independent of political ones, naturally impelled him. He seems to have spent the year 1844 in great retirement, not even interfering at the election which followed the death of his old friend and colleague, Joshua Scholefield. Mr. Scholefield died on July 4th, in his seventieth year, and his son, Mr. W. Scholefield, was proposed for his vacant seat by Mr. W. Mathews, the other candidates being Mr. Spooner and Mr. Sturge. The polling took place on the 13th of July, when, to the surprise of every one, Mr. Richard Spooner at last obtained the reward of his perseverance, and was returned at the head of the poll as the first and only Conservative who ever represented Birmingham.

So far as I can trust my memory, Mr. Attwood spent a part of this year at Ryde and the remainder at Harborne. In December he had a severe attack of influenza, and when it passed away the first symptoms of the fatal disease (*Paralysis agitans*) which terminated his life after so many long years of suffering, made their appearance in one of his fingers. I can find but few traces of him during the earlier part of 1845, He spent the spring and early summer in London, and on the

30th of June, 1845, he married at St. John's, Paddington, his second wife, Elizabeth, only daughter of Joseph Grice, of Handsworth Hall, a lady who nursed him for the remainder of his life with the most devoted care and affection. After his marriage he spent a short time in Germany, where he appears to have been favourably impressed with the condition of the inhabitants as compared to that of the masses in England. In a letter, written from Aix la Chapelle on the 12th of July, he notes with interest the cathedral and relics of Charlemagne. I can well remember also, as an illustration of his kindness to children, that he brought home for me a pretty little snake, which he had caught in Germany, and which I afterwards turned loose upon Barming Heath. In the autumn of this year, to the surprise and regret of the neighbourhood, he left Grove House, Harborne, where he had resided for nearly twenty-five years, where he had seen his children grow up, and where he had witnessed such brilliant scenes and triumphs. He first removed to Scarborough, where he occupied a small house, still remaining unaltered, called "Grove Villa," looking upon the viaduct and the sea. This was his principal residence for the greater part of a year, and I can remember that his physical strength was still comparatively unimpaired, as he was able to walk across the north sands to Selby Mill and back. Once, when he was walking with Mrs. Attwood in this neighbourhood, a lark, pursued by a hawk, took refuge on his breast. This pretty incident has since often struck me forcibly, as emblematic of the character, which he bore throughout his life, of a protector of the oppressed and helpless. On another occasion, Mrs Attwood tells me, when they were at Moor Park, in Surrey, a wild squirrel came and sat upon his foot. It seemed as if the very brutes instinctively appreciated the benevolence of his heart. During his stay at Scarborough he gradually withdrew himself more and more from public affairs, and when urged by an old political friend, Mr. John Betts, to take part in the Anti-Corn Law agitation he was compelled to decline travelling for that purpose. Mr. Betts wrote several letters to him on the subject, and to these he returned the following reply:—

Grove Villa, Scarborough, 6 Decr., 1845.

MY DEAR SIR,—I thank you sincerely for your letter of the 2nd inst., and for the generous and friendly sentiments which it contains, and which, I assure you, are most cordially reciprocated by me

Pray do me the favour to express to the gentlemen who are seeking a repeal of the Corn Laws, my sincere regret that distance from Birmingham and other circumstances should prevent my taking any part in their proceedings. My sentiments, however, upon this great subject, continue unchanged I am of opinion that the people of England will never obtain any solid prosperity or safety until the Corn Laws are repealed. Those unjust laws were passed for the concealed object of protecting the landed interest against the contemplated effects of the *Money Laws* of 1819, and to a certain extent they have succeeded in that object; for it cannot be doubted that they have tended to *keep up* the prices of agricultural produce, and to protect the landed interest from that extreme *depression of prices*, and that general misery and distress, which the *Money Laws* have inflicted upon the manufacturing and commercial interests of the country. The *landed interest* have been hitherto *bribed*, as it were, by the *monied interest*, to co-operate with them in humbling the manufacturing and commercial interests, in aggrandising the value of *money*, and in breaking down the value of *labour*. The owners of land will shortly be brought to a community of suffering with the unhappy *owners of labour,* and they will then throw their weight into the scale of the people, and they will put forth the political power which they yet possess in repealing the money laws of 1819 (Discord between the *oppressing classes* at last gives hope to the *oppressed classes*.) Until this latter grand object is effected in *good faith*, it is in vain for the industrious classes to toil early and late and eat the bread of carefulness. They will reap only disappointment and ruin as their reward. So long as the landowners and the Government can obtain their *paper* rents, taxes, and salaries *in full* and in *standard gold*, there is no limit to their oppressions upon the people. The very distraction of the poor is made the aggrandisement of the rich. But when the landowners shall be brought down to the metallic level of 1793, they will have no resource left but to co-operate with the industrious classes in resisting that fraudulent and grinding oppression under which the people have been suffering for nearly 30 years.

Wishing most sincerely all health and happiness to you and your family,
I remain, my dear Sir,
Your faithful friend and servant,
THOMAS ATTWOOD.

About the end of the spring of 1846 Mr. Attwood removed from Scarborough to York, where he occupied an old-fashioned house close to Micklegate Bar. Here we all lived through the summer of 1846, though Mr. and Mrs. Attwood travelled in the course of the autumn. During his stay at York my grandfather fully appreciated the beauties of the Minster, as well as of the walls and bars and other antiquities of that fine old city; but the interest which he took in such subjects was of a general and not a special nature. It was the same with his taste for natural history. Men, and not books, stones, or animals, had been the chief objects of his study. Everything with him was secondary to the one grand aim of promoting the happiness of mankind.

Nevertheless, he had so lofty and simple a way of discoursing upon history and antiquities, so admirably lowered to the capacity of a child, that what I heard him say upon these subjects I have never forgotten.

I may note here that during the year 1832 his popularity was so great in York that an engraving of him (of which Mr Moore has given me a copy) was published in that city.

In the autumn of 1846 Mr. Attwood removed from York to High Harrogate, where he took a small house and remained about six months.

I can find but a single letter on the Curreney, preserved amongst his papers for 1846; but the following one from Sir Archibald Alison is interesting, as showing, as many passages in the *History of Europe* do, that his views upon that subject were shared by the great historian of the Tories:—

"*Sheriff's Office, Glasgow, March* 4, 1847.

"DEAR SIR,—I beg to return you my best thanks for your kind and gratifying Letter regarding my work on the Currency, to which an extraordinary pressure of business has prevented me hitherto answering.

It is peculiarly pleasing to me to find my labour approved and conclusions supported by a Gentleman so eminently qualified to form a correct opinion on the subject, and who has made it the object of such long-continued and profound study.

Should you be interested in the effects of a contracted Currency and free trade in grain on the *present* condition of the *Roman Campagna*, which is a most important subject, you will find it fully treated by me in an article styled "The Roman Campagna," *Blackwood's Magazine*, April, 1846.

Interest here by Bankers is up to 6 *per cent.*, a state of things I never recollect before. It was predicted in the Preface to the third Edition of my Currency Pamphlet, and affords but a melancholy proof of the effect of imported grain and exported gold.

Believe me, Dear Sir, With much Respect,
Your faithful servant,
A. ALISON."

In the spring of 1847 Mr. Attwood left Harrogate and returned to the neighbourhood of Birmingham. Here he resided for more than a year in a house called "Fern Lodge," on the Heathfield Road, Handsworth. Although he thus revisited the scenes of his triumphs, where his name was a household word, he continued to live in great retirement, and as the fact of all political excitement being forbidden him was generally known, but few of his former friends came to see him. Amongst these I recollect Mr. Muntz and General Bem. The enormous beard of the former, worn at a time when close shaving was universal, was calculated to make a great impression on a child, and the newspapers were soon afterwards filled with accounts of Bem's gallant exploits in the Hungarian War. During his stay at Fern Lodge Mr. Attwood's physical strength remained pretty good, and he was able to take walks of tolerable length, besides attending regularly at Handsworth Church. In one of these walks I remember that he found a fine specimen of *Prionus coriarius*, a somewhat rare beetle in most parts of the country, and at once knew that it was not a common species.

It was at the election for North Warwickshire in 1847 that Thomas Attwood appeared in public for the very last time. To the disgust of his Radical friends, he voted upon that occasion for the Conservative candidates, Newdegate and Spooner. I had a holiday for the purpose of accompanying him to the poll, but my mother becoming alarmed at the reports of the dense crowd, I was left behind at Mr. Mathews' house in Calthorpe Street, a fact which I have since regretted, for as he stepped out of his cab the famous shout of "Attwood for ever" was raised for the last time, and the sight might have enabled me to realise, in some slight degree, the stirring scenes of '32. As we drove back to Handsworth I remember the walls of Birmingham being placarded with "Thomas Attwood has voted for Newdegate and Spooner." This was, of course, a triumph for the Conservatives; but Radicals naturally thought differently, and attributed his last vote to the failure of his mental powers.

At this election, infirm health compelled Mr. Matthias

Attwood to retire from the representation of Whitehaven, after a Parliamentary service of nearly thirty years, and Mr. John Attwood was unseated upon a petition as member for Harwich.

Soon afterwards, Mr. Attwood's elder daughter, Mrs. Wakefield, left Fern Lodge to join her husband in New Zealand, but, at his kind and special request, I remained in England with him. I think it was in November of this year that Mr. and Mrs. Attwood went to Great Malvern for a few weeks, and took me with them. Edward Gibbon Wakefield was then staying at Dr. Wilson's hydropathic establishment, busily engaged in maturing his scheme for the foundation of the Canterbury Settlement, and then it was that I had the privilege of seeing these extraordinary men together, though, of course, I was too young to appreciate their conversation. Though both ranked as Radicals, or, at least, extreme Liberals, they differed greatly in other respects, and it would, I think, be difficult to determine whether the foundation of the Birmingham Political Union or the systematic colonisation of South Australia and New Zealand were the greater or more original design. Attwood was utterly incapable of understanding the magnificent and far-sighted views of Wakefield on colonial subjects. In fact, so far as colonisation was concerned, his opinions were not one whit in advance of those of the most bigoted Tory peer or squire of his day. He believed, in common with the "respectable" people of the country, that it was the duty of the English race to increase and multiply, to crowd and starve, in one small island of the globe, whilst they abandoned its larger and fairer territories to a few poor savages. It should be remembered, nevertheless, that he always firmly maintained that the soil of England was fully capable of supporting its population, provided only that a just system of government were adopted. Both these able men have resembled each other in their fate (owing, possibly, in the case of the one, to his own fault) of having their splendid services overlooked or denied by an ungrateful country. But, whatever the public may choose to think, it is fitting that justice should be done to their memories by their own relatives. Without detailing minor services, I believe that Thomas Attwood saved England from revolution, whilst E. G. Wakefield rescued New Zealand from the grasp of France. But, just as the credit of passing the great Reform Bill is popularly given to Grey, Russell, Althorp, or any one but its real hero, so the glory of the colonisation of New Zealand has been but grudgingly accorded to him who bore the brunt of it.

During the course of the year 1847 Mr. Attwood resumed his pen upon the subject of the Currency, and at least four letters from him appeared under the signature of "An Old Correspondent" in the *Morning Posts* of May 7th, May 17th, June 2nd, and June 17th, 1847. He also wrote the following letters:—

(Thos. Attwood to Lord George Bentinck, M.P., enclosing his pamphlet of 1826, called "The Late Prosperity, &c.")

Birmingham, 1st Nov., 1847.

MY LORD,—Upon looking over my pamphlets on the Currency, I find in one such a remarkable analogy between the circumstances which attended the great *panic of* 1825 and those of the present period, that I am induced to send it to your Lordship, in the hope that you may find it useful under the great duties which I foresee are devolving upon you.

I have the honour to be, my Lord,
Your Lordship's humble servant,
THOMAS ATTWOOD.

(Thos. Attwood to the same, enclosing his letters of 1847, in re Ireland and the Duke of Wellington, and in re Lord Ashburton and the "Birmingham Philosophers," also his papers of 1822 on the "Doubling of the National Burdens.")

MY LORD,—On the 1st instant I took the liberty of forwarding to your Lordship, by post, a pamphlet on the Currency, published by me in 1826, explaining the *sole* cause of the panic of 1825, and of all the anomalous distresses which have afflicted this unhappy nation ever since the Peace of 1815.

I now beg leave also to trouble your Lordship with 2 or 3 other papers of mine, which I hope may possibly be useful, in the present very gloomy state of things. . . .

The following letter seems to be the very last which Mr. Attwood wrote on public affairs:—

To G. F. Muntz, Esq., M.P
Handsworth, 27 March, 1848.

MY DEAR SIR,

I have been thinking that the present state of things in England, and on the Continent, gives a golden opportunity for the insertion, on the Books of the House of Commons, of a notice to the effect of the enclosed Resolutions.

I think that no honest man could vote against the first; and I think also that none but "*bold, bad men*" could vote against the two others. The worst that such men as Inglis, Bentinck, and Plumptree could do, would be to run away from the subject!!

If you should not think it prudent to insert the notice yourself, you will perhaps do me the favour to place the Resolutions in the hands of Wm. Scholefield, or R. Spooner, or Cayley, or of some other proper person, who may possibly think right to undertake the duty, bearing in mind that the Resolutions may at any time *be withdrawn from the Books of the House*, if their withdrawal should become advisable. If I am not mistaken, the very insertion of the notice upon the Books would at this time produce an immense effect upon the nation.

I am, my Dear Sir,
Yours ever faithfully,
T. ATTWOOD.

P.S.—The Salaries of the Ministers and Judges in 1797 were £2,500 a year each; they are now £5,000 each The Pay of the Soldiers was in 1797 *only 6d. per day;* it is now 1s. 2d. *per day;* and the same is the case with the Navy!! The present pay of the French Soldier is only 4d. per day!!

Resolved—

1st.—That this House, having upon many occasions expressed its determination to persevere at all hazards, and every sacrifice, in restoring the ancient metallic money of the country, and in consequently breaking down the general prices of property and labour ultimately to the ancient level which existed prior to the year 1797, it is but just and right that the *monetary burdens* of the nation and of individuals should, as far as possible, be reduced correspondently with this reduction of the *monetary means*.

2nd.—That with this object, this House will shortly proceed to enquire in what degree the salaries of the Ministers and Judges, and of other Government officials, and the pay of the army and navy, have been increased since the year 1796, and in what degree such expenses of the nation can be properly, justly, and safely reduced; and also that this House will shortly proceed to enquire how far the National Debt, mainly contracted during the existence of artificial money, can be honestly, justly, and safely reduced, and how far the mortgages, and other fixed *monetary charges* attaching to landed property, can also be honestly and efficiently reduced, so as to render equal justice to all parties, and prevent the injury and ruin of some classes of the community, for the unjust and surreptitious aggrandisement of other classes.

3rd.—That seeing how the diminution of the artificial money of the country tends to diminish the means and the inducements necessary to the employment of labour, and consequently to throw labour out of employment, by breaking down remunerating prices, and crippling the means of purchase among the community, and thus arresting the great processes of production and consumption throughout the country, this House will shortly proceed to enquire what measures can be safely and prudently adopted for the purpose of counteracting this fatal operation, and of securing, as far as practicable, to all classes of labourers, workmen, and tradesmen, the permanent means of being fully and beneficially employed in the mutual production, distribution, and consumption of each other's commodities

Without entering into the question of the justice or expediency of the foregoing resolutions, there is, to my mind, something very pathetic about this final despairing effort of Thomas Attwood, which I think must be the last thing he ever wrote upon public affairs. Life was over for him, but the one ruling wish of it was still uppermost in his mind, and that was to remedy by any means in his power (what he considered to have been) the cruel and fraudulent wrong committed against the industrial classes by Peel's Bill of 1819. In opposing that measure he had vainly expended the whole strength of his life, and he now entered his farewell protest against it. It was, indeed, the last feeble stroke of the dying lion.

On the 11th of July, 1848, Mr. Attwood removed from Handsworth to Allesley, where he had taken a pretty, old-fashioned stone house near to the church. Here the state of his health compelled him to retire into deeper privacy than ever. Soon after his arrival Mr. Newdegate visited him, but the necessity for perfect quiet having been explained I do not think that any one of note ever called upon him after this. Towards the end of the year he wrote the following letter of condolence to his daughter in New Zealand, upon the death of her child:—

Allesley, near Coventry,
13 *Decr.,* 1848.

MY VERY DEAR ANGELA,

Your letter of the 22nd August has given me the greatest distress, but I trust that God Almighty, in His mercy, will comfort and console you under the heavy affliction which you have sustained. No one is better fitted than yourself to submit with humble deference to the Divine Judgment upon this distressing occasion. If the dear little Angel had been left with me, and I had found myself unable to save her, I think that the sight would have broke my heart As it is, I trust in the Divine Mercy that she is gone into a state of eternal happiness and joy, where no troubles of our transitory life can ever reach her again.

Her dear little brother is, I am happy to say, quite well and happy. We brought him a few days ago from Mr. Noble's school at Worcester, and he will return there in about six weeks. All the rest of our family are quite well. Rosabel is coming home from Kent and Hertford, where she has been staying, and I expect that Bosco will bring her here in about a week and then take Evelyn back with him.

Pray give my kindest remembrances to your husband, with most sincere wishes for his health and happiness. I am concerned to hear that his brother, the colonel, has been so unwell.

I remain, my dearest Angela,
Your ever affectionate father,
THOMAS ATTWOOD.

I do not think that Thomas Attwood can have written many letters of any sort after this, which is the latest I have found preserved. Long before I left him his hand shook so much that he was scarcely able to raise a glass of wine to his lips, and for several years before his death he was obliged to leave off signing his cheques. Little remains to be added concerning his subsequent life. Gradually he became more and more helpless, and the whole of his duties of every kind devolved upon his wife, who never left him for an instant. During the first few years of his residence at Allesley his physical strength remained comparatively unimpaired, and he was able to walk for some distance round the neighbourhood, where he became very popular amongst the farmers, a class which he had ever done his utmost to serve. As a striking instance of his innate conservatism I may mention that he was strongly opposed to any alienation of the "Lammas" lands round Coventry, which most persons, even then, were beginning to regard as a nuisance. Another instance, in which he was undoubtedly mistaken, was his opposition to the Exhibition of 1851, which he regarded as a new-fangled and foreign idea of Prince Albert. He was now living upon the road along which he had passed in triumph on the memorable 28th of May, 1832, when the whole distance of sixteen miles, between Coventry and Birmingham, was lined with shouting crowds; but the recollection of that great day, which would have filled an ordinary man with pride for the rest of his life, never seems to have afforded him any particular pleasure; he was so cruelly mortified at his failure to cause general prosperity to follow in the wake of his success. The progress of his complaint was so gradual that it is difficult to recollect the stages of it. I remember accompanying him on his last long walk, which was to a place called Eastern Green, about two-and-a-half miles from Allesley. During the earlier stages of his illness he was chiefly attended by Mr. Prichard, of Leamington; but as the malady progressed he paid longer and longer visits to Umberslade Hall, where he seemed to derive temporary benefit from the skill of Dr. Edward Johnson, who then kept a water-cure establishment there. He had inherited the strong constitution of his family, which would not give way to the attacks of disease without an obstinate resistance, and, in consequence, he suffered severely. Mrs Attwood informs me that, during the whole course of his long.and trying illness she never heard him make a complaint, save that once, when informed (I think by Sir Benjamin Brodie) that his complaint was incurable, he simply said, "It is early to be prevented from doing any more good to any one." In the midst of his sufferings he invariably preserved his kind and courteous address to all, and that exquisite consideration for others which, in the days of his fame, had justly rendered him the most popular man in the Midland counties.

His sons were prevented from visiting him frequently by their business engagements, but Aurelius Attwood always made a point of spending Christmas with him, cheering the melancholy household with his genial wit. To these visits I always looked forward with pleasure, though the festivities consisted only of roasting oysters upon Christmas Eve and visiting the ringers in the belfry afterwards. On these occasions also Thomas Attwood used to repeat, in a grand and solemn voice, some favourite lines on Christmas, from *Hamlet*, until he became too feeble to be asked to do so. Whilst he was lingering on in this deep retirement it was his fate to survive several of his near relatives and more than one of his illustrious opponents. Sir Robert Peel died on the 2nd of July, 1850, and I remember that I was with my grandfather when the news arrived. His relations with Peel had extended over many years, and seem at one time (1825) to have been of an intimate and confidential nature, though, owing to the stiffness and pride of Peel, he seems never to have been on friendly terms with him. Indeed, whilst doing justice to the talents and good .intentions of Peel, he firmly believed that no individual had ever inflicted so much misery upon his country, in spite of advice persistently offered him to the contrary. Nevertheless he used no bitter expressions, but joined in the manifestations of regret which were universally exhibited at the sudden end of the great statesman.

On the 11th of November, 1851, Matthias Attwood died at his house at Dulwich, the first of the brothers to join the majority. He was by far the wealthiest, and, next to Thomas, the most politically famous of the Attwoods, having been one of the last members for Boroughbridge and the first member for Whitehaven, His parliamentary career had extended over nearly thirty years, and though not a brilliant speaker he was always listened to with attention and respect, as a solid and useful member of the House, who never spoke on subjects which he did not thoroughly understand. For many years his relations with his brother had been of an estranged character; but whatever reasons his family may have had to complain of his conduct, it is certain that the public had none, for his political career had been almost as disinterested as that of his relative. A consistent Tory by conviction, he wanted nothing to please the great leaders of his party but a renunciation of his Currency doctrines; and these he never affected to compromise or conceal in the slightest degree. In defence of them he had fearlessly encountered both Peel and Huskisson, and, according to Alison, had emerged from the conflict upon no unequal terms. Possessed of parliamentary ability, considerable wealth, and great business talents, besides having much influence in the City, it may be reasonably assumed that he could easily have obtained a title had he wished for one; but he was as simple and unostentatious in his mode of life as the rest of his family. He was the chief founder of some of the most important and successful undertakings in the country, amongst which may be mentioned the General Steam Navigation Company, the National Provincial Bank of Ireland, and the Imperial Continental Gas Association. He is said to have been the head of no less than seven City Companies, but was chiefly connected with the Merchant Taylors. He was the trusted friend and associate of Sir Moses Montefiore, whose signature is appended to the following resolution of condolence sent to his son:—

Copy of a Resolution passed at the Meeting of the Board of the Imperial Continental Gas Association on the 13th Novr., 1851.

"The Presidents and Directors, previously to commencing the business of the Board, feel it incumbent on them to record their deep regret at the loss they individually and the Association as a body have sustained by the death of their highly respected and esteemed President and Chairman, Matthias Attwood, Esq.

Mr. Attwood in every way entitled himself to be regarded as a friend to this establishment. He was one of the original founders of it; during the period of depression and adversity which succeeded, he patiently and perseveringly adhered to it; and to his counsel, advice, and exertions may in a great degree be attributed its subsequent prosperity.

To his affectionate and devoted son, M. Wolverley Attwood, Esq., the inheritor of his father's talents, energy, and attainments, the Board beg to offer their sincerest sympathy, and their earnest hope that he may be supported under the present afflicting dispensation.

MOSES MONTEFIORE,
Chairman."

A similar resolution was passed by the Directors of the General Steam Navigation Company.

Matthias Attwood was buried in Norwood Cemetery. I have an oil-painting of him, said to be by Sir Thomas Lawrence, which used to hang in the dining-room at Dulwich Hill.

Previous to his removal to Dulwich he had resided for many years at Streatham Manor House.

On the 14th September, 1852, occurred the death of the great Duke of Wellington, an event which must have excited the most profound reflections in the mind of Thomas Attwood, for Wellington had been the most obstinate of all his opponents, was popularly credited with a desire to disperse the famous meetings on Newhall Hill by military force, and had even ordered a warrant to be prepared for the arrest of Attwood, Muntz, and Salt, though he shrank from the impending storm of popular indignation and abstained from putting it into execution. I do not think that Thomas Attwood was ever much influenced by pride and vain-glory, those overmastering passions of many great men; but if he ever was, it must have been one of his proudest recollections that he, a simple citizen, had organised a force which the conqueror of Napoleon was afraid to assail. I think it may be said, without exaggeration, that Attwood was the only man who had ever dared the Iron Duke to do his worst, and that the Duke feared to accept the challenge. At this date it is interesting to recall the fact that there *was* a time when the subject of this memoir was not considered unworthy to contest the palm of popularity with the Hero of Waterloo. A curious proof of this is afforded by the circumstance that, in or about 1832, the name of Wellington Street in Birmingham was changed by acclamation into Attwood Street, though a compromise was afterwards effected, and the street which once bore these names now goes by the name of Pershore Street.

I was at school at the time of Wellington's death, but I remember that Aurelius Attwood went up to London to see his magnificent funeral on November 18th. In the course of the year 1852 a correspondence took place between Mr. James Jaffray, editor of the *Birmingham Journal*, Mr. T. C. Salt, and G. de B Attwood, respecting the desirability of publishing a memoir of Thomas Attwood. Mr. Salt urged the project with affectionate warmth and earnestness ; but apparently it was never carried into execution, although it seems that Mr. Jaffray was willing to defray all the expenses of publication. However, G. de B. Attwood was thereby induced to write the brief account of the famous nine days preceding the reinstatement of Earl Grey which I have inserted in its proper place.

In August, 1853, Algernon, fourth son of Thomas Attwood, married Emma, only daughter of John Foulkes, of Elwy House, Wrexham.

I cannot recollect the exact date, but it was in April or May, 1854, that I saw Thomas Attwood for the last time, when I left his kind and generous roof to go to New Zealand. He was sitting in the dining-room at Allesley, a mere wreck of his former self, and scarcely able to shake hands with me at parting. He lived to see the Crimean War, but was, I imagine, too ill to follow the course of its operations with interest ; and perhaps it was well that it was so : for, had he been what he once was, a victorious war with Russia, followed by an inglorious peace, without insistance upon the independence of Poland and Circassia, would have broken his heart.

The mantle of his foreign policy, however, had fallen upon his brother Charles, who strenuously exerted himself at a number of important meetings, held at Newcastle-on-Tyne, to induce the population of the North to urge the Government to a vigorous prosecution of the Russian war.

George Attwood, the eldest of the family, died at Edgbaston Priory on the 24th May, 1854, in the seventy-seventh year of his age. He was the only one of the seven sons who had been sent to college, and, curiously enough, he was the only one of an ordinary and unintellectual disposition amongst them. Yet, as if Nature had determined to grant him some compensation, he bore when at University College the reputation of being the handsomest man in Oxford of his day. He was intended for the Church, but deafness prevented him from taking Orders, an unfortunate circumstance, for all his business speculations were unsuccessful.

On the 24th April, 1855, George de Bosco, the eldest son of Thomas Attwood, preceded him to the grave, at the early age of forty-seven, leaving a family of six children. I have already narrated the stirring events of his early career, but for many years past feeble health and the cares of a family had compelled him to devote himself exclusively to his business as Secretary to the Bank of British North America. That, in this comparatively humble capacity, he had been as successful in obtaining the respect and esteem of his Directors as he had once, not unreasonably, aspired to be in securing the applause of his constituents in a more distinguished sphere of action, the following minute shows :—

"*Bank of British North America,*
7, St. Helen's Place,
London, 26 April, 1855.

"At a Meeting of the Court held this day, Sir Andrew Pellet Green, K.C.H., in the Chair it was unanimously resolved to place the following upon the Minutes, and to transmit a copy of the same to the Branches, and to all Banking Establishments in correspondence with this Bank :—

'The Court met as usual on Tuesday, the 24th inst., and proceeded to the business of the day ; the Secretary had begun to read the Minutes of the previous Court, when he was most suddenly arrested by the hand of death.

In recording this very solemn and melancholy event, the Court would desire to express their deep sympathy with the bereaved family of Mr. Attwood, and the sincere regard which, collectively and individually, they entertained towards him.

Mr. Attwood took part in the formation of this Bank, having been one of the original Committee, and subsequently, on the 21st November, 1836, he was appointed Secretary.

During a period of nearly 20 years he devoted himself most assiduously to the duties of the office, exhibiting in their discharge a singular equanimity of temper, and the most strict truthfulness and integrity.

In his unexpected removal from the midst of them, the Directors feel that the Institution has been deprived of the services of a valuable officer, and that they have lost the society of an esteemed personal friend.'

A. P. GREEN,
Chairman."

Mr. de Bosco Attwood was by no means destitute of poetic taste. His famous Union Hymn was very popular in 1832, and has been quoted by Martineau, who, however, gives him no credit for the authorship. He subsequently printed, for private circulation only, a pretty piece entitled *Musings in the Morning Express Train from Brighton to London*, and another on the Battle of the Alma.

In the later part of the year 1855 Rosabel, younger daughter of Thomas Attwood, was married at Barming Church, by the Rev. Henry Demain, to H. W. Demain Saunders, Manager of the Union Bank of Australia.

The end was now rapidly approaching, and but little remains to tell. In October, 1855, Thomas Attwood gave up the house at Allesley and removed to Ellerslie, Great Malvern, where Dr. Walter Johnson at that time received a small number of patients, and here, on the 6th of March, 1856, in the seventy-third year of his age, he terminated his, possibly mistaken, but singularly patriotic, laborious, and disinterested life.

Let his shortcomings have been what they may, I am persuaded that a more heroic and unselfish spirit never returned to its Creator. He attached but little weight to the dogmas of different creeds, and he abhorred all cant; but in the most essential attribute of Christianity—love of one's neighbour—no professional saint or philanthropist ever surpassed him. Owing to his liberal opinions, he was at one time accused by some of the coarser of his political opponents of being an

Atheist. Even, however, his famous utterance, "The people don't want priests and religion, but beef, bread, and beer," which gave such great offence to the respectable Tories of the time, may be interpreted so as to satisfy the requirements of modern Christianity.

Pretty good evidence of his real religious sentiments may be collected from the letters, speeches, and poems inserted in this book.

His Radical politics were, of course, very unacceptable to the Established clergy of his day, and amongst the few letters he preserved I can only find one from a clergyman, and that is a cold and stiff note from Archbishop Vernon Harcourt But it is greatly to his credit, and of a piece with the rest of his character, that he never allowed the behaviour of the ministers of the Church of England to affect, in the slightest degree, his faithfulness to the Church herself. His patriotic schemes had been frowned upon by the dignitaries of the Establishment—they had been welcomed with enthusiasm by Nonconformists and Roman Catholics; but he never for a moment permitted this difference of treatment to influence his religious opinions. As he had repeatedly promised, he lived and died a member of the Church of England, and attended her services regularly as long as his strength permitted. I can well remember that this was the case at Allesley, although the ascent from his house to the church was steep and trying for an invalid. It would be easy to dilate at length upon the beauties of his character, but I prefer that this should be done by others, in no way related to him, whose speeches I shall presently quote.

He was buried in Hanley Churchyard, within sight of the residence of his widow, The Boynes, near Upton-on-Severn. A plain slab of polished granite, bearing no political allusion, but simply the dates of his birth and death, marks his grave. In the days of his fame he had written in an album belonging to Miss Pearman, of Tennall Hall, the following remarkable sentence:—"Whenever it shall please Almighty God to call me to the grave the greatest compliment which my friends can pay me will be to inscribe upon my tomb, 'HERE LIES

THE FOUNDER OF POLITICAL UNIONS.' But this was written in the flush of success, when he had hoped to restore prosperity to his country by means of Political Unions, and I do not know that he retained the wish in his later years.

He died in almost Spartan poverty. The silver cup presented by 20,000 workmen of Birmingham, the gold chain and medal presented by the Birmingham Political Union, the gold box presented by the Corporation of London, and his old house in the Crescent, which realised only about £800, were all the property left by him who had been for a time the most powerful man in the kingdom, whose word had made and unmade Ministries.

The following leading article upon his death appeared in the *Birmingham Journal* or some other newspaper of similar politics:—

"It would seem difficult for any Englishman, it would seem impossible for any inhabitant of this town, to hear of the death of Thomas Attwood without some lively emotion and some serious reflection.

An eminent man has passed from among us: a singularly pure and disinterested patriot has been withdrawn: a leader of the people has departed—the leader of the people when its life was most vigorous and intense, and when its power was most mightily manifested—the chief representative and foremost man of the English nation during the most stormy, the most interesting, and the most momentous period of recent English history—the founder and leader of the Political Union—the hero of the Reform Bill—the most potent wielder of English democracy that has appeared in these latter days.

In such a man all England has an interest; his departure must arrest for a moment the attention of every earnest and thoughtful Englishman. But far deeper is the impression which it must produce upon the inhabitants of this town, when they reflect that this eminent Englishman was a citizen of Birmingham, that this leader of the people of England was originally and conspicuously the leader of the people of Birmingham, that Thomas Attwood was more especially their own Attwood, that the Political Union was a society belonging to this place, that the hero of the Reform Bill was their own particular hero, that it was from Birmingham that Mr. Attwood wielded the democracy of England, that under his guidance, Birmingham, for the first and for the last time, marched in the van of England, stood conspicuously forth in English History, and bore the greatest part in achieving the greatest political revolution of these latter times.

For a leader of the people, Mr. Attwood possessed many admirable endowments and remarkable qualifications, and in many respects towered above most of those who have attained that distinction. Perhaps his greatest quality was the purity and disinterestedness of his patriotism;

herein he was very seldom equalled and never surpassed. Neither Agis nor the Gracchi, not the martyr king of Sparta, not the martyr brothers of Rome, exceeded him in unselfish and untainted devotion to the welfare of the people. This utter indifference to self-aggrandisement, this entire forgetfulness of his own interests in those of his country, placed him immeasurably above O'Connell This disinterestedness was accompanied and seconded by a native and inherent magnanimity such as seldom exists in public men. He was as free from everything small and petty as from everything sordid ; and his benevolence fully came up to his magnanimity. There never breathed a man more tenderly sensible to human suffering, and more earnest and ready to relieve it. All these qualities were heightened and deepened by an intense fervour, which impregnated his whole nature, and gave him a ready access to the popular heart.

These qualities pervaded his deeds and his words. As a speaker, he was earnest, forcible, fervid, impressive, and sometimes solemn and magnificent He was a born poet ; in him the imagination was strongly developed, imparted potency and impressiveness to his oratory, and lent it even an occasional grandeur. The faults and excellencies of his oratory were pretty exactly the faults and excellencies of his character—excellencies very precious in the eyes of the people, but in very small esteem with Parliament—faults which help to win the favour of a great popular assembly, but of which the House of Commons is specially intolerant.

He entered the House of Commons in December, 1832, the hero of the Reform Bill, the most popular and powerful man in England ; he retired from Parliament in 1839, weary and disappointed. His Parliamentary failure may have been somewhat owing to excessive vehemence of manner, and unrestrained violence of expression, and to his incessant and not always seasonable or skilful advocacy of his monetary views. But it was still more emphatically owing to the nobleness of his nature, to the disinterestedness of his patriotism, to his intense abhorrence of party selfishness, to his utter disdain for mere party interests, to his entire incapacity for, and hearty detestation of, the not very exalted manœuvres, and the not very creditable intrigues of which too much of parliamentary life is made up.

He outlived his position ; he outlived in some sense his popularity ; but he never outlived the affection and admiration of the followers whom he had inspired, and the people he had led. He will be gratefully remembered by his countrymen. He was by no means free from faults and infirmities. But where through all history shall we find a popular leader more disinterested, more magnanimous, and more benevolent? He can hardly be called a great statesman, nor was he perhaps a successful politician, as party counts success. But he was an illustrious patriot, a great tribune of the people, and in the highest sense of the phrase he was an eminently successful politician. He was the hero of the Reform Bill, the leader in the greatest revolution in these latter days, and that a peaceable revolution. He did a great work, and the work of his hands has been established. He will abide in the grateful remembrance of his countrymen, and will occupy no petty place in English history."

These lines were written by Mrs. Attwood, March 6th, 1856:—

> "Love strong in death :—The voice was faint and low,
>   'Not better, never better more, dear wife,
> God's will is mine, willing to stay or go,
>   Kiss me, again, now kiss me.' So from life
> Passed unto God a man of antique mould,
>   Stainless and incorruptible, whom power
> Left poor, and strife left loving ; for the old
>   Heroic virtue was his shield, and dower
> The sense of duty : there was wrong to right,
>   And he must right it if he could or die ;
> And so he toiled and won that hard-fought fight,
>   And having won it, laid down silently
> All power and fame, and with clean hands and heart
>   Lived patiently and bore with manly pride
> The quick forgetfulness that is a part
>   Of the mere popular breath soon blown aside.
>
> Years passed, and slowly, gently, God's good hand
>   Fell, parting him from all of active life,
> From all of good or work he hoped or planned,
>   From patriot schemes and the world's stirring strife—
> A memory to his friends, a treasure past
>   All price to *one*, till when his hour was come,
> And the great loving heart was cold at last,
>   In a March morn's grey dawning summoned home,
> He, who unflinchingly had borne and done
>   His life's toil, died. The March sun with red ray
> Rose not for him, on tear-dimmed eyes it shone—
>   His was the dawn of Heaven's eternal day."

CHAPTER XXV

A Tory account of Attwood's political career—Meeting at the Town Hall, Birmingham, to honour his memory—Testimonies of Messrs. Muntz, Spooner, Edmonds, Dawson, Hill, and others to his great services—The committee determine to erect a statue in his honour—Inauguration of the Attwood statue—Conclusion.

SHORTLY before Thomas Attwood's death the following article appeared in the *Morning Herald* of January 22nd, 1856, and I think it is worth while to reprint it as it gives an account of Attwood's political career from a Tory point of view, and also throws considerable light upon his Currency doctrines. It is curious to note that the writer persisted in believing that Attwood had been a Tory at the commencement of his public life.

"Birmingham has vindicated its previous character for determined resistance to the pernicious monetary legislation of the late Sir Robert Peel.

Those who have paid attention to this question will recall to mind the part taken through many years by Mr. Thomas Attwood, and his partner Mr. Spooner, the present member for North Warwickshire.

Mr. Attwood, who through all his former life had ranked as a Tory, became so indignant with those of his party who adhered to the monetary crotchets of the bullionists, carried out, unhappily, by Sir Robert Peel, that he raised the cry of Reform in Parliament, mainly, as he was accustomed to avow, for the purpose of obtaining a House of Commons so independent of the former ruling parties—Tory or Whig—that a fair consideration might be obtained for this most influential of social questions, in its bearing upon the material comfort of the industrial classes.

The Whigs had seized upon this lamentable instance of departure from the political consistency of Toryism, and in every way strengthened the hands of an opponent who was so clearly playing their game; for if the Tories had been more remarkable for one line of policy than another, it was for their readiness to provide a sufficiency of the instruments of commercial interchange, and to encourage the 'live and let live' principle. Well might Mr. Attwood turn aside with disappointment when he found the rising leader of the party to which he had long adhered, throw himself into the meshes of the bullion committee of 1810, originating, as it too evidently did, in the political purpose of staying the progress of the war, by forcing upon the

Government a premature return to cash payments, in the midst of our large subsidies and growing taxation, direct and indirect.

The late Sir Robert Peel, on his return from the Chief Secretaryship in Ireland, as a rising public man, became chairman of the Commons' committee on Currency in 1819, from which his well-known legislation proceeded The late Mr. Matthias Attwood, in his place in Parliament, was unceasing in powerfully as truthfully denouncing this impracticable Bill on all occasions of public pressure which occurred between 1820 and 1826—a course in which he was subsequently aided and materially aided by Mr. Cayley, the talented member for the North Riding of Yorkshire; while Mr. Thomas Attwood as strenuously applied himself in Birmingham to the same end. Baffled, however, in his more ordinary means of influence, he at length formed the notorious Political Union and its extensive ramifications; and by the extraordinary influence he thus acquired over the many, worked out that great and hazardous change which was said to carry him and his more Radical colleague, Mr. Scholefield, into the House of Commons on the shoulders of the people. This revolution in our social system, whether for good or for evil, soon taught this popular favourite how futile are all human calculations.

Mr. Attwood very early found, to his sorrow, that the increased democratic element infused into the State had more securely forged the metallic fetters of monetary legislation than before.

Not because the mass of the people approved the legislative errors which their leader denounced, but because the new members returned to the Reformed Parliament gave almost implicit confidence to the late Sir Robert Peel as the paramount authority on the subject. The members of Earl Grey's Administration having smiled upon the Reform movement were not very likely to concede a question so peculiarly their own as bullionism. The Government used the power obtained by the Reform Bill movement as a means of consolidating their sectional influence, and made it the basis of corporate and other so-called reforms, which were so arranged as to procure them for years to come the political suffrages of the operative classes. Mr. T. Attwood became so fully convinced of the abortion of his personal efforts to stem the torrent that he retired from Parliament in disappointment and disgust, that his benevolent though misdirected efforts had been unavailing. . . ."

During the twelve years of Thomas Attwood's illness an uneasy feeling seems on several occasions to have pervaded the minds of his friends that it was anything but creditable to the Liberal party that the town of Birmingham should have remained so long without any public monument in his honour, but no practical steps were taken towards providing funds to erect one. When, however, the news reached the town that their beloved old member was actually dead, a considerable number of the inhabitants at once awoke to the fact that great disgrace would be reflected upon the public spirit of the Midlands should they suffer to pass away unhonoured one who had done, and sacrificed so much for them.

Accordingly a public meeting was convened on the 21st April, 1856. I subjoin the following slightly abridged report from the *Birmingham Mercury* of April 22nd, 1856.

"ATTWOOD MEMORIAL.

An enthusiastic meeting of the inhabitants of Birmingham was held in the Town Hall yesterday at noon, 'To determine the manner in which this town will pay its debt of honour and gratitude to our late illustrious townsman, Thomas Attwood' About 3,000 people were present. The Mayor presided, and there were also present on the platform—G. F. Muntz, Esq., M.P.; William Scholefield, Esq., M.P; Aldermen Cutler, Muntz, Baldwin, and Hawkes; Councillors Walker, Truman, Holland, Pollard, Stinton, Hicks, Aspinall, Turner, Norman, Goode, Boyce, Smith, J. Lloyd and Jackson; the Rev. P. Sibree, and Messrs T. C. Salt, W. Mathews, George Dawson, J. Webster, J. Betts, Tyndall, Allen, Downing, Fielding, E. Taunton, T. Aston, G. A. Ashford, Maber, Biggs, J. A. Lander, J Hall, C. Perry, T. Griffin, J. Green, H. Jenkins, L. Watkins, Hobley, W. R. Lloyd, W. Taunton, T. Stainbridge, and M. Green

The working classes mustered in good numbers, and many of the members of the old Birmingham Political Union displayed the medal of the association on their breasts.

The Mayor commenced the business by reading several letters of apology for non-attendance from several gentlemen Richard Spooner, Esq., M.P., regretted it was out of his power to attend the meeting to pay respect to his friend, the late much lamented and greatly esteemed Thomas Attwood, as a most important question relative to education was coming on for discussion on Monday evening, from which he could not absent himself. He observed that though he differed from Mr. Attwood on most important political subjects, that difference never for a moment interrupted their friendship, and he was convinced that a more honest politician never existed (Cheers) The benefit of all classes, but chiefly the industrious classes, was the great object he ever kept in view—(Hear, hear),—his sole aim was to promote the welfare of the country; the only reward he claimed was the approval of his fellow-countrymen, and the consciousness that he had done his duty. Mr Spooner concluded by expressing the pleasure he should feel to join in any testimonial the meeting might agree to. (Cheers.) The next letter was from Matthew Davenport Hill, Esq., the Recorder, who bore testimony to the invaluable public services of his departed friend Mr Attwood, and said he laboured not merely for his town but for his country. His fame was recorded for ever in the history of England, and required no other monument; but it behoved them to show to the world they would not suffer their great and good townsman to pass away from amongst them without bearing witness by some memorial that they were not insensible to his talents and his virtues The Mayor said he had also received letters apologising for non-attendance from Thomas Thornley, Esq., M.P., and the Mayors of Wolverhampton and Walsall Since he had been in the committee room of the Town Hall that morning a deputation had waited upon him from the United Brothers Society, by whom he had been requested to read to the meeting this letter:—

'*Golden Eagle Inn, Swallow St*

'DEAR SIR,—It is the intention of the Order of United Brothers to assist as far as possible the objects of your meeting. Deputations from three Lodges have been appointed to organise a subscription amongst all the members of this association.

Yours obediently,
W. MILLS.'

(Cheers.)

Having informed them of the communications he had received, he felt it incumbent upon him to make a few remarks concerning the various reasons which had led him as the chief magistrate of that town to call a public meeting of the townsmen of the late Mr. Attwood. Shortly after the great man's death, gentlemen of various political creeds suggested to him that some mark of respect was due to so eminent and good a man. (Hear and cheers.) He thought it his duty, therefore, to convene a meeting of influential inhabitants by circular. The result was that it was deemed advisable to take the opinion of Mr. Attwood's fellow-townsmen as to what should be done in respect to his memory. (Hear, hear.) Their meeting that day proved that though dead he was not forgotten. (Cheers.) He (the Mayor) was no orator, but he could sincerely express his conviction that if ever an honest man lived, that man was their lamented townsman. (Cheers.) He was glad to see so many of the working classes there to-day, for they more than all others owed a debt of gratitude to Thomas Attwood they could never repay Trace back twenty-five years ago, see how incessantly he laboured for the working classes, and recall to mind what he gained for them by his patriotic exertions. (Hear, hear.) Other gentlemen on the platform knew Mr. Attwood more intimately than he did, whom he would call upon to address the meeting, after venturing to hope that he had not departed from propriety as Mayor of this borough in convening that assembly, assuring them that political feeling had not swayed him in the matter, for if Mr. Attwood had entertained opinions diverse to those he advocated, he should still have felt it his duty to do all that lay in his power in recognition of a great and good man's character. (Cheers.)

G. F. Muntz, Esq., M.P., rose to move the first resolution, which with the others will be found in our advertising columns. He was greeted with loud and long-continued applause, on the subsidence of which he said that many of those present, and he could wish they were a larger number, must recollect Thomas Attwood in what he called his glory; and they must also recollect that their departed friend and himself worked cordially together. (Cheers.) It had been said most justly by the Mayor and Mr. Spooner, that Mr. Attwood was essentially an honest man. He could subscribe to that most heartily. He never heard him express an opinion of any sort or kind which was not thoroughly honest, and never heard him advance anything political which was not entirely and immediately connected with the people at large. (Hear, hear.) He always used to say, 'My dear fellow, it is the people, the working men, who ought to be cared for; we can take care of ourselves, they cannot help themselves, they are trampled upon in all ways, and when they cannot get their regular wages they cannot get bread, beef, or beer, or anything necessary for their comfort and happiness. No man knows better than you know that a single week's wages lost to the working man, and all his own and his wife's and children's comfort and happiness are lost also.' His object was to see every working man—industrious, sober, and honest, for he always made that exception—his object was to see every such working man at all times in such a position that, instead of having to run after masters, masters should run after him, and that he should earn more than was required for the immediate wants of his household. He laboured hard to accomplish those ends. What he did for the country was perhaps more than many estimated; but what he would have done if he had had the power was infinitely greater still. (Cheers.) They had had, since his labours, times of prosperity and adversity, but a large portion of the adversity had been relieved by his exertions, as compared with what existed previously If Thomas Attwood had carried out his will, the honest and industrious would now be in a position to more than support themselves and families. That being the case, should they not recollect their duty towards such a man? and should they not try to mark that recollection in some substantial way, in order to encourage other men to be faithful to their interests, and to exert themselves in their cause? If the rising generation saw that after all Thomas Attwood had done for his fellow-countrymen they neglected to substantially evince their reverence for his memory, there would be no very great inducement for a man to imitate his laudable career Mr Attwood had no private interest to benefit, no personal triumphs to achieve, nothing to look for and work for but the good of the people at large. (Hear, hear, and cheers.) He was indefatigable, zealous, painstaking, and eminently wise. With some parties he got into discredit, but what man besides a fool or a rogue would be on good terms with everybody? (Hear, hear.) To gain all persons' expressed goodwill a man must connive at the rogue's rascality, and laugh at the fool's foolery. (Hear, hear.) Mr. Attwood would not brook either roguery or foolery, and therefore sustained considerable ill-usage. By the people at large he was, however, beloved, and lived in their hearts still (Hear, hear.) Although some few around him recollected their lamented townsman in his glorious days, still there were many present who knew him only by report. When a man's good character was reported by the working people of any country they might depend upon its correctness. Working men remembered only the character of men who had been faithful towards them; and those who did not know Thomas Attwood but by what they heard of him might take the working man's warranty that all the statements were true of him which were made by men who had the gratification of knowing such a man, and loving his many estimable qualities. (Applause.) He had never seen such a worthy man during his connection with public life—a period of forty years.

W. Mathews, Esq., seconded the resolution. He declared his ardent admiration for the noble simplicity and intelligence displayed by Mr. Attwood throughout his political career. It would be unwise and injudicious on his part to detain them by any selfish retrospect of private regard, however much his desire might lead him to that line of argument, because it was not in the indulgence of this retrospection that he should forward the object of to-day. Public men were public property, and if there was anything inconsistent in their public acts, it was not by allusions to their private life he could claim their sympathy and attention. He should therefore stand before them simply as an admirer of Thomas Attwood in his political capacity, and should endeavour to appreciate him in his public career, to criticise his public acts, and to see how far he was justified in recommending any claim upon them to acknowledge those public acts by some public testimony of his services. He was quite aware that in addressing himself to this topic he laboured under some disadvantage. He was an older man than many assembled there, and was addressing men who only knew Mr. Attwood by reputation, who were boys when his political career was in active usefulness. Their recollection of his grand exertions could hardly be so active as that of those who acted with him; but yet he very well knew that the men of Birmingham were generous sympathisers with all disinterested exertions in their favour; and he had no apprehension of any shortcoming on their part to bear testimony to a man who had no shortcomings in his public life. (Applause.) He knew their venerated townsman for more than forty years, his acquaintance having begun with him when a boy. He looked to him as his senior in years and very much his senior in wisdom; and his admiration for him never ceased from their earliest intimacy till his death. (Hear, hear.) There was a dignity, a straightforwardness, a noble simplicity of patriotism about him he never saw manifested by any public man. (Loud cheers.) A double object was a matter he could not comprehend. He had but one object in view—the public good in general, and the good of Birmingham men in particular. (Applause.) His public career began at twenty-one years of age, and he filled the post of chief officer of this town soon after attaining his majority. With untiring, unwearied vigilance—without hope of reward—without fear of enmity—without affection for mortal man, except for the public good—did Thomas Attwood pursue the object of his heart. (Cheers.) All present who were associated with the deceased patriot during his long political career would bear him out that the statement he had just made was in nowise exaggerated. (Hear, hear.) He would not weary them with details, but go on to say that Mr. Attwood continued so to act till at last he, like many other wise men in this country, found that the House of Commons was perfectly unfitted for the Constitution, and perfectly unqualified in all respects to attend to the public good. Therefore a reformed Parliament became absolutely necessary for the welfare of the country. Nothing would more emphatically prove how well he organised Birmingham to carry out this great object than the fact that by the efforts of Birmingham alone was this great measure carried; and that but for Birmingham and Birmingham men they might have been without a Reform Bill till this moment. (Loud cheers.) He held long consultations with their dead friend concerning the formation of this

SPEECH OF W. MATHEWS.

movement Mr. Attwood organised the Political Union, directed its moral force, controlled its vehemence, checked its immoderate impulses, and through its means carried triumphantly the object it was founded to obtain. (Cheers.) In this great work he had most unmistakably the support of Birmingham men. When danger became great—when the Whigs wanted to get into power, and found that they could not obtain power without some pressure from without, they joined the Political Union (Hear, and laughter.) They ought never to have left it. (Hear, hear.) When the hour of danger was over, and they saw an easy entrance before them into political life without the instrumentality of those great powers which had placed them where they were, the Whigs then left the Political Union, and from that time to this he had never ceased to hate the Whigs. (Loud cheers.) They reaped the harvest others had sowed, and denied the labourers their well-deserved reward. (Applause.) When the Reform Bill was carried came the temptation. Mr. Attwood was then at the zenith of political power, and in the height of his popularity. He (Mr. Mathews) saw letters from twenty towns in England lying on the patriot's table, offering to return him as their member to Parliament He might have gone to Parliament with a fame superior to O'Connell's ; and if he had consented to truckle to the Whigs, there was no position he could not have obtained (Loud applause) He was true to his nature, true to his trust, and true to his destiny. (Prolonged cheering.) He worked in the House of Commons with the same diligence he had worked when out of it ; but found his exertions less effectual than before. His health began to give way ; and at the earnest entreaty of his family he retired from his public post, with the consciousness that he could do no more for the public good than he had done His honourable friend Mr Muntz succeeded him, and he had proved a worthy successor—(applause) —and one who, he trusted, lived in their esteem, and would ever continue to live there. (Loud cheers) It was not for him to tell the men of Birmingham the form their commemoration of their eminent dead townsman should take. He was convinced Birmingham men would do justice to his memory Whatever might be the nature of the testimonial—a statue, a monument, or an institution—he was convinced it would be paid for. (Applause.) If, as it was said, the spirits of the departed honoured those localities they most loved, sure he was that the shadow of their venerated friend was at that moment contemplating with a listening ear and a grateful heart the demonstration being made in his favour ;—(Hear)—and sure he was that the testimony which that large meeting had evinced would be to him a more fitting requiem than any other sounds of praise, inasmuch as the assemblage was congregated in that noble building—a fitting temple—where so many of his political triumphs were displayed, and so frequently his political exhortations were made to the people of Birmingham (Hear, hear)

Mr George Edmonds, on presenting himself to support the resolution, was greatly cheered He craved their indulgence in consequence of illness, and said he could not absent himself on such an occasion. He had been closely connected in personal friendship with the late Thomas Attwood since the month of February, 1817, when the first great meeting was held on Newhall Hill on the subject of Reform. They were met in that hall, it was said, to pay a debt. If it had been a debt upon simple contract, they might have pleaded the statute a great many years ago. (Laughter.) If it had been a debt under seal, more than twenty years had elapsed since the debt was proved, and moreover the creditor was dead. (Hear, hear.) He really did not wish to cast reflections upon the people of Birmingham, because he must bear a part in them, perhaps, for allowing this patriot to die without having at least paid him some poundage on his debt before he departed. (Hear, hear.) Well, then, let them endeavour to wipe out any stain that might attach to them for their cold-heartedness and neglect. He could tell them that Mr. Attwood, whether considered privately or publicly, was a man to be beloved by all who knew him, in whose hearts he remained embalmed with all the sweetness that could fall upon a disposition possessing qualities most noble, and at the same time most amiable and condescending. (Cheers.) No man so markedly combined what was called the *suaviter in modo* with the *fortiter in re*, as Thomas Attwood. He was unflinching in his purpose, but in the manner in which he prosecuted his great cause, he contrived to seduce every heart into compliance with his wise arrangements. (Cheers.) He might be suffered to draw their attention to one simple object which their revered friend accomplished. He was a purely historical being to most of those present, nearly a quarter of a century having elapsed since his labours, but it was not too late to ask what were their obligations to this great man. He would tell them that, if in this century they were to judge of a man by the effects of his conduct, no man existed more entitled to their gratitude in a high degree than Thomas Attwood. (Cheers.) It was by the power of his character, the wisdom of his arrangement, that that great measure the Reform Bill was passed. Mr Attwood was the *primum mobile* who led on and succeeded in that grand object. By the passing of that Act, 56 rotten boroughs were sent down to the infernal regions at one blow. (Hear, cheers and laughter.) Those 56 rotten boroughs sent twice that number of rotten members to the House of Commons. (Hear, hear.) In the very height of enthusiastic feeling, when he first started in politics, he never dreamt of such a great benefit as that. He should have been thankful to accept the enfranchisement of Birmingham, Manchester, and a few great towns, as a wonderful thing coming from the Tories of that day. What else was produced by that Bill?—32 other boroughs, that had some population, but were merely in the hands of individual aristocrats, who sent their servants to Parliament, and who ought to have sent them in livery—(Hear, hear)—32 of those by that Bill were sent to follow the others in the downward road. (Cheers and laughter.) In addition (though there was a difference of opinion as to the manner in which the benefit was conferred) 65 new members were given to the counties at large That he conceived to be an important benefit, notwithstanding objections, because it brought a great number of persons to bear upon the politics and proceedings of the House of Commons. (Hear, hear). Lastly, there came the creation of 42 new boroughs, consisting of the great towns of the empire, and applying to a population of about 2½ millions, 800,000 electors. This was accomplished by the simple Act which Thomas Attwood was the great instrument of passing. (Loud cheers.)

(Mr Edmonds then proceeded to narrate the history of the Reform Bill, and of the perils to which Mr. Attwood had been exposed, at considerable length, and concluded by appealing to the meeting to exhibit heartily their appreciation of his services.)

Mr. George Dawson next came forward. He observed that there was a reason probably why they would hardly expect him to take part in the meeting, yet he thought that was the very reason why he should. He never had the pleasure of seeing Mr. Attwood, who was politically dead before he came to Birmingham. He counted himself happy to have come to the town in which that man lived—(cheers);—and he also counted himself happy to have continued the spirit of the work in which that man laboured. When Mr Attwood was in his glory he was a schoolboy shut up in a schoolroom surrounded by tall London walls. As the tide of the sea found its way into the smallest creeks, so did Mr. Attwood's name find its way into his schoolroom. The scholars took sides ; and he was glad to say he joined the Liberal party. There were Conservatives among them. They were gentlemen's sons, and he and his party were snobs (Laughter and cheers) One or two sharp battles were fought, and he was delighted to inform them it was then, as it ever should be to the end of the world, the Liberal party conquered and their opponents ran away. (Cheers and laughter.) Now for the very reason that he never saw the man it was befitting that he should join in such a meeting as that. Belonging to another generation, it was proper he should state their estimate of this great man. Unlike those who had spoken to-day, he was not led away by personal considerations for Mr. Attwood. He was one of the few men in this world who were loved. A man was not loved for doing his duties properly, washing his face and keeping out of debt, but for large-heartedness, geniality of manners, kindness to all, forgetfulness of himself, always studying other people and their interests instead of his own. As far as he could learn, Mr. Attwood never bored others with himself. (Cheers.) He consecrated himself thoroughly to others. He was loved because he had a large heart, admired and respected because he had a large brain, and used his large gift well. (Cheers.) It was difficult to find an opportunity to do honour to a really just and good man, for sorry he was to say that honours, so thick and plentiful in this country, were apt to fall upon the heads of the least worthy people. (Cheers.) To win honours in this day it was necessary to be incapable, fit only to make a muddle, to land England in the mire, and to lower her fame. (Loud cheers.) It was some pleasure to pay tribute to a real Englishman like Mr. Attwood. He was like the old Roman who left his garden to save his country, and when his country was saved went back to his garden. Thomas Attwood was a thoroughly honest man, a fearless man, a wise man, a brave man. He helped the people to get liberty, and saved them from anarchy. It seemed to him that God was not well pleased with England at this time He formerly gave us great men by the score , now He hardly provided us with one. What was now to be done? Great generals were scarce, great admirals not known, great statesmen few indeed, House of Peers deadly, House of Commons only lively and excitable when it has a bit of Sabbath-mongering or Maynoothing—(cheers and laughters) ;—but if it is a question of continuing the work of Thomas Attwood, the House of Commons, like a beaten horse at a race, is nowhere at all. (Laughter and cheers.) Mr.

Dawson went on to say that there was no great Englishman at the present day, that he revered Thomas Attwood because he was the last great Englishman who had been given us, and bore tribute to his manifold virtues and excellencies.

Mr J Betts briefly supported the motion, which, like all the others, was carried with acclamation.

Mr. T. C. Salt observed that no man ever lived a life of purer devotion to the cause of the people than had done Thomas Attwood. (Cheers). He had retired with their blessing, though not on their tongues, yet lying warmly on their hearts. Justice had not been done to his great merits—he had not secured the recognition which was his due during his lifetime. The people whom he had done so much to serve, almost seemed to have forgotten him; and now, instead of lying among Birmingham people, who at heart loved him so much, he lay beneath the turf of a hallowed, but, as yet, unhonoured grave, in a remote country churchyard. He (Mr. Salt) desired to recall to their mind some of the glories of the memorable Reform era, and he could not do that better than by bringing before them a few extracts from the speeches of the man whom they had that day met to honour. (Cheers.) He would, in the first instance, read to them the noble declarations with which Mr. Attwood had opened and closed the career of the Political Union. He had addressed the people of Birmingham at the commencement of the Union in these terms :—' It may be thought that because I come forward now, I shall be ready, come weal, come woe, to lead you through the dark and dreary scenes which are approaching. As far as the law will justify me, I will go with you. When I say I will go with you as far as the law will allow, I declare to you most solemnly that I will not go one inch further. I know that a great crisis is approaching. I will do all I can to avoid that crisis. But if this nation is ordained to go through the ordeal of political convulsions, I will not interfere, except legally and peacefully. I wish you to bear this in mind; when those dreadful circumstances arise, you will come to me and say, "Lead us." My friends, I will not lead you. I will go with you as far as the law will justify me, but if the elements of peace, law, and order are disorganised, I will go with you no further.' (Loud cheering.) This had been Mr. Attwood's warning. The result had been one of the most glorious in the history of any country. At the close of the Political Union, in August, 1832, Mr. Attwood had used these words :—' Other nations have achieved great and glorious revolutions by the sacrifice of their best blood. It has been left to England to effect a real revolution, more glorious than any recorded in the history of nations, by the moral power of public opinion, by the force of peaceful and legal exertions, without the shedding of one drop of blood, without one single circumstance arising which either the patriot, the philosopher, or the Christian can regret' He had led them through all these trials and dangers to a triumph not stained by one crime. (Loud applause.) . . . In reference to the memorial, he (Mr. Salt) thought it should harmonise with the life and character of the man. A statue, a mere tribute to the vanity of an individual, would not harmonise with his life. The memorial must be something which would tend to the benefit of the people. A park for the people would do most honour to Attwood—(applause);—or, if not a park, it should be something of a charitable nature—something to relieve distress, or increase the comforts and happiness of the working classes. (Cheers.) A memorial of this sort no doubt pre-supposed a large subscription. A large subscription they ought to have. (Hear, hear) There must be subscriptions from other places besides Birmingham ; for Attwood had been the benefactor of the whole nation, and Birmingham was not the whole nation. (Applause.) Mr Salt concluded by moving the appointment of a committee for the purpose of receiving subscriptions, and of deciding on the character of the memorial.

W. Scholefield, Esq, M.P, who was received with loud applause, came forward to second the resolution. He remarked that the life of Attwood had been, as they were well aware, one continued series of acts of devotion to his country ; but the crowning act of his life had been that connected with the great struggle for Reform. (Cheers) He (Mr. Scholefield) had not then been of age to mix in political matters ; and, like many present, had not an intimate practical acquaintance with that particular season of his life. Happily, however, for them, Attwood had risen to the dignity of a historical person, and it was to history that they should refer for a knowledge of those noble deeds which had immortalised his name. (Loud cheers) The people had at last been aroused to what it had been conceived was a great imperfection in the representative system of this country. They had cried aloud for Reform, and that Reform had been refused. For once, the customary prudence of the aristocracy of this country had failed them, and they had forgotten what was due to those over whom they were placed Attwood, however, had told them what was necessary to save both the people and the aristocracy from the coming anarchy He had raised the banner of Reform, but with it also the banner of the Constitution. He had determined to save King, Lords and Commons. He had raised the battle cry ; but his battle cry had not been like some of which they had heard on the Continent—his battle cry had not been war to the knife, but 'Peace, Law, and Order.' (Cheers.) These had been his memorable words—words too often forgotten in this country from that day to this The town of Birmingham had taken a leading part in the agitation. There had been some truth in the remark of his friend Mr. Mathews ; but he (Mr. Scholefield) could not attribute to Birmingham the entire glory of passing the Reform Bill. He would, however, say that without Birmingham the Reform Bill would not have been secured, and Birmingham would not have had its share in obtaining that Reform Bill had it not been for Attwood. (Cheers) It was to Attwood, mainly, that the honour belonged of achieving the success on which they now congratulated themselves, and if, at the moment of achieving that success, the question had been raised of honouring Attwood, there was not a district but would have sent in its thousands. (Cheers) For a time his great merits had been lost sight of, and he (Mr Scholefield) must say that he shared with his fellow-townsmen and fellow-countrymen at large in the feeling of shame which belonged to them for not recognising Mr. Attwood's great claims But that time was now past, and they could only take shame to themselves that they had not acted as became them. His lamented death had now revived the sleeping love of his countrymen ; the Mayor had, to his honour, taken a prominent part in calling upon them to redeem, to some extent, the lost time, and it was to be hoped they would now do their duty. (Cheers.) He hoped that this town would come forward freely and liberally with its contributions. (Cheers.) Although it was customary to call the people fickle, he knew it was not so. He knew that they were alive to the claims of true patriotism, great public services, and unspotted private worth such as were exemplified in the character of their friend Mr. Attwood. (Loud applause.)

Mr. Joseph Webster bore testimony to the great merits of Mr. Attwood. With respect to his character, he would say that he had never lost a private friend, and never had a public enemy. (Loud applause.)

Mr. Taunton, of Coventry, had worked with Mr. Attwood in times when it was dangerous to express Liberal sentiments, and he had come there to do what he could in rendering justice to the memory of a man who had rendered services to his country which they could not over-estimate. (Cheers.) The time, he felt, was fast approaching when they would require the services of such men as Attwood. There was corruption going on in every department of the State, and there must soon be a reunion of all the honest men of the community to bring about those changes which were so absolutely necessary to the well-being of the people. He called on them to afford substantial proof that they esteemed the memory of such a man as Attwood, and for himself he would promise to do all in his power in his own locality. (Applause.)

Mr. Hill, a working man, said that when the Union was established he had been but a boy of 16. He had, however, taken a deep interest in its proceedings, and felt it his duty to do what he could to forward the great and good objects in view. He remarked that it had not been Mr. Attwood's fault, or that of any member of the Council, that Reform had not been carried further. They had been cheated, but the fault had not been Attwood's. (Applause.) . . . It had always been to him a matter of regret that they had not done their duty to Attwood. He called on them to do it now. He had done his part. He had cheerfully subscribed his mite, and he hoped that every man amongst them would do the same. (Cheers.)

Mr. Alderman Baldwin said that although he had never agreed with Mr. Attwood on money matters, he had respected him as a man thoroughly sincere at heart. Looking at the man's character, he did not believe that any one ever had a greater desire to promote the interests of mankind generally. (Cheers.) When they found a man like Mr. Attwood, whose friends and relations had been hostile to the cause he had at heart, come out and work so devotedly for the people, they would be wanting in their duty if they did not do their utmost to honour his memory. He concurred with Mr Salt that the monument should partake of a character which should not only be a lasting memorial of his worth, but also a benefit to the working classes.

Mr. Alderman Cutler expressed the pride he felt in taking even the smallest share in the proceedings of that meeting. In speaking of the power wielded by the late Mr. Attwood, and the wisdom and discretion he displayed, he said he challenged history to point out, from the earliest Saxon times down to the present day, a single instance where a man possessing so much power as Thomas Attwood had wielded it with so much honour to himself and advantage to the nation. (Cheers.) Referring to the method of raising funds for the memorial, he thought that the various societies of the town might do much. The working men, he felt assured, would be glad to contribute their pence to so worthy an object. (Applause.)

Mr. Mackay expressed in brief terms his high admiration of their departed benefactor. He felt persuaded the working men would willingly contribute, and he urged them to do so, for small amounts in sufficient numbers would reach a great sum. (Cheers.)

Mr. Ashmore stated that in the year 1834 or 1835, he had waited on the late Mr. Attwood at Harborne, when he told him, with tears in his eyes, that Poland was lost, that Hungary would follow, and though he were not alive to see it, the blood of England would be spilt and the treasure of England expended in a great struggle with Russia. All this had taken place. Mr. Attwood, however, not anticipating the French alliance, had calculated on a severer struggle than had occurred. The speaker then related an instance in which Mr. Attwood had been applied to for the purpose of obtaining a young man a situation in the Excise. Mr. Attwood had replied that he had never asked a favour of Government, and should not do so, for it might be expected that in return he should vote against the liberties of his countrymen. (Cheers.)

The Mayor said he had the gratification of announcing that upwards of £200 had been subscribed in the hall. (Loud applause.)

G. F. Muntz, Esq., M.P., in moving a vote of thanks to the Mayor, took occasion to make an explanation respecting the connection between Mr. Attwood and himself. He remembered that when Mr. Attwood had retired from the representation of Birmingham, he (Mr. Muntz) had been charged with having entered into an arrangement with Mr. Attwood to become his successor. The fact was, that before any one knew Mr. Attwood was going to resign, he had written him (Mr. Muntz) a long letter, expressing extreme disgust at the want of honour and ability in the existing Government, stating that he felt no good would ever arise from it, that his peace of mind was so interfered with that he was anxious to retire, and that he knew of no one who he was so anxious should succeed him as he (Mr. Muntz). He had written back that he was busily employed, and had no wish to enter Parliament, and urging Mr. Attwood to reconsider the matter. Mr. Attwood had written to him again upon the subject, but he had positively declined, and it was only when he was reminded that he had pledged himself in case of any difficulty to be at their service, that he had consented. He had thought it only fair to both of them to make that statement. As to Mr. Attwood making an arrangement with him, the supposition was out of all character. He (Mr. Muntz) had not entertained the slightest intention or expectation of succeeding him. After paying a tribute to the praiseworthy steps taken by the Mayor in promotion of the movement, Mr Muntz concluded by proposing that the thanks of the meeting should be tendered him.

The Mayor briefly acknowledged the compliment, and the meeting dispersed about three o'clock."

I have had much pleasure in transcribing at considerable length the foregoing speeches, for, taken together, they constitute a body of impartial testimony to the merits of Thomas Attwood such as could with difficulty be collected concerning the vast majority of public men. But I regret to add that the generous efforts of the Committee were but ill seconded by the people at large. When I reflect upon the thousands which are raised without difficulty for the purpose of doing honour to princes, dukes, bishops, deans, and other men, who, so far from ever having done anything for the public gratuitously, have either spent their whole lives in drawing huge salaries from the public purse, or have inherited vast ancestral estates,—when I call to mind that £50,000 was subscribed by his friends for Richard Cobden,—when I think of the enormous sums squandered upon Albert Memorials, I feel ashamed to record that the Committee found considerable difficulty in raising the paltry sum of £800 to perpetuate the memory of Attwood. Such, however, is the gratitude of the people! All persons, whatever their politics, must admit that the aristocracy know better how to reward *their* champions. With this sum it was decided to erect a statue of Thomas Attwood, and the execution of the work was entrusted to Mr. Thomas, sculptor, and Messrs. Branson and Gwyther, contractors. The formal inauguration took place on the 7th June, 1858, with considerable ceremony. The Mayor, Sir John Ratcliff, followed by the Corporation and a number of sympathisers, walked in procession from the Town Hall to the site of the monument in Stephenson Place, New Street. Mr. Muntz, who had so generously exerted himself to do justice to the memory of his friend, did not live to take part in the ceremony, but upon the platform were present George Edmonds, William Mathews, and Aurelius and Algernon Attwood. Amongst the ladies assembled at the windows overlooking the site were Mrs. Attwood and Mrs. William Mathews. After a few preliminary remarks, the Mayor read the following address drawn up by the Committee:—

"*To the Mayor, Aldermen, and Burgesses of the Borough of Birmingham.*

The committee entrusted with the duty of erecting a memorial of the late Thomas Attwood, in dedicating it to the public for ever, desire to state the circumstances under which the work was undertaken, and the spirit in which it was carried out. There are few politicians of any kind who now deny the manifold blessings which the Reform Bill of 1832 has conferred on the country. Under that measure, and mainly by its instrumentality, commerce has been set free; penal laws have been modified; liberty, civil and religious, has been advanced; and that freedom of thought and speech to which the Reform Bill contributed, have made a still wider reform in the representation of the people safe and practicable. To Thomas Attwood the country was indebted for an agitation, resulting in the Bill which, on this day seven-and-twenty years ago, received the Royal Assent, and from which these individual and national blessings have flowed. The party prejudices then prevailing, the aversion to change, the mistaken and unworthy fear of the people, and the self-interested opposition which the Bill encountered, roused a spirit of indignation throughout the country which was either salutary or dangerous, according to the direction given to it. The popular faith, which all history verifies and strengthens, that God raises up men to meet every emergency, received another confirmation. As Birmingham was the centre of the agitation for Reform, so did it furnish the man fitted to control and direct it; honest and incorruptible, unselfish in his aims, and genial in his nature, Mr. Attwood won the confidence and the love of the people. While his stirring eloquence and his fervent enthusiasm aroused the feelings of the populace, his calm judgment gave to them a safe and useful direction. At this distance of time it is impossible to realise the influence which Mr. Attwood exercised. It is scarcely a figure of speech to affirm that the destiny of his country—at any rate, the fate of popular freedom—for a time was in his keeping, and all honour is due to the memory of him whose patriotic and beneficent influence not only saved the country from anarchy, but speeded the great work of human freedom and human happiness. As unselfish as he was enthusiastic, he accepted no honour or reward; but when his good work was done, he betook himself to the performance of the ordinary duties of life, leaving the struggle for office and its fruits to those who care for them In testimony of their admiration of so much patriotism, and in the belief that the lesson which such a life teaches cannot fail to influence the future of many who study it, a number of the contemporaries of Mr. Attwood, and many who knew him only by the fame of his good deeds, have erected this statue to his memory. The memorial so designed, and so admirably executed by the distinguished sculptor, Mr. Thomas, they now dedicate to the public for ever, as a record of and a stimulant to public virtue.—Dated this 7th day of June, 1859.— T. R. T. Hodgson, Chairman, J. H. Cutler, Deputy-Chairman, T. Aspinall, Treasurer; W. M. Cooper, Secretary. Members of the Executive Committee: George Edmonds, John Jaffray, W. Mathews, John Betts, S. A. Goddard, John Webster, William Mills, E. Gwyther, T. C. Salt."

The disrobing of the statue was then commenced, and the

work received the sanction of the assembled crowd, whose loud applause showed that they were well satisfied with the memorial. The royal standard was elevated at the moment when the statue was uncovered. The Mayor formally accepted the custody of the statue on behalf of the Corporation of Birmingham, and after speeches by Mr. George Edmonds and Mr. William Mathews, the proceedings terminated amidst applause. At night, thirty or forty gentlemen dined at the Navigation Inn, Edgbaston, to commemorate the inauguration of the statue. Mr. J. A. Langford, author of *A Century of Birmingham Life*, proposed the toast of the evening, "The Immortal Memory of Thomas Attwood," and observed that few men were more worthy of the honour and gratitude of a country than was the man whose memory they had met to celebrate. He had been one of the most self-denying and noble patriots who had ever laboured for his country's welfare, and the work he and his compeers had accomplished would ever remain a glorious part of the history of their country.

Considering the comparatively small sum expended on the Attwood Memorial, the statue has always appeared to me to be a creditable one, and I should imagine that both sculptor and contractors must have liberally interpreted the terms of their undertaking. "The figure is nearly nine feet high, and cut from a fine block of Sicilian marble. The base is of freestone, and the shaft of grey granite, the height of the whole being twenty-two feet. Mr. Attwood is represented in the act of addressing a meeting. The very posture of the outstretched arm shows that his eloquence was not of the fiery inflammatory kind; even the hand conveys the idea that he is appealing to reason rather than passion. The left hand holds a roll, on which is inscribed the word "Reform," and this rests on the Roman fasces (emblematic of the unity of the people and the supremacy of the law), on the bands of which are the words "Liberty, Unity, Prosperity."

The site of the statue is certainly one of the best in Birmingham, where it at once attracts the eye of arrivals by the London and North Western Railway, and looks upon the street which has so often re-echoed with tremendous shouts in Attwood's honour, and which witnessed his crowning triumph. The inscription seems to have been judiciously selected, and merely asserts an incontrovertible fact. There may be Tories who still consider Attwood to have been a dangerous politician, who first opened the floodgates to anarchy and communism; there may be many of all political creeds who consider his notions on the Currency to have been pernicious and absurd; and there are doubtless many who give all the credit of his great deeds to those persons of rank and fortune who reaped the reward of them. But that he was the founder of that mighty organization, in opposition to which the victor of Waterloo was but as a brittle reed, no one can possibly deny. Without, therefore, entering into the question, whether the momentous secret of the irresistible power of peaceful combination were first divulged by Attwood for the ultimate benefit or otherwise of the human race, the statue bears upon its shaft the simple inscription, so similar to that which he once wished to be written on his tomb, of "THOMAS ATTWOOD, FOUNDER OF THE BIRMINGHAM POLITICAL UNION."

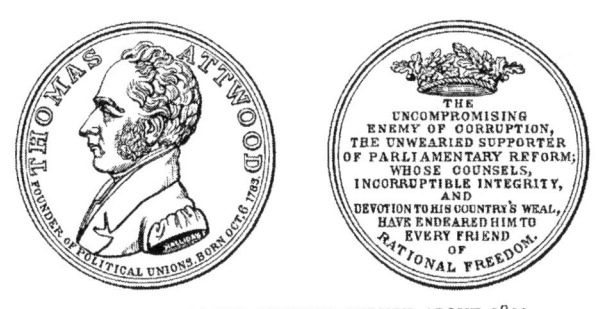

MEDAL OF THOMAS ATTWOOD STRUCK ABOUT 1832.

BIBLIOLIFE

Old Books Deserve a New Life
www.bibliolife.com

Did you know that you can get most of our titles in our trademark **EasyScript**™ print format? **EasyScript**™ provides readers with a larger than average typeface, for a reading experience that's easier on the eyes.

Did you know that we have an ever-growing collection of books in many languages?

Order online:
www.bibliolife.com/store

Or to exclusively browse our **EasyScript**™ collection:
www.bibliogrande.com

At BiblioLife, we aim to make knowledge more accessible by making thousands of titles available to you – quickly and affordably.

Contact us:
BiblioLife
PO Box 21206
Charleston, SC 29413

Printed in Great Britain
by Amazon.co.uk, Ltd.,
Marston Gate.